Multicultural Psychology

Understanding Our Diverse Communities

FIFTH EDITION

Jeffery Scott Mio

California State Polytechnic University, Pomona

Lori A. Barker

California State Polytechnic University, Pomona

Melanie M. Domenech Rodríguez

Utah State University

John Gonzalez

Bimidji State University

NEW YORK   OXFORD

OXFORD UNIVERSITY PRESS

Oxford University Press is a department of the University of Oxford.
It furthers the University's objective of excellence in research, scholarship,
and education by publishing worldwide. Oxford is a registered trade mark of
Oxford University Press in the UK and certain other countries.

Published in the United States of America by Oxford University Press
198 Madison Avenue, New York, New York 10016, United States

For titles covered by Section 112 of the US Higher Education
Opportunity Act, please visit www.oup.com/us/he for the latest
information about pricing and alternate formats.

Library of Congress Cataloging-in-Publication Data

Names: Mio, Jeffery Scott, 1954- author. | Barker, Lori A., author. |
  Domenech Rodriguez, Melanie M., author.
Title: Multicultural psychology: understanding our diverse communities /
  Jeffery Scott Mio, California State Polytechnic University, Pomona, Lori
  A. Barker, California State Polytechnic University, Pomona, Melanie M.
  Domenech Rodriguez, Utah State University, John Gonzalez, Bimidji State
  University.
Description: Fifth edition. | New York, New York : Oxford University, [2020]
Identifiers: LCCN 2018053190| ISBN 9780190854959 (paper back) |
  ISBN 9780190854973 (loose leaf)
Subjects: LCSH: Multiculturalism. | Multiculturalism—Psychological aspects. |
  Multicultural education. | Mental health education. | Ethnopsychology.
Classification: LCC HM1271 .M555 2020 | DDC 305.8—dc23
LC record available at https://lccn.loc.gov/2018053190

Printing number: 9 8 7
Printed by Sheridan Books, Inc., United States of America

To my unofficial professional mentors, Joseph Trimble, Derald Wing Sue, and Stanley Sue, who have taught me by example and encouragement what it means to be a multicultural psychologist.
—JSM

For AZ, as you launch into the next phase of this amazing journey called life.
—LAB

To my maternal great-grandmother, paternal grandmother, mother, father, and two children. As individuals, you have enriched my life in innumerable ways. As members of one family, you have collectively helped me understand my place in the world.
—MMDR

To my wife Nanako: my life partner and my most influential multicultural teacher.
—JG

Brief Contents

Contents

About the Authors

Dr. Jeffery Scott Mio is a professor in the Psychology and Sociology Department at California State Polytechnic University, Pomona (Cal Poly Pomona), where he also serves as the director of the MS in Psychology program. He received his PhD from the University of Illinois, Chicago, in 1984. He taught at California State University, Fullerton, in the Counseling Department from 1984 to 1986 and then at Washington State University in the Department of Psychology from 1986 to 1994 before accepting his current position at Cal Poly Pomona.

Dr. Mio has taught multicultural psychology since 1985. He is a fellow in Division 1 (Society for General Psychology), Division 2 (Society for the Teaching of Psychology), Division 9 (Society for the Psychological Study of Social Issues), and Division 45 (Society for the Psychological Study of Culture, Ethnicity, and Race) of the American Psychological Association (APA) and a fellow of the Asian American Psychological Association (AAPA) and the Western Psychological Association (WPA). He was honored with the Outstanding Career Achievement for Teaching and Training award from APA's Minority Fellowship Program, the Outstanding Teaching award from WPA, and the Distinguished Contribution award from AAPA. He served as president of both Division 45 (2002–2003) and WPA (2010–2011) and was the executive officer of WPA (2016–2017). His research interests are in the areas of teaching multicultural issues, the development of allies in multicultural psychology, and how metaphors are used in political persuasion.

Dr. Lori A. Barker is a professor in the Psychology Department at California State Polytechnic University, Pomona (Cal Poly Pomona). She received her BA in psychology from Yale University and her PhD in clinical psychology from the University of California, Los Angeles (UCLA). After receiving her degree, Dr. Barker spent one additional year at UCLA as a National Institute of Mental Health postdoctoral research fellow. Dr. Barker is a licensed clinical psychologist with a private practice in Riverside, California, called the Center for Individual, Family, and Community Wellness.

Dr. Barker is a fellow of the Western Psychological Association and a recipient of their Outstanding Teaching award. Other awards include Outstanding Advisor, Psi Chi Western Region; Outstanding Advisor, Office of Student Life, Cal Poly Pomona; Professor of the Year, Psi Chi, Cal Poly Pomona Chapter; and Cal Poly Pomona Diversity Champion. Her primary areas of interest include multicultural psychology and community psychology. Her research focuses on factors that influence the effectiveness of multicultural education and diversity training programs, as well as the psychological impact of multicultural factors on U.S. presidencies. Her most recent book is *Obama on Our Minds: The Impact of Obama on the Psyche of America* (Oxford University Press, 2016). Dr. Barker regularly gives presentations, workshops, seminars, and keynote addresses for community and professional organizations.

Dr. Melanie M. Domenech Rodríguez is a professor of psychology at Utah State University (USU); she began her appointment at USU in 2000. Dr. Domenech Rodríguez has been actively engaged in programs of parenting intervention research in Mexico, Puerto Rico, and Michigan, examining the effectiveness of GenerationPMTO. Her research has been funded by the National Institute of Mental Health and the National Institute of Child Health and Human Development.

At USU, Dr. Domenech Rodríguez teaches multicultural psychology to undergraduate students and diversity issues in treatment and assessment to graduate students in psychology. Dr. Domenech Rodríguez is a licensed psychologist in Utah. She obtained her doctoral degree at Colorado State University in 1999. She completed a postdoctoral fellowship with the Family Research Consortium–III at the University of Washington. Dr. Domenech Rodríguez is a fellow of the American Psychological Association and the Association for Psychological Science. She has received awards for mentorship (MENTOR award from the Society for the Clinical Psychology of Ethnic Minorities, APA D12S6), research (Emerging Professional award from the Society for the Study of Culture, Ethnicity, and Race, APA D45), service (Star Vega Distinguished Service award from the National Latina/o Psychological Association), and the advancement of diversity issues in psychology (Carol Atteneave Award for Diversity, Society for Family Psychology, APA D43). She is a past president of the Society for the Clinical Psychology of Ethnic Minorities and the National Latinx Psychological Association. She is president of Psi Chi, the international honor society in psychology. Dr. Domenech Rodríguez was born and raised in Puerto Rico and has two children.

Dr. John Gonzalez is Ojibwe from White Earth Anishinaabe Nation and a professor of psychology at Bemidji State University in northern Minnesota, where he also received his undergraduate degree in psychology. He received his PhD in clinical psychology from the University of North Dakota. He has taught multicultural psychology since 2005.

Dr. Gonzalez has served as program chair (2007) and then treasurer (2010–2014) for the Society for the Psychological Study of Culture, Ethnicity, and Race (APA's Division 45) and as historian for the Society of Indian Psychologists. Dr. Gonzalez was selected as a University Faculty Scholar in 2015 and was also honored as the American Indian Post-Secondary Teacher of the Year by the Minnesota Indian Education Association in 2017.

Dr. Gonzalez's professional interests are in cultural psychology, which attempts to understand people as cultural beings through their own indigenous psychological perspectives; multicultural psychology, which considers people's cultural, historical, and sociopolitical contexts; and community psychology, which actively works to enhance the strengths and quality of life in communities.

Dr. Gonzalez's research interests are in the areas of mental/behavioral health disparities for indigenous people and people of color. He has worked with indigenous communities utilizing local cultural knowledge and values in developing suicide and substance abuse prevention programs. Dr. Gonzalez also investigates microaggressions and racial experiences of American Indians in education and health care. He regularly provides presentations, workshops, seminars, and invited lectures in these areas.

Preface

Throughout the years that we have taught courses on multicultural psychology and attended conference presentations and workshops on this topic, what has stuck with us are the stories people felt compelled to tell. In fact, the genesis of this book was a student's reaction paper that was so moving we felt it had to be published. Thus, we planned this book around stories (narratives or anecdotes) that illustrate important aspects of scientific studies and other professional writings in the field of multicultural psychology. The personal stories from our students have generally not been edited for grammar, although some markedly ungrammatical phrases and sentences were modified to make them a bit more grammatical. We did this to maintain the flavor of their stories from the heart, which seemed to illustrate the academic points we are trying to make.

In general, science tells us that anecdotes are not sufficient evidence to prove one's point. Although we agree with that stance from a scientific perspective and do not substitute anecdotes for scientific investigation, we do use anecdotes as central points around which to build our case for multicultural issues based on science. In addition, multicultural psychology emphasizes the value of integrating quantitative and qualitative methods to accurately capture the richness of diverse cultures and communities. Thus, rather than substituting for science, our anecdotes are prototypes for scientific investigation. For example, science tells us that there are differences in the way in which men and women communicate. We illustrate those differences by presenting anecdotes highlighting the common experience women have of sometimes being shut out of conversations, particularly ones that are about "male" topics. Science tells us that there are various stages or statuses of racial identity, and we present some prototypical anecdotes that illustrate how those statuses of racial identity affect one's perceptions and life experiences. Science tells us that clients of color may have very different reactions to European American therapists, and we present an anecdote that conveys a typical reaction to a European American therapist who did not approach a family of color in a culturally sensitive manner. Again, these stories are meant not to replace science, but to enrich science—to add texture to the clean (and sometimes sterile) lines of science.

Organization of the Book

This book is organized around the emphasis that we place in our undergraduate multicultural courses and arose out of a perceived need we saw in the field. The initial books on multicultural psychology were written for graduate students, because organizations governing graduate curricula required that such courses be taught. As multicultural psychology began to become popular at the undergraduate level, several genres of undergraduate texts were developed. One genre adapted the basic structure of graduate texts to the undergraduate level. The result was a focus on therapy with specific populations of color. The more advanced texts in this genre also had one or two chapters that dealt with other populations of diversity, such as women; lesbian, gay, and bisexual populations; and people with disabilities. Another genre of undergraduate texts was infused with international issues in psychology. Finally, other texts had more specific foci, such as multicultural communication or issues of racism. Our undergraduate courses focus more on many issues covered in other books (e.g., differences in worldviews, differences in communication, issues of racism, racial/cultural identity development, and immigration) than on therapy with specific populations of color or on international issues in psychology. We also have chosen to integrate issues specific to populations of diversity throughout our chapters rather than covering such issues in separate chapters.

In Chapter 1, we define relevant terms and discuss the overall importance of multicultural psychology and how it came into prominence. Historically, many researchers in the field have identified three forces in psychology: psychoanalysis, behaviorism, and humanism. Some feel that multicultural psychology is the fourth force in our field. Moreover, an understanding of the cultural context is essential as we view behavior from the biopsychosocial perspective. Initially, researchers in the field of psychology attempted to describe general issues of human behavior and treated all individuals as if they were the same. Because the field was overwhelmingly European American, individuals in communities of diversity saw these "general issues" as being imposed on them and at times irrelevant to their lives. Thus, they began to define themselves, and from their varied definitions emerged a deeper understanding of human behavior.

In Chapter 2, we explore issues involving research and testing. We build on the notion that the history of psychology was dominated by a European American standard by explaining that sometimes the European American standard is not relevant to communities of diversity and can even be damaging to them. For example, if we were to find that some groups diverge from a European American standard, we might describe those groups as deviant, deprived, or deficient. In one historical case described in this chapter, the researcher was interested in the differences between African Americans who performed well academically and those who did not perform well. That study was rejected by reviewers because it did not compare the African American students with European American students. The researcher wondered why one needed a European American comparison group when the entire purpose of the study was to examine African Americans. There is also a preference for quantitative analysis in science because it is believed that qualitative studies introduce too much bias or are not generalizable enough. However, bias can be introduced in quantitative analyses as well, through the choice of what to study, through the way in which one's measures are converted into numerical responses, through the interpretation of those results, and so on. Therefore, we discuss qualitative analyses, particularly as they apply to communities of diversity. Finally, we apply issues of research methodology to our understanding of psychological testing.

In Chapter 3, we discuss various kinds of worldviews. First, we discuss issues of etic versus emic perspectives. In multicultural psychology, the etic perspective attempts to develop theory by finding similarities across different cultures, whereas the emic perspective emphasizes meaningful concepts within cultures that may not translate across cultures. Among the most important distinctions in the multicultural literature is the distinction between individualism and collectivism. That is because these perspectives are infused in societies, so one's cultural context may be from an individualistic society or from a collectivistic society. Different cultural groups may also have different values, such as the importance of the past, present, or future. Again, we discuss how diverse communities can have very different worldviews from those of their European American majority counterparts. We added a section on the worldview of today's youth.

In Chapter 4, we examine differences in communication. We first present rules of conversation that have been identified by linguists and psycholinguists. There are some regularities in conversations within various groups, but there are many examples of differences among groups. For example, people in some groups feel more comfortable standing closer to their conversational partners than do people in other groups. Another key distinction in multicultural communication is the distinction between high- and low-context communication groups. In high-context groups, less is said because the context carries with it much of the communication, whereas in low-context groups, more must be said because there may be different rules governing contextual communication that may be applied to the situation. We explore differences in communication that have been identified in diverse communities. We pay particular attention to gender differences in communication: men tend to use more direct methods of communication, and women tend to use more indirect methods; women also use *softening* methods so that their opinions do not seem so harsh. We also present communication styles by older adults, and also communication styles by younger adults. We finish this chapter by discussing bilingual communication, including both cognitive and social consequences.

In Chapter 5, we discuss issues involving immigrants and refugees. Often, people do not make a distinction between these two populations. However, there can be some very important differences psychologically. For example, immigrants choose to come to the United States, and they prepare for that transition by studying this country and its traditions, learning English, deciding where to settle, and so on. In contrast, refugees come against their will. They often must escape from their countries of origin to save their lives, do not know where they will ultimately settle (often going from country to country until a final host country can be found), and encounter many hardships and even trauma in their transition. However, beyond those initial differences, immigrants and refugees can encounter many similar issues, such as language barriers, changing family roles, and problems with employment. We conclude this chapter by discussing models of acculturation, some of which may also apply to American-born individuals, such as some American Indian populations.

In Chapter 6, we focus on issues involving racism. First, social psychologists make a distinction among stereotypes, prejudice, discrimination, and racism. All of these are forms of group categorization, but stereotypes relate to similarities we perceive within the categorized group, prejudice relates to our feelings about the categorized group, discrimination relates to our behaviors toward the categorized group, and racism relates to our institutional practices against the categorized group. Racism is also related to other *isms* (e.g., sexism, heterosexism, ableism) in that they all involve institutional practices that systematically disadvantage those who are on the downside of power. Although overt racism is largely a thing of the past, modern forms of racism still exist. We apply these issues of racism to contemporary issues, such as the U.S. government's response to the Dakota Pipeline issue near the Standing Rock Reservation in North Dakota and the government's response to Hurricane Maria, which devastated Puerto Rico. One way to overcome racism and other isms is to understand issues of European American privilege and other privileges of power. In so doing, one can become an advocate or ally for those who are unfairly disadvantaged by institutional practices.

In Chapter 7, we look at issues of identity. People who are familiar with developmental psychology know that this is one of the central questions that arises in adolescence. In multicultural psychology, one must explore not only issues of who one is and what aspirations one has, but also how those issues relate to one's racial/cultural identity. We discuss models of identity development, beginning with African American identity development, then European

American identity development, and finally a general racial/cultural identity development model. This final model also includes other forms of identity, such as multiracial identity development and gay/lesbian identity development. Our previous editions had not included an American Indian identity development model, but this has been corrected in this edition. We conclude this chapter by discussing issues of multiple identities. For example, an African American heterosexual woman who is a mother and a professor has a racial identity (African American), a sexual identity (heterosexual), a gender identity (woman), a parental identity (mother), and an occupational identity (professor). These are only a subset of potential identities; other identities include but are not limited to religion, ability, region, and marital status. At different times, one or a subset of these identities may come to the fore, and we need to understand how we can balance these different demands. Moreover, being secure within all our multiple identities means that when we emphasize one identity over another, we are not less of the other but rather are emphasizing the one identity in response to contextual demands.

In Chapter 8, we discuss health issues. Health and health behaviors are related to one's worldview and the context within which one develops. For example, different groups of people of color encounter differential care in a health-care system where policies and behaviors are still affected by remnants of racism. Much of that may be a result of poverty, because people with better health insurance are treated better than are those who are compelled to use public assistance programs. To the extent that there remain differences in socioeconomic status among different groups in this country, there remain differences in health-care opportunities. However, even with the barrier of poverty removed, structural barriers remain, such as language and access. Change can occur if we increase the number of health-care providers for people of color and address structural barriers in the health-care system. We finish this chapter with the example of sickle cell anemia, a disorder that affects primarily African Americans in this country and that is relatively ignored by the health-care system. Thus, there still appears to be racism within the system.

In Chapter 9, we deal with issues involving mental health, both diagnostically and therapeutically. We point out that the main classificatory system in the mental health field—*The Diagnostic and Statistical Manual of Mental Disorders*—tends to ignore issues of culture. That is because this document is based on a medical model that emphasizes disorders existing within an individual as opposed to those in the environment. We describe how many large-scale studies that have examined mental disorders have underrepresented populations of color. Thus, although we can come to some conclusions about the prevalence and course of disorders in communities of color, those conclusions must remain tentative. Also, some disorders may be specific to some cultures. These are called *culture-bound syndromes* and may be fundamentally different disorders or different expressions of similar disorders across cultural groups. An example of culture-bound syndromes that may be unique to the United States (and European American women in particular) is eating disorders. In therapy, many people of color either underutilize mental health services or terminate treatment prematurely because of discomfort with their therapists. Their discomfort may be caused by various barriers to treatment, such as cultural (value) differences, class differences, and language problems. To overcome these barriers, we must develop culturally sensitive approaches to treatment. Development of such approaches began with the publication of the multicultural competencies by the American Psychological Association in 2003. We conclude by discussing the effectiveness of cultural matching between the therapist and the client and other forms of culture-specific therapies that have been developed over the years.

Finally, in Chapter 10 we discuss general issues in increasing our multicultural competence. We must be aware of our cultural attitudes and understand how they may be different from attitudes of other cultures. In coming to understand our differences, we may encounter what we call the *Five D's of Difference*: distancing, denial, defensiveness, devaluing, and discovery. The first four D's of Difference involve negative reactions we might experience in an effort to hold on to our own more secure patterns of behavior. However, the fifth D of Difference involves a positive reaction that we may experience by understanding how the difference expressed by the other culture may enrich our lives. Part of the reason for the four negative reactions to difference may be what we call the *Three S's of Similarity*, which are simple, safe, and sane. When we prefer our own more secure patterns of behavior to the different ones we might encounter in another culture, our secure patterns feel more simple, make us feel safe, and keep us sane as opposed to confused. We offer suggestions to help you improve your multicultural competence, such as learning about other cultures before you encounter them; knowing about basic values, beliefs, and practices; not being afraid to ask questions; traveling to other places; becoming an ally; and making a decision to develop an attitude of discovery and courage.

We hope that you enjoy this book and learn a little bit more about yourself and others. We have certainly learned a little about ourselves in writing this book and are excited about that discovery. The field of multicultural psychology is relatively new, and it will undoubtedly change with the demographics of our country and the emergence of new and important issues. We intended to give you the tools to address and understand these emerging issues. The rest is up to you.

New to This Fifth Edition

One of the additions we made to this edition is in how we identify ethnicities in our book. Although this may seem merely cosmetic to some people, it reflects important underlying issues. The ethnicity we referred to as *White* in the past is now identified as *European American* in the current edition. This is because all those who identify as White have European roots, much as the broad group we identify as Asian or Asian American has roots in Asia. Thus, European American, Asian American, African American, and Latin American have all been placed on equal status.

The second change we made to an ethnic group is to refer to Latinos and Latinas as *Latinx* or *Latinxs* in keeping with current trends. Part of the reason for this change is that this new term provides a gender-neutral way of referring to people of Latin American descent (Salinas & Lozano, 2017). When the terms American Indian, European American, Asian American, or African American are used, they do not identify a gender of the referent, so Latina or Latino stands in stark contrast to these other supposedly equivalent terms. Moreover, Latinx is a way of working against the heteronormative conception of a binary gender selection of male or female (Santos, 2017). There is a growing trend of individuals not wanting to conform to this binary choice. This stance is most associated with individuals who are transsexual and in transition from one gender to another, but it is also a growing trend among those whose sexuality is more fluid. For these reasons, the National Latino/a Psychological Association has announced that it has officially change its name to the National Latinx Psychological Association (National Latinx Psychological Association, 2017).

We have added a new author, John Gonzalez, an Ojibwe American Indian psychologist and member of the White Earth Anishinaabe Nation. His perspective and work on the racism and identity development chapters have improved the book.

We have added a new section on American Indian identity development.

The issue of worldviews of women is greatly expanded.

There is expanded coverage on the worldviews of people of color, those in poverty, and youth given the Parkland student protest movement.

There is expanded coverage of recent examples of racism, including the Standing Rock protest; the Neo-Nazi protest in Charlottesville, Virginia; the shooting of Philando Castile; the racist incident at Starbucks; and Hurricane Maria in Puerto Rico.

The concept of WEIRD has been added to the worldviews chapter.

There is a new section on social media in communication.

The health chapters have been updated with new research.

Acknowledgments

A book of this sort cannot be completed without the help of many people. First and foremost, we would like to thank students, family members, friends, and colleagues for helping to provide us with stories and anecdotes that illustrated theoretical and research points we made throughout the book. As we mentioned at the beginning of this preface, the genesis of this book was one such personal story, so we are grateful to those whom we have quoted. We would also like to thank the following reviewers for their helpful comments:

Danice Brown
Southern Illinois University–Edward

Wen-chi Chen
Western New Mexico University

Eric John David
University of Alaska Anchorage

Kevin Eames
Covenant College

Allyson Graf
Elmira College

Lauren M. Haack
University of San Francisco

Kim Harding
Indiana Institute of Technology

Melissa Heerboth
Mercyhurst University

Carole Hetzel
Cardinal Stritch University

Callista M. Lee
Fullerton College

Christina Lee
Las Positas College

Christine Ma-Kellams
University of La Verne

Silvia Mazzula
John Jay College of Criminal Justice

Rocio Meza
University La Verne

Pamela Mulder
Marshall University

Trina Seefeldt
Metro State University of Denver

Winston Seegobin
George Fox University

Josephine Shih
St Joseph's University

Helen Taylor
Bellevue College

Monnica Williams,
University of Louisville

We also thank those reviewers who choose to remain anonymous.

Thank you also to those mentors and colleagues—particularly those active in Division 45 of the American Psychological Association, including Derald Wing Sue, Stanley Sue, Thomas Parham, Joe White, Martha Bernal, Allen Ivey, Lillian Comas-Díaz, Patricia Arredondo, Janet Helms, and Joseph Trimble—who helped shape our ideas throughout the years. Thanks also to Jenni Kolsky Goldman for her generosity in assigning her photography class to take most of the pictures in the first edition. Thanks to Tom Zasadzinski for numerous additional photographs in the second, third, fourth and fifth editions.

Jeffery Scott Mio
Lori A. Barker
Melanie M. Domenech Rodríguez
John Gonzalez

CHAPTER 1

What Is Multicultural Psychology?

Photograph by michaeljung/Shutterstock

Learning Objectives

Reading this chapter will help you to:
- understand the general definition of multicultural psychology;
- identify basic tenets of multicultural theory;
- know which strategies are appropriate for applying equality versus equity;
- recognize the differences among the terms culture, ethnicity, and race;
- distinguish between tolerance for diversity and a true multicultural mindset; and
- know a basic history of the field of multicultural psychology.

My whole life is a multicultural experience. I first learned to love and appreciate different cultures from my parents, who immigrated to the United States from the island of Barbados in the West Indies. I believe their openness to people from all walks of life came from their experiences as immigrants to this country, and they passed that on to me, my brother, and my sister.

Growing up with parents from a different country automatically made me aware that there are different cultures. Although I couldn't hear it, other people often commented that my parents spoke with an accent. I noticed that we ate different food. The differences were also apparent in the various groups with which we socialized. For example, we lived in a predominantly White neighborhood, but on the weekends we drove across town to the Black neighborhood to attend a Black church. Every weekend our house was full of people. My parents often invited their West Indian friends over to eat, play games, and tell stories. They also often befriended immigrant students from the local university they knew were far away from their families. We entertained students from all over—Latin America, Asia, Africa—and everybody was treated the same.

I also learned to love and appreciate different cultures from our family vacations. My parents took us on trips to different countries. Of course, they took us back to Barbados to learn about our West Indian roots, as well as to other Caribbean islands. We also traveled to Canada and Mexico. Again, in all our travels, I never saw my parents look down on or belittle anything or anybody in another culture. It was always seen as an adventure, an opportunity to see, do, and learn something new. And that has stayed with me for life. When I was old enough, I started traveling on my own.

My next primary multicultural experience was in high school. I attended a small, private, parochial school. The population was predominantly White (60%), but 40% other. By "other" I mean Cubans, Filipinos, Samoans, Koreans, Chinese, East Indians . . . you name it, we had it. In my closest circle of friends, one girlfriend was African American, one Cuban, one Bolivian, one Filipina, and one Chinese from Singapore. Talk about a United Nations! We all hung out together and everybody dated everybody else, no matter the background.

The utopia truly ended after high school. Some of the White people who were my friends throughout high school slowly distanced themselves from me and started hanging out only with other White people. I guess they saw that the rest of the world was not like our little oasis and succumbed to the pressure of the dominant outside culture, adopting its racist, prejudiced attitudes. I ended up feeling hurt and betrayed by them. Deep down, I learned not to trust White people. The innocence of youth was gone. But those few negative experiences did not outweigh the positives. I still feel most comfortable in a diverse environment, and my circle of friends, family, and colleagues continues to be very diverse. I notice that the similarities are not necessarily in the color of our skin but in our attitudes. I tend to associate with people who also value and respect cultural differences.

And now my love for other cultures has turned into a life mission. In my work as a teacher, researcher, and clinician, I try to teach others the value of learning about and interacting with people from different cultures.

—LAB

This story relates some of the life experiences of one of the authors of this book, Lori A. Barker (LAB). The experiences of the other three authors also reflect their multicultural backgrounds. Jeffery Scott Mio (JSM) is from a family whose grandparents immigrated to the United States from Japan, Melanie M. Domenech Rodríguez (MMDR) straddles life in the United States with her Puerto Rican roots, and John Gonzalez (JG) is Ojibwe, raised on the White Earth Indian Reservation in northern Minnesota.

Throughout this book you will read many unique stories of people whom we identify by pseudonyms. Motivated by these and other personal stories shared with us over the years by students, colleagues, family members, and friends, we have woven this material as illustrations into the fabric of theories, concepts, and research findings to create a textbook that uses a narrative approach to multicultural psychology. The use of oral history and personal life stories has a long tradition in the field of psychology. Personal narratives are particularly important in the study of people from diverse groups (Ponterotto, 2010). Atkinson says, "Telling our story enables us to be heard, recognized, and acknowledged by others. Story makes the implicit explicit, the hidden seen, the unformed, formed, and the confusing clear" (as cited in Ponterotto, 2010, p. 7). That is what we hope the stories included in this book do for you: that they bring multicultural psychology to life. The book's topics include, among others, worldviews, communication, immigration, acculturation, racism, identity, and physical and mental health. We hope you enjoy this more personal approach.

> I am more convinced each day that telling our stories to each other is the way we learn best what our collective life is all about, the way we understand who we really are, how our stories are intertwined, what this reality means for us now, and what it portends for the future.
>
> —Dr. Terrence Roberts, psychology professor and one of the "Little Rock Nine" who integrated Central High School in Little Rock, Arkansas, in 1957 (T. Roberts, 2009, pp. 10–11)

What Is Multicultural Psychology?

In the story that opens this chapter, LAB describes how her experiences interacting with people from many backgrounds eventually led her to a career in multicultural psychology. Her story might give you some indication as to what the field of multicultural psychology is about, but let us get more specific. In this chapter we introduce you to the field of multicultural psychology and to concepts that will be discussed in more detail in the following chapters.

Let us begin with a basic definition of the term **multicultural psychology**. First, let us define *psychology*. Most likely you already had a class in introductory or general psychology, where psychology was defined as the systematic study of behavior, cognition, and affect. In other words, psychologists are interested in how people act, think, and feel and in all the factors that influence these human processes. Therefore, you can probably guess that multicultural psychology involves examining in some way the effect of culture on the way people act, think, and feel. On the one hand, culture is an external factor because it influences the events that occur around us and our interactions with other people, but on the other hand, culture influences our internal processes, such as how we interpret the things going on around us.

> **multicultural psychology**—the systematic study of behavior, cognition, and affect in settings where people of different backgrounds interact.

The prefix *multi-* means "many," and the suffix *-al* means "of" or "pertaining to." Therefore, the term *multicultural* means pertaining to many cultures. If we put the term multicultural together with the term psychology, we can conclude that multicultural psychology concerns the systematic study of behavior, cognition, and affect in many cultures.

That is a good place to start, but the term is more complicated. What about the final component? We have not yet defined *culture*.

I am White and I have no idea about my culture. I am Polish, Dutch, Cherokee Indian, Mexican, Italian, and a couple of more things that I do not remember and have not discussed with my family since elementary school. There is not much religion on either side of my family. Even both of my step parents do not have that much religion on either side.

Everyone in my different families (real parents and step parents) celebrates all of the basic big holidays on the calendar. We all get together and celebrate Christmas, Easter, and Thanksgiving. But without the religious aspect. It seems kind of weird to me to celebrate Christmas and Easter when we are not religious. But I guess any time you can get most of your family together it is worth a celebration.

I got married five years ago to my beautiful Christian wife. We do not discuss religion that much. On holidays when we are with her family, we pray before eating and give our thanks. On Christmas and Easter we all go to church together. My wife's family shows culture this way. My wife and her whole family are Italian. It seems to me that they have a culture that is loud and a culture that wants everyone around them to know that they are Italian. I see a lot of culture with my wife's family. Whether it is because of their religion or their nationality that I did not grow up with.

I still to this day do not see or know my culture. I always thought that White people did not have a culture because it seemed to be the norm. When I married my wife I saw that White people did have culture. Just not my family.

—Vince, 30+-year-old European American (multiracial) student

Culture is a complex term. Defining it is difficult, because although we use it all the time, we use it in so many ways. For example, in describing his experiences with his different families,

Vince used the word culture to refer to countries, holidays, religions, family traditions, and interpersonal interactions. These represent many of the different meanings of the term culture.

You may also note that Vince described himself as *White*, although he had a very mixed heritage. At times, we will identify those individuals whose ancestors came from Europe as White, and at times we will refer to such individuals as *European American*. The terms may be seen as interchangeable in most cases. Our experience has been that when we refer to White students as European American, many say, "I am not from Europe." They do not make the connection that when we refer to people whose ancestors originated in Asia, we label them *Asian Americans* even if they were born in the United States. For those of us who teach and research topics in the multicultural domain, the term European American is more common, but we recognize that for most people, White is the more common term.

When someone asks what culture you are from, how do you reply? Do you tell them your nationality (e.g., Chinese, El Salvadoran)? Do you tell them where your ancestors were from (e.g., "I'm Polish on my dad's side, but Swedish on my mother's")? Do you refer to your racial group (e.g., "I'm Black"), or do you use a specific ethnic label (e.g., "I'm African American")? If you answer in one of these ways, you are like most people, who, when asked about culture, reply by stating their race, ethnicity, or country of origin (Matsumoto, Kasri, Milligan, Singh, & The, 1997, as cited in Matsumoto, 2000).

Sometimes we use the word culture to mean various types of music, art, and dance. For example, when people refer to the cultural life of a city, they usually have in mind artistic opportunities, such as access to a good museum and a good symphony orchestra or the quality of the plays that come to town. At other times we use the term culture to refer to such things as food, clothing, history, and traditions. For example, American Indian[1] culture is associated with powwows, sweat lodges, talking circles, and the like. These activities represent traditions that tribes have passed down from generation to generation and are ways in which the people connect with their cultural heritage, purify themselves, and express ideas and solve problems. At still other times we use the term culture in reference to the regular or expected behaviors of a particular group. We might use the term *teen culture* to refer to the particular way adolescents act, talk, and dress. It signifies that adolescents behave differently from people of other age groups.

Kroeber and Kluckhohn (1952/1963) and Berry and associates (J. W. Berry, Poortinga, Segall, & Dasen, 1992) described six uses of culture in everyday language: (a) *descriptive*, the specific behaviors and activities associated with a culture; (b) *historical*, a group's heritage and traditions; (c) *normative*, the rules that govern the behavior of a group; (d) *psychological*, which emphasizes behavioral processes, such as learning and problem solving; (e) *structural*, which reflects the organizational elements of a culture; and (f) *genetic,* which refers to the origins of that culture.

---

1   Various terms have been used to categorize indigenous peoples of the Americas. Common terms are *Native Americans, American Indians, Native American Indians,* and *aboriginals.* The two most common terms are Native Americans and American Indians. We have chosen to use the term American Indians because some European American people who want to resist classification based on racioethnic grounds have said, "I was born here in America, so I am Native American, too." Moreover, individuals of Mexican descent may also validly use the term Native American because many of their ancestors lived in the Western regions of the United States when those regions were still part of Mexico. According to our friend and colleague Joseph E. Trimble, the term American Indian is the least confusing and most accurate, so we have adopted that convention. However, we recognize that many American Indians still prefer the term Native American, and some prefer their specific tribal affiliation. We are using the term American Indian merely as a convention for this book.

Let us use Mexican culture as an example. To talk about Spanish as the primary language is a descriptive use of culture. To talk about the holidays the people celebrate, such as Cinco de Mayo and El Día de los Muertos, is a historical use. To talk about traditional gender roles and machismo is a normative use. To talk about the process of learning a new language or adjusting to a new culture is a psychological use. To talk about the importance of the extended family is a structural use. Finally, to talk about the combined influence of indigenous and Spanish (European) people on Mexican physical appearance is a genetic use.

culture—the values, beliefs, and practices of a group of people, shared through symbols, and passed down from generation to generation.

Culture refers to systems of knowledge, concepts, rules, and practices that are learned and transmitted across generations. Culture includes language, religion and spirituality, family structures, life-cycle stages, ceremonial rituals, and customs, as well as moral and legal systems. Cultures are open, dynamic systems that undergo continuous change over time; in the contemporary world, most individuals and groups are exposed to multiple cultures, which they use to fashion their own identities and make sense of experience.

—American Psychiatric Association, 2013

So far, our discussion covers the ways in which we use the term culture in our everyday language. How do psychologists define culture? Psychologists have struggled to develop a concise definition of culture. Atkinson (2004) summed up the debate by saying that culture "consists of values and behaviors that are learned and transmitted within an identifiable community . . . and also includes the symbols, artifacts, and products of that community" (p. 10). Matsumoto and Juang (2008) also listed several definitions of culture before presenting their own working definition. They defined *human culture* as "a unique meaning and information system, shared by a group and transmitted across generations, that allows the group to meet basic needs of survival, pursue happiness and well-being, and derive meaning from life" (p. 12). In other words, culture usually refers to a particular group of people and includes their values, or guiding beliefs and principles, and behaviors, or typical activities. Those values and behaviors are symbolized in the things that the group of people produces, such as art, music, food, and language. All those things are passed down from generation to generation. In summary, we could define **culture** as the values, beliefs, and practices of a group of people, shared through symbols and passed down from generation to generation.

Narrow and Broad Definitions of Culture

The field of multicultural psychology distinguishes between narrow and broad definitions of culture. A narrow definition of culture is limited to race, ethnicity, and/or nationality. This use of the term is probably the more common one.

In contrast, a broad definition of culture includes "any and all potentially salient ethnographic, demographic, status, or affiliation identities" (Pedersen, 1999, p. 3). In other words, any of the important or meaningful ways in which we identify ourselves can be viewed as a culture. D. W. Sue, Ivey, and Pedersen (1996) gave the following broad definition of culture: "any group that shares a theme or issue(s)" (p. 16). Therefore, language, gender, ethnicity/race, spirituality, sexual preference, age, physical issues, socioeconomic status, and survival after trauma all define cultures. Under this broad definition, we can have simultaneous membership in more than one culture.

Some psychologists argue that a broad definition of culture is not particularly helpful. Should something such as gender be included? Do men and women really have separate and distinct cultures? If this definition is taken to its extreme, anything could be considered a culture. Let us use the deaf community as an example.

If we define a culture as a distinct group of people characterized by shared customs, behaviors, and values, would the deaf community fit that definition? Backenroth (1998) thinks so. She argued that deaf people share a common language (sign language); have their own schools, churches, and social organizations; have common experiences and a common way of interacting with one another and with hearing people; and therefore have a distinct culture. Other authors agree that persons with disabilities, such as individuals who are hearing impaired, besides being distinguished by their physical impairment, share other psychological and sociological characteristics (Clymer, 1995; M. H. Rose, 1995). Following is a description of deaf culture by a deaf person:

> Deaf culture for me is about the complexity of deafness. Life as a deaf person, life stories, and destinies. Deaf culture for me is not theatre, art and so on per se. These ways of expression are not particular for deaf people. However, the content in these different ways of expression can illustrate the Deaf culture, deaf people's lives. For example, the American artist Harry Williams, now deceased. He was painting violins without chords, separated violins, like two worlds. This example is a clear expression of the Deaf culture, not art per se but the content in art. The particular traits that deaf people in comparison to hearing people in society, for example the language, music, the pictures and so on, are typical deaf cultural expression . . . well, o dear it is so difficult to describe this in words but easy to experience.
>
> —Anonymous research participant (cited in Backenroth, 1998)

Do you agree with a broad or a narrow definition of culture? As we stated earlier, although some psychologists disagree, most multicultural psychologists subscribe to a broad definition of culture that includes statuses and affiliations such as gender, physical ability, religion, and sexual orientation. This broad definition of culture includes a wide range of **diversity** that encompasses differences beyond race, ethnicity, and nationality.

diversity—acknowledgment of individual human differences that go beyond race, ethnicity, and nationality, such as age, gender, sexual orientation, religion, socioeconomic status, and physical ability.

Culture and Worldview

S. Sue (1977) defines a **worldview** as "the way in which people perceive their relationship to nature, institutions, other people, and things. Worldview constitutes our psychological orientation in life and can determine how we think, behave, make decisions, and define events" (p. 458). In other words, different cultural groups perceive, define, and interact with their environment in different ways based on their past learning experiences (D. W. Sue et al., 1996). People from different cultures may see or experience the same thing but interpret it in drastically different ways. An example of this is seen in the differing ways in which the European American and African American communities reacted when O. J. Simpson was acquitted after his criminal trial of the murders of his ex-wife, Nicole Brown Simpson, and her friend, Ronald Goldman.

worldview—a psychological perception of the environment that determines how we think, behave, and feel.

Time Magazine calls October 3, 1995, one of "Eighty Days That Changed the World" (Poniewozik, 2003). At 10:00 a.m. that day the world paused to watch the verdicts in the O. J. Simpson criminal trial.

O. J., a former NFL football star and popular celebrity in both the White and the Black communities, was accused of brutally murdering his ex-wife, Nicole Brown Simpson, and her friend, Ron Goldman. The world was captivated by the case, and many watched the daily courtroom drama. When it came time for the jury forewoman to read the verdicts, some networks went to a split screen where on one side they showed crowds gathered at various spots in the African American community, and on the other side they showed groups gathered at popular spots in the European American community. When the "not guilty" verdict was read, African Americans jumped, shouted, and cheered as if they had won the Superbowl, while European Americans looked shocked and stunned. Some cried while others expressed outrage.

The media commented on the differing reactions of the two communities in the weeks and months following the verdict, including a documentary on CBS called *O. J. in Black and White* (CBS News, 1996). Many struggled to explain the drastically different reactions. Reactions to the O. J. verdict for both African Americans and European Americans go all the way back to slavery. In the South, Black slaves far outnumbered White slave owners. Therefore, White slave owners used violence, fear, and intimidation to keep Black slaves in line. Once slavery was abolished, Whites, fearing for their safety, developed new tactics to keep large numbers of ex-slaves in line. The Ku Klux Klan accomplished this task through the continued use of violence, fear, and intimidation, but so did the justice system. African Americans were often falsely accused and convicted of crimes for which they were not guilty or given harsher

What is culture? *Photograph by Tom Zasadzinski*

sentences when they were guilty. Even today, statistics indicate that African Americans are more likely to be arrested, imprisoned, shot and killed by the police, and given harsher sentences, including the death penalty, than are European Americans (Sampson & Lauritsen, 1997; P. B. Smith, 2004).

Backtrack to 1992 and the verdicts in another famous trial of four European American police officers accused of beating Rodney King, an African American. The beating was caught on videotape and aired on television over and over in the following weeks. African Americans hoped that for once the system would work in their favor. After all, hadn't everyone seen the videotape? When a majority European American jury found the four European American officers not guilty, all hope was lost. African Americans reacted, not just to the verdict, but to centuries of unjust treatment. The Rodney King beating verdict was simply the straw that broke the camel's back, the match to the gasoline. African Americans (and others) in Los Angeles and other communities expressed their hurt, disappointment, pain, and rage by rioting for three days.

In 1995, when O. J. was acquitted, with the help of an African American defense lawyer and a predominantly African American jury, many African Americans said, "Finally! We beat them at their own game!" Hope was restored. In contrast, when the system they invented no longer worked in their favor, European Americans cried foul and said the system was flawed. (adapted from Barker-Hackett, 1995)

The drastically different responses of the African American and European American communities to the verdicts in the O. J. Simpson trial illustrate the different worldviews of these two communities. Remember, worldviews are shaped by past experiences. The jubilation of the African American community and the outrage of the European American community can truly be understood only in the historical context of centuries of unjust treatment of African Americans by European Americans, particularly within the justice system.

In the following excerpt, an African American woman describes reactions to the O. J. Simpson case among the clients in her beauty salon.

I remember how people divided, so much that I couldn't even express myself for fear of losing clients. I'm sure it was because he was so famous that it got the notoriety it did, but for the White and Black people, it was more than that: it was a Black man, killing a White woman, and the possibility of him not getting a fair trial.

At the time, all my clients were White, and each day, with the TV on, we all watched the proceedings. I think what blew me away was how everyone had decided so quickly that he was guilty. But what really shocked me was how people were angry because he was financially able to afford a good defense team, which was not usually the case in past trials involving Black defendants who usually ended up with public defenders. I'll never forget when I spoke up and stated that it's great that he can afford a good attorney, someone responded, "It doesn't matter, he's guilty." That client never booked with me again, and it was at that time I decided that I would not discuss my thoughts with my clients, or react to their statements. When they'd ask me point blank, though, I would say, "He's innocent until proven guilty." Of course they would say, "Yes, but what do you think?" "I don't know, like they don't know. I need to hear the evidence before I can make such a judgment."

If O. J.'s wife would have been a Black woman, I don't think it would have been as publicized, and I don't believe the White world would have even watched the trial. Racism

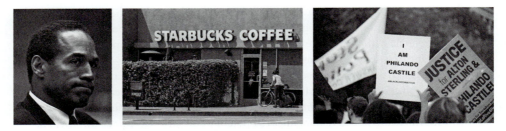

Individuals from different backgrounds perceive and interpret events in dramatically different ways.
Photographs courtesy of Eric Draper/Associated Press; Rena Schild/Shutterstock; Karl_Sonnenberg/Shutterstock

and discrimination against all (cultures, women, gays, etc.) will always play a role in judgment in a society where "White privilege" is placed as what is right. White people will act as though they love you, but when it boils down to it, if you piss off the White man . . . you're just another Black man, woman, etc.

—Cecelia, 50+-year-old African American student

Two more recent cases demonstrate the different worlds in which people of color (particularly African Americans) and European Americans live. On July 6, 2016, in a routine traffic stop for a broken tail light, a police officer shot and killed Philando Castile, who was reaching for his driver's license as the officer had instructed (Louwagie, 2016). Castile initially alerted the officer to the fact that he had a license to carry a gun and did not want the officer to be alarmed if he saw one. This case gained national attention because Castile's girlfriend captured the immediate aftermath of the shooting and posted it to social media. Later, footage from a police dashboard camera revealed that Castile was indeed being calm and cooperative, yet the officer quickly escalated the situation and shot Castile to death. Moreover, the officer indicated by police radio before the stop that he was stopping the car because he thought that the driver looked like a robbery suspect (Mannix, 2016). Governor Mark Dayton was shaken by this incident and said, "Would this have happened if the driver were White, if the passengers were White? . . . I don't think it would have" (Louwagie, 2016). The officer was acquitted in the ensuing trial, despite clear evidence that contradicted the officer's account of the incident (Stahl, 2017).

Most African Americans do not experience such dramatic circumstances as the ones surrounding Philando Castile's case. However, most African Americans see the world quite differently from their European American counterparts. On April 12, 2018, two African American men (Donte Robinson and Rashon Nelson) were waiting for a business associate for a meeting at a Starbucks coffee shop. They had been in the Starbucks for less than 5 minutes when one of the men asked for the key to the restroom. The manager of the Starbucks said that the restroom was for customers only and she called the police, saying that the African American men were causing a disturbance (Madej, DiStefano, & Adelman, 2018). The business associate, Andrew Yaffee, who is European American, arrived to see his associates being taken out of the Starbucks restaurant in handcuffs. He tried to explain that the men were waiting for him for a business meeting, but the police took the two men to the police station for processing (Horton, 2018). Even after the details of this case were made public, the Philadelphia police chief defended his officers for following proper procedures. It was only after a massive nationwide outcry of the underlying racism of their actions that the chief apologized (Calvert, 2018). As Melissa DePino, who posted the video of the police arresting the two men, stated on Twitter,

> @Starbucks The police were called because these men hadn't ordered anything. They were waiting for a friend to show up, who did as they were taken out in handcuffs for doing nothing. All the other white ppl are wondering why it's never happened to us when we do the same thing. pic.twitter.com/oU4Pzs55Ci
>
> —Melissa DePino (@missydepino), European American activist

All three cases—O. J. Simpson, Philando Castile, and the Philadelphia Starbucks incident— illustrate differences in worldview, where individuals from different backgrounds perceive and interpret events in dramatically different ways.

These stories demonstrate differences in worldview between communities. This next story illustrates how an individual's worldview can change over time and with varying experiences.

> A topic that stuck with me this week was the example of how different people perceive law enforcement through worldview. The example in class mentioned how differently someone in a White neighborhood might react to a police officer as opposed to some- one in an African American neighborhood. I found this topic interesting because, as a young Latina, I was raised in a predominantly African American neighborhood, but also attended school and spent a great majority of my time as a teenager in a predomi- nantly White neighborhood, allowing me to witness both sides of this spectrum. The example in class stated that while people in White neighborhoods would most often associate law enforcement with good aspects and helpful qualities, people in an Afri- can American neighborhood would most often associate them with bad qualities and making a situation worse, for themselves and in general. I personally feel that I have witnessed and experienced both.
>
> I grew up in a neighborhood where most people were in a gang and, as in most gang run towns, I witnessed many people get arrested or get in trouble with the law. At such a young age, I did not fully get the concept of having to pay for your crimes. From my view, I just saw it as taking away people I knew and cared for. Whenever a fight would break out, most people would just let it play out because the police were seen as making it worse. If someone did call the police, they were seen as a "traitor" or a "snitch" for most likely getting someone arrested. Avoiding the police at all costs was just a known practice among everyone in the neighborhood, not a piece of advice we said out loud to each other.
>
> At eleven years old I started school in a predominantly White neighborhood where I would spend the day from seven in the morning until four in the afternoon. After a few years I would often sleep over at a friend's house on weekends to hang, or so that I would not have to wake up so early on Monday morning for school. As a result, I started to spend much time with my White friends and their families, some weeks even more time than I spent with my own family. The more I started to associate myself with them, the more I felt like them, and my view of law enforcement changed. A memory I associate with this is when one weekend while at a friend's house, my friend and I were playing in her front yard when a man who appeared to be drunk and homeless walked by and attempted to talk to us. Her mother ushered us inside and

proceeded to call the cops. They arrived quickly, arrested the man, and I could not help but actually feel relieved as her mother thanked them for their service.

—Lucy, 30+-year-old Latinx student

These differences in worldview—whether between communities, between individuals, or within an individual—all illustrate the need for a field like multicultural psychology. We hope that further reading of this book will increase your understanding of these different perspectives and how they occur. Worldview will be discussed in more detail in Chapter 3.

What Is Race?

Previously we said that most people use the word culture to refer to their race, ethnicity, or nationality. The terms culture, race, and ethnicity are often used interchangeably, but their meanings are distinctly different and their usage is often confusing. Atkinson (2004) calls them "three of the most misunderstood and misused words in the English language" (p. 5). Since they are vital to a discussion of multicultural psychology, we must try to define them and clear up some of the confusion. Let us begin by defining *race.*

biological concept of race—the perspective that a race is a group of people who share a specific combination of physical, genetically inherited characteristics that distinguish them from other groups.

sociocultural concept of race—the perspective that characteristics, values, and behaviors that have been associated with groups of people who share different physical characteristics serve the social purpose of providing a way for outsiders to view another group and for members of a group to perceive themselves.

The term race is used in two main ways—as a **biological concept** and as a **sociocultural concept**. Zuckerman (1990) said, "To the biologist, a race, or subspecies, is an inbreeding, geographically isolated population that differs in distinguishable physical traits from other members of the species" (p. 1297). Biologically speaking, a race is a group of people who share a specific combination of physical, genetically inherited characteristics that distinguish them from other groups (Casas, 1984). From this biological perspective, human beings are divided into the main racial groupings used in the United States today—Black, White, Asian, Latinx, and American Indian.

As long ago as ancient Egypt, human beings attempted to describe and classify themselves ("Historical Definitions," 2011). The scientific notion of race as a biological construct was first developed during the Age of Enlightenment. It became very popular during that time and in the centuries that followed to create taxonomies of the human species. By the late 19th century, several of these classification systems existed, the simplest with only 2 categories and the most complex with 63 (Darwin, 1871).

Most of these early taxonomies placed humans in categories based on superficial phenotypic characteristics, such as skin color, hair texture, shape of nose, shape of eyes, and size of lips. One of the most influential categorizations, which still influences conceptualizations of race today, came from Johann Friedrich Blumenbach (1752–1840), who placed human beings into five categories based on the shape of the skull: the Caucasian, or white race; the Mongolian, or yellow race; the Malayan, or brown race; the Ethiopian, or Negro or black race; and the American, or red race. Blumenbach believed that physical factors such as skin color and skull shape interacted with environmental factors such as geographic location, exposure to the sun, and diet to produce the different racial groups (Blumenbach, 1775/1795/1865).

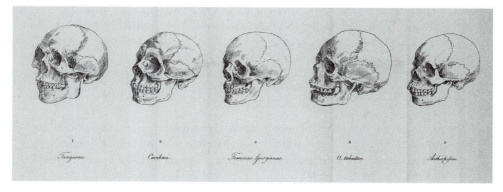

Blumenbach's five races, from *De generis humani varietate nativa* (*On the natural varieties of mankind*, 1775).

By the 18th century, scientists began to include behavioral and psychological characteristics in their classifications of race. The Great Chain of Being, an idea from Christian Western Europe in the medieval era, was the belief in a hierarchical structure of all life. Those nearest the top of the hierarchy were considered closest to perfection, or to God ("Great Chain of Being," 2011). This idea crept into racial categorizations in which Christian Europeans were placed at the top of the chain. Characteristics assigned to groups lower in the chain were often derogatory and demeaning. Thus, society assigned a value to these characteristics, which eventually led to notions of racial inferiority and superiority and to justification of the unfair treatment of different racial groups ("Historical Definitions," 2011), such as the enslavement of Black Africans. Such beliefs were widely spread and passed down from generation to generation, so that today, groups such as African Americans still struggle to combat stereotypes about their racial inferiority.

The inclusion of behavioral and psychological characteristics in the taxonomies, along with the value judgments placed on these characteristics and the resulting differential treatment of various human groups, led to the sociocultural construct of race. The assignment of dispositional and intellectual characteristics to the racial groups was not completely arbitrary. It came from observations (albeit biased ones) of the behavior of the different groups. The sociocultural meaning of the term race also came from the migration of various groups to different parts of the globe. Because of the resulting geographic isolation and inbreeding, these groups developed not only similar physical characteristics, but also their own unique set of values, beliefs, and practices—in other words, different cultures.

Today, results of genetic studies indicate that the physiological differences among racial groups are superficial and that as human beings we have far more genetic similarities than differences (Latter, 1980; Zuckerman, 1990). Variation within different racial groups is far greater than is variation among the groups (Jorde & Wooding, 2004). Estimates indicate that 88–90% percent of genetic variation occurs within local populations, whereas only 10–12% is between populations (Angier, 2000). This means that two people from different groups may share more similarities than two people from the same group. Most respected scholars currently acknowledge that human beings came from the same beginnings in Africa and that genetic differences among groups can be explained by patterns of migration and adaptation as groups moved farther away from that point of origin (Angier, 2000; Begley, 1995; Diamond, 1997). The American Anthropological Association concluded that "race is not a legitimate biological or genetic construct; rather, it is an ideology used to justify the domination of one identifiable group of people by another" (American Anthropological Association, 1999, as cited in J. Miller & Garran, 2008, p. 15). In other words, there really is only one biological race . . . the human race (Atkinson, 2004; Fish, 2002).

Although a biological definition of race has little evidence to support it, once the broad categories were drawn and the idea of significant genetic differences among groups was propagated, the term took on sociocultural significance.

> The concept of race has taken on important social meaning in terms of how outsiders view members of a "racial" group and how individuals within a "racial" group view themselves, members of their group, and members of other "racial" groups. . . . Thus, the *term* race survives despite the lack of a scientific basis because it continues to serve one purpose or another for those who use it. (Atkinson, 2004, p. 8)

Helms (1990) called such purposes the psychological implications of racial group membership.

Thus, race, rather than being a biological fact, is a sociocultural concept. This means that the term exists because it has become useful in our interpersonal, group, and societal relationships. Atkinson (2004) noted that its sociocultural use continues because it provides people a way of organizing the world and reducing complexity, and for some groups it provides a vehicle for identity and empowerment. Because of confusion between the two definitions of race, there has been much debate in the psychological literature about the appropriateness of its use (e.g., Helms & Talleyrand, 1997; Yee, Fairchild, Weizmann, & Wyatt, 1993; Zuckerman, 1990).

The term **ethnicity** is often used interchangeably with race and culture. Technically, ethnicity refers to the combination of race and culture, because ethnicity is determined by both physical and cultural characteristics (Atkinson, 2004; Phinney, 1996). Individuals may be from the same racial group but come from different cultures, leading to their particular ethnicity. For example, Black people are all of African descent but now live all over the world in various cultures. Racially they are *Black*, but depending on what part of the world they grew up in, they are from different cultures, leading to separate and distinct ethnic groups. Thus, we have Afro-Cubans, Afro-Brazilians, and African Americans. That is why racial categories can be confusing. If a Black person from Cuba is filling out a survey in the United States and is asked to check his or her race, which one does he or she check—Black or Latinx? He or she is both. To select just one is misleading and inaccurate. The following story illustrates this dilemma:

ethnicity—a combination of race and culture.

> In my country, we also have lots and lots of ethnicity groups, and one ethnicity group may physically look like another group (e.g., Javanese and Sudanese), or very different (e.g., Chinese and Javanese). It is considered very rude, even it may be interpreted as a racial slur, to directly ask a person, "What are you? Are you Chinese?" We are expected to be able to infer a person's ethnicity from the person's physical appearances, or the dialect he/she speaks, or the accent he/she has. I rarely, if ever, encountered a form in Indonesia where it asked me to fill in my ethnicity. Yes, it is an issue, but we never think it should be explicitly put on paper.
>
> The first few weeks after I got here [to the United States], I was in this class where a student handed out a survey questionnaire for us to fill in. I filled out all questions

in the demographic sheet without any problem, except the question that asked about my ethnicity. There were several choices there (Asian, African American, Caucasian, Chinese, Hispanic, etc.). I was quite confused to have a question like that in front of me. I think of myself as "Chinese-Indonesian" . . . what's the difference between "Chinese" and "Asian?" . . . Besides, I don't see myself as either of those, I'm Chinese-Indonesian. I remember thinking at that time, "Wouldn't anyone in this room get offended with this question?" I felt quite weird because I never had to put "what I am" on a piece of paper, in a category. Luckily one of the choices was "Other," so I just checked that one. Although thinking that I am an "Other" was quite unsettling, but I just didn't think I fell into any other categories. I suppose I can always put myself as "Chinese," but "Chinese" is different from "Chinese-Indonesian." I don't even speak Chinese fluently.

—Maya, 20+-year-old Chinese Indonesian student

It should also be recognized that people have more than one identity. We have an identity related to each major demographic characteristic—race, ethnicity, social class, gender, age, religion, sexual orientation, and so on. We are simultaneously members of each of these groups, and each identity influences the other. For example, the experiences of a Black, gay male cannot be fully understood by examining each of these identities independently. As a male, he is in the dominant group, but by being gay and African American he may experience both homophobia and racism. Navigating each of these identities constitutes a unique experience. Change one identity and you change the person's experience (a European American gay male versus a European American heterosexual male, etc.) To fully understand a person's experience, we must look at the interactions between these identities. This is known as the *intersection of identities*, or **intersectionality** (see Chapter 7) (Crenshaw, 1989; Gopaldas, 2013).

intersectionality—the meaningful ways in which various social statuses interact (e.g., race, gender, social class) and result in differing experiences with oppression and privilege.

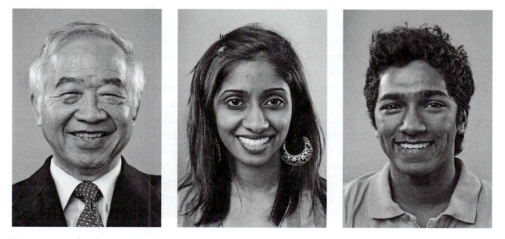

To some people, the concept of race is biological, whereas to others, it is a social construction.
Photographs by Daxiao Productions/Shutterstock

Multicultural Psychology and Related Fields

Our goal has been to define *multicultural* psychology. So far, we have broken the term down into its components, stating that psychology is the systematic study of behavior, cognition, and affect; multi- and -al mean pertaining to many; and culture refers to the values, beliefs, and practices of a group of people that are shared through symbols and passed down from generation to generation. If we put all that together, we can define multicultural psychology as the systematic study of all aspects of human behavior as it occurs in settings where people of different backgrounds interact. Multicultural psychologists are concerned with "the psychological reactions of individuals and groups caught up in culturally heterogeneous settings" including the "behaviors, perceptions, feelings, beliefs, and attitudes" that result from living in such conditions (Bochner, 1999, p. 21).

Our definition of multicultural psychology states that the field is interested in what happens when people of different backgrounds interact with one another. Bochner (1999) defined **culture contact** as "critical incidents where people from different cultural, ethnic, or linguistic backgrounds come into social contact with each other" (p. 22) and described two broad categories of contacts: (a) contacts that occur between members of a culturally diverse society or between people of many different backgrounds who live and work together on a daily basis; and (b) contacts that occur when people from one society visit another country, for purposes such as business, tourism, study, or assistance (e.g., Peace Corps). Multicultural psychology is interested in both types of cultural contact, although it emphasizes the first type.

> **culture contact**—critical incidents in which people from different cultures come into social contact with one another either (a) by living and working with one another on a daily basis or (b) through visiting other countries on a temporary basis, such as for business, tourism, or study.

Several terms in the literature are similar to multicultural psychology. **Ethnic minority psychology** is the study of "issues relevant to racial and ethnic groups that have been historically subordinated, underrepresented, or underserved" (para 1, American Psychological Association, 2018). Although this term is still used, there was movement in the field away from ethnic minority psychology to multicultural psychology sometime during the 1990s (Iijima Hall, 2014). This shift took place for several reasons. One reason was to strengthen ties and develop allies across the various racial/ethnic groups. Another was to move beyond race and ethnicity and be more inclusive of other identities related to gender, religion, sexual orientation, etc. (Franklin, 2009). In addition, the term *minority* has come to have a negative connotation when referring to people of color. This is not statistically accurate. When looking at the global population, people of color make up a statistical majority. Even within the United States, in five states people of color constitute the majority, and census projections predict that by the year 2044, the United States as a whole will be a *majority-minority* country (U.S. Census Bureau, 2015). The term minority also carries a negative connotation and implies that one group is of lesser status than another, which can lead people in these groups to feel less powerful. In short, the term multicultural psychology is seen as more inclusive, more accurate, and more empowering.

> **ethnic minority psychology**—the study of issues relevant to racial and ethnic groups that have historically been marginalized, oppressed, and underserved.

Other related terms represent different subdisciplines within the field of psychology. **Cultural psychology** is concerned with how local cultural practices shape psychological processes. In other words, cultural psychology studies what

> **cultural psychology**—the study of how unique practices within a culture shape behavior, cognition, and affect.

is unique within a culture. In contrast, **cross-cultural psychology** is interested in cultural comparisons and searching for the universality of psychological processes, or what is similar or different across cultures (Heine & Ruby, 2010). Although some might disagree, multicultural psychology can be seen as the broad umbrella under which these other areas fall.

cross-cultural psychology—the search for universal principles of human behavior, cognition, and affect, or for what is common across cultures.

Multiculturalism as a Philosophy

The idea of multiculturalism goes beyond the field of psychology. The term applies to settings in which more than one culture exists and represents a set of beliefs about how those groups should coexist (Heywood, 2007; Parekh, 2000). As a philosophy, multiculturalism has influenced a wide range of disciplines, including education (e.g., Banks & Banks, 2004), political science (e.g., Parekh, 2000), and medicine (e.g., Wear, 2003). It is a complex concept that has been discussed in many ways, without consensus about what it entails (Fowers & Davidov, 2006; Parekh, 2000). Nonetheless, the basic assumptions of multiculturalism can be summarized as tolerance, respect, inclusion, sensitivity, and equity (see Table 1.1).

Today, the term *tolerance* has come to mean a fair, open, and objective attitude toward people and ideas that differ from yours (Dictionary.com). This often refers to religious tolerance, or allowing individuals of different faiths to practice their beliefs freely and openly. However, many people believe that simple tolerance is not enough and that there is a need to move beyond tolerance to other ideals. One student expressed some of the limitations associated with using tolerance as a goal of multiculturalism.

> I thought it was interesting that we talked about the word "tolerance" in class because I have always thought that the word "tolerance" is not a very good word for creating and encouraging equality among people. I feel like you have to deal with it, stand it, but you don't have to understand or like it. It is interesting to think that we want to create "equality" in our country but there is still a lot of racism and prejudice, and not a very good attitude toward fixing it, especially if we are using terms like "tolerance"

TABLE 1.1   **Multiculturalism as a Philosophy: Basic Assumptions**

Tolerance: A fair, open, and objective attitude toward people and ideas that differ from yours

Respect: To value, appreciate, and show regard or consideration for differences

Inclusion: Active efforts to reverse the historical exclusion of certain groups in society

Sensitivity: Awareness that cultural differences exist and taking these differences into account in our interactions

Equity: Equal access to opportunities and resources; this includes providing extra assistance to those who have historically not been given equal access

Empowerment: Helping members of marginalized and mistreated groups stand up for their rights

Social justice: Efforts aimed at providing equal distribution of rights, privileges, opportunities, and resources within a society

Social change: Widespread change in the institutions, behaviors, and relationships within a society rather than respect. I think we should be teaching respect of people's culture, and choices rather than "tolerance." To me, that word is just a half-hearted attempt to make good.

—Shelby, 20+-year-old mixed European American/Latinx student

As Shelby points out, tolerance implies putting up with something we really do not like. What would the world be like if we simply tolerated one another? Tolerance should be the minimum goal, a starting point. Dr. Joseph White (2001) stated the goal should not be tolerance but *mutual enrichment*. Putnam (2007) agreed: "Tolerance for difference is but a first step. To strengthen shared identities, we need more opportunities for meaningful interactions across ethnic lines where Americans (new and old) work, learn, recreate, and live" (p. 164). Although tolerance is a basic value of multiculturalism, we must move beyond it and learn to respect, value, and appreciate differences.

Inclusion refers to the realization that certain groups have historically been excluded from participation in mainstream society. Therefore, active efforts must be made to reverse this exclusion. For example, the purpose of the Americans with Disabilities Act (1990) is to prevent discrimination against individuals with physical and mental challenges. Under this law, public buildings must include structural accommodations so people with disabilities have access, and employers may not discriminate against individuals with disabilities in their hiring practices. Multiculturalism also stresses the importance of *sensitivity* to the values, beliefs, and practices of varied groups. For example, sensitivity to issues of gender means using gender-inclusive language, such as chair of the board instead of chairman, or understanding when a woman misses work because her child is sick. Finally, *equity* means that all people should have equal access to the same resources and opportunities, such as quality housing, food, education, and health care.

> I have learned that the language we use to promote multiculturalism can be problematic and that we must replace terminology as "teaching tolerance" with the words "fostering appreciation." You see, people who sense that they are being "tolerated" don't feel welcome, but people who know that they are being "appreciated" feel that they have an honored place at the table.
>
> —Dr. Mark S. Kiselica, psychology professor (as cited in D. W. Sue & D. Sue, 2013, p. 14)

Equity and *equality* are not the same thing, although both are related to the idea of fairness. The concept of equality harkens back to the basic American ideal that all men are created equal. It is the belief that everyone has equal access to resources and opportunities and can take advantage of them if they choose. Equality assumes everyone starts at the same level. Equity, however, recognizes that not everyone has equal access. Historically, some individuals have been excluded or lack the knowledge, finances, or training necessary to take advantage of these opportunities. Therefore, equity means providing remedies for the past injustices to level the playing field. Examples include providing classes in English as a second language in schools and targeting scholarships to students from poor families. Equality says that per-student funding at every school should be the same; equity says that students who come from less should get more to help them catch up. Equality is fairness as uniform distribution, whereas equity is fairness as justice (Kranich, 2005; Mann, 2014).

Multiculturalism as a philosophy goes beyond simple belief in concepts such as inclusion, sensitivity, and equity. It is also important to take action to ensure these ideas become reality. In other words, it is not enough to talk about the issues; we must actively work to reduce behaviors such as discrimination and oppression. From this action-oriented perspective, multiculturalism also involves the ideas of *empowerment, social justice,* and *social change* (Banks, 2010; Gorski, 2010).

Empowerment means helping individuals from marginalized, disenfranchised, and mistreated groups stand up for their rights and fight for equal treatment. It means putting pressure on people in power to share that power. Social justice means working toward equity, where every citizen is treated fairly and has equal access to the rights, privileges, opportunities, and resources available within society. Achieving these goals requires widespread social change. Gorski (2010) noted that social change occurs through transformation of the self, social institutions, and society. In terms of self, this means individuals work to reduce and eliminate personal prejudices and discriminatory behaviors. On a social institutional level, this means implementing policies and practices in schools, corporations, government, etc., to ensure everyone receives fair treatment. On a societal level, it means creating an environment that is inclusive, in which differences are valued and respected, where all members can live, work, and thrive

Equality treats everyone the same, regardless of circumstances, whereas *equity* considers differing needs. We must have equity before we can achieve true equality. *Illustration by Mary Quandt*

side by side. In other words, multiculturalism is more than a philosophy; it is a "social, intellectual, and moral movement" (Fowers & Davidov, 2006, p. 581), where these basic values are seen as goals to be achieved.

These values—respect, inclusion, sensitivity, equity, empowerment, social justice, and social change—represent core values in the field of multicultural psychology, and you will see them infused throughout this book. In considering these values, you might ask, as scientists, aren't psychologists supposed to be objective? If psychologists espouse certain values, doesn't that make them biased? Yes, as scientists, psychologist do their best to reduce the effects of bias on their research. However, multicultural psychologists acknowledge that complete objectivity is impossible and believe that scientists should be open about the values that drive their work. (This idea is discussed further in Chapter 2). All fields of study are founded on a core set of values, but the values are not always explicitly understood or communicated. For example, physicians take the Hippocratic oath to do no harm. Lawyers in the United States operate under the motto "innocent until proven guilty." Even in science, the goal of being objective includes a value judgment. Therefore, multicultural psychology is explicit about the values it espouses and how these values guide theory, research, and practice in the field.

Do We Still Need the Field of Multicultural Psychology?

After the election of Barack Obama as the first African American president of the United States, a question arose as to whether we now live in a postracial society (e.g., Cillizza, 2014; Mio, 2016; S. Steele, 2008; Thernstorm, 2008). In other words, did Obama's election prove that race is no longer a significant issue? Have we progressed to the point where differences such as race, gender, and sexual orientation no longer matter? If so, would that mean we no longer need a field like multicultural psychology? Research results confirm that people's belief in the racial progress of America increased following Obama's election (Kaiser, Drury, Spalding, Cheryan, & O'Brien, 2009), but let's take a closer look at the evidence.

Although he never said so directly, Obama essentially portrayed himself as a postracial candidate (Cillizza, 2014; Mio, 2016; S. Steele, 2008). This message was first conveyed in his keynote address at the Democratic National Convention in 2004. Obama said that, as the son of a White mother from Kansas and a Black father from Kenya, he embodied the diversity and opportunity of America. He also expressed the belief that America no longer had to be a country divided along political and racial lines and in the values of unity and equality.

> Tonight we gather to affirm the greatness of our nation not because of the height of our skyscrapers or the power of our military, or the size of our economy; our pride is based on a very simple premise, summed up in a declaration made over two hundred years ago: "We hold these truths to be self-evident, that all men are created equal." . . . It is that fundamental belief—I am my brother's keeper, I am my sister's keeper—that makes this country work. It's what allows us to pursue our individual dreams, yet still come together as a single American family: "E pluribus unum," out of many, one. . . . There's not a liberal America and a conservative America; there's the United States of America. There's not a Black America and White America and Latino America and Asian America; there's the United States of America. . . . We are one people, all of us pledging allegiance to the Stars and Stripes, all of us defending the United States of America. (Obama, 2004)

Obama embodied a *racial idealism* and his election signaled a hope that America could put its racist past behind (S. Steele, 2008).

Even as Obama painted himself as a unifying force for the country and as his election was touted as proof of racial progress, other evidence indicated that race (and other forms of diversity) continued to be a major dividing factor in the United States. There were many reports of racist incidents during Obama's campaigns and presidency, including racial epithets scrawled on homes, racist campaign slogans and signs, figures of Obama hung from trees, crosses burned on lawns, death threats against Obama supporters, and chants of "assassinate Obama" (e.g., Associated Press, 2008; Goodale, 2012; Merida, 2008). Other evidence comes from statistics regarding the continued disparities between groups in education, income, employment, health, civic engagement, and social justice (National Urban League, 2014). Additional signs of discord include the cases of Philando Castile discussed earlier in the chapter, as well as those of Trayvon Martin, Michael Brown, Eric Garner, Freddie Gray, and Sandra Bland. Tensions in the United States were also illustrated by the racist remarks that flooded the Internet after a Mexican American boy sang the national anthem at the finals of the National Basketball Association (C. Rodriguez, 2013), a

Cheerios commercial depicted an interracial family (Goyette, 2013), and an Indian American woman won the Miss America pageant (Botelho, 2013; Judkis, 2013). These events signify that the United States still has a way to go in embracing its multicultural identity.

Events during the campaign, election, and presidency of Donald Trump also provide evidence of continued tensions around issues of diversity in the United States. When Donald Trump first declared his candidacy, most people did not take it seriously. He was an unconventional, controversial candidate who broke all the rules. However, Trump defied the odds and went all the way to cinch the Republican nomination and beat Hillary Clinton for the presidency. Social analysts and research results indicate Trump won by appealing to poor and working-class European Americans who felt disenfranchised during Obama's presidency. Trump appealed to people's economic anxieties, cultural fears, and class rebellion (Cox, Lienesch, & Jones, 2017; Wead, 2017; Zakaria, 2017). Author, activist, and CNN commentator Van Jones called it *whitelash*, or the backlash of European American voters against a Black president, against minorities in general, and against a changing country (Patel, 2016).

This whitelash was vividly illustrated when one of the largest White supremacist rallies in decades took place in Charlottesville, Virginia, in August 2017. The Unite the Right rally was organized by Jason Kessler, a White nationalist, and advertised as a protest against the City of Charlottesville's decision to remove a statue of Robert E. Lee, a civil war hero. The rally promotors said the protest was about free speech and the freedom to honor and preserve the history of the Confederacy. Right-wing groups from all over the country gathered in Charlottesville, including Neo-Nazis and the Ku Klux Klan. On Friday night, they marched on the University of Virginia's campus, carrying burning tiki torches and chanting slogans such as, "White lives matter" and "blood and soil." The next morning, the alt-right groups gathered again for their planned rally and were met by a large group of counterprotesters. Violence erupted between the two sides throughout the morning while local law enforcement allegedly stood by and did nothing. The violence went on for two hours and culminated when 20-year-old James Alex Fields drove his car into a crowd of counterprotesters, injuring 19 and killing 1, 32-year-old Heather Heyer (Faucet & Feuer, 2017; Moskowitz, 2017; Pearson, Cloud, & Armengol, 2017). People in the United States and across the globe were astonished and disturbed to see images harkening back to the postslavery Jim Crow era and the civil rights movement. Individuals who were alive at that time expressed dismay that the United States seemed to be moving backward instead of forward (Carey, 2017; Mitchell, 2017).

Some people have critiqued Donald Trump's campaign slogan, Make America Great Again (McGirt, 2016; Smiley, 2016). Radio and television host Tavis Smiley (2016) asked,

> To what specific period of American greatness are you wanting us to return? When Black folk suffered segregation after slavery? When women had no right to vote or control their own bodies? When gay brothers and lesbian sisters felt ceaseless hate? When we stole land from the Native Americans? When we sent Japanese families to internment camps? When America lynched Mexicans? I just need Trump to give me some clarity on the time period he wishes to travel back to. (para. 5)

Overall, the policies of the Trump administration communicate a lack of support for multicultural issues, including anti-immigration, eroding protections for the LGBTQ community, support of police brutality, and dismantling of affirmative action (BBC News, 2017; J. Keller & Pierce, 2017; On the Issues, n.d.). His attitudes and beliefs are evident not only in his political agenda, but also in statements he has made, such as saying Ghazala Khan, the mother of slain

U.S Army captain Humayun Khan, did not speak while standing beside her husband at the Democratic National Convention because she was forbidden to do so because they are Muslim, or insinuating that federal judge Gonzalo Curiel was biased in the case against Trump University because he was Mexican (even though Curiel is an American citizen, born in the United States). Trump consistently argued that Obama was not born in the United States. He initially refused to denounce the support of White nationalist and former Ku Klux Klan leader David Duke during his campaign. He stated that a Black Lives Matter protester deserved to be beaten and that Trump supporters who beat up a Latinx man were simply passionate and got carried away. He was caught on tape making sexist remarks about women, such as commenting that when you are a star you can grab women "by the p***y . . . you can do anything." He has referred to women as fat pigs, dogs, and slobs and he admitted that women made it on his show *The Apprentice* because of their sex appeal (Lusher, 2016; O'Connor & Marans, 2016). In response to the violence in Charlottesville, he claimed responsibility lay with "all sides," equating hate-mongering right-wing groups with antiracism counterprotesters (Faucet & Feuer, 2017; Moskowitz, 2017; Pearson, Cloud, & Armengol, 2017).

Some may dismiss Trump as a single individual or the alt-right as a fringe group that does not represent the majority of people in the United States. Nonetheless, enough people agreed with Trump's views to vote him into office and an atmosphere was created in which extreme right-wing groups have become "emboldened, angrier, and more militant" (Moskowitz, 2017, para. 7). Thus, it seems we need a field like multicultural psychology now more than ever.

Population statistics confirm the United States is a multicultural society. According to the U.S. Census Bureau (Cohn & Caumont, 2016), the population of the United States is currently 61.3% European American (not Hispanic or Latinx), 13.3% Black or African American, 5.7% Asian, 1.3% American Indian or Alaska Native, and 0.2% Native Hawaiian or Other Pacific Islander. The census no longer includes Hispanic as a racial category in acknowledgment that people from all racial groups may have Hispanic or Latinx origins. As a result, 17.8% of the population responded that they were Hispanic or Latinx. Although the population of most groups increased since the 2010 census, the largest increases were in the Asian and Hispanic/Latinx groups. Census projections indicate that the European American population will decline and the other racial/ethnic groups will grow to the point where all groups of color combined will outnumber the European American population. According to the Pew Research Center, this change will occur by the year 2055 (Cohn & Caumont, 2016), but the U.S. Census Bureau (2015) projected it will happen even sooner, by the year 2044. In other words, sometime in this century, the United States will become a majority-minority country. Five states already have majority-minority populations—California, New Mexico, Hawaii, Texas, and Nevada—and several more are poised to do so in the near future, including Maryland and Georgia (DeVore, 2015; Maciag, 2015; D. Poston & Saenz, 2017). The youngest members of the U.S. population—those under the age of 1—reached majority-minority status (50.4%) in 2011 (U.S. Census Bureau, 2012a).

This increasing diversification is a result of two primary forces—immigration rates and differential birthrates (Cohn & Caumont, 2016; D. W. Sue & Sue, 1999). Since the Pilgrims arrived at Plymouth Rock, the population of the United States has been greatly influenced by immigration. According to the Pew Research Center, approximately 14% of the U.S. population is foreign born, up from just 5% in 1965. In the past 5 years, nearly 59 million immigrants have come to the United States, most from Latin America and Asia (Cohn & Caumont, 2016). Unlike the early immigrants to this country, mostly White Europeans who easily assimilated into mainstream culture, current immigrants are from more visible racial and ethnic groups that are not as easily assimilated (Atkinson, 2004).

People of color also have higher birthrates. According to the Centers for Disease Control and Prevention (2016), in 2015 the average number of births per 1,000 women was 9.7 for American Indians or Alaska Natives, 10.7 for European Americans (not Hispanic/Latinx), 14.0 for Asians or Pacific Islanders, 14.2 for Blacks (not Hispanic/Latinx), and 16.3 for Hispanics/Latinxs. In addition, the number of babies born to parents from different racial backgrounds is also on the rise; multiracial births went from 1% of all births in 1970 to 10% in 2013 (Pew Research Center, 2015). These statistics indicate that the numbers of people of color are increasing at a faster rate than that of European Americans and help explain what R. Rodriguez (2002) refers to as the *browning of America*.

The first Indian American to win the Miss American pageant, Nina Davuluri, was the target of racist attacks. *Photograph courtesy of Nick Lisi/AP/Corbis*

Multiculturalism as the Fourth Force

Paul Pedersen (1990, 1991), a leading multicultural psychologist, proposed that multiculturalism is the **fourth force** in psychology. What does he mean? In psychology, the term *force* is used to describe a theory that has a huge influence on the field and precipitates a **paradigm shift**, or major change, in the way people think about human behavior.

The notion that multiculturalism is the fourth force suggests that this perspective will have just as big an impact on the field of psychology as the first three forces—psychoanalysis, behaviorism, and humanism (Table 1.2). Pedersen (1990, 1991) does not see multiculturalism as replacing the other three theories, but as adding a fourth dimension to psychology to supplement and, ideally, to strengthen the other three. According to Pedersen, labeling multiculturalism the fourth force "explores the possibility that we are moving toward a generic theory of multiculturalism that recognizes the psychological consequences of each cultural context, where each behavior has been learned and is displayed . . . and calls attention to the way in which a culture-centered perspective has changed the way we look at psychology across fields and theories" (1999, p. xxii).

I have always viewed Miss America as the girl next door, but the girl next door is evolving as the diversity in America evolves. She's not who she was 10 years ago, and she's not going to be the same person come 10 years down the road.
—Nina Davuluri, Miss America 2013 (Botelho, 2013)

multiculturalism as the fourth force—the idea that multicultural psychology is so important that it will fundamentally change the direction of the field of psychology, as psychoanalysis, behaviorism, and humanism did.

paradigm shift—a major change in the way people think about a field.

The notion that multiculturalism is the fourth force [creating a paradigm shift in psychology] suggests that this perspective will have just as big an impact on the field of psychology as the first three forces.
—Paul Pedersen, a leading multicultural psychologist

TABLE 1.2 **Multicultural Psychology as a Fourth Force**

Force	Name of theory	Key theorists
First force	Psychoanalysis	Freud
Second force	Behaviorism	Pavlov, Thorndike, Watson, Skinner
Third force	Humanism	Rogers
Fourth force	Multiculturalism	Sue, Pedersen, White, Ivey, Bernal, Trimble

In other words, calling multiculturalism the fourth force challenges us to acknowledge that (a) all behavior occurs in and is impacted by a cultural context; (b) until recently, this fact has virtually been ignored by the field; and (c) once we understand the nature and contribution of culture, this understanding will dramatically alter and expand the way we study and understand behavior. Pedersen and other multicultural psychologists believe it is no longer possible for psychologists to ignore their own culture or the cultures of their clients and research participants. A multicultural perspective makes our understanding of human behavior more clear and meaningful, rather than more obscure and awkward. According to Pedersen (1999), "The main goal of [multicultural psychology] is to convince general psychology that culture is an important contributor to the development of human behavior, and to our understanding and study of it" (p. 6). Thus, identifying multiculturalism as the fourth force in psychology attempts to place it at the center of the field.

Understanding the Cultural Context of Behavior: The Biopsychosocial Model

One of the major tenets of multicultural psychology is that all behavior occurs in a cultural context. Therefore, to fully understand human behavior, we must understand its cultural context. Culture influences everything.

The **biopsychosocial model** helps explain the effect of culture on behavior. This model grew out of behavioral medicine and health psychology and focuses on an understanding of the psychological, social, and biological factors that contribute to illness and that can be utilized in the treatment and prevention of illness and the promotion of wellness (Engel, 1977; G. E. Schwartz, 1982). Although the model originally focused on an understanding of physical illnesses, it is also very useful in understanding psychological illnesses. Let us take a closer look at this model.

biopsychosocial model—a model of human behavior that takes into consideration biological, cognitive-affective, social-interpersonal, social institutional, and cultural factors.

On the morning of May 5, 2004, David Reimer retrieved a shotgun from his home while his wife, Jane, was at work, took it into the garage, and sawed off the barrel. He then drove to the nearby parking lot of a grocery store, parked, raised the gun, and shot himself. He was 38 years old. What led David to such despair that he decided to end his own life?

Press reports cited an array of reasons for his despair: bad investments, marital problems, his twin brother's death two years earlier. Surprisingly little emphasis was given to the extraordinary circumstances of his upbringing. This was unfortunate, because to truly understand David's suicide you first need to know his anguished history, chronicled in the book, *As Nature Made Him: The Boy Who Was Raised as a Girl,* by John Colapinto (2000).

David Reimer was one of the most famous patients in medical history. He was 8 months old when a doctor doing a routine circumcision accidentally removed his entire penis. David's parents were referred to a leading expert on gender identity, psychologist Dr. John Money, who recommended a surgical sex change from male to female and the administration of female hormones to further feminize David's body. David became the ultimate experiment to prove that nurture, not nature, determines gender identity and sexual orientation. His twin brother, Brian, provided a perfect matched control.

Dr. Money continued to treat David and, according to his published reports through the 1970s, the experiment was a success. David, who had been renamed Brenda, was portrayed as a happy little girl. The reality was far more complicated. "Brenda" angrily tore off dresses, refused to play with dolls, beat up her twin brother, and seized his toy cars and guns. In school she was relentlessly teased for her masculine gait, tastes, and behaviors. The other children would not let her use either the boys' or the girls' restroom, so she had to go

in the back alley. She complained to her parents and teachers that she felt like a boy. Brenda was also traumatized by her yearly visits to Dr. Money, who used pictures of naked adults to "reinforce" Brenda's gender identity and who pressed her to have further surgery on her "vagina." Meanwhile, Brenda's guilt-ridden mother attempted suicide, her father lapsed into alcoholism, and the neglected twin brother, Brian, eventually descended into drug use, petty crime, and clinical depression.

When Brenda was 14, a local psychiatrist finally convinced the parents to tell Brenda/David the truth. David later said about the revelation, "Suddenly it all made sense why I felt the way I did. I wasn't some sort of weirdo. I wasn't crazy."

David went through the painful process of converting back to his biological sex, yet was still very troubled and attempted suicide twice in his 20s. He eventually married, but he was not easy to live with, given his explosive

David Reimer was raised as Brenda after a botched circumcision. *Photograph courtesy of Reuters/CORBIS*

anger, fears of abandonment, feelings of sexual inadequacy, and continued depressive episodes. At about the age of 30, David received help from a rival psychologist of Dr. Money, Dr. Milton Diamond at the University of Hawaii, but he continued to have difficulties. In the spring of 2002, his twin brother died of an overdose of antidepressant medication. Then, in the fall of 2003, David was cheated out of $65,000 by an alleged con man. The last straw seemed to come on May 2, 2004, when after 14 years of a difficult marriage, David's wife told him she wanted a separation. Two days later, David ended his own suffering. (adapted from Colapinto, 2004, and "David Reimer," 2004)

Many factors contributed to David Reimer's suicide. The biopsychosocial model helps put those factors into perspective. The biopsychosocial model says that behavior can be understood on many levels (see Figure 1.1). The first is the *biological level*. At the most basic level, our behavior is influenced by our physiological and genetic makeup. When we lack certain nutrients, our body sends us signals that something is out of balance and must be corrected. For example, if we do not have enough fluids in our body, we feel thirsty and are motivated to drink. If our body lacks fuel, we feel hungry and we eat. The behaviors of eating and drinking are linked to basic biological needs. Our behavior is also influenced by our genetic makeup.

There was evidently a strong genetic component to David Reimer's depression. His mother and brother suffered from depression, and his father may have as well. It is possible that his father was self-medicating his depression through alcohol abuse. Research clearly indicates that depressive disorders tend to run in families (M. D. Keller et al., 1986). Perhaps David Reimer inherited a biological predisposition to depression from one or both of his parents. His unusual life circumstances brought it out for him and for his brother.

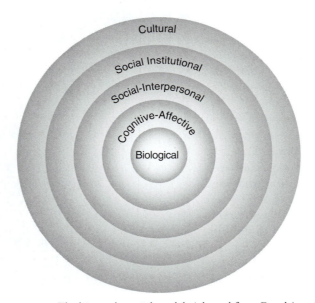

FIGURE 1.1   The biopsychosocial model. Adapted from Engel (1977) and Myers (1986).

The second level of the biopsychosocial model is the *cognitive-affective level.* Cognitions refer to our thoughts but include all our basic mental processes, such as memories, perceptions, and beliefs. *Affect* refers to feelings or emotions. This level examines the effect our thoughts and feelings have on our behavior. The connection between one's mental or psychological state and physical health has long been established. For example, we know that when we are stressed, our immune system is weakened and we are more likely to get sick. You have probably had the experience of coming down with a cold during or immediately after a particularly stressful week at school.

The cognitive-affective level is the level at which most people understand and think about mental disorder, because most of what we know and study in the field of psychology occurs at this level. Currently, the most popular theory of depression is the cognitive theory, proposed by Aaron Beck (1967, 1970). Beck proposed that depression is associated with and maintained by negative thinking patterns. Beck noticed that depressed people exhibited what he labeled the **negative cognitive triad**, or a negative view of the self, the world, and the future. He also noticed that depressed people made many *cognitive errors*, or distortions of reality. One example of a cognitive error is *overgeneralization*, wherein a person draws global conclusions about his or her worth, ability, or performance on the basis of a single fact.

> **negative cognitive triad**—Beck's label for the negative view depressed individuals tend to have of themselves, the world, and the future.

For instance, David Reimer may have concluded that because he did not have a penis, he was less of a man and would never be able to have a normal, happy, satisfying married life. According to Beck, such negative and distorted thoughts lead to negative or depressed feelings. Once people get caught in this negative cycle, it is very hard for them to get out. Even after David met and married Jane, he was still plagued by feelings of low self-esteem and sexual inadequacy.

The third level of the biopsychosocial model is the *social-interpersonal level*, which focuses on the impact of social relationships on our behavior. For example, the various approaches to marriage and family therapy emphasize that the problems of individual family members are the result of the interpersonal dynamics of the entire family system, or the unique pattern of interactions among family members. There was an interpersonal component to David Reimer's depression. His family relationships likely influenced his depression as he interacted with his alcohol-abusing father, his guilt-ridden mother, and his neglected brother. In addition, David was the recipient of relentless teasing and cruelty from his peers, which likely also had affected the development of his depression.

The fourth level of the biopsychosocial model is the *social institutional level.* Social institutions are large, complex, relatively stable clusters of social relationships that involve people working together to address some basic human or societal need (Sullivan & Thompson, 1994). Examples of social institutions include the military, the government, the educational system, and large corporations. At this level of analysis, psychologists try to understand how behavior is influenced by our interactions with these large organizations. For example, a man may become depressed because his company downsizes and he loses his job. A businesswoman may become depressed because she is juggling the demands of both career and family.

David Reimer's case was influenced by the family's interactions with the health-care system, first with the botched circumcision and then with the referral to and advice of Dr.

Money. At the time of the accident, David's parents were described as "teenagers barely off the farm" (Colapinto, 2004). It is not hard to imagine their fear and confusion and the influence that a powerful authority figure such as Dr. Money, with the backing of the medical establishment, had on their decision-making. Anyone who has had a serious medical problem and had to navigate the health-care system can attest to how stressful this can be.

The final level of the biopsychosocial model is the *cultural level*. At last! You may have been wondering when culture would factor into this model. As we have discussed, culture reflects the values, beliefs, and practices of a group of people, and all behavior occurs in a cultural context. Let us go back to our previous example of the depressed businessman and let us say he is African American. He may feel that he was let go because of racism, a belief about the inferiority of African Americans that continues to pervade our society. What about the businesswoman? Although our cultural beliefs about the role of women have changed to incorporate the idea that women can have careers outside the home, we have not entirely abandoned the belief that women should be the primary caretakers of children. Women in America are caught between these two sets of beliefs.

David Reimer's case was influenced by the cultural attitudes of the time. In the 1960s and 1970s, when David was growing up, traditional gender roles still predominated in our society. The belief was that David had to be either male or female, which could be dictated by his genitals and how he was treated. However, when Brenda/David did not fit the traditional ideas of how a girl ought to behave—wearing dresses, playing with dolls, walking and talking a certain way—he was ridiculed by his friends. As an adult, David equated masculinity, or being a "real man," with having a penis and being able to sexually satisfy his wife. Where did his ideas about masculinity and the proper husband role come from? They came from the larger society. What would have happened to David if he had been born into a different culture? Do you think his circumstances would have been different? What do you think would happen to him if he were born today?

Figure 1.1 depicts the biopsychosocial model as concentric circles, with the biological level in the center and each level a larger ring until the last and largest, the cultural level. The biological level is the most basic level at which we can analyze and understand behavior, and the levels become larger and more complex, with each level influencing the last. As the final level, culture influences all levels. Thus, the biopsychosocial model reminds us that all behavior occurs within a cultural context. A complete analysis of David Reimer's suicide must consider on all levels, from his biological predisposition to depression, to his negative thinking patterns, to his family dynamics and treatment by peers, to the health-care system and cultural beliefs about gender roles. All of these worked together, seemingly against David, to lead him to that moment when he raised a shotgun and took his own life.

After learning about the biopsychosocial model, a student shared the following:

During the first two years of college, I was struggling with family issues as I found myself hard to get along with my parents. The constant bickering had made me feel stressed and overwhelmed. I was not able to concentrate on school work and was automatically put into a bad mood when I returned home from work or school. This got in the way of making time to do my assignments and readings as I would just want to go out and be with my friends instead of being at home. As time progressed, studying became less important to me and in a way I hated it as well. This would be an example of an effect on behavior on a social-interpersonal level, because I feel that a good relationship with my family and support would have had a more positive effect on my grades.

Another reason why I feel I did poorly is because I was working more than thirty hours a week, and my work environment was stressful. I had problems with employees and going to work became stressful as I was dealt more work. I feel like my progress in school was affected on a social institutional level as well because constant thoughts of work and stress would be on my mind while in school. Not only did family and work have an effect on school grades but also my cultural background was an issue, as there were many pressures put upon myself for begin born in a Korean family. Many Asian parents pressure children into hard work and good grades, and if these expectations were not met, you would be looked down upon. Being born in the States it was hard for me to understand this type of mentality, but as I grew older, I began to understand more and more why many Asian cultures are this way. Sometimes I felt like if I wasn't pressured so much by my family and friends, I would have done better in school.

—Lily, 20+-year-old Korean American student

Lily does a nice job of analyzing her academic struggles using the biopsychosocial model. She begins at the social-interpersonal level and then moves to the social institutional and cultural levels. The first two levels could also be used to explain her situation. From a biological point of view, some people would say perhaps she struggles in school because of a learning disability. At the cognitive-affective level, the difficulty she experienced studying for classes could be attributed to her internal feelings of stress, pressure, and being overwhelmed. Lily went on to say that the biopsychosocial model increased her understanding of how behavior is influenced by relationships with others, the institutions in which we function, and cultural attitudes. She said, "The next time I feel or do a certain thing, I think that this model will help me break down the reasons to my behaviors, and to become more positive within each level." We hope it does the same for you.

The Basic Tenets of Multicultural Theory

One major premise of multicultural psychology is that all behavior occurs in a cultural context. What are some other major ideas that shape the field?

The field of multicultural psychology evolved primarily from the areas of clinical and counseling psychology and work that was done on conducting counseling and psychotherapy with diverse populations. D. W. Sue et al. (1996) outline the basic tenets of a theory of multicultural counseling and therapy (MCT). Although some aspects are specific to treatment, the theory includes general principles that are the foundation of multicultural psychology.

D. W. Sue et al. (1996) laid out six basic assumptions of MCT, which are summarized in Table 1.3. The first proposition says that MCT theory is a *metatheory* of counseling and psychotherapy. This means that it is a generic theory that provides a framework for understanding all other therapeutic approaches, both the traditional ones (i.e., psychoanalytic, behavioral, humanistic) and the nontraditional ones, such as indigenous forms of healing. No one approach is viewed as inherently good or bad; each simply represents a different worldview.

TABLE 1.3   **Basic Assumptions of a Theory of Multicultural Counseling and Therapy (MCT)**

Proposition 1	MCT is a metatheory of counseling and psychotherapy.
Proposition 2	Both counselor and client identities are formed and embedded in multiple levels of experiences (individual, group, and universal) and contexts (individual, family, and cultural milieus). The totality and interrelationships of experiences and contexts must be the focus of treatment.
Proposition 3	Development of cultural identity is a major determinant of counselor and client attitudes toward the self, others of the same group, others of a different group, and the dominant group. These attitudes are strongly influenced not only by cultural variables but also by the dynamics of a dominant–subordinate relationship among culturally different groups.
Proposition 4	The effectiveness of MCT theory is most likely enhanced when the counselor uses modalities and defines goals consistent with the life experiences and cultural values of the client.
Proposition 5	MCT theory stresses the importance of multiple helping roles developed by many culturally different groups and societies. Besides the one-on-one encounter aimed at remediation in the individual, these roles often involve larger social units, systems intervention, and prevention.
Proposition 6	The liberation of consciousness is a basic goal of MCT theory, which emphasizes the importance of expanding personal, family, group, and organization consciousness of the place of self-in-relation, family-in-relation, and organization-in-relation. This emphasis results in therapy that not only is ultimately contextual in orientation but also draws on traditional methods of healing from many cultures.

Source: Sue, Ivey, and Pedersen (1996).

The second proposition says that both client and counselor have multiple identities at the individual, family, group, and cultural levels. These identities are dynamic, and the salience of one over the others varies across situations and across time. For example, LAB is an African American, female, Christian, heterosexual individual. These are four of her primary identities, and they are listed in their most typical order of importance. However, in some situations the order switches and another identity becomes more salient; for example, when she is with only African Americans, her gender may become more important. To fully understand a person, we must understand all layers of his or her personal identity. (The concept of multiple identities is discussed further in Chapter 7.)

The third proposition of MCT theory says that cultural identity plays a major role in one's attitudes toward the self, others in the same group, others in different groups, and the dominant group. One's cultural identity is shaped by a variety of forces, and it typically develops as one progresses through a series of stages, moving from a lack of awareness of culture and its impact, to encountering cultural issues and reflecting on oneself as a cultural being, to some form of internalization and integration of multiple cultural perspectives. (We discuss issues of cultural identity in detail in Chapter 7.)

The fourth proposition says that therapy is most effective when the therapist takes into account the culture of the client when defining issues, setting goals, and developing treatment strategies. One of the main goals of multicultural training is to help therapists expand their repertoire of helping skills so they can find the best match between the client's culture, the client's presenting problems, and the interventions.

Proposition 5 expands on this idea by saying that therapists must go beyond the traditional helping role of one-on-one therapy and be willing to integrate other things, such as indigenous forms of helping and community resources. Going to therapy carries a great stigma in some cultures; therefore, many people who need help do not seek services. Many people are more comfortable going to their pastor or priest. Perhaps psychologists could coordinate with clergy in making referrals, provide training for clergy to enhance their counseling skills, or provide counseling in church settings where individuals feel more comfortable. Consider a Chinese person who comes to a Western therapist for help but who is also seeing a traditional Chinese herbalist. By opening the lines of communication and cooperation, the therapist and the herbalist could work together to coordinate the client's treatment. (The issue of culture and mental health treatment is discussed further in Chapter 9.)

Finally, Proposition 6 of MCT theory discusses the *liberation of consciousness*. Multicultural counseling and therapy emphasizes that psychologists must break out of the traditional mode of thinking, open their minds, and expand beyond a Western, individualistic perspective to incorporate aspects of the family, group, organizations, and society. That means placing the person in context and understanding self in relation to all these other groups. These ideas should sound familiar because they were discussed in connection with the biopsychosocial model.

Some aspects of MCT theory are specific to counseling and psychotherapy. Nonetheless, the theory also includes general principles that form the basis of multicultural psychology. One principle is the idea that culture provides the context for all behavior. Another is that each person has a cultural identity that is made up of many dimensions and layers. This cultural identity is shaped by larger cultural forces and by interactions with other groups, particularly the dominant group, and influences an individual's attitudes, feelings, and behaviors. We must expand our minds beyond traditional Western ways of thinking and try to understand and incorporate non-Western concepts and ideas. These premises are the meat and potatoes of multicultural psychology. The following quotation captures the essence of multicultural psychology:

> Indeed, cross-cultural and multicultural literature consistently indicates that all people are multicultural beings, that all interactions are cross-cultural, and that all of our life experiences are perceived and shaped from within our own cultural perspectives. (American Psychological Association, 2003, p. 382)

critical consciousness—the ability of individuals to take perspective on their immediate cultural, social, and political environment, to engage in critical dialogue with it, bringing to bear fundamental moral commitments including concerns for justice and equity, and to define their own place with respect to surrounding reality, constitutes an important human faculty.
—Mustakova-Possardt's (1998, p. 13) interpretation of Paolo Freire (1973)

Breaking away from traditional Western ways of doing things may give one insight into treating clients from other cultures. *Photograph by FS Stock/Shutterstock*

Historical Background

In this section, we highlight some historical events that influenced the field of multicultural psychology. This is not a comprehensive historical review but simply a description of a few key events to give you a sense of the way the field developed and the primary areas of theory, research, and practice in multicultural psychology. This section will give you a background for topics covered in more depth in the rest of the book. (For a more in-depth history of multicultural psychology, see Leong, 2009.)

Dubious Beginnings

The birth of psychology as a scientific field of study is traditionally regarded as having occurred in 1879 with the founding of the first psychological laboratory in Leipzig, Germany, by Wilhelm Wundt (Goldstein, 2005). Wundt's laboratory soon became a magnet for individuals wanting to become psychologists. Individuals who studied there went on to establish their own laboratories in countries around the world, including the United States. Wundt and his colleagues studied psychophysiological processes they called **structuralism**. Through a process called **structural introspection**, research participants reported on their own mental experiences. The researchers measured things such as sensation, perception, reaction times, imagery, and attention (Wade & Tavris, 2003).

structuralism—the first formal approach to psychology that attempted to examine the contents of people's minds.

structural introspection—the method that structuralists used to examine the contents of people's minds.

ethnical psychology—the study of the minds of "other races and peoples."

The intense examination of individual differences and quest for heritable traits leading to greater survival of the species eventually led to research on racial group differences. Early names for this area of research included *ethnical psychology* and *racial psychology* (Guthrie, 1998). Haddon (1910) defined **ethnical psychology** as "the study of the minds of other races and peoples, of which, among the more backward races, glimpses can be obtained only by living by means of observation and experiment" (p. 6). Robert Guthrie (1998), in his book *Even the Rat Was White,* argues that this research was highly influenced by the popular notion of racial superiority and an underlying desire by White Europeans to lend scientific credibility to such beliefs. Early studies compared racial groups not only on psychophysiological measures but also on intelligence and personality.

Guthrie (1998) described an early joint expedition by anthropologists and experimental psychologists sponsored by the Cambridge Anthropological Society to the Torres Strait in the South Pacific in 1889. The researchers used Wundtian methods of psychophysics to examine hearing, vision, taste, tactile acuity, pain, motor speed and accuracy, fatigue, and memory in native peoples of that region. The researchers concluded that the inhabitants were far less intelligent than their examiners. Guthrie also described another early psychophysiological study that took place at the World's Congress of Races, which convened at the St. Louis World's Fair in 1904. Several prominent psychologists in attendance tested approximately 1,100 individuals from 22 groups. Again, the researchers concluded that some of the racial groups made many errors and took a long time to perform the tasks and looked similar to people with mental deficiencies. Guthrie cited other early researchers who drew similar conclusions about the racial inferiority of certain groups.

Alfred Binet and Theophile Simon are credited with the development of the first standardized intelligence test in France in 1904. The most famous revision of the Binet–Simon test was done in the United States in 1916 by Lewis Terman of Stanford University. Although the test has been revised several times since then, the Stanford–Binet is still one of the most widely used intelligence tests, and Terman is considered one of the leading and most influential early psychologists. Terman standardized his intelligence test on a sample of about 1,000 children and 400 adults. All the children were European American native Californians. This did not stop Terman from drawing negative conclusions about the mental ability of Blacks, for example, that they are not capable of abstract thinking and should be placed in special education classes (Terman, 1916). Based on his later testing of a sample of Mexican and American Indian children, Terman concluded that individuals from these cultures were genetically inferior (R. J. Cohen & Swerdlik, 2002).

Guthrie (1998) claimed Terman's test was biased in favor of European American middle-class culture. Test takers were asked to interpret middle-class proverbs such as "One swallow does not make a summer"; to repeat sentences based on the ability to speak the English language, such as "The early settlers had little idea of the great changes that were to take place in this country"; and to discriminate between "prettiness" and "ugliness." It is not difficult to imagine children of color struggling with such tasks. Terman's conclusions were not unusual for the time. Other researchers comparing the mental abilities of European Americans and members of ethnic groups reached similar conclusions (Guthrie, 1998). Standardized testing of ethnic groups continues to be a controversial issue and is discussed in more detail in Chapter 2.

The results of such studies were used to support popular notions of racial inferiority and to support ideas and policies such as limitation of education and occupational opportunities for people of color. For example, Terman recommended that Blacks be placed in special education classes and trained for manual labor. Arguments of racial inferiority, buffered by questionable research practices, also fueled the **eugenics** movement (Guthrie, 1998), which advocated that certain groups should not be allowed to procreate because they would pass on negative or deficient genes.

> **eugenics**—a movement that maintains that only "good genes" should be passed from generation to generation and that "undesirable" groups should be dissuaded from reproducing.

Psychologists of color were virtually nonexistent until the 1930s, when the first Black students began to enter graduate programs. These students protested the negative image of Blacks portrayed in the psychological literature and frequently dedicated their theses and dissertation research to refuting beliefs about Black mental inferiority, or the *deficit model*. Examples of dissertation titles during this period include "Analysis of Test Results from Third Grade Children Selected on the Basis of Socio-Economic Status" by Howard Hale Long (PhD, 1933, Harvard University), "Non-Academic Development of Negro Children in Mixed and Segregated Schools" by Inez Beverly Prosser (PhD, 1933, University of Cincinnati), and "A Socio-Psychological Study of Negro Children of Superior Intelligence" by Martin David Jenkins (PhD, 1935, Northwestern University; all cited in Guthrie, 1998). Similarly, Sanchez (1932) reviewed intelligence testing among Mexican American children and refuted findings about their low IQ test scores (as cited in Iijima Hall, 2014). Thus, the work of early psychologists on racial group differences and the response of psychologists of color to their racist conclusions can be considered the early roots of multicultural psychology. (For a more detailed history on issues of race, culture, and ethnicity in psychology, see Duckitt, 1992; Freedheim, 2003; Holliday & Holmes, 2003; and Iijima Hall, 2014).

We Begin to Define Ourselves

Research among psychologists of color soon turned to the effects of forces such as racism, discrimination, and poverty on individuals from ethnic backgrounds. A landmark study in this area was conducted by Kenneth and Mamie Clark in 1939. The Clarks, a husband-and-wife team, conducted a study in which they showed a sample of African American and European American children Black and White dolls or pictures of Black and White children and asked a series of questions such as "Which doll is prettiest?" "Which doll is the smartest?" "Which doll is ugly?" and "Which doll is dirty?" The Clarks found that African American children tended to attribute more positive characteristics to the White dolls or pictures. They concluded that such responses indicated the low self-esteem of African American children and that those negative self-perceptions were the result of racism and discrimination. Their results played a key role in the 1954 Supreme Court decision in *Brown v. Board of Education* that resulted in the desegregation of schools. Guthrie (1998) stated that this demonstrated the role psychology could play in producing significant social change and that "there is no doubt of the impact of the Clarks' work for the betterment of American society" (p. 152).

In 2005, 18-year-old high school student Kiri Davis conducted her own version of the Clark and Clark doll study. The results were the same (Media That Matters, n.d.; search "Kiri Davis: A Girl Like Me" to watch her documentary on www.YouTube.com). On his CNN nightly news show, Anderson Cooper also conducted a replication of the classic study (Billante & Hadad, 2010). Again, the results were the same.

Although many years have passed since the Clarks' original study, as the following story confirms, society continues to struggle with the same issues today.

> As we watched the online video during class it took me back to a similar childhood experience. It was Christmas day and I was around seven or eight. We got home after our Christmas party at my grandma's house and we came to find our presents from Santa Claus. That Christmas both my sister and I received the same doll that was very popular. It was a changing diaper one and it would stain the diaper after feeding it so you could change it again. I loved it from the first time I saw it on the commercial. But when I opened mine I found out it was the African American version. I feel so bad now, but I actually started crying because I wanted the White one. I made my parents go return it and it's even sadder to know the truth behind it. It turns out my parents got us the darker one because it was on sale as opposed to the lighter one that was at full retail price. It sucks doesn't it? Now that I think about it I was so dumb. It's just that when you're younger you think that being lighter is prettier. Why? I honestly don't know. I think the media has a major influence on the way we see things. And look at the media; all over the majority of the people in advertisements are White. Any other ethnic background looks ridiculous or unattractive in advertisements.
>
> —Irma, 20+-year-old Latinx student

Irma questioned where her own preference for lighter skin came from as a child. In the following narrative, Valerie gave some insight into this topic after watching Kiri Davis's documentary.

> One of the topics that caught my attention this past week was the Kenneth and Mamie Clark doll study. The video clip of the remaking of this study was especially interesting because you see these African American females talking about how some of their family members bleached their skin in an effort to be lighter. I believe that in most cultures lighter skin means "better"; people with lighter skin in any culture are seen as prettier and of higher socioeconomic status. I'm Latina and I've personally experienced this in my family; I'm the darkest out of my two siblings and my family

continuously makes fun of me. Family and even friends tell me, "Tu eres del lechero," meaning my real dad is the milkman because I don't look anything like my light-skinned siblings. I know they are joking around, but after a while it hurts and gets annoying.

Also, I identify with the girl on the video that said that she grew up being the "ugly one" of her sisters because she was darker; in my family I feel that way, too. My sister always gets way more compliments of how pretty she is, that her color skin makes great contrast with her black hair, etc. Additionally, I remember an incident when I was crossing the border from Mexico to the U.S. I was around seven years old and again the color of my skin made the border patrol question my legal status in the U.S. They kept us about 1–2 hours questioning my siblings if I was really their sister. The funny part was that I was the one in question, not my lighter skin siblings. Did I look too Mexican/dark to be a U.S. citizen? Did they think I was trying to cross illegally or something?

—Valerie, 20+-year-old Mexican American student

The Clarks' work also had a significant effect within the field of psychology in that it sparked further research in the area, most notably, research on racial and ethnic identity, which continues to be one of the most dominant topics in the multicultural literature (Parham, 2001). In 1970, Joseph L. White published the first article on African American psychology in *Ebony* magazine, and in 1971 William Cross published a model on *nigrescence*, or the "Negro-to-Black conversion experience" in which he described five stages African Americans go through in the development of their racial identity. Cross proposed that African Americans begin in a stage where they identify primarily with European American culture and see their Blackness as negative. Their progression through the stages is sparked by some significant, moving, or startling event that makes it impossible to avoid issues of race. Following this event, Cross believed, many Blacks enter a stage in which they immerse themselves in their Blackness and devalue anything that is European American. The final stage is one of acceptance and comfort, both with one's own culture and with the dominant culture.

Cross's article sparked a long line of work on ethnic identity. Most notable in the group are Thomas Parham and Janet Helms (1981), who operationalized Cross's stages into the Racial Identity Attitude Scale, one of the most widely used and cited measures of racial identity. This scale has been adapted for use with a wide range of other populations, including European Americans (e.g., Helms, 1995b) and gays and lesbians (e.g., Walters & Simone, 1993). The work of these individuals also influenced the development of other models of racial and ethnic identity. We have dedicated an entire chapter to this topic, so you will read much more about it in Chapter 7.

Another movement in the field involved the complete rejection of psychological theories and concepts based on European American frameworks. Psychologists of color turned inward and developed models designed specifically to increase understanding of and the ability to intervene in their own communities. This movement began in the 1970s and gained momentum in the 1980s. For example, the Afrocentric perspective in psychology is represented by psychologists such as Akbar (1981), Baldwin (1981), and Azibo (1989), who developed their own theories of African American mental health, mental disorder, and personality.

Gender Differences

Once upon a time in psychology there was no such thing as gender differences. That might seem unthinkable to you, because today people make millions of dollars from the idea that men and women are from different planets, but there was a time when gender differences were not

Women may have different ways of moral reasoning than men do. *Photograph by baranq/Shutterstock*

discussed in the field of psychology. If they were, women usually got the short end of the stick.

In the early 1970s, during the resurgence of the women's movement in the United States, Carol Gilligan was a graduate student at Harvard University working with Lawrence Kohlberg. Kohlberg (1968, 1976) proposed six stages of moral reasoning based on research he conducted over a span of 12 years with 75 boys who ranged in age from 10 to 16 years old when the study began. Kohlberg used stories to test the boys' reasoning on several moral concepts. He was more interested in the reasoning behind his participants' answers than in what they would actually do. Based on his findings, Kohlberg concluded that children's moral reasoning changes with age and maturity, following his six stages in progressive order.

Gilligan (1982/1993) found that men tended to base their moral choices on abstract principles, such as justice and fairness, whereas women tended to base their choices on principles of compassion and care. In other words, women tended to be more relationship oriented than men. According to Kohlberg's stages, this meant that women looked less moral than men because their responses did not fall into Kohlberg's higher levels of moral reasoning. Rather than concluding that women were not as moral as men, Gilligan suggested that women think and speak differently about relationships. Gilligan did not make strong claims about the cause of the differences but acknowledged that they "arise in a context where factors of social status and power combine with reproductive biology to shape the experience of males and females and the relations between the sexes" (Gilligan, 1982/1993, p. 2). In other words, factors at the biological, social-interpersonal, and cultural levels interact to result in the differing reactions of men and women to moral dilemmas.

Lesbian, gay, and bisexual individuals are beginning to define themselves rather than allowing the dominant culture to define them. *Photograph by Sean Pavone/Shutterstock*

Gilligan (1982/1993) criticized psychology for the "repeated exclusion of women from the critical theory-building studies of psychological research" (p. 1). Thanks in no small part to Gilligan and other leading women psychologists, research standards have changed. Women must now be included in studies, and gender differences must be examined for research to be considered good science. Another influence of Gilligan and others is that the psychology of women is a respected and growing field. We know that to truly understand the human condition, we must include humans from all backgrounds in our research samples. This was not always the case.

Lesbian, Gay, Bisexual, and Transgender Issues

The lesbian, gay, bisexual, and transgender movement is another important part of the history of multicultural psychology and illustrates how psychology has handled another aspect of human diversity.

Variations in sexual identity were initially considered mental disorders. The *Diagnostic and Statistical Manual of Mental Disorders* (*DSM*) is published by the American Psychiatric Association and contains the diagnostic criteria professionals use to determine whether someone has a mental disorder. (The *DSM* is discussed in more detail in Chapter 9). The first edition of the manual (*DSM-I*) was published in 1952 and classified homosexuality under the broad category of *personality disorders*, as well as the subcategories of *sociopathic personality disorder* and *sexual deviation*. Other conditions in this category included transvestitism, pedophilia, and sexual sadism (American Psychiatric Association, 1952). In the next edition (*DSM-II*, American Psychiatric Association, 1968), homosexuality was no longer associated with being sociopathic, but was still listed among the sexual deviations (Drescher, 2015).

Two years later, in 1970, gay activists protested at the American Psychiatric Association convention and demanded that homosexuality be removed from the *DSM*. These protests motivated various committees within the association to deliberate the validity of the diagnosis. At the annual convention in 1973 the debate came to a head, with both sides vigorously arguing their positions. In the end, the vote was swayed by a particular definition of mental disorder, which stated the condition must cause significant distress or be associated with significant impairment in social functioning. The majority concluded homosexuality did not fit these criteria and could therefore not be considered a mental disorder. In December 1973, the American Psychiatric Association Board of Trustees voted to remove homosexuality from the *DSM*. Dr. Laura Brown, an out lesbian and one of the pioneers of feminist therapy, stated that on that day in 1973, she was "cured" of her "mental illness" (L. S. Brown, 2011). Members who opposed the decision of the Board of Trustees called for a vote from the entire membership of the American Psychiatric Association. Of the 20,000 members, 58% voted to uphold the decision by the Board of Trustees to remove homosexuality from the *DSM* (Drescher, 2015).

Despite this victory, the belief that homosexuality was a mental disorder persisted. Subsequent printings of *DSM-II* did not list homosexuality specifically, but did include the diagnosis *sexual orientation disturbance*, which described homosexuality as a mental disorder if the individual was distressed by his or her attraction to the same sex and wanted to change. In *DSM-III* (American Psychiatric Association, 1980), sexual orientation disturbance was replaced with *ego-dystonic homosexuality*. Both diagnoses were criticized for legitimizing *conversion therapy* (the practice of trying to change a person's sexual orientation) and for pathologizing other types of identity issues, such as a person being unhappy with his or her racial background. Eventually, these diagnoses were also removed. In the next three versions of the manual (American Psychiatric Association, 1987, 1994, 2000), the idea of homosexuality as a mental disorder was subsumed under the diagnosis *sexual disorder not otherwise specified*, a general category used when the person's symptoms did not fit neatly into any of the other categories of sexual disorders or dysfunctions. One example given in the *DSM* for this diagnosis was "persistent and marked distress about one's sexual orientation" (American Psychiatric Association, 1987, p. 296). Some people still considered this a method for diagnosing homosexuality as a mental disorder and the example was finally removed from the most recent edition—*DSM-5* (American Psychiatric Association, 2013).

The issue of gender identity is undergoing a similar transformation. A growing population of individuals identify as something other than the gender they were assigned at birth. Most well known are those individuals who identify as *transgender*, or the opposite of their biological sex. Transgender identity has received substantial attention in the media recently through trans celebrities such as Caitlyn Jenner, Laverne Cox, and Alexis Arquette and television shows such as *I Am Jazz* and *Becoming Us*.

Transgender identify first came to the forefront in 1952 when an American, George Jorgensen, went to Denmark as a man and returned to the United States as a trans woman—Christine Jorgensen. Jorgensen underwent what eventually became known as gender reassignment surgery and her case was published in the *Journal of the American Medical Association* (Hamburger, Sturup, & Dahl-Iverson, 1953). Most medical professionals, including psychiatrists, were critical of the procedure being performed on people they believed were mentally ill with disorders originally labeled *transsexualism* or *transvestitism*. No such diagnoses appeared in the *DSM* until the third edition in 1980. The *DSM-III* contained two diagnoses related to gender—gender identity disorder of childhood and transsexualism for adolescents and adults. A third diagnosis was added in *DSM-III-R* (American Psychiatric Association, 1987)—gender identity disorder of adolescence and adulthood, nontranssexual type. These diagnoses were collapsed in *DSM-IV* and *DSM-IV-TR* into the single category of gender identity disorder with different criteria for children, adolescents, and adults. As with homosexuality, controversy surrounded these diagnoses and whether they should be considered mental disorders. Again it was argued that variations in gender identity should only be considered mental disorders if the condition caused significant distress or interfered significantly with social functioning. Thus, in *DSM-5*, the name was changed to *gender dysphoria* with emphasis on the level of distress the individual experiences based on the discrepancy between his or her assigned gender and experienced gender (Drescher, 2015).

The evolving controversy over whether sexual variations should be diagnosed as mental disorders illustrates that, unlike other medical diagnoses, mental disorders are social constructs and change as society changes. The controversy also illustrates the inherent tension in the diagnosis of mental disorders between the need for access to care, which requires a medical diagnosis, and trying to reduce the stigma associated with mental disorder (Drescher, 2015). In other words, an official diagnosis may be needed to determine, provide, and pay for the most appropriate course of treatment, but receiving a diagnosis may result in labeling, which can result in negative consequences that follow the person for the rest of his or her life.

Despite its own checkered past with regard to LGBT issues, the American Psychological Association (APA) has taken a strong stand in support of the LGBT community and has targeted many resources toward their well-being. In 1975, the APA adopted a resolution that stated, "homosexuality per se implies no impairment in judgment, stability, reliability, or general social or vocational capabilities" and encouraged mental health professionals to lead the way in removing the stigma attached to homosexual identity (Conger, 1975, p. 633). In 2012, the APA published "Guidelines for Psychological Practice With Lesbian, Gay, and Bisexual Clients" to promote the health and well-being of people who identify as lesbian, gay, and bisexual and to provide therapists with tools to conduct affirmative research, education, and practice with these populations (American Psychological Association, 2012).

The Rise of Multiculturalism

As we have seen, the field of psychology has traditionally been dominated by European American males in theory, research, and practice. Members of diverse groups, such as African Americans, women, and the LGBT community, have traditionally been left out or viewed as inferior. The same can be said for other groups, such as people with disabilities and those of diverse religious backgrounds. The broader climate of social change, which addressed the issues of underrepresented, oppressed, and disadvantaged groups during the 1950s, 1960s, and 1970s (e.g., the civil rights movement, the War on Poverty), also affected the field of psychology. Over time, psychology and psychologists have been pushed to become more inclusive. Following are some examples of those efforts.

One way to examine how individuals in the field of psychology have dealt with multicultural issues is to look at the history of its primary professional organization, the APA. With a membership of over 100,000, APA is a large and powerful organization that sets the standards for the practice of psychology and represents the field in society at large. Historically, APA has the reputation among diverse groups of having to be pushed to acknowledge and address their needs. (For a more detailed account of APA's handling of ethnic minority issues, see Comas-Díaz, 1990). One response is for groups to break away from APA and form their own organizations.

Various historical influences convinced Black psychologists to make such a move. These historical influences included the assassination of senator Robert F. Kennedy and the civil unrest in many major U.S. cities in the mid-1960s. Moreover, very few African Americans were being trained in the top psychology programs in the country. Between 1920 and 1966, the 10 most prestigious psychology departments in the United States had awarded only 8 PhDs to African Americans from a total of 3,767 doctorates; 6 of those 10 departments had not awarded a single PhD to an African American (Albee, 2003, as cited in Freedheim, 2003). The following is a firsthand account of the inception of the Association of Black Psychologists (ABPsi) at the APA National Convention in 1968 by Dr. Joseph L. White, the father of Black psychology:

> Blacks were being called "dumb," and "stupid," and "inferior." Now they were talkin' about my mama and them, so I had some personal feelings about that. We all did. So it was a personal thing. We held a meeting to talk about how we didn't like what was going on in psychology. People started givin' sermons, and testifyin', and hootin' and hollerin'. As the "Black Grapevine" went into effect and folks heard about what was going on, more people started to come. Estimates range from 80 to about 200 Black psychologists and their allies who participated in those first meetings.
>
> As the meetings grew bigger we realized we needed a bigger space, so we approached the person in charge of logistics for the conference to ask for a meeting room. At first we were told no. Well you know White folks don't plan anything without having a contingency plan, so we knew they had to have a room, so folks started gettin' upset. Then we were told we'd have to wait in line to get a room. Well Black folks reacted like we'd been waitin' 400 years and The Man acted like we'd been waitin' 5 minutes. Then folks got angry and we had what you call a communication breakdown. People started cursing. Someone called the man a mother f— and that we were gonna kick some a——. It got really heated so we had to take a break. We were told to come back in 5 minutes. In 5 minutes they had a meeting room for us on the first floor of the Hyatt Regency with cokes and refreshments and everything.

On the final day of the APA conference, members of our newly formed ABPsi executive council had a meeting with the executive council of APA. The members of ABPsi presented APA with a "challenge to change" that outlined a series of issues that demanded APA's immediate attention, including increased efforts to recruit African American students in psychology, greater representation of African American psychologists in APA, development of a means to provide mental health services to the African American community, and recognition of the Black power and identity movement as a credible tool for fighting racism. . . . So, we made demands on APA, they responded, and we formed ABPsi, and ABPsi has been goin' ever since. (Joseph L. White, personal communication, July 25, 2004)

After the founding of ABPsi in 1968, other diverse groups followed suit and formed their own organizations. Examples of other special-interest professional associations include the Association of Women in Psychology, the Asian American Psychological Association (AAPA), the National Latinx Psychological Association, and the Society of Indian Psychologists. When these groups began forming their own professional associations, APA recognized it needed to become a more inclusive organization. More detailed accounts of the history of ethnic groups in the field of psychology are given for African Americans (Holliday, 2009), Asian Americans (Leong & Okazaki, 2009), Latinos (A. M. Padilla, 2009), American Indians and Alaska Natives (Trimble, Clearing-Sky, & Sapa, 2009), and Native Hawaiians (McCubbin & Marsella, 2009).

The APA has also dealt with multicultural issues through its organizational structure. In 1979, APA established the Office of Ethnic Minority Affairs to handle issues related to cultural diversity, such as expanding the roles of psychologists of color (Holliday & Holmes, 2003). This office still exists, along with the Committee on Ethnic Minority Affairs and the Public Interest Directorate, all components of the APA governing structure that demonstrate the representation of interests of people of color in the organization today; in addition, the previous chief executive officer of APA was an African American psychologist, Dr. Norman Anderson (J. M. Jones & Austin-Dailey, 2009).

The membership of APA is also organized into various divisions, each representing a particular area of interest. Currently, there are 54 divisions,

Dr. Joseph White, known as the "Father of Black Psychology" and a founding member of the Association of Black Psychologists. *Photograph courtesy of Joseph White*

several of which deal with issues of diversity. Some of those divisions address specific cultural groups (e.g., Division 35, Society for the Psychology of Women); others reflect broader areas of interest but have a history of paying significant attention to minority-related issues (e.g., Division 9, Society for the Psychological Study of Social Issues). See Table 1.4 for a list of these divisions.

In 1986, the APA Council of Representatives voted to establish Division 45, the Society for the Psychological Study of Culture, Ethnicity, and Race, the main division for psychologists interested in multiculturalism. In her description of this event, Comas-Díaz says, "This historical event signaled the mainstreaming of ethnicity, race, and culture, and their interactions with other diversity variables into psychology" (2009, p. 400). She describes the threefold purpose of Division 45 as follows:

> (1) advance the contributions of psychology as a discipline in the understanding of issues related to people of color through research, including the development of appropriate research paradigms; (2) promote the education and training of psychologists in matters regarding people of color, including the special issues relevant to the service delivery issues relevant to ethnic minority populations; and (3) inform the general public of research, education and training, and service delivery issues relevant to ethnic minority populations. (Comas-Díaz, 2009, p. 400)

Division 45 publishes its own journal, *Cultural Diversity and Ethnic Minority Psychology* (Educational Publishing Foundation), as do many of the other divisions. Other associations also publish their own journals, including the National Latinx Psychological Association, the Asian American Psychological Association, and ABPsi.

Another seminal event in the rise of multiculturalism was the inauguration of the National Multicultural Conference and Summit. The National Multicultural Conference and Summit is a joint effort between four APA divisions—Society of Counseling Psychology (Division 17), Society for the Psychology of Women (Division 35), Society for the Psychological Study of Lesbian, Gay, Bisexual, and Transgender Issues (Division 44), and Society for the Psychological Study of Culture, Ethnicity, and Race (Division 45). The purpose of the conference is to bring together "scientists, practitioners, scholars, and students from psychology and related fields, to

TABLE 1.4 **Divisions of the American Psychological Association Concerned With Diversity Issues**

Division 9	Society for the Psychological Study of Social Issues
Division 17	Society of Counseling Psychology
Division 27	Society for Community Research and Action: Division of Community Psychology
Division 35	Society for the Psychology of Women
Division 36	Psychology of Religion
Division 44	Society for the Psychological Study of Lesbian, Gay, and Bisexual Issues
Division 45	Society for the Psychological Study of Culture, Ethnicity, and Rule
Division 48	Society for the Study of Peace, Conflict, and Violence: Peace Psychology Division
Division 51	Society for the Psychological Study of Men and Masculinity

Note: Information on each of these divisions can be obtained by visiting the American Psychological Association website at http://www.apa.org

inform and inspire multicultural theory, research, and practice" (National Multicultural Conference and Summit, 2015). The first summit took place in 1999, when leaders in the field came together in Newport Beach, California, to discuss how psychology could address the "growing mental health needs of historically marginalized groups and disenfranchised individuals" (National Multicultural Conference and Summit, 2015). Approximately 500 people attended the first meeting. Since then summit has grown into a biennial conference with more than 800 attendees.

Evidence for the rise of multiculturalism in psychology is also seen in the various documents and policies adopted by APA. The *Ethical Principles of Psychologists and Code of Conduct* (American Psychological Association, 2017a) is the main document guiding the profession of psychology. It defines the boundaries and responsibilities of the profession. The document is divided into four sections; the main two are the general principles, which describe the ideals and aspirational goals for the profession, and the ethical standards, which are the enforceable rules of conduct for psychologists. Statements regarding the need for psychologists to pay attention to culture were first included in the document in 2002. In the current version, General Principle E, "Respect for People's Rights and Dignity," states the following:

> Psychologists are aware of and respect cultural, individual, and role differences, including those based on age, gender, gender identity, race, ethnicity, culture, national origin, religion, sexual orientation, disability, language, and socioeconomic status, and consider these factors when working with members of such groups. Psychologists try to eliminate the effect on their work of biases based on those factors, and they do not knowingly participate in or condone activities of others based upon such prejudices. (American Psychological Association, 2017a, p. 4)

The code also states that psychologists must obtain training, experience, consultation, or supervision to ensure the provision of competent services to diverse populations and that the specific characteristics of the individual, such as linguistic or cultural differences, should be taken into account when interpreting the results of psychological tests. This is especially important when critical decisions are made from those results, such as placement in educational programs. The code did not always include such statements. The fact that they are now included indicates that multiculturalism is supported, at least in principle, from the top down in the field of psychology.

The ethics code is updated periodically to reflect changes in the field and in society as a whole. The APA engaged the help of representatives from the various ethnic professional organizations (ABPsi, the Asian American Psychological Association, the National Latinx Psychological Association, and the Society of Indian Psychologists) to address concerns raised by these groups regarding inclusion of cultural issues in the next revision of the code (Morse & Blume, 2013).

In 1973, at an APA conference on training in psychology in Vail, Colorado, APA made a landmark decision that graduate training programs must include courses on multicultural issues (Comas-Díaz, 2009; Korman, 1974). To be considered for APA accreditation today, graduate programs must comply with Domain D of the APA *Guidelines and Principles for Accreditation of Graduate Programs in Professional Psychology* (2013). Domain D Is titled, "Cultural and Individual Differences and Diversity," and says programs must demonstrate systematic efforts to attract and retain students and faculty from diverse backgrounds, provide a supportive and encouraging learning environment for diverse Individuals, provide training opportunities for working with diverse populations, and implement "a thoughtful and coherent plan to provide

students with relevant knowledge and experiences about the role of cultural and individual diversity in psychological phenomena as they relate to the science and practice of professional psychology" (p. 10). This standard must be demonstrated in the program's faculty, students, policies, curriculum, and field placements (APA, 2013; Vazquez-Nuttal et al., 1997). Another important conference was the Dulles conference in 1977. Under the joint sponsorship of APA and the National Institute for Mental Health, this was the first official national gathering of psychologists of color, titled Expanding the Roles of Culturally Diverse People in the Profession of Psychology. The purpose of the conference was to explore ways in which psychologists of color could become more actively, effectively, and meaningfully involved in APA activities (Comas-Díaz, 2009).

After the Vail and Dulles conferences, many multicultural psychologists began to develop theory, conduct research on, and advocate for multicultural competence, or the training of psychologists to work with diverse populations. This resulted in publication of the multicultural competencies that operationalized the specific attitudes, knowledge, and skills psychologists need to work effectively with people from differing backgrounds (e.g., D. W. Sue et al., 1992; D. W. Sue, Carter, et al., 1998). It was not until 2002, almost 30 years after the Vail conference, that the APA Council of Representatives formally adopted a set of multicultural guidelines, which were subsequently published in their journal, the *American Psychologist*, in 2003, and titled *Guidelines on Multicultural Education, Training, Research Practice and Organizational Change*. Even APA acknowledged the significance of the publication of this document: "This approval was hailed as a cardinal event, as it represented a major accomplishment in the 4-decade multiculturalism movement in psychology dating from the first mention of cultural diversity at the Vail Conference" (American Psychological Association, 2008). This document was revised in 2017 and renamed *Multicultural Guidelines: An Ecological Approach to Context, Identity and Intersectionality*. The goal of the document is to present practice guidelines to help the practitioner, educator, researcher, and consultant strive to identify, understand, and respond to multicultural content in a helpful, professional way" (American Psychological Association, 2017b, p. 96). (See Table 1.5 for a summary of the guidelines.) This document signals another landmark event in the rise of multiculturalism in the field of psychology.

The following story illustrates the struggles faced in implementing multicultural training standards. In one of his previous faculty positions, one of the authors (JSM) proposed including multicultural psychology as a major area of study for the comprehensive exam in his department's graduate program in clinical psychology. However, the clinical faculty voted the proposal down.

> Stunned, the DCT [director of clinical training] and I met, wondering what happened. Weeks later, he suggested that I try to make the proposal again, giving my colleagues the benefit of the doubt that perhaps they misunderstood my request. I stated my case even more clearly and passionately than before, also emphasizing APA's commitment to this area and its requirement that cross-cultural/multicultural content be infused into all graduate programs in psychology. This time, I thought for sure, my colleagues would understand and pass the proposal. However, to my surprise, the response was even more heated than before. I heard comments like these: "Cross-cultural psychology is too limited an area to be considered a major topic area for prelims." "There is nothing to cross-cultural psychology." "We allowed it to be a required course—what more do you want?" "Cross-cultural psychology is unimportant." "Haven't we already dealt with this? No means no!"

TABLE 1.5   **Multicultural Guidelines: An Ecological Approach to Context, Identity, and Intersectionality**

Guideline 1. Psychologists seek to recognize and understand that identity and self-definition are fluid and complex and that the interaction between the two is dynamic. To this end, psychologists appreciate that intersectionality is shaped by the multiplicity of the individual's social contexts.

Guideline 2. Psychologists aspire to recognize and understand that as cultural beings, they hold attitudes and beliefs that can influence their perceptions of and interactions with others as well as their clinical and empirical conceptualizations. As such, psychologists strive to move beyond conceptualizations rooted in categorical assumptions, biases, and/or formulations based on limited knowledge about individuals and communities.

Guideline 3. Psychologists strive to recognize and understand the role of language and communication through engagement that is sensitive to the lived experience of the individual, couple, family, group, community, and/or organizations with whom they interact. Psychologists also seek to understand how they bring their own language and communication to these interactions.

Guideline 4. Psychologists endeavor to be aware of the role of the social and physical environment in the lives of clients, students, research participants, and/or consultees.

Guideline 5. Psychologists aspire to recognize and understand historical and contemporary experiences with power, privilege, and oppression. As such, they seek to address institutional barriers and related inequities, disproportionalities, and disparities of law enforcement, administration of criminal justice, educational, mental health, and other systems as they seek to promote justice, human rights, and access to quality and equitable mental and behavioral health services.

Guideline 6. Psychologists seek to promote culturally adaptive interventions and advocacy within and across systems, including prevention, early intervention, and recovery.

Guideline 7. Psychologists endeavor to examine the profession's assumptions and practices within an international context, whether domestically or internationally based, and consider how this globalization has an impact on the psychologist's self-definition, purpose, role, and function.

Guideline 8. Psychologists seek awareness and understanding of how developmental stages and life transitions intersect with the larger biosociocultural context, how identity evolves as a function of such intersections, and how these different socialization and maturation experiences influence worldview and identity.

Guideline 9. Psychologists strive to conduct culturally appropriate and informed research, teaching, supervision, consultation, assessment, interpretation, diagnosis, dissemination, and evaluation of efficacy as they address the first four levels of the Layered Ecological Model of the Multicultural Guidelines.

Guideline 10. Psychologists actively strive to take a strength-based approach when working with individuals, families, groups, communities, and organizations that seeks to build resilience and decrease trauma within the sociocultural context.

Source: American Psychological Association (2017b).

You might think that this happened in the 1970s when the idea was still relatively new to those teaching in the profession. Or that those professors were "old fogies" who were trained under an antiquated system, anyway, so of course they would be against new ideas. What would you say if I told you that this happened to me in 1989? The surprising thing was that two of the most vocal opponents to the proposal were relatively new and young professors, so even the old-fogies excuse cannot be applied. This incident convinced me that I should be looking elsewhere for employment, and even though I received tenure from the university later, I gave it up to leave such an environment. (adapted from Mio & Awakuni, 2000, pp. 1–2)

As this story and others like it illustrate, the multicultural movement has met serious resistance. Several authors cite reasons for resistance to multiculturalism. D. W. Sue, Carter, and associates

(1998) identify what they call "the seven deadly resistances" (p. 28). These are arguments raised by the power structure against integrating multiculturalism into training programs, such as the contentions that current theories are generalizable to all populations and that conceptually sound multicultural standards do not exist. Mio and Awakuni (2000) wrote a book titled *Resistance to Multiculturalism: Issues and Interventions,* in which their main premise is that resistance to multicultural issues is rooted in various forms of racism. But they do not leave us without hope. They also outline what they think are effective ways of addressing such resistance, such as self-awareness, openness, and self-examination; knowledge and understanding of European American privilege; and knowledge and understanding of ethnic identity models.

These stories of the structure, policies, and publications of APA illustrate a long and slow struggle toward the acknowledgment and inclusion of multicultural psychology. Despite continued discussion and examination, APA is now clear in their commitment to multicultural issues, as evidenced in the following statement by former APA president, Gerald P. Koocher:

> As psychologists, we recognize the ever-increasing racial, ethnic, and cultural diversity of America and the need to incorporate respectful understanding of group differences in our professional practice, research, and teaching. As an organization, APA recognizes the critical need to attend to diversity in our own house and make certain that our policies and publications appropriately reflect affirmative steps toward inclusive thought and action. (Koocher, as cited in American Psychological Association, 2008)

In addition, the APA Task Force on the Implementation of the Multicultural Guidelines stated,

> Psychology has established multiculturalism as an integral and driving force in the field through adoption of the Multicultural Guidelines. . . . By adopting the Multicultural Guidelines as APA policy, the field of psychology has validated and emphasized the critical role that culture plays in education, training, research, practice, and organizational change. . . . Psychology's directive to develop cultural competency is clear. By infusing cultural competency throughout psychology, the field is better positioned to meet the needs of a growing and diverse U.S. society and is better able to respond to the needs of a global community. (American Psychological Association, 2008)

Franklin (2009) summarized the major themes that emerged from the history of multicultural psychology. They are (a) the central role of culture, history, pride, and resilience in the experiences of historically marginalized and underrepresented groups; (b) the deep impact of the indignities of discrimination and negative treatment on these groups; (c) the influence of the deficit model in ethnic minority literature and research, along with the lack of legitimate attention paid to the cultural reality of people of color, as catalysts for confronting mainstream psychology; (d) the role of diverse professional organizations in challenging the status quo; (e) the transition from ethnic minority psychology to multicultural psychology in an effort to seek allies and be more inclusive; and (f) questions regarding the future of the multicultural movement and whether it has remained true to its original mission.

Comas-Díaz (2009) stated that multicultural psychology has "raised the consciousness of psychologists of all colors," "shifted the mainstream psychological paradigm" (p. 407), and better equipped us for the challenges of a global society. We look forward to sharing more with you about this exciting and vibrant field in the remainder of this book.

Food for Thought

Whether multiculturalism truly is the fourth force in psychology remains to be seen. You are free to draw your own conclusions about that. We cannot deny, however, that culture is a critical factor in the way human beings think, feel, act, and interact. The field of multicultural psychology seeks to study that factor, with the ultimate goal of increasing our understanding of ourselves. We hope this chapter has whetted your appetite, because in the following chapters we will introduce you to more specific areas of theory, research, and practice in the field of multicultural psychology.

Summary

Multicultural psychology is the systematic study of all aspects of human behavior as it occurs in settings where people of different backgrounds encounter one another. Essential to an understanding of multicultural psychology are such terms as race, ethnicity, and culture, as well as issues and controversies related to those terms.

A brief historical perspective shows that racism permeated the field from its early beginnings in research on individual and racial group differences and in the response by psychologists of color and women to bias in that research. Some psychologists suggest that multiculturalism is the fourth force in psychology, meaning that it will have as big an effect on our understanding of human behavior as did psychoanalysis, behaviorism, and humanism.

The main premise of multicultural theory is that all behavior occurs in a cultural context. Multicultural issues have gained greater acknowledgment and inclusion in the field of psychology over time, but not without resistance and struggle, as evidenced by the various policies and practices of the APA.

Critical Thinking Questions

1. What were your early experiences with racial and ethnic differences? What were your early experiences with other aspects of difference? How have those early experiences shaped you into the person you are now?
2. Have you ever been to foreign countries and felt out of place? Have you ever been to other regions of the country and felt out of place? Have you ever been to different areas of your own city that made you feel out of place? How have you handled those situations?

CHAPTER 2

Multicultural Issues Involving Research and Testing

Photograph by HBRH/Shutterstock

Learning Objectives

Reading this chapter will help you to:

• understand research and testing issues when studying multicultural issues;
• identify basic tenets of quantitative and qualitative approaches to measurement;
• know which strategies are appropriate for investigating diverse populations;
• explain how to conduct quantitative and qualitative studies;
• recognize the differences between quantitative and qualitative approaches; and
• distinguish among the different ways of measuring the equivalence of measures.

Korchin (1980) noted that researchers tend to question the generality of findings only when the research involves ethnic minority populations. Korchin mentioned that once he and his colleague had conducted research on why some African-American youths had made extraordinary achievements. A paper from the research was submitted for publication and rejected. One reviewer had indicated that the research was grievously flawed because it lacked a White control group. Why was a White control group necessary if the interest was in African Americans? More critically, Korchin asked why we do not require studies of Whites to have an African-American control group. In other words, we ask that ethnic minority research show its pertinence to other groups or more general phenomena, but we fail to make the same requests when the research involves White populations. (S. Sue, 1999, p. 1072)

As this quotation from Stanley Sue suggests, the scientific study of psychology is only as good as those who apply and interpret it. Researchers in psychology try to apply scientific methods in the attempt to be objective in discovery. As most researchers in the multicultural arena would agree, however, whereas our methods may aim for objectivity, our results and interpretations are laden with subjective values. In this chapter we examine multicultural issues relating to the ways in which psychological research has been conducted and to psychological testing.

Research Methods in Psychology

The General Research Model

The standard way of applying science to psychology is to have a pool of potential research participants and to assign each participant to either a control group or an experimental group. Each individual has an equal chance to be in the control or the experimental group. The control group either does not receive any treatment or receives a typical treatment, whereas the experimental group is given a regimen designed to make some significant difference (Figure 2.1). This difference is determined by comparing the results from the experimental group with the results from the control group.

To apply this general method to a concrete example, let us say that we are interested in finding out whether a new medication will relieve the symptoms of depression. The control group in this instance is given a placebo—typically a sugar pill—and the experimental group is given the experimental medication. No one knows whether he or she is receiving the sugar pill or the medi-

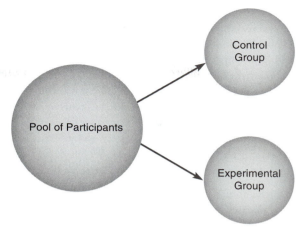

FIGURE 2.1 Assignment of research participants to a control or experimental group.

cation, and each individual has an equal chance of being in the control or the experimental group. After a period of time, we compare the groups to see whether those individuals who received the medication are measurably less depressed.

Although medical examples are the clearest form of experiments with people, let us explore an example more relevant to psychology. Suppose we are interested in finding out whether a new method of teaching history will result in students learning the subject better. With this new method, students act out historical events. The control group comprises the students learning history in the standard way, and the experimental group consists of the students acting out historical events. At the end of the academic year, students are tested about their knowledge of history, and we compare the scores from the two groups. If the new method is more effective for teaching history, the students in the experimental group will have higher scores on the history test than will the students in the control group. If the new method is less effective, the experimental group will have lower scores. If the new method does not make a difference, the students in the two groups will have approximately equal scores.

Now, what if we are interested in finding out whether students of color learn as much as their European American counterparts when both learn with the new method? We can compare the scores of students of color with the scores of European American students to see whether their scores are higher, lower, or the same. That seems to be an easy comparison. However, a wealth of evidence from the modeling literature suggests that children learn more when they can identify with models displaying the behaviors (Bandura, 1977, 1986, 1997; Eron, 2000; Eron, Huessman, Lefkowitz, & Walder, 1996; Eron, Walder, & Lefkowitz, 1971). Therefore, to the extent that history learned in America is dominated by European American events, what can we conclude if we find that European American children have higher scores than their counterparts of color? After all, the children will be portraying the European explorers, conquerors, and settlers in American history.

The European American Standard

J. Jones (1993) discussed that the dominant research paradigm in American psychology is to see European American as the standard against which all others are measured. Thus, if people of color are measured as different from the European American standard, that difference is seen as deviant or deficient. You may recall that when researchers studied children from inner-city environments several years ago, they characterized the children as coming from "culturally deprived" environments. We find it interesting that this phrase came from European American liberals who were trying to empathize with these children, and they did not realize they were perpetuating the notion that a European American middle-class background was the correct environment and that anything different from that environment was culturally deprived. Derald Wing Sue had originally given his influential book the title *Counseling the Culturally Different* (D. W. Sue, 1981; D. W. Sue & Sue, 1990, 1999). However, *different* implied that those who were not in the majority were different from the standard in society, so by 2003 the authors changed the title of the book to *Counseling the Culturally Diverse* (D. W. Sue & Sue, 2003, 2008, 2013, 2016). As D. W. Sue and Sue (2003) put it,

> the phrase "culturally different" begs the question: "Different from what?" In almost all cases the comparison standard is related to White Euro-American norms and has the unintended consequence of creating a hierarchy among different groups (race, culture, ethnicity, etc.) in our society. (p. xv)

In other words, the diverse groups that come closer to the European American standard are considered higher in the hierarchy of groups and more acceptable to the majority, whereas the groups that are farther from the norm are deemed less acceptable. In contrast, *diverse* implies that there are multiple perspectives or norms, with none being necessarily better or more desirable:

> In reading the text, more detail was given with regard to "The White Standard." Growing up, we took these standardized tests, we received and sometimes celebrated our "standing" in whatever the lineup was. And as I was reading this particular section, I thought about exactly what we were celebrating or reacting to. And it appears to be true that the standard to which we were held was indeed "the White standard." And it wasn't just scholastically. Our school was located in South Los Angeles and the schools with which we were compared were . . . predominantly White. Then I recall how involved and absolutely passionate our 8th grade teacher was about promoting excellence. Mr. [name] made it a point to use his networking to get us into math competitions, national spelling bees, and even cheerleading competitions all over Southern California. The culture shock and the inferiority we felt was nothing less than obvious. But he didn't do it to make us feel poorly about ourselves. He did it to defy just that—the White Standard to which we were being held. We were intelligent kids who needed a push and he gave it to us.
>
> —Alexandria, 20+-year-old Latinx student

Internal Versus External Validity

We began this chapter with a quotation from one of Stanley Sue's articles (S. Sue, 1999). The purpose of that article was to discuss the tension between internal and external validity. *Internal validity* refers to causal inference. In the experimental studies we discussed earlier, the procedures were designed to help make an inference that a change in procedure leads to a change in behavior. In the drug study, for example, a change in the medication (placebo versus medication) resulted in a change in depression; in the teaching study, a change in the method of teaching (standard teaching method versus students acting out history scenarios) resulted in a change in student learning. In other words, internal validity suggests that our changes make a difference.

The reason researchers randomly assign potential research participants to experimental and control groups is to have more confidence that the changes in procedures *cause* differences in behavior. Suppose we allow students to choose whether they want to act out history or to learn history the usual way. If we find differences in learning, can we infer that they result from the differences in teaching methods? Probably not. That is because those students who choose to learn by acting out history may be more extraverted, so we may be measuring differences between extraverts and introverts, not between acting out history and standard teaching models. Researchers expend substantial effort to ensure that studies are internally valid. If one cannot make any inference that one's changes result in differences, the study will be useless, no matter how interesting or important the topic is.

External validity refers to the generalizability of the results we obtain. If we conclude from one study that our methods are effective, do those methods generalize to other studies? In many psychological studies, introductory psychology students participate in studies and researchers conclude that "people" behave in similar manners. Is that inference justified? Sometimes yes and sometimes no. For example, if we were to study attraction and dating behavior, introductory psychology students might be good research participants because they are at the age when such issues are very important, if not dominant. However, if we were interested in poverty or grief, introductory psychology students might not be the best population to study.

External validity may be—and often is—at odds with internal validity, as Campbell and Stanley (1963) indicated in their classic publication:

> Both types of criteria are obviously important, even though they are frequently at odds in that features increasing one may jeopardize the other. While internal validity is the sine qua non, and while the question of external validity, like the question of inductive inference, is never completely answerable, the selection of designs strong in both types of validity is obviously our ideal. (p. 5)

As S. Sue (1999) indicated, even though psychologists have recognized that both internal and external validity are important, the notions that internal validity is indispensable in experimental design and that external validity is "never completely answerable" have influenced the field to markedly favor internal validity over external validity. S. Sue called this "selective enforcement of scientific principles." As he so eloquently put it,

> The phenomenon of selective enforcement of scientific criteria is apparent. We criticize research for problems in internal validity. Yet, we pay relatively little attention to external validity. Whether in research papers submitted for publication or research grant proposals submitted for funding, ethnic minority research is primarily scrutinized for internal validity problems. This is appropriate. Yet much of research, whether or not it is focused on ethnics, is not criticized for external validity problems. In experimental studies, the discrepancies between internal and external validity are brought into bold relief. Rigorous and sometimes elegant experimental designs allow us to make causal inferences. However, because of their rigor and need to control for extraneous variables, they frequently involve small numbers of participants, foregoing issues of sampling and representativeness. (S. Sue, 1999, p. 1073)

Thus, when a researcher submits a study examining the effectiveness of a psychological treatment for depression, anxiety, or other forms of psychopathology, the study is typically reviewed for threats to internal validity and the proper application of statistical procedures, not for the degree to which the treatment can be generalized to all populations. Yet if you were in therapy for the treatment of one of these disorders, it would probably be more important for you to know whether the treatment will work for you than to know whether the study was conducted correctly. Scientifically, it is important that studies are conducted correctly, but practically, people want to know whether things will work.

Quantitative Versus Qualitative Research

Suppose you were given the following set of questions and were told to answer each one according to your preference:

At a party do you
    a. interact with many people, including strangers?
    b. interact with only a few close friends?

Do you
    a. initiate conversations?
    b. wait for others to begin talking to you?

Do you prefer to have
    a. many friends but only a little bit of time for each one?
    b. a few friends but more time to spend with each one?

Do you find it
    a. easy to speak with strangers?
    b. difficult to speak with strangers?

Are you
    a. easily approachable?
    b. somewhat reserved?

Note that all "a" answers are extraverted forms of answers and all "b" answers are introverted forms. If you were to answer 20 such questions, we would be able to calculate how introverted or extraverted you are. Thus, if you had 5 "a" answers, you would have an extravert score of 5, and if someone else had 12 "a" answers, he or she would have an extravert score of 12. From those scores, we could conclude that you are more introverted and the other person is more extraverted.

Quantitative Approaches

The example on extraversion illustrates how a question can be turned into a meaningful number. You may have taken tests that ask you to circle a number to indicate what your preference is or what characterizes you best, such as the following:

Did you like this movie?

    1   2   3   4   5   6   7

    I did not like it at all   *I liked it a lot*

Do you consider yourself creative?

    1   2   3   4   5   6   7
    Not at all   *Quite a bit*

Research that involves turning questions into meaningful numbers that can be compared with other numbers is called quantitative study. Our entire system of statistics is based on comparing numbers to make inferences about differences between groups or individuals.

Thus, in our earlier example involving the effectiveness of an antidepressant medication, we can ask the individuals to rate on a scale from 1 to 10 how depressed they are after treatment, with 1 meaning *not depressed at all* and 10 meaning *deeply depressed*. If the medication (experimental) group yields an average score of 3.7 and the placebo (control) group yields an average score of 6.2, we can conclude that the medication was effective in relieving the depression. This general approach is known in science as **logical positivism** (Costa & Shimp, 2011; Georgaca, 2001; Hoshmand, 1994; Morrow, Rakhsha, & Castañeda, 2001; S. P. Schwartz, 2012; Unger, 1995).

> **logical positivism**—a scientific approach that attempts to measure "truth" or real phenomena through methods of numbers and statistical analyses.

Students are very much aware of such evaluation techniques. Most professors assign a given number of points for tests, projects, papers, participation, and the like, and students who accumulate a higher number of points receive higher grades in the course. Although this method is generally accepted and yields accurate comparisons, there can sometimes be injustices or inaccuracies in this system. At some point, someone else probably received a higher grade in a course than you did. You may have thought that you understood more of the material than the other person did, so you may have felt that you suffered an injustice. However, you may have also benefited from this system, because you may have received a higher grade than someone who understood more in a particular course than you did. One source of difference is class participation credit. Extraverts tend to get higher participation credits than introverts, so even though an introverted person may know the material better, an extraverted person may receive a higher grade.

Even more interesting is a situation in which two people both receive an A grade, yet one individual just barely received the A and perhaps received it only because of extra-credit work or luck, whereas the other individual knew enough of the material to be able to teach the course. If both received point accumulations of 95 of 100 or both received A grades, we will lose the subtleties of meaning behind those numbers or grades. To understand such subtleties, we must employ qualitative research methods.

Qualitative Approaches

When people are asked whether they prefer to interact with many people at parties or just a few close friends, they often say, "Well, it depends on the party." If you looked at the extraversion–introversion questions at the beginning of this chapter, you likely felt that your answer would depend on the situation. If the party was lively, with lots of interesting people, you would probably be more interested in meeting several people. However, if there were many people to whom you could not relate, you probably would stick closely to your friends. If you were standing in a line and some strangers were engaged in a conversation about a topic that was of interest to you, it would probably be easier for you to be drawn into the conversation. If you were sitting in an airport in front of the gate and people were reading books around you, it would be difficult for you to talk to strangers.

These examples suggest that collecting only numerical data may result in the loss of some important information and/or may ignore contextual variables that could affect how we respond. Qualitative approaches to research can be employed when a researcher determines that gathering strictly numerical answers to questions results in the loss of essential information (Denzin & Lincoln, 2007a, 2007b; J. Elliott, 2005; Grbich, 2007; Hill, Thompson, & Williams, 1997; Liamputtong & Ezzy, 2005; Maxwell, 2004; Morrow et al., 2001; Phillon, He, & Connelly, 2005; Rissman, 2007; Seale, Gobo, Gubrium, & Silverman, 2004; Silverman, 2004; Silverman & Marvasti, 2008; Yin, 2004). There are different kinds of qualitative data collection, such as case studies, structured interviews with open-ended questions, focus groups, and analyzing discourse (texts or narratives). Some people have used qualitative research to generate ideas for quantitative research, whereas others have used it as the goal of the research to give people an in-depth understanding of the phenomenon being examined. Our use of narratives in this book is a kind of qualitative application, because we are trying to convince you of some underlying truths or themes experienced by people who have been touched by multicultural issues.

For example, Constantine, Kindaichi, Okazaki, Gainor, and Baden (2005) applied qualitative methods to examine how Asian international women adjusted to the United States and college. Using these methods, they were able to determine six prominent domains from their research participants: living in the United States, differences between their original cultures and the United States, English language issues, discrimination experienced, peer and family networks, and strategies for cultural coping. Without this qualitative procedure, one might assume that issues such as academics (because the subjects were international students in college), individualism versus collectivism, and homesickness might have been prominent themes. On the basis of these assumptions, researchers may have developed measures of these presumed themes. Participants responding to these measures might then have reified the importance of the themes. Although issues of academics, individualism, collectivism, and homesickness did arise, they were embedded within the larger themes that Constantine et al. identified. Thus, Constantine et al.'s (2005) study provided us with a richer—and more accurate—understanding of the issues with which these women dealt.

The examples at the beginning of this section showed how context can play a part in people's responses to research questions. However, contextual variables are not the only things that are lost in quantitative methods. If the choice is between preferring to interact with many people at a party and preferring to interact with just a few, if on the whole you prefer interacting with many people, your answer would be classified as extraverted. You may know someone who always prefers to interact with many people (the life of the party), and that person's response would also be classified as an extraverted answer. Is it fair to give both of you one point for this question? Qualitative research methods can help us understand the degree to which a question is applicable to someone, or they can give a sense of the profound differences between two respondents.

Finally, qualitative methods are often used when it is difficult to convert a question into a numerical response. Aesthetic questions are difficult to convert into numerical responses, particularly when respondents are asked to compare objects that are markedly different. For example, how would you convert to a number the joy you experience when you see a very close friend for the first time in years? How does that joy compare with the joy you experience when you finish a lengthy project that involved many frustrations and obstacles? You may try to quantify those experiences, but are the numbers resulting from that conversion meaningful?

Researchers examining communities of color have employed qualitative techniques more and more. For example, Vo-Jutabha, Dinh, McHale, and Valsiner (2009) examined how Vietnamese adolescents developed their ethnic identities within and outside of their own ethnic enclaves. Quantitative methods do not immediately jump out at researchers for examining such a question, so they must explore what issues are important to these adolescents using qualitative methods. This is not to say that quantitative techniques have been discarded, but that a trend is evident in the use of qualitative techniques. As Mio (2002) stated,

> As those of us in the multicultural arena know, measures on scales have helped us to understand elements of culture reasonably well, but this methodological approach has limited our understanding of culture, or at least the questions we can ask, for these questions must be reduced to quantifiable responses. Thus, in recent years, many multicultural researchers have drifted away from the logical positivistic methodology of numerical values that are statistically manipulated and analyzed and toward the more ethnographic and qualitative research methodologies used by our anthropology cousins. (p. 506)

A concept that is gaining interest in examining cultural differences is the *intersubjective approach* (Chiu, Gelfand, Yamagishi, Shteynberg, & Wan, 2010). This approach treats individuals within societies as quasirational arbiters of societal norms, so their collective wisdom is most likely close to the norm of society. This approach has three premises: (a) people often act based on their perception of the beliefs and values of the wider society; (b) the immediate environment plays a role in one's perception of the broader society's beliefs and values, so not everyone in a society has the same intersubjective perception; and (c) intersubjective perceptions are sometimes distinct from one's personal beliefs and values. Therefore, if people behaved in a competitive manner even if some believe in cooperation, they may be behaving competitively because they felt that is what society would have dictated in their situation. A researcher using the intersubjective approach would know by interviewing these individuals whether they were acting according to their personal beliefs or on the basis of how they perceived society expected them to behave.

One reason qualitative methods have not been widely employed is, frankly, that they are much more difficult to employ than quantitative methods. They typically use far fewer research participants and require more time to gather information because of the interview format of data collection. As noted in the section on quantitative approaches, our entire system of statistical inference is based on quantitative, logical positivistic methods of inquiry. If we interview one or just a few individuals from a community, can we confidently generalize our results to the entire community or social group? How representative is that one individual or one community? A response from researchers who employ qualitative methods may be that we should not be confined only to questions that can be answered in numerical form. Moreover, how representative are the research participants in quantitative studies? We cannot be certain about the representativeness of our samples unless the samples cover the entire populations about which we are attempting to make inferences.

Clarke, Ellis, Peel, and Riggs (2010) feel that our Western bias toward the logical-positivistic approach unfairly places researchers who are challenging our existing knowledge in a defensive position while ignoring the limitations of logical positivism. They contend that qualitative researchers have had to justify their rejection of norms and standards in favor of alternative positions, yet quantitative researchers are never forced to justify their assumptions. According to Clarke et al. (2010), "The dominance of positive-empiricism (particularly in the USA) means that qualitative approaches occupy a marginal position in the field. . . . [It] also means that there is virtually no reflective discussion of the assumptions and benefits of quantitative approaches" (p. 76).

If quantitative researchers are forced to justify their assumptions as qualitative researchers are, there can be more open dialogue between the two camps.

Another reason qualitative methods have not been widely employed is that there is not agreement on the best ways to interpret the information we receive. For example, as we will see in the next chapter, meanings of words, phrases, concepts, and so on may change from culture to culture or even from subgroup to subgroup. Triandis and associates (Triandis et al., 1986; Triandis, Bontempo, Villareal, Asai, & Lucca, 1988) discussed the difficulty in measuring *self-reliance* across cultures. In individualistic cultures, self-reliance is related to the pursuit of one's own goals and has a flavor of being in competition with others. In collectivistic cultures, self-reliance is related to not burdening others and there is no sense of competition. (We also discuss individualism and collectivism in the next chapter.) The different meanings pose a difficulty in quantitative methods of inquiry, because what does a 6 on a 10-point scale mean when respondents rate themselves on a scale measuring self-reliance in a collectivistic culture as opposed to self-reliance in an individualistic culture? In contrast, if we interview individuals in both cultures about the term and come up with a sense of how each culture can be characterized with respect to self-reliance, are we examining the same concept? Because of the growing use of qualitative methods of data collection, the APA launched a new journal dedicated to qualitative methods (*Qualitative Psychology*) in 2014.

An example of the kinds of articles published by this new journal is the article by Belmonte and Opotow (2017), who used a qualitative approach to understand how archivists examine information about context and social justice, among other variables, to catalog such disparate topics as the AIDS epidemic, histories of lesbian individuals, and the World Trade Center attack on September 11, 2001. Such cataloging helps researchers to track information in these areas. Closer to multicultural psychology is an article by Nadal et al. (2016), who used a qualitative method to discuss microaggressions (to be discussed in Chapter 6).

Equivalence of Measures

Many researchers have discussed the problem of equivalence between measures developed in one culture and their translations to another culture (Brislin, 1986; Brislin, Lonner, & Thorndike, 1973; F. M. Cheung, 1985; Lonner, 1979; S. Sue & Sue, 2000). These issues involve the concepts of *functional equivalence, conceptual equivalence, linguistic equivalence*, and *metric equivalence*. **Functional equivalence** refers to items that can be functionally instead of literally equated. For example, if we were to inquire about a child's knowledge of and conclusions about fairy tales, we might select *Beauty and the Beast* if we were testing children in this country, whereas if we were testing children from a different background we might select a well-known fairy tale from the child's country of origin.

functional equivalence—the equating of items on a test or a survey functionally as opposed to literally.

Conceptual equivalence refers to terms or phrases whose meanings are culturally equivalent. For example, Marsella (1980) found that the term *depression* does not exist in some cultures, but if one were to describe a condition wherein an individual experiences fatigue and slowness of thought, the symptoms could be identified by those cultures. Thus, although the *term* depression does not exist in those cultures, the *condition* of depression does.

conceptual equivalence—refers to a term or phrase that is a culturally meaningful equivalent of the term being examined.

Linguistic equivalence refers to how the test items are translated. Most people have accepted the standard that measures must be back-translated instead of merely translated. *Back translation* is a procedure whereby the measure is translated into the target language and then translated back to the original language. If the back translation is the

linguistic equivalence—the translation of a term that carries with it similar meaning from one language to another.

same or nearly the same as the original, then the translation is acceptable for study. However, sometimes the back translation is very different from the original phrasing, so a different translation must be sought. There is a joke from the Cold War about a computer that was designed to read every book in Russian to see whether any secret codes were being transmitted in the text. To test the computer, the American scientists had the computer translate "The spirit was willing but the flesh was weak." The computer whirred and translated the item into Russian and then back into English, and the result was "The vodka was good but the meat was rotten."

Finally, **metric equivalence** refers to numerical scores between cultures. Some cultures may be risk-averse and not select the extremes of the possible answers. For example, in a culture that tends to be risk-averse, research participants presented with a 7-point scale may select 6 as the highest score, so the researcher may have to make 6 in that culture

metric equivalence—numeric scores that are generally equivalent from one culture to another.

the equivalent of 7 in a culture that uses the full range of the scale.

Even with these precautions, a researcher's work may not be done. K. Fernandez, Boccaccini, and Noland (2007) indicated that 10% of the U.S. population over the age of 5 speaks Spanish at home, and of these individuals, nearly half indicate that their English proficiency is not very good. Moreover, according to the U.S. Census Department, this percentage will rise to 13.3% by 2020, with 21.3% of U.S. households speaking a language other than English at home (Ortman & Shin, 2011). Therefore, many individuals may need special accommodations in a testing situation. The authors proposed a four-step approach to selecting appropriate tests, including identifying translated tests, identifying research using these translated tests, confirming that the research applies to the client at hand, and determining the level of research support for using the translated test with that client. Acevedo-Polakovich et al. (2007) further indicated that the clinical interview portion of the testing situation should determine the person's immigration history, contact with other cultural groups, acculturative status, acculturative stress, socioeconomic status, and language abilities and that attention must be paid to measure selection and assessment planning and translation and the use of interpreters. Beyond language issues, Fields (2010) suggested that when conducting assessments about mental health, one must go beyond merely taking into account certain cultural beliefs an individual may have by engaging in a *cultural exchange* with the interviewee. To what extent might this render an instrument fundamentally different when going from one culture to another?

Qualitative Approaches and Gender

Qualitative approaches to inquiry are not limited to multicultural issues. In fact, for years, research from the feminist literature has included qualitative methods. In her groundbreaking work, Carol Gilligan (1982/1993) discussed the differences between boys and girls based on interviews with them about their reasoning through moral dilemmas. Here is one such interpretation:

> Most striking among these differences is the imagery of violence in the boy's response,
> depicting a world of dangerous confrontation and explosive connection, where [the girl]

Men and women can respond to research questions different from each other. *Photograph by Syda Productions/Shutterstock*

sees a world of care and protection, a life lived with others whom "you may love as much or even more than you love yourself." Since the conception of morality reflects the understanding of social relationships, this difference in the imagery of relationships gives rise to a change in the moral injunction itself. To Jake, responsibility means not doing what he wants because he is thinking of others; to Amy, it means doing what others are counting on her to do regardless of what she herself wants. Both children are concerned with avoiding hurt but construe the problem in different ways—he seeing hurt to arise from the expression of aggression, she from a failure of response. (p. 38)

Much more depth can be derived from this analysis than can be obtained from an interpretation of quantitative differences in choices among alternative courses of action when children are given moral dilemmas to evaluate. Gilligan not only posits the reasoning behind the choices the children make in their course of action but also asserts what their different forms of imagery (or worldviews) are in guiding their choices. One might disagree with Gilligan's interpretations, but would have to come up with an alternative set of interpretations of the meanings of children's worldviews, which again would require more depth of interpretation than can be derived from an analysis of different numerical averages. Other researchers have provided us with guidance on using qualitative methods in examining issues of gender (Ceballo, 2017; Hesse-Biber & Leavy, 2003; Hesse-Biber & Yaiser, 2003; Holder, Jackson, Ponterotto, 2015; Seale et al., 2004; ten Have, 2004).

Qualitative Approaches and Older Populations

Because they have more life experience, older populations are more aware of contextual variables when considering questions. Hays (1996, 2007, 2009, 2016) developed a model of inquiry with older individuals of color that she calls *ADDRESSING*. This acronym stands for (A) age and generational influences, (D) developmental and acquired (D) disability, (R) religion, (E) ethnic and racial identity, (S) social status, (S) sexual orientation, (I) indigenous heritage, (N) national origin, and (G) gender. When developing research programs designed to measure older populations, researchers should include or at least consider all these variables. For example, many researchers lump all Asians together when conducting research comparing different populations of color with one another or with European Americans. However, Asians from Hong Kong may respond quite differently than Asians from the Philippines.

> I was serving on a jury, and it was striking how much the individuals on the opposite side of the issue actually seemed to hate each other. I thought that farmers tried to help other farmers where they could, but this wasn't happening in this case. The suit that each was pressing against the other seemed rather trivial, but they were determined to

make the other pay or at least suffer. Then it struck me—one of the guys was from Belgium and the other was from Germany. The Belgian was obviously not over World War II and wanted to extract all that he could out of this German farmer.

—Sam, 40+-year-old Japanese American professor

Older individuals may prefer data collection forms different from those preferred by younger individuals. *Photograph by xmee/Shutterstock*

As this quotation indicates, the Hays model is not restricted to studying populations of color. Here, national origin is an important factor along with generational influences, in view of the fact that many older Belgians still harbor resentment toward Germans. It is hard to imagine that 50 years from now, older Belgians will still harbor those feelings, because their generation will have had a markedly different experience with people of German origin. Similarly, many older Koreans might still harbor resentments toward people of Japanese origin because of the hardships caused by World War II (S. C. Kim, 1997; Sung, 1991), whereas it is doubtful that Korean American adults will harbor such resentments toward Japanese Americans 50 years from now.

Iwamasa and her colleagues (Chin, Mio, & Iwamasa, 2006; Hilliard & Iwamasa, 2001; Iwamasa & Sorocco, 2002) indicated that elderly individuals, particularly Asians, may feel more comfortable with qualitative studies than with quantitative studies. When elderly research participants filled out items with numerical responses, they failed to see the relevance of those items and wondered why they had to answer the questions three times (pretest, test, and posttest). However, they seemed to enjoy the focus-group study in which they participated because they were able to share stories with their contemporaries, and the questions being asked seemed to stimulate their fellow participants. When Iwamasa and her colleagues gave elderly Asian American participants open-ended questions, they found that the answers were more extensive when the questions were asked and answered orally than when the questions were asked in written form and required responses in writing. Thus, part of the advantage of these qualitative techniques of data gathering seems to lie in the communal interaction in which the participants are able to engage.

Experimental Designs

Two common research designs are cross-sectional and longitudinal designs. *Cross-sectional designs* gather data across different age groups. For example, if we wanted to know whether people become more conservative as they grow older, we might collect data from individuals in their 20s, 30s, 40s, 50s, 60s, and 70s and see whether the participant responses are more conservative in later age groups than in earlier age groups. One problem with this kind of research is that it may not accurately characterize the progression of political thought. Younger people may feel more liberal about some issues, and older people may feel more conservative about them.

The *longitudinal design* follows a certain set of individuals over time. Thus, to find out about liberal and conservative attitudes, we might want to collect data on 20-year-old individuals and then follow them for 60 years to see whether their attitudes become more conservative. A disadvantage of this research design is the length of time it takes to collect and analyze the data. Researchers must have the vision to design such a study when they are very young, the funding to sustain the research, and the patience to wait 60 years for the results. Over the course of the study, some participants may pass away, and researchers may also pass away. Another disadvantage of this research is that the cohort of individuals may be unusual. For example, individuals who grew up during the Great Depression may have an entirely different worldview than individuals who grew up during the civil rights movement.

Research in aging has long advocated sequential designs in studying elderly populations (Nesselroade & Labouvie, 1985). The *sequential design* is a combination of the cross-sectional and longitudinal designs. Researchers collect data on multiple cohorts of individuals and follow them over time so that by the end of the study, all age groups may be represented. For example, we might design a study collecting data on individuals in their 20s, 30s, 40s, and 50s and follow those four cohorts for 30 years (Figure 2.2). Thus, individuals in the first group will ultimately represent ages from 20 to 50 (assuming some individuals were 20 years old when they first began the study), individuals in the second group will represent ages from 30 to 60, individuals in the third group will represent ages from 40 to 70, and individuals in the fourth group will represent ages from 50 to 80. Although this design still requires the researcher to actively collect data for a long time, it requires much less time (30 years) than a strict longitudinal design (60 years) in this example.

In the sequential design, the researcher will be able to compare data from multiple groups at similar ages. For example, if we want to see how liberal or conservative individuals are at age 45, we can look at three groups: the cohort whose data were collected in their 20s, because 20 years later, many of these individuals will have become 45 years old; the cohort whose data were collected in their 30s, all of whom will have become 45 years old 20 years later; and the cohort whose data were collected in their 40s, which will have many individuals whose data at age 45 will be available. If a cohort is unusual, the data collected from it will differ from the data from other cohorts. However, if the data are more a function of age than of cohort, the results will be similar across the cohorts.

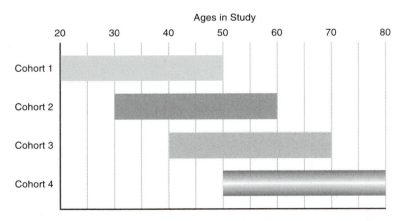

FIGURE 2.2   Overlap of age ranges in each of the cohorts in a 30-year study.

Collaborative Problem Solving

As we move toward an interdependent world, the ability to engage in collaborative problem solving becomes more important. In the first report of its kind, the Organisation for Economic Co-operation and Development (2017) examined collaborative problem solving across the globe. Researchers examined 15-year-old children solving problems across 52 countries. The collaborative problem-solving tasks involved three types of problems: (a) a jigsaw problem, where individuals within a group are given different pieces of information and they are to put their information together to come up with a unified answer; (b) a consensus-building task, where the group must consider different points of view and avoid what social psychologists call *groupthink*; and (c) negotiation tasks, where group members have different opinions or perspectives but must come up with the best possible solution to their problem. If you are interested in studying these domains further, they are popular topics in social psychology textbooks and courses.

Researchers at the Organisation for Economic Co-operation and Development found that girls across all countries scored significantly higher than boys did, although the results of another study just a few years earlier (Organisation for Economic Co-operation and Development, 2013) indicated that boys individually had better problem-solving skills than did girls. It seems that the problem-solving skills of girls as a group far exceeded their individual problem-solving skills when such skills were used to conduct a collaborative problem-solving task. The researchers (Organisation for Economic Co-operation and Development, 2017) also discovered that disadvantaged children placed more importance on teamwork than did advantaged children. These studies involved worldwide samples, and children in the United States did not fare poorly. In fact, although the United States was not among the highest performing countries, it was in the upper half. Moreover, children from the United States performed much better on the collaborative tasks than their individual scores in science, reading, and mathematics predicted. Thus, with regard to a skill that is becoming more important for the future, the performance of U.S. children as a group exceeds that of U.S. children as individuals.

Psychological Testing

Psychologists have long been engaged in various types of testing, including intelligence testing, personality testing, and diagnostic testing. Multicultural issues and challenges arise in all these types of tests. More than ever before, psychologists must be aware of these issues (Paniagua, 2014).

Intelligence Testing

> When I was young, I remember being called to the school counselor's office. Someone I had never met began giving me a test that I later recognized was an intelligence test. One of the items was "What is the Vatican?" I didn't know what it was. After the test, I asked the examiner what it was, and she told me. Since I was raised Buddhist and I was only a child, how was I supposed to know what the Vatican was? I remember thinking that the item was really unfair.
>
> —Jeremy, 40+-year-old Japanese American professor

As this story indicates, the way in which we measure intelligence can be a reflection of cultural knowledge, not what Spearman (1904, 1927) would call *general intelligence*, or *g*. Many standardized intelligence tests, such as the Stanford–Binet Intelligence Scale (Thorndike, Hagen, & Sattler,

1986) and the Wechsler Intelligence Scales for Children (Wechsler, 1991), use cultural knowledge as a part of the overall measurement of intelligence. This practice is based on Alfred Binet's long-held belief that such information was a direct measure of intelligence (Binet & Simon, 1905). This so-called direct measure contrasted with a movement headed by Sir Francis Galton to measure intelligence indirectly through sensory acuity (Galton, 1883). Galton measured intelligence by examining things such as visual acuity, how high a pitch people could hear, and how accurately people could detect different weights. Although the cultural knowledge method of measuring intelligence has proven to be much more successful and meaningful than the sensory acuity method, it is still vulnerable to subjective assessments of what is important to know and what is not.

Measuring intelligence has been a psychological pursuit at least since the time of Binet and Galton. We all have encountered people who we feel are smarter than or not as smart as we are, so this question seems to have some inherent interest. However, historically, people may have biases or assumptions about issues of intellect that influence the science they conduct. A famous case is that of Cyril Burt. Burt contended that Blacks were intellectually inferior to European Americans as determined by his scientific investigations. Burt, a prominent figure in educational psychology, was influential in his day, and people accepted his findings without question. Part of the reason for that unquestioning acceptance may have been that his findings were consistent with the general racism of the time. Years later, however, many researchers determined that Burt based his findings on his own assumptions and the genetic theory of intelligence that he was supporting, not on actual data analysis (Dorfman, 1978; Gillie, 1977; Kamin, 1974).

More recently, Herrnstein and Murray (1994) published a controversial book titled *The Bell Curve: Intelligence and Class Structure in American Life.* One of their central theses was not controversial: smart people generally do better than those who are not as smart. However, their other central thesis was controversial: individuals of color are not as smart as European American individuals, so people of color should be trained for more service-oriented and physical labor occupations, whereas European Americans should be trained to do more intellectually challenging work. The authors go on to state that an appeasing *custodial state* should be created so that individuals who are less intellectually able will not rise up in opposition to being suppressed:

> In short, by *custodial state*, we have in mind a high-tech and more lavish version of the Indian reservation for some substantial minority of the nation's population, while the rest of America tries to go about its business. In its less benign forms, the solutions will become more and more totalitarian. Benign or otherwise, "going about its business" in the old sense will not be possible. It is difficult to imagine the United States preserving its heritage of individualism, equal rights before the law, free people running their own lives, once it is accepted that a significant part of the population must be made permanent wards of the state. (Herrnstein & Murray, 1994, p. 526)

Although many have attacked Herrnstein and Murray for their apparently racist stance (e.g., Gould, 1996; Samuda, 1998), what Herrnstein and Murray (1994) really seem to ignore is that they take our measures of intelligence as unquestioned. As the story at the beginning of this section indicated, there may be systematic reasons that some individuals do not score as highly on intelligence tests as others do. If a group of individuals not in the mainstream is asked about items that are common in the mainstream, should we be surprised that they do not score as high as people who are exposed to those items? The solution to this problem is not to simply add questions that are common to this subgroup and not to the mainstream, but to try to find measures that truly get at some essence of intelligence. This pursuit is very difficult, however, because nearly every set of items is layered with cultural influence.

Another issue in measuring intelligence is that different cultures may value different contributions to what is called intelligence. Okagaki and Sternberg (1991) interviewed European American parents, Mexican American parents, and Asian immigrant parents about what they felt contributed to their children's intelligence. Asian parents reported that noncognitive factors, such as motivation and social skills, were more important than cognitive skills, such as problem solving and creativity; Mexican American parents valued cognitive and noncognitive skills equally; and European American parents valued cognitive skills more. Armour-Thomas (2003) posited this explanation:

> Although not ruling out other explanations, it is possible that the observed ethnic differences in intellectual performance may be attributed to different cultural values about what it means to be intelligent. If this is the case, an intelligence measure may be assessing different notions of valued intellectual abilities in different racial and ethnic groups and, in so doing, invalidating its results for these groups. (p. 363)

As Herrnstein and Murray's (1994) quotation about a custodial state indicated, a great deal is at stake when measuring intelligence. In fact, intelligence tests, aptitude tests, achievement tests, and other forms of placement tests have been referred to as *high-stakes testing* because the results of the tests have real implications for getting into schools, applying for jobs, setting the tone for how people respond to you, and so forth. For example, most college students have had to take college entrance exams such as the Scholastic Aptitude Test (SAT). If students receive high scores on these exams, their chances of getting into their colleges of choice are enhanced. If they receive low scores, their chances are diminished. Thus, the stakes are high for students taking these tests.

> High-stakes testing is more common than most people stop to reflect on. Looking back on life I realize this testing started when I was just a little girl and tested to get into the GATE program in elementary school. The tests continued throughout my schooling and even outside of school, such as testing for my driver's permit and, ultimately, my driver's license. The tests continued throughout high school, including the exit exam, the SAT test, and the placement tests once I was admitted to college. Even in regards to jobs these tests have been prevalent, such as the drug tests and background tests.
>
> Thinking about high-stakes testing reminds me of when immigrants had to take difficult literacy tests to enter into the United States so many years ago. I remember learning in my high school class that the creators of these tests were the elite and that the tests often contained elaborate language that even many Americans wouldn't fully comprehend. Even if it is not to that past extent, there are still literacy tests that are in favor of [native] English speakers.
> —Kaylene, 20+-year-old biracial (Latinx/European American) student

How did you feel when you took such tests and when you received your results? Intelligence tests have considerable impact. If you score high on intelligence tests, your teachers may give you more opportunities to succeed or may interpret some of your failures as a function of your not trying hard enough or of other factors getting in the way of your success. If you score low on intelligence tests, your teachers may assume that you do not know the answers, so why should they spend time on you? They may attribute your failures to what they perceive as your lesser abilities instead of other factors getting in your way. If you experience a lifetime of such assessments, you may tend to succeed or fail depending on expectations (Rosenthal, 1991, 1994; Rosenthal & Jacobson, 1968). Chapter 6 begins with a story related to teacher expectations.

Intelligence, Context, and Older Adults

In considering intelligence and aging, Labouvie-Vief (1985) discussed how our Western view of mature intelligence resides outside context and observed that we regard consideration of contextual variables to be less mature or less intelligent. Labouvie-Vief noted, "According to such deficit interpretations, one might argue, of course, that the concrete bias of the uneducated and/or the old reflects an inherent restriction on abstract thinking" (p. 516). However, she cited an interaction reported by Luria (1976) to question the degree to which we cling to our own (or at least Luria's) conceptions of intelligence and ignore cultural and contextual variables:

> Subjects often assimilate the information presented in the problem to their own ways of conceptualizing reality; they construct new premises and correctly operate upon those. The following excerpt from Luria's study will serve as a good example. Three subjects were first shown a picture of a saw, an ax, and a hammer and then asked if a "log" belonged to the same category (i.e., tools).
>
> **EXPERIMENTER (E):** Would you say these things are tools? All three subjects
> (S-1, S-2, S-3): Yes.
> **E:** What about a log?
> **S-1:** It also belongs with these. We make all sort of things out of logs—handles, doors, and the handles of tools.
> **S-2:** We say a log is a tool because it works with tools to make things.
> **E:** But one man said a log isn't a tool since it can't saw or chop.
> **S-3:** Yes you can—you can make handles out of it! . . .
> **E:** Name all the tools used to produce things . . .
> **S-1:** We have a saying: take a look in the fields and you'll see tools. (Luria, 1976, pp. 94–95)
>
> If presented with the same task, city-educated subjects will almost inevitably exclude "log" from the category of tools, and from this fact Luria argues that the uneducated display a deficit in classificatory behavior. Yet one also senses here a different dimension; these Uzbekistan peasants appear engaged in a bantering argument about the proper definition of "tool," rejecting any one concrete definition and arguing for a more flexible and perhaps even creative stance. And indeed, although the experimenter attempts to guide the subjects towards a "correct" definition of tools, one is hard put to judge who is more "rigid" or "concrete"—the subjects or the experimenter! (Labouvie-Vief, 1985, p. 517)

In other words, the experimenter had a conception of intelligence and was trying to measure that conception through a predetermined metric. When the elderly research participants brought their experience to bear on the situation, showing flexibility in their thinking, the experimenter rejected this flexibility in favor of an "objective" definition of *tool*. Which person is displaying more intelligence?

Alternative Conceptions of Intelligence

Sternberg (2002) related a research project by Cole, Gay, Glick, and Sharp (1971), who studied the Kpelle tribe in Africa. They were trying to sort objects conceptually:

> In Western culture, when adults are given a sorting task on an intelligence test, more intelligent people typically will sort hierarchically. For example, they may sort names of different kinds of fish together, and then place the word "fish" over that, with the name "animal" over "fish" and over "birds," and so on. Less intelligent people will typically sort functionally. They may sort "fish" with "eat," for example, because we eat fish, or they may sort "clothes" with "wear" because we wear clothes. The Kpelle sorted functionally—even after investigators unsuccessfully tried to get the Kpelle spontaneously to sort hierarchically.
>
> Finally, in desperation, one of the experimenters (Glick) asked a Kpelle to sort as a foolish person would sort. In response, the Kpelle quickly and easily sorted hierarchically. The Kpelle had been able to sort this way all along; they just hadn't done it because they viewed it as foolish—and probably considered the questioners rather unintelligent for asking such stupid questions. (pp. 503–504)

As you can see, our limitations in measuring intelligence may be the limitations of both how we measure intelligence and how we understand intelligence.

> The son of one of our regular customers came fishing with his father. His father was bragging about how intelligent his son was. He was going to MIT and was in the process of developing his own math system or something like that. I watched his son hook his hook onto one of the eyes of his fishing pole and go to get some bait out of the bait tank. While he was away, the wind had blown his hook off of the eye, and his hook was flapping in the wind. When he came back, he looked at the eye where his hook should have been, and when it wasn't there, he started looking at every eye, wondering where his hook was. Any idiot should have known that his hook was flapping in the wind, but this so-called genius didn't seem to have any common sense.
>
> —Anthony, 20+-year-old Japanese American boat worker

As the story indicates, there are different ways of being intelligent. The "genius" did not seem to be able to figure out a simple problem, and he thus appeared to be of less than average intelligence to Anthony.

Most of how we have measured intelligence in the past has been what Sternberg and his colleagues would call *analytic intelligence* (Sternberg, 1985, 1988, 1995, 1997, 1999, 2002, 2003; Sternberg, Ferrari, Clinkenbeard, & Grigorenko, 1996; Sternberg, Grigorenko, Ferrari, & Clinkenbeard, 1999). Sternberg's general model suggested that intelligence is not made up of a single factor, g, as Spearman (1904) had suggested. Instead, it is made up of at least three components: analytic intelligence, creative intelligence, and practical intelligence. Intelligence tests and academic achievement tests have measured primarily analytic intelligence because it is the easiest component to measure. Analytic intelligence depends heavily on memorization and calculations based on learned formulas. Thus, individuals who excel in creative and practical forms of intelligence are not identified by our standard measures (Wagner, 2000).

When I was a student in high school, I was always interested in comparing scores on tests, especially on important tests. My older brother scored in the 1500 range on the SATs, while I didn't quite [do] as well with only a 1060. I always wondered how this was possible because we attended the same schools growing up, and had pretty much the same teachers. Where he had the ability to read a book and memorize the information, I had to study material for hours and use different types of methods in order to get the information to stay long enough to remember it for an upcoming test. At the time I just thought that he was smarter than me, but now I know that he excelled in analytic intelligence, which tests like the SATs measure above creative and practical intelligence. This is mainly because analytic intelligence is the easiest to measure.

—Monica, 20+-year-old European American student

Taking up a new, cognitively demanding activity—ballroom dancing, a foreign language—is more likely to boost processing speed, strengthen synapses, and expand or create functional networks.

—Sharon Begley, *Newsweek* magazine, January 10, 2011

As a test of this triarchic theory of intelligence, Sternberg and his colleagues (Sternberg, 2012, 2014; Sternberg et al., 1996, 1999; Sternberg, Rayner, & Zhang, 2013) measured children who excelled only in analytic intelligence, only in creative intelligence, only in practical intelligence, in all three areas, or in none of the three areas. They then gave these children matching or mismatched instructions for performing a task. For example, children who excelled only in analytic intelligence performed better when given analytic instructions than when given practical instructions, children who excelled in practical intelligence performed better than did children who excelled in analytic intelligence when given practical instructions, and so forth. These results confirmed that differing forms of intelligence produce measurably different performances in different contexts.

A different conception of intelligence was proposed by Gardner (1983, 1993, 1999). Whereas standard intelligence tests generally measured a verbal component (with mathematical abilities subsumed under this verbal component) and a nonverbal component of intelligence, Gardner proposed that intelligence comprises seven intelligences: (a) linguistic, (b) logical-mathematical, (c) spatial, (d) musical, (e) bodily-kinesthetic, (f) interpersonal, and (g) intrapersonal. He later added an eighth intelligence: naturalistic intelligence (Gardner, 1999; Table 2.1). The following is an example of one of Gardner's forms of intelligence:

Creativity may be seen as a type of intelligence.
Photograph by Tom Zasadzinski

I went to a Stevie Wonder concert last night. Man, that guy is a genius! During one part of the concert, he just came out by himself with his guitar and asked people to shout out their names and occupations. Right then and

TABLE 2.1 Gardner's Eight Types of Intelligence

Type of intelligence	Examples of intelligence
Linguistic	Reading and understanding a book; understanding oral presentations; writing term papers for a class
Logical-mathematical	Solving mathematical problems; understanding advanced calculus; logical reasoning processes
Spatial	Developing a cognitive map of a route; doing mental rotations; estimating whether objects will fit into certain spaces
Musical	Playing a musical instrument; composing music; appreciating the construction of music
Bodily-kinesthetic	Playing athletic events; learning new dance steps; being able to control one's bodily movements
Interpersonal	Being able to talk easily with others; detecting changes in emotional states of others; understanding others' motives
Intrapersonal	Being attuned to our own emotional states; understanding our own abilities; knowing how to change ourselves
Naturalist	Understanding patterns of nature; being able to survive in naturalistic settings

Source: Gardner (1999).

there, he composed songs using these people's names and jobs. I've never been so impressed by anyone in my life!

—Dave, 20+-year-old European American student

In reading the story about Stevie Wonder's musical genius, a student had this reaction:

Out of the eight, I would definitely like to look into the musical one more. I believe that musical talent takes a lot of energy and intelligence. The story about Stevie Wonder really stuck out to me during class. Growing up, my dad always played his music around the house and in the car. I grew up listening to "oldies" and definitely learned to love it. The talent those artists had back then couldn't be defined as anything but musical intelligence. The way Stevie Wonder could just improvise his music like that must have been truly an amazing experience to see. Sometimes I wish I were born into that music generation so I could see how it was firsthand.

—Pamela, 20+-year-old Asian American student

Although intelligence test purists might identify Gardner's linguistic and logical-mathematical intelligences as the only true measures of intelligence, classifying the other forms of intelligence as merely learned abilities, Gardner would hold fast to the notion that these are true forms of intelligence. Dave would certainly agree that he was in the presence of genius when he saw Stevie Wonder.

Overall, I have found through Sternberg and Gardner that I don't have to [have] analytical intelligence to be intelligent; that I can be intelligent in other ways. Reflecting on the approaches that these two psychologists have come up with has made me feel more secure about myself, more intelligent, and has made me appreciate other approaches about intelligence more. I believe when it comes to defining who is and who is not intelligent that we as a whole society need to redefine it, because so many people are left feeling unintelligent because they were not able to pass or do well on a test and this is unfair, sad, and a tragedy.

—Carrie, 20+-year-old biracial (Latinx/European American) student

Personality and Diagnostic Testing

Much of personality and diagnostic testing is subject to the same problems of general study discussed earlier in this chapter. If we were to use a test to determine the personality characteristics of an individual or the level of depression that an individual is experiencing, then we would have to make sure that the test is measuring the same or very similar characteristics. The measuring instrument should have functional, conceptual, linguistic, and metric equivalence. Because so many personality and clinical tests are developed in the United States, the greatest amount of energy expended in addressing equivalence issues has been devoted to linguistic equivalence, particularly Spanish. Thus, many instruments, such as the Minnesota Multiphasic Personality Inventory (MMPI, Hathaway & McKinley, 1967; MMPI-2, Butcher, Dahlstrom, Graham, Tellegen, & Kaemmer, 1989), have been translated into Spanish (Dana, 1993; Montgomery, Arnold, & Orozco, 1990; Velasquez, Callahan, & Young, 1993; Whitworth, 1988).

In examining the literature on the MMPI applied to different people of color, Zalewski and Greene (1996) found that although few group differences existed, it was premature to suggest that single norms could be applied to all cultural groups. However, they did find that factors such as socioeconomic status, education, acculturation, and intelligence were more important in determining MMPI profiles than was cultural group membership. Ultimately, if differences *were* found based on one's identification with one's group membership, then a separate group membership test would have to be administered to give meaning to any interpretation of the MMPI profile.

Moreland (1996) identified one of the central questions regarding personality testing and populations of color: Do we look at group personalities to characterize a set of people (such as nations or specific groups of people of color), or do we pay attention only to individual personalities that we measure? Some countries or groups value certain characteristics, and those characteristics may be distinguished from characteristics valued by other countries or groups. For example, countries can be classified as generally more collectivistic or generally more individualistic (Hofstede, 1980; Triandis, 1995). However, when we characterize a country or a group,

Some see bodily-kinesthetic and musical abilities as distinct forms of intelligence. *Photographs by Tom Zasadzinski*

we may be confirming certain stereotypes about individuals from those countries or groups and not appreciating the rich variation within the groups. Because most personality assessment tools have been developed in the United States and other Western countries, how much do these assessment tools apply to individuals from other cultures?

Perhaps the most difficult question to address when applying tests and other measures to populations of color is the problem of bias. We have been discussing the difficulties in making these instruments as equivalent as possible, to eliminate as much bias from the tests as possible. However, there are at least two other kinds of bias: *bias of the user* and *bias in the usage* (Helms, 1995a). **Bias of the user** refers to the introduction of bias into the interpretation of the test by the user of the test. If the user has a predetermined assessment of a group of individuals, then the test results may be interpreted to confirm that bias. For example, Adembimpe (1981) found that African Americans were more likely to be diagnosed with schizophrenia when presenting the same symptoms as their European American counterparts, who were more likely to be diagnosed with bipolar disorder. In the clinical psychology realm, schizophrenia is considered the more severe diagnosis with a worse prognosis for recovery. Paniagua (2001) indicated that populations of color are seen by the majority group as being more pathological because the majority group does not value the lifestyles and norms of people of color as much as they value their own.

> **bias of the user**—a bias in the interpretation of a test when the test user has a particular perspective or bias that may disadvantage a person or group.

In contrast, **bias in the usage** of a test refers to how a test is used. For example, if a teacher uses a test of verbal fluency—which may be a good test for native English speakers—to determine who in a first-grade class will be section leader, the use of that test may be biased if the test is administered in an area with many children whose parents are monolingual in a different language. Eventually, these children may become as fluent in English as their European American counterparts, but at this very early age, most of them will not be as fluent in English. Thus, they will lose out on an early experience in leadership, not because they lack leadership ability, but because of another factor. Sometimes bias in the usage of a test is unconscious; sometimes, however, the bias is intentional and conscious.

> **bias in the usage**—a bias introduced when a test is used in an inappropriate manner, such as being administered in a language in which the test taker is not fluent.

Summary

Psychologists have conducted research with populations of color in many ways, and challenges can arise in these research studies. Traditionally, multicultural studies were conducted by measuring differences between European American populations and comparison groups of people of color. Such a comparison may not make any sense if the target of study is the group of people of color being studied. For example, if we want to know why some American Indians maintain a strong tie to their tribal reservation and others do not, there is no need to have a European American comparison group. However, in the past, many mainstream researchers insisted on European American comparison groups when the topic of study concerned people of color.

Important differences exist between quantitative data and qualitative data. Quantitative data are data that can be transformed into numbers so that averages of one group can be compared with averages of another group. Qualitative data are more difficult to collect and to

Food for Thought

Most students have taken tests such as the SAT to get into college, so you probably know the importance of high-stakes testing whether or not you were consciously aware of the term for this kind of test. You got into the college or university where you are in part because of the SAT score (or some other entrance test) you received and/or you did not get into another college or university in part because your score was not high enough.

As you can see, tests of this nature can have a major impact on your life and can even be life-changing events. Think about how you might feel if you were to go to a different country and be given a test that would affect your status in that country. You might gain some insight into the importance of psychological assessment.

interpret. However, qualitative data may be more meaningful in studies of groups of people of color, comparisons between women and men, and studies of elderly populations.

One problem in studying different groups is the issue of equivalence. This problem is particularly important when the material in a study must be translated into a different language. There are at least four problems of equivalence: functional, conceptual, linguistic, and metric equivalence.

Research projects have differing designs. The two most common are cross-sectional and longitudinal designs. The cross-sectional design collects data all at once across age groups, and the longitudinal design collects data at one point in time and follows the original group across time to collect data across all age groups. A combination of these two designs is the sequential design, which collects data across age groups and follows the research participants over time. Because some research participants are older than others, data that are the equivalent of data from a longitudinal design can be collected in a much shorter period of time.

Finally, multicultural issues arise in psychological testing. Intelligence testing, personality testing, and clinical assessment are subject to the same kinds of difficulties and challenges as other kinds of studies. Even if these tests are constructed carefully, their use can be biased. An added challenge is that sometimes these tests involve high-stakes testing: the results of the tests may have a major impact on individuals' lives, so particular care should be taken when using such tests.

Critical Thinking Questions

1. Have you ever been certain about something? If so, how did you know it was true? How did you go about proving its truth?
2. Have you ever been associated with a group that was the object of a research study (such as your gender, your ethnicity, your religious group)? If so, what did you think about the conclusions of the research? Did they apply to you or not?
3. Have you ever been compared unfavorably with someone or with a group that had an advantage over you? How did that make you feel? Can you construct a study that is more fair?
4. Did you ever perform poorly on a test and feel that if your teacher had just interviewed you, he or she would have come away with a much better picture of your abilities?
5. Have you ever felt that you were being unfairly measured against someone else's standards?

CHAPTER 3

Cultural Differences in Worldviews

Photograph by Kdonmuang/Shutterstock

Learning Objectives

Reading this chapter will help you to:

- understand why imposing a worldview on diverse populations can be problematic;
- identify the components of a WEIRD population;
- know which strategies are appropriate for individualistic versus collectivistic cultures;
- explain different components of worldviews;
- recognize the differences among the worldviews of diverse populations; and
- distinguish between the emic and etic approaches to understanding cultures.

She asked me if she took one pill for her heart and one pill for her hips and one pill for her chest and one pill for her blood how come they would all know which part of her body they should go to?

I explained to her that active metabolites in each pharmaceutical would adopt a spatial configuration leading to an exact interface with receptor molecules on the cellular surfaces of the target structures involved.

She told me not to bullshit her.

I told her that each pill had a different shape and that each part of her body had a different shape and that her pills could only work when both these shapes could fit together.

She said I had no right to talk about the shape of her body.

I said that each pill was a key and that her body was ten thousand locks.

She said she wasn't going to swallow that.

I told her that they worked by magic.

She asked me why I didn't say that in the first place. (Colquhoun, 2002, p. 14)

Different people with different experiences often see the world in disparate manners. People who live in cold climates may see the world quite differently than those who live in warm climates; individuals who live in crowded cities may see the world differently than those who live in rural environments; people who are of one ethnicity may see the world differently than those of another ethnicity. The above prose was written by Glenn Colquhoun, a medical doctor from New Zealand, and this is a recounting of a real-life interaction he had with a Maori woman. The modern medicine model did not fit into her worldview, and she was not satisfied with his explanations of how pills worked until he explained how they worked

---

worldview—a psychological perception of the world that determines how we think, behave, and feel.

in a manner that she would understand—magic. In this chapter we will examine some of the ways in which people have different **worldviews**, which reflect the ways in which the world is filtered through one's experiences and teachings.

Different Perspectives for Looking at Cultures

The chapter-opening story illustrates a major topic in the multicultural arena—the distinction between the *etic* and the *emic* perspectives on cultures. These terms derive from the linguistic terms *phonetic* and *phonemic* (Pike, 1967). The **etic** approach attempts to find commonalities across cultures. It examines cultures from the outside to build theories that develop universal aspects of human behavior. The

etic perspective—an attempt to build theories of human behavior by examining commonalities across many cultures.

emic approach examines only one culture from within that culture. This approach attempts to derive what is meaningful among group members (Bernal, Cumba-Aviles, & Rodriguez-Quintana, 2014; Bernal & Domenech Rodríguez, 2012; Berry et al., 1992; Brislin, 1980; Jahoda, 1982; Mestenhauser, 1983; Mio, 2013; Reynolds, 1999). U. Kim and his colleagues (U. Kim & Berry, 1993; U. Kim & Park, 2006; U. Kim, Yang, & Hwang, 2006) call the emic approach the *indigenous and cultural psychology* approach to investigation. D. W. Sue and Sue (2016) call the etic approach a culturally universal perspective, whereas the emic approach is a culturally specific perspective.

emic perspective—an attempt to derive meaningful concepts within one culture.

Imposing a Worldview

Although both approaches are necessary, J. W. Berry (1969) cautions against **imposed etics**, by which he means the imposition of an outsider's worldview on a different culture. Sometimes observers assume that behaviors or concepts are universal or have the same meaning they do in the observers' culture. For example, Colquhoun, in the opening story, initially demonstrated imposed etics when he tried to impose on the Maori woman his own value of modern medicine. He believed that the modern medicine notion of receptor sites should be understood by all, but instead, the Maori woman

imposed etics—the imposition of one culture's worldview on another culture, assuming that one's own worldviews are universal.

thought he was making something up. However, who is to say that our modern notions of medicine are correct? In the ancient Greek times of Hippocrates, after whom the Hippocratic oath is named, doctors believed that our personalities were determined by the body humors of blood, phlegm, yellow bile, and black bile. Currently, we talk about neurochemical transmitters and receptor sites. In the movie *Star Trek IV: The Voyage Home* (Nimoy, 1986), Dr. McCoy was in a hospital and saw someone who was about to have his appendix removed. Dr. McCoy said, "How barbaric!" and gave the patient a pill that fixed his appendix.

Mischel's (1958, 1961) studies represent a historical example of imposed etics. Mischel was interested in studying **delay of gratification**. He set up studies wherein children had a choice between a less desirable reward that they could have immediately (such as a small piece of candy or pretzels) and a more desirable reward that they could have if they waited until the next day (such as a large piece of

delay of gratification—the ability to wait for a more desirable reward instead of taking a less desirable reward immediately.

candy or marshmallows). He found that European American children at the Stanford Day Care Center predominantly chose to wait for the more desirable reward, whereas African American children in the inner city of Oakland chose to take the less desirable reward immediately.

Mischel concluded that African American children in the inner city did not know how to delay gratification, but that if we could teach them to delay gratification, they could work themselves out of the inner city.

However, alternative interpretations to this conclusion suggest that the African American children were behaving adaptively for a number of reasons based on their experiences: the experimenter could have been lying to them and would not show up the next day; the children may have been hungry, so the small piece of candy was more meaningful to them immediately; the experimenter could be robbed the next day; the experimenter's car could break down, so he might not show up; and so forth (Mio & Awakuni, 2000; Mio & Iwamasa, 1993; Mio & Morris, 1990). Therefore, even though Mischel's studies were well intentioned, they were still an example of imposed etics: Mischel thought he was studying delay of gratification (or lack thereof), whereas the more meaningful concept for the children was adaptive behavior.

A former student wrote about his frustrations with some of his colleagues when doing a group project. He felt that students were more interested in getting A grades than in learning something useful. He previously talked about how frustrating it was when people who thought they were doing more work than their share would take it on themselves to tell professors about those students who were not pulling their weight. He framed his interpretation in terms of imposed etics:

> Because our society as a whole is more individualistic, we impose etics on those who may not be motivated the same way. In the group setting, we assume that everyone wants to get an A on a project. And if you want to get an A then you will participate. If you aren't participating, then you obviously do not care about your grade. As a member of the group, I will make sure that you are not rewarded and, more importantly, I will not be punished.
>
> —Jamaal, 20+-year-old African American student

Even when there is some overlap or connection between ideas from different cultures, there may be cultural variations. A colleague told us of the connection between Freud's Oedipal complex and a Japanese variant of this story:

> There was an old article (1980s?) about the Ajase complex. It told of a Japanese psychiatrist in the 1920s or '30s who was pondering Freud's Oedipal complex. He concluded that the Oedipal complex was based on a Western family structure, and so, came up with the Ajase complex. Ajase is a mythical character as was Oedipus. The story of Ajase speaks to the close Mother–Son relationship in an Asian family (especially a Japanese family?). In fact, the myth does not even mention Ajase's father explicitly, just Ajase resolving his relationship with his mother (his mother did not have Ajase out of love for Ajase, but out of love for her husband and family duty as well—Ajase was torn apart when he realized this truth). This Japanese psychiatrist went to Vienna to present his thesis to Freud, himself. As I recall Freud's reaction, he found this cross-cultural variation of the Oedipal complex fascinating and read the thesis.
>
> I think the Ajase complex speaks to the need for culture-specific assessment of Freudian theory and of Ericksonian theory as well (Kohlberg could also be included).
>
> —Yasue, 60+-year-old Japanese American professor

At first blush, this Ajase complex seems similar to the Oedipus complex. However, the Ajase story does not include a jealousy of one's father, a fear that the father would cut off the boy's penis, or an underlying sexual connection between Ajase and his mother. Instead, the story seems to underscore the cultural value of not sticking out or being too prideful. Ajase thought he was special and thought he was central to the family structure, so he was devastated to discover that he was conceived as a result of family obligations.

Understanding Differences From Within

As discussed in Chapter 2, *self-reliance* is a good example of how different countries can conceptualize terms differently. Triandis and associates (Triandis et al., 1986, 1988) found that individualistic countries conceive of self-reliance as related to the pursuit of one's own goals, whereas collectivistic countries conceive of it as related to not burdening others. We will be discussing individualism and collectivism much more extensively later in this chapter, but, briefly stated, people in individualistic cultures tend to place individual rights over the rights of the collective, whereas people in collectivistic cultures tend to place collective rights over the rights of the individual. Each culture has some elements of the other (i.e., individualistic cultures have some elements of collectivism and collectivistic cultures have some elements of individualism), but on balance, there are identifiable tendencies in most cultures (see Triandis, 1995). The emic definitions of self-reliance give completely different flavors to the term and an insight into the countries defining the term.

S. Sue and Sue (2000) give another example of emic differences between individualistic and collectivistic societies in defining a term:

> For example, one aspect of good decision making in the Western [individualistic] cultures may be typified by an ability to make a personal decision without being unduly influenced by others, whereas good decision making may be understood in Asian [collectivistic] cultures as an ability to make a decision that is best for the group. (p. 3)

Again, we see that the individualistic definition of the term (*good decision-making*) involves a reflection of individualism: independence; the collectivistic definition of the term involves a collectivist value: paying attention to others.

A former student wrote about how gayness was understood in the Philippines before Western religious concepts took over the country:

> I believe also that lesbians, gays, and bisexuals have a connection with religion and spirituality. Beyond the privileges discussed in class, early shamans of almost every tribe and nation were almost always homosexual (though I have read that some were bisexual). In ancient Greece and Rome, many priests dressed in matron's gowns and paraded as women in certain festivals, and priestesses of certain deities wore belts that had a phallus shape in front for certain rites. The notion is that these are people who are in between norms of usual interaction or in between genders; they can be both. Thus, they were perceived also as being able to traverse in between the normal and paranormal worlds. In the Philippines, they were once called babaylan (priests, most likely gay men or wounded warriors and sickly men) and catalonan (priestesses, most likely lesbians or infertile women). It was not until the arrival of Christianity that these people were demonized and labeled as sinful. In many early societies, homosexuals are delegated the positions of spiritual leaders primarily for two things: one, because they

cannot or will not aid in the propagation of the tribe; and two, because they are seen to be not one, not another, yet both. This is a mysterious quality that was attributed to and associated with special abilities. In modern day India, a special class of eunuchs who dress in feminine garb are believed to be able to curse or bless people because of this very reason. Thus, homosexuality has a long and intriguing yet hidden history.

—Trevor, 20+-year-old Chinese Filipino student

Male and Female Perspectives

If one needed evidence regarding the perceptions of men and women, one need look no further than 2017. The year began with the Women's March on January 21, which was "possibly the largest [protest march] in U.S. history" (Vick, 2017, p. 32), through *Wonder Woman* in the middle of the year (Docterman, 2017), and ended with women breaking their silence for being sexually harassed and being selected as *Time* magazine's "Person of the Year" (Felsenthal, 2017).

The Women's March was spurred by the inauguration of Donald Trump as president of the United States. Trump's surprise victory came in November 2016, just weeks after admitting that he had abused and harassed women because of his fame. Since his inauguration was to be on January 20, 2017, organizers of the Women's March scheduled their protest for January 21. Estimates of the crowd size in Washington, DC, ranged between 250,000 and 750,000, and across the country, the lowest estimate was 3.2 million protesters (Vick, 2017).

The film *Wonder Woman* received the largest opening for a film by a female director (Patty Jenkins), with over $100 million the first weekend of its opening, and it was also the first superhero blockbuster movie given to a female director (Docterman, 2017). Success for this film was not guaranteed because previous "blockbuster" superhero movies did not produce the anticipated large box office revenues (*Batman v Superman* and *Suicide Squad*), nor were they reviewed favorably by film critics. Moreover, according to Docterman, "Hollywood executives have been skeptical about whether female superheroes can succeed at the box office" (p. 52).

Women gathered by the hundreds of thousands to protest the inauguration of Donald Trump as President of the United States and to demonstrate their unity and empowerment. *Photo by bakdc/ Shutterstock*

For years, women—and many men—have accused men of sexual abuse and harassment. As many in Hollywood had indicated, Harvey Weinstein's abuse had been an open secret (Zacharek, Docterman, & Edwards, 2017). However, women were reticent to go public with these accusations for fear of ruining their careers or breaking settlement agreements. Finally, Ashley Judd told the *New York Times* of the abuse (Kantor & Twohey, 2017), and the newspaper uncovered a long history of Weinstein's abuse and paying off women in nondisclosure agreements. Action was swift, as Weinstein's own company, Miramax, fired him, and he has since been unwelcome at all Hollywood movie studios. This was the dam breaking, with numerous women coming forward to give their accounts of abuse they had endured over the years. A #MeToo Twitter campaign began a couple of years before the Weinstein revelation, but the movement exploded when Hollywood stars began using it, prompting women of all professions to reveal abuse they had encountered. At the time of this writing, it appears that this movement will change how society treats victims of this kind of abuse and disciplines the abusers.

Men and women clearly have different worldviews. Some (Bendahan, Zehnder, Pralong, & Antonakis, 2015; Riggio, 2017a) connect the abuse to power differentials between men and women. Riggio (2017b) warns that we must pay attention to how we engage in nonverbal behavior in this new understanding of differing worldviews. Gone are the days when men can excuse their behaviors or dismiss women's perceptions by imposing their male etics; women's emics must be considered in our interactions.

Wonder Woman was a huge hit and was the first superhero blockbuster directed by a woman. *Photo by Kathy Hutchins/Shutterstock*

Ashley Judd and Rose McGowan (pictured here) were Hollywood actresses who gave public interviews about the sexual abuse they experienced from Harvey Weinstein, stimulating the movement against such kinds of abuse. *Photo by Kate Geen/Shutterstock*

A former student discussed how she perceives safety and noted that many men in her life do not see it the way she does and call her paranoid:

> Many times at night, when I am walking to my car, I carry my keys in my hand and keep looking around, making sure nobody is too close to me. I get a sort of nervous feeling when I am by myself at night and it never really dawned on me until we went over women's worldviews that very few men, if any, have ever done that. I have been known to carry a bottle of pepper spray on me and every once in a while I get teased for being overcautious by some of my male friends, but I know it's because they have never really experienced how it feels to be a relatively small, defenseless person.
>
> I am currently writing a report about the effects of society blaming the victim on victims of sexual assault. It's upsetting to me that so many people can blame female victims of sexual assault by saying that they were either out where they shouldn't be or dressed inappropriately or in some way, shape, or form had it coming to them. Now I am not saying that every man feels this way or even most men, but for any man who has ever thought that just disgusts me. I mean, what right does a man have to blame a female for sexual assault when he has never known how it feels to be as defenseless as a woman feels on a day to day basis?
>
> —Kerry, 20+-year-old European American student

In addition to the issue of sexual harassment identified previously, man and women have very different experiences in the field of work. Halpern and Cheung (2008) and F. M. Cheung and Halpern (2010) interviewed 62 powerful women in China, Hong Kong, and the United States, asking about their experiences both climbing the corporate ladder and while they were at the top. These women were at the chief executive officer or college administrator level, so they were in charge of major institutions while looking at the world through gender lenses. Even though these cultures were quite different from one another—particularly comparing the United States to the other two cultures—they have similar gender statistics. Women comprise 46% of the workforce in the United States, 45% in China, and 42% in Hong Kong. Of the people who have college degrees, 57% are women in the United States, 44% in China, and 54% in Hong Kong. Moreover, at a time when having children is optimal, our corporations and institutions of higher education expect the greatest amount of personal sacrifice to climb the respective institutional ladders. Thus, it is not surprising that only about 2% of the chief executive officers of the Fortune 500 (and also the Fortune 1000) companies in the United States are women. This statistic is comparable to that for our European counterparts: 2.8% of the chief executive officers in the United Kingdom and 3% of those in the European Union are women.

Halpern and Cheung (2008) found that women at these lofty levels often had to choose between having

"Denim Day" has become a symbol protesting violence against women. *Photograph by Tom Zasadzinski*

children or climbing the corporate/institutional ladder. In the popular press, the media described this phenomenon as the *mommy track* versus the *career track*. The women who chose to have children had to be especially creative in being able to combine these two aspects of their lives. Traditionally, men did not have to make the same choices because they married women who were not in the workforce and stayed at home and raised their families.

One of the authors (JSM) recalls watching a *This Week With David Brinkley* news program in which they were discussing the problem that president Bill Clinton faced in filling the post of attorney general. Two consecutive potential nominees had to withdraw because it was revealed that while they were advancing in their law firms, they had employed undocumented nannies to care for their children. David Brinkley asked why it was so difficult to fill this post. Sam Donaldson said, "Why is there such a 'nanny' problem? In the old days, we didn't have nanny problems." Cokie Roberts tersely replied, "That is because men married their nannies."

This issue reemerged in the 2010 California race for governor. Meg Whitman, who had been the chief executive officer of eBay for several years, was running nearly even with Jerry Brown when it was revealed 6 weeks before the election that she had hired an undocumented worker as her housekeeper. Shortly thereafter, Brown had a double-digit lead over Whitman and ended up winning the election handily.

On the one hand, the emic perspective involves differences between cultures in interpreting concepts and terms. On the other hand, the etic perspective attempts to find commonalities across cultures. Landrine, Klonoff, and Brown-Collins (1995) stated, "'Truth' is understood as both the emic and the etic data, or as the emic data alone, but not as the etic data alone" (p. 62).

Connecting the distinction between the emic and etic perspectives with J. W. Berry's (1980) notion of imposed etics, students are encouraged to think of times when they felt misunderstood by someone else. Such a situation can be conceptualized as imposed etics in that one person probably felt that the other person's behavior was based on one sort of motivation, whereas it was in fact based on another sort of motivation. Have you ever felt misunderstood by someone and then found, when you talked it over with that person, that the misunderstanding was just a matter of the two of you interpreting the situation differently?

Well-Meaning Clashes

Emics and etics refer to larger societies, or at least subcultures, as opposed to individual differences in interpretation. However, our collective individual interpretations can lead to greater societal differences. Brislin (2000) pointed out that in some cultures (e.g., the United States), belching after eating is considered rude, whereas in other cultures, belching is a compliment to the chef on the excellent food. In Japan, people are expected to sip their tea loudly to indicate to the host that the tea is delicious, whereas in the United States, people are supposed to sip their tea or coffee quietly.

Much of our adaptation to other countries involves learning the emic rules of conduct. Brislin (2000) talked about *well-meaning clashes*, which are cultural differences in interpretation that are not meant to harm others but that cause problems because there are different emic interpretations of situations or concepts. Cushner and Brislin (1996) developed several such scenarios. Here is one of them:

> After a year in the United States, Fumio, from Japan, seemed to be adjusting well to
> his graduate-level studies. He had cordial relations with his professors, interacted
> frequently with other graduate students at midday coffee breaks, and was content with

his housing arrangements in the graduate student dormitory. Fumio's statistical knowledge was so good that professors recommended that certain American students should consult him for help in this area. He seemed to be excluded, however, from at least one type of activity in which many other of the American graduate students participated. This was the informal gathering of students at the local pub (bar) at about 5:00 on Friday afternoons. People did not stop and invite him to these gatherings. Since he was not invited, Fumio felt uncomfortable about simply showing up at the pub. Fumio wondered if the lack of an invitation should be interpreted as a sign that he was offending the American students in some way. (p. 202)

As one can see, Fumio was acting according to his own cultural perspective, which demanded that one be invited to a social gathering, whereas the American cultural perspective was that since this was an informal gathering, anyone could show up. Because he was not invited, Fumio wondered whether he was being purposely excluded from the event.

After hearing this story, a former student wrote the following in her reaction paper:

My boyfriend, Carl, told me a story about a foreign exchange student from Japan. She was in one of his classes. She had only been in the United States for a couple of months and did not have very much confidence in the way that she spoke English. She came to class every day, sitting quietly in the back of the classroom for most of the quarter. Carl saw her every day looking sad and sitting alone. After a few weeks of class had passed, he decided to say hello to her. He had been watching a Japanese television program on his satellite and had learned how to speak certain words in Japanese. He said hello to her in Japanese, and as soon as the words came out of his mouth her face lit up and she smiled and said hello back to him. Every day for the rest of the quarter Carl said hello to her in Japanese and every day she returned the greeting by saying hello and with a smile. At the end of the quarter, she told him how appreciative she was that he took the time to say hello to her every day. He was the only friend that she had in America at the time. Throughout the quarter he introduced her to more people. She now has several friends and no longer sits in the back of the classroom alone.

—Amy, 20+-year-old European American student

Research suggests that the notion of worldviews is complex, even in examining just two major cultures compared with one another. Obasi, Flores, and James-Myers (2009) conducted a study examining over 1,800 participants of African and European ancestry. Their analysis suggested that there were seven major dimensions distinguishing these broad groups: materialistic universe, spiritual immortality, communalism, indigenous values, tangible realism, knowledge of self, and spiritualism. Their resultant Worldwide Analysis Scale produced consistent results affirming their seven dimensions across different administrations of their instrument.

How much do men understand women's worldview regarding safety? *Photograph by Tom Zasadzinski*

Individualism Versus Collectivism

We touched on the concepts of **individualism** and **collectivism** in Chapter 2 and earlier in this chapter. In this section, we will discuss these concepts in more detail. Perhaps the most respected name in this area is Harry Triandis (Triandis, 1989, 1995). As the basis for understanding these terms, Triandis (1995) explains,

> Collectivism may be initially defined as a social pattern consisting of closely linked individuals who see themselves as parts of one or more collectives (family, co-workers, tribe, nation); are primarily motivated by the norms of, and duties imposed by, those collectives; are willing to give priority to the goals of these collectives over their own personal goals; and emphasize their connectedness to members of these collectives. A preliminary definition of individualism is a social pattern that consists of loosely linked individuals who view themselves as independent of collectives; are primarily motivated by their own preferences, needs, rights, and the contracts they have established with others; give priority to their personal goals over the goals of others; and emphasize rational analyses of the advantages and disadvantages to associating with others. (p. 2)

individualism—a social pattern in which individuals tend to be motivated by their own preferences, needs, and rights when they come into conflict with the preferences, needs, and rights of a group or collective in which the individual is a member.

collectivism—a social pattern in which individuals tend to be motivated by the group's or collective's preferences, needs, and rights when they come into conflict with the preferences, needs, and rights of the individual.

As a way of measuring individualism and collectivism, Triandis (1995) asked people to rate the degree to which they agreed with various statements that relate to the terms, such as the following:

a. One should live one's life independently of others.
b. It is important to me that I do my job better than others would do it.
c. My happiness depends very much on the happiness of those around me.
d. I would sacrifice an activity that I enjoy very much if my family did not approve of it.

If you agree with the first two statements, then you hold an individualistic perspective; if you agree with the second two statements, then you hold a collectivistic perspective.

A student discussed how her collectivistic upbringing can put a lot of pressure on her, but she did not feel that this pressure was burdensome:

> My family breathes and lives on the words, "family always comes first—we must take care of each other." My parents have seen firsthand how the strength of a family can withstand any obstacle—these are not merely words of wisdom; it is a means of survival. To begin, my father immigrated from Mexico and my mother immigrated from El Salvador when they were both only 18 years old. Even when she had nothing to her name and barely any food or clothes to wear, my mother would work days and nights only to be able to send money back to El Salvador for her mother and sisters. While her mother and sisters knew about how much she was struggling to make ends meet here in America, it was expected that my mother would send back almost 60% of her weekly

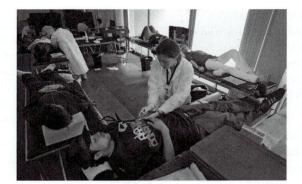

Collective behavior can help all. *Photograph by Tom Zasadzinski*

checks back to El Salvador—because it was for the betterment of her family. With the money that she and her brothers were able to send back to El Salvador, her little sisters and mother were able to survive and were even able to send one of their sisters to school. Naturally, when I first heard this story as a little girl I asked her "why she would do so much for people that are so far away—and why couldn't they pay for their own things when you had to?" Her answer was simple and later I felt embarrassed for even questioning; she said calmly, "Because they are my family, and family always takes care of each other. And one day when you go to La Universidad we will all do the same for you. We will have to make sacrifices, but we will do it gladly so that you can make something of yourself; so that maybe one day you will be able to help us when we are old and tired." While this may sound like a lot of pressure to put on a little girl, it is not—simply because of the fact that these have been the same words that I have heard and lived by my entire life and I understand the role that I play for the betterment of my family; my parents have always led by example, and have done the same for us. My mother always says, "En la union esta la esfuerza," which translates to "in union there is strength."

—Jeannie, 20+-year-old Latinx student

Yet another student compared her collectivistic upbringing with that of some of her European American friends:

Growing up in a Mexican and Sicilian home I was very much brought up in a collective society environment. Every action I made, I thought about how will this affect my family? I still do as a grown woman. I used to get teased by my friends when I was younger endlessly for this. "Marissa, why do you let your family control your life?" my friend Rebecca would ask. I reply, I didn't, and thus an argument would ensue about how I was going to be a little girl my whole life. A lot of my friends who were mostly White didn't understand. Though, on the other side I didn't understand how they made decisions every day without thinking about their family first. If they wanted to do something, they just did it. No questions asked, just freedom of their own choice.

I was jealous at times but then I realized how close I was with my entire family, including extended family, and watched how my friends' families were not as close. They only had their immediate family unit. For the most part there was no value for their elders.

> Most people start by being collectivists, attached to their families. They become detached from them in different degrees and learn to be detached from collectives in different situations.
> —Harry Triandis, individualism–collectivism researcher

They were put away in retirement homes while my grandmother lived with us. There was fighting over who would take care of their elderly; my family simply did it. . . . To me, growing up in that collective unit was not suffocating, but reassuring that I will always have people around me who love, respect and cherish who I am in this life and who I have yet to become.

—Melissa, 20+-year-old Latinx student

The Individual and Society

Triandis (1995) also made a distinction between *idiocentrism* and *allocentrism*. He believed that individualism and collectivism were ways of characterizing the dominant perspectives of societies, whereas idiocentrism and allocentrism were ways of characterizing individuals. Thus, if an individual is **idiocentric** in an individualistic society, then his or her perspective will be in concert with society's perspective. However, if an individual is **allocentric** in an individualistic society, then his or her perspective will be at odds with society's perspective.

Because individualism and collectivism reflect a society's dominant modes of interaction, most people in societies are consistent with the society's perspective (i.e., individualistic societies have more idiocentric individuals in their respective societies, and collectivistic societies have more allocentric individuals in their respective societies). However, a certain percentage of people find themselves mismatched with respect to their society's perspective. Triandis (1995) calls these people **countercultural individuals**:

> **idiocentrism**—individualistic tendencies that reside within an individual. Individualism refers to the society, whereas idiocentrism refers to an individual.

> **allocentrism**—collectivistic tendencies that reside within an individual. Collectivism refers to the society, whereas allocentrism refers to an individual.

> **countercultural individuals**—idiocentric individuals residing in a collectivistic culture or allocentric individuals residing in an individualistic culture.

> Thus, in collectivist societies there are idiocentrics, who look for the earliest opportunity to escape the "oppression" of their ingroups, and in individualistic societies there are allocentrics, who reject individual pursuits and join gangs, clubs, communes, and other collectives. The idiocentrics reject conformity to the ingroup and are most likely to leave their culture and seek membership in individualistic cultures. They are also very likely to criticize and object to their culture. (p. 36)

A former international student from Hong Kong agreed with the notion of idiocentrism and allocentrism:

> I have found the concept of idiocentrism and allocentrism to be interesting because it directly relates to my experience here in the United States. . . . It is interesting because that is exactly how I feel after coming here to study. I was considered a more individualistic person in Hong Kong; though I lived with my parents, I was independent and responsible. I took care of myself and I had my own personal life and my parents did not have to worry about me. Quite often I kept in touch with my siblings and we had family gatherings from time to time.

However, living in the States for more than five years, I have found that though I have not changed, compared to my friends' lifestyles here I am a collective person. I think that as an individual, I have the freedom to make my own decisions and have my own life, and I have to be responsible for my life. For my family, even though I do not have to take care of them, at least basic things like keeping in touch with them have to be done. However, my friends who live here seem to not feel this way. They say they have a busy schedule and they do not have time to do that. For those who live with their parents, they say they usually go home late, so they have their dinner alone or eat out with friends before going back home. It is amazing when I have found that most of my friends who live with parents have their own television in their bedrooms, they watch TV in the bedroom and would not think of watching TV in the living room with their siblings and parents.

—Veronica, 20+-year-old Hong Kong immigrant student

In a widely cited study, Hofstede (1980) examined individualism and collectivism across 39 countries. The United States ranked highest in individualism, with Australia, England, Canada, the Netherlands, and New Zealand rounding out the top 6 countries. These countries are typically classified as Western countries. In fact, 15 of the most individualistic countries are what we would consider Western countries, because all are in Europe or are predominantly White former British colonies (the United States, Canada, Australia, and New Zealand). South Africa ranked 16th in individualism, followed by two more European countries, Israel and Spain. The highest ranking individualistic Asian country was India, at 21. Of the 19 lowest ranking individualistic countries (i.e., the countries that scored in the collectivistic direction), only 3 were European countries (Turkey, Greece, and Portugal), with all other countries coming from Asia, Latin America, and the Middle East.

masculine–feminine dimension—a continuum of authority from hierarchical (masculine) to egalitarian (feminine).

Hofstede (1980) also categorized countries according to what he termed a **masculine–feminine dimension**, depending on what he felt were power distances. A country in which there was a great deal of power distance between people who were high in authority and people who were not in authority was labeled a masculine country; a country in which there was less power distance between these two points in the authority hierarchy was labeled a feminine country. Triandis (1995) later renamed this dimension a horizontal–vertical dimension. Figure 3.1 depicts this dimension.

At the beginning of this section (p. 81), we noted four statements from the scale that Triandis (1995) devised to measure the degree to which people are horizontally individualistic ("One should live one's life independently of others"), vertically individualistic ("It is important to me that I do my job better than others would do it"), horizontally collectivistic ("My happiness depends very much on the happiness of those around me"), and vertically collectivistic ("I would sacrifice an activity that I enjoy very

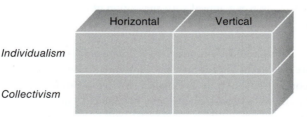

FIGURE 3.1 Triandis's (1995) individualism–collectivism and horizontal–vertical dimensions.

much if my family did not approve of it"). In other words, the horizontal dimension places everyone at or near the same level, so the horizontally individualistic statement sees everyone as being equal and having an equal opportunity to live independent of others, whereas the horizontally collectivistic statement sees one person's happiness as being a shared (collective) experience. The vertical dimension deals with hierarchical structures of societies, so the vertically individualistic statement reflects competition, with each person trying to outdo others, whereas the vertically collectivistic statement reflects the requirement that the individual accede to the collective's desires and the belief that family is more important than the individual. I half-jokingly say to my students that in the United States, we are more horizontal in our greetings, so students may say hello to me by saying things like, "Hey there, Dr. Mio" or "How's it goin', Dr. Mio?" or simply "'Sup?" However, in Latin American countries, one might say to friends and peers, "¿Como estas?" or "¿Que tal?" but one would never greet an elder or a professor in such an informal manner, instead saying "¿Como esta usted?," which is a formal greeting.

Many of our students are intrigued by the vertical dimension. Although it applies to their lives, they have never had a word to categorize their experiences. The following are some of the reactions we have received from students:

> Over the weekend I had something really funny happen between two of my friends. My friend, Ralph, who is White, was talking about his family and how not close they were to each other and how he did not love his father. My other friend, Tammy, who is Asian, was there also. She did not understand how someone could say that kind of stuff about their own family. I guess she and her family are very close and they do not disrespect each other even when they are not around. She was not upset, I think it just showed the differences of the cultures. . . . I have always seen the Asian culture as a collectivistic culture and this backs up my beliefs.
>
> —Connie, 20+-year-old European American student

> I am from a Filipino background where everything is centered on the family. For example, a family member's achievement in work, school, etc. can be looked at as the family's accomplishment. In other words, successes and failures from each family member are representative of the family as a whole. One way that I see this as an advantage is that because the family works together, each member encourages, supports and helps the others. So in this type of family there is great social support. The disadvantage to this is that when one member of the family fails at something, the family as a whole is also seen as a failure as well. So there is increased pressure to do well and accomplish goals. And this in turn may put a strain on the relationship between parent and child.
>
> A second advantage (vertical collectivism) is the fact that when parents become older and their own children grow up, their children take them into their homes and care for them, compared to other families where the parents are set up in retirement homes or their own homes (where they care for themselves) or convalescent homes (where other people care for them). The disadvantage to this is that when parents are living in the homes of the children, boundaries are unclear. The relationship changes from parent/child to parent/adult child. And when the transition isn't smooth there could also be a strain on their relationship.
>
> —Ann Marie, 20+-year-old Filipina American student

As Ann Marie indicated, there can be disadvantages to the collectivistic perspective, particularly the vertical collectivistic perspective. Because part of this orientation involves respect for one's elders and for individuals in authority, one may feel victim to the desires of people in authority. The following student talked about the breakup she had with her boyfriend because she did not believe her mother would approve of the relationship:

> For the past four years I was in a relationship with an older (out of the norm) Mexican American man that my family knew nothing about. Every day of those four years, it was like I was living another life. I had to hide my relationship with the man I loved because deep down inside, I knew that my family would never understand why I would get involved with someone so much older than me. In the first couple of years into our relationship, I didn't care of the fact that I had to sneak around just to be with him. My individualistic side of me only cared about my own happiness, and my happiness revolved around him. He opened my eyes to a different light and a new life. A life that I happened to fall in love with. It was because of him why I am the way I am today.
>
> Towards the last year of our relationship, we had hit the ceiling. . . . Because we came from a very collectivistic culture, hiding our relationship from our families started to really hurt us. Near the end of our relationship, he wanted for us to come out to both our parents about our relationship. I was torn. I did not know what to do. All I knew was I loved that man but I didn't have the heart to break my family's heart, especially my mother. My individualistic side of me wants to say, "Screw it! I'm in love with that man, it is my life, and I'll do whatever [what] will make ME happy!" But at the same time, my collectivistic side of me is saying, "I don't want to disappoint my family. They've done so much for me. All they want is for me to be with a man who's more suitable for me."
>
> Even though my individualistic side of me is more dominant, I had to end our relationship for the sake of my family's happiness. Some people might say I'm a coward for not stepping up and living my own life. But all I know is, I can't allow my own selfishness [and] break my mom's heart. I love my mom and she has sacrificed too much for me so that I'm able to have all the things I need and want. The least I can do for now is, do my best to be a good person to make her proud of me.
>
> —Alisha, 20+-year-old Chinese/Indonesian immigrant student

Another student whose family is from a different part of the world had undergone the same kind of agony that Alisha did. She was dating a man who was unacceptable to her family of origin and struggled between what her family was telling her and what her heart was telling her:

> Trust me; this decision was probably the hardest one I have ever had to make. My family and I fought night after night for months straight about who was right and who was wrong. Quite frankly, it got me nowhere. I felt so alone even though I had someone who loved me more than this world right beside me. I felt like no one understood what I was going through in the challenges I was facing trying to choose between my family and him. "Why did I have to choose?" I kept saying to myself and, "Why did

I?" I mean honestly, it was either my family being selfish as hell trying to get me to marry someone who fell under their criteria of who I should be with or it was me, wanting only what I wanted no matter what anyone else thought of it. Until this day, I still do not know what the answer to that is. . . .

I kept thinking that if I made my family go through all of that embarrassment in our country and be put to shame by the Lebanese community (remember my mom works for our government) and what they would say about us, somewhere down the line my relationship would be hit with a disaster and when I would try to come back to my family all they will have left to say to me is, "I told you so." My mom cried all summer. My family, who is extremely close, fell apart because of me and my own selfishness and it is so hard to get rid of that guilt I have within me. After constant battles, I decided to leave for a month and go be with him in Seattle where my family could not attack me every minute. Although I was trying to run away, it was hard for me to be happy there with him knowing all the anxiety and anguish I was putting my family through back at home.

All of my friends kept telling me, "You are not doing anything wrong! Your family is the one who is wrong," but tell that to my heart. . . . No one understood why it was such a big deal because they are not Lebanese and their mother does not work for their country's government. It was a battle in itself trying to explain to them why the issue was such a big deal. All in all, after so much heartache from so many things, I realized that my family is the most important in this world to me and without them, I would not have even made it this far. To sacrifice my love for all they have given me is worth every penny in my opinion. A good man may be hard to find, yet there are more out there, but a family you only have ONE of and they are not replaceable.

—Anna, 20+-year-old Lebanese American student

How would you have reacted if you were Alisha or Anna? Remember, individualism and collectivism are general terms that describe general feelings or choices when personal and collective choices are in conflict. The vertical collectivistic choices that Alisha and Anna made were not without the anguish of their idiocentric feelings. If you had selected a path that was more idiocentric, this would not mean that you did not feel allocentric tugs at your heartstrings.

S. Sue and Morishima (1982) presented a clinical case that reflected the power of vertical collectivism. A Chinese American woman married a man born in Hong Kong. Everything was going well in their marriage until her husband's parents immigrated to the United States and lived with them. No matter what the woman did, her parents-in-law (particularly her mother-in-law) criticized her efforts. She wanted her husband to ask his parents to back off, but he did not feel that he could confront them. This situation nearly resulted in their divorce. When we present this case to our classes and ask students how they might handle the situation, many have said things like, "I'd tell my mother-in-law to mind her own business," "I'd tell my mother-in-law that if she didn't like how I did things, she could do them herself," and "I would kick them out of my house." These "solutions" would definitely have led to a divorce in this particular case. We will discuss how the therapist resolved this dilemma in the next chapter, because it relates to issues of communication. However, for purposes of this chapter, this case illustrates how influential vertical collectivism is in guiding lives. As a hint to how the case was resolved, the therapist used vertical collectivism in her intervention.

Guilt Versus Shame

In individualistic societies, **guilt** is a prominent negative emotion. In fact, psychoanalytic theory places guilt as one of the fundamental ways of punishing ourselves for violations of cultural expectations (Brenner, 1982). According to psychoanalytic theory, our behaviors are a result of the *compromise formation*. In this formula, the id wants to express a drive (sexual or aggressive), the ego employs a defense mechanism to express that drive, and the superego evaluates the defense mechanism. If the defense mechanism expresses the drive in a socially appropriate manner, then we feel good and fulfilled; if the drive is expressed in a socially inappropriate manner, then we are punished through depression or anxiety. Guilt is at the core of both depression and anxiety.

Collectivistic (particularly Asian) societies tend to place more emphasis on **shame** as a motivating negative emotion (Shon & Ja, 1982; D. Sue, Mak, & Sue, 1998; D. W. Sue & Sue, 2016; Yeh & Huang, 1996). Whereas guilt is more of an individualistic notion in which someone does something wrong and feels guilty about it, shame is a more collectivistic concept wherein the offending behavior is a reflection of one's upbringing or community. As Shon and Ja put it, "Shame and shaming are the mechanisms that traditionally help reinforce societal expectations and proper behavior. The East Asian concept of *tiu lien* (loss of face) embodies the social concept of shame" (p. 214). This distinction between guilt and shame seems to resonate with many of our Asian students:

> guilt—a prominent negative emotion in individualistic cultures that involves an individual's sense of personal regret for having engaged in a negative behavior.

> shame—a prominent negative emotion in collectivistic cultures that involves an individual's sense of regret for having engaged in a negative behavior that reflects badly on his or her family and/or upbringing.

> Thinking about the concept of shame, I remember that we have a phrase that is similar to "shame on you," but the pronoun "you" is replaced with "people." It applies in situations where one has made a mistake. This phrase clearly indicates the notion that the mistake not only aroused guilty feelings but also brings shame to the family, and it is commonly used for children so as to let them know they should not make mistakes again and should prevent "loss of face" in the family.
>
> —Veronica, 20+-year-old Hong Kong immigrant student

Western cultures emphasize guilt, whereas Eastern cultures emphasize shame. *Photograph by LeventeGyori/ Shutterstock*

Face Saving, Face Giving, and Social Support

As the preceding discussion indicates, shame is related to the concept of loss of face. An important social skill in collectivistic/Asian societies is the ability to help those with whom one is interacting to save face if they make a social mistake (Leong, 1998; Redding & Ng, 1982; D. Sue, Mak, & Sue, 1998; Zane & Ku, 2014; Zane & Yeh, 2002). For example, in the study by Zane and Ku (2014), the authors found that Asian American college students who were more concerned with issues of saving face disclosed less to therapists in an analogue therapy situation than did those students who were not concerned with issues of saving face. Because self-disclosure is an essential part of the therapy process, Zane and Ku's results provide insight into why the long-observed phenomenon of Asian and Asian American clients dropping out of therapy prematurely might be a result of face concerns (B. S. Kim, Atkinson, & Umemoto, 2001; B. S. K. Kim et al., 2003; S. Sue, Fujino, Hu, Takeuchi, & Zane, 1991; S. Sue & Zane, 1987).

Most people are aware of the notion of **losing face/ saving face**. One strategy to avoid losing face is to not stick out from the collective or otherwise leave oneself open to criticism from the group (Kitayama & Markus, 1999; Kitayama, Markus, Matsumoto, & Norasakkunkit, 1997; Kitayama, Snibbe, Markus, & Suzuki, 2004; Kitayama & Uchida, 2003; Markus & Kitayama, 1991). The following is a humorous example of how a student of ours came to understand his father's need to save face:

> **losing face/saving face**—loss of face involves being publicly revealed for negative behavior; face saving involves being able to protect one's public persona.

> A perfect example is when I was deciding what to choose as my major for college. Let me digress for a bit and point out that the Indian culture is a collectivist culture (however, I see it becoming more and more individualistic recently) while I am almost fully individualistic. To my parents, one must do what is best for the family—no questions asked. Coming back to the college situation, you can see how this posed a problem for me. My father wanted me to do something that would benefit the family in some way (whether practically or simply for the family's honor, which is a very legitimate reason in India). I had originally chosen architect engineering . . . but soon realized that math was not my forte; I changed to psychology and my dad almost had a brain aneurism. He saw psychology as such a low-level subject that he was basically saying that anyone can do psychology. Needless to say, the arguing went on for weeks and I even took him to see my high school counselor, after which he finally gave in. I later realized that it was the family's honor that was at stake because he made me promise that if I did psychology I would have to get straight A's and get a PhD; this way he can still say that his son is a doctor.
>
> —Pervez, 20+-year-old Indian American student

In contrast, most people are not aware of the notion of **face giving/giving face** (Lim, 1994; Ting-Toomey 2005; Ting-Toomey & Cocroft, 1994). Face giving is extolling the virtues of another in public. In collectivistic societies, it is generally inappropriate or deemed to be overly drawing attention to oneself to talk about one's accomplishments. It is much more culturally appropriate to be humble about one's accomplishments and allow someone else to let others know about them. This allows one's self-esteem to be uplifted without seeming to toot one's own horn. For example, let

> **face giving/giving face**—extolling the virtues of another person in public. It would be considered boastful and individualistic if the individual did this himself/herself.

us say that you have won a prestigious award but you are in a setting where most people do not know about the award. In the United States, you might say something like, "I was honored and humbled to win this award." Even though you say that in a demure manner, Asian groups still see it as inappropriate bragging. In Asian groups, it is much more appropriate to say nothing about your award, but because some people may know about it, someone else is expected to announce to the group that you have won the award. You can then express your humility about receiving it. This other person is engaging in face giving.

Notice that in face giving, your collective still knows about your award, your esteem is raised in the group, and your own self-esteem is increased. Kitayama and Markus (2000) discussed this in terms of how one gains happiness and subjective well-being through one's social relations. They suggest that in individualistic societies, good feelings are "owned" by individuals and people connect with others by discussing their good feelings with one another. This is seen as a personal property that the two interacting individuals may share with each other. In East Asian cultures, happiness and good feelings are the property of the interpersonal atmosphere, so the feelings are in the relationship between the two interacting individuals, not within each individual. Thus, one can see the importance of face giving in collectivistic societies. If one brags about one's own accomplishments, there is a bad feeling in the air; if one gives face to another, there is a good feeling in the air, and the two are drawn closer together through the process of empathy.

I (JSM) have a personal story that underscores the notion of giving face. In the Japanese and Japanese American communities, there is a notion of *the rule of three*. When we are complimented, we are not supposed to accept the compliment until the other party insists three times that we did something well or looked particularly good, and so forth. My grandmother— *Ba-chan*, which means "grandmother" in Japanese—used to stay up all night before New Year's Day to have the sushi for our New Year's celebration be as fresh as possible. She made excellent sushi, yet she would never accept compliments for her sushi. I recounted this in the *Asian American Psychologist*:

> My grandmother was famous for her sushi. She really made the best sushi around. Every year, people would compliment her on her sushi, and she refused their compliments, saying how tired she was and that it wasn't her best effort, etc. Our guests and my grandmother would do this dance every year, with my grandmother finally accepting their compliments [after their third compliment] and insisting that they take some food home. One year, after all of our guests left, my grandmother said, "My sushi must not have been very good this year." We all said, "Oh, no, Ba-chan, it was delicious. Why would you say that it wasn't very good?" She replied, "Our guests didn't insist enough this year." (Mio, 2008, p. 9)

Face giving is a common practice in Asian cultures.
Photograph by Phil Date/Shutterstock

Are We WEIRD?

In examining cultures across the world, one must wonder whether the Western way of thinking is unusual. In a series of publications, some researchers concluded that we really are WEIRD, an acronym standing for Western, educated, industrialized, rich, and democratic (Henrich, Heine, & Norenzayan, 2010, 2016; D. Jones, 2010). To the extent that most psychologists, hence psychological researchers, are from Western-oriented countries—particularly the United States—the research that emerges from these countries is biased toward individuals who fit the WEIRD profile. In fact, Arnett (2008) calculated that 95% of the empirical papers published in the six top journals in psychology were published in Western countries (68% from the United States and 27% from the United Kingdom, Canada, Australia, New Zealand, and the rest of Europe). However, the continents of Asia, Africa, and South America have a much larger population than the continents of North America, Europe, and Australia. Hence, much of our knowledge is WEIRD in that it has been conducted on a minority of people in the world—a minority that is predominantly individualistic as opposed to collectivistic in orientation. How do you think that this might affect the way in which we perceive the world?

Value Orientation and Worldviews

Kluckhohn and Strodtbeck's Value Orientation Model

As D. W. Sue and Sue (2003) have pointed out, Kluckhohn and Strodtbeck (1961) presented a model of worldview based on value orientation. They identified four dimensions and examined how different groups responded to those dimensions. Table 3.1 presents these dimensions and value orientations.

Past, present, and future **time focus** are self-evident. However, the other value orientations probably need explanation. In the **human activity** dimension, *being* refers to being what you are, which is fine. *Being and in becoming* means that you are motivated to become something more than what you are right now; you must nurture your inner self to realize your potential. *Doing* refers to the value of activity. If you work hard, you will eventually be rewarded.

In the **social relations** dimension, *lineal orientation* is related to our earlier discussion of a vertical relationship, in which there is a hierarchy of authority. *Collateral orientation* suggests that we should respect the opinions of our family and our friends when encountering problems, so

time focus—an orientation that values a particular time perspective. Some cultures value the past, some value the present, and some value the future. Although all cultures value all three, some cultures value one of these perspectives more than do other cultures.

human activity—the distinction among being, being and in becoming, and doing. *Being* refers to an individual's being accepted just as he or she is. *Being and in becoming* refers to an individual's evolving into something different and presumably better. *Doing* refers to an individual's being valued for the activity in which he or she is engaged.

TABLE 3.1   **Kluckhohn and Strodtbeck's Value Orientation Model**

Dimension	Value orientations		
1. Time focus	Past	Present	Future
2. Human activity	Being	Being and in becoming	Doing
3. Social relations	Lineal	Collateral	Individualistic
4. People/nature	Subjugation	Harmony with nature	Mastery over nature

Source: Kluckhohn and F. L. Strodtbeck (1961).

social relations—the distinction among lineal, collateral, and individualistic. *Lineal orientation* is a respect for the hierarchy within one's family. *Collateral orientation* is essentially the same as collectivism. *Individualistic orientation* is the same as individualism.

people/nature relationship—how people relate to nature, be it subjugated to nature, in harmony with nature, or mastery over nature.

this term is related to our earlier discussion of collectivism. *Individualistic orientation* is the same as individualism.

Finally, **people/nature relationship** refers to how people relate to nature. *Subjugation to nature* refers to one's submission to external forces, such as God, fate, and biology. *Harmony with nature* suggests that people should try to be in harmony with nature, allowing nature to be dominant in some circumstances and trying to overcome nature in other circumstances. *Mastery over nature* refers to trying to conquer and control nature.

These dimensions can differ across different racial/ethnic groups, as Kluckhohn and Strodtbeck (1961) demonstrated. In a more explicit comparison among differing racial/ethnic groups, Ho (1987) examined the values (worldviews) of the dominant groups typically discussed in the United States (see Table 3.2).

An examination of Table 3.2 indicates that there seems to be much more similarity among worldviews of populations of color than there is between any one of those groups and the middle-class European American worldview. One might speculate that people of color's somewhat common worldviews are at least partially influenced by their experience of racism within the United States.

In a wonderful example of American Indian value orientation, Trimble (2003) discussed a classroom exercise he conducted with his students. This exercise demonstrated to students that attachment to personally valued items is ephemeral for many American Indians, particularly in the Pacific Northwest. It also demonstrates how one might feel when left out of a collective activity. Because of the ephemeral (or permanent) nature of our attachment to objects, the exercise helps to demonstrate the time orientation dimension discussed in Kluckhohn and Strodtbeck's (1961) study.

To demonstrate the value of sharing—and the nature of the Potlatch system of the northwest coast tribes in Canada and the United States—I ask students to bring something of value to the next class meeting and inform them that they may have to give it

TABLE 3.2   Ho's Depiction of Value Orientation Comparison Among Racial/ Ethnic Groups

Area of relationship	Middle-class European Americans	Asian Americans	American Indians	Black Americans	Hispanic Americans
People to nature/ environment	Mastery over future	Harmony with past–present	Harmony with present	Harmony with present	Harmony with present
Time orientation	Future	Past–present	Present	Present	Past–present
People relationships	Individual	Collateral	Collateral	Collateral	Collateral
Preferred mode of activity	Doing	Doing	Being-in-becoming	Doing	Being-in-becoming
Nature of man	Good and bad	Good	Good	Good and bad	Good

Source: Ho (1987).

to someone else. At the beginning of that class, I arrange the students in a circle, and one by one I have them place their valued possession in the circle's center. Students then are asked to pick out their valued possession and give it to someone else in the circle, someone whom they respect and wish to honor for their value to the group (the instructor does not participate in the distribution process). Outcomes differ from one class to another. On some occasions, a few students do not receive recognition or gifts, and discussion can become spirited as they attempt to deal with being overlooked. Discussions invariably gravitate to the difference between the reciprocity norm and sharing one's possessions without expecting to receive anything in return. (Trimble, 2003, p. 230)

Can you imagine giving someone one of your prized possessions? Can you imagine doing this and not receiving anything in return? As these questions imply, people in the United States seem to have an attachment to material possessions. Is this true throughout the world? Yes and no. Oishi and Schimmack (2010) examined the literature on *subjective well-being*, or how contented or happy people of various nations felt about their life circumstances. People in richer countries tended to be happier than people in poorer countries, but once the average annual income per capita exceeded $15,000–$20,000, other factors determined happiness, such as trusting fellow citizens, feeling individual freedom, and having close social relationships. Therefore, even though the United States is the richest country in the world on a per capita basis, its citizenry does not report the highest levels of well-being; that crown goes to Venezuela. Thus, even though the United States in the past decade or so has tried to unseat Hugo Chavez, Venezuela's president, one reason he has remained popular and in power is that the people of Venezuela are among the happiest in the world.

Derald Wing Sue's Worldview Model

Derald Wing Sue is one of the most prolific and influential authors in the multicultural arena. In fact, he and his two brothers (Stanley and David) have all contributed heavily to this literature. Some time ago, Derald Wing Sue (1978) proposed a model of a person's worldview that examined the intersection of **locus of control** and **locus of responsibility** (see Figure 3.2). Both dimensions vary along an internal–external continuum. Thus, a person can have an

locus of control—the focus of control over outcomes of one's life, be it internal or external control.

locus of responsibility—the focus of responsibility for one's position in life, be it internal feelings of responsibility or external, societal responsibility.

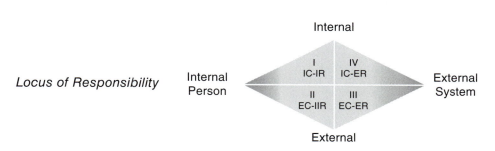

FIGURE 3.2   Derald Wing Sue's (1978) worldview model. From "Eliminating Cultural Oppression in Counseling: Toward a General Theory," by D. W. Sue, 1978, *Journal of Counseling Psychology, 25.*

internal locus of control, an external locus of control, an internal locus of responsibility, or an external locus of responsibility. When crossed, these two dimensions yield four forms of worldview.

People with an *internal locus of control* and an *internal locus of responsibility* (IC–IR) world-view, or Quadrant I in the model in Figure 3.2, believe that they have control over their lives and that their position in life is based on their own attributes. This is the dominant view in the United States. We can control our own lives because of our own abilities. The American dream is based on this worldview, and those who fail may fall victim to problems such as depression and guilt because they believe that they have no one but themselves to blame for their failures.

People with an *external locus of control* and an *internal locus of responsibility* (EC–IR) world-view, or Quadrant II in the model, have little control over their lives, yet accept the dominant society's view that they are responsible for their position. D. W. Sue and Sue (2003, 2008, 2013, 2016) cite Stonequist's (1937) concept of the **marginal man** (person) to describe these individuals. They feel caught between two worlds, yet they do not see racism as having any relevance to their position in life.

marginal man—Stonequist's concept of how one feels when one is caught between two worlds.

People with an *external locus of control* and an *external locus of responsibility* (EC–ER) worldview, or Quadrant III in the model, have little control over their lives and feel that the dominant societal system is against them. This is a recipe for disaster, and individuals often give up trying to succeed. Seligman's (1982) notion of learned helplessness is often associated with this quadrant. This concept suggests that people can become depressed because they have learned that no matter what they do, something bad will happen, or that they cannot predict their environment, so life seems meaningless. When a system of racism constantly assaults people, they often give up and develop a worldview in which they are powerless to make changes.

Finally, people with an *internal locus of control* and an *external locus of responsibility* (IC–ER) worldview, or Quadrant IV in the model, believe that they have strong personal abilities and could control their lives if the system of oppression and racism were not preventing them from realizing their full potential. D. W. Sue and Sue (2016) suggested that these individuals take pride in their ethnicities and strongly identify with their own ethnicity and that of others who see the injustices in the world.

Nagata and Takeshita (1998), in their examination of Japanese Americans who were interned during World War II, reported the reactions of some of their Nisei (children of Japanese immigrant parents) research participants: "It [the internment] affected me, my self-esteem, that they would think that of me. . . . You feel like 'I'll show you that you're wrong!' That's part of what drove me to do what I did" (p. 599). This participant volunteered for the U.S. Army to fight in the war effort. Thus, his feeling of disempowerment from a racist system drove him to prove that he had some degree of control over his life. One's experience with racism determines whether one develops an EC–ER worldview or an IC–ER worldview. Nagata and Takeshita's discussion continued:

> "Seeing the evacuation notice, I couldn't believe it, you know," recalled an interviewee. "They can't do that to me. I'm an American! That was a natural response of most of us Nisei." However, as a disempowered ethnic minority group who experienced consistent and significant stressors related to discrimination from before the war, Japanese

Americans had already drawn upon their cultural strengths and values in times of need. Such previous exposure to past discrimination helped some Nisei to cope. One interviewee noted that he was not entirely surprised by the internment decision, given the level of prejudice that existed at the time, and pointed out that well before the war, Japanese Americans in his community were treated as second-class citizens, restricted to the back-row seating in movie theatres, and barred from certain barber shops, swimming pools, and churches. Perloff (1983) found that individuals who felt least vulnerable prior to being victimized expressed the most difficulty in coping with negative life events, while those who felt most vulnerable had the least difficulty coping with their victimization. Based on this finding, one might hypothesize that for some Nisei, an already established sense of vulnerability may have interacted with Japanese cultural values to enhance coping ability. (pp. 599–600)

Thus, many individuals who had little exposure to racism seemed to take the internment experience very hard and developed an EC–ER worldview. The people with this worldview had the most difficult time adjusting to internment and may have even developed depression or other forms of difficulties at the time of removal from their homes. In contrast, many people who had actively experienced the racism around them seemed to understand that this was an oppressive system against which they had to resist, and they seemed to develop an IC–ER worldview, knowing that they had their own abilities and that those abilities must be used to fight the system of oppression or to prove their worth to their oppressors. The effects of the Japanese American internment experience can still be felt today (Nagata, 1990a, 1990b, 1993, 1998; Mio, Nagata, Tsai, & Tewari, 2007).

Ethnic Minority Worldview

We discuss issues of racism and related terms more extensively in Chapter 6, but here we address the issue of ethnic minority status in the development of an individual's worldview. As D. W. Sue's (1978) model suggests, this issue is very important in shaping one's view of the world.

As Janet Helms and her colleagues indicated, the major groups considered ethnic minority groups in the United States are identifiably different from the White Anglo-Saxon Protestant majority (Cook & Helms, 1988; Helms, 1992, 2001; Helms & Cook, 1999). They refer to the dominant ethnic minority groups as **ALANAs** (African Americans, Latinxs, Asian Americans, and Native Americans) or **VREGs** (visible racial/ethnic groups) to avoid the term minority, because that term implies "an inescapable psychological reminder of the disempowered status of individuals who are not White" (Helms & Cook, 1999, p. 28). Moreover, the term minority is inaccurate in areas where ALANAs are the numerical majority. Similarly, *majority* is used to describe European Americans, whether or not they are a numerical majority group. Thus, the terms ALANA and VREG can be used in contrast to White Anglo-Saxon Protestant, but on equal footing.

> **ALANA**—Helms's acronym for African Americans, Latinxs, Asian Americans, and Native Americans.

> **VREG**—Helms's acronym for members of visible racial/ethnic groups.

Some individuals are referred to as *White ethnics*: individuals whose families have either recently emigrated from Europe or held on to their country-of-origin identification. A good example of the latter use of the term can be seen in celebrations of St. Patrick's Day in the United States. People of Irish background "put on their Irish hats" and engage in more Irish activities and mannerisms than they normally display. What distinguishes European American ethnics from ALANAs or VREGs is that European American ethnics can blend into society and be indistinguishable from European Americans who have been in this country for several generations. However, ALANAs cannot blend this way because their physical features (e.g., skin color, hair texture, shape of eyes) distinguish them from the European American population. Therefore, ALANAs may experience racism or even just be thought of as different from the norm, which, in turn, can have a profound influence on their worldviews.

In a benign example of different worldviews, an African American colleague talked about her daughter's closest friend in her day-care school:

> It's interesting. . . Allie's best friend at her day care is Rebecca. Allie is the only African American child in the day care, and Rebecca is the only Asian American girl, and somehow they seem to know that they are the most different from the other children, so they have become close. I don't know if the other children or the day care workers actually treat them differently, but they just seem to know that they are different.
>
> —Linda, 30+-year-old African American professor

This feeling of being different is learned quickly. M. J. T. Vasquez (2001) recounted her first day in elementary school:

> When I first entered elementary school in the first grade, I cried daily for weeks and weeks. My mother was very distressed, assuming separation anxiety. She had not expected this, since during the first 6 years of my life, I had been versatile in staying with any number of extended relatives; my parents had assumed that entering school would be an easy adjustment. Although what I felt may have been partly "separation anxiety," the experience of entering a White majority school, with not a single teacher or administrator of color, led to my world feeling suddenly unsafe. It was not the color difference but the attitudes of those with power toward those of us of color (primarily Hispanic, since there were very few Asian students, and Black students attended a segregated school). The subtle and not-so-subtle negative attitudes were clear. We were ignored, spoken to more curtly and harshly than the White children, and some of the children of color (mostly boys, as I recall) were treated harshly (e.g., knocked down on the playground) and called racial epithets. I remember feeling incredible empathy for Latino children who were abused on the playground and felt an immediate identification with and protection of those like me. I remember feeling the pain of loss of positive regard at both a personal and a group level but had no words to describe the loss and sadness and lack of safety and resulting anxiety that emerged. (pp. 66–67)

With experiences like those, ALANAs learn quickly that the world is different for them than it is for European Americans. These differences are reinforced by media presentations of the world (Cortés, 2000). We once witnessed an exchange in a predominantly European American area of the country that illustrated the different worldviews of European Americans and ALANAs:

WHITE WOMAN: How was your spring break?
LATINX MAN: It was nice. I was able to hang out with my friends. However, we were stopped by the police, which kind of bummed me out.

WHITE WOMAN: Why were you stopped?

LATINX MAN: The usual reasons.

WHITE WOMAN: What do you mean by that?

LATINX MAN: The cops just stopped us because we were Mexican. Every time my friends and I drive around together, we get stopped. We weren't doing anything except driving and laughing and talking together, but we got hassled.

WHITE WOMAN: But they can't do that! Police are not supposed to stop people for no reason.

LATINX MAN: We always get stopped for no reason. They see our dark color and they stop us.

WHITE WOMAN: But that can't happen! That's not fair!

LATINX MAN: But it is my world.

However, Castellanos and Gloria (2007) used cultural worldviews to help Latinx students succeed in college. This effective use of strengths-based worldviews will be revisited in our chapter on cultural differences in communication.

As many authors have indicated, major motion pictures can have a huge influence on our perspectives and identities (Greenwood & Long, 2015; Tan & Visch, 2018; Young, 2012). Essentially, these authors indicated that such films invite audience members to co-create a world with the filmmakers in creating a vision of imaginary worlds with implications for real life. Greenwood and Long (2015) go so far as to say that movies can give adolescents life lessons and character role models and help them understand social relations. However, as Erigha (2016) pointed out, African American filmmakers have been systematically shut out of the world of science fiction. This has the dual effect of keeping such filmmakers from some of the most lucrative positions in Hollywood and not providing children with representation of powerful African Americans. For this reason, the 2018 release of *Black Panther* is seen as a major breakthrough in American cinema.

As we will discuss in Chapter 6, there is a notion of *White privilege* in American society. White privilege means that people of European American heritage can assume that characterizations and images of them will appear widely in American society. People of color—particularly African

The film *Black Panther* is seen as a breakthrough in American cinema. *Photograph by Marvel/Disney/Kobal/Shutterstock*

Americans—cannot assume the same thing, particularly with respect to positive images. Ryan Coogler, the African American director of *Black Panther*, indicated that when he was growing up and it came time to wear a costume for Halloween, there were no superhero costumes representing someone who was Black (T. Johnson, 2018). In proudly reflecting on the impact of his film, Coogler stated,

> An entire generation of children will not know what it feels like to not see themselves reflected back on costume racks, coloring books or movie screens. We're at a pivotal time where these characters and stories are coming not out of permission or obligation, but necessity. (Ryan Coogler, director of *Black Panther*, as cited in T. Johnson, 2018)

The commercial success of *Black Panther* and the inclusion of the Black Panther in the subsequent Marvel superhero movie (*The Avengers: Infinity Wars*) solidified the image of this character as a positive role model with which African American children—and children of all races and ethnicities—can identify.

Worldview of Women

As we discussed earlier, women's worldview is different from men's, especially regarding safety and work expectations. We discuss sexism a bit more in Chapter 6, but for now, let us examine how issues of sexism and other kinds of societal expectations can color a woman's worldview:

> I remember at a very young age being taught that men came first and the needs of women came last. I was told that what women had to say really had no importance compared to what the men had to say, but as they instill this value onto me, I always believed that this was not fair, and as I grew up I learned that not everyone holds this to be true. I became very independent and tried to succeed in everything and yet I knew in my heart that there were still disadvantages for women that were not out in the open but kept under lock and key. I still believed that we were moving in the right direction for change. When something like this [an experience of sexism she encountered] happens, I am able to understand a little more clearly why women fought so hard to earn their rights to be equal. It is such a sadness to know we have come a long way, but to realize there are some people not willing to change is a greater sadness.
> —Bonnie, 20+-year-old Latinx student

Women are often shaped by society's standards of beauty, which are applied to women and not to men. This is particularly true for girls and women of color:

> Unfortunately, I've seen Black children who try to make their skin white by painting their skin with white paint. In addition, I've heard Black children say that they wanted "White girl" hair because they are tired of their "monkey braids." I don't think that this negative socialization is affecting only Black children. I think that this negative socialization is affecting all minority children. When my sister was younger (we are biracial; half Mexican and half white), she asked our dad why he didn't marry a White woman. My sister added that she wished he had married a White woman because my

sister wanted blonde hair and blue eyes; she wanted to look like Barbie. It is this way of thinking that creates general "beauty" rules/guidelines in our society. Children are growing up thinking that White is beautiful. It is extremely depressing.

—Lois, biracial (Latinx/European American) student

Other issues help to shape women's worlds. Iwamasa and Bangi (2003) discussed mental health issues related to women, including a higher incidence of depression, postpartum depression, and eating disorders. Eating disorders affect women more than men because thinness is considered an important component of feminine beauty. Woodside and Kennedy (1995) indicated that eating disorders are relatively rare among men, so this is predominantly a women's issue. Halpern et al. (2007) examined why science and mathematics fields are often not in women's worldviews. McLean and Beigi (2016) examined barriers to leadership roles for women. Eagly (2009) found that when engaging in prosocial behavior, women differ from men in that their helping behaviors tended to be directed to emotionally supportive and sensitive behaviors that are mostly directed toward those who are close to them, whereas men tended to direct their helping behaviors toward the collective as a whole and use their strength and courage.

Mio and associates (Mio et al., 2003) discussed the impact that violence can have on women's views of the world. It is interesting that violence against men is more often perpetrated by strangers, and violence against women is more often perpetrated by their partners. Thus, women encounter violence in settings where they would expect to find the most love and protection. Imagine how that can change one's worldview. Moreover, women encounter sexual harassment in the workplace much more than men do. As Koss and associates (Koss et al., 1994) would say, there is no safe haven for women because violence against them can occur at home, in the workplace, and in the community. Kerry's story near the beginning of this chapter illustrates that men often have no concept of the feelings of vulnerability in women's lives.

At the other end of the emotional spectrum, there are gender differences in humor (Crawford, 2003; Crawford & Gressley, 1991; T. E. Ford, Boxer, Armstrong, & Edel, 2008; R. A. Martin, 2007; Mio, 2009; Mio & Graesser, 1991; Rappoport, 2005). For example, R. A. Martin found that men tended to prefer formal jokes, whereas women tended to prefer humorous anecdotes. One consistent finding is that men tend to prefer more aggressive forms of humor (Mio, 2009; Mio & Graesser, 1991; Rappoport, 2005). Overall, men tended to engage in more jokes and humor than women do. Mio and his associates (Mio, 2009; Mio & Graesser, 1991) speculated that humor was one of the few positive ways in which men could express emotion in public, so humor is more important to men than to women. In contrast,

Women's and men's worldviews often differ. *Photograph by Rawpixel.com/Shutterstock*

women have a variety of ways with which to express emotions, so humor does not occupy a special attraction for women.

Worldview of Lesbian, Gay, Bisexual, and Transgendered Individuals

The worldview of lesbian, gay, bisexual, and transgendered (LGBT) individuals still contains a large element of fear and danger (Herek, 1995, 2000). Because of heterosexism (discrimination by heterosexuals against nonheterosexuals), LGBT individuals do not feel safe in the current environment:

> I can't have a picture of my partner on my desk without people wondering who it is or grilling me about my relationship with her. I can't walk hand in hand with my partner without fear of someone yelling obscenities at me or even beating me up or worse. It is hard to explain how much fear I have just being myself because I can't control what someone else might do or how someone else might react.
>
> —Lonnie, 30+-year-old European American lesbian professor

Some LGBT individuals also believe that they are always on display or are a source of curiosity. Therefore, they can never feel completely at ease around straight individuals. A lesbian woman on our campus talked about how uncomfortable she was participating in an exercise involving targeted and nontargeted individuals at a campus-sponsored cross-cultural retreat. In this exercise, everyone stands on one side of the room, and when one is in a targeted group (e.g., women, people of color, LGBTs, individuals coming from a lower socioeconomic background) identified by the moderator, he or she must go to the other side of the room. After each targeted group is identified, its members are reunited with the main group. The purpose of this exercise is to give everyone the experience of being in a targeted group so that they can empathize with people who are in targeted groups (Barker-Hackett & Mio, 2000). As a woman in a discussion group said,

Many lesbian, gay, and bisexual individuals congregate in groups to feel safer. *Photograph by KathyHyde/ Shutterstock*

> When I had to go to the opposite side of the room when [the moderator] said that all LGB individuals had to be targeted, it was really irritating to look back at the main group. I saw how people were craning their necks to see who was gay on campus. When I was in other targeted groups, people didn't seem nearly as curious as to who was on the opposite side. It only happened when the issue of gayness came up.
>
> —Fawn, 30+-year-old European American lesbian student services worker

Some LGBT individuals know that they are living in the context of a straight world. However, they wish that their straight friends could understand a worldview from the LGBT perspective:

> I am going to start off by saying that I love, care, and cherish my close friends; they are a multicultural blend that I would do anything for. They range from European American to Asian American as well as a mixture of straight and gay individuals, but for the most part my close friends are straight. Yes, they all know that I am gay and they fully accept me for who I am; then again, I am not the type of person that would shove my sexuality down someone's throat or make them feel uncomfortable around me. So, why do I bring them up?
>
> I firmly believe that they need to mix things up when it comes to going clubbing or just to hang out, meaning gay clubs or hangouts. It seems that all we do is hang out at straight clubs the majority of the time, which is not a problem for me. However, I would like for them to at least go to gay clubs once in a while just so I can mingle or be around people that I can relate to or have an interest within.
>
> I did mention my thoughts and feelings on this matter, adding that I enjoy their company, although I would like to see them take an interest in my "gay culture" just as I have taken an interest in being part of [their] straight community. I explained that it is important for me to retain them as close friends as well as it is important for me to remain true to myself.
>
> —Miguel, 30+-year-old biracial (Latinx/German) gay student

Many LGBT individuals report that others feel that their sexual orientation is their entire identity. It is easy to imagine that an African American woman might have an identity as a woman separate from her African American identity (and separate from her combined African American woman identity), but LGBT individuals often are seen only through the prism of their sexuality:

> When I first joined this organization and people found out I was gay, they introduced me to [names of three other gay men]. At our next meeting, I got introduced to them, again. Year after year, I got introduced to the same three guys, as if people were saying, You gay guys hang out over here and don't bother the rest of us. No one would bother asking me about what my other interests were and that I might have something in common with them instead of these three guys. Yes, these guys were nice and I enjoyed interacting with them, but I would have liked it if someone were to take some interest in me other than simply knowing that I was gay.
>
> —Van, 40+-year-old American Indian professor

Two issues that underscored the view of a hostile world toward LGBT individuals were the Pentagon's "Don't Ask, Don't Tell" (DADT) policy and the opposition to same-sex marriage. Although DADT was overturned by a vote in the U.S. Senate in 2010 and fully repealed/implemented in 2011 (Bumiller, 2011), repealing this law required herculean efforts. Still, influential senators such as the 2008 Republican nomination for president, John McCain, warned that the military was going to be harmed grievously if DADT was overturned, despite many reports that there would be minimal disruption to the military in implementing this repeal

(Belkin, 2013; J. C. Johnson & Ham, 2010; J. L. Lee, 2013; Parco & Levy, 2013; Parrish, 2010). Although such predictions had not come to pass in the first year of its implementation according to an official Department of Defense study (Parrish, 2012), the opposition to DADT's repeal was an indication of how some people still viewed LGBT populations (Belkin, 2013). Although as of this writing it seems that DADT is safely in place in the military, the LGBT community still feels under attack with the current attempt to ban transgender individuals from the armed forces (C. O'Brien, 2017). President Trump announced in July 2017 that the military should ban transgendered individuals from serving in the military and in the Homeland Security department, and he signed this executive order in August 2017. This ban has been stayed by the federal courts as of this writing (Keneally, 2017), but efforts such as these continue to create a hostile environment for LGBT individuals.

With respect to same-sex marriage, according to a *Washington Post*–ABC News poll taken in 2014, 56% of people polled supported same-sex marriage, whereas only 38% opposed it. This is essentially a reversal of these percentages over the previous 10 years (Capehart, 2014; Chokshi & Craighill, 2014). Beyond polls, researchers have also documented the trend toward acceptance of same-sex marriage, particularly among younger Americans (Baunach, 2012; A. B. Becker, 2012a, 2012b). This general acceptance in the broader society, along with the Supreme Court's earlier decisions about limited acceptance of marriage equality, led to the Supreme Court's historic decision to make same-sex marriage the law of the land (Liptak, 2015). However, despite the growing cultural support for marriage equality, there is still consistent resistance, particularly along religious and/or political lines (Baye, 2012; Nagourney, 2013; *New York Times* Editorial Board, 2013). At the time of this writing, the Supreme Court is considering whether LGBT individuals have the right to common services such as having a wedding cake made in their honor (Ambrosino, 2017). Such considerations again create a hostile environment for LGBT individuals and affect their respective worldviews. As a student of ours said,

> When I decide to come out to someone, I still have to be very careful. Even though polls show that the majority of people support marriage equality, there are still around 40–45% who are against this, and I don't know how they are going to react to me. I need to be sure I will be safe when I come out to people.
>
> —Kiera, 20+-year-old European American lesbian

Some LGBT individuals must operate in an environment in which they do not know whether they will be accepted or rejected by their families (Hancock, 2003). On the one hand, if they are rejected by their families of origin, think of the worldviews that may result: Because people whom they love and trust the most rejected them, they may end up not trusting anyone or at least having a very difficult time trusting people in the world. On the other hand, those who accept them may be considered a *family of choice* as opposed to their *family of origin*, and their worldview may be tremendously more loyal to the family of choice.

Ever since Bruce Jenner announced to the world that he was transgendered and will henceforth be called Caitlyn Jenner (Bissinger, 2015), the topic of transgendered individuals has been of interest in the broader society. However, there are still not many role models for both genders. For example, there is not an equivalent female to male model for women in transition to men as the model that Caitlyn Jenner provided for men transitioning to women provided. Thus, transgendered individuals are still searching for how to develop their respective worldviews, as Carl stated:

I've asked myself countless times, "What does it mean to be transgender?" My answer changes dramatically once every year. But from the moment I learned that word, "transgender," I felt something tugging inside me: the desire to embrace and express my masculinity, and furthermore, to embody that masculinity. I've wondered why I understand myself to be a man, and a rather effeminate man, rather than a woman— perhaps a somewhat masculine woman. After all, I am not a traditional vessel of manhood. I like the color pink. I cry in front of other people. And unlike many so-called male role models on TV, I believe strongly in softness, kindness—solving confrontations with diplomacy instead of "justified" violence. What, then, is manhood? What makes me a man? Undoubtedly, I'm aesthetically attracted to marks of manhood and wear them like a nice hat, but what I think makes me transgender is my great desire for a deeper voice, for slimmer hips, for my physical existence to be perceived as a masculine entity. I felt uncomfortable in my female body. Now, with the help of hormone therapy, I'm comfortable with this body of mine, which I largely perceive as male.

Fascinatingly, though, some transgender men have no desire for hormone therapy or a traditionally male body. Some transgender men relate to maleness and masculinity in other ways— there are a thousand and one ways to relate to maleness, be them cultural or biological. That is at the crux of the transgender question. To be transgender, you only have to relate to the other world of the other gender. You can be very creative in how you bridge the worlds together. Transgender people are re-inventing a thousand and one ways to be a man or a woman. Every combination of gendered aspects is possible. The transgender world becomes more diverse every day.

Carl, 20+-year-old European American Transgendered Student

Worldview Based on Social Class

The worldview based on social class can vary widely depending on how many resources people have. You might recall from your introductory psychology courses that Abraham Maslow had a theory based on a hierarchy of needs (Maslow, 1968, 1970), where one must address one's basic needs (e.g., food, water, safety) before addressing higher needs such as self-esteem, aesthetics, and self-actualization. People who are in the upper class and are financially secure can feel freer to pursue ways to self-actualize—or realize their highest potential as a person—whereas those who are in the lower classes necessarily are concerned with putting food on the table and a roof over their heads. Such pursuit of very different needs necessarily will lead to different views of the world. My (JSM) sister-in-law was a teacher who had a very well-off friend. The friend invited her to spend a week in Las Vegas with her during the school year. My sister-in-law said she could not go while classes were in session and she could not afford to spend an entire week in Las Vegas. Her friend's response was, "Oh, you don't need to work; you can afford this trip." My sister-in-law's friend had no concept of the need for most people to work for a living.

To address issues of social class, W. M. Liu and his colleagues (Colbow et al., 2016; W. M. Liu, Colbow, & Rice, 2016; W. M. Liu, Latino, & Loh, 2017; W. M. Liu, 2011, 2013) developed a scale to measure the degree to which therapists are conscious of issues of social class when seeing clients. This scale examines issues of materialism, social class behaviors, and lifestyles. Materialism involves issues such as money, possessions, and other valued objects. Social class behaviors involve issues such as etiquette and accents. Finally, lifestyles deal with leisure time, such as going to museums, concerts, ballets, theater, and so on. W. M. Liu (2011) discovered that therapists who had a social class consciousness were perceived as better, more empathic therapists.

Poverty can have a lasting effect on one's worldview. The American Psychological Association, APA Working Group on Stress and Health Disparities (2017), conducted a comprehensive evaluation on how low socioeconomic status affected individuals. Such individuals live with much more daily stress, mainly because they do not have the resources to address these stressors. Those living in poverty have a higher probability of dealing with crime in their neighborhoods, and by definition, they do not have the resources to be able to move to safer neighborhoods. Moreover, the well-known phenomenon of low-income neighborhoods being *food deserts* (Dubowitz, Ncube, Leuschner, & Tharp-Gilliam, 2015), where there are no stores that sell nutritious foods, can lead to obesity (because of the consumption of high-fat, processed foods such as potato chips and cookies) and other health-related problems. Such factors lead to decreased life expectancy (Chetty et al., 2016) and poor subjective well-being (A. E. Clark, D'Ambrosio, & Ghislandi, 2016). Poverty, coupled with race (Boylan, Jennings, & Matthews, 2016; Matthews et al., 2017), can lead to decreased life expectancy because of cardiovascular stress.

Mio and Fu (2017) discussed how poverty colors one's worldview throughout one's life. Thus, even when an individual gets out of poverty later in life, he or she may still have an impulse to feel that spending any amount of money is extravagant or wasteful. Lott and Bullock (2007) discussed how teachers might treat students who they know live in poverty with low expectations, discount the opinions of the students and/or their parents, or apply other kinds of stereotypes to the students. To the extent that elementary school has a lasting impact on one's development, these experiences cannot help but impact these children's worldviews.

At the other end of the spectrum, Joseph Stiglitz (2012), who served as president Bill Clinton's chairman of the Council of Economic Advisors, among other government posts, and received the Nobel Prize for Economics, warned against the trend toward widening the wealth gap between the upper levels of economic social class and the lower levels of social class. This gap has widened to the point where "the top .1 percent receive in a day and a half about what the bottom 90 percent receives in a year" (Stiglitz, 2012, p. 4). As Stiglitz pointed out, when people who are poor have even less disposable income, they will no longer be able to purchase the products that the people who are rich and own companies are trying to sell. An oft-quoted statement from Henry Ford (H. Ford & Crowther, 1922) says that he raised the minimum wage of his workers to $5.00 per day—an amount that was extremely generous for that era—so that his workers would have enough money to buy his cars.

An example of different worldviews from people of substantially different economic classes comes from Paul Krugman (2012), another Nobel Laureate of Economics. He reported that when people were protesting the upper 1% of wage earners and that the bottom 99% wanted more economic justice, rich investors at the Chicago Board of Trade unsympathetically yelled at the protestors to get jobs and threw applications for McDonald's restaurants at them. Another example of the mentality of people in the upper reaches of income in the United States occurred when 2012 Republican presidential candidate Mitt Romney commented that he made "some" money in speaker's fees the previous year, but it "wasn't very much" (Burns, 2012). Romney—who is clearly in the upper reaches of income in the United States—in fact had made over $374,000 in speaker's fees that year. This prompted Republican opponent Rick Santorum to declare that Mr. Romney was out of touch with average people. As an indication of how out of touch Romney's statement was, his $374,000 alone placed him in the upper 1% of income earners in the United States. Contrast these examples with those of people who may not have jobs or are struggling with minimum-wage jobs trying to support families and you can see how such people have fundamentally different worldviews.

Youth and Worldview

As many of us who are older remember, we lived in a world where nuclear war between the United States and the Soviet Union was a real possibility. We viewed the world as dangerous, and *drop drills* were routine. In a drop drill a teacher would say, "Boys and girls, drop!" and children were to duck under their desks, face away from the window, and cover their eyes and the backs of their heads. This drill was to protect children from a nuclear blast in the hopes that some would survive an atom bomb dropped in their proximity, far enough away that they would not be killed by the initial blast but close enough that the concussive wave caused by the nuclear weapon might cause the building to collapse and/or the windows to blow into a classroom.

Today's youth have a different kind of worldview. They live in a world where there is a real possibility that a shooter could roam the hallways of their schools and shoot as many people as possible. Cameron Kasky, a student at Marjory Stoneman Douglas High School in Parkland, Florida, who survived the mass shooting that occurred on that campus on February 14, 2018, called his generation the mass-shooting generation (C. Alter, 2018). Alternatively, this generation has also been called Generation Columbine (Toppo, 2018) because the Parkland, Florida, shooting was the 208th shooting since Columbine (M. Roberts, 2018). Thus, the world of these students involves routine locker searches, bulletproof backpacks, and active-shooter drills (Toppo, 2018). The 2018 school shootings occurred in 41 different states and Washington, DC, and they have touched every region of the country except Alaska. However, the last shooting in Alaska occurred just outside of the studied period, and a high school student from Alaska reported that students there prepare more for mass shootings than they do for earthquakes, although Alaska is one of the states that is most highly susceptible to earthquakes (O'Harra, 2018).

School shootings may even be considered inevitable by some students in this generation. Paige Curry interviewed a student who escaped the Santa Fe, Texas, shooting that occurred on May 18, 2018 (a shooting that came after the compilation of the school shootings between Columbine and Parkland):

> I've always kind of felt like eventually it was going to happen here, too.
> —Santa Fe, Texas, student who escaped mass shooting

> "Was there a part of you that was like, 'This isn't real, this is—this would not happen in my school?'" the reporter asked.
>
> The young girl shook her head: "No, there wasn't."
>
> "Why so?" the reporter asked.
>
> "It's been happening everywhere," she said. "I felt—I've always kind of felt like eventually it was going to happen here, too." (M. Fernandez, Fausset, & Bidgood, 2018)

Despite this generation's worldview as Generation Columbine, the mass-shooting generation, or whatever label is applied, this generation also has an empowered feeling that no previous generation has (or at least the few previous generations). Kasky began the #NeverAgain movement on Twitter to curb gun violence. He, Emma Gonzalez, Alex Wind, Jaclyn Corin, and David Hogg used their social media skills to organize school walk-outs, a major march, and

Emma Gonzalez has emerged as one of this generation's most prominent voices against gun violence. *Photograph by Steven Ferdman/Shutterstock*

various other events protesting gun violence (C. Alter, 2018). Curbing gun violence is very difficult because of the Second Amendment and strong support for gun ownership in this country. However, these students were successful in getting the Florida legislators to pass a bill banning bump stocks (a device that turns a semiautomatic rifle into an automatic rifle that can deliver bullets like a machine gun), impose a waiting period between when someone buys a gun and being able to carry it out of the store so a background check can be completed on the purchaser, raise the minimum age for purchasing a weapon, and allow the police to confiscate guns from individuals with mental illness. This bill was signed into law by Florida's governor, Rick Scott, who was previously against such measures. Gonzalez has become a symbol of this resistance. She previously did not have a Twitter account, but 11 days after she opened one, she had more followers than the National Rifle Association (C. Alter, 2018). It is yet to be determined whether this movement's early success will lead to long-term political power, but if it does, it will transform the mass-shooting generation label to a can-do label.

Summary

Worldviews come in many forms. The world looks different depending on whether a person is looking at behavior and concepts from within a culture or from without. The emic perspective is the perspective from within a culture, and this perspective seems to be more important than the etic perspective, or the perspective from outside the culture being examined. Although both perspectives are important in advancing our scientific knowledge of cultures, often those who view a culture from without impose their own worldviews on the behaviors of the culture being observed. This can lead to wildly different (and wrong) interpretations of the behaviors.

Perhaps one of the most important distinctions between cultures is the individualism–collectivism dimension. Individualistic societies place more importance on individual rights, whereas collective societies place more value on the desires of the collective. This dimension also exists in conjunction with the horizontal–vertical distinction. Thus, a society can be horizontally individualistic, vertically individualistic, horizontally collectivistic, or vertically collectivistic,

---

Food for Thought

When one of the authors (JSM) attended a conference for deaf people, he felt uncomfortable and out of place. All around him, people were using American Sign Language, and although he knew some signs and phrases, the deaf people were signing so fast that he could not keep up with them. As he described this situation, "The silence was deafening." Obviously, these people had no intention of harming him—they were merely communicating with one another. Still, he felt out of place and even a little frightened, because his worldview was so different from that of the people around him, or, rather, the dominant worldview was so different from his own. In thinking about the issues raised in this chapter, recall a situation in which you had a markedly different view of the world from those around you. You probably felt a little uncomfortable or afraid. That is a normal feeling until one begins to understand and appreciate the dominant worldview. If you did some reading about this situation or the people in it, you probably felt a little more comfortable and less afraid the next time you encountered it. Did you gain some insight into someone who has entered your world?

---

depending on the degree to which it is hierarchically structured. The individualism–collectivism distinction has important implications for how one experiences some negative emotions. Individualistic societies tend to place more importance on guilt, whereas collectivistic societies place more importance on shame. Collectivistic societies also tend to place more emphasis on face saving and face giving.

Kluckhohn and Strodtbeck (1961) presented a model that examines various dimensions of viewing the world. In combination, cultures, groups, or subgroups can be understood in terms of these value orientations. According to Kluckhohn and Strodtbeck's model, racial/ethnic groups in the United States seem to have worldviews that are much more similar to one another than they are to the middle-class European American worldview. This situation is perhaps a result of similar experiences with racism. Derald Wing Sue's (1978) model of worldview seems to combine Kluckhohn and Strodtbeck's model with racism. As Janet Helms and her colleagues indicated, the issue of racism is very important in the development of the worldviews of ALANAs, because these views are identifiably different from the views of the people around whom this society was developed. Women and men develop differing worldviews because of their experience with sexism and other issues that affect women more than men. The worldviews of LGBT individuals may differ from those of non-LGBT individuals, particularly about issues of safety, given the current situation in the United States. Contemporary issues such as the resistance to DADT and same-sex marriage underscore their concerns of a hostile environment. People who are in fundamentally different social economic classes see the world in fundamentally different ways. Finally, the youth of today have been dubbed "the mass shooting generation" or "Generation Columbine" because of the number of mass shootings on school campuses. However, through social media, this generation is organizing to prevent such shootings in the future.

Critical Thinking Questions

1. Have your actions ever been misconstrued by another person or a group of people because their assumptions differed from yours? If so, how did that make you feel? What steps did you take to correct their misconception?
2. Have you ever misperceived someone else's actions because you applied your own assumptions, which were different from the other person's? If so, how did you resolve the problem?

3. Would you characterize yourself and your family as allocentric (collectivistic) or as idio-centric (individualistic)? Do you fulfill society's expectation regarding this dimension?

4. What advantages and disadvantages does your worldview on collectivism and individual-ism have when you interact with the society at large?

5. Have you ever engaged in face giving? Has anyone ever given you face? What kind of connection did you feel with that person after the face giving?

6. If you are a person of color, do you feel you stand out because of your ethnicity/race in certain situations? If you are European American, do you tend to notice when a person of color is around? How do you feel about this dynamic?

7. Have you ever pretended that you were a superhero of a different race? How did that make you feel?

8. If you are a woman, to what extent is your view of the world markedly different from that of men? If you are a man, to what extent is your view of the world markedly different from that of women?

9. If you are an individual who is LGBT, how does your worldview differ from that of people who are straight? If you are straight, how does your worldview differ from that of LGBT individuals?

10. If you are an individual who is economically very well off, have you ever tried to live among poor people or volunteered at a soup kitchen?

11. To what extent have constant active-shooter drills affected the way you view the world?

· CHAPTER 4 ·

Cultural Differences in Communication

Photograph by michaeljung/Shutterstock

Learning Objectives
Reading this chapter will help you to:
- understand conventions of conversation;
- identify the different components of communication;
- know which strategies are appropriate for communicating with diverse populations;
- explain some cognitive complexities between monolingual and bilingual communicators;
- recognize the differences between high- and low-context communication; and
- distinguish between communication among older adults and younger adults.

I was talking with a guy who is pretty "Americanized." His mother was still very influenced by Japanese traditions. He was telling me that his mother was worried that his brother was not going to come to the wedding of a family friend. He wasn't even going to send a wedding gift. This guy said, "Mom kept saying, 'I don't know what I'm going to do,' and I kept saying, 'Well, that's how he is. You know how he is, so don't worry about it.' However, she kept saying, 'I don't know what I'm going to do.' Why do you think my mom wouldn't give it up?" I said, "Well, if she is very traditionally Japanese, she was telling you indirectly that she wanted you to tell your brother that he should send a wedding gift." This guy said, "Oh, is *that* what she was saying?! Now it makes sense. No wonder why she kept repeating herself."

—Jeremy, 40+-year-old Japanese American professor

As this story indicates, there are different ways of communicating, and it seems that in the United States, overt, direct communication is required. Although most people can understand or interpret implications and other forms of indirect communication, some contexts or some people require direct communication. In this chapter we discuss issues of communication that can differ across cultural groups and genders.

cooperative principle—a psycholinguistic term that assumes that we strive to communicate with one another sincerely and effectively when we engage in a conversation.

Conversational Rules

Grice (1975) proposed a set of conversational rules that guide people's conversations (see Table 4.1). Grice suggested that we all engage in what is called the **cooperative principle**, that is, we strive to communicate with one

TABLE 4.1   **Grice's Conversational Maxims with Norman and Rummelhart's Additions**

Maxim	Brief definition
Quality	Tell the truth.
Quantity	Say about as much as is appropriate for the situation.
Relevance	Stick to the topic.
Manner	Speak to your partner in an appropriate manner.
Relations with conversational partner	Take advantage of your past relationship with your conversational partner; fill in others who may not be privy to your mutual understandings.
Rule violations	Identify when you are breaking one of the conversational maxims.

Sources: Grice (1975); Norman and Rummelhart (1975).

another sincerely and effectively. He proposed four maxims that guide such conversations: *quality*, *quantity*, *relevance*, and *manner*.

The **maxim of quality** suggests that whenever we engage in a conversation, we strive to be truthful. Because you and I are engaged in a cooperative conversational relationship, you expect me to tell you the truth or give you my honest opinion on the topic we are discussing. If you can never be certain that I am telling you the truth, you may choose to break off our conversation. Alternatively, if you do not know that I am telling you a lie, we are not engaged in a cooperative relationship: I am manipulating you.

> **maxim of quality**—a communicative presumption that suggests that we tell each other the truth when we engage in a conversation.

The **maxim of quantity** suggests that each of us should contribute an appropriate amount to our conversation. In normal conversations, two speakers are generally expected to contribute equally. Have you ever tried to talk with a partner who dominated the conversation, never allowing you to contribute? Did that irritate you? If so, you were irritated because your conversational partner violated

> **maxim of quantity**—a communicative presumption that suggests that we contribute an appropriate amount of talk when we engage in a conversation.

the maxim of quantity. However, in some contexts, it is appropriate for one person to dominate the conversation. For example, on talk shows or in television interviews, it is appropriate for the interviewee to contribute more to the conversation than the host or interviewer, who asks only brief questions to move the conversation forward. This is also true in therapy, where the client is expected to contribute more to the conversation than the therapist, who mostly listens. What other contexts can you think of in which one partner is supposed to dominate the discussion?

The **maxim of relevance** suggests that we strive to remain on topic. If we suddenly start talking about baseball during a discussion of multicultural psychology, we are violating the maxim of relevance because our utterance does not relate to the topic, even though it may be truthful and of an appropriate length. Some people may go into long digressions when talking, and you may wonder whether they are being relevant.

> **maxim of relevance**—a communicative presumption that suggests that our discussion is relevant to the conversation.

Often these people get back on track and say something that ends up being relevant to the topic, but by the time they get there, they have violated the maxim of quantity. A former graduate student discussed this situation when describing the way that her supervisor conducted their supervision sessions:

It is so frustrating to have supervision with Jay. He gets off on such tangents, I wonder where he is going. Even when I ask him a yes-or-no question, or ask him directly whom I should call if I have a question about child abuse, he goes off on some story about what this reminded him of or why it is important for me to get training or something, and ten minutes later, he still hasn't answered my very direct question. He may say something that is somewhat relevant, but it is hard to get through our supervision meetings without wanting to tear out my hair.

—Lilly, 20+-year-old Mexican American student

maxim of manner—a communicative presumption that suggests that we are clear in our language and that we pay attention to normal standards of conversation, such as not shouting at someone who is right in front of us.

Finally, the **maxim of manner** suggests that people should be clear in their communication and pay attention to normal standards of conduct. This is the broadest maxim and can include a wide range of issues. For example, you would not discuss quantum mechanics with a 3-year-old, nor would you speak in a disrespectful manner to someone in a position of authority. You would not talk in an intentionally obscure manner, nor would you shout to someone standing 2 feet in front of you. In the United States, the appropriate distance between two people engaging in a typical conversation is about 1½ feet. It would violate the maxim of manner to stand 6 inches from that person's face, and it would also be a violation if you were to stand 10 feet away. A former colleague described an interesting formality when he made a presentation in Germany:

I went to Germany the summer after I served as the interim department chair. After my talk, there was a question–answer period. The director of the institute began this period by asking me a question. This guy and very few others asked me questions. After a while, I noticed that some of the other professors were passing notes down the aisle, but they never asked me any questions. When my talk was over, I asked the director of the institute why it was that the other professors were not engaged in the question–answer period. He told me that they actually were engaged, but in Germany, only people at the same level or higher could ask questions, and since I was the director of my institute, only he and a few other directors could ask me questions. The younger professors were writing questions they wanted asked, and they passed these questions down to those who could address me.

—James, 40+-year-old European American professor

Such a formal system may not exist in the United States, but we often have informal rules similar to the one described by James. If you work in a large corporation, you may have been told that you must take any questions to your supervisor because the manager or director of the organization cannot be bothered by every question from every employee. In the United States, however, there is more of an egalitarian tradition. People are considered equal, so asking people of different hierarchies is not violating the maxim of manner. In fact, on our own campus, the president of our university includes the student body president in regular meetings with students on campus. These meetings are called "Pizza with the Presidents," and the university pays for pizzas to draw as many students as possible to gather in an informal manner to hear the two presidents make opening statements. After that, students are encouraged to ask the presidents any questions on their minds, and sometimes these questions can get heated and disrespectful, such as why student tuition was raised or why a certain controversial speaker was paid to make a presentation on campus. The two presidents see such questions as appropriately holding their feet to the fire to be accountable for decisions they make. Does your campus conduct events that equalize the power between students and your campus's president or chancellor?

Norman and Rummelhart (1975) added two maxims to Grice's (1975) conversational rules: *relations with conversational partner* and *rule violations*. The maxim of **relations with conversational partner** suggests that we should rely on our previous experience with our partners in our conversations. If we were talking to you about multicultural psychology, we would know that you know something about the topic, so we could talk about something within the area knowing that you would be able to follow what we are saying. However, if we were talking with someone who knew nothing about multicultural psychology, we might have to give a brief sketch of the area before we could discuss a specific topic. If you had an inside joke with a friend, you could use telegraphic language to refer to the inside joke and apply it to the present situation, but if you were with people unfamiliar with the inside joke, you should fill them in before making the comments or let them know later why the situation was so funny.

relations with conversational partner—a communicative presumption that suggests that we use our previous relationship with our conversational partner so that we do not have to repeat shared experiences.

A colleague at another university wrote an email to a listserv:

> I asked my students to think of a joke that would translate across all cultures. A student in the back shouted, "That's what she said!" and the entire class burst out in laughter. Does anyone know what this means?
>
> —Jack, 60+-year-old American Indian professor

Obviously, my colleague did not know the inside joke that today's students tell. Here is an example of a formal joke about relations with conversational partners:

> A new prisoner was eating his first dinner in the prison cafeteria. After a few minutes, someone shouted out, "23!" and everyone laughed. The new prisoner was confused, but he went on eating. Someone else shouted out, "102!" and everyone laughed. The new prisoner was still confused, and finally when someone shouted out, "495!" and everyone laughed, the new prisoner went to an older prisoner and asked what was happening.
>
> The older prisoner said, "Well, son, we used to tell a bunch of jokes, but as time went on, the joke-telling portion of our dinner got pretty long, and everyone couldn't tell their favorite joke. Therefore, we decided to number our jokes, and to save time, someone just has to should out the number of the joke and everyone would know what joke it was and laugh."
>
> The younger prisoner said, "That's great! Is there anywhere where I can learn these jokes?"
>
> The older prisoner said, "Sure, they are all cataloged in the prison library."
>
> The next day, the younger prisoner went to the prison library and studied all of the jokes. By the time dinner came around, he was ready to be the life of the party. After

a few minutes, he shouted out, "51!" Dead silence. He thought, "Gosh, I thought that joke was pretty funny." Undeterred, he shouted out, "273!" Again, no one laughed. Desperate, he began shouting all of the funniest jokes in the catalogue, "522!" "594!" "735!" but after each number, no one laughed.

Frustrated, the younger prisoner went up to the older prisoner and said, "I can't believe this. These were the funniest jokes in the catalog. Why didn't anyone laugh?"

The older prisoner put his arm around the younger prisoner and said, "Well, son— some people can tell jokes and some people just can't."

rule violations—a communicative presumption that suggests that we signal our conversational partners when we are about to engage in a violation of one of the other maxims.

The maxim of **rule violations** suggests that when violating one of the other maxims, one must signal that violation. For example, if we want someone to interpret an utterance as ironic, or the opposite of what the literal utterance means, we must signal it with a voice inflection or some other means. We are sure that you all have been in a boring lecture or at a boring party when someone has said, "This is *real* interesting." The emphasis on real, done with a voice inflection or stress, signals that you should interpret the utterance not literally, but ironically. Some people draw quotation marks in the air when they want others to interpret an utterance ironically instead of literally or to disregard the utterance. For example, someone might say "The 'experts' say you should do this . . ." and draw quotation marks in the air with their fingers when he or she says "experts," which means that you should disregard the advice that the experts are giving. You may be aware of this joke:

> An English professor says, "Some people mistakenly believe that double negatives always mean the opposite. For example, if I were to say, 'This is not unlike the situation last week,' I mean by the double negatives of 'not' and 'unlike' to mean that the current situation is exactly like the situation last week. That is well and good, but sometimes a double negative can be an intensifier. Thus, if I were to say, 'One should never, never stick one's finger into a light socket,' I really mean that one should not do this under any circumstance. However, there is never an instance where a double positive is anything but an intensifier. In other words, double positives always intensify the positive meaning of something and never mean the opposite or something negative."
>
> A student in the back of the room says, "Yea, right!"

Clearly, the professor in this story has never heard of sarcasm. We might note that this is a humorous violation of the maxim of manner, but also an illustration of how in the United States we allow such violations of hierarchies, and under many circumstances, students and their professors can be at the same level of hierarchy.

As one can imagine, different cultures can have different conversational rules, but they likely have similar general maxims that guide their behaviors. The greatest variation occurs in the maxim of manner because differ rules govern what is an appropriate or an inappropriate manner. This is particularly true for many cultures that attend to hierarchical communications, such as the German culture that James encountered. We turn next to these nonverbal aspects of language.

Nonverbal Aspects of Language

One of the greatest differences among cultures is the way in which nonverbal communication is used. Sue and Sue (2003, 2008, 2013, 2016) categorize nonverbal communication into *proxemics, kinesics, paralanguage,* and *high- and low-context communication.* Because high–low context communication is such an important issue in the multicultural literature, we present it in the next section.

Proxemics

Proxemics deals with personal space. When people interact with one another, they maintain a standard range of distance between them. The range of distance varies depending on the context, such as a close, intimate relationship or a public lecture (E. T. Hall, 1966, 1976). As we noted earlier, in

proxemics—personal space in conversations.

normal conversations the distance between two conversational partners is usually about 1½ feet. According to Hall, the acceptable distance is 1½ to 4 feet. However, numerous researchers have found that conversational partners in other cultures tend to stand or sit closer to each other when interacting than do those in the United States and other Western countries (Dolphin, 1999; Matsumoto, 2000). Goldman (1980) found that individuals in the United States feel more uncomfortable when someone stands too close than when he or she stands too far away. I (JSM) recall being at a sporting event and feeling uncomfortable when I saw two sports reporters standing extremely close to one another. I remember thinking how interesting it was that *I* was the one who was feeling uncomfortable in just observing these two people standing so close to one another when they were talking to each other. I then realized that in the context of televised sporting events, they had to stand close to one another to both be in the camera shot on television. After I realized the context, I felt much more comfortable about their distance from one another. A student of ours talked about her discomfort about her personal space being violated when she visited her parents' home country of Korea:

> When we talked about how we have cultural norms that govern personal space, I remembered my visit to Korea last winter. I despised Koreans for having no personal spaces. When I was taking [the] bus or subway, people not only violated my personal space, they were touching me. I hated how my arms had to touch other people's arms. Most of the public transportations were so crowded that I sometimes felt the person behind me breathing. Also, there was one time a Korean grandmother [who] asked me to give my seat to her. She could have just asked and I would have given it to her. She literally put her face in front of my face and told me to move. She spat at me a little and I got really mad. I even told her that nobody talks to me this close, but she did not seem to care at all. I really liked Korea except for there was no personal space and no saying sorry or excuse me. I still do not get that. Even though Korea is a culture that has high respect for elders and has straight rules, I do not know why they do not say sorry or excuse me. I also realized even my close family members in Korea were sitting too close to me when we chat. Although they were my aunts and cousins, I really felt uncomfortable and tried to move as far as I could. I think my family in America adopted the American personal space. When my mom and I talk, we try not to violate each other's personal spaces. I think we know each other's boundaries. It is interesting how my parents unconsciously adopted the American culture.
>
> —Stella, 20+-year-old Korean American student

Remland, Jones, and Brinkman (1991) studied three European countries (the Netherlands, France, and England). Although some differences were found for pair interaction, such as

Asians tend to stand farther away from each other while talking than their American counterparts. When talking with someone from a different culture, a person can find it difficult to determine a comfortable talking distance. *Photographs by Stuart Jenner/Shutterstock and g-stockstudio/Shutterstock*

distance (more distance between Dutch participants, less distance between French pairs, even less distance between English pairs in declining distance) and body orientation (French participants more directly across from each other than Dutch or English participants), no differences were detected when gender and age were examined. In other words, culture was the dominant influence in proxemics in these countries. Some early researchers questioned the importance of culture in influencing proxemics (Fortson & Larson, 1968; Mazur, 1977; Shuter, 1977), but more recent studies have confirmed this importance (Mindess, 1999; N. M. Sussman & Rosenfeld, 1982; Wolfgang, 1985).

Sue and Sue (2003, 2008, 2013, 2016) gave a practical reason that proxemics is an important topic in multicultural studies. When an individual from a culture that prefers smaller distances between speakers comes in contact with an individual from a culture that prefers larger distances, the first individual might misinterpret the second one's warmth, sincerity, or motive. Imagine a person from a close culture trying to stand closer to a person from a distant culture, who keeps moving away. The person from the close culture may feel that the other individual is not a warm person or is trying to hide something, whereas the person from the distant culture may feel that the other individual is trying to become overly personal or invasive. I (JSM) once greeted an African American friend whom I had not seen in a while. When I reached out to shake his hand, he pulled me closer and gave me a hug, saying, "Come over here like you really know me!" The friendship was close enough that he felt comfortable telling me why he was hugging me, and I felt comfortable enough to give him a hug back. Imagine how it would have seemed if he had tried to give me a hug and I had pulled away. He has "trained" me, so now I just immediately hug him whenever I see him.

Kinesics

D. W. Sue and Sue (2003, 2008, 2013, 2016) define **kinesics** as aspects of communication that deal with bodily movements. This is a wide-ranging category that includes "facial expressions, body movements, gestures, and conversational regulators" (Andersen, 1999, p. 245). One kinesics aspect that has been studied extensively is eye contact or gaze duration. Matsumoto (2000) reported that eye contact can be an indication of either aggression or nurturance, depending on the

Kinesics—bodily movement in conversations, including hand gestures, facial expressions, and eye contact.

context. He cites the animal literature as a suggestion of a genetic, animalistic basis for the relation between gaze duration and dominance (see also Matsumoto & Juang, 2012). Most of us can remember being told as children that it was impolite to stare at someone. However, equally embedded in our minds are phrases such as *gazing lovingly into someone's eyes* or *casting a loving glance*, which indicate that eye contact or gazes can also indicate affection or care. Moreover, there is even evidence that love can be distinguished from lust by evaluating eye gazes (Bolmont, Cacioppo, & Cacioppo, 2014).

As one might expect, people of different cultures seem to engage in varying levels of eye contact. Some early researchers found that people from Arabic cultures tend to gaze longer and more directly than do people from the United States (E. T. Hall, 1963; Watson & Graves, 1966). Within the United States, African Americans gaze less directly than their European American counterparts do (LaFrance & Mayo, 1976). American Indians tend to make even less eye contact (Richardson, 1981) and prefer a side-by-side orientation to a face-to-face orientation. A friend and colleague of ours, Joseph Trimble, once told us,

> When I am interacting with my White colleagues, I sit or stand across from them and interact with them in a manner that is comfortable for them. However, when I visit my friends on the Lakota reservation, I find myself standing side by side with them, looking at my feet and kicking at the ground. We rarely look at each other, but we have very good and deep conversations. (Joseph Trimble, personal communication, January 1999)

Now, whenever I (JSM) see Joseph at conferences, I make sure we stand side by side.

However, not having a great deal of eye contact is different from avoiding eye contact. According to van Meurs and Spencer-Oatey (2010), there are cultural differences in avoidance of eye contact when there is a conflict. Many researchers (e.g., Bond & Hwang, 1986; Ohbuchi & Takahashi, 1994) labeled this a *neglect style* of dealing with conflict. East Asians tend to have less eye contact under conditions of conflict than their counterparts in the United States. We say *tend to have* because there are large variations in both populations, and among those in the West, van Meurs and Spencer-Oatey reported that British managers had a more avoidant style of managing than their Dutch counterparts.

D. W. Sue and Sue (2003, 2008, 2013, 2016) discuss smiling as an important part of kinesics. In general, smiling is an indication of happiness, liking, and other positive feelings. However, Asian cultures may also use smiling as a way of discharging uncomfortable feelings. Ekman (1972) conducted a series of experiments in which he showed American and Japanese students highly stressful videotapes (e.g., of a surgical operation) and secretly videotaped their facial expressions. Half of the time the research participants watched the stressful videotapes alone, and half of the time they watched the videotape with an older, high-status experimenter. The American participants showed facial expressions of disgust, fear, and other negative affects when they watched the film alone or with the experimenter. However, the Japanese participants displayed these negative expressions when watching the videotape alone, but they smiled in the presence of the high-status experimenter. That was because they did not want to offend the experimenter by seeming to disapprove of the task the experimenter was asking them to perform. Thus, although facial expressions of emotion may have some universal application, as evidenced by the similar expressions of the American and Japanese participants when viewing the videotapes alone, the social setting may be an important determinant of the kinesics displayed in a particular situation. D. W. Sue and Sue (2013) connected this tendency for Asians to smile when discharging negative emotions with a misunderstanding that arose in the aftermath of the Rodney King verdict during a confrontation between African Americans and Korean grocery store owners:

> African Americans confronted their Korean-American counterparts about exploitation of Black neighborhoods. African Americans became incensed when many Korean American store owners had a constant smile on their faces. They interpreted the facial expression as arrogance, taunting, and lack of compassion for the concerns of Blacks. Little did they realize that a smile in this situation more rightly indicated extreme embarrassment and apprehension. (p. 215)

Kinesics may be determined by the general influences of individualism and collectivism. They tend to be more synchronized in collectivistic cultures (Andersen, 1999; Argyle, 1975), whereas in individualistic cultures, people are allowed to do their own thing and not coordinate their movements with others as much. Matsumoto (1991) speculates that "collective cultures will foster emotional displays of their members that maintain and facilitate group cohesion, harmony, or cooperation, to a greater degree than individualistic cultures" (p. 132).

Paralanguage

D. W. Sue and Sue (2003, 2008, 2013, 2016) refer to **paralanguage** as a category that involves the use of nonverbal vocal cues in communication, such as loudness of voice, silences, and rate of speech. Perhaps the aspect of paralanguage that lends itself to the most cultural variation of meaning is silence. In the United States, silences are often signals for the receiver of a message to contribute to the conversation. When silences last too long, people in the United States often become uncomfortable. Many of you have probably heard the expression *pregnant pause*, which indicates the discomfort one feels when the conversation has come to a halt and there is an extended period during which neither conversational partner contributes to the conversation.

paralanguage—nonverbal vocal cues in conversation, such as loudness of voice, silences, and rates of speech.

However, E. T. Hall (1966, 1976) found that silences mean different things in different cultures. For example, some cultures (Russian, Spanish) view silence as agreement among the conversational partners. Asian cultures view silence as a sign of respect for elders. For American Indians, silences are a way of gathering one's thoughts, so breaking the silence merely disrupts their train of thought. As Richardson (1981) advised when seeing American Indians in a therapy situation,

> Do not lean toward the client and commence giving the "third degree" or studying him or her with piercing eyes. Do not be upset with long pauses, but, on the other hand, do not try "seating out the client" to see who can be the winner. A loud and overbearing manner is exceedingly irritating and makes Indians feel subservient, and this will cause them to shut you out as they clam up and remain quiet. (p. 236)

The forms of nonverbal communication we have mentioned are important contributors to conversations between partners, but one of the most important and underappreciated aspects of nonverbal communication is the distinction between high- and low-context communication, which we will now examine.

High- Versus Low-Context Communication

A daughter from a higher-class family [in Malaysia] fell in love with the son of a lower-class family. The son approached his parents and told them that he wanted to marry the girl from a higher-class family. His mother said she would approach the girl's family to see if it were acceptable to them. She made an appointment with the girl's mother and went to the home on the proper day. She was greeted by the mother and was shown into the sitting room. Refreshments were brought in consisting of tea and bananas. The two mothers talked about the weather and other things, but they never mentioned their children. After a period of time the boy's mother thanked her hostess politely and left. Upon returning home she told her son that the marriage was unacceptable and, therefore, not possible. (Shon & Ja, 1982, p. 216)

How did the mother from the lower-class family know that the mother from the higher-class family disapproved of the marriage? It is because she used the context of the situation to understand the other mother's wishes. In Malaysia, tea and bananas do not go together, so the mother from the higher-class family was giving the other mother the message that their children should not go together. E. T. Hall (1976, 1999) called this **high-context communication** (HC), which means that much of the communication is carried either by the context of the situation or by societal rules that are internalized. Conversely, **low-context communication** (LC) is language dependent: the language itself is the crucial aspect of the communication, and context does not carry as much meaning. E. T. Hall (1999) explains:

> **high-context communication—** communication in which the context conveys much of the meaning.

> **low-context communication—** language-dependent communication, in which the words carry most of the meaning and context plays a lesser role.

> A high-context (HC) communication or message is one in which most of the information is either in the physical context or internalized in the person, while very little is in the coded, explicit, transmitted part of the message. A low-context (LC) communication is just the opposite; i.e., the mass of the information is vested in the explicit code. (p. 47)

Although no culture is exclusively HC or LC, cultures fall on a continuum between high and low context. Communication in the United States tends to be at the low-context end of this continuum (German Swiss, Germans, and Scandinavians are at the lowest end, according to E. T. Hall (1976)), and many Asian countries tend to be at the high end. E. T. Hall connects the Asian dependence on context to the Chinese written language, which is over 3,500 years old and has not changed much in the past 3,000 years. Thus, other countries whose written languages are derivations of the Chinese language (e.g., Japan, Korea) are HC countries.

One advantage of HC is that it allows individuals to avoid confrontations. In the example of the Malaysian mothers, notice how the mother from the higher class does not have to directly state her wish that their two children not marry. Also, the mother from the lower class does not have to be embarrassed by being told to her face that her son is not acceptable to the other family. Although in the United States we might prefer this clarity, direct questioning in HC countries is considered a sign of immaturity because it causes both parties to lose face (Andersen, 1999). Incidentally, although we do not know how this situation was ultimately resolved, it is possible that in the long run, the mother from the upper-class family gave her consent to the marriage. As S. Elliot and associates (S. Elliot, Scott, Jensen, & McDonough, 1982) found, people who talked less and allowed context to communicate more were seen as more attractive in collectivistic cultures. Thus, if these mothers had additional contact in the future, the mother from the upper-class family may have come to see the mother from the lower-class family as more attractive because she could read contextual cues. For those of you who are romantics, there is hope that love conquered all in this case.

As indicated earlier, HC helps one to save face. What is saving face? According to Ting-Toomey (1994), "Face involves the claimed sense of self-respect or self-dignity in an interactive situation" (p. 3). Thus, saving face is preserving one's dignity when interacting with another person or when being viewed or evaluated in a public context. The topic of HC communication helping to save face elicited the following reaction from one of our students when direct communication embarrassed her and made her lose face:

> I went to Australia when I was 15 years old. It was my first time leaving my own place [Hong Kong], and I had no experience of talking with people from different cultures. In Australia, people talk to each other in a very direct way just like Americans do. I did not feel comfortable when they talked that way. For example, I lived with a host family when I first arrived in Australia. My host family usually went to bed very early. One day, I took a shower around ten, and I did not know it was very noisy when I took the shower. The next day my host family told me not to take showers so late. They could not fall asleep because of the noise the shower made. I felt they talked to me in a very direct way, and they made me feel embarrassed. I also felt they were rude because I thought they could tell me this in a more gentle, unobvious, and subtle way. However, I still kept saying sorry to them. Moreover, I thought that they were angry with me. I finally realized it was not true after years of contact with people from low-context societies. It is their culture that leads them to communicate in a very direct way. I feel uncomfortable because I was raised in a collective culture, and we never communicate in such a direct way. People who communicate directly in my culture would be labeled as impolite and not well raised. I think the major reason is they do not save others' faces. Therefore, people in my culture do not like such direct people. I finally understand there are two types of communication, and this concept will help me a lot in my real life when I communicate with Americans.
>
> —Li-Chiang, 20+-year-old Hong Kong immigrant student

With respect to HC communication, a joke among Japanese Americans is that when they visit non-Japanese families for dinner, they go home hungry. That is because of the Japanese concept of *enryo*, a term meaning to hold back or to suppress one's desires. Thus, in Japanese American families influenced by *enryo*, if one is hungry and is offered more food, one must say no. The food must then be offered again, and again the answer must be no. If the food is offered a third time, it is appropriate to accept the food while also complimenting the cook on how tasty the food is. This is related to the rule of three discussed in Chapter 3. However, when Japanese Americans visit the homes of people from other cultures and are offered food, when they refuse the food the first time, the food is taken away, even though the visitor may still be hungry.

A coauthor of this book (LAB) is an African American woman whose brother is married to a Japanese American woman. She used to get irritated when her sister-in-law continued to offer her food even when LAB had said she was full and did not want any more to eat. LAB's thought was, "I just said no—why are you offering me food again?" However, after some time, she came to realize that her sister-in-law was just following the Japanese tradition of offering the food multiple times just in case she (LAB) was holding back and being polite in the Japanese tradition. Thus, LAB has now learned how to be definitive in saying no the first time she refuses the food.

As you may recall, in Chapter 3 we discussed a family-therapy case presented by S. Sue and Morishima (1982) that involved a mother-in-law from Hong Kong who was unreasonably critical of her daughter-in-law's efforts. Her attitude caused extreme marital distress for the daughter-in-law and her husband and nearly precipitated a divorce. The husband would not intervene on his wife's behalf because he did not want to show disrespect to his own mother. As promised, we will now discuss the therapeutic intervention that was chosen and that seemed to resolve this conflict. The therapist discovered that the mother-in-law had an older brother whom she respected and who lived about 50 miles away. The therapist suggested that the daughter-in-law contact this uncle and explain the situation to him. He recognized the seriousness of the situation, so they planned a dinner in which he was invited to eat with the family. After the dinner, the uncle told his sister that the daughter-in-law looked tired and unhappy and wondered whether she was working too hard. His sister (the mother-in-law) immediately recognized that he was criticizing her and that she needed to stop being so demanding of her daughter-in-law. To signal to her brother that she had received the message, she acknowledged that her daughter-in-law was doing her chores well and working very hard. Later, the daughter-in-law reported that her mother-in-law had noticeably reduced her criticisms, had begun praising the daughter-in-law's work, and had even begun helping with the household chores.

Notice how this intervention took advantage of HC communication. Neither the uncle nor the mother-in-law had to directly confront the other about the situation. That allowed the mother-in-law to save face and also understand what a serious effect her criticisms were having. It is interesting that, by praising her daughter-in-law, the mother-in-law was also able to maintain her higher status in the relationship, but she realized that this status also came with the responsibility to be fair and to give positive feedback as well as negative feedback. Finally, this example demonstrates the importance of vertical collectivism because the mother-in-law did not challenge her older brother's authority.

When I presented this case to one of my classes, it resonated with a student from the Philippines, who said that his family has been engaging in family therapy all along without knowing it. He said that when family conflicts arise, a respected intermediary intervenes. Being older is not the important factor here. Rather, the family recognizes certain individuals for having strengths in various areas. When a dispute arises, they turn to the individual with strength in that area and follow his or her counsel. Another student whose parents immigrated from Hong Kong asked her parents how they would solve this marital problem. She reported that her parents solved it in a manner nearly identical to that of S. Sue and Morishima (1982).

Direct Versus Indirect Communication

Related to high- versus low-context communication is *direct versus indirect communication*. Most people know that **direct communication** is literal and assertive communication. It is related to low-context communication in that the message is contained in the language used.

direct communication—blunt communication that is literal and to the point.

indirect communication—
communication that relies on context
and the receiver's ability to draw
inferences.

Indirect communication relies on both context and the receiver's powers of inference. To illustrate the difference between these two forms of communication, let us say that someone wants a window closed. Direct speech would say, "Close the window." Indirect speech would say, "Are you cold?" P. Brown and Levinson (1978) indicated that indirect speech acts are used because they convey a degree of politeness in communication. As such, they are universal.

Both indirect communication and high-context communication resonated with a student of ours. She related this rather amusing anecdote to us:

> I come from a culture that values indirectness. I remember when I was getting married; it is customary for the bride to look sad and depressed. She should let her family feel that she is not happy leaving home. If a bride smiles and shows that she is happy it is an indirect way of saying she does not value her family and she would forget them if she leaves home. I cried and acted so sad. My younger sister however took it a step further; she ran away from home the night before her wedding. I remember my father huffing and puffing and screaming, "If she does not want to marry we would just cancel it—nobody is forcing her." I laughed so hard secretly because I knew she wanted so badly to get married but she was trying to show that she was a "good girl." I always resented the indirect way of doing things because we always have to refuse things and gifts when it is offered to us for the first time and luckily people would continue to insist. God knows how difficult it was for me when I migrated to the USA. I kept insisting my friends eat more or take something I offered them when they said no. They resented it and thought I had no boundaries.
>
> —Adjoa, 40+-year-old Ghanaian immigrant student

Yum (1999) acknowledged that indirect communication may be a universal component of all languages. However, she cited wide cultural variations in preference for direct or indirect communication styles. As we discussed in Chapter 3, people in many Asian countries are concerned with saving and giving face. Therefore, it should not be surprising to find that indirect speech is prevalent in Asian countries (Katriel, 1986; Lebra, 1976). Lebra (1976) indicated that this level of indirect communication can be extremely subtle. Lebra reported that a woman communicated discord with her mother-in-law based on slight irregularities found in the mother-in-law's flower arrangement. Table 4.2 summarizes Yum's comparison of North American and East Asian forms of communication (p. 83).

After reading this section of the book, one of our students reflected on how she sometimes violated the cooperative principle, engaged in indirect communication, and could have avoided a conflict with a friend of hers:

> This chapter in the book reminded me of the times when I violated the cooperative principle which says we should be honest and communicate effectively. For example, I used to be very indirect with people and never really said how I felt. When my best friend lived with my mom and me for the summer, it became tense because my friend would sleep until 2 pm and be in her pajamas watching TV, while the house was a mess. Mom would then complain to me (although she also gave [my friend] indirect messages)

TABLE 4.2 **Comparison Between North American and East Asian Orientations to Communication Patterns**

East Asian orientations	North American orientations
1. Process orientation: Communication is perceived as a process of infinite interpretation.	Outcome orientation: Communication is perceived as the transference of messages.
2. Differentiated linguistic codes: Different linguistic codes are used depending on the persons involved and situations.	Less differentiated linguistic codes: Linguistic codes are not as extensively differentiated as in East Asia.
3. Indirect communication emphasis: The use of indirect communication is prevalent and accepted as normative.	Direct communication emphasis: Direct communication is a norm despite the extensive use of indirect communication.
4. Receiver centered: Meaning is in the interpretation. Emphasis is on listening, sensitivity, and removal of preconception.	Sender centered: Meaning is in the messages created by the sender. Emphasis is on how to formulate the best messages, how to improve source credibility, and how to improve delivery skills.

that [we were] lazy and did not pull [our] weight around the house. In turn I would give my friend "subtle" hints that she needed to help around the house. I'd say things like, "Uh! How can this house be such a mess!" or I would go around the house cleaning like crazy and move her things and put them in different spots where they would not be seen. I would even wait for her to take her shoes off so I could put them in the closet when she wasn't looking (that was my form of high-context communication).

Eventually, I got tired of giving her all these indirect messages and one day, I finally yelled at her that I wasn't her maid. Needless to say, that made our relationship strained (she had no idea how I felt). If I had learned that I should be honest with her about my feelings (using the quality maxim) and not give her dirty looks or roll my eyes at her or give her the "silent treatment" (that was my paralanguage) when she did something I did not like, I could have avoided the blow up and the strained [relationship] that followed.

—Melanie, 20+-year-old Mexican American student

Ethnic Minority Patterns of Communication

Researchers have conducted a great deal of research comparing Asian and East Asian forms of communication with Western forms of communication because of the general interest in collectivistic versus individualistic cultures. Most of the foregoing information deals with this comparison. A few other researchers have examined differences in communication patterns among other ethnic minority populations in the United States. Sometimes generalizations cannot be applied to all people in a group, but the following are general trends identified by some researchers. First, however, one of our students gave the following observation about different cultures and behavior:

This weekend I was with a friend of mine in an elevator, and the example of elevator etiquette and culture unfolded before us. My friend and I got in the elevator, followed by a Latino family. Then we went two floors down and another Latino family got on the elevator. Couple more floors and a European American couple quickly said "We'll wait" and another couple floors and a couple of Asian guys got right in the elevator. When we finally got to the first floor my friend (who is not in this class) said, "Wasn't that funny? All those different people's reactions when the elevator doors would open? That one couple wouldn't come in and those Asian guys got right in?" I laughed and told her that this was an example of personal space and different cultures, particularly people from high population density areas. We laughed about it.

—Nikki, 20+-year-old European American student

African Americans

Ribeau, Baldwin, and Hecht (1999) identified seven issues of importance when their African American participants interacted with European Americans: (a) negative stereotyping, (b) acceptance, (c) personal expressiveness, (d) authenticity, (e) understanding, (f) goal attainment, and (g) power dynamics. Note that these issues are not different from those of other groups. However, they are more important when European Americans interact with African Americans and serve as the context within which the communication occurs.

Ribeau and associates (Ribeau et al., 1999) found that African Americans are particularly attuned to issues of negative stereotyping. They identified two types of **negative stereotyping**: (a) typical kinds of stereotyping, which cast African Americans in a negative light, and (b) indirect stereotyping, which limits discussion to "African American topics" such as music or athletics. For example, I (JSM) recall that when Eddie Murphy first made it big in Hollywood, a European American talk show host was obviously struggling to ask Murphy relevant questions. He finally asked, "What are you doing with all of your money, now? Are you buying cars?" Murphy responded, "That's a very White question to ask." When he said that, I thought back and realized that this talk show host had never asked his European American guests who had made it big what they did with their money or whether they bought several cars with their sudden wealth. Related to negative stereotyping is **acceptance**. Some African American participants indicated that they did not feel accepted by their European American conversational partners.

Many African Americans prefer to speak from the heart and not the head, which Ribeau and colleagues (Ribeau et al., 1999) call **personal expressiveness**. Because of the history of African Americans in the United States, many African Americans do not show this open expression to their European American conversational partners until a sense of trust has been established. Connected with this issue is **authenticity**. One of Ribeau and associates' research participants expressed his frustration about "so many phony conversations—White people trying to impress African Americans with their liberalness" (p. 150). Orbe (1999) suggested that one of the difficulties is in trying to figure out what is authentic or sincere and what is merely politically correct. Orbe reported one research participant struggling with this problem: "I guess that I have found it very difficult to distinguish when they [Whites] are sincere versus when they are trying to be politically correct. . . . I struggle with that" (p. 231).

negative stereotyping—according to Ribeau and associates (Ribeau et al., 1999), stereotyping that casts African Americans in a negative light, or that limits discussion to "African American topics" such as athletics and music.

acceptance—the feeling that one is accepted as an equal in the conversation.

personal expressiveness—speaking from the heart and not the head.

authenticity—being truthful and not trying to be merely politically correct.

Understanding is also important to many African Americans. Often a barrier to understanding is one's lack of experience with racism or even with other African Americans. If an African American conversational partner does not feel that his or her European American partner has had sufficient experience with African Americans, he or she may feel that understanding cannot take place. As one of Ribeau and associates' (Ribeau et al., 1999) partici-

understanding—according to Ribeau and associates (Ribeau et al., 1999), the sense that a conversational partner has enough experience to truly understand the African American experience.

pants indicated, "If people don't share the same life experiences, they can't be expected to truly understand each other. If Whites haven't been exposed to Blacks, there will be a 'fear of the unknown'" (p. 150). This is related to the story about Eddie Murphy and the European American talk show host. The host had obviously not interacted with many African Americans (he was relatively new in the industry at that time) and did not know what kinds of topics would be relevant to African Americans. Each African American is different, so there is no generic African American topic; if the host had just done a little research to find out what kinds of topics interested Murphy, he could have asked Murphy a more relevant question than what kinds of cars Murphy bought with his money.

Goal attainment is the sixth issue identified by Ribeau and associates (Ribeau et al., 1999), and it refers to the goal of mutual understanding between the two conversational partners. Part of the problem in communication may be that the two partners have different emic definitions of the concepts discussed. I remember seeing an 11-year-old African American boy in therapy many years

goal attainment—according to Ribeau and associates (Ribeau et al., 1999), this refers to the goal of mutual understanding between two conversational partners.

ago. He told me that sometimes he makes money by *hustling*. When I asked him what he meant, he told me that hustling was the term used for standing around in grocery store parking lots and offering to help older people put their groceries into their car trunks. Sometimes the boy would get tips for this assistance. (I was relieved when I heard this definition.)

Finally, Ribeau and his associates (Ribeau et al., 1999) discussed how **power dynamics** are in effect when interacting with African Americans. This category is divided into two subcategories: powerlessness and assertiveness. Powerlessness is the feeling of being trapped or manipulated by one's conversational partner or otherwise unable to express oneself freely. To overcome feelings of powerlessness, some African Americans engage in overly assertive verbiage, *code switching*, or *doing the dozens*. Code switching is switching from the Queen's English to Black English or other forms of African American coded language. It is something of a game in which the speaker says things that his or her European American conversational partner either does not understand or misinterprets; the speaker then knows internally that he or she has control of the conversation. This is what E. P. Johnson (1995) and Orbe (1999) would refer to as *playing the part* or *SNAP! culture*, in which a person changes in a snap (with a snap of the

power dynamics—according to Ribeau and associates (Ribeau et al., 1999), this refers to powerlessness and assertiveness in conversations with African Americans. Sometimes, African Americans can feel powerless when conversing with European American conversational partners. In response, they may *code switch*; that is, they may switch from the mutual conversational rules to African American rules, such as Black English or other such verbiage. In code switching, African Americans can regain a sense of control over the conversation.

Conversational dynamics can differ when African Americans speak with other African Americans as opposed to European American individuals. *Photographs by Golden Pixels LLC/Shutterstock and wavebreakmedia/Shutterstock*

finger indicating this instant transformation). Doing the dozens is a game in which some African Americans (particularly males) engage. In this game, they attempt to one-up their conversational partners by putting them down or making fun of them (e.g., "yo mama" jokes). Ribeau and associates (Ribeau et al., 1999) emphasize that this is by no means universal among African Americans, but it is popular among many, and most African Americans at least understand the game being played.

Within the African American community, another type of power dynamic is in play. Neal-Barnett, Stadulis, Singer, Murray, and Demmings (2010) discussed how many African American adolescents try to "keep their friends in line" by accusing them of *acting White*, which means that these targets of the accusation do not engage in Black English or try to excel in school. According to Neal-Barnett et al., this accusation "is one of the most negative accusations one African American adolescent can hurl at another" (p. 103). Certainly, a version of the epithet of acting White was hurled at Barack Obama early in his political career when he was accused of "not being Black enough" or similar kinds of accusations by his critics (Ifil, 2009). For example, Ifil reported that Robert Johnson, an African American supporter of Hillary Clinton during the 2008 political campaign, called Obama a sellout and compared Obama to Sidney Poitier's character in the movie *Guess Who's Coming to Dinner* because Poitier's character wanted to date a European American woman.

Latinxs

Relatively few researchers have examined communication styles among Latinxs as different from those of their European American counterparts. In one of the few such studies, E. T. Hall (1966) found that Latinxs tend to be from a *contact* culture, whereby they tend to touch their conversational partners more (see also Andersen, 1999; Dolphin, 1999). E. T. Hall's classification has been reaffirmed by others (S. E. Jones, 1994; M. L. Patterson, 1983). Related to contact is emotional expressiveness, with contact cultures expressing more interpersonal warmth and low-contact cultures being more interpersonally cool (Andersen, 1999). From her clinical experience, Falicov (2014) affirmed that Latinxs engage in more contact when they communicate with others.

When I was first getting to know my (Latino) friend, he would invite me to his home for large family barbeques and parties and what not, and I remember it caught me off guard when each one of his relatives hugged me or kissed me on the cheek when I was introduced to them. These were people I was meeting for the first time and they were hugging me; I remember feeling very uncomfortable, like they were invading my personal space. It took me quite a while to get used to greeting his family in that manner; I don't remember exactly how long, but ten years later now, I think nothing of it.

The reverse was also interesting, when my friend and I were first starting to hang out, I would invite him to my home for our family get-togethers, which are much smaller by comparison. I remember how shocked he was that my family was so small and that I only had one cousin. I also remember him thinking that my family disliked him because as I introduced him to everyone they would simply shake his hand. No hugging or kissing on the cheek. It took me a long time to convince him that my family didn't dislike him and that it was simply a cultural thing. I had to explain to him that that was just the way my family greets new people they are meeting for the first time and that it was nothing personal, they greeted everyone new like that.

—Shelly, 20+-year-old European American student

A biracial student who read about contact culture was struck by the difference between him and his biracial friend. The student was raised mostly by his European American mother and said that his Mexican American father did not really retain the Mexican part of his culture. However, his friend was raised mostly by his mother, who was Latinx:

When I first met my friend [Chaz] I noticed that when he would be engaged in a conversation that he would always be all "touchy feely" with the person who he was talking to; I always thought it was just the way he was. I didn't realize that it was this way for his entire family and his culture. Most of the time I just noticed him being "touchy feely" with females who he was engaged in a conversation with, so I just assumed that he was flirting with them, but then I noticed that he was like that to males that he was engaged in a conversation with. After reading the text book I learned that most Latino/na are "touchy feely" when they are engaged in a conversation, because that is their culture. Chaz is half Mexican and half White. He was brought up by his mom who is one hundred percent Mexican, and therefore he grew up in the Latino culture.

—Denny, 20+-year-old biracial (Mexican/European American) student

Latinx people tend to touch each other while talking more than do people in other cultures. *Photograph by Diego Cervo/Shutterstock*

One interesting aspect of Latinx—particularly Mexican and Mexican American—communication is the use of proverbs, sayings, and metaphors

(Aranda, 1977; Aviera, 1996; Campa, 1947; Castellanos & Gloria, 2007; Comas-Díaz, 2006, 2014; J. M. Sellers, 1994; Weisman de Mamani, Gurak, & Sura, 2014; Zormeier & Samovar, 1999). These proverbs, or *dichos*, are used to transmit important cultural values. J. M. Sellers (1994) identified some prototypical proverbs used to transmit the values of collectivism, fatalism, present-time orientation, being orientation, and family:

Collectivism
Better to be a fool with the crowd than wise by oneself.
A solitary soul neither sings nor cries.
He who divides and shares is left with the best share.

Fatalism
God gives it and God takes it away.
He who is born to suffer will start from the cradle.
Submit to pain because it is inevitable.

Present-Time Orientation
Don't move the water; the river is already flooding.
There is more time than life.
Don't do today what you can put off until tomorrow.

Being Orientation
He who lives a hurried life will soon die.
He who gets drenched at dawn has the rest of the day to dry out.
He who wants everything will lose everything.

Family Values
A tree that grows crooked cannot be straightened.
Better to die on your feet than to live on your knees.
A man is king in his home.

Higher Education
Castellanos and Gloria (2007) have used this notion of *dichos* to help Latinx students succeed in higher education. These *dichos* include the following:

Where there's food for one, there's food for many. (encouraging students to help one another)

A person who's close to a good tree receives good shade. (encouraging students to seek a good mentor)

What one learns well will never be lost. (encouraging students to pursue research opportunities and professional development)

L. Vasquez (2000) indicated that these proverbs, sayings, or *dichos* are powerful when used properly in therapy. They are so ingrained in many Mexican American minds that when they are relevant either to what is preventing clients from acting or to what an appropriate perspective can be for a situation, therapy can move rapidly.

As everyone congratulated my friends on their new business venture, the president of the Hispanic Chamber of Commerce Association made a comment; he said, *"Dime con quien andas y te dire quien eres"* which translates [to], "Tell me who you associate with and I'll tell you who you are." As he said this everyone nodded in agreement. He went on to say in Spanish, "We want associates who want to invest in a future, people who want to succeed, not those who make excuses. We consider this a family of contacts where like-minded people may do business together." At the end of his speech, everyone cheered and clapped and they systematically went around the room and introduced themselves and their businesses to my friends. In a way, it reminded me of an induction ceremony and the dicho was sort of creed everyone followed.

—Alicia, 20+-year-old Ecuadorian American student

American Indians

As we discussed earlier, an important aspect of American Indian communication is silence (Richardson, 1981). Another thing to keep in mind when interacting with American Indians is that often time is considered in terms of eras instead of chronology. Kluckhohn and Strodt-beck's (1961) notion of present-time orientation does not capture the significance of this value. In American Indian terms, the present time can be years, decades, or even centuries, because the current time can signify a phase in the development or progress of their people. In therapy, this concept of time can clash with the chronologically governed time of a therapy session. Often, Western-trained therapists see being late to a session as a form of resistance (Greenson, 1967). However, to the American Indian client, getting to the therapy session around the time of the scheduled appointment is within the present time when he or she is seeking help. Finally, as we have previously discussed, American Indians tend to engage in less eye contact, and direct eye contact with someone who is an elder is considered a sign of disrespect (Garwick & Auger, 2000; D. W. Sue & Sue, 2003, 2008, 2013).

Communication Patterns of the Elderly

Few researchers have examined how elderly individuals differ from nonelderly individuals in communication styles. Because of the increased use of the health-care system, many researchers have examined how medical professionals must communicate with the elderly (Christenson, Buchanan, Houlihan, & Wanzek, 2011; Moberg & Rick, 2008). For example, Pennbrant and Trolihaettan (2013) found that involving relatives with medical instructions increases the confidence in these instructions and a higher compliance with the medical regime being described, and Ballantyne, Yang, and Boon (2013) found that in dealing with patients with limited English abilities, medical professionals needed to ask what the patient heard when receiving medical instructions. Nonmedical studies have involved factors such as the amount of respect given to elderly individuals when interacting with them (Giles, Khajavy, & Choi, 2012) and examining how elderly individuals interface with new electronic devices and applications (Bruder, Blessing, & Wandke, 2014). Moreover, Underwood (2010) found that normal-functioning elderly individuals did not differ in the sophistication of their conversational interactions from their younger counterparts.

Some interesting studies have concentrated on how grandparents interact with their grandchildren. Much of the interest in this area has been stimulated by the relatively recent increase in grandparents taking responsibility for much of the care of their grandchildren for various reasons:

child abuse or neglect in the parents' home, divorce, and/or working parents (Jendrek, 1994; McKay, 1989, 1993, 1999; McKay & Caverly, 1995). The major motivation of grandparent–grandchild interaction is the desire by the grandparents to transmit knowledge based on their lives and family history (Nussbaum & Bettini, 1994). This is in keeping with Erik Erikson's (1950/1963, 1964) notion that a life-stage motivation in older ages is to pass on wisdom to subsequent generations. Nussbaum and Bettini note that grandchildren are quite interested in this kind of knowledge as well. McKay (1999) stated that it is very important for elderly individuals to be able to share their family histories: "These individuals have a lifetime of wisdom and experience to impart; to be unable to do so is a loss not only to the listener, but to the teller as well" (p. 179).

Many of our students relate to the notion of the importance placed on communication from grandparent to grandchild and vice versa:

> My grandfather would often use the term *"Pobre pero honesto"*—he took pride in being an honest man. He would repeatedly say, "I don't have much but I have my dignity." My grandfather just turned 92 and he still is poor but honest. I love my grandfather for all the sacrifices he made for his family and for the values that he instilled in all of us. It's his selflessness that inspires me to better myself as an individual. I want to pass on the torch of knowledge to my nieces and nephew so that they can be even better than me.
>
> —Sarah, 20+-year-old Mexican American student

Elderly individuals enjoy interacting with their grandchildren and passing on information. *Photograph by KPG Payless2/Shutterstock*

> My family moved here from the Philippines when I was only 6 months old, so I was pretty much raised here. It is a Filipino tradition to take care of our grandparents and great-grandparents when they get older so when our family moved here my great-grandparents moved in with me, my mom, and my dad. They lived with us until they passed away a few years ago. I'm sad to say that even though I was taught to always respect my elders there were many times growing up when I began to see them as more of a hassle. I know that this is very sad to say because I loved them both very much, but because I was raised in an American culture I felt like

I did not really relate to them. I am somewhat disappointed in myself for feeling this way because I constantly took it out on my great-grandparents, especially my great-grandmother. I felt that when she would ask me about my day, or what I had done that weekend, or even if I was hungry that she was just trying to control me and get into my business. Now I know that she was just interested in what was going on in my life because she was old and didn't have much going on in her life so her family was everything to her. I should have treated her better because she took care of me from the day I was born, and I feel like the way I repaid her was by being mean. The sad thing is, is that the only time I realized how great she is was when she was already gone. I know that this is so cliché, but it is true. You really never appreciate the people you love until they are gone. I want to get back to my roots of respecting my elders so I am going to start spending more time with my grandmother. She is getting old, and to that stage where she's beginning to become lonely and she has feelings of being useless. My great-grandmother went through this stage and I didn't realize it because I was too busy being a high school student.

—Celeste, 20+-year-old Filipina American student

McKay (1989, 1993, 1999) found that grandchildren also enjoyed hearing stories about their parents when their parents were children. Can any of you relate to this?

Communication Among Younger Adults

One rising difference in communication patterns between younger adults and older adults is the use of social media. Barack Obama knew the power of the Internet and used it not only to raise campaign contributions but also to motivate his supporters to work in his favor (Carr, 2008). He even inspired others to post support for him, such as Obama Girl's "I Got a Crush on Obama" and Will.i.am's "Yes We Can Obama Song" posted on YouTube. Throughout his presidency, Obama used social media such as Twitter, YouTube, and Facebook to garner support for his policies and to keep his supporters—and the general public—informed ("Social Media Case Study: How Barack Obama Became President," 2017).

Donald Trump continued the use of social media, particularly Twitter, in his campaign to be elected president. This was predicted even before his election in 2016 (V. Jones, 2015). During his primary and presidential campaigns, Trump insulted his opponents and expressed many thoughts using Twitter that no previous candidate would dare utter out loud. Many defenders of Trump said that he would be "more presidential" once he became president. However, his Tweets continued to lack decorum. President Trump defended his use of Twitter, saying that it is a modern-day way of communicating directly with the public (LeBlanc, 2017) and circumventing *fake news*, referring to the media who challenged his tactics and policies.

> My use of social media is not Presidential—it's MODERN DAY PRESIDENTIAL.
> —Donald J. Trump, July 1, 2017

Why do modern presidents engage in so much social media? Perhaps it is because it is how younger adults communicate. As many people who have studied politics have understood, younger adults are the most difficult class to motivate to vote (Brennan & Cook, 2015). Because young adults use social media so much more than older adults do, using this form of communication is an attempt to reach younger adults.

Prevalence of Social Media

How much time do young adults spend on social media? How much time do you spend on social media? According to the most extensive study to date, the answer might surprise you. Teenagers spend nearly 9 hours per day consuming media (Kaiser Family Foundation, 2010; Tsukayama, 2015). *Consuming media* includes watching online videos, listening to music, and engaging in other forms of technology. However, the study by the Kaiser Family Foundation, which is cited by all researchers in this area (e.g., American College of Pediatricians, 2016; Coyne & Padilla-Walker, & Holmgren 2018; Zhao, Qiu, & Xie, 2012), was conducted in 2010, before the existence of Snapchat and Instagram. Instagram has now replaced Snapchat as the most used form of social media, surpassing both Snapchat and Facebook (Riley, 2018). Although Facebook might be seen as a dominant social media platform by most Americans, only 51% of teenagers between the ages of 13 and 17 report that they use Facebook, compared with 72% who report that they use Instagram and 69% who report that they use Snapchat (Riley, 2018). Lower-income teens use Facebook more than higher-income teens, indicating that the platform may be more accessible to people of all income levels, whereas Snapchat and Instagram require more expensive phones to use.

Positives and Negatives of the Use of Social Media

Why do young people use so much social media? As Bayer, Ellison, Schoenebeck, and Falk (2016) indicated, college Snapchat users enjoyed being able to share mundane experiences with individuals whom they trusted. Although it was not designed for in-depth social support, the platform allows people to share parts of their lives with others, such as what they are eating, something that made them laugh, or something that caught their interest. These students felt that this form of social media was more enjoyable than other forms of communication. Jessica discussed the kind of enjoyment she gets from using social media platforms, which is different from that of her mother:

> My parents grew up in the era where there was no Internet and social media platforms such as Instagram, Snapchat, and Facebook. When they were young adults they did not have the luxury of communicating with their friends and family by the touch of a button. My mom is so bad at texting that I can never understand what she is saying because of her excessive typos. She doesn't use the same social media platforms as me and therefore does not have the same accessibility to contact her friends and family. With the help of social media I can virtually engage with my friends by Snapchatting them or posting a picture to Instagram. This form of communication can aid in the development of lifelong friends. Unlike my parents who don't keep in contact with their high school friends, social media has made it so much easier for me to thrive in my friendships.
> —Jessica, 20+-year-old European American student

A criticism of today's social media usage is that such forms of communication can cause shallow thinking, called the *shallowing hypothesis* (Annisette & Lafreniere, 2017). Annisette and Lafreniere found that individuals who used texting or social media frequently were concomitantly less likely to be reflective in thought. This has implications for lowering moral standards because one is less likely to understand the implications of one's actions if one is less likely to reflect on one's thoughts.

One of the most negative aspects of social media can be the bullying that some children receive. According to the American College of Pediatricians (2016), over half of the adolescents surveyed said that they have been bullied through social media, and over a quarter said that they have been repeatedly bullied. Unfortunately, the overwhelming majority of these individuals have not told their parents. Even more unfortunate is that this form of bullying has been linked to suicidal ideation and even behavior.

Because social media is a peer-to-peer form of communication and because nearly anyone can start a blog or plant information on the Internet, information coming from any web-based communication is without an editor (C. G. Prado, 2017). C. G. Prado asserted that this serves to render consumers of this form of information gathering indifferent to any evidence in support of the information. Thus, opinions are placed on equal footing as evidence. Pingree, Stoycheff, Sui, and Peifer (2018) posited that the use of social media has led consumers of news to be complacent because news and Twitter are considered trivial.

The Silver Lining

Because of the negatives associated with social media, it is easy to discount this form of communication as shallow and trivial. However, major social movements have been organized through social media. As discussed in Chapter 3, the high school students at Marjory Stoneman Douglas High School organized a national movement against gun violence in schools using social media. Other forms of important social movements have also been organized through social media. Bogen, Bleiweiss, and Orchowski (2018) credited Twitter's #NotOkay campaign with bringing sexual victimization to the forefront of public consciousness and changing long-standing policies, almost overnight. Similarly, Keib, Himelboi, and Han (2018) credited the #BlackLivesMatter campaign with being highly effective in bringing violence against African Americans to consciousness. Gleason (2018) contended that teenagers now think in terms of effective hashtags for national campaigns. Thus, great social movements can be influenced by current social media technology.

Gender Differences in Communication

> Sometimes I'll go to parties and I'll be in a conversation with a group of people, and I've noticed that men will not only dominate the conversation, but they will also look at you like you're stupid if you have an opinion on a "male" topic. I know that I've had it happen to me many times when the topic was related to sports or cars. I may not be an "expert" on these topics, but I believe that my opinions are not stupid.
>
> —Sylvia, 20+-year-old Filipina American student

Women's communication occurs within a context of sexism. Sylvia's experience should not be surprising. How many times do you find yourself in a class in which the first question or comment is made by a European American male student? In a classic experiment, Broverman and associates (Broverman, Broverman, Clarkson, Rosenkrantz, & Vogel, 1970) asked both male and female mental health professionals to check off the personality characteristics of mentally healthy adult women, mentally healthy adult men, and mentally healthy adults. The characteristics listed were bipolar, such as *very subjective–very objective, very submissive–very dominant*, and *feelings easily hurt–feelings not easily hurt*. Male and female mental health professionals agreed markedly on their ratings. Broverman and colleagues found that the characteristics for mentally healthy men and mentally healthy adults were in almost perfect agreement, whereas the characteristics for mentally healthy women and mentally healthy adults were in disagreement. Thus, women could not be perceived to be both mentally healthy women and mentally healthy adults. For example, when asked what mentally healthy women should be, the research participants responded that women should be submissive, whereas when asked what mentally healthy adults should be, the participants responded that people should be dominant.

Broverman et al.'s (1970) study of characteristics associated with men and women has been replicated in a worldwide study by J. E. Williams and Best (1982, 1994). They sampled college students (as opposed to mental health professionals) internationally and found amazing agreement about "male" and "female" characteristics among the 30 countries they studied. Men were characterized as active, aggressive, individualistic, loud, rational, and tough, whereas women were characterized as affectionate, dependent, gentle, sensitive, submissive, and weak. It is interesting that assessments of these characteristics varied from country to country. Whereas Broverman et al. suggested that adult male characteristics were seen as more mentally healthy than adult female characteristics in the United States, respondents in other countries varied in their assessment of the desirability of these characteristics.

Another personality dimension that is associated with gender differences is the field dependent–independent distinction. Those who are field independent function in the world autonomously, not relying on external validation of their own perceptions, whereas those who are field dependent do use these external frames (Goodenough, 1978). This area of psychology was initially based on Witkin's (1949) examination of how people judged objects in space. People generally use a combination of visual and bodily cues to assess the degree to which an object is upright, and Witkin found that men tended to use their internal bodily cues more than women did, whereas women tended to use visual cues more than men did. Witkin et al. (1954) extended this perceptual tendency to personality traits, and this dimension was taken as proven in the personality literature. However, in an interview with Susan Fiske, Hackney (2005) reported how misleading this "truth" of psychology could be. Rather than calling it field dependent or field independent, Fiske suggested that if we were to call it *field sensitive or field insensitive*, the positive versus negative connotation of this gender difference would be in the opposite direction in which it had been understood. Have you ever witnessed (or been a victim of) men saying that what women talk about is unimportant, but what men talk about is important? It seems that only men make judgments such as this.

Lakoff (1975) found that women used **tag questions** more often than their male counterparts. Tag questions are questions added to a statement of assertion. An example of a tag question is "This class is interesting, don't you think?" The tag question ("don't

That's such a girl thing to say.
—Bart Simpson, famous cartoon son

tag questions—questions added to a statement of assertion, such as "This is good, don't you think?"

Men and women have different communication styles.
Photograph by WAYHOME studio/Shutterstock

you think?") allows the conversational partner to agree or disagree with the assertion ("This class is interesting"). Traditionally, tag questions have been interpreted as an indication of weakness or passivity on the part of the speaker (Paludi, 1998). However, Paludi indicated that another interpretation of tag questions is that they connote warmth by inviting the other individual to engage in a conversation.

Another form of communication more commonly used by women than by men is **qualifiers** (Carli, 1990; Wood, 1994, 1999). Qualifiers are words or phrases that soften statements, such as "I may be wrong, but I think this class is interesting." The phrase "I may be wrong" is a quali-

qualifiers—words or phrases that soften statements, such as "I may be wrong, but . . ."

fier. One interpretation of this usage is that women are less confident about their topics of discussion or are otherwise passive, but another interpretation is that women use this style of communication to convey warmth and politeness.

Wood (1994, 1999) has written extensively about gender differences in communication. She found that women tended to use more indirect forms of communication, whereas men tended to use more direct communication; women disclosed more about themselves than men did; women tended to match their experiences with the experiences of others to show understanding and empathy, whereas men tended to try to compete with or outdo their conversational partners; and women tended to use more tentative judgments, whereas men tended to be more assertive and confident in their speech, among other similar kinds of differences. These conclusions were confirmed by Gay (2012). Moreover, Gay found that when men used *female speech*, they tended to lose status among conversational partners. In summarizing Hoyenga and Hoyenga's (1979) review of gender and communication, Gay wrote, "They report that 'feminine communication styles' are associated with less intelligence, passivity, and submissiveness, while 'masculine styles' evoke notions of power, authority, confidence, and leadership" (p. 395). Table 4.3 presents examples of the kinds of speech that women and men tend to use, based on the findings of Wood and Gay.

These findings are about general differences between men and women, and they do not apply to every man and every woman. We presented this concept in one of our classes as a point of discussion, and one woman in the class said that she and her husband engaged in behavior opposite what the comparison suggested. However, most students agree with these observations. One of our students observed male–female differences in communication on the television show *The Apprentice*:

> In The Apprentice, contestants are put into two competing groups, which most of the time is usually a male and a female group. You can see right away how different the males and females interacted within their own group. After being given a task, the male

TABLE 4.3   **Examples of the Kinds of Speech That Women and Men Might Use**

Women might say . . .	Men might say . . .
How sad; I know how you feel.	You wimp!
Is it cold in here?	Close the window.
I experienced the same thing that you did.	You think that is something, listen to what happened to me . . . (this can be either good or bad)
This is only my opinion, but I think this stuff about gender and communication is pretty interesting.	This stuff is freakin' awesome.

group took no time to socialize; instead they were more assertive and task oriented. Their communication was direct and often involved a lot of argument and interruption between sharing of ideas. On the other hand, female groups tried to include all the members' thoughts and opinions on pending decisions. However, whenever conflict rose within the group, the females hesitated on being straightforward about their problems. It seems like dealing with the problems was by spreading gossip behind each other's back. Somehow in the end the male group always won.

Given the fact that males are socialized to be more direct and aggressive, I wonder if this is what fuels their power and success? Because of this, I sometimes feel that men act a bit too arrogant, especially in conversations with women. I have seen men act as if they are the ones who know better, and perhaps this attitude, whether conscious or unconscious, can sometimes make them feel superior to women.

—Valerie, 20+-year-old Chinese American student

The point that men will often equate disclosure with vulnerability resonated with one student. These are the kinds of gender differences found in industrial/organizational studies (Riggio, 2013):

I am one for details when I talk to someone. I need detailed directions, I want details when someone is describing something to me, and I love it when someone tells me details from a movie or a conversation that they had had with someone. My husband thinks that details are trivial and it drives him crazy when I ask him to try and remember the details of a conversation or something else. He is the type that believes one should just get to the point of the conversation, and that's it, nothing more. . . .

I had a friend share with me things that she had been experiencing and we talked for almost an hour or two. It brings us closer together when we share those experiences with one another and we can help each other out with problems. Her husband said he doesn't understand how women could stay on a phone for so long and talk about what he called "nothing." I asked her to ask him what he talks to his friends about when he talks and he told her to tell me that they just talk about what things have happened to them that they have either done better than someone else or they usually compare experiences, but the conversation doesn't last for an hour. He also complained that his wife discloses too much information, something my husband has told me that I do, too. He seems to feel that people shouldn't know too much about you and your life because you never know when they can use it against you. That idea kind of goes along with the masculine talk idea that personal disclosure can make one vulnerable.

—Abigail, 30+-year-old European American student

Wood (1999) emphasized that gender differences in communication are more a product of socialization than of biology. There seem to be two sources of such socialization: family communication and communication between playmates. Paludi (1998) suggested that this socialization occurs very early because parents respond measurably differently to boys and girls. Will, Self, and Datan (1976) found that differences in socialization happened even when people only *thought* they were interacting with a boy or a girl. They dressed an infant in pink and referred to it as *Beth* and dressed the same infant in blue and referred to it as *Adam*. The research participants played with the infant measurably differently—for example, offering Beth a doll and Adam a toy train.

Bilingual Communication

At a very young age of 5, my father sent my brother and me to Mexico to learn how to speak "proper" Spanish. I attended kindergarten through third grade in a private school that taught only in Spanish. At the age of 9, my father sent for us, and we continued school here in Southern California in classes which were taught in all English. It was a difficult transition due to the fact that I hardly knew the English language, but after a year I managed to grasp the most important words to be able to communicate with my peers at school. At home, where I was able to speak Spanish with my parents, I felt a lot more comfortable because I didn't have to struggle to get a point across.

—Penny, 20+-year-old Mexican American student

Most people in the world are bilingual or multilingual (Matsumoto, 2000; Matsumoto & Juang, 2012; Snow, 1993; Whitney, 1998). There are various ways in which people can become bilingual. Some people grow up in societies in which two or more languages are pervasive and in which one must know multiple languages to survive (e.g., Switzerland and Quebec); some are bilingual because their native language is not the official language of the country (e.g., Zulu speakers in South Africa who needed to learn English and Lithuanian speakers who needed to learn Russian before the fall of the Soviet Union); some are bilingual because they immigrated to a country that speaks a different language (e.g., Spanish or Cantonese speakers who immigrate to the United States); some are bilingual because of colonization (e.g., Aymara speakers in South America, where Spanish was imposed on them); some are bilingual because of education and extensive travel (e.g., those in the United States who learn French and have the opportunity to travel to France); some are bilingual for economic or professional reasons (e.g., Korean business-men who learn English to do business with American companies); and some are bilingual because they grew up in households that spoke two languages. When the second language does not replace the native language, this is called **additive bilingualism** (J. W. Berry et al., 1992; W. E. Lambert, 1977). When the second language replaces the native language, this is called **subtractive bilingualism** (J. W. Berry et al., 1992; W. E. Lambert, 1977). Subtractive bilingualism is also called **language attrition** (Snow, 1993). Language attrition occurs when a language is used infrequently, even when the first language is well ingrained.

additive bilingualism—the acquisition of a second language that does not replace the native language.

subtractive bilingualism—the acquisition of a second language that replaces the native language.

language attrition—equivalent to subtractive bilingualism.

Vietnamese was my first language and over time I was able to assimilate into the surrounding culture and learn English as well. However, as my English advanced my Vietnamese waned until it just didn't run deeply enough for my parents to be able to effectively communicate with me. I always thought that my parents didn't ever have much to say to me. In truth, my relationship with my parents sucked growing up. We hardly ever talked, and it wasn't until recently that I was able to have conversations with them. In a recent dialogue, my mom and I sat and talked about when we were growing up and she said something that just brought so much clarity to me first but also to the struggle of the parents who have to raise their children up in an unfamiliar culture. She said, "Back then, it wasn't that we didn't want to teach you or that we didn't have anything to teach you, but because we only spoke Vietnamese and didn't know English and you only spoke English and didn't understand Vietnamese well enough we lacked the framework by which we could instruct you and guide you." My parents went through a lot over the years and I am proud of them today.

—Tommy, 20+-year-old Vietnamese American student

Becoming aware of subtractive bilingualism or language attrition can enable people take steps to prevent such attrition. Upon reading about this topic, the following student vowed to prevent it from happening:

When I was younger I used to speak and write Thai more fluently but now I notice that my American accent is thicker and my vocabulary is shrinking. I used to go to my temple every weekend to learn how to read and write Thai and participated in extracurricular activities that involved Thai art and playing Thai classical music, both in which I excelled. I entered art contests and won first place. I also traveled to Thailand with my Thai band and had the honor of playing for the queen of Thailand. Now I am not involved in the Thai community and rarely go to my temple.

I used to believe that I had a hard time assimilating into the American culture when I was younger because I was more involved with my Thai culture than with my American side. However, a few years ago it seemed like I did a good job integrating both cultures into my life. Now I am leaving my Thai side and my American side is taking over. I am glad that I had learned about this in class because it made me aware of my actions and thought process. Now I can try to incorporate my Thai culture back into my life, since it is very valuable to me and I would horribly regret it if I were to let it slowly drift away.

—Billy, 20+-year-old Thai American student

native bilingualism—the ability to speak two languages from birth, acquired because both languages are spoken in the household.

When two languages are used in the household so that people become bilingual from birth, this is called **native bilingualism** (Snow, 1993). There are both cognitive and social consequences of bilingualism (W. E. Lambert, 1967, 1977, 1980).

Cognitive Consequences of Bilingualism

Early studies indicated that bilingual children performed more poorly than their monolingual counterparts did (see W. E. Lambert, 1977, and Matsumoto, 2000, for reviews of these early studies). However, W. E. Lambert and his colleagues criticized those early researchers for not controlling for social class or educational opportunities (W. E. Lambert, 1977; W. E. Lambert & Anisfeld, 1969; Peal & Lambert, 1962). When studies were controlled for these factors, W. E. Lambert and Anisfeld (1969) and Peal and Lambert (1962) found that bilingual children performed better on various measures of intelligence. Price-Williams and Ramirez (1977) suggested that this performance might be the result of increased levels of cognitive flexibility among bilingual individuals.

Bialystok and Craik (2010) examined the advantages and disadvantages of being bilingual. They found some costs of being bilingual, such as having smaller vocabularies, having more tip-of-the-tongue experiences, and generating slightly fewer words in a timed task (called *semantic fluency tasks*) than did individuals who are monolingual. However, bilingual individuals demonstrated better performance in nonverbal tasks that required conflict resolution. For example, most people are familiar with the Stroop effect, in which it is difficult to name the color of the ink if the word is the name of a color different from the color of the ink. People who are bilingual demonstrate less interference in Stroop tasks. Put another way, bilinguals perform better than their monolingual counterparts. A surprising and significant difference, however, is that being bilingual seems to give some degree of protection against cognitive decline. In examining 91 monolingual and 93 bilingual individuals who had been diagnosed with dementia, Bialystok and Craik found that bilingual individuals contracted the dementia more than 4 years *later* than those who were monolingual.

C. Baker (2013), Kroll, Bobb, and Hoshino (2014), and Verkoeijen, Bouwmeester, and Camp (2012) also examined aspects of bilingualism. C. Baker concluded that knowing two languages is a benefit to individuals if both languages are well learned. However, problems can occur in the classroom if the second language is not as highly developed as the home language. Verkoeijen et al. (2012) found that studying in the language of origin and testing in the second language helped students learn material more deeply as opposed to learning only surface features of the list of words to be remembered.

There is evidence that acquiring a second language changes the brain location of certain concepts or at least causes a change in category clustering of concepts. Grabois (1999) studied native Spanish speakers, expert speakers of Spanish, Spanish learners, foreign-language Spanish learners, and native English speakers. Native Spanish–speaking participants were monolingual Spanish speakers who spoke Spanish from birth. Participants who were expert speakers of Spanish were native English speakers who lived in Spain for at least 3 years and achieved a level of expertise in the Spanish language. Spanish learner participants were native speakers of English who were advanced learners of Spanish and who were studying abroad in Spain for 1 year. Foreign-language Spanish learners were enrolled in advanced Spanish-language courses and had been learning Spanish for about 2 years. Native English–speaking participants did not have any expertise in Spanish. Grabois examined how these participants responded to sets of words that related to emotional terms (*love, happiness, fear,* and *death*). The closer on the continuum participants were to native Spanish–speaking participants, the more similar their clusters of responses were to those of the native Spanish–speaking group. In other words, clusters of participants who were expert speakers of Spanish looked much more like the native Spanish–speaking clusters than did the foreign-language Spanish learner participant clusters. From a cognitive perspective, this finding suggested that the actual mental structure changes according to one's proficiency in the second language.

Kroll et al. (2014) concluded that bilingualism changes brain structure. Researchers in neuroimaging studies that have examined the brain when bilingual and monolingual individuals are engaged in general cognitive tasks revealed that bilingual individuals seem to be able to think more efficiently than their monolingual counterparts. For example, when viewing a nonverbal conflict, although the anterior cingulate cortex areas are activated in both types of individuals, bilingual anterior cingulate cortex activation is more focused in its activation. These researchers speculated that this efficiency may be behind the protection against dementia that Bialystock and Craik (2010) discovered previously. Subsequent research (Rossi, Cheng, Kroll, Diaz, & Newman, 2017) confirmed changes in brain structure through magnetic resonance imaging analysis.

> When I try to figure out words that I don't know in English, I think of Spanish words that are written similarly. This happens quite a bit when I see a word in English that is spelled the same way in Spanish. If I am thinking in English I sometimes don't know the word. However, if I switch to Spanish, the meaning of the word often comes to me right away. My brain is wired to think in Spanish first and then English. Like I count in Spanish and spell in Spanish.
>
> —Andres, 30+-year-old Mexican American professor

Although popular wisdom has it that children acquire second languages faster than adults do, systematic investigation proves otherwise (Snow, 1993). This is true for both formal and informal acquisition of the language (Snow, 1983, 1987; Snow & Hoefnagel-Höhle, 1978). However, older learners may be more "fossilized" in their native languages, so accents from their first language will persist into their second languages (Krashen, Long, & Scarcella, 1982). Thus, an older learner's mastery of the second language may be inferior to that of a younger learner.

O. Garcia and Kleifgen (2010) suggested that the political debate has disadvantaged individuals who are not quite bilingually fluent. They are often referred to as being of *limited English proficiency*. Even the less judgmental *English-language learner* label has a somewhat negative connotation in that it suggests that these people are in the process of learning English but will not become fluent. O. Garcia and Kleifgen prefer the term *emergent bilinguals* because these individuals will ultimately become proficient in two languages. In this worldwide economy, bilingual abilities will become increasingly important.

In looking at the statistics of emergent bilinguals, O. Garcia and Kleifgen (2010) reported that from 1979 to 2008, the number of emergent bilinguals in the United States increased from 1.3 million to 2.7 million, or 107%. Moreover, during this same time frame, the number of individuals who became fluent in two languages increased from 2.5 million to 8.1 million, or 220%. Of these emergent bilinguals, 77% are of Latinx descent and 13% are of Asian/Pacific Island descent. Thus, it is important that we pay attention to this growing segment of our population. O. Garcia and Kleifgen reviewed the positive aspects of being bilingual beyond what Bialystok and Craik (2010) did, and they concluded that bilinguals have a greater analytic orientation to language (called *metalinguistic awareness*); have a greater flexibility of perceptions and interpretations to describing the world, resulting in greater creativity; and are better at gauging communicative situations, such as if someone is hesitant about a suggestion or merely thinking through the suggestion. This creative flexibility can lead to playfulness with languages:

> As a consequence of speaking more languages, I always feel that my native language is more of a playground than a prescriptive canvas. I like to play with words, and change things according to what I like. For example, in Italian (my native language) the verb for "to meow" is "miagolare" . . . so many vowels!! It seems almost impossible to pronounce. One day, while addressing my very vocal cat, I wanted to tell it in Italian "Can you meow less"? Very spontaneously, I decided to change the verb "miagolare" into "miagare" thus eliminating a bunch of sounds from it . . . To me it sounded perfect! And so much easier to pronounce. The nice thing is that I introduced the new verb to my parents who found it funny enough. To date, they also started using "miagare" instead of "miagolare."
>
> —Emilia, 30+-year-old Italian immigrant professor

Social Consequences of Bilingualism

Speaking multiple languages has an effect on one's identity (J. W. Berry et al., 1992). In fact, ability to speak the language reflective of one's racial/ethnic group is a dimension or a component of some racial identity models (Bernal, Knight, Ocampo, Garza, & Cota, 1993; Isajiw, 1990; Mendoza, 1989; Phinney, 1992; Sodowsky, Lai, & Plake, 1991; Suinn, Ricard-Figueroa, Lew, & Vigil, 1987; Zea, Asner-Self, Birman, & Buki, 2003). If you speak a particular language you may feel an instant connection with someone else who speaks that language or you may have observed people who seem to have such a connection with one another when they are speaking their native language.

Tsai, Ying, and Lee (2001) found that in their Chinese American sample, the people who knew a great deal about Chinese culture and were proficient in the Chinese language had higher self-esteem than did those who did not have such knowledge and abilities. Tsai and associates suggest that this increased self-esteem may be used to counteract racism and discrimination. However, the researchers noted that because their sample was taken from the San Francisco Bay area, which has a large Asian/Pacific American population, the results may apply only to people from that region. You can imagine that if you have a friendship network in which it is the norm to speak the language of your country of heritage, someone who does not speak that language could feel excluded from the group at times, which may in turn have a negative effect on his or her self-esteem.

Some people who have immigrated to the United States have chosen to primarily or completely use English because of their life circumstances. This can come at a cost. For example, a woman who emigrated from Russia felt that her basic personality changed because she only interacted with English speakers:

> When I was in Russia, I was perceived to be a very clever person because I was always quick with a joke or a quip. However, now that I am in the United States, no one perceives me to be clever because it takes me a little while to translate what I want to say into a clever introjection, and by the time I think of what to say, someone else has already said what I wanted to say. This makes me kind of sad because I enjoyed being perceived as quick with a quip.
>
> —Ivana, 20+-year-old Russian student

When I related this story to a Japanese immigrant, she affirmed that she felt different speaking only in English, although she did not feel that it was a personality difference. Instead, she felt that she was more passive, waiting to respond to others as opposed to initiating conversations.

In the short run, giving up one's language of origin may make it easier to fit into one's social environment when that environment does not support the language of origin. You may remember your childhood, when anyone who deviated from the predominant group was teased and ridiculed. One of our students wrote about how she tried to eliminate any evidence of her difference from her peers:

> The issue of acculturation is extremely interesting to me, especially since I am not an American citizen. I was born and raised in Munich, Germany, and didn't set foot on American ground until I was eleven years old. As we discussed in class on Wednesday, my quick assimilation into the new Californian life supports the fact that children adapt very quickly to their new environment. In my case this was primarily driven by the fact that I just wanted to fit in!

Maintaining one's native language can be a source of connection with others who also speak that language.
Photograph by Jaggat Rashidi/Shutterstock

In Germany I had stood out my entire life for being Eurasian (my father is Japanese, my mother German), and the taunting and constant questions were still too fresh in my mind. I was relieved to see that being Asian was of very little consequence in my Arcadia elementary class, since the majority of the other children stemmed from an Asian background. Hence, I was determined to fit in and appear "American" in every way. I asked my mother to pack me sandwiches instead of the Tupperware dishes filled with German or Japanese leftovers. I refused to wear some of the clothes I had brought over, simply because they didn't quite look like everyone else's. I learned to speak English (accent-free) over the next year, achieved primarily by watching countless episodes of Full House and I Love Lucy. The end product resulted in my mother scolding me for "becoming completely Americanized" and trying to hide the parts of me that were the most special.

—Judy, 20+-year-old German/Japanese student

In other reaction papers, Judy indicated that she wished she knew more about her background, particularly her Japanese background. Her mother imparted much of her German knowledge, but her father was not very communicative about his Japanese background. Thus, while Judy was in Germany, even though her classmates knew she was Eurasian and identified her as Japanese, her lack of knowledge about her Japanese heritage left her with a sense of loss. Had she known more about her Japanese heritage and had she known some Japanese words, her teasing classmates might have expressed interest in her instead of taunting her. When she came to America, she tried to eliminate all aspects of her German heritage so that she would fit in with other Asian and Eurasian children in her school. We never asked her whether she retained her German language, but it would be interesting to know the degree to which she still feels German.

Summary

Grice (1975) identified some conversational conventions that make face-to-face communication a cooperative endeavor. These conventions go beyond the content of the communication and to extraverbal issues such as turn taking, politeness, and relationships between the two conversational partners. In this chapter, we dealt with many of these extraverbal issues. D. W. Sue and Sue (2003) identified some of these areas as proxemics, kinesics, paralanguage, and high- and low-context communication factors. We discussed some aspects of proxemics, kinesics, and paralanguage, but much of this chapter dealt with high- versus low-context communication.

Communication is more than just language. Words constitute much of the basis of our communication with one another, but they do not make up the entirety of what is being communicated. Societies that depend more on words than on the context within which the words are transmitted are called low-context communication societies. Alternatively, societies that depend more on the context to convey a message are called high-context communication societies. In general, Western societies tend to be LC and Asian societies tend to be HC. Connected with the LC–HC distinction is the distinction between direct and indirect communication. HC societies in particular use indirect communication. Part of this connection is that indirect communication in conjunction with contextual messages allows people to avoid conflict. In Asian cultures, this form of communication also allows people to save face.

There are many specific cultural differences in communication. High-context communication is associated with Asian cultures. African Americans vary in their communication styles, primarily in ways that examine the authenticity of their conversational partners, particularly when their partners are European American. Thus, they are attuned to issues such as stereotyping, honesty, and power. Latinxs tend to be from contact cultures. Thus, they touch their conversational partners more and are more emotionally expressive. The use of metaphors, proverbs, and sayings (*dichos*) is also common in Latinx—particularly Mexican American— communication. American Indians appreciate silences more and are governed by a time orientation of eras as opposed to chronology. Moreover, side-by-side conversations and less eye contact are more common among American Indians.

Elderly individuals may use language in ways that vary from the ways in which young and middle-aged adults use language. Most of the research in this area has been on grandparent– grandchild communication and revealed that Erik Erikson's notions of transmitting knowledge and wisdom govern this kind of communication. Grandparents are particularly interested in telling the story of the family, and grandchildren are particularly interested in hearing these kinds of stories.

Gender differences are particularly interesting. Women, more than men, tend to use qualifiers and other forms of communication that indicate tentativeness. One interpretation of this tendency is that women are less confident in their communication. However, another interpretation is that women are more inviting and polite in their communications, so they soften their words to allow their conversational partners to agree or disagree with them. It is important to note that women's conversations occur within the context of general societal sexism. Thus, some interpretations of "women's language" may be negatively assessed by men, such as feeling that women are field dependent as opposed to field sensitive.

Researchers in earlier studies indicated that bilingualism reduces one's ability to function in society. However, more recent studies have demonstrated that a second language seems to add to cognitive flexibility and ability. Snow (1993) pointed out that bilingualism can be achieved in many ways, such as learning a second language beyond one's native language, having a second language imposed on one, and learning two languages from birth because two languages are spoken at home. It is surprising that being bilingual may help protect people from cognitive decline, and Bialystok and Craik (2010) found that age of onset of dementia is later for individuals who are bilingual than for those who are monolingual. Moreover, O. Garcia and Kleifgen (2010) documented the increase in emergent bilinguals in this country. W. E. Lambert (1977) indicated that there are at least two consequences of bilingualism: cognitive and social. Besides cognitive flexibility, one cognitive consequence of bilingualism seems to be that clusters of concepts are influenced such that these clusters are a combination of the native language and the acquired language. Social consequences seem to be connections with others who also speak the language, contributions to one's identity, and ethnic pride.

Food for Thought

We all have a sense of the conventions of everyday speech. Did you ever watch the television series *Seinfeld*? Many episodes had as their central premise a violation of a conversational rule. Do you remember the episode of the close talker? How about the soft talker who got Jerry to wear a puffy shirt on national television because Jerry could not hear what she was saying and he inadvertently agreed to do so? We cannot really verbalize what conversational rules are, but we can certainly recognize when they are violated. On situation comedy shows, those violations are funny; in our everyday lives, they make us feel uncomfortable. Think about times when you may have violated conversational conventions—for instance, talking louder to a person who does not understand English. After reading this chapter, you may be more conscious of how you interact with others in conversation.

Critical Thinking Questions

1. Have you ever been in a conversation with someone who violated one of the cooperative principles (e.g., the person kept talking and did not let you join in the conversation or stood uncomfortably close to you)? If so, how did that make you feel?
2. Can you recall ever being in a conversation with two (or more) people who seemed to have some inside information to which you were not privy? Did their conversation seem to leave you out of their discussion? If so, how did you signal to them that you did not know what they were talking about?
3. Do you consider yourself a high-context or a low-context communicator? How have your conversations gone with those who tend to be your context opposite?
4. Do you tend to have a direct or an indirect communication style? How does it feel when you are in a conversation with someone who uses the opposite style of communication?
5. When you are in a conversation with someone from a different racial or ethnic group, are you aware of different styles of communication?
6. Do you maintain physical contact with your conversational partners, or do some conversational partners physically touch you when they talk with you? How does this make you feel?
7. When interacting with elderly individuals, do you notice that they tend to like to transmit information about the past? When interacting with your grandparents, do they pass down family stories, particularly about your parents?
8. How does your use of social media differ from your parents or even your older siblings or cousins?
9. Do you notice any differences between the ways men and women talk?
10. Have you studied different languages? How fluent are you in those other languages?
11. Seek out people who have learned English as a second language. To what extent did they feel that English replaced their native language, or to what extent did they feel that they were able to retain their native language?

CHAPTER 5

Immigrants, Refugees, and the Acculturation Process

Photograph by Juanmonino/Getty

Learning Objectives

Reading this chapter will help you to:

- understand phases of migration;
- identify common experiences of migrants;
- know which strategies are appropriate for working with immigrants versus refugees;
- explain how the refugee experience is much different from the immigrant experience;
- recognize the differences among models of acculturation; and
- distinguish among the different contexts in Bronfenbrenner's ecological model.

The modern history of immigration into the United States began in 1492 when Columbus landed on "American" soil. In the period between 1490 and the signing of the U.S. Constitution in 1776, there were massive waves of migration from Spain, England, Germany, Scotland, Ireland, and other European countries. There was also massive importation of slaves from Africa. Census data are available from 1850 to the present day and reflect high percentages of foreign-born persons in the United States. In the decades between 1850 and 1930, the foreign-born population of the United States fluctuated from a low of 9.7% to a high of 14.8% of the total population (U.S. Census, 1999). The percentage of the total population that was foreign born decreased steadily every decade between 1940 (8.8%) and 1970 (4.7%) and then began increasing again in 1980 and rose steadily each year, until it reached 12.9% in 2010 (U.S. Census, 1999, 2003, 2012). The United States is a nation of immigrants. Immigrants' countries of origin have greatly fluctuated. For example, in 1965, 80% of immigrants were White. In 2015, only 15% of immigrants were White and the majority hailed from Latin America (47%) and Asia (26%; Hugo Lopez, Passel, & Rohal, 2015).

　　With shifts in the type and number of immigrants, the attitudes in the United States and their accompanying immigration policies have dramatically changed over the years, privileging some groups (e.g., Cubans in the 1960s) and hindering others (e.g., Mexicans today). In a recent survey of U.S. adults, 45% said immigrants make our society "better" and 37% say they make it "worse" (Hugo Lopez et al., 2015). These views differ across age, gender, ethnicity, education, and political affiliation. Men, younger age, Latinxs, and individuals with bachelor's degrees or higher have more favorable attitudes than women, older groups, and people with some college or less education (Hugo Lopez et al., 2015). In the present time, partisan affiliation plays a role in perceptions. Fewer Republicans (31%) than Democrats (55%) or Independents (45%) have favorable attitudes toward immigration. It is important to recognize that these partisan politics are very time and context bound. For example, the 1864 Republican platform, which is the stated policy of the party, declared 11 points for the quadrennial election. The 8th point stated, "Be it resolved, that foreign immigration, which in the past has added so much to the wealth, development of resources and increase of power to the nation, the asylum of the oppressed of all nations, should be fostered and encouraged by a liberal and just policy" (Republican Party, 1864).

What is certain is that immigration continues to be an important part of human behavior. Immigration is ubiquitous in the United States now and for all our modern history. And immigration affects us all, from our own family or personal histories to the transformation of our communities. The impact of immigration and current policies can be deeply felt, as evidence in this writing published in the *Huffington Post* and authored by an undocumented college student living in the United States:

> As a junior, I am halfway done with my college career. The thought of pausing my education because I won't have the financial means to continue became my most worrying thought. But then I realized how trivial a thought that was. What I really felt was anger, especially when I began to read what some news stories had to say about the Dreamers, and the narrative they spun of "good immigrants." News reports said we deserved better because it was not ultimately our decision, that our parents were the ones that broke the law. I realized that no program or "protection" that the government offers us is worth enough to criminalize our parents, our neighbors, those who made the difficult decision to leave their home country to find the opportunities their own country could not offer. I am not better nor am I worse than the other 10.2 million undocumented immigrants that were not granted this protection in the first place. I am not the "Good Immigrant." I am not the "Dreamer." Our parents, our families, those who made the decision to come to a country in which they are criminalized, they are the original dreamers. Not us. Our entire undocumented community deserves to step out of the shadows, not only a selected few. My mother deserves to go to work and run errands without the fear that she may get stopped by ICE and not see her children again. She deserves to not be afraid anymore. DACA was never the solution, neither is any legislation that does not protect all of the undocumented community. I do not want to defend DACA, and although it granted me privilege and opportunities, I want the same for the rest of my community. The end of DACA will not be the end of an era, but the beginning of a new one. An era where we fight for all 11 million, not just the "good" few. (Brenda, 2017)

These thoughts from a youth affected by the Deferred Action for Childhood Arrivals nicely capture the complexity of immigration policies and the impact they can have on individuals and families. This narrative invites us to ask deeper questions: Who are immigrants? Who are undocumented immigrants? How do immigrants, refugees, and/or "illegal aliens" intersect in experiences and societal definition/treatment?

Immigrants and Refugees

According to Hong and Ham (2001), the term *migration* includes two phenomena: (a) the flight of refugees from their own countries because of the threat of persecution, imprisonment, or death and (b) the voluntary departure of individuals from their own countries to some other country. According to How et al. (2018), *refugees* and *immigrants* have very different experiences when they arrive in their new host country. Their stories of acculturation and stress may differ because of the differences in how they decided to migrate to a new country. Mbutu describes this difference:

> Growing up in Senegal, I have always thought that I would never leave my homeland. When I reached the age of 17 years old, my father decided to bring me to the USA where he resided. Before leaving Senegal, I had about a year of preparation, learning some basic words in English, getting my school documents ready, and saying goodbyes to my friends and family members. Knowing that I was going to immigrate to the USA enabled me to early on prepare myself in order for me to be able to have a smooth transition. This is what many of the immigrants' journey is like before they immigrate to a country, which differs completely from a refugee's experience.
>
> —Mbutu, 20+-year-old African student

Immigrants

Immigrants usually have some time to consider their migration. Their decision may be based on their desire to improve the lives of their families. Adult immigrants may be employed in their own country and want to apply their knowledge, expecting that the host country will be able to provide them a higher salary and more success than their country of origin can afford them. Other adults may have trade or professional skills and are eager to be employed. Immigrants may have a job waiting for them or at least have some assistance in finding a job (How et al., 2018).

immigrants—people who move to another country voluntarily. The decision to move can take weeks, months, or even years, which allows these people to prepare for the move and to begin the acculturation process before the move.

Social support networks may be more readily available to immigrants than to refugees, both in the host country and in their country of origin, so that contacts are maintained with family members from their own country even after they leave. In that sense, immigrants may have consistent social and economic support so that they do not feel completely alone in a new host country. With their migration usually planned, immigrants tend to seek out other support systems within their own cultural group, which serve as additional safe havens and extended families.

Immigrants are more likely than refugees to have opportunities to plan their exit from their host country, arrange for orderly transportation to their chosen place of residence, pack their belongings, and say goodbye to family and friends. They may be able to ship items to their arrival place if family members or friends will be there to receive them. Family and friends may be present to welcome immigrants to their new home and to help them learn to function within their new society (How et al., 2018; Hong & Ham, 2001).

Some immigrants will have the opportunity to return to their home country periodically for visits. They may even choose to return home if the host country is not what they thought it would be. In their elderly years, immigrants may return to their home countries, remain settled in their host country, or exercise the third option of spending significant time between the host and native countries (Bolzman, Fibbi, & Vial, 2006).

However, immigration experiences vary widely. Some immigrants may flee because of extreme social insecurity resulting from drug trafficking or high rates of interpersonal violence in their native countries. These immigrants may experience harsh trauma during migration, which has lasting effects for individuals and their adaptation to a host country (Sládková, 2014). Furthermore, migration may entail adaptation to multiple contexts, as was the case in a sample of Honduran migrants who faced adaptation to both Mexico (during the journey) and the United States (on arrival; Sládková, 2014).

Immigrants may not feel completely at home with either their host culture or their original culture.

Refugees and Asylum Seekers

Like immigrants, **refugees** leave their homelands. Unlike immigrants, refugees move because they are at risk of being seriously harmed for their race, religion, political opinion, nationality, or other group status (U.S. Department of Homeland Security, 2017). **Asylum seekers** are a special class of refugee who either already reside in the United States or are at a U.S. port of entry asking to be allowed in (U.S. Department of Homeland Security, 2017). The Vietnamese man described at the beginning of this chapter left his home because of the Vietnam War. He and his wife and children attempted to leave together, but were separated as they ran for their lives. He does not know whether his wife and children are dead or alive. As did most refugees, he left with no belongings except the tattered clothes on his back.

refugees—people who are forced to move from their homelands because of war or political oppression. The decision to move is almost immediate, taking days, hours, or even minutes, which does not allow these people to prepare for the move or to begin the acculturation process because they do not usually know which country they will finally settle in.

asylum seekers—a special class of refugee who either already reside in the United States or are at a U.S. port of entry requesting admittance.

In contrast to most immigrants, this refugee did not want to leave his home. His sudden departure did not allow him to say goodbye to friends and family, and he could not stay behind. Often family members who leave together do not stay together. Some die during flight, and their bodies are left behind without proper burial. In 2016, the numbers of deaths from people fleeing their countries was estimated at 7,927. That same year, there were 398 persons dead or missing on the U.S.–Mexico border alone (*Missing Migrants Project*, 2017).

People often have mistaken ideas about who refugees are and where they come from. The president of the United States, in consultation with the Congress, determines the number of refugees that will be allowed into the country in a given year. In 2015, the United States allowed 70,000 refugees and in 2016 the number increased to 85,000 (Mossaad, 2016). Although the number may sound large, it represents only 0.26% of the U.S. population in that same year. In 2017, the new administration reduced the allowed admittances to 50,000 (Zong & Batalova, 2017). Refugees admitted to the United States mostly hail from Asia or Africa, a trend that has held since 2004 (Zong & Batalova, 2017).

The path to possible citizenship for refugees is long and certainly plays a role in the adaptation to the new culture and context. Refugees must first be admitted into the United States, a process that takes 18 months to 3 years. After that, they must wait 1 year before applying for lawful permanent resident status. Once they are granted lawful permanent resident status, refugees wait a minimum of 5 years before they can apply for naturalization. It is a long and complicated process. In addition to the exposure to trauma or violence in their countries of origin, refugees experience significant distress in the process of applying for refugee status (Kirmayer et al., 2011; Schock,

Rosner, & Knaevelsrud, 2015). This stress is added to the already high risk for posttraumatic stress disorder, depression, chronic pain, and other somatic complaints (Kirmayer et al., 2011).

Because refugees' flights are often unplanned, during their migration they may experience resistance, and sometimes violence, from individuals who are not welcoming and who are ignorant about refugees' cultures. Vietnamese refugees are a prime example. They represented the enemy to people in the United States who remembered the Vietnam War, so some people were afraid of the Vietnamese refugees who came to America. Vietnamese refugees also endured overcrowded camps (How et al., 2018; Wong, Kinzie, & Kinzie, 2009) and an unfamiliar social system. They were at the mercy of the host culture, suffering emotionally as well as physically. Because of their lack of experience with the host culture, many refugees relied on rumors within the refugee community to obtain relevant information about the host culture. Reality often clashed with rumors, resulting in a distrust of others that kept refugees from seeking medical help, even when their lives were at stake. Even after they were able to settle into the new host country, most of these refugees, especially the older ones, had few skills with which to find and maintain employment. With no family to depend on for communication and support networks, they usually settled for jobs with under-the-table pay and terrible working conditions.

Often, students are unaware of the hardships their parents endured when coming to the United States. However, courses such as this stimulate their curiosity, and either they ask their parents about their migration history or the stories their parents told them bring their experiences into sharper focus. One student came to the realization of her father's hardships after class discussion:

> I always thought that my dad was an immigrant because, well, he "immigrated" from Vietnam. Although he had told me stories about how hard it was to come to America, I just associated it with the will for freedom and the will to create a better life for themselves and for their family. I can honestly say that I did not know the difference between a refugee and immigrant. I knew that they were leaving their country, but I did not know the purpose or meaning of it. My dad told me that he and three of his siblings, two younger brothers and a younger sister, had to leave Vietnam because of the war that was occurring. They were still fairly young, around their mid-teens and early twenties. He actually told me two stories but I'm not sure how they link together. They had to pay a lot of money to people that would smuggle them over in boats. When the boat was in the middle of nowhere, the smugglers robbed the passengers of whatever valuables they had, but my dad had hidden his money into the seam of his shorts. The details are quite fuzzy, but my dad and his siblings made it safely to America.
>
> My dad and his siblings somehow ended up in St. Paul, Minnesota, and we were sponsored by a middle-aged White American couple. They attended church, went fishing, and other activities that their sponsors introduced them to. They worked minimum-wage factory jobs to get by each day. My aunt was a young teenager and was able and encouraged to go to school by her three brothers who worked to support each other. They shared a one-bedroom apartment, where my aunt got the only room and my dad and his brothers slept in sleeping bags on the living room floor. They did not have the luxuries of eating out, wearing nice clothes, or a comfortable living environment. My dad told me that they shopped at thrift stores for clothes because they could not afford to buy new clothes. The extra money that they did have, they allowed

my aunt to buy new clothes or supplies for school. They felt that it was better for one of them to be able to get an education than for all four of them to be working in low-paying, dead-end jobs.

—Carley, 20+-year-old Vietnamese American student

Berry (1988, 1991) discussed the notion of a *refugee career* (Table 5.1) and identified six stages of this career: (a) predeparture, (b) flight, (c) first asylum, (d) claimant, (e) settlement, and (f) adaptation. *Predeparture* refers to the conditions that force refugees from their homelands, such as wars, revolutions, and natural disasters. *Flight* refers to the period of transit away from the home country. This is a period of maximum uncertainty, during which the refugees do not know where they are going. They know only that they must flee their homes and communities. Whereas immigrants plan their departures over the course of months or years and know where they are going, refugees often make their decision to leave in a matter of days or even hours. Carley's story about her father nicely demonstrates Berry's model.

First asylum refers to the first place the refugees settle where they feel safe. Conditions in these places of asylum vary widely, however, from safe and relatively good to woefully under-funded and unhealthy. For example, after the Cuban revolution in the late 1950s, most Cuban refugees fled to the United States, particularly to the Miami area (Kitano, 1999). This was not only the first asylum area, but also their settlement area. These refugees were generally well-off and were able to shelter their money in the United States before they fled Cuba. Most refugees today do not have such luxuries. Indeed, later waves of Cuban refugees did not have the same experience! (Portes & Clark, 1987).

More than 4 million people live in refugee camps. Refugees are men, women, and children. In 2016, more than 3.5 million children who were refugees did not attend school (United Nations High Commission for Refugees, 2017). In 2017, hundreds of thousands of refugees from Mosul were crowded into makeshift refugee camps in Syria. These camps are a first asylum and were designed only for tens of thousands of people, so there was a dangerous shortage of food, water, and medicine (World Health Organization, 2017).

Claimant refers to a country that grants asylum. At this point, there is a possibility that the refugees can be deported or repatriated. Often, refugees are permitted to stay in the initial country for only a limited time. If they exceed the time limit, they are subject to deportation. *Settlement* refers to a country's formal acceptance of refugees who want to settle there. Finally, *adaptation* refers to the adjustments that refugees make to their new host country. This process is referred to as *acculturation* later in this chapter.

TABLE 5.1   **Berry's Six Stages of Refugee Careers**

Stage	Brief description
Predeparture	Conditions that force refugees to flee their homelands
Flight	The period of transit away from the homeland
First asylum	First place where refugees settle
Claimant	The first country of potential resettlement
Settlement	The country of settlement
Adaptation	Adjustment to the new country of settlement

Source: Berry (1988, 1991).

Because refugees generally flee extremely difficult circumstances, they often experience posttraumatic stress disorder (Kirmayer et al., 2011). Frequently, refugees experience deaths in their families, threats of violence or death, separation from important family members, and other forms of trauma. Trauma and adaptation intersect in complex ways. Refugees exposed to trauma and loss can experience symptoms of posttraumatic stress disorder and prolonged grief disorder, which vary according to adaption to the new culture. For example, for Mandean refugees in Australia, disruptions in social support and cultural practices predicted symptoms of posttraumatic stress disorder. Adaptation difficulties since relocating predicted prolonged grief disorder, and exposure to traumatic loss predicted posttraumatic stress disorder/prolonged grief disorder comorbidity (Nickerson et al., 2014).

When discussing issues regarding refugees, many students gain more respect and appreciation for people who had to flee their circumstances and go to a world quite different from the one they knew. This student felt humbled by realizing his parents' ordeals:

> My parents and I are a refugee family. My parents were escaping persecution from the Communist Cambodian government during Pol Pot's evil regime where a genocide of Cambodians was taking place. Fortunately, we took refuge in a camp in Thailand. There at the refugee camp is where I, the oldest child, was born. . . . Less than a year later, my family and I ended up in Louisville, Kentucky, where my brother was eventually conceived. My parents told me that a church sponsored a cohort of refugees. Fortunately, my family was one of them. I couldn't imagine the difficulties and racism that my parents had in the acculturation process. A year later, we moved to California, where I suppose the acculturation process was a little easier due to a more diverse environment; but I cannot say for sure since I was too young to recall.
>
> The film [on refugees we saw in class] gave me a glimpse into my parents' life and I have never been so humbled. I have always considered myself to be "first-generation" American because of the fact that I immigrated when I was less than a year old. American culture had more of an impact in my life than my culture of origin. Therefore, my acculturation process has been facile. But after viewing the film and reflecting about my parents, I sympathetically realized why my parents never acculturated.
>
> —Channock, 20+-year-old Cambodian American student

Channock's story highlights a developmental dimension to the migration process. Channock's parents were asylum seekers when they arrived in Thailand. Asylum seekers have left their native country and await a decision by a host country on their refugee status (Sanchez-Cao, Kramer, & Hodes, 2013; U.S. Department of Homeland Security, 2017). Channock was an accompanied minor and thus experienced a protective factor for adaptation. Alternatively, unaccompanied minors experience developmental disruptions that threaten their educational, economic, social, and psychological well-being. There are well-documented impacts on mental health for such minors (Sanchez-Cao et al., 2013). The numbers of unaccompanied refugees who are minors have recently been at the highest levels ever recorded, at well over 98,000 (United Nations High Commission for Refugees, 2015).

Refugees often hope to return to their country of origin. However, a lack of financial and social resources, as

> The film [on refugees we saw in class] gave me a glimpse into my parents' life and I have never been so humbled. . . . I sympathetically realized why my parents never acculturated.
>
> —Channock, student in one of our multicultural courses

well as the perceived threat in their own country, makes return an unattainable dream for most of them. For the most part, they are left in the host country with other people of their ethnic group, as a type of extended family. They usually live in neighborhoods that are ethnically homogeneous, so that they are able to fulfill their needs without having to go too far outside their respective communities. This arrangement represents a double-edged sword. On the one hand, living within their communities allows them to settle in their new land with relative ease. On the other hand, it may delay the acculturation process

Internal political conflicts can cause people to flee their home countries and seek asylum in other countries. *Photograph by Tom Zasadzinski*

in the long run (McGoldrick, 1982). According to Ryan, Dooley, and Benson (2008), the overwhelming majority of research about refugees has not been about culture learning, ethnic identity, or economic integration, but about mental health issues.

Common Experiences of Immigrants and Refugees

We have seen that there are many differences between immigrants and refugees, even when we consider only the reasons behind their migration. Just as important, however, are the potential similarities in the experiences of these groups once the individuals begin their lives in their new country.

People in the host country often do not distinguish between immigrants and refugees and use a convenient label to support a discriminatory stance. In other words, if it is convenient to label the targeted group as *immigrants*, then immigrants and refugees are lumped together under that label to support a person's stance that we should curb immigration. If it is convenient to label the targeted group as *refugees*, then immigrants and refugees are lumped together under that label to support a person's stance that tax dollars should not go toward supporting people fleeing from their countries of origin—freedom should be their payment.

The history of Asian migration to the United States has been riddled with resistance and racism toward the migrants (Mio et al., 2007). First, the Chinese were recruited to the United States to help build the railroads from the West through the Rocky Mountains in the mid-1800s. However, after these tracks were built, the U.S. Congress passed the Chinese Exclusion Act of 1882 to prevent more Chinese from immigrating to the United States. In the early 1900s, there was the "Gentleman's Agreement," in which Asian countries agreed not to allow their citizens to immigrate to the United States. This "Gentleman's Agreement" became codified through the Immigration Act of 1924, which allowed tens of thousands of immigrants from European countries to immigrate to the United States but only 100 immigrants from Asian countries, although "no one of discernible Asian ancestry was allowed to immigrate to the United States" (Mio et al., 2007, p. 346). This allowed British ex-patriots who lived in Asian countries to immigrate to the United States, while keeping Asians from doing so. One result is that people of Asian ancestry are treated as perpetual foreigners, even if they were born in the United States (S. J. Lee, Wong, & Alvarez, 2009). A student of ours wrote about this:

> I was born in America and have been a citizen here all my life. This doesn't change the fact that immediately when many people see me they stereotype me as a foreigner. I hate feeling like I am an outcast in my own home. If America is such a "melting pot" of cultures, why is it so hard to be accepted by the majority?
>
> —Patrice, 20+-year-old Chinese American student

Now let us take a closer look at some of the common experiences that immigrants and refugees face in their host country. Foremost among these experiences are problems with language barriers, support networks, changing family hierarchies, new family roles, employment, and education.

Language Barriers

> When I moved here to California I was scared. I did not have the basics to communicate with others. I was just 11 years old and it was hard to deal with not knowing English. I always seemed to be doing everything wrong. I did not understand there was a way of communication and sometimes it seemed like the teachers were mean. I had that concept of meanness until I had a teacher who was bilingual. She helped me so much; my self-esteem was low and she always tried to encourage me to do my best. I remember I just wished I was back in Mexico where I was outgoing and more myself. I did not know how much my way of communication meant to me. While I was learning English it seemed harder because I did not understand that it seemed emotionless.
>
> Learning English seemed to take forever. I was frustrated. I wanted to go back to Mexico. My only break was when I came home. I did not have to struggle to get my point across. After a few months I got to understand small parts of the language. However, what made it worse was that in sixth grade my new teacher did not speak any Spanish. It hurt me to depend on others to translate. It was hard to do work without knowing English. I was busy thinking how to learn faster. I did not notice that I was already understanding others' conversations. I was scared "what about if I was wrong?" [i.e., that I might misinterpret what was being said]. Until one day, at recess this kid hit me. Our teacher called us and asked us what had happened. The kid knew English, so he told his version of the story. He blamed me. I was so mad that I interrupted him and said that did not happen. Both of them were shocked; even though I was mumbling, I got to tell my version of the story. I just remembered that day was one of the happiest days in my life.
>
> Communication with others who speak English as their first language seemed to be a struggle. Now, it does not seem that way. Every time I get to talk to someone just in English, it makes me proud of who I am. Now I do not need translators in my life. I do, however, remember this friend who said that I spoke so fast that it was hard for her to understand the whole conversation. I notice I do this when I am nervous or stressed. I work every day to improve in communicating in English. It is funny sometimes how I start talking in English and I end up talking in Spanish. This usually happens with my family or closest friends who are bilingual. When I get home from a busy day, just knowing I get a break from English makes me smile. I never imagined that my life would be as different as when I was in Mexico.

I notice that when you do not understand each other, it is hard to have a relationship with others. However, it is not impossible. When I was in middle school, I had a friend who was from Taiwan. She did not speak English or Spanish, but we had a friendship. I still do not know how we communicated with each other, but I know it was fun. We did a lot of drawings and hand signals. It got easier when she started to know English. One day she told me that she wishes that I knew her language or she knew Spanish. Language is so important that we sometimes do not think of it.

—Dora, 20+-year-old Mexican American student

I don't know what my culture really is. I have mostly Asian friends, but they all speak as I do, English. I speak Mandarin to my mom but never to anyone else. I communicate to my younger brother in English, and he talks to our mom in Mandarin also. I only became aware of myself after I was set up on a blind date with someone who speaks Chinese. I talked to her in Mandarin, but I was very uncomfortable because the only person I talk to in Chinese is my mom. The date was a disaster because she never talked at all, and I was very frustrated at the fact that the person who fixed me up was not aware that I am pretty Americanized. Well, the fact that I was born in Taiwan doesn't mean much, but the fact that I was raised here in Los Angeles and didn't hang out with foreigners means much more. After that I never called that girl again and she never called me either. I realized only recently, after encountering a non-English-speaking person, that the very least someone has to be is English-speaking.

—Terry, 20+-year-old Taiwanese American student

People who come from other countries encounter language barriers that are sometimes hard to overcome. Differences in how individuals deal with the communication problems are apparent within the older and the younger generations. As if the words were not hard enough to learn, the directness of the American culture clashes with the indirectness of certain other cultures to create an awkward and guarded relationship between people. Whereas the younger generation adapts more readily to the direct ways of this society, older people find the directness rude and insensitive, which increases their dependence on the younger generation for communication.

Even people who can communicate reasonably well in English may experience some sort of loss. Recall the Russian immigrant from Chapter 4 who spoke very good English. She talked about her loss of personality when she immigrated to the United States because she was not as quick-witted in English as she was in Russian, so people here in the United States did not perceive her to be witty.

Many individuals who migrate from one country to another have little or no exposure to the host country's language. This is especially true of people from developing countries who migrate to more developed countries, such as the United States. How can we expect a person to succeed when that person does not know how to speak effectively with other people on a daily basis? Older immigrants may have a harder time acquiring a new language (Chiswick & Miller, 2008). They may rely on their children or the younger generation to communicate with people outside their community, a dependence that affects both older people and younger ones. Older people may feel alienated, insecure, distrustful, and useless, whereas the youth may feel overly responsible for their parents. Some of the youths, as exemplified by the Asian male quoted earlier, begin to lose a sense of the importance of their native tongue. Fluency in the English language becomes the mark of a better person within these groups, and whether someone is a refugee or an immigrant, the less pronounced the accent, the more privilege that person achieves.

acculturative stress—changes in individuals' thoughts, feelings behaviors, or attitudes as a result of exposure to a new culture.

bicultural stress—changes in individuals' thoughts, feelings behaviors, or attitudes as a result of exposure to a new culture while trying to maintain one's culture of origin.

Whenever individuals feel unsuccessful within the mainstream society because of language barriers, they move into the part of the country, town, or city where most of "their own" live. This trend is apparent when we see that specific ethnic groups occupy certain towns or cities. These areas become safe havens for most immigrants or refugees and others might be experiencing **acculturative stress** or **bicultural stress**. Acculturative stress refers to changes in individuals' thoughts, feelings behaviors, or attitudes as a result of exposure to a new dominant culture whereas bicultural stress refers to that same process while trying to maintain one's culture of origin (Romero & Piña-Watson, 2017).

Whereas immigrants, who are usually prepared to migrate, may have some knowledge of the host country's language, refugees, who had no plans to migrate, are thrown into confusion and burdened with humiliation. This situation is a result not only of their inability to speak the new language, but also of the lack of social support networks who are willing or able to translate so that they can function and live in the new cultural context.

Support Networks

In August of 1988, my parents migrated to the United States. They lived in Tijuana, Mexico, with a cousin of my father's while my parents tried to figure out how they were going to come to this country. My mother was six months pregnant with me and my parents wanted to come to the United States as soon as possible so that I will be born and be a U.S. citizen. It was very difficult to find a decent job in Tijuana, so my parents decided to come to the U.S. with only $5 in their pocket. My parents had contacted an uncle of mine who lived in Los Angeles and my uncle offered for my parents to live with them until my parents found a place to live. When my parents arrived in California, they came to the city of San Ysidro and from there my uncle picked them up and took them to live with him. After a couple of days, my uncle did not want my parents with him anymore so my parents were in the streets for about 2 weeks. With the $5 that my parents had, they bought canned food and ate what they could. A short time after that, my mother wasn't feeling well, so my father took her to the hospital and that same day my father went to a pharmacy to pick up some baby products for my mother and he ran into one of his cousins. She offered for my parents to stay with them until they had me and when they find a place to live. My father found two jobs: one in a mattress factory, and the other was as a butcher in a supermarket. My father only had four hours of sleep a day. A month later, I was born. I was born premature and the doctor told my parents that I had a 10% survival rate. I was in an incubator for 2½ months. My parents couldn't afford to pay the hospital bill after I was born and a social worker helped my parents file for welfare to pay the bill. My parents drove to the hospital daily to see me. Luckily,

I survived and was taken home by my parents. My parents were so blessed to have had me because they had the support system they needed and they made it through without asking for too much. Now, my parents have steady jobs and I have two younger siblings. My parents migrated here to the U.S. only for us to have a good life, to have the life they never had. I thank my parents from the bottom of my heart for migrating here and I know they suffered through enough pain and trouble, but now they have a better life than they had 21 years ago. Without my parents, I don't know where my siblings and I would be.

—Faviola, 20+-year-old Mexican American student

Whether an individual is an immigrant or a refugee, support networks become one of the most important factors within a societal context to assist the acculturation process. Although employment, language, roles, and education may be important, lack of support networks can be the greatest source of stress.

As we have noted, immigrants usually have more ready support networks than refugees do. Although that is the case, we must further consider the country from which the immigrant comes and the generation traveling to the new host country. Many Asian immigrants are typically cut off from their families in their country of origin, both socially and emotionally (Hayashino & Chopra, 2009; Hong & Ham, 2001). Although their trip to America or some other host country may be planned, they usually do not have the financial resources to stay in contact with family overseas on a consistent basis. Many immigrate as single individuals, lacking the extensive support system that they had in their country of origin. Other social interactions or friendships take a longer time to establish (Hong & Ham, 2001).

According to various researchers (Hayashino & Chopra, 2009; Hong & Ham, 2001), the lack of a support network leads to social isolation and stress for many immigrants, particularly when they encounter difficult situations. We may assume that the farther one's country of origin is from the host country, the harder it is to maintain contact with family members left behind. Whenever problems of any kind arise, the isolation and stress caused by the lack of support systems may lead to anxiety, depression, and marital conflict.

Although community resources are available, immigrants and refugees fear being turned away or humiliated because of their difficulty with English and their different ways of behaving, and they rarely reach out for help. Because limited community resources target individuals who speak English as a second language, most immigrants and refugees remain isolated. They may spend the rest of their days alone and unaware of available help. This lack of desire to reach out may stem not from total ignorance of available resources, but from previous experiences of alienation from the majority population. Technology and social media have played an important role in supporting the integration and well-being of refugees (Alencar, 2017; Díaz Andrade & Doolin, 2016).

Among immigrants and refugees, *perceived* quality of social support may be a more accurate predictor of psychological distress than the quantity of social support (Hovey, 2000). Therefore, larger social networks may not offer more support than another resource that the person believes can offer better support. Immigrants, who usually have a more positive view of their move, will have a more positive perception of support than will refugees, who did not want to migrate in the first place. These perceptions are an extra factor that should be considered within the context of supportive networks.

Family Hierarchies

While migrating individuals struggle with language and maintaining social contact, changes are also taking place within their family structure. Decision-making power and the family hierarchy may dramatically shift.

> Pablo and his family immigrated to the United States when he was only 5 years old. They were originally from Mexico and they wanted to succeed in the land of opportunity. Pablo was the youngest in the family and acculturated the fastest, but the family struggled seemingly more as they found out that the land of opportunity had rules one had to follow for success. Pablo's parents did not speak English and had difficulty finding jobs. Pablo witnessed his older brothers and sisters grow in different ways as the country "ate them alive." Pablo also saw how the family struggled because his father expected the same respect as head of household, although his mother became the primary breadwinner in the home. This created an obvious rift in the home as his older brothers lost respect for their father who could not hold a job. In order to attempt maintenance of peace in the home, Pablo's mother still cooked, cleaned, and cared for the children while she worked full-time outside of the home. Eventually, Pablo's two older brothers joined a gang, one older sister married early and moved out of the home, and Pablo moved out of the home to attend college.
>
> I go by "Paul" now. I don't like to talk about my family in first person because I don't feel like we are the same people we were before we moved here. I'm in college trying to get a doctorate degree. Everything has changed. I have no contact with my father and my mother died from a broken heart.
>
> —Paul, 20+-year-old Mexican American student

In the United States, primarily individualistic and egalitarian principles prevail. That may cause problems in the realm of family hierarchies and organization for immigrants and refugees entering the country. Although the United States is known as a country driven by individualism, patriarchy still exists in many ways within the family, if not within the society as a whole. Some migrating individuals, however, come from countries that consider the mother the head of the family. People from Western cultures tend to share the U.S. view of hierarchy and individualism, but some revere the mother most within the family. Meanwhile, individuals from the Eastern societies tend to be collectivistic, but some are still very patriarchal in beliefs. In light of all these differences, how can we begin to understand changes that take place in an individual's life after they move or flee to the host country?

For example, although Mexican families stress affiliation and cooperation (Falicov, 2005), those values are supported with clear hierarchies.

Latinx families generally have more structured family hierarchies than do their Western counterparts.
Photograph by Monkey Business Images/Shutterstock

Parents and children try to achieve smooth relationships that avoid conflict. Respect for parents is a must, but in Mexican families, the mother commands much authority. For these groups, the status of the children is low and the status of the parents is high. Although a patriarchal view persists, more complex dynamics exist, with a wide range from patriarchal to egalitarian and many combinations in between (Falicov, 2005; Hong & Ham, 2001).

Whereas Americans attempt to maintain romantic ties even after having children, most immigrant couples begin to lose romantic ties and focus more on the parental dyads. The process of acculturation disrupts this hierarchy for most families as the children begin to command equal time and independence from parental decisions. The parents' views of how things were in the old country begin to conflict with the children's views of how things should be now that they are residing in a country that values individualism and egalitarianism. Women, who traditionally are lower in the hierarchy than their husbands and partners are, begin to demand equality, particularly after they gain employment. (Dual incomes are often necessary for the family to survive.) Daughters demand the same treatment as sons after learning about feminism and equal rights.

Most families migrating to the United States include grandparents who are regarded as the *root of the oak*, commanding as much respect as the parents, if not more. Yet the elderly people who migrated or fled to a new host country must also endure the changes in hierarchy. Outside responsibilities, the necessity that all members of the family be employed, and less respect for the old ways combine to lessen the importance of the elderly within U.S. culture (Lewin, 1948). Within the U.S. culture, elderly individuals are encouraged to remain independent regardless of ailment, whereas in other countries, the elders are viewed as part of the nuclear family.

Within the hierarchy are roles in the family subsystems that usually change. Many family members resist those changes, if only to maintain some stability, and find that other members rebel and eventually leave the system.

New Family Roles

Ed and Nancy (adopted American names) migrated from Japan in search of a better life for their son, whom Nancy was carrying at the time. After Nancy had the baby, Ed found it difficult to make ends meet with his salary as a factory worker. Initially, when Nancy suggested that she find work, Ed was enraged. He announced that he was the man and he should work while she took care of the baby. Besides, he thought that it would be ridiculous for other family members to help raise the child, even though they had aunts who were willing to help care for Mitchell, their newborn son. Finally, Ed relented and "allowed" Nancy to work. Nancy began to work 40-hour weeks while Ed's hours at work were cut in half. Nancy had to work overtime to help support the family. After work, she would pick Mitchell up from her aunt's house, bathe him, and then make dinner. At times, she would be so exhausted that she would doze off while they ate dinner. Eventually, she began to fight with Ed because even though he would come home from work earlier in the day, he would not pick up Mitchell and would wait for Nancy to come home to make dinner while he napped. Nancy and Ed fought for the most part around issues of Ed's refusal to take on any role that would equate him with a woman. He screamed about his father who worked for the family and his mother who did everything at home. He blamed Nancy's American friends for "poisoning her mind," making her believe that she should "talk back" to her husband. Nancy screamed about the fact that she did not "just" stay home, and that they were no longer living in Japan. She insisted that things must change before it was too late. Mitchell was 10 when Nancy divorced Ed. Ed eventually returned to Japan and remarried. Nancy is a single mother who vows to raise Mitchell with values of respect for his partner as an equal.

—Jaymie, 30+-year-old biracial (Filipina/Black) student

Along with changes in the family hierarchy come changes in roles. Men who are used to being the breadwinners are exposed to a society that allows for stay-at-home dads. Though fathers who decide to stay home are still somewhat underappreciated in this society, in other countries this role *cannot* exist. Furthermore, men must give up their role as sole breadwinner in the household when their wives must enter the workforce to meet the family's needs. Women's role of housewife and mother changes to that of *supermom*, who cleans the house, cares for the children, and works 40-hour weeks. Sometimes, the father must accept additional roles in child care and housekeeping, sharing those responsibilities with his partner.

Grandparents who migrate in their later years become strangers in the home. Their children and grandchildren are busy with their own lives, so the grandparents begin to associate with other seniors who share their values and circumstances and with whom they feel comfortable. Although they sometimes assume the role of babysitter for the younger children while parents work, they are not revered as they once were in their country of origin.

Children of immigrant families have more household responsibilities than they did in premigration days because both parents are now working (Hong & Ham, 2001). They also become translators for their parents publicly, especially if the parents struggle with the language of the host country.

If the family has boundaries that are too rigid to adapt to the demands of their new situation, dysfunction can occur and relationships break down (Hong & Ham, 2001). Role changes between partners and the children may cause marital conflict. Children as family translators have too much power, and from a family-therapy perspective (Hayashino & Chopra, 2009; Hoffman, 1981; Nichols & Schwartz, 1998), there is a violation of generational boundaries. What this means is that adults *should* be at a higher level in the family hierarchy than children, but because the children have more power around language issues, they enter into the adults' level of power.

For most families, the demands of changing roles present difficulties that eventually modify the family system. If families cannot adjust to these changing roles, they may face dissolution. For most of us, it is easy to say that change is necessary to maintain cooperation and avoid conflict, but for families who migrate with deeply rooted beliefs, such change is not an easy process. In a sense, it is impressive that so many families *are* able to adapt to these changes.

Employment

My wife and I thought how wonderful it will be to move from a third-world country to the United States. I had a degree as a chemical engineer and my wife was willing to stay home and care for our three young children. Most of our family lived here in the U.S. and have told many stories of how much easier it was to get jobs. One thing I didn't consider was how my degree was "no good" because I earned it from elsewhere other than the U.S. They said I need re-certification, which was a nicer way of saying that I needed to go back to school and learn "their way." Well, I couldn't do that because we had no money, and we had three children. My wife was unemployed and the rest of our family had to work to maintain their own household. I work at an ARCO gas station now and we've gotten robbed twice. I want to feel hopeful, but it has gotten harder and harder. I guess I just have to be thankful that I have a job. I want to go back "home," but we feel like it will be harder since most of our family is here.

—Andy, 30+-year-old Asian immigrant student

Reasons for immigration are clustered into four main categories: economic, social, political, or environmental. Within these broad areas, there are factors that push people away from their countries of origin and others that pull people into a new host culture. Employment opportunities are considered a pull factor.

Once they are settled in the United States, however, prolonged low-income employment or underemployment can take its toll. Lacking English-language skills and enjoying only limited social support, most immigrants and refugees are forced to find employment in diverse communities that are also limited in growth and income. Immigrants who have sufficient financial resources attempt to establish local businesses, but must do so in high-crime neighborhoods. Some groups, such as Korean Americans (Hong & Ham, 2001), have financial assets tied up in their small businesses, which prevents them from moving into more favorable businesses or neighborhoods. Other groups settle into factory jobs and other low-paying, intensive manual labor that requires many hours.

Not only do these individuals face limited employment opportunities, but also, once they do find employment, their premigration experiences, limited English, and physical characteristics become reasons for employers to discriminate against them. Promotions are nearly impossible, even for those who have held prestigious positions in their countries of origin. Degrees held by immigrants before their move are not as marketable in the United States, and they are forced to accept jobs with much lower status. Decline in status lowers self-esteem and increases disillusionment, and these factors can eventually cause family distress. For some individuals who have some social or familial support, further education to obtain equivalent credentials is possible. For others, the necessity of making ends meet makes such opportunities impossible. Most migrating people recognize that they must attend English classes to move forward with employment, but they cannot always do so. According to Gans (2009), although both immigrants and refugees suffer downward mobility as a result of limitations in employment opportunities, immigrants may suffer more because of the significant differences between their employment in their country and their lack of ability to attain similar status in the United States. For refugees, migration to another country involves issues dealing more with their survival and personal freedom than with simply trying to pursue a better life. They most likely lost their jobs and social status before leaving their host country (Gans, 2009).

Individuals who are unable to master the English language are easily taken advantage of and discriminated against by employers and other employees. These individuals may be forced to accept conditions that do not meet minimal legal standards, but their lack of education and their need to feed their families force them to tolerate such treatment and working conditions. Some immigrants who are able to establish businesses are leery of taking their small businesses outside the ethnic communities because they know that thriving within a bigger cosmopolitan setting is nearly impossible. Although some do dream that their established businesses within smaller, diverse communities are only a stepping-stone to a well-accepted and profitable venture, such dreams rarely become reality. To clinicians and other laypeople, these people present a picture of resilience, determination, content, and noble self-sacrifice (Hong & Ham, 2001). Yet beneath such external appearances can lie severe stress, doubt, and frustration (Hong, 1989; Hong & Ham, 2001).

Education

Today's immigrants have both higher levels of education and a greater likelihood of living in poverty than did immigrants in the 1970s (Hugo Lopez et al., 2015). Immigrants are more educated than in decades past. Immigrants hold about the same number of bachelor's degrees as and a greater number of advanced degrees than U.S.-born individuals (Hugo Lopez et al., 2015). Large differences exist between groups, however, with Asian and African immigrants showing superior academic attainment compared to Latinxs (Waters & Pineau, 2015).

Higher levels of education do not always guarantee good economic outcomes for the first generation. Degrees may not transfer between the country of origin and the United States, relegating highly trained professionals to menial positions, either short-term or permanently. Although this can affect the mental health and well-being of immigrants, it is important to understand that one of the primary reasons that immigrants move is to provide their children with greater opportunities.

Data show that immigrants today, much like their European counterparts from earlier generations, bring with them ambition, an extraordinary work ethic, and a willingness to sacrifice for the benefit of future generations. Immigrants even report a greater belief in the American Dream compared to U.S.-born persons! And their sacrifice pays off. The educational attainment of the children of immigrants is very strong and occurs regardless of their parents' educational preparation (Waters & Pineau, 2015). In fact, the second generation surpasses, on average, the educational attainment of U.S.-born people who are third generation and beyond.

Unfortunately for some groups, those gains are not maintained. A close look at third-generation Mexican Americans reveals stagnation in gains. It is not easy to understand why these gains are not maintained. At one level, it is difficult to track third-generation Mexican Americans, especially when their parents may have married across diverse groups and the third generation may not continue to identify as being of Mexican origin. There may be a suppression of attainment because intermarriage rates in Mexican Americans are higher for individuals with higher income and education, so the *ethnic attrition* is occurring systematically (Waters & Pineau, 2015). Mexican American children are exposed to prejudice and discrimination, both at the individual level (e.g., personal attacks, taunting) and at the institutional or structural level (e.g., poorer access to high-quality schools and teachers; Alba et al., 2014; Telles & Ortiz, 2008). In addition, differences in legal status and parental involvement in their children's education have been noted as important explanations for the lagging attainment into the third generation.

Parental involvement in academic achievement is an interesting construct to consider as researchers study multicultural psychology. Parental involvement in U.S. schools is considered good when parents attend parent–teacher conferences, reach out to teachers at other times, check their children's homework, and volunteer at the school. But for Latinx parents, parental involvement appears to mean something different. For Latinx parents, parental involvement may be more tied to communication of parental expectations for educational attainment, monitoring of their children's activities, and their parenting styles than to specific activities to advance academic achievement.

The reasons for the differences in how immigrant parents and U.S. teachers and schools understand good parental involvement may be complex. One of us (MDR) lived in Puerto Rico for a year and her young children attended school there. She vividly recalls being stopped at the gate and being asked to leave her children there because parents were not welcome in the school. This was in sharp contrast to her experience in the United States as an active parent volunteer in the classroom and a school board member. Such differences in local practices may profoundly shape the behavior of first-generation immigrants who may not even know the rules in U.S. schools. Furthermore, it is also difficult for parents with a limited or different education to support their children in completing homework. MDR has repeatedly attempted to help her children complete math homework over the years, but the instruction practices are dramatically different in the United States today than they were in Puerto Rico in the 1970s and 1980s. Despite holding a doctoral degree, MDR was only able to successfully help her children in mathematics through multiplication. Imagine what the experience must be for a parent with much less educational attainment.

Although we highlight the preceding issues as major considerations in attempting to comprehend the experiences of immigrants and refugees, they are only some of the many issues that relate to the process of acculturation. How individuals adapt to the differences between their country of origin and their host country may determine their success. In defining the success of immigrants and refugees, we should not look at the success of individuals who have lived in the United States all their lives.

Some migrating individuals equate success with fulfilling basic needs, such as food and shelter. Long-time citizens of this country also face unemployment and obstacles in attempting to achieve the American Dream while we keep our gates open to others. However, individual-level arguments regarding the suitability of immigration policies ignore larger social and political forces that create the incentives for immigration such as job opportunities (Camarota & Jensenius, 2009) not only for low-income earners, but also for professionals who are in low supply and high demand in the United States. Furthermore, negative attitudes toward immigration ignore important gains made by society at large, often at the cost of immigrants. For example, the Social Security Administration estimated a $12 billion infusion into Social Security, offering substantial protection to the program (Goss et al., 2013).

At an individual level, it is important to also consider that if some people have the greater advantages of family and social support, knowledge of the language, and educational and occupational opportunities and still struggle to succeed within this culture, imagine how difficult it must be to pursue the American Dream for individuals who are not as privileged and who lack basic language skills and cultural knowledge.

Because an individual's level of acculturation can determine his or her success, we will take a more elaborate look at what is involved in the acculturation process. In the next section, we apply the process of acculturation to *natural citizens* as well as to immigrants and refugees.

Acculturation

I just recently got a job as an assistant social worker. This job entails visiting the elderly from different backgrounds (socioeconomic status, culture, etc.) who are suffering physical ailments, some of which are debilitating. I am to assess their psychosocial support and their coping with their illness and provide resources upon request. I am also to provide "suggestive counseling" whenever patients (the term they use) are emotionally affected by their physical ailments. Most of these patients are depressed, some are alone, and this job is a test of keeping my boundaries. I visit these patients, at the very most, twice.

One of my patients was a Vietnamese man, who lived alone in a one-bedroom apartment, within a senior citizens' complex. This man meekly welcomed me into his very well-kept home. When I spoke to this man on the phone, prior to my arrival, he told me that he spoke very little English. Amazingly, when I began to assess him and started asking him questions, I found that he spoke English very well! I told him this and he shyly laughed. He mentioned afterwards that he has been here since 1986 and that he was a refugee from the Vietnam War and had escaped from jail, went from Malaysia to the Philippines, and finally into the United States. Anyhow, he was amazed at how many resources he could be given as a senior citizen with Medi-Cal. Apparently, he has been paying someone $50 each time he had to visit his doctor! This is a service he can get for about $.75 per ride from the county!

The most surprising aspect of my visit with this old man was a comment he made after I complimented his English. He said that he has not spoken English like he was speaking it with me. He said that he was surprised himself at how well he spoke the language. He suggested that it might be because I was not asking him to repeat words and I wasn't acting as if he was deaf and speaking in volumes that could have ruptured his eardrums. He described that for the most part, whenever he attempted to speak to people, they would always talk to him loudly and overly accentuate his words as if he was, in his words "stupid." White people did this for the most part, according to him, and this made him feel "less than a person." Therefore, he really stopped talking to people altogether. He said that "no one" would want to speak to an old, stupid man like him anyway. I held back the tears as I listened to him and couldn't even imagine not speaking to anyone due to fears of feeling "stupid." I couldn't imagine being all alone as this man was, and keeping everything he had to say to himself. After he said all this, he looked at me, smiled, and said, "Thank you for being my solace. Since 1987, you are the first person to talk to me." This was a man who thought that he did not speak English well. I told him that I was glad that he felt better and that I would be coming back to confirm if he indeed received all the services that we had set up that day. We stood up and before I knew it, this man took my hand and had it about two inches from his face, then gently put it down. After seeing the quizzical look on my face he told me that if I called him back, he probably would not remember my name, or my voice. He said that when people called on the phone, he gets scared about his English and blanks out sometimes. He told me that when I call next time, to say that I was the one whose hand he smelled. He said that this, he would remember. He said, "I may not remember your name, but I will always remember your scent. For an old man like me, anything you remember is always good." As I walked away, he put his arms together, as if in prayer and bowed. I smiled and did the same.

—Jaymie, 30+-year-old biracial (Filipina/Black) student

The process of acculturation can indeed be difficult—spanning myriad experiences across people and over time that have important social, economic, and psychological impacts. Here is another story that attests to this complexity.

My family lived in the Philippines until I was about 12 years old. Coming to America brought about mixed emotions because of stories we heard about the American people. First of all, we always saw Americans who looked like Ken and Barbie dolls, so we assumed that this is how they all looked. This somewhat prepared us for how different we would look beside them. Secondly, America was supposed to be a great country of opportunity and success. Everything that happened in between was never considered.

My sister was 8 years of age and my brother 5 when we settled in America. The main reason we came was due to my father's job in a prestigious firm that was based in Michigan. We chose to live in California due to the numerous relatives we had residing in the state. My family immediately went through changes within the year that we had arrived. Due to these changes, and the incomplete and unrealistic stories we were told, my brother, my sister, and I became more different than we were alike.

I wanted to be American. I stayed in front of the television for hours at a time, attempting to rid myself of the Filipino accent. I was determined to stay out of the sun, so I could be more "White," and adopt the Californian accent. Most of my friends were White during high school, and my father was very proud.

My sister "hung out" with Filipinos and Asians. She insisted on being Filipino only, denying any other cultural parts that were a part of our own family, much less others. For the most part, she refused to eat like Americans, act like Americans, or be among Americans. She dated only Filipinos and Asians and never really looked at any other ethnic groups as dating partners.

My brother became a loner. He didn't associate with any ethnic/cultural group in particular. As a matter of fact, he prided himself on being different. He would go out of his way to be different from "the norm" of what a Filipino AND an American should be. Although he never got in trouble, he always made sure that he was noticed for being apart from everyone.

Now as adults, it is somewhat surprising that I am the one who took it upon myself to learn about my culture and my "different selves." I retained the language and cultural beliefs. My sister married an Asian man and my brother remains an "enigma" and continues to go "against the waves."

Although as a family, we went through many hardships and struggles, we were thankful that we had other family members to rely on when things became difficult. We were prepared to come to America, if not to survive, to live a dream. Those dreams changed as soon as we settled, but were revived as we grew to realize that holding on to our family was just as important as "fitting into" a society that struggles to accept us.

—Sylvia, 20+-year-old Filipina American student

These two stories are similar in that they relate the hardship and struggles of people in a host country that differs greatly from their native country. However, we must also appreciate the differences in these people's experiences of adaptation and **acculturation.**

> **acculturation**—experiences and changes that groups and individuals undergo when they come in contact with a different culture.

Acculturation, the process by which people change as a result of intercultural interactions, is clearly evident in immigrants and refugees because of the sharp differences in language, beliefs, values, and practices between groups. Acculturation is also seen within national groups, as is the case in cross-ethnic interactions within the United States. People who reside in the host culture can also experience acculturation and acculturative stress. We focus our discussion on immigrants and refugees to help us make meaningful comparisons involving the acculturation process and facilitate further examination of multicultural topics.

We are all aware of how difficult it is to grow up and face developmental, societal, and economic changes in our own multicultural society. Can we, then, begin to imagine how hard it is for people who grew up in a different country with different norms? Can we imagine the acculturation process that occurs in a new host country? We must consider language, norms, education, family systems, and more, as well as the confusing and sometimes heartbreaking experiences immigrants and refugees must endure. Some might argue that people can stay where they are and avoid this process, but that defies our human history, which is one of constant motion. From the first humans to inhabit the earth, people have been migrating to new lands in search of better living conditions.

Acculturation refers to the experiences and changes that groups and individuals undergo when they come into contact with a different culture (Brislin, 2000; G. C. N. Hall & Barongan, 2002; Hovey, 2000; Yeh, 2003). Tseng and Yoshikawa (2008) reported acculturation was most often conceptualized, measured, and analyzed at the individual level; acculturation measures are used to assess individuals' levels of acculturation, and then individuals' acculturation levels are analyzed in relation to individual-level outcomes such as physical and mental health status, social and emotional well-being, and educational achievement. Depending on the changes people go through, their stress levels will differ. Furthermore, Hovey (2000) found that *acculturative stress,* which is the tension and anxiety that directly results from and has its source in the acculturative process, is unrelated to the level of acculturation, such that a person who is less acculturated may not experience any more or less stress than one who is more acculturated.

Note that acculturation is a *process* as opposed to an *outcome.* In other words, people who immigrate to the United States are acculturating or adjusting to their new host country as opposed to trying to achieve a certain level of acculturation as an end point. Moreover, the host country (in our case, the United States) is also undergoing a process of adjusting to immigrants. For example, as the number of Latinx and Asian groups has increased on the West Coast, more and more Latin American (primarily Mexican) and Asian restaurants have opened, and some restaurants are even specializing in *fusion cuisine,* which is a mixture of United States, Latin American, and Asian flavors. It is very important for psychologists to note that nearly all research on acculturation treats the variable as a static predictor or outcome. There is very little longitudinal research on acculturation, so little is known about how individuals acculturate over time and how these patterns of change relate to health and well-being. This presents a great opportunity for psychology students who are looking for topics to research.

Acculturation is usually assumed to apply to diverse groups whose immigration to the United States is relatively recent, such as Latinxs and Asian Americans (G. C. N. Hall & Barongan, 2002). However, we should keep in mind that because there are major differences between the dominant cultural group and both African Americans and American Indians, members of these two groups also may go through an acculturation process. In these cases, we see how racism and discrimination can affect the acculturation process even for those who are natural citizens of this country. Although immigrants and others who have moved here have been an important part of U.S. history, the topic of acculturation has only recently been addressed.

Acculturation is a bidirectional process (S. J. Schwartz, Unger, Zamboanga, & Szapocznik, 2010). While groups are trying to acculturate to the host culture, the success of their adjustment is at least partially dependent on how the host culture reacts to them; that is, when new immigrants arrive, they undergo a process of change, but so do the people who come in contact with them. If a group experiences discrimination, the acculturation process is impeded. According to John Berry, who is considered the father of psychological research on acculturation, "There is evidence that discrimination is often the most powerful predictor of poor psychological and sociocultural adaptation" (Sam & Berry, 2010, p. 479). This is also the position taken by Schwartz et al. (2010).

Enculturation can be considered the other side of the acculturation coin. Through enculturation, individuals retain or deepen their learning of their own cultural norms (B. S. Kim & Abreu, 2001). There is much less research into enculturation, yet researchers in one meta-analysis reported that enculturation did not predict negative mental health outcomes such as depression, anxiety, psychological distress, and negative affect. However, enculturation did predict positive mental health outcomes, specifically self-esteem, satisfaction with life, and positive affect (Yoon et al., 2013). This finding is important because individuals connecting with their culture of origin may build important resilience in the process.

The United States is diverse. Compared to other countries that have ethnic and linguistic diversity, the United States falls squarely in the middle (Morin, 2013). That diversity may be welcome to some, but for others, it creates confusion, fear, distrust, and hatred. Even with increasing research into acculturation and the processes immigrants and refugees go through, most people still must be educated about the inevitable experiences of people who move from a familiar environment to a new one that contrasts dramatically with the old one.

"Old" and "New" Immigrants

People who curse the continuing flow of immigrants into this country usually know little about issues of migration and acculturation. Their ignorance goes back to earlier periods of immigration, when fear and denigration of immigrants were prevalent, especially in the 19th century (G. V. O'Brien, 2003). According to G. V. O'Brien, the predominant concern then was whether the country could *adequately assimilate* the large number of people who were moving into the United States, especially between 1880 and 1920.

In the 19th century, differentiation between "new" and "old" immigrants began as a primary rationale for restricting entrance into the nation, and many other fears magnified the "threat" posed by immigrants (G. V. O'Brien, 2003). Both the new and the old immigrants were unwelcome because people in the United States feared that their jobs were being threatened. Furthermore, the new immigrants were regarded as physically, mentally, and morally inferior to the older immigrants (G. V. O'Brien, 2003). As reported by many studies, new immigrants were viewed as retarded, as less intelligent, and frequently as occupants of mental institutions. Immigrants were objectified and associated with waste, animals, and catastrophic events (G. V. O'Brien, 2003). Diseases and crime were known to spread from areas where immigrants lived, which contributed to the already exaggerated fears about immigrants. This concern is an example of the ultimate attribution error (see Chapter 6 in this volume): The diseases and crime were blamed on the immigrants rather than on the social conditions.

Today, most concerns of U.S.-born people focus on the job market and how immigrants are willing to work for low pay and thus may take jobs away from U.S.-born people. Not much research and mention have been made regarding changes in the countries of origins of immigrants as affecting immigrant behavior and the acculturation process. For example, changes in countries related to technology, language studies in schools, and media access can affect an individual's ability to adapt and integrate into the host country. And people in the United States still protest the mixing of the races, which was also a concern in previous eras. But have things fundamentally gotten better? Most people would say yes. Research suggests that explicit prejudice expressions are reduced in general and have given way to the expression of implicit prejudices. These implicit prejudices have real effects on decision making and on the health and well-being of the people who experience them.

The focus of most research on immigrants has been on the image of immigrants and the fears of residents of the host country. Not enough research has been done on the experiences of migrating individuals before, during, and after their move. This type of examination might help U.S. citizens understand why people from other countries continue to act the way they do, even after they have moved to the United States. Understanding the acculturation process might also shed some light on stereotypes, prejudice, discrimination, and racism (see Chapter 6).

Models of Acculturation

Traditionally, researchers in the field have identified the process of adjusting to a new culture as being assimilated into that culture. These researchers contended that immigrants or refugees maintain their original cultures for the most part, then their children begin to transition to acquiring the norms and values of the host culture while they lose their connection to their parents' culture, and then the grandchildren of the immigrants or refugees lose almost all connection with their grandparents' culture. By the third or fourth generation, there is almost no hint of the original culture in favor of the norms and values of the host culture (Gordon, 1964; Warner & Srole, 1946; see Kitano, 1999). However, most researchers now feel that there are different ways of acculturating. They have examined models of acculturation to foster understanding of the processes that individuals undergo before, during, and after their move to the United States. (Keep in mind that the classifications in this model [and others] are processes rather than end points.)

Acculturation of Immigrants

John Berry laid the foundations for research on acculturation within psychology (Brislin, 2000; B. S. K. Kim, 2009; Leong, 2001; S. J. Schwartz et al., 2010). J. Berry's (1990, 1997) original model is presented in Table 5.2.

> My parents were born in India and came to America about 25 years ago. Even though I was born and raised in California, I am still aware of my Indian culture as well as the American culture. My cousins, on the other hand, are of the third generation. Their grandparents immigrated here and their parents were raised here. My cousins are of the "straight line" model. They know nothing of the Indian culture that their grandparents brought with them. They consider themselves to be American, nothing else. There's nothing wrong with this, but in my belief, there should be a healthy balance of both cultures. Teach the good from both. When my aunt and uncle go out to the Indian cultural events, my cousins are clueless on what they are experiencing and I always find myself explaining to them every detail.
>
> —Sanjay, 20+-year-old Indian American student

Immigrant parents are often conflicted as to how traditionally versus how Westernized their children should be raised in the United States. *Photograph by R. Gino Santa Maria/Shutterstock*

TABLE 5.2   Berry's Model of Acculturation

Status	Brief descriptions
Assimilationist	An individual who has given up his or her identity of origin in favor of identifying with the host culture's values and beliefs
Separationist	An individual who identifies with his or her identity of origin and rejects of all the host culture's values and beliefs
Marginalist	An individual who does not identify with either his or her original culture or the host culture
Integrationist	An individual who combines (integrates) aspects of his or her own culture and the host culture

Source: Berry (2017).

Are Sanjay's cousins' actions "bad"? That may depend on whom we ask. According to J. Berry's model, Sanjay's cousins may be representative of the **assimilationist** in U.S. society. The cousins have adopted values of their host culture, and it is apparent that they have basically given up the beliefs and values of their native country. They have essentially become Americanized, and possibly in their own minds that has made their transition easier. They may believe that they will be more accepted if they are like everyone else. Assimilationists can also be said to believe in guilt by association, in that they think that they will increase their level of privilege if they are closely associated with the majority culture. However, is that true?

assimilationist—an individual who blends completely into the host society, taking on the values of that society and rejecting his or her original values.

> Tina moved to the United States as a teenager due to economic difficulties her family had in their native country. She is the oldest of three children, and her parents depended on her as the responsible person for her siblings. They relied on her to care for her siblings while they worked, as a dual income was necessary for the family to survive. Tina attended a high school, where she was definitely a minority, and she found herself searching for others who "looked like her." She insisted on speaking her native language with her friends in and outside her school, and especially at home. She made sure that her brother and sister were able to speak their own language and became especially upset when she noticed that her sister associated more with White Americans. She religiously followed traditions from her own country while she refused to celebrate more American traditions. She really did not associate with more "Americanized" folks besides those she worked with, unless she absolutely had to do so. She fraternized only with individuals who moved in a particular circle. That circle encompassed an area composed of only people from her own country.
>
> —Jaymie, 30+-year-old biracial (Filipina/Black) student

Some of us may applaud Tina's strict commitment to pursue and follow her own beliefs and her refusal to assimilate into the majority culture. However, some may wonder how Tina can ever become successful in the United States if she refuses to follow any of its traditions, especially if she intends to stay. According to J. Berry's model, Tina's case is representative of

separationist—an individual who refuses to take on any values of the host society, hanging on to his or her original values completely.

the **separationist**. Separationists refuse to observe any traditions of their host country. They strongly maintain beliefs and values of their country of origin and are unwilling to identify with any other culture, even though they are confronted with the values of the host country on a daily basis. Tina and others like her may have observed and experienced discrimination because of their ethnic and cultural backgrounds. Whereas others prefer to join the majority to avoid the wrath of society, Tina chose to stay separate from the majority as much as she could for the same reason. Although Tina belongs in a different group than others who assimilate, hate and fear exist within both groups because of the experiences that they have been through.

> Joe was born and raised here in the U.S. Though his parents brought him up in a very strict, traditional home, Joe never really "felt like he belonged in his own cultural/ethnic group." He also did not like White people very much, so he really did not associate with many of them.
>
> So, Joe grew up in a predominantly Asian neighborhood, but he never really agreed with many of the norms of his culture. When Joe was about 16, he joined a Chinese gang. One of the things his gang did on a daily basis was to rob stores around his neighborhood. Chinese Americans in his area feared Joe and his gang, for they were known to hurt people. Joe and his gang also participated in drive-by shootings in other areas, and especially gang wars or "color wars." Joe never finished high school, though at the age of 32, he was able to leave the gang. Even after Joe left the gang, he did not pursue his education. Joe is now 40 years old, and he chose to be a proponent of anti-gang campaigns. He never finished his education and he makes just enough money to get by.
>
> —Jaymie, 30+-year-old biracial (Filipina/Black) student

marginalist—an individual who does not adopt either the host society's values or his or her original values.

Joe is representative of J. Berry's **marginalist** category. Marginalists are alienated individuals who neither adopt values of the host culture nor hold on to the values of their own culture. These people, as shown by Joe's story, must create their own group, with separate norms and a different value system, which some of us may not completely understand. This group paints the classic picture of rebellion. They turn their backs on society, just as they feel that society has turned its back on them. They choose a family that accepts them regardless of where they come from. Although marginalist groups are considered the outcasts of society, they still come together by having something in common. Besides the common experience of not belonging, they may share common ethnic backgrounds, religion, beliefs, and so on.

The last group is the **integrationists or biculturals**. These individuals are able to make the best of both worlds. They hold on to their own values, beliefs, and culture while learning about and adapting to their host culture. Integrationists are the individuals who are deemed most likely to succeed (David, Okazaki, & Saw, 2009). They also seem to be the most well-balanced and the happiest of the four main groups. Although they can function in the host society, they are still able to relate to their own people without

integrationists or biculturals—individuals who hold on to their original values while also learning and adopting the values of the host culture.

difficulty. We could suppose that integrationists are more readily able to deal with people from other ethnic groups because they have adopted a flexibility of association.

It could be that these acculturation groups are not necessarily stable, meaning there may be fluidity in a person's status. More specifically, at age 14, someone may be grouped with marginalists, who choose to give up their own cultural beliefs while refusing to adopt those of the host culture. The changes that this same person experiences can later allow him or her to go from being a marginalist to being an integrationist. It could also be that a person is associated with more than one group in his or her lifetime. This fluidity suggests that there are more variables to consider when looking at the processes immigrants and refugees must go through to appropriately acculturate into their host culture.

Whenever people ask me, "What nationality are you?" I would always respond by saying that I'm Korean but hardly ever Korean American. When I think about it, I always thought my blood and my appearance as Korean but my attitude American. I find myself being proud of being Korean and being born in the United States. As a Korean American, I spend time with my Korean friends and with my "Americanized" friends. When I spend time with my Korean friends, I usually abide to Korean culture such as the youngest pours drinks for older people, bowing to elders, speak respectfully to their older peers, etc. When I spend time with people outside of my Korean friends, I feel myself being casual and not having to keep up with the Korean culture. Having to deal with two different cultures creates confusion. There are times I forget that I'm the youngest with my Korean friends or sometimes I forget that I need to be more respectful to people who are older than me. Sometimes whenever I forget, people take that as an offense. To be honest with myself, I get a bit uptight or uncomfortable having to keep up with Korean culture. At the same time, when someone younger than I does not treat me with some respect, it makes me feel that they should give me some respect if they are Korean. I think I might have some identity issues.

California to some, can be very confusing. I always thought of California as a melting pot of a bunch of different races and cultures. It is because of this that people start developing their own culture and identity by living in California. I think I'm at that point of understanding where I stand with my peers and with myself being Korean American. I have visited Korea a few times and whenever I'm there, people are able to point out that I'm from America. Just the way I speak Korean or the way I dress. If I'm in America, people say I'm Korean, but people in Korea say that I'm American. This makes me a bit confused sometimes. It's hard to say who I am because even at the age of 23, I'm still trying to figure out my place in the world and with myself. At this point I would give myself the title as Korean American just because my blood is Korean but my attitude is American. Being a person from two different cultures sometimes gives me more to appreciate. For now I think I'm comfortable with that.

—Kenny, 20+-year-old Korean American student

Acculturation of Diverse Populations

LaFramboise proposed a model of acculturation from her American Indian perspective that was designed to describe the acculturation process of U.S. diverse populations (LaFramboise, Coleman, & Gerton, 1993). Similar to J. Berry's model, LaFramboise's model (Table 5.3) includes *assimilationists,* who are also defined as people who completely absorb the dominant culture.

TABLE 5.3   LaFramboise and Associates' Model of Acculturation

Status	Brief description
Assimilation	Absorption into the dominant culture
Acculturated	Competence in a second culture without complete acceptance
Fusion	The process of combining one's culture of origin with the host culture, creating a somewhat new culture
Alternation	The process of alternating between one's culture of origin and the host culture depending on what the context dictates
Multicultural	Distinct cultural identities are maintained with a single multicultural social structure

Source: LaFramboise, Coleman, and Gerton (1993).

Although assimilationists believe that complete absorption into the dominant culture ensures acceptance, they may experience rejection from the members of their own cultural group. Assimilationists also lose their original cultural identity, which may later cause guilt and isolation.

LaFramboise and associates (LaFramboise et al., 1993) defined individuals who are competent in a second culture without completely accepting it as being **acculturated.** This group seems to mirror integrationists in that people are able to show competence within the dominant culture. The difference is that individuals who are classified as acculturated are always identified as members of the minority culture, and they are relegated to a lower status and not completely accepted, even given their capabilities. M. M. Chao, Chen, Roisman, and Hong (2007) might call these individuals *bicultural essentialists* who believe that there is an essential quality to their ethnicity. Such individuals may experience more difficulties in switching between cultures than they consciously realize.

acculturated—competent in host culture but maintains own cultural identity as more essential.

Another group defined by LaFramboise and associates (LaFramboise et al., 1993) is characterized by **fusion.** This idea is similar to the melting pot theory, wherein individuals come together to form a new, homogenous culture from parts of the different cultures. Fusion differs from J. Berry's assimilation group because aspects of multiple cultures are integrated into a new culture. Cultures of origin are not distinct and identifiable (LaFramboise et al., 1993). Fusion can sometimes be used as an excuse to not see color or other differences among people, which some people may argue is the perpetuating principle behind continuing racist acts. In Chapter 6, you will learn about color-blindness.

A group that seems to have similarities with Berry's (1990, 1997) integrationist model is the **alternation** group (LaFramboise et al., 1993). This group regards two cultures as equal. An individual does not have to choose between the two cultures and can alter his or her behavior to fit the context. LaFramboise et al. (1993) see this group as the optimal one, just as J. Berry (1990, 1997) describes the integrationist group as his most positive one. Though the alternation group is optimal and many people would wish to be able to adjust themselves according to context, this kind of life is not easy. It is not always possible to maintain positive relationships, even when an individual

alternation—competence in both the host culture and one's original culture such that one is able to apply the values and behaviors that are appropriate for the situation.

can adapt and adjust accordingly. However, there does seem to be some evidence that individuals can master this process (Devos, 2006).

The **multicultural model**, according to LaFramboise et al. (1993), involves cultures with distinct identities joined together within a social structure. Individuals from one culture cooperate with those of other cultures to serve common needs. This is different from the melting pot notion in that each subculture can maintain its identity while living among others without necessarily assimilating or completely adopting the others' cultures. This group may be more accurately described by Jesse Jackson's[1] pluralistic quilt idea, in which each culture can be seen apart from the others, yet they are all joined within the same blanket. This is the optimal and most extreme definition of the multicultural model. When there is interaction, however, there also tends to be mutual influence, and cultures of origin tend not to be distinctly maintained. Thus, the multicultural group is difficult to achieve in practice (LaFramboise et al., 1993).

> **multicultural perspective**—the perspective that there are multiple groups within a society and all groups are mutually appreciated.

The Berry and LaFramboise models of acculturation help us to determine the ways that people adapt to this society. These models could apply not only to immigrants and refugees but also to members of minority cultures who are trying to adapt successfully. However, as stated previously, the process of acculturation and the success of immigrants who are attempting to adjust to a new culture can be determined by their experiences before, during, and after their arrival in the host country.

The Migration Process

There are three phases of migration to consider when speaking of immigrants and refugees: *premigration, migration,* and *postmigration* (Hong & Ham, 2001). The **premigration period** refers to the time before individuals leave their country of origin. We must consider the established set of values, beliefs, and familial relations imposed on individuals by the norms of their culture. Disruption of set patterns and norms can affect each person differently, sometimes depending on his or her age at the time of departure to another country. Immigrants' experiences during the premigration period determine how readily able they will be to tolerate outside experiences and, at times, an imposed set of norms. In the premigration period, we must also consider rituals that are looked on as *abnormal* in the host country; after migration, individuals often do not feel that they have the freedom to practice rituals that have been an important part of their lives. These individuals usually must reestablish their rituals in certain diverse communities where they are welcome.

> **premigration period**—the time before migration, when the acculturation process can begin to take place.

> **migration period**—the period when a group is migrating from the country of origin to the host country. This includes the period immediately before the migration, when the final feelings about moving are experienced and leave is taken from family and friends from the country of origin.

The second phase, **migration,** refers to the experience of leaving the country of origin. This phase includes the feelings of the migrating individuals when they are close to

---

1   In his 1988 presidential campaign, Jesse Jackson described "a quilt of many colors" sewn by his grandmother. He said that a single patch of color was not large enough to provide warmth, but that when it was combined with other patches of color, the result was a quilt that could keep someone warm and safe.

departure, saying goodbye to family members and friends, and then traveling. While they are departing, they have the opportunity to really think about the decision they have made, finalized by their departure. Some people may feel fear and apprehension, and others may avoid having expectations for fear of disappointment. The separation from what is known, safe, and comfortable may bring about feelings of isolation, loss, trauma, and sometimes suicidal ideation (Hovey, 2000). Still, people who leave their countries of origin often do so in search of something better than what they have had, so they are somewhat prepared for the unknown. Immigrants have usually been prepared by social networks of people who already reside in the host country, so the shock of relocation is lessened.

The **postmigration** phase refers to the continued stress experienced by immigrants, specifically related to new societal and cultural contexts. An individual may experience feelings of ambiguity and confusion because of the desire to hold on to his or her own cultural beliefs while living in a country that holds different and sometimes opposing cultural views. The postmigration period is when language, new roles and hierarchies, education, and employment begin to change. Individuals who are unable to change during the postmigration period may suffer financially, emotionally, and/or mentally.

If we refer to our two chapter-opening stories of the Vietnamese man and the immigrant family from the Philippines, we can see how the phases of migration become an important aspect to consider in predicting the outcome of their lives. Generally, the differences in the outcomes of their stories are rooted in the way immigrants left their native countries and the resources they had when settling into their host country. Unfortunately, when we talk about adaptation, acculturation, and cultural issues, no single concept can explain how some people end up living here successfully, whereas others continue to struggle for the rest of their lives.

Some people ask, "If one person were to successfully adapt within the host culture but also hold on to the most important cultural beliefs from their country of origin, could they be promised success?" Given that a glass ceiling exists for many people who were born into this society, can we honestly say that immigrants have a chance regardless of whether they assimilate or adopt a multicultural perspective?

We continue to ponder such questions because there is a lack of research on familial relations and outcome of migration (Kaslow, 1996). In addition, we have only recently begun to really push for multicultural research, which involves the study of topics ranging from migration to racism. For now, we can focus on the information that we have learned from past researchers. How can we determine how certain individuals become "more successful" in their lives after migrating to a new country?

Ecological Context and Fit

As one approach, consider some researchers' suggestions of a necessary ecological fit for migrating individuals (Falicov, 1998, 2005; Hong & Ham, 2001). By **ecological fit** or **ecological context,** we mean the degree to which there is a match between the sociocultural environment in the migrant's culture of origin and the country to which he or she is immigrating. Tseng and Yoshikawa (2008) suggested that an ecological perspective opens up our conceptualization of acculturation to include process of change at the social setting, social network, organizational, institutional, community, and policy levels. Several layers of ecological context must be considered, and we

ecological fit/ecological context— similarity of the social and cultural environments between an immigrant's country of origin and new host country.

cannot stress enough how important an individual's context is as he or she moves from the smallest layer or system of ecological context to the largest. Modified from Bronfenbrenner's (1979) model, the layers are *microsystem, mesosystem, exosystem,* and *macrosystem* (Figure 5.1). These layers are relevant to acculturation because of possible stressors that exist within each layer and that may dictate an individual's degree of acculturation.

The **microsystem** includes relationships among family members. These relationships primarily involve the immediate family living in the same household. The **mesosystem** extends to relationships outside the family but is limited to the school, the workplace, extended families, and the community in which one lives. The **exosystem** involves the major societal institutions, such as the media, the government, and laws. Finally, the **macrosystem** encompasses the cultural norms and societal rules that determine the overall exchanges and interactions of the society in which we live. These four systems are interrelated, which means that things occurring at the smallest level of context can affect what occurs in the largest context (Hong & Ham, 2001).

When we observe the migration process, we can imagine how a person's ecological fit is disrupted. Immigrants and refugees are moved from a familiar environment in

microsystem—a layer of context that includes relationships among family members living within one household.

mesosystem—a layer of context that includes relationships in the immediate area outside the family, such as schools, work, the extended family, and the community in which one lives.

exosystem—a layer of context that includes major societal institutions, such as the media and the government.</ MN

macrosystem—a layer of context that includes the cultural norms and societal rules that determine rules of conduct.

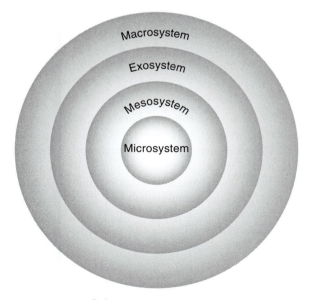

FIGURE 5.1.   Bronfenbrenner and Morris's (1998) ecological model.

which the rules of the government and their communities are well defined. During their flight or migration, their context changes, and all that they are familiar with becomes unknown. As they go through the different stages of migration (premigration, migration, and postmigration), they will experience changes within the different layers or systems. Such changes are inevitable because of the different belief systems and cultural norms that exist in their host country.

We can begin to see how the different systems are composed of a person's family, language, roles, and beliefs, but the geographical context also becomes an issue. In considering individuals outside the majority culture, intersecting layers of issues must be discussed within the same context. We cannot describe the reasons an individual has for leaving his or her country of origin without describing the changes that individual must endure. Additionally, the changes come from imposed rules within the host culture and affect rules learned from the country of origin. The changes that take place during and after migration, sometimes drastic, result in culture shock and acculturative stress. Most minority culture members must make a choice between holding on to their own culture and adopting the majority culture.

More specifically, certain migrating groups experience more culture shock and acculturative stress than others do. How can we explain that? Again, we go back to the question of which variables are to be taken into consideration when looking at a healthy acculturation process.

In consideration of the acculturation process, we should begin with the reason behind the need to migrate to another country. Although we noted earlier that the acculturation process is not limited to immigrants and refugees, most of our discussion related to the issues of migrating individuals. Individuals who undergo the process of acculturation and are natural citizens of this country do not experience the stressors of premigration and migration. They may share some postmigration experiences of immigrants and refugees, mainly involving stereotypes, prejudice, and discrimination.

Immigrants and refugees face the challenge of holding on to their own beliefs while they attempt to succeed in their host country. They must learn a different language and adapt to different roles to remain physically and mentally healthy. They must deal with the changes that their children undergo and how those changes modify their family structure. They learn to accept their limitations and sharpen their skills so that they can maintain a certain lifestyle most befitting the American Dream.

Summary

Immigrants and refugees have much in common, but they also have important unique experiences. Immigrants and refugees come from foreign lands and face challenges adapting to a new language and customs. However, there are some important psychological differences. Immigrants decide to come to the United States for economic, political, and/or personal reasons. They plan to immigrate to the United States, and that planning process can take years. Thus, the acculturation process starts before immigrants arrive. They learn about U.S. culture and norms, decide whether those norms are consonant with their view of the world, and carefully decide where in the United States they will settle. Often, they have family and friends here who can assist in their immigration process or at least help them with the kinds of norms and services that can be of assistance.

Food for Thought

Most of you attend colleges and universities with immigrants and refugees who have recently settled in the United States. Colleges and universities may have special offices that support multicultural and/or international students and offer specific programs, such as guest speakers or movie events. Take advantage of these offerings. If you know any immigrants or refugees, ask them whether they might be willing to tell you why their families came to the United States. Were they immigrants or refugees? Note that some people came to the United States as small children and might not know all the circumstances that brought them here. If you engage in a conversation with an immigrant or a refugee, you might want to ask them whether their parents feel a need to talk about their reasons for coming to the United States. More often than not, people want their stories heard, and you and your colleagues might be able to learn something from their parents.

In contrast, refugees have very little time to decide to leave their homelands, often only a few hours. They may not want to leave but perhaps oppose those in power and must flee political upheaval or the threat of death. They do not know where they will finally settle because their overriding motivation to leave is to save their lives. After they leave their homelands, they typically are held in refugee camps that are overcrowded and unsanitary. Throughout the process of leaving (before, during, and after), refugees often experience a great deal of trauma, such as seeing family members and friends die or going through extreme hardships of transit. As a result of these circumstances, the acculturation process cannot begin before the refugees arrive in their host countries.

Once in their host countries, both immigrants and refugees must acculturate to their new surroundings; that is, they must adjust to the new country, with its unfamiliar customs and values. Among the challenges they face are language barriers, new family roles, employment opportunities, and educational opportunities. Often, children learn the new language much faster than do the parents and are able to interact with the social agencies of the new country. This gives the children more power than their parents have and leads to a disruption of the family hierarchy.

Researchers have developed models of acculturation that identify various resolutions of acculturation, such as maintaining two cultural competencies, holding on to the traditional culture, blending the two cultures, or being confused about cultural issues. The degree to which immigrants and refugees successfully adjust to their host culture depends on the degree to which they can successfully negotiate the blending of their traditional values with the new values of their host cultures.

Critical Thinking Questions

1. What is the history of your family in the United States? What hardships did your family experience when coming to the United States? What were the conditions of your family's ancestral homeland before they arrived?
2. If you are an American Indian, what hardships did your family encounter when it came in contact with European Americans/Whites? What were the conditions of your family's ancestral home before it came in contact with European Americans/Whites?

3. If your family immigrated to the United States, did it settle in an area known for immigrants from your family's country, or did it settle in an area that was widely integrated?

4. If your family immigrated to the United States, did your ancestors speak English, or did they have to learn English after arriving here? If they spoke a non-English language, what issues did your family encounter?

5. What roles within your family changed after your family arrived in the United States?

6. How would you characterize yourself according to the acculturation models? Are you different from others in your family? If so, what are the differences?

CHAPTER 6

Stereotyping, Prejudice, Discrimination, and Racism

Photograph by Tyler Olson/Shutterstock

Learning Objectives

Reading this chapter will help you to:

- understand the differences among stereotyping, prejudice, discrimination, and racism;
- identify components of overt versus covert racism;
- know which strategies are appropriate for combatting racial microaggressions;
- explain components of modern forms of racism;
- recognize the differences between a color-blind racial ideology and a color-conscious ideology; and
- distinguish between European American privilege and allied behaviors.

There's an old story about an elementary teacher. Her name was Mrs. Thompson. And as she stood in front of her fifth-grade class on the very first day of school, she told the children a lie. Like most teachers, she looked at her students and said that she loved them all the same.

But that was impossible, because there in the front row, slumped in his seat, was a little boy named Teddy Stoddard. Mrs. Thompson had watched Teddy the year before and noticed that he didn't play well with the other children, that his clothes were messy, and that he constantly needed a bath. And Teddy could be unpleasant. It got to the point where Mrs. Thompson would actually take delight in marking his papers with a broad red pen, making bold X's and then putting a big "F" at the top of his papers.

At the school where Mrs. Thompson taught, she was required to review each child's past records, and she put Teddy's off until last. However, when she reviewed his file, she was in for a surprise.

Teddy's first-grade teacher wrote, "Teddy is a bright child with a ready laugh. He does his work neatly and has good manners . . . he is a joy to be around."

His second-grade teacher wrote, "Teddy is an excellent student, well-liked by his classmates, but he is troubled because his mother has a terminal illness and life at home must be a struggle."

His third-grade teacher wrote, "His mother's death had been hard on him. He tries to do his best, but his father doesn't show much interest, and his home life will soon affect him if some steps aren't taken."

Teddy's fourth-grade teacher wrote, "Teddy is withdrawn and doesn't show much interest in school. He doesn't have many friends and he sometimes sleeps in class."

By now, Mrs. Thompson realized the problem, and she was ashamed of herself. She felt even worse when her students brought her Christmas presents, wrapped in beautiful ribbons and bright paper, except for Teddy's. His present was clumsily wrapped in the heavy brown paper that he got from a grocery bag.

Mrs. Thompson took pains to open it in the middle of the other presents. Some of the children started to laugh when she found a rhinestone bracelet with some of the stones missing, and a bottle that was one quarter full of perfume. But she stifled the children's laughter when she exclaimed how pretty the bracelet was, putting it on, and dabbing some of the perfume on her wrist.

Teddy Stoddard stayed after school that day just long enough to say, "Mrs. Thompson, today you smelled just like my mom used to." After the children left she cried for at least an hour. On that very day, she quit teaching reading and writing and arithmetic. Instead, she began to teach children.

Mrs. Thompson paid particular attention to Teddy. As she worked with him, his mind seemed to come alive. The more she encouraged him, the faster he responded.

By the end of the year, Teddy had become one of the smartest children in the class, and, despite her lie that she would love all the children the same, Teddy became one of her "teacher's pets."

A year later, she found a note under her door from Teddy, telling her that she was still the best teacher he ever had in his whole life.

Six years went by before she got another note from Teddy. He then wrote that he had finished high school, third in his class, and she was still the best teacher he ever had in his whole life.

Four years after that, she got another letter, saying that while things had been tough at times, he'd stayed in school, had stuck with it, and would soon graduate from college with the highest of honors. He assured Mrs. Thompson that she was still the best and favorite teacher he ever had in his whole life.

Then four more years passed and yet another letter came. This time he explained that after he got his bachelor's degree, he decided to go a little further. The letter explained that she was still the best and favorite teacher he ever had. But now his name was a little longer—the letter was signed Theodore F. Stoddard, M.D.

The story doesn't end there. You see, there was yet another letter that spring. Teddy said he'd met this girl and was going to be married. He explained that his father had died a couple of years ago, and he was wondering if Mrs. Thompson might agree to sit in the place at the wedding that was usually reserved for the mother of the groom. Of course, Mrs. Thompson did.

And guess what? She wore that bracelet, the one with several rhinestones missing. And she made sure she was wearing the perfume that Teddy remembered his mother wearing on their last Christmas together.

They hugged each other, and Dr. Stoddard whispered in Mrs. Thompson's ear, "Thank you, Mrs. Thompson, for believing in me. Thank you so much for making me feel important and showing me that I could make a difference."

Mrs. Thompson, with tears in her eyes, whispered back. She said, "Teddy, you have it all wrong. You were the one who taught me that I could make a difference. I didn't know how to teach until I met you."

This story has been used repeatedly and in a wide variety of settings to inspire people—especially teachers—with the power of a single individual's influence on others' lives. Although the story is fictional, it illustrates what can happen when we help individuals in need and open them up to a world of possibilities. This version of the story traveled around the Internet several years ago and has been published on Barbara and David Mikkelson's website (Mikkelson & Mikkelson, 2005). According to the Mikkelsons, the story was written by

Elizabeth Ballard (now Elizabeth Ungar) for *Home Life* magazine in 1976. She combined two incidents—one she had heard of and one from her own life. In the first, a boy gave his Sunday school teacher a gift of perfume and a broken rhinestone bracelet. In the second, Ms. Ballard herself gave a box of handpicked pecans to her elementary school teacher. Her teacher stifled laughs from Ms. Ballard's classmates by saying that she was about to make some fruitcakes, and pecans were exactly what she needed to complete her baking. Thus, in a way, given how many lives Ms. Ballard has touched by writing this story, the essence of the Teddy Stoddard story is true.

As mentioned, this story is used primarily as a poignant way of motivating teachers to inspire their own students. It appears in various forms on numerous websites (http://lessonslearnedinlife.com/three-letters-from-teddy; http://makeadifferencemovie.com/index.php; Silance Ballard, n.d.). These websites number in the tens of thousands and contain different versions of the story. Why has the story become so popular? What is it about this story that resonates with people?

Besides demonstrating that teachers can make a difference (or, more broadly, that people can make a difference) in other people's lives, this story also demonstrates how wrong we can be when we make judgments about others without knowing their stories or personal histories. Let us explore this notion further.

attribution theory—a theory that attempts to determine the cause of a behavior. Two major dimensions are internal–external and stable–unstable.

One of the more important theories in social psychology is **attribution theory** (Kelly, 1967, 1973), which describes how people explain the causes of human behavior. Attribution theory suggests that we use two primary dimensions to develop judgments (attributions) about others' behaviors: the internal–external dimension and the stable–unstable dimension. When combined, these two dimensions yield four possible explanations of another's behaviors: internal–stable, internal–unstable, external–stable, and external–unstable. For example, if you were to see Bobby hit Jimmy, you might say that Bobby is an aggressive child (an internal–stable attribution), that Bobby was in a bad mood (an internal–unstable attribution), that everyone hits Jimmy (an external–stable attribution, since this is external to Bobby), or that Jimmy just hit Bobby, so Bobby reciprocated (an external–unstable attribution; Table 6.1).

According to Lee Ross (1977), we have a tendency to overuse dispositional (internal–stable) attributions and to underestimate external causes for behaviors. Thus, of the four attributions,

fundamental attribution error—the tendency to overestimate dispositional (internal, stable) causes of behaviors and to underestimate external causes of behaviors.

we tend to believe that Bobby is an aggressive child before we believe any of the other three possible explanations of his behavior. This tendency is called the **fundamental attribution error** (Ross, 1977). Our assessment may or may not be an error, but if we ignore possible external reasons for certain behaviors, then we may be committing this error. For example, Bobby may be an aggressive child, so our

TABLE 6.1   Attribution Theory: Four Kinds of Attributions for Bobby Hitting Jimmy

	Internal	External
Stable	Internal–stable: Bobby is an aggressive child	External–stable: Everyone hits Jimmy
Unstable	Internal–unstable: Bobby was in a bad mood	External–unstable: Jimmy just hit Bobby

attribution of him as an aggressive child may be accurate. However, if he is *not* an aggressive child and we fail to take into account that Jimmy just hit him, we would be committing the fundamental attribution error if we were to assume that Bobby is aggressive. The tendency to commit the fundamental attribution error may be more of a Western error, because there are some indications that Eastern Asians do not have this tendency (Choi, Nisbett, & Norenzayan, 1999).

Let us consider the Teddy Stoddard story once again. How many of you automatically thought that Teddy Stoddard was a European American child? That was our immediate reaction, too. Mrs. Thompson (whom we might also have assumed to have been European American) turned this child's life around and made him a productive member of society. However, let us engage in a thought experiment: suppose that Teddy Stoddard was an African American child and Mrs. Thompson was European American. What might have been the result? Mrs. Thompson might have responded in a different manner, still compassionate and caring, but different. She might have thought, "Oh, what a shame that this child has had such a hardship! I should not be so hard on him. Maybe I will grade his papers with a bit more leniency."

We bring this up because in the story, Mrs. Thompson reacted to Teddy as an individual, and she gave him a kind of encouragement that resulted in his blossoming into a success story. In our thought experiment, Mrs. Thompson sees Teddy as a representative of all African American children. Her caring for him might have resulted not in his flourishing but, rather, in his recognizing that not all European American people are bad and that some will treat him with more kindness than others do. He might not necessarily have flourished intellectually but, rather, might have been more forgiving toward European Americans who treated him with less compassion. One of the challenges that people of color face is that the European American culture tends to engage in another kind of attributional error: the **ultimate attribution error**. Thomas Pettigrew (1979) coined this term to mean that when attributions are directed toward individuals who represent a particular group, the internal and stable attributions are ascribed to the group members instead of just to the individual. Again, in the case of Bobby hitting Jimmy, if Bobby were an

> **ultimate attribution error**—the tendency to ascribe the cause of a behavior to dispositional characteristics of the group rather than to an individual member.

African American child, an ultimate attribution error would be to say, "African American children are so aggressive," instead of limiting the aggression to Bobby. A student related the following story that discussed both the fundamental attribution error and the ultimate attribution error:

> After being in this class, I have begun to see the things that people say differently. We are so quick to judge and think the worst of people. We rely upon heuristics that are engrained in society that tell us how to evaluate people based on the way that they look and act. And we are so quick to accept these faulty evaluations as truths, and we will fight to hold on to them in spite of information contrary to our beliefs.
>
> One of the biggest problems I think we have is that we lack the ability to include context into our evaluations of others. If someone is on welfare, then they must be lazy, and if they would just get out there and work hard like the rest of us they wouldn't be relying on government handouts. Never mind that the person might be a single parent, working two minimum wage jobs, and may be even harder working than we are to provide for their family. We lack context. If a person of color says that the system is rigged against them, we tell them that they're using it as a crutch, playing the victim,

and holding themselves back. Never mind that the reality is that the system is rigged, and that Whites have it better in almost every way compared to people of color. We lack the ability to look beyond what we see in front of us. The people we see are only that. We see cardboard cutouts of who people are when we pass them on the streets. We see a thin piece of their existence that lacks any depth and insight to the person, who they are, and what their life might just be like. And we judge them on that lack of depth, even when we consider it for ourselves. When we are having a rough day and we are rude to a worker at the supermarket, we know that's not us and that it's only in the context of the day. When we're the worker at the supermarket that has a rude customer, we think that's all that they are, that rudeness must encompass all of their existence, and if there's another external cue that we use to justify that feeling towards them, we'll probably use that too.

—Eldred, 20+-year-old European American student

The ultimate attribution error can be applied to any group that can be targeted for discrimination. Have you ever heard one woman's behavior attributed to all woman? One LGBT person's behavior attributed to all LGBT persons? One person's behavior from a religious minority attributed to all people from that religion? This is how the ultimate attribution error can undermine entire groups of people.

Categorizations of Race and Ethnicity

I have a European American friend who has for most of her life lived in a "White" community. I, on the other hand, have grown up with people of all ethnic backgrounds. When I met her, my first thought was that we would get along great. We had common interests and similar taste. The more we spent time together the more I realized she expressed herself as being superior. . . .

I recently bought a Louis Vuitton purse. For people who know about this couture brand, these bags are quite costly, ranging from $300 to $3,500 dollars. When I received my bag I was ecstatic about my purchase and called everyone I knew to share the good news that I had one of the most popular couture bags in Southern California. When I called my friend "Brooke" (not her real name) she was quiet for a second. When she finally spoke she said that it was impossible for me to buy such a costly bag. She said that whoever sold it to me had ripped me off and sold me a knockoff. I had explained that the bag I purchased was at a price of over $600 and that it was definitely real. What was mostly heartbreaking about this situation was that she laughed at me, on the phone, and started chanting to her dorm friends, or anyone who would listen, that her friend had just been made a fool and had a fake bag. It was as if I had no common sense and most of all didn't have the funds to have an item such as this.

A few weeks ago, I was talking with Brooke and she made an indirect comment that Mexican people are mostly poor. It didn't occur to me that I was included in this category of people until she stated that I couldn't afford something that only wealthy people could afford. Or should I say that only "White" people could afford. I have come to the realization that there are many people like Brooke. These people look at minority groups as not having the ability to live up to a higher standard of living.

—Laurel, 20+-year-old Mexican American student

Was Laurel's story one of stereotyping, prejudice, discrimination, or racism? Most social psychologists make a distinction among these forms of racial/ethnic categorization. D. G. Myers (2013) describes the differences as follows:

- **Stereotype**—a generalization about a group or its members based on categorization. A stereotype can be an accurate reflection of a group's norm; can be an overgeneralization, applying the norm to every member of the group or not allowing for variation about this norm; or can be simply inaccurate. Stereotypes are cognitive categorizations of people made based on some demographic characteristic and do not necessarily convey positive or negative evaluations. For example, to say that Asians tend to be more collectivistic than European Americans is an accurate stereotype. To insist that all Asians are collectivistic is an overgeneralization. However, to say that Asians are collectivistic is not to make a positive or a negative assessment of Asians based on this categorization. Stereotypes are considered the *cognitive component* of categorization.

  stereotype—a generalization about a group or its members based on their categorization.

- **Prejudice**—a judgment about a group or its members based on their categorization. This judgment may be positive or negative, but it is typically thought to be negative. For example, someone may be prejudiced against Asians because they are collectivistic and tend to suppress individual freedoms or not express individualistic creativities. Prejudices are considered the *evaluative component* of categorization.

  prejudice—a negative judgment about a group or its members based on their categorization.

- **Discrimination**—a negative behavior toward a group or its members based on their categorization. For example, an Asian individual may not be selected for an assignment because it is assumed that this individual's collectivistic tendencies will not allow him or her to be creative enough. Discrimination is considered the *behavioral component* of categorization.

  discrimination—a negative behavior toward a group or its members based on their categorization.

- **Racism**—discriminatory behavior that has institutional power behind it. This applies to people with institutional backing (those on the upside of power) who discriminate against individuals on the downside of power. For example, an individual may discriminate against an Asian individual and be backed by institutions of power. Most social psychologists feel that racism is a routine mistreatment of individuals on the downside of power, meaning that the mistreatment is part of institutional practices. Racism is considered the *institutional component* of categorization.

  racism—discriminatory behavior that is backed by institutional power.

The description of racism also applies to other *isms*, such as sexism, ageism, ableism, heterosexism, and anti-Semitism and other forms of religious discrimination. Institutional practices of the dominant society tend to suppress members of the nondominant parts of society. A former student wrote about her encounter with ageism:

> In my community psychology class, every student had to do eight hours of community service. I did my community service at a convalescent home. It was interesting. While

I was changing the decorations in the lunchroom, I noticed that there was an elderly woman who was crying and screaming. None of the other workers or nurses seemed to pay any attention to her. I also noticed that she was speaking in both English and Tagalog (the national language of the Philippines). This went on for about 20 minutes until finally one of the workers went to take the lady to her room. I asked that worker if the lady, Monica, could sit next to me while I was working. When Monica came over to sit next to me I asked her if she was Filipina, and I asked if she spoke Tagalog. She said yes and we started to have a conversation about the Philippines. She sat next to me for about an hour talking without screaming and crying. This was really amazing to me. Here was someone who just needs someone to talk to about something that she could relate to. It was amazing to see that just knowing a little bit about the Philippines and knowing only a few words would be an icebreaker between Monica and me. To me this just goes to show that understanding an individual's culture and background can do a lot. I hope that perhaps the elderly lady, Monica, for that hour felt really good having someone to talk to.
—Jessica, 20+-year-old biracial (Mexican/European American) student

The practice of isms may not be intentional, and once it is exposed, members of the dominant group may be motivated to change the behavior to be more fair. However, until exposure takes place, the practice may have an element of suppression. For example, most universities heavily weigh teaching and research productivity for the purposes of making tenure decisions. Members of the dominant group may feel that this emphasis is fair because it applies to all individuals equally. However, many faculty of color and indigenous faculty may have been hired to help recruit and advise students of color and engage those respective communities. Furthermore, many indigenous scholars engage in community/tribally based research, which requires additional protocols in the research process and adds substantial time to the review and dissemination of research findings. As such, these activities necessarily take away from their ability to publish as much as their European American colleagues or publish in more "prestigious" journals—because many indigenous scholars tend to publish their work in journals that are more likely to be read by practitioners and providers in the community. Therefore, when compared with their European American colleagues, they may not be evaluated favorably. However, if such inequities are pointed out and if the institution is motivated to be fair, community activities may be given some value in the tenure process, and articles published in some ethnically focused journals should be considered as scholarly as those in more prestigious journals.

Did you notice that *stereotyping* and *prejudice* are internal activities? If I hold a stereotypic attitude toward you, or even a prejudicial one, but keep that attitude or feeling to myself, you are not hurt. It is not until my attitude is expressed either behaviorally (discrimination) or institutionally (racism) that you get hurt. It is difficult to get stereotypic or prejudicial attitudes out of our system because many of them are products of years of "learning" or exposure. However, if we can become aware of such attitudes and work to counteract them, we will not hurt others. Once we act on them, we have crossed the line to discrimination and/or racism.

As a humorous example of categorization and assumptions based on the status of an individual, I (JSM) ask my students to imagine that I had some thoughts and feelings about students who sit in the front of a class (*front-sitters*) versus students who sit in the back of the class (*back-sitters*). I tell them that I may have certain thoughts about front-sitters, such as that they ask more questions during lecture and back-sitters ask fewer questions during lecture.

However, students do not know whether I feel positively toward front-sitters and negatively toward back-sitters or if it is the other way around. On the one hand, if someone were to ask more questions during lecture, I may feel that they are more involved in class and the topics we are covering; thus, I may have a more favorable opinion of them. On the other hand, I could feel that the questions get in the way of my lectures, and I am not able to get through all the material that I wanted to cover. In this case, I may feel more negatively toward students who ask a lot of questions. Students simply do not know whether I feel more positively toward front-sitters or more negatively toward front-sitters. I point out that my assumptions about front-sitters and back-sitters—that they ask more and fewer questions, respectively—are stereotypes and that my opinions of front-sitters and back-sitters are prejudices. However, unless I act on them, students will never know what my stereotypes and prejudices are with regard to where they sit in the class, so my opinions of them do not hurt (or advantage) them. They are not hurt by my categorizations until I actually act on them, which is discrimination. If students complain to my department chair, my dean, and/or my college president that they are being disadvantaged because they are front-sitters (or back-sitters), and if those leaders all support my discrimination, then this becomes an ism where there is institutional support for my discriminatory behavior.

Racism in the News

Stories about race and racism have always been present in our society as part of the news cycle. However, with the advent of social media, the voices of social activists are more difficult to ignore and society is becoming more aware. For example, police brutality has long been considered a problem and a form of racism for communities of color. Over the decades and in recent years, several incidents have received national attention, primarily involving the beating and/or killing of unarmed Black and American Indian men and women by police. They include the stories of Rodney King in Los Angeles; Eric Garner in New York; Marlene Pinnock in Los Angeles; Michael Brown in Ferguson; Jason Pero on the Bad River Indian Reservation; Tamir Rice in Cleveland; Freddie Gray in Baltimore; Paul Castaway in Denver; Benjamin Whiteshield in Oklahoma City; Zach Bearheels in Omaha; Philando Castile in Minneapolis; and Sandra Bland in Texas, just to name a few (Craven, 2017; Hansen, 2017; Hennesy-Fiske, 2014; Landers, Rollock, Rolfes, & Moore, 2011; Pearce, 2014; Queally & Semuels, 2014; von Drehle & Altman, 2014; Winton, Mather, & Serna, 2014). Most of these incidents include video recordings that clearly show the person was unarmed and not a threat at the time. However, of the officers involved, few were convicted for any wrongdoing or even charged with a crime. Why are we discussing police brutality and shootings in terms of racism? Remember, the definition of racism is discriminatory behavior that is backed by institutional power. In this instance, law enforcement is part of the criminal justice system (institution) that engages in the mistreatment of people of color and indigenous people. Furthermore, this mistreatment occurs at disproportionate rates relative to the population. In other words, African Americans, American Indians, and Latinxs are more likely to be incarcerated and/or on probation and parole than are European Americans. There are more African American men in jail, on probation, or on parole today than there were enslaved before the emancipation proclamation (Alexander, 2012). In fact, a direct link exists between the police and the criminal justice system dating back to the enforcement of Jim Crow laws as well as slavery and, thus, institutional laws, policies, and practices that create advantage for some people and mistreatment for individuals on the downside of power.

Two recent series of events provide striking examples of racism in our society. The first occurred on the Standing Rock Indian Reservation in North Dakota with the protest to stop the Dakota Access Pipeline (DAPL). The DAPL is designed to ship oil from oil fields in western North Dakota to Illinois. Opposition and concern about the DAPL began in 2010 (Dalrymple, 2016; Nauman, 2012), but reached a flashpoint and the national news in 2016. The DAPL crosses the Missouri River less than a mile north of the Standing Rock reservation and within the boundaries of the Treaty of Fort Laramie of 1868. The pipeline's construction sparked fear among the tribe that their primary source of fresh water could be contaminated if an oil spill were to occur. (Originally, the DAPL was to travel north of Bismarck, North Dakota, about 50 miles to the north of Standing Rock, but the proposed route was altered because the mostly European American residents in that area had also expressed concern over the potential for water pollution in the event of a spill.) In the spring of 2016, the Sacred Stone Camp was established by Lakota youth near Cannon Ball, North Dakota, on the northeast edge of Standing Rock, to protest and attempt to stop construction of the DAPL. Over the next several months, approximately 10,000 people, mostly American Indians, visited the camp to show support (Whyte, 2017) and conduct peaceful protests to stop the pipeline's construction. In response, the local sheriff and the governor of North Dakota mobilized the police force in riot gear and militarized armored vehicles to protect the construction site. In addition, local, regional, and nearby state police agencies sent their forces to assist with the response. Unrest broke out as protesters attempted to block access to the construction site, and the police responded with the use of tear gas, pepper spray, and even water cannons in the subfreezing temperatures (Hawkins, 2016). At one point, the DAPL company engaged a private security force, which used dogs that attacked and mauled the protesters (Peralta, 2016). Scenes from Standing Rock were eerily similar to images from the civil rights–era marches and protests.

In stark contrast is the response of authorities to the Unite the Right rally by White nationalists and White supremacists in Charlottesville, Virginia, one of the most memorable news stories of 2017 (Astor, Caron, & Victor, 2017; Ellis, 2017). On the night of August 11, 2017, about 250 mostly young European American men carrying torches marched through the University of Virginia campus chanting slogans such as, "Blood and soil!," "You will not replace us!," and "Jews will not replace us!" In the center of campus, near the statue of Thomas Jefferson, they were met by about 30 students—students of color and European American students. The marchers circled the students and began to yell "White lives matter!" Chaos ensued and fights broke out between the two groups. Only one university police officer was present and there were no city or state police along the route of the march. The following day, thousands of White nationalists and White supremacists gathered for the official rally, many of them carrying shields and clubs and a large number carrying pistols and rifles. In addition, about three dozen members of a militia joined the crowds, dressed in full camouflage and carrying semiautomatic rifles and pistols. Law enforcement was on hand this day, but stationed in places that did not prevent contact between the White nationalists and the counterprotesters who also gathered. Small skirmishes began to occur, and within an hour, full conflict broke out between the groups when the White nationalists charged through the line of counterprotesters. Fighting continued for nearly an hour before the police declared an unlawful assembly. The day ended with a White nationalist driving his car into the crowd, injuring 17 people and killing 1 woman (Heim, 2017). The fact that thousands of White nationalists and White supremacists marched is clearly an indication that racism exists, even though they have the right to do so under the First Amendment. However, in this case the response by law enforcement to the marchers is more troubling. For example, only three White nationalist marchers were arrested, although hundreds of them arrived at the march carrying shields, clubs, and firearms, items usually not associated with peaceful protest. Many people have argued that if African Americans had attempted to march carrying weapons, the police would have immediately responded with force. In fact, the police have responded with force to peaceful protests of Black Lives Matter marches (D. Smith, 2018; Prager, 2017; Yan, 2017). The initial response of the president of the United States, Donald Trump, stating "There were good people on both sides," appeared to be one of sympathy for the White nationalists (Bennett, 2017; Rafferty, Sotomayor, & Arkin, 2017). This type of differential treatment and reaction by authorities indicates how racism works in society.

One of our European American students recounted a story that underscored how racism still existed in an overt manner when she was in elementary school and her African American babysitter was stopped by the police:

> One day I was roller-skating and we were crossing the street and he held my hand. We were a block or so down the street when the police pulled up, grabbed [Conner], my babysitter, and pushed him against the car. The other officer pulled me to the side and said, "Don't worry, you're safe now," and I started screaming and crying, "What are you doing to my brother?" Conner got really upset, understandably, and so the cop unstrapped part of his gun holder, which scared me so much. The whole time I was telling them to stop but they didn't listen. My neighbor, who

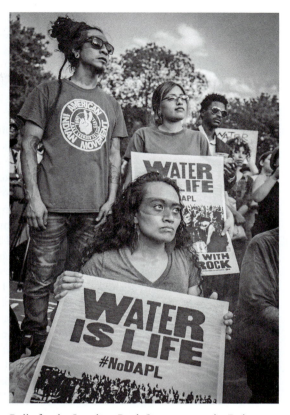

Rally for the Standing Rock Sioux to stop the Dakota Access Pipeline. *Photograph courtesy of Pacific Press/ Getty Images*

White supremacists and White Nationalists marching in Charlottesville, Virginia. *Photograph courtesy of Anadolu Agency/Getty Images*

happened to be Latina, came down the street and told the cops that Conner was my babysitter. The cops just stopped what they were doing, got in the car, and drove off.

No apologies. I had a serious distrust of police after that and was well aware from then on that there is a serious problem in our society with racism.

—Nikki, 20+-year-old European American student

In the following story, one of our students describes being stopped by a police officer. The student believes the officer thought he was Black when he stopped him.

I had driven to a bar in "Jacksonville" with a friend. After a few hours and a couple of drinks with other friends we decided to leave. As I pull out of the bar driveway onto the street I see a police car traveling the opposite direction. The police [officer] turns around and pulls me over. The officer, who looked to be Asian descent, asks for my license, registration, and insurance. As I am looking for the documents the officer asked me if I had been drinking. I know the officer saw me leave the bar, so I decided to tell him that I had a couple of beers. At the time I was living in "Springfield" with my parents and the officer sees on my license and asks me if I still lived in Springfield. At this point I am scared of getting a DUI and I had no idea if I was legally drunk or not. The officer comes back to my car, hands me my documents and tells me to have a good evening. As my friend and I drove home, I could not understand how "lucky" I got that the officer did not request a field sobriety test. My friend had made a comment that I was pulled over for "D.W.B." I asked what that was, and he replied, "Driving while Black." My friend pointed out that my car was a Lexus with dark tinted windows and 20-inch wheels. My friend said that Jacksonville has a fairly large Black population relative to the surrounding cities and that he was almost sure that is why we were pulled over. I now think that the police had stereotyped the car I was driving, the city I was in, and the town in which I lived. When I was someone different than what he expected, I was let go. Now, if I was a Black male in the car I truly think that I would have had to at least take a field sobriety test.

—Terry, 20+-year-old European American student

Stereotype Threat

Suddenly I was in the middle of this test with the question laid out before me and I started to panic. What if I couldn't write a good essay? What if I couldn't pass this most basic test? I think I spent most of the 75 minutes trying to talk away my anxiety rather than concentrating on the questions. I finished that test knowing that I didn't do my best on it. And then it hit me . . . could this be stereotype threat? Is this the fear that I would be confirming a stereotype that Asians "no speakie goodie ingerish"? Is this what I have been reading about in class? . . . Am I now feeling the insidious nature of racism? I am starting to wonder if taking this class is making me paranoid or more aware. Or maybe giving me a healthy dose of both. (Asian/Pacific Island female college student; Mio & Barker-Hackett, 2003, p. 15)

This paragraph was part of a weekly reaction paper assignment written by a former student. She was one of the brightest students in her graduate program, but she was overcome with self-doubt when she had to take a writing test that our university required for graduation. All students had to pass this test before they could receive a degree. Just before the exam, she looked around her and saw several Asian students who spoke English as a second language. She was aware that most of these students did not pass this test the first time they took it, and she was concerned that she would be lumped together with them and be stereotyped negatively.

Claude M. Steele (1997) has written extensively about what he termed **stereotype threat**—the threat that individuals belonging to a group that is negatively stereotyped will confirm that stereotype when confronted with a difficult task that purports to measure differences in abilities. For example, C. M. Steele and Aronson (1995)

stereotype threat—a fear that one will confirm the negative stereotype of a group to which one belongs in an area in which the individual excels.

reported on freshman African American students who were extremely accomplished in English, as measured by their verbal scores on the Scholastic Aptitude Test, who were given the Graduate Record Examination subject test in English. The subject test was 4 years beyond their education level, but the students did not know that it was designed for students who were far more advanced than they were at the time. Still, these African American students performed just as well as their European American counterparts when both groups were led to believe that the test was simply a very difficult test that was being administered because they had previously proven how accomplished they were. When the students were led to believe that the test would measure differences between Blacks and European Americans, however, African American student performance decreased.

The same pattern was demonstrated for women taking mathematics tests. Freshman women who had received extremely high quantitative scores on their Scholastic Aptitude Test were given the Graduate Record Examination subject test in mathematics. Again, these women performed as well as their male counterparts did when they were led to believe that the test was simply a very difficult one. However, when they were led to believe that the test might measure gender differences in mathematics, the women's scores decreased. This pattern also seems true with respect to gender differences in political knowledge (McGlone & Neal, 2003).

C. M. Steele (2001) stated that stereotype threat occurs under specific circumstances. First, an individual must excel in an area that is contrary to the stereotype. In the areas examined in C. M. Steele's earlier studies, African Americans are not stereotypically considered to excel in English in comparison with their European American counterparts, women are not considered to excel in math in comparison with their male counterparts, and women are not considered as interested in politics as men are. And, as exemplified in the preceding story, Asians—especially Asians who are learning English as a second language—are not considered fluent in written or oral English skills.

Second, the stereotype must be negative. Verbal and mathematical skills are highly valued, and deficits in those areas are considered negative; politics are important in that they relate to how the country is run. For example, Derald Wing Sue, one of the most respected researchers in multicultural psychology, jokes about his inability to dance, saying that Asians are not really expected to dance well. Thus, although that is a negative stereotype about Asians, deficits in dancing are not threatening, because dancing is not a highly valued skill in mainstream America. However, if one does not speak English well in this country, he or she is considered less intelligent.

Third, the area in which the individual excels must be important to him or her. The African American and female research participants in C. M. Steele's earlier studies excelled in English and mathematics, respectively, in high school, and the students valued those skills. They were at the top of their high school classes and received much recognition for their accomplishments. The Asian student taking the writing test was in a graduate program learning to become a

Fear of confirming a stereotype can inhibit performance.
Photograph courtesy of oliveromg/Shutterstock

therapist, an occupation in which verbal fluency skills are important.

Finally, the test of the individual's skills must be challenging. Clearly, tests 4 years beyond one's current training would be challenging. In the example of the Asian student, the writing test was not difficult and merely involved developing a written argument about a topic, but because failing the test would mean not receiving a degree from the university, it was a high-stakes test.[1]

C. M. Steele (2001) reasoned that the internal dialogue of victims of stereotype threat goes something like this: "Oh, no! I thought I was bright in this area, but now I am not performing well. I wonder if the stereotypes are true. Could it be that I have hit the limits of my abilities? Is my failure in this area only confirming the negative stereotypes that people have about me and people like me?" Contrast this internal dialogue with that of someone who is not threatened by such a negative stereotype: "Gosh, this test is hard!" The internal dialogue for the latter individuals is not as complex as the internal dialogue for those who are threatened by negative stereotypes. The internal dialogue for such threatened individuals adds a greater amount of stress, which interferes with their ability to perform.

C. M. Steele (2001) suggested that no one is immune from negative stereotypes. He cited a study conducted at a major university on European Americans and African Americans. The negative stereotype for European American athletes is that they are not as naturally athletic as their African American counterparts, and the negative stereotype for African American athletes is that they do not think as well as their European American counterparts. The researchers of this study told half of the group of athletes that a certain miniature golf course measured one's true athletic abilities, and they told the other half that the course measured one's ability to engage in complex planning. As predicted by the stereotype threat theory, the European American athletes performed worse than their African American counterparts when told that the course measured true athletic abilities, and the African American athletes performed worse than their European American counterparts when told that the course measured complex planning abilities.

In an amusing example of how Steele himself fell victim to stereotype threat (C. Steele, 2012), he discussed a meeting he had with the dean of his college. Steele was the chair of the Psychology Department at Stanford, and Stanford had just restructured so that the college that previously included psychology, Humanities and Social Sciences, had merged with the College of Sciences to form the College of Humanities and Sciences. The dean of the new college was a scientist, and Steele was well aware of the history of psychology and its struggle to be recognized as a real science. The Psychology Department had requested a new magnetic resonance imaging

---

1 Students are allowed to take this written test multiple times to pass it and receive a degree. However, failure on this test even once is a blow to the self-esteem of a student who is bright, so even the brightest students feel pressure when taking the test.

machine for the study of areas of the brain that are activated under different conditions. The dean was curious about how psychologists use magnetic resonance imaging and, out of intellectual curiosity, asked Steele how psychologists use this piece of very expensive equipment. Steele laughingly recalled his somewhat tongue-tied attempt to explain how in psychology, scientists really do conduct sophisticated studies using magnetic resonance imaging. He noted that his performance was inhibited by his perceived inferiority as a psychologist trying to explain science to someone whose discipline was in the "hard" sciences.

What kinds of negative stereotypes apply to you? How would you respond? Have you ever been in a situation in which you were performing an activity that might support a negative stereotype about a group to which you belonged? Did your fear of confirming the stereotype interfere with your performance? If so, then you have firsthand experience of stereotype threat. According to C. M. Steele and his colleagues (Murphy, Steele, & Gross, 2007; C. M. Steele, 1997, 2001; C. M. Steele & Aronson, 1995), the signal of the threat can be subtle. For example, Murphy et al. (2007) signaled the threat subtly by showing women students of math, science, or engineering courses videotapes of such courses with either a balance of men and women or the number of men far outnumbering that of women. Remember, stereotype threat happens only if you have high ability in a particular area, performing well is part of your identity, and the task you are doing is difficult (or there is pressure on you to perform exceptionally well on the task).

In recent years, the focus of stereotype threat has been on how to eliminate or at least minimize this effect on performance (e.g., A. I. Alter, Aronson, Darley, Rodriguez, & Ruble, 2010; Casad & Merrit (2014); Forbes & Schmader, 2010; Regner et al., 2010; Sawyer, Major, Casad, Townsend, & Mendes, 2012; Shapiro, 2013; Shapiro, Williams, & Hambarchyan, 2013; Walton & Spencer, 2009). For example, A. I. Alter et al. replicated the stereotype threat effects when testing Black grade school children and college students in mathematics. However, when they reframed the task as a challenge, as opposed to a threat, students' performance was not negatively impacted. Have you ever encountered a difficult task, but when you reframed it as a challenge you performed better than you thought you would? Armenta (2010) discovered that positive stereotypes can boost performance under stereotype threat conditions. He also found that individuals who had high ethnic identities were positively or negatively affected by the stereotype, depending on whether the stereotype was positive or negative, whereas people with low ethnic identities were not affected by the stereotype. Walton and Spencer, in their extensive evaluation of numerous studies totaling nearly 18,000 research participants across five countries, found that under conditions of reduced psychological threat, students who were stereotyped performed better than nonstereotyped students. Have you found a positive stereotype about your groups to give you the confidence to perform better?

The Development of Negative Stereotypes

A biracial student wrote in one of her weekly reaction papers the following story about being stereotyped as a hoodlum:

> After working out at [name of fitness center] in Sherman Oaks I noticed two security guards. They were both White males. One was on his walkie-talkie, and I just knew he was on the radio about us. I turned to my friend and said, "Oh gosh, here we go, I bet they have something to say . . ." I turned the corner and the other security guard put his radio away, and walked up toward me. With his eyes toward my basketball, he asked, "Is that the property of [name of fitness center]?" I said, "No, there is no

basketball court, or basketballs at that facility. I'm sure [name of fitness center] didn't call you and complain about it."

So, he followed me as I continued to walk toward the parking lot. I was bouncing the ball in the outdoor area. He said, "Don't bounce your ball on our floors." I was pretty upset, and I replied, "Am I disturbing the stores that are all closed, and the people that are not shopping or eating? Is it wrong to bounce my ball on your floors of dirty concrete and old pieces of gum? My ball is cleaner than your floor. I am disturbing no one." He stood quiet. Suddenly, there was a Black security guard. When I looked back the other security guard was walking away, now at a far distance.

I couldn't figure out what had happened. I felt picked on, and belittled. I felt like I was some hoodlum who hadn't accomplished anything in life, and was destructive, as this is how I was treated. I realized that it just doesn't always matter who I am. People such as those guards will only see my outsides. I did notice their confusion from the way I spoke. My speaking probably wasn't what they expected from a Black person in sweats and a bandana. But, my way of speaking wouldn't outweigh my color, probably.

—Terri, 20+-year-old biracial (African American/Filipina) student

Another student told us about how a classmate stereotyped her ability to drive because she is of Asian descent:

Just this year, I recently encountered someone who had actually passed judgment verbally to me because I am Asian. In Fall Quarter, I was in class and I was given the option of going on a field trip for extra credit. The professor told me and my other classmates that we should carpool to get to the site. My friend (also of Asian descent) and I were asked by one of our classmates if we would like to carpool with him, but he told us, "I don't trust you guys driving." So we asked him why and he answered, "It's obvious . . . it's because you both are Asian." I have never had anyone flat out tell me that they did not trust me driving because of my race. People have joked about it but they end up getting in the car with me anyway and don't say a thing about how I drive. My friend and I ended up not carpooling [with him] because we were so offended by his comment. It makes me upset that I could not even defend myself or back myself up by saying that I have never received a ticket or gotten in an accident before. I took his comment to heart and felt so upset that someone could think that of me just because I am Asian.

—Michaela, 20+-year-old Japanese American student

How are negative stereotypes developed? Why do people hold such views? There are at least two ways in which such stereotypes are developed. One is somewhat benign and the other is somewhat malicious.

Hamilton and his colleagues have discussed how negative stereotypes can develop from normal cognitive processes (Hamilton, 1981; Hamilton, Dugan, & Trolier, 1985; Hamilton & Gifford, 1976; Hamilton & Rose, 1980; Hamilton & Sherman, 1989, 1994, 1996; Hamilton & Trolier, 1986). Essentially, this perspective suggests that people of color (and other numerical and identifiable minorities) are labeled with negative stereotypes because of an overestimation of negative behaviors that occur with their minority status. Hamilton says that when two minority events co-occur, there is a natural cognitive process that takes notice of that co-occurrence. Because special note is taken, the overestimation occurs. Hamilton states that negative events are not as frequent as positive events in our lives. If an person of color—who is in the statistical minority and by definition is less frequently encountered by the majority population—engages in a negative behavior, the observer sees two minority events happening together and registers that co-occurrence. Hamilton calls this overestimation **illusory correlation**, because the observer sees a correlation between the two events that does not really exist. Thus, if European Americans and Latinxs have engaged in the same percentage of shoplifting in the past, store managers and workers may feel that Latinxs engage in a greater amount of shoplifting (illusory correlation) because the co-occurrence of the minority group (Latinx) and the minority behavior (shoplifting) in the past had a greater impact on perception.

illusory correlation—an overestimation of the co-occurrence of two minority events.

As evidence for this stance, Hamilton and his colleagues conducted several studies that demonstrated the relative ease with which illusory correlation can occur (Hamilton, 1981; Hamilton, Dugan, & Trolier, 1985; Hamilton & Gifford, 1976; Hamilton & Rose, 1980; Hamilton & Sherman, 1989, 1994, 1996; Hamilton & Trolier, 1986). They conducted these studies even without using people of color as experimental stimuli. Research participants received descriptors of two groups of people (Group A and Group B). Participants received 16 descriptions of positive behaviors and attributes and 8 negative descriptors for Group A. They also received 8 descriptions of positive behaviors and attributes and 4 negative descriptors for Group B. Thus, the participants received half as many descriptions of Group B as they did of Group A, and there were half as many negative descriptions as there were positive descriptions. In other words, both Group B and negative behaviors/attributes were minority events. Later, when the participants were asked to recall all the positive and negative events for both Groups A and B, they recalled about twice as many positive descriptors as negative descriptors for Group A (an accurate recollection), but they recalled about equal amounts of positive and negative descriptors for Group B (an overestimation of negative descriptors). Illusory correlation has been confirmed by other researchers in the field (Ratliff & Nosek, 2010; Risen, Gilovich, & Dunning, 2007; Sherman et al., 2009; M. R. Smith & Alpert, 2007; Van Rooy, Vanhoomissen, & Van Overwalle, 2013).

One way of understanding Hamilton's series of studies is to view illusory correlation as a form of Tversky and Kahneman's well-known **availability heuristic** (Tversky & Kahneman, 1973). A heuristic is a mental shortcut or rule of thumb used for making calculations or assessments of sometimes complex circumstances. Availability is a specific kind of heuristic in which the perception of frequency, importance, or probability of an event is based on the ease with which the event comes to mind. In their original study, Tversky and Kahneman asked their research participants whether there were more words that began with the letter *k* or words with the letter *k* in the third position. Many more participants said that there were more words that began with the letter *k* even though there are three times as many words with *k* in the third position. Tversky and Kahneman suggested that because our minds are organized in something of a lexicon (dictionary-like) manner, it is easier to "look up" words that begin with the letter *k* than it is to look up words that have *k* in the third position. This relative ease in coming to mind was therefore translated

availability heuristic—a mental shortcut whereby the importance, frequency, or credence of something is exaggerated because it comes to mind easily.

into an assessment that there were more words that began with the letter *k*. If the co-occurrence (illusory correlation) of two minority events is noticed or registered more, it will come to mind more easily than the co-occurrence of two majority events or a majority and a minority event, so the co-occurring minority events will be judged to be more numerous or probable. Risen et al. (2007) suggested that illusory correlation can occur with a single co-occurrence if the group is rare and the behavior is unusual enough. Incidentally, Daniel Kahneman received the Nobel Prize for Economics in 2002 for his work with Amos Tversky because their work helped us understand how people allow heuristics to interfere with their economic decisions. Unfortunately, because Amos Tversky passed away in 1996, he was not able to share the honor with his friend and colleague.

As Tversky and Kahneman's (1973) study on the letter *k* demonstrates, sometimes the availability heuristic can lead us to wildly disparate conclusions. Could it be that stores and shops are overlooking a number of shoplifters because they are overly focused on customers of color? Quite possibly. The U.S. General Accounting Office (2000) found that this has been the case with screening airline passengers for possible drug trafficking: "Black and Hispanic men and women were about 4 to 9 times more likely than White men and women to be X-rayed after being patted down or frisked" (p. 13). Despite this disparity, women of color were *less* likely to be found with illegal drugs. According to the U.S. General Accounting Office, "Hispanic women, for example, were 4 times as likely to be X-rayed as White women were, but they were about two thirds as likely to have contraband found during an X-ray" (p. 15). This study concluded that the U.S. Customs Service would be more efficient if it did not engage in such biased racial profiling.

As we saw in the earlier story by Terry, many people recognize this racial profiling as "driving while Black" or "driving while Brown." A student of ours related this story:

> The first week I arrived in this country, I was stopped by the police. He said I matched the description of someone spotted with a gun. He searched me and found nothing. I then inquired what the description was. The man they were looking for was Hispanic. The only matching aspect of our descriptions was that we were both wearing blue jeans.
>
> —Godfrey, 20+-year-old Zimbabwean immigrant student

Because Godfrey was driving, the police would not have seen his blue jeans, so it seems they were targeting him because of the color of his skin. Again, racial profiling is *inefficient* because the police must spend some amount of time with an innocent person while the person who committed the crime is allowed more time to escape.

An extreme version of racial profiling was told to us by a former graduate student:

> There was a commotion down the street from my apartment. There was a party, and someone shot off a gun. It took the police over an hour to get there. I was standing outside just to see what was going on. The police came up to me and questioned me about if I saw anything, and they eventually asked me if I had a gun. I said no, but I continued to watch what they were doing. They stopped every single ethnic minority person who walked by, despite the fact that the gun shot was at a party where there were almost exclusively White students and the alleged gunman was White.
>
> —Ramón, 20+-year-old Mexican American student

A former student who was conducting a literature search in preparation for a class project was astonished by the amount of documented racial profiling:

> This project has really opened my eyes and made me sick. I can't believe that racial profiling is as prevalent as it actually is. I just don't want to believe that people automatically think someone is guilty or suspicious just because their skin color is slightly different. I guess it's one of those things that has developed in America and appears to be beyond control. They have made it illegal but it still exists; what can we do to change it?
>
> —Scott, 20+-year-old European American student

The less benign and more malicious reason negative stereotypes are developed is the need of people in power to justify the suppression of those who do not have power (Aronson, 1990; Mio, 2003). This stance is based on **cognitive dissonance theory** (Festinger, 1957). According to Festinger, attitudes follow behavior. Cognitive dissonance theory suggests that when two cognitions are in conflict (dissonance), people are motivated to reduce that dissonance, as they would be motivated to reduce hunger or thirst. Thus, if we were to observe ourselves behaving badly toward another person or a group of people,

> **cognitive dissonance theory**—when two cognitions are in conflict, a person will be motivated to change one of them to reduce the unsettled feelings caused by the discrepancy.

we might engage in the following internal dialogue: "I am a good person, but I behaved badly toward that other person. That person must have deserved such bad treatment." This reduces the dissonance and leaves us feeling justified in engaging in such negative behavior. As Aronson (1990) stated in his presidential address to the Western Psychological Association Convention, psychoanalytic theory suggests that if we felt hostility toward another individual, we should get the hostility out of our systems, and thus the process of catharsis would reduce our hostility toward that individual. However, cognitive dissonance theory predicted the opposite (and more correct) result: "If we hurt someone, it does not produce a release of hostile energy—on the contrary, it causes us to try to justify our actions by derogating our victim; this impels us to feel more hostility toward him, which opens the door for still further aggressions."

Racism

> Many people are familiar with the horrific case of Emmett Till (Williams, 1987). Till was a 14-year-old African-American boy from Chicago visiting his cousins in Mississippi. He was murdered, and his body was desecrated by Roy Bryant and J. W. Milam for simply saying "Bye, Baby" to Bryant's wife when leaving a general store. This was a famous case of racism made even more despicable by the fact that a defense lawyer addressed the all-White jury by concluding, "I'm sure that every last Anglo-Saxon one of you has the courage to free these men in the face of that [outside] pressure" (Williams, 1987, p. 52), and it took the jury one hour to find Bryant and Milam not guilty. They later acknowledged committing the murder because they were offended that Till would not beg for mercy for having flirted with Bryant's wife.
>
> —Jeremy, 40+-year-old Japanese American professor

Overt forms of racism are rarer nowadays. *Photograph by John Gomez/Shutterstock*

The historic Black–White relationship has set the context within which racism has been discussed in the United States. The first African slaves in the United States arrived in 1619, when 20 slaves were sold to settlers in Virginia (Kitano, 1999). By 1860, shortly before the Civil War, nearly one-third of the population in slave-owning states and the District of Columbia were slaves (4 million of 12.1 million total population; Black, 1996). Although only 25% of the population owned slaves, the overwhelming majority of individuals in slave-owning states supported the practice for economic reasons. Moreover, according to Black, "slavery also provided even the poorest of Whites with a sense of superiority over the African population, a superiority based on skin color" (p. 58). For centuries, European Americans tried to justify slavery, then segregation, and then general mistreatment of African Americans in the United States. Consequently, institutional practices developed over the years disadvantaging African Americans and other people of color.

Wise (2008, 2013) identified various laws that were explicitly designed to advantage European American individuals over African American individuals. For example, in response to the Great Depression, one of President Roosevelt's Fair Deal programs was called *job insurance*, also known as unemployment insurance. This program gave money to individuals who were laid off from work for a period of time until they could find another job. However, to pass this legislation, President Roosevelt had to make a deal with Southern politicians to exclude people who worked in agriculture or those who were domestic workers in private homes from receiving unemployment insurance. Although these exclusions did not overtly identify race as the reason for this policy, the effect was racist, because the overwhelming majority of people working in agriculture or as domestic workers were African American, and over 80% of all African Americans in the country worked in these two areas. Another part of the Fair Deal was the Federal Housing Authority loans. This program was designed to help people buy their first houses, but for the first 28 years of the program (1934–1962), 98% of the recipients were European American, because the loan applications from people of color were almost routinely denied. Finally, as an example of legal discrimination, Wise identified the GI Bill for soldiers returning from World War II. This program was designed to reintegrate soldiers returning from the war into society by giving them things such as low-interest mortgage loans, low-interest start-up loans for business, and money and living expenses to attend colleges and universities. However, the overwhelming majority of recipients were European American, and people of color were excluded from these benefits. Wise further pointed out that when government assistance programs are given to European Americans, they are called *benefits* or *earned insurance*, but when such programs are given to people of color, they are termed *welfare* or *handouts*.

Another example of overt racism in the United States comes from World War II. As most people know, Americans of Japanese ancestry in seven U.S. states (California, Idaho, Utah, Arizona, Wyoming, Colorado, and Arkansas) were *interned* (a euphemism for *imprisoned*) during the war (Nagata, 1993, 1998). Following the attack on Pearl Harbor, the U.S. government felt that these people were a threat to national security and moved them to concentration camps in the interior of the country. These Japanese Americans and resident aliens were transported with little warning, and *evacuation sales* were forced on many of them. The following story, which occurred in 1942, describes such a sale:

> We had two restaurants, and they were being taken away from us. In only a few days, I had to sell everything I could or else lose all that we had. I had to do this alone, because my husband was taken away the day the evacuation order was given because he was considered a community leader. All of these Americans came to our community to get the best deal they could. They didn't care that our lives were being taken away from us. I remember trying to sell one of our refrigerators for $10. A White woman said, "That refrigerator isn't worth $10. I wouldn't give you more than $5 for it." She was so uncaring; they were so uncaring. Our lives were being ruined, and all they cared about was taking away our possessions for as little money as they could.
>
> —Makiko, 80+-year-old Japanese American grandparent (translated from Japanese)

Our Japanese American student who encountered the stereotype of Asians not being good drivers believed that these stories of racism were ancient history. However, she encountered a taste of racism herself and began to relate to Makiko's story:

> When my grandparents told me all of their stories where they were always discriminated [against], I could never relate to them because I have grown in such a multicultural community. My family is even multi-ethnic, so our family does not discriminate against anyone. Unfortunately, I experienced my first taste of racism and discrimination last year. I was headed to Big Bear with a Japanese American club on campus and we stopped off in [Redwood] where we got something to eat. I did not know this, but Redwood is predominantly Caucasian, so walking into Carls Jr. felt a little awkward for the whole club. Everyone was staring at us and we could hear the teenagers saying things like "Chinks" and "Japs." None of them said anything directly to us, but we could hear the snickering and the way everyone was looking at us. When we decided to leave, some people drove past us bowing with their hands together in front of them and they yelled, "Go home, Chinks!" . . . That moment made me realize that my grandparents had to go through this every day for most of their lives.
>
> —Michaela, 20+-year-old Japanese American student

Overt racism can also be hidden from the public. A former student told this story of when he was in the workforce:

> I worked at an office that was almost exclusively White. I was in the office of our personnel manager who had a stack of White applicant files to the company and a stack of minority applicant files to the company. This guy looked right at me and said, "The law says that I must carefully consider these minority applicants. You are a witness that I have carefully considered them," and then he threw the stack of minority applicant files into the trash can. I couldn't believe he did that right in front of me.
>
> —Gary, 30+-year-old biracial (Asian Indian/Mexican) student

Overt racism is often thought to be a relic of our past and not relevant to modern discussions of racism. In general, overt forms of racism are not as common as they used to be and the public does not condone them. Modern forms of racism are much more subtle and difficult to detect. We must be aware of them so that we can eliminate their influence on our everyday lives.

> Our department was in the process of interviewing candidates for a tenure-track faculty position. As was our custom, each candidate interviewed with two faculty members at a time. On this particular day, I was paired up with one of our newest and youngest faculty members, a European American male. The candidate was also a European American male, but he was older, probably in his mid- to late-forties. We met in my office for the interview and, as the senior member of the team, I took the lead in asking the questions. I soon noticed that, although I asked most of the questions, the candidate directed all of his answers to my colleague. The candidate would not look at me, would not have eye contact with me, and even turned in his chair so he was facing my colleague. At the end of the interview, I stood up to shake the candidate's hand and say goodbye, but he turned his back and walked out the door and down the hallway without acknowledging me. I looked stunned, and so did my colleague, who turned and looked at me, a little red in the face, and just shrugged his shoulders. In the faculty meeting when we discussed the candidates, I shared this story and my colleague spoke up and confirmed that he experienced the interaction the same way I did. Interestingly, some other faculty members seemed to have been making excuses for his behavior, and one of the faculty members was even supportive of hiring him. However, fortunately, he had alienated many of the other female faculty members, too, and our department decided against making an offer to him.
>
> —Linda, 30+-year-old African American professor

This story illustrates a subtle (or not so subtle) racist interaction that had costs for both the recipient and the offender. For the recipient, it was yet another slight in a long list of such insults. We all desire to have positive interactions, and each negative one stings. This interaction is an example of a racial microaggression, which will be discussed later in this chapter. For the offender, the obvious cost was that he was not offered a position in the department. A less apparent cost was that if this individual was completely unaware of how racist he appeared in the interview, then he is destined to continue to offend others and be prevented from furthering his professional career.

Our students have related many encounters with modern forms of racism:

> As a Mexican American female, I am always conscious of my racial identity, even though I have assimilated into the dominant culture. In American society, racial labels are very important. Everybody has to fit into a category. These categories allow people to generalize certain characteristics to a group. These stereotypes are often inaccurate. Recently, I was shopping at the Riverside Galleria, when an older White lady approached to ask me a question. Mistakenly, she confused me for a worker. It was an honest mistake until she questioned my ability to speak English. I was very offended by her preconceived notion. She presumed that because I am Latina, I must not speak English correctly. She did not realize how offensive her comment was and did not bother to apologize. On the other hand, I contemplate why this is a frequent

encounter. As a minority, I am always pointed out that I am not part of the dominant society. I have done what society has asked me to do and assimilated. In the process, I lost my ancestral past. . . .

Recently I went to [name of upscale department store] with my mother to purchase her a perfume. A White female was working in the counter and refused to help me by pretending to be busy with paperwork. I stood at the counter for 3 minutes and no service. I finally left the counter and asked someone else to help me. The other salesperson was just as rude as the original clerk. Their behavior made me very uncomfortable and angry. At first, I just wanted to leave and not buy anything. I thought, Why should I spend my money here? But I did not leave. I was not going to let their discrimination break my spirit. My mother, on the other hand, was saddened by the experience. She refused the perfume I bought her because it was tainted by hate.

—Juanita, 20+-year-old Mexican American student

When I first got the job I am currently at I had many problems with people talking about me and trying to keep me down. I am a very proud and intelligent person. I always held my head high no matter where I am and I believe they were very intimidated by that. Especially because I talked like I had some sense. Sometimes some of my co-workers would ask me if I was mixed because I don't talk "Black," whatever that is supposed to mean. Even other African Americans tell me I talk White and that really upsets me because when they tell me that they are only bringing themselves down. When an African American tells me I talk like I am "White" just because I speak intelligently, it makes them look like they're unintelligent. Can't an African American speak intelligently without being told they are acting "White"?

—Ariel, 20+-year-old African American student

In the past, racism was overt and vicious; in the modern world, racism is disguised and subtle. To stop it, we must be able to identify modern forms of racism and make others aware of the ways in which they perpetuate it. Main forms of modern racism are *overt/covert racism*, *aversive racism, color-blind racial ideology*, and *racial microaggressions*.

Overt Versus Covert Racism

Ridley (1989, 1995) discussed the distinction between *overt* and *covert racism*. **Overt racism** is *old-style* racism, in which those in the majority openly engaged in hostile and aggressive acts against people of color without fear of reprisal. Such acts included slavery, lynchings, and legal segregation (J. M. Jones, 1997). J. M. Jones's important book took a Black–White perspective, so those examples of overt

overt racism—discriminatory behavior in which people in the majority engage in open, hostile acts of aggression against racial minorities consciously and unapologetically.

racism are consistent with that theme. Hostility toward Blacks, the devastation of the American Indian population and the later boarding-school policy that took American Indian children as young as 5 years old hundreds or thousands of miles away from their parents and tribes and "educated" them in Western ways (McDonald & Chaney, 2003; Tafoya & Del Vecchio, 1996, 2005), the internment of Americans of Japanese descent during World War II (Mio et al., 2007; Nagata, 1990a, 1990b, 1993, 1998), and social oppression of Latinx by the Immigration and Naturalization Service (now called Immigration and Customs Enforcement; Garcia-Preto,

1996, 2005) are just a few examples of how overt racism has affected the broad spectrum of people of color in the United States. Although overt racism may be thought to be a thing of the past, many of our students have reported being the victim of overt racism or seeing it firsthand:

> I have personally been detained for reasons of DWB [driving while Black]. So often in fact that it was one of the first things I discussed with my son when teaching him how to drive. "Always wear your seatbelt, signal long before you intend to turn, and when approached by the police, keep your hands on the steering wheel until instructed to move, and then do so slowly."
>
> I have been given many excuses for being stopped including "you appeared to be weaving back there," and "we've had a rash of robberies in the area and are stopping everyone." But now and then a police officer will just come outright and state "this doesn't look like a car that you would own." Most of the time I simply sit quietly because if you speak up, you're asking for a ticket, or worse.
>
> —Mike, 40+-year-old African American student

> My best friend Theresa has been dating an African American man for the past year. You would think that it wasn't a big deal, except she is White and her mother will not accept the relationship. . . . Obviously, this is very difficult for my friend. She cries almost once every week and often questions her relationship with her boyfriend. It is not his fault, however, there are times when she feels guilty, responsible for her mom's tears and disappointment. I personally have spent hours talking to her, reassuring her that her mom is wrong, that she is ignorant. At times I wonder if she will ever accept the relationship, what it would take for her to understand that she is racist?
>
> Theresa's mother does not believe that she is a racist, nor that she is ignorant. When I come over to the house she yells at me, asking me what kind of friend I am to support this. Then she usually follows with questions about what kind of men I date and when I plan to start dating "Blacks." It gives me the sickest feeling, I look at her with such shame. This is a woman that I once looked at as a second mother, never knowing her racist views. Now I am embarrassed to know her.
>
> —Barbara, 20+-year-old European American woman

covert, intentional racism— discriminatory behavior that is intentional but is covered up so that one can deny his or her racism.

Ridley (1995) identified *covert racism* as a modern form of racism that seems subtle and even deniable. According to Ridley, covert racism can be either *intentional* or *unintentional*. **Covert, intentional racism** occurs when individuals are aware that they are acting in a racist manner but try to disguise their true intent with a plausible story.

Many people believe that affirmative action draws covert, intentional racists. Certainly, there are individuals who want to eliminate affirmative action for principled reasons, such as the ideal of equality for all and the belief that favoring one group over another necessarily discriminates against the group not being favored. However, other individuals oppose affirmative action as a covert, intentional way of impeding the progress of people of color.

As discussed in Chapter 1, the election of Barack Obama as president of the United States, twice, was not proof that racism no longer existed (Ifil, 2009, Mio, 2016). Instead, the seeds of a whitelash were sown that culminated in the election of Donald Trump eight years later (Coates, 2017).

Mio (2016) pointed out that modern forms of racism such as covert, intentional racism were used to discredit President Obama almost immediately. First, some people did not believe that President Obama was born in the United States. They contended that Hawaii was not a state when Obama was born. However, when they discovered that Obama was born in 1961 and Hawaii became a state in 1959, they posited that he was secretly born in Kenya, although Hawaii produced a birth certificate for Obama and there was a newspaper report of his birth in 1961. In fact, Orly Taitz, a woman who took the issue of Obama's citizenship to extremes, was accused of falsifying a birth certificate for Obama in Kenya. The birth certificate was clearly falsified because it included many mistakes, such as saying it was issued by "The Republic of Kenya," which is not consistent with how birth certificates were issued in Kenya at the time Obama was born. Taitz was fined $20,000 for her frivolous lawsuit by a U.S. District Court judge (Turley, 2009) Although these are clearly ploys to discredit President Obama, conservative talk radio and television hosts continued to perpetuate such rumors, such that a significant percentage of Americans believed the discrediting information (Zuma, 2010).

> A Black man can't be president of America. However, an extraordinary, gifted, and talented young man who happens to be Black can be president.
> —Cornell Belcher, pollster for Barack Obama

A second attempt to discredit President Obama was to call him a *closet Muslim* because he spent several years as a youth growing up in Indonesia, a predominantly Muslim country. This criticism put President Obama in a difficult position because he both respected the Islamic religion and wanted to repair relations with Muslim countries that had been frayed as a result of U.S. policies, but he also had been a member of a Christian church for over 20 years. This issue was highlighted against a backdrop of growing animosity toward Muslims in this country (Ghosh, 2010; L. Miller, 2010; Zakaria, 2010), characterizing them as anti-American, terrorists, and the like. Although such attempts to discredit President Obama by claiming he was not born in the United States or that he is a closet Muslim are "outlandish" (J. Alter, 2010) and fueled by conservative commentators such as Glenn Beck (Baird, 2010; Begley, 2010), about one-quarter of the American public now believes these discrediting attempts. Sears (1988) would call such

Many people hoped that the election of Barack Obama as president of the United States would signal a postracial period in the United States, but detractors use modern forms of racism such as covert, intentional racism to oppose him. *Photograph by Action Sports Photography/Shutterstock*

symbolic racism—an issue that does not overtly involve race but is used to promote racism through issues that are associated with one racial group and not the European American majority group, even if this association is not real or is exaggerated.

attempts **symbolic racism**: issues that are resisted on the basis of race, but race is not technically discussed. Voter identification laws are considered another example of covert, intentional racism. Since 2006, 33 states have passed and implemented voter identification laws, citing concerns of illegal voting. However, every independent, scholarly study indicates that actual voter fraud is almost nonexistent (see the Brennan Center for Justice in the New York University of Law for an extensive list of studies, reports, and court rulings, https://www.brennancenter.org/analysis/resources-voter-fraud-claims). For example, Levitt (2014) conducted a comprehensive study of state and national elections from 2000 to 2014, in which over 1 billion votes were cast. He found only 31 documented cases of people intentionally attempting to vote illegally; thus, the chances of someone committing voter fraud is less than .0000000031! An individual has a greater chance of being struck by lightning (1 in 3000), bitten by a shark (1 in 3.7 million), attacked by a bear (1 in 2.1 million), or being struck by a meteor (1 in 1.6 million)! If voter fraud is not a problem, then why are such voting laws being implemented? And what does this have to do with racism? In a recent study, Hajnal, Lajevardi, and Nielson (2017) found that strict voter identification laws have a differential impact on racial groups. They used actual voting data for different racial groups between 2006 and 2014 and thus were able to see the effect before and after voter identification laws were implemented. In general, a gap already exists between European American voter turnout and people of color, for many historical reasons. However, when strict voter identification laws were implemented, the gap increased significantly. The White–Black turnout gap increased from 2.9 to 5.1 points in general elections and from 2.5 to 11.6 points in primary elections after strict voter identification laws were passed. For Latinx voters, the gap was 4.9 to 13.2 in general elections and 3.4 to 13.2 in primary elections. For Asians, the turnout gap was 6.5 to 11.5 points in general elections and 5.8 to 18.8 points in primary elections. These differences in voter turnout equate to hundreds of thousands of people. American Indian voters are also negatively impacted. Many Native voters only have tribe-issued identification cards, which are a federally recognized form of identification, although many local polling stations would not accept them because the voter identification laws do not list them as valid forms of identification (Brewer, 2016). On the surface, voter identification laws seem to make sense. However, as the studies above indicate, they negatively impact people of color and indigenous people. Moreover, recent legal challenges and the rulings by U.S. 4th Circuit Court of Appeals over North Carolina's voter identification law stated that the law was purposefully discriminatory, targeting people of color to disenfranchise their right to vote (Herbet & Lang, 2016). The above discussion of affirmative action is an example of symbolic racism, so symbolic racism and covert, intentional racism overlap substantially.

Ridley (1995) felt that **covert, unintentional racism** is much more insidious and pervasive than covert, intentional racism. Such racism may be expressed by anyone—even people who would consider themselves enlightened. However, covert, unintentional racism is generally expressed by individuals who are unaware of the racist traditions of this country and perpetuate such racism without thought. A story that one of us (JSM) tells in regard to covert, unintentional racism involves a discussion he had with a high school friend:

covert, unintentional racism—discriminatory behavior that is unintentional but serves to perpetuate ongoing racist acts or traditions.

We were wondering who would be quarterback for the high school the following year, after Vince Ferragamo graduated. (I was in Ferragamo's graduating class, but I was worried for my friend's class the next year.) He suggested the name of an African American at the school, and I asked, "How could he be quarterback?" My friend said that this guy had a great arm, was fast, and could make quick decisions, but I still wondered how he could be quarterback. I had heard that Blacks could not be quarterbacks, and I blindly accepted this view, not knowing why people were saying such things. . . . I did not know that Blacks could become quarterbacks, as there were no professional Black quarterbacks at that time and very few on major college football teams. Boy, was I naive! (Mio & Awakuni, 2000, p. 22)

Another example of covert, unintentional racism came right after the 2002 Winter Olympics. Asians are often viewed as forever alien. Michele Kwan was one of America's best female figure skaters. She was born in the United States. In fact, her parents were born in the United States, so her family has been part of the American tradition for decades. During the 1998 Winter Olympics, when Tara Lipinski unexpectedly beat Michelle Kwan for the gold medal, a headline on the MSNBC website read,

American Beats Out Michelle Kwan

The headline implied that Kwan was not American. Four years later, on February 22, 2002, when Sarah Hughes beat out Kwan for the gold medal, the *Seattle Times* (a newspaper in Washington State, which at the time had the only governor of Asian descent in the continental 48 states) displayed this headline:

Hughes Good as Gold: American Beats Out Kwan, Slutskaya

Again, the headline implied that Kwan was not American. After being flooded with angry letters, the editorial staff of the *Seattle Times* recognized its error and apologized. Initially, the newspaper explained the error by offering the rationale behind the headline: it did not want to repeat Hughes's name in the subheadline, so it replaced "Hughes" with "American." However, the public saw the explanation as an excuse and demanded that the newspaper take full responsibility for the error. The paper then issued a second, more sincere apology.

American Indian people face many similar examples and constant reminders of this type of racism in society. For example, the use of American Indian mascots, nicknames, and logos by sports teams continues to cause outrage and controversy. One of the most notorious examples occurred after the killing of Osama bin Laden, when the following message was transmitted to then President Obama in his situation room:

Geronimo E-KIA

As it turned out, Geronimo was the codename given to bin Laden by the U.S. military and *E-KIA* stands for "Enemy Killed in Action." This is problematic on several levels. First, many American Indian tribes consider Geronimo a hero. To use his name for the world's most notorious terrorist is extremely insulting. Second, the underlying message portrays and reinforces the idea of American Indian people as the forever enemy of the United States, which has historical significance. Third, using Geronimo as the codename for bin Laden negates and ignores the fact that, percentage wise, American Indians serve in the military more than any other racial group (Grover, 2015; Schilling, 2014), dating back to the Civil War. Ironically, in the post 9/11 era, which marked bin Laden as the world's most wanted terrorist, 18.6% of the American Indian population has served in the military compared to only 14% of the general population.

Ridley feels that covert, unintentional racism is perhaps the most damaging of all forms of racism because it is practiced by well-intentioned individuals who do not see themselves as racist at all. They are not motivated to change their behaviors or perceptions because they do not equate themselves with obvious, overt racists of the past or the present.

The Response to Hurricane Maria: A Case of Covert, Unintentional Racism or Covert, Intentional Racism?

In the previous edition of this book, we discussed how the government's slow response to Hurricane Katrina may have been a case of covert, unintentional racism. President George W. Bush's praise of Federal Emergency Management Agency director Michael Brown ("Brownie, you're doing a heck of a job"; https://www.CNN.com, 2017), despite clear indication that the agency was not responding quickly, caused many to believe that the response was a case of racism, whether intentional or not. This criticism struck President Bush particularly hard because he viewed himself as a compassionate, nonracist individual.

Over a decade later, another hurricane revealed a possible case of covert, unintentional racism, although many felt that it was more of a case of covert, intentional racism (Arrigoitía, 2017; Holmes, 2017; J. A. Pearson, 2017). This case involves the response of president Donald Trump's administration to Hurricane Maria, which devastated Puerto Rico. Earlier in the year, Hurricane Harvey had flooded the city of Houston and Hurricane Irma had devastated many areas of the state of Florida, and the response of the Federal Emergency Management Agency was immediate. Within a few days, President Trump visited these areas and oversaw their rebuilding in relatively quick manner. For example, power was knocked out in Houston and many areas of Florida, but within days, power was restored (Reyes, 2017). In contrast, President Trump did not visit Puerto Rico until 2 weeks after the hurricane hit the island.

President Trump uses Twitter nearly every day to comment on many different matters. Hurricane Maria hit on September 5, 2017, after the National Football League season had begun, and at the time, President Trump seemed obsessed with criticizing players who knelt during the National Anthem to protest treatment of African Americans in the United States, particularly treatment by the police. Even after national attention turned to the devastating effect of Hurricane Maria on Puerto Rico, President Trump continued to post tweets in criticism of the football players. President Trump first tweeted about Puerto Rico 5 days after the hurricane hit. However, the tweet did not express compassion toward the Puerto Rican people—who are all American citizens—but criticized Puerto Rico for its massive debt and poor infrastructure (Lluveras, 2017; Reyes, 2017; Varela, 2017).

The seemingly uncaring attitude toward Puerto Rico pervaded the Trump administration. Elaine Duke, the homeland security secretary, said that Puerto Rico exemplified a "good news story" 11 days after Hurricane Maria hit the island because many supplies were sitting on the dock in the port of San Juan, Puerto Rico. However, millions of people in the interior of the island had not received any assistance. They had no power, no food, and no drinkable water. The fact that the supplies were sitting on the dock meant that they were not being distributed to people in need (Arrigoitía, 2017). In Secretary Duke's defense, President Trump complained that the Puerto Rican people did not want to work for their own recovery, but wanted everything to be done for them, despite plenty of evidence to the contrary (M. T. Garcia, 2017).

Many observers (M. T. Garcia, 2017) felt that President Trump was trying to invoke the lazy Mexican stereotype to characterize the Puerto Rican people.

When President Trump finally visited Puerto Rico to bring attention to the plight of its people, he undermined the recovery effort by again discussing Puerto Rico's debt, its poor infrastructure, and the fact that it was surrounded by water, so it was difficult to get relief to the island (Lluveras, 2017). President Trump also refused to waive the Jones Act, which prevented ships from foreign countries from providing relief to Puerto Rico for several days after the hurricane hit (Reyes,

Many felt that President Trump flipping paper towels into a crowd in Puerto Rico underscored his insensitivity to their real plight in the aftermath of Hurricane Maria. *Photo by AP/Shutterstock*

2017). Finally, President Trump asserted that Hurricane Maria was not a "real tragedy" like Hurricane Katrina because the death toll on the island was much lower than the death toll in New Orleans (Holmes, 2017). At the time, the reported death toll was far below 100, but by the end of November, it had reached 1,230 (Carrero, 2018). Moreover, in what seemed to some a flippant move, President Trump tossed paper towels into a crowd of people who were there to hear his remarks about the tragedy (J. A. Pearson, 2017).

On the one hand, some people believe that the Trump administration's response to Hurricane Maria was a case of covert, unintentional racism; on the other hand, others might assess it as a case of covert, intentional racism. Many people have connected President Trump's response to Hurricane Maria with his seeming animosity to all people of color, as evidenced by the previously mentioned criticism of African American football players kneeling in protest during the National Anthem (Reyes, 2017; Varela, 2017); his lack of knowledge of basic African American history (a statement made by President Trump implied that Frederick Douglass is a current figure who is gaining acclaim, although in fact Douglass lived over 100 years ago; Holmes, 2017); his assertion that judge Gonzalo Curiel could not judge Trump fairly merely

We only came here to try to help a few thousand because nobody had a plan to feed Puerto Rico, and we opened the biggest restaurant in the world in a week. That's how crazy this is.

—Jose Andres,
celebrity chef

Jose Andres, celebrity chef, who served over 2.2 million hot meals and sandwiches in only the first 5 weeks after Hurricane Maria hit the island *Photograph by Eric Rojas/ New York Times*

because Curiel is of Mexican descent; his presidential campaign based on building a wall between the United States and Mexico and deporting all undocumented immigrants; and his criticism of Khzir Khan, a Gold Star father whose son was killed in Iraq while protecting his unit (J. A. Pearson, 2017). J. A. Pearson wrote, "Broadly speaking, a racist combines negative prejudicial biases with sufficient power to leverage action against targeted groups." To be classified as covert, unintentional racism, an action must be truly unintentional, and if the underlying racism is brought to the surface, the person engaging in the action will take immediate corrective action. To be classified as covert, intentional racism, the covertness of the action provides "plausible deniability" that racism was the true intent, but when the underlying racism of the action is brought to the surface, the person does not engage in corrective action. How do you assess the response to Hurricane Maria?

As another example of unintentional racism, students at Cal Poly Pomona have the opportunity to visit historic civil rights–era locations in the Deep South during the school's spring break. Students who have made this pilgrimage have reported to me how emotionally meaningful the trip has been. However, the most striking injustice they feel is when they visit graves in the Deep South. The graveyards are segregated by race, with the European American portion being neatly manicured and maintained, whereas the African American portion is overgrown with weeds. As part of their experience, the leader of this pilgrimage asks all the students to care for the African American portion of the graveyards they visit. Students are happy to do so, feeling that it is a small gesture they can make toward combatting racism.

Aversive Racism

aversive racism—covert, unintentional discriminatory behavior practiced by individuals who would deny being racist and who would be appalled to realize that they were engaging in racist acts.

Gaertner and Dovidio (1986) discussed **aversive racism**, a form of racism practiced by individuals who believe that they are not racist at all and who would find it offensive or aversive if they were thought to be racist. When their unconsciously racist views surface, these individuals cite logical or common-sense reasons for their views and thereby deny that they are racist. This form of racism is related to Ridley's covert, unintentional racism.

Dovidio (2001) and Dovidio and Gaertner (2000) reported support for their aversive racism concept. For example, when making hiring decisions between African American and European American candidates, individuals who scored high on the authors' aversive racism scale hired European American candidates rather than their African American counterparts. When given the opportunity to discuss their decisions, aversive racists focused on the strengths of the European American candidates and the weaknesses of the African American candidates. Another group of aversive racists hired more European American candidates than African American candidates, but although the candidates' qualifications were opposite those of the first set of candidates, the second group's reasoning also focused on the strengths of the European American candidates and the weaknesses of the African American candidates. In other words, hiring decisions were based on the opposite qualifications, yet the two groups always favored the European American candidates and had "logical" reasons to back up their decisions. Figures 6.1 and 6.2 show Mio's (2003) depictions of data from Dovidio and Gaertner's (2000) study.

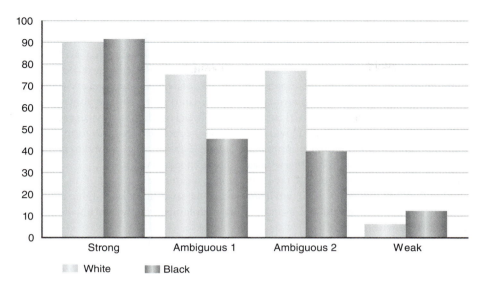

FIGURE 6.1 Representation of Dovidio & Gaertner (2000) data on aversive racism—probability of being hired. In Ambiguous 1, the European American candidate was strong on Criterion A and weak on Criterion B, whereas the African American candidate was weak on Criterion A and strong on Criterion B. In Ambiguous 2, the European American candidate was weak on Criterion A and strong on Criterion B, whereas the African American candidate was strong on Criterion A and weak on Criterion B. However, the European American candidate had a higher probability of being hired in both ambiguous situations.

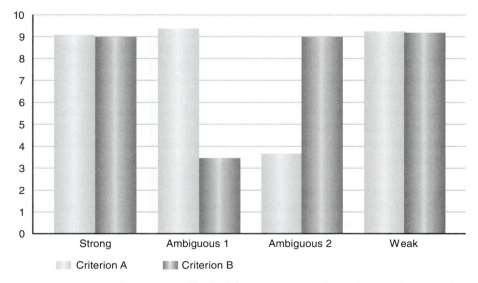

FIGURE 6.2 Ratings of importance of both of the criteria in Dovidio & Gaertner (2000) study.

Aversive racism has been repeatedly found to be a useful conceptualization for many modern forms of racism (de França & Monteiro, 2013; Dovidio & Gaertner, 2008; Dovidio, Gaertner, Penner, Pearson, & Norton, 2009; Henkel, Dovidio, & Gaertner, 2006; A. R. Pearson, Dovidio, & Gaertner, 2009; Penner et al., 2010; Rodenborg & Boisen, 2013). Henkel et al. (2006) interpreted the response to Hurricane Katrina in terms of aversive racism. Penner et al. (2010) found that African American patients consistently had less positive reactions to services they received from non–African American physicians than to services they received from African American physicians. Dovidio et al. (2009) concluded that this form of modern racism is so pervasive that it behooves us to educate people about its effects and to find ways to combat such discrimination from otherwise well-intentioned individuals.

Some aversive racists may excuse racist symbols as meaningless or part of tradition, with no intent to create a hostile racist environment. One student talked about an African American friend who encountered aversive racists explaining confederate flags flying all around a small town:

> My friend, who is African American, is so excited to finally be finished up and is ready to go out and work as a full-blown doctor. He was offered a couple of different jobs and was telling me about how vastly different two of them were. For instance, he was offered a job in southern Georgia. He was explaining to me how different he felt from everyone else in that town because he was the only Black person around anywhere. He told me he felt like everyone was looking at him strangely, "as if they had never seen a Black man before." He himself never saw another Black or ethnic person in that town during the couple of days he was there. But, he did tell me he saw confederate flags hanging everywhere throughout the town on buildings, cars, in restaurants, and even inside the place where he was interviewing. He said this also made him feel really uncomfortable. Also, after his interview he told me that another doctor came up to him and told him not to worry about all the confederate flags hanging throughout their town. "It is just tradition around here," the doctor told my friend. "It doesn't mean anything though so don't worry about it," he said. This was another red flag for my friend not to take this job even though he was offered it. This made me realize, once again, that we still have a long way to go. It seems that racism will never be eradicated but it can certainly be decreased more, especially in areas where there isn't much diversity. It almost seems like the doctor who told my friend not to worry about the confederate flags was almost excusing the town's racist mentality by saying that it is just part of their tradition. This scares me. How can racism become a tradition? Sadly, it does for some.
>
> —Guadalupe, 20+-year-old Mexican American student

Mujcic and Frijters (2013) illustrated another example of aversive racism. In their ingenious study, the authors asked European American and African American patrons to attempt to ride public transit using an expired bus pass. Individuals were instructed to board the bus and insert their bus pass. Because the pass had expired, the meter would make a sound and a red light would flash. The authors asked the riders to inform the driver that they had a very important appointment about a mile down the route and ask whether they could please ride for free, just this once. All riders told the same story at random places around the city. The results were astonishing: 72% of the time, the driver allowed the European American person to ride for free, but only 36% of the time did he or she allow the African American person to ride for free. A difference was even observed when the bus driver was African American: 83% of European Americans received a free ride, whereas only 68% of African Americans received a free ride. The authors then added a twist and had the riders wear military uniforms indicating they were veterans. In this case, European American veterans rode for free 97% of the time, but the African American veterans only rode for free 77% of the time. We have no reason to doubt that the bus drivers were good, decent people who believe they are not racist or engaging in racism. In fact, they could easily justify denying the African American riders a free ride, because their bus passes had no more fare. However, at the same time, they provided discriminatory gifts to the European Americans and gave them a free pass. This example illustrates how insidious aversive racism can be.

Although the following story is an example of aversive sexism rather than aversive racism, the principle is the same. The story was told by a colleague in a department with two different disciplines. One division had a gender balance, whereas the other division was all male. The names of the colleague and the department have been withheld to protect both from reprisal.

> My department was conducting searches a few years ago. The other division had two positions for which it was searching. One of the positions was a "generalist" position, and the other position was a "specialty" one. The top two candidates for each position were a man and a woman. The generalist candidates differed in that the woman was finishing up her dissertation and the man had a postdoctoral position. The woman had one publication and several conference presentations, and her references said that she was a very promising candidate. The man, who had received his PhD several years before, had a few publications and a contract for a book. The specialty candidates differed in that the man was finishing up his dissertation. Although he did not have any publications, he had several conference presentations, and his references said that he was a very promising candidate. The woman, who had received her PhD several years before, had a few publications, had already published a book, and had received two fairly substantial grants. Amazingly, the chair of the search committee recommended that we offer the generalist position to the male candidate because he was a proven individual, and he also recommended that we offer the specialty position to the male candidate because he was a promising individual. Despite the fact that all of the women from my division of the department voiced their opposition to this ranking of candidates, the chair of the search committee stood his ground, feeling that he had made the right choices. It wasn't until a man from our division voiced his opposition to this ranking that the chair of the search committee agreed to reconsider the rankings. Sexism is alive and well in modern academia.
>
> —Lonnie, 30+-year-old European American woman

Racism and the Biopsychosocial Model

As we have demonstrated, racism is not just one thing; it exists in several forms. Many arguments about race occur because of misunderstandings about its different forms. The biopsychosocial model discussed in Chapter 1 can help with understanding the different types of racism (see Figure 1.1).

Remember, the biopsychosocial model has five levels—biological, cognitive-affective, social-interpersonal, social institutional, and cultural. With regard to racism, let's begin at the cognitive-affective level, which addresses thoughts and feelings. Stereotyping and prejudice exist at the cognitive-affective level and are the building blocks of racism at the individual level. As mentioned previously, *stereotypes* are expectations or generalizations about a person's behavior based on membership in a group. Therefore, stereotypes reflect beliefs one holds regarding individuals who belong to different groups. When evaluations are added to stereotypes, they become *prejudice*, which refers to judgments—positive or negative—about someone based on their membership in a particular group. More specifically, racial prejudice or racial bias involves attitudes toward a particular person or group because of race, So, an individual person can harbor racist thoughts and feelings.

When an individual acts on those negative thoughts and feelings, racism becomes interpersonal. The social-interpersonal level of the biopsychosocial model examines the dynamics of social relationships. Generally, when people use the term racism, they are referring to *interpersonal racism*, or negative treatment of someone simply because he or she belongs to a particular racial group. As mentioned previously, this is the definition of *discrimination*. When a landlord refuses to rent an apartment to a family because of its race, an employer decides not to hire an applicant because of her race, or a sales associate follows a customer around a store because of his race, this is discrimination, or racism at the social-interpersonal level.

Racism also exists at the social institutional level. In Chapter 1, *social institutions* were defined as complex networks of social relationships designed to fulfill a function in society. Examples of social institutions include the educational system, law enforcement, government, organized religion, and corporations. *Institutional racism* occurs when the policies and practices of a social institution result in the differential treatment of particular racial groups. Examples of institutional racism include racial profiling by law enforcement, biased sentencing by the criminal justice system, and racial bias in educational standardized tests. Institutional racism also occurs when interpersonal racism is backed by institutional power. For example, when an individual landlord refuses to rent an apartment to an individual family, that is interpersonal racism (discrimination). However, when social institutions, such as government housing policies and bank lending practices, support landlords, homeowners, and real estate agents who engage in such practices, making it more difficult for people of color to live in certain areas, it becomes institutional racism.

Racism has existed since humans began to divide themselves into categories and became engrained in the fabric of the Western world during more than 400 years of the Atlantic slave trade. Racist ideologies continue to exist, despite scientific evidence that as humans we are more genetically similar than different (see Chapter 1). Because such beliefs have been around for so long, they have become the norm—like the proverbial water to the fish. Practices that have roots in racism go unnoticed because they are so commonplace. This is *cultural racism*. Blaut (1992) defined cultural racism as the belief that one's own culture is inherently superior to another. He argued that although most people no longer believe in biological racial superiority, they still believe in cultural superiority, more specifically, European cultural superiority. Other racial/ethnic groups are seen as having the *capacity* to be equal in terms of intelligence, appropriate social behavior, etc.; they just have not had the *opportunity* to do so. Therefore, Europeans are justified in their discrimination against other racial/ethnic groups until those groups develop to the same level as Europeans. From this perspective, the differences between groups are based on culture, not biology. We (the authors) argue that this type of thinking has gone beyond the individual level and is so widespread that it has moved to the cultural level. In Chapter 2 we discussed how the term *culturally deprived* was used to describe children of color from the inner city. This term was used by well-meaning European American liberals who did not realize they were perpetuating the belief that the European American middle-class environment was the correct environment, and anything different was deprived. A similar problem occurs with the terms *developing countries* and *third world countries*. What standard is being used? White/European culture. These terms are used in everyday language without awareness of their implications and illustrate the concept of cultural racism.

The concept of *cultural racism* is similar to *implicit racial attitudes*, or ideas and opinions individuals hold about race of which they are unaware. People can harbor racist attitudes that are outside their conscious awareness, but still impact their behavior. For example, an employer who refuses to hire an applicant of color may genuinely believe the applicant is less qualified and may not realize that the race of the applicant influenced his decision (Dovidio & Gaertner, 2004; Gaertner & Dovidio, 1986). A large body of research supports the idea of implicit bias (see Fazio & Dunton, 1997; Fazio & Olson, 2003; Greenwald & Benaji, 1995). (For more information on implicit bias, visit the Project Implicit website at https://implicit.harvard.edu/implicit/.)

Understanding that racism occurs on different levels helps explain some of the arguments people have regarding racism. For example, when people use their personal lack of racial prejudice ("I'm not a racist!") as evidence that racism is dead, they are talking about racism at the cognitive-affective and social-interpersonal levels. In other words, they do not believe they harbor any racist beliefs, and they do their best to treat everyone equally. People also argue that racism is dead because they have never experienced racist treatment, nor have they witnessed anyone else being treated that way. Even some people of color will say, "I've never experienced any racism." However, just because you are not racist, have not experienced racism, and have not witnessed racism does not mean it is gone. We have presented recent examples of racism at the cognitive-affective and social-interpersonal levels in personal stories from students. In addition, social institutional and cultural racism were apparent in recent news stories. Some people cite the election of Barack Obama as the first African American president of the United States as evidence that racism is dead. However, much of the rhetoric around his election and presidency, as well as the subsequent election of Donald Trump, serves as examples that we continue to struggle with racism on numerous levels.

> Nowadays we seem to have a lot of racism but very few racists.
>
> —James M. Blaut (1992)

Color-Blind Racial Ideology

In recent years, the concept of a **color-blind racial ideology** has gained attention (Apfelbaum, Pauker, Sommers, & Ambady, 2010; Apfelbaum, Sommers, & Norton, 2008; Awad, Cokley, & Ravitch, 2005; Bonilla-Silva, 2003; Bonilla-Silva & Dietrich, 2011; R. C. L. Chao, Wei, Good, & Flores, 2011; Guinier & Torres, 2007; Holoien & Shelton, 2012; Knowles, Lowery, Hogan, & Chow, 2009; Neville & Awad, 2014; Neville, Awad, Brooks, Flores, & Bluemel, 2013; Neville, Spanierman, & Doan, 2006; Plaut, Thomas, & Goren, 2009; Tynes & Markoe, 2010; Worthington, Navarro, Loewy, & Hart, 2008). This ideology essentially suggests that often people attempt to pretend that race and racism will not exist if people ignore race or ethnicity. According to Neville et al. (2013), color-blind racial ideology contains two dimensions: color evasion and power evasion.

color-blind racial ideology—an attempt to pretend that race and racism will not exist if people ignore race or ethnicity. This ideology has two components: color evasion and power evasion.

When I look at people, I don't see color. People tell me that I am White, and I have to believe them because so many people tell me I am White, but I don't see my color.

—Stephen Colbert, famous television satirist

The color evasion dimension asserts that there are no differences in the way in which people are treated based on their color. The power evasion dimension asserts that any differences in accomplishments are completely based on the individual's own work and not due to any advantages of color built into the system.

When people engage in color evasion, they often say things such as, "I don't see race," "I don't see color," and "we are all the same." Part of the motivation behind this stance is a discomfort in discussing racial or ethnic issues. As a result, these individuals may choose to have fewer interracial interactions to avoid their discomfort. However, people cannot help but notice the race or ethnicity of other people with whom they engage. A former European American female student of mine once said to me, "Jeff, when I look at you, I don't notice that you are Asian." My response to her was, "When I hear that, my reaction is that it is like me saying to you, 'When I look at you I don't notice that you are a woman.' *Of course* I notice you are a woman."

When people engage in power evasion, they often say things such as, "Racism is not important in today's society," "Everyone has an equal chance to succeed," and "Reverse racism is more prevalent than racism in today's society." Such attitudes fuel more racial animus in these individuals, and they are less competent in interacting in today's multicultural society. A former European American male student of mine, on reading Peggy McIntosh's article about her invisible backpack of European American privileges, denied that most if not all of her European American privileges applied to him, and he did not believe they existed in today's society. Fortunately, I did not have to respond to him because his astonished classmates quickly challenged his assertion. It is also not surprising to me that he had difficulties in his clinical placement the following year.

Have you encountered individuals who do not believe that racism exists in today's society? You may even have had these kinds of ideas yourself because you were told that being "colorblind" was the correct way to think. A police television show I saw years ago had a scene where the female policewoman shamefully admitted to her husband when she stopped an innocent African American man that day that she could not help but notice that he was African American. Her husband responded, "That is not automatically wrong—it is one of the colors we come in."

Internalized Oppression

For many years, E. J R. David has been writing about **internalized oppression** (David, 2008, 2009, 2010, 2014; David & Derthick, 2014; David & Okazaki, 2006, 2010) This concept is not new; various researchers have discussed it dating back to the classic study by K. B. Clark and Clark (1939; also see Bailey, Chung, Williams, Singh, & Terrell, 2011; Bearman, Korobov, & Thorne, 2009; L. S. Brown, 1986; Duran & Duran, 1995; Freire, 1970; Gainor, 1992; Hanna, Talley, & Guindon, 2000; Lipsky, 1977, 1987; L. M. Padilla, 2001, 2004; Parmer, Arnold, Natt, & Jansen, 2004; Poupart, 2003; Prilleltensky & Laurier, 1996; Pyke, 2010; Rosenwasser, 2002; Ross, Doctor, Dimito, Kuehl, & Armstrong, 2007; Szymanski & Kashubeck-West, 2008; Tappan, 2006; Thomas, Speight, & Witherspoon, 2005).

internalized oppression—people who are colonized and/or oppressed may automatically accept the superiority of the oppressor.

Internalized oppression is implicit in the first stage/status of racial identity development models (see Chapter 7). When individuals are trying to fit in with the majority population or the population in power (as is the case for countries that have been colonized), their first stage/status of identity development is to suppress their cognitive, behavioral, and emotional tendencies that may differ from those of the population in power in favor of the tendencies of those in power.

As a Filipino American, David is particularly conscious of how the colonization of the Philippines has affected the mentality of Filipinos, who see Filipino tendencies to be inferior and European American tendencies to be superior. This can be as subtle as preferring lighter-skinned people or as overt as consciously rejecting the opinions of Filipinos, who are seen as immigrants as opposed to being born in the United States. David and Derthick (2014) discussed a narrative of a Filipino man who characterized how internalized oppression affected him:

> As much as I've spent thinking deeply about internalized oppression, and as aware of it as I am, I am sure I still have it and my daily life is still affected by it, whether I am aware of it or not, and even if I don't want it to. For example, I still find myself laughing at FOB [fresh off the boat—a derogatory categorization of new immigrants] jokes until I remind myself of how wrong it is. I still have a tendency to feel embarrassed whenever I hear other Filipinos speak English with a thick Filipino accent. I still find myself ignoring the opinions of Filipinos who are not very Americanized. . . . It's like my automatic responses to some Filipino things are negative, until I catch myself, think more, then reconsider. (Filipino American man cited in David and Derthick, 2014, pp. 15–16)

Similarly, American Indians struggle to navigate in a society where the oppressor is still in power, which leads to the rejection of their values, knowledge, beliefs, and ceremonies (Gonzalez, Simard, Baker-Demaray, & Iron Eyes, 2014). The dominant image and message about American Indians is negative—they are seen as savage, as alcoholics living on government handouts, and as a vanquished people of the past, forever defeated in Western movies. For Native people, this results in the stealing of identities. One of the authors (JG) shares part of the story of his own internalized oppression.

> I remember growing up on White Earth in the 70s. My dad, Jim "Ironlegs" Weaver taught us how to sing and dance—we went to powwows every summer. We had sweats behind our house. But, back then, hardly anybody was doing sweats or ceremonies, it seemed like nobody was singing or dancing and going to powwows, except our family and maybe a few others. I looked around the Rez and started to wonder why. When I would go hang out with cousins and friends, they would tease me. I started to question my own identity. Instead of going to powwows and doing ceremonies, it seemed like being Indian meant partying and doing drugs. I strayed from the sacred Circle. I wanted to be like the other Indians on the Rez. I had to go through some rough times and learn the hard way before I freed myself and found my way back to our Anishinaabe ways so that I could heal. (John Gonzalez, cited in David, 2014, p. 14)

The extreme levels of poverty, unemployment, and lack of opportunity in American Indian communities, particularly in rural reservation communities, reinforce these ideas for Native youth, which may contribute to the high levels of suicide (Whitbeck, Sittner Hartshorn, & Walls, 2014).

Thus, just as many forms of modern racism affect people who are European American unconsciously and/or implicitly, internalized oppression affects people of color unconsciously and/or implicitly, even when people are sophisticated about issues of racism. Moreover, such oppression directly hurts people who engage in it.

Racial Microaggressions

As we have been discussing throughout this chapter, modern forms of racism are subtle and sometimes unconscious. Certainly, Ridley's (1995) conception of covert, unintentional racism, Gaertner and Dovidio's (1986) aversive racism, and Neville and Awad's (2014) color-blind racial ideology are unknown to those who engage in such forms of racism. When these forms of racism are pointed out to the individuals engaging in the practices, they will either deny that they were being racist or strive to adjust their behavior immediately.

Derald Wing Sue and his colleagues have examined these forms of modern racism and come up with what they call *racial microaggressions* (Burrow & Hill, 2012; M. L. Jones & Galliher, 2014; Nadal, 2011; Nadal, Griffin, Wong, Hamit, & Rasmus, 2014; Owen, Tao, Imel, & Wampold, 2014; D. W. Sue, Bucceri, Lin, Nadal, & Torino, 2007; D. W. Sue, Capodilupo, et al., 2007; D. W. Sue, Lin, Torino, Capodilupo, & Rivera, 2009; D. W. Sue et al., 2008; D. W. Sue & Sue, 2008, 2013; Torres-Harding, Andrade, & Romero-Diaz, 2012; J. Wang, Leu, & Shoda, 2011;). A racial **microaggression** is a small slight or offense that may be intentional, but is mostly unintentional and does not harm the target of the offenses in any major way; however, it can accumulate and become burdensome over time. D. W. Sue and colleagues categorized racial microaggressions into three categories: *microassault*, *microinsult*, and *microinvalidation*.

> **microaggression**—a small slight or offense that may be intentional but is mostly unintentional and does not harm the target of the offenses in any major way, but can accumulate to be burdensome over time.

According to D. W. Sue and his associates, a **microassault** is similar to our conceptions of old-fashioned racism. These are "blatant verbal, nonverbal, or environmental" attacks that are intentionally discriminatory or biased (D. W. Sue & Sue, 2013, p. 154). Racial epithets and discriminatory hiring practices fall into this category. If people who engage in microassaults have any sense of conscience, they engage in such behavior only when there is some degree of anonymity, when they are in the presence of like-minded individuals, or when they simply lose control and blurt out their underlying feelings. Because of its anonymity, the Internet is a fertile ground for such behavior. A former student who started her own blog reported on her experiences:

> **microassault**—a blatant verbal, nonverbal, or environmental attack that is intentionally discriminatory or biased.

> I couldn't believe it! I had so many racist comments it wasn't funny. When I blogged about being supportive of affirmative action, so many people wrote racist comments laced with swear words. They only did this because they had pseudonyms and I couldn't identify who they were or direct an email to them individually. I thought this was just this one issue, but it happened every time I wrote about multicultural issues. It got so bad that I decided not to blog about this topic anymore.
>
> —Kelsey, 20+-year-old European American student

Another example of a microassault is when people want to tell a racist joke but then check to make sure that someone who could be the target of the joke is not around to hear. Finally, an example of the third condition under which someone might engage in a microassault was given in by D. W. Sue and Sue (2013) when they identified the case of Michael Richards's comedy club rant. Michael Richards played Kramer on the *Seinfeld* television series. He was performing a comedy routine and was allegedly drunk. His routine was not going well, and he began ranting about two African Americans in the audience. He then used racial epithets (e.g., the "N-word") to insult the couple and all African Americans.

A **microinsult** is an unintentional behavior or verbal comment conveying rudeness or insensitivity. For example, Laurel's story, recounted earlier, in which she bought a Louis Vuitton purse and her European American associate could not believe that a Mexican American woman could purchase such an expensive item, is an example of someone engaging in a microinsult.

microinsult—an unintentional behavior or verbal comment conveying rudeness or insensitivity.

During the 2008 Democratic presidential nomination campaign, then senator Joe Biden described then senator Barack Obama as "articulate and bright and clean" in a manner that suggested that people do not expect African American presidential candidates to be clean and intelligent. This was a microinsult that both illustrated the concept and underscored how unintentional it was because Senator Biden thought that he was complimenting Senator Obama. After Obama won the presidential nomination, he asked Senator Biden to be his running mate, so although Biden's comment was a microinsult, Obama saw that Biden was trying to be complimentary.

A **microinvalidation** is related to a microinsult in that it is generally unintentional and out of the awareness of the perpetrator, while also being dismissive of the experience of people of color. A microinvalidation excludes, negates, or dismisses the perceptions of the target person. For example, if an American Indian were to say that he did not get a job because of racism, a person who says, "I know the person who is hiring and I do not believe he is racist; maybe you just misperceived his reasoning for not hiring you" is engaging in microinvalidation.

microinvalidation—an action that excludes, negates, or dismisses the perceptions of the target person.

In a study conducted by one of the authors (JG), a participant shared an experience of a microaggression:

> I was taking a weight training class. On the first day, the instructor told us to make groups. Right away the six White girls in the class made a circle and left me and an international student standing by ourselves.
>
> —Carli, 20+-year-old American Indian student (cited in Gonzalez et al., 2012)

For example, I (JSM) once encountered a microinvalidation that I will never forget. I found a recipe for spanakopita (Greek spinach and cheese pie). When I was in Chicago as a graduate student, I loved spanakopita, and was excited to try the recipe. I went to the grocery store and looked for two items that I never bought before: phyllo dough and feta cheese. After looking around the store for a while trying to find the items on my own, I asked a grocery store worker where the phyllo dough was. When she did not understand me, I said, "I'm not sure if it is pronounced 'feel-o' or 'file-o' but it is a dough to make spinach cheese pie." When she still did not know what I was looking for, I then asked where the feta cheese was. It was obvious to me that she did not know what phyllo and feta were, but instead of admitting to her own ignorance, she said, "You have a funny accent. I can't understand what you are saying."

A student of ours wrote about her experiences involving subtle racism:

> The concept of microaggressions was not new to me, but I had never heard of the term before. (In fact, neither has this computer as the word is underlined in red.) The funny thing about it is that often microaggressions are passed off as a joke or downplayed. I want to add to some of the examples of microaggressions. I was chosen for a Wider Opportunity through Girl Scouts in my senior year [of high school] to live for 2 weeks with the Amish in Pennsylvania. Out of 50 girls chosen, 48 were White. There was one African American girl and I was the only Mexican American. The funny thing was all the girls roomed in assigned pairs and they put the two minorities together. We got along great, but we called them on it and asked why they chose the only two non-White girls to room together and they admitted to putting us together on purpose because they thought we'd understand each other. That was all that was said and we thought it was outrageous and hilarious at the same time, but looking back I think it was a form of microaggression, even though I'm not sure which category it would fit under or maybe it's a microinvalidation. . . . I think so much of microaggressions go ignored or are thought of as not important. Unfortunately it is now a more popular version of racism, because blatant racism is no longer tolerated.
>
> —Renatta, 20+-year-old Mexican American student

Hernandez, Carranza, and Almeida (2010) examined people of color who are mental health professionals. These professionals were aware of the concept of microaggressions and discussed the ways in which they coped with them. Although confrontation with the perpetrator was one method used to cope with the problem, it was only one of eight such measures. In fact, confrontation was fourth on the list of most commonly used coping strategies. The first strategy was to identify the key issue involved and decide how to respond. If the perpetrator was simply naive, then education might be the best strategy; if the perpetrator was more abusive, then confrontation might be needed. This strategy, self-care, and seeking mentoring were employed by all participants in the study. The order of the strategies from the next most used to the least used strategies was organizing public responses, spirituality, keeping records and documenting experiences tied with confrontation, and seeking support from European American allies. The authors did not suggest that one should ignore microaggressions, but that one should find ways to cope with them.

Microaggressions Broadly Defined

The foregoing examples of microaggressions are racial microaggressions. Microaggressions can be perpetrated against any group on the downside of power, just as the concepts of general racism can be applied to any group that can be targeted. Thus, sexism, heterosexism, ageism, ableism, and the like can be subtly expressed in the form of microaggressions. For example, when someone constantly refers to an indefinite person as *he*, that person is engaging in a sexist microaggression; when someone assumes that people are either married or single and does not consider gay or lesbian partnerships, that person is engaging in a heterosexist microaggression; or when someone does not believe that a person in a wheelchair has career aspirations and should be content to work in a repetitive job with no future advancement, that person is engaging in an ableist microaggression. What other examples of nonracial microaggressions can you produce?

White Privilege

One of the most powerful treatises on the depth of unconscious European American racism in this country was proposed by Peggy McIntosh (1988, 1995). Lonnie's story about how the all-male search committee ranked the female candidates second in both searches clearly illustrates **male privilege**. Not only was the search committee chair biased in favor of male candidates, but also he ignored all the female voices that protested his decision, whereas he listened to the lone male who voiced his opinion. **White privilege** is similar to male privilege in that many unearned advantages are given to European American individuals without examination. If society truly is fair, such advantages should not exist. McIntosh (1995, pp. 79–81) presented many instances that might otherwise be unexamined but that underscore the advantages of being European American in this society:

- I can avoid spending time with people whom I was trained to mistrust and who have learned to mistrust my kind or me.
- I can turn on the television or open to the front page of the paper and see people of my race widely and positively represented.
- I can talk with my mouth full and not have people put this down to my color.
- I am never asked to speak for all the people of my racial group.
- If my day, week, or year is going badly, I need not ask of each negative episode or situation whether it has racial overtones.

A biethnic female student wrote in one of our courses on multiculturalism about her reaction to reading McIntosh's (1995) treatise on White privilege:

> When we discussed Peggy McIntosh's subtleties of racism, I especially liked "I am never asked to speak for all the people of my racial group." I notice that a lot of people do ask me to give the "Asian female" perspective, like I know what the Asian female perspective is. I am a fourth-generation Japanese and Chinese female, who does not for the most part know the language, customs, superstitions, culture tales, [or] traditions of both the Japanese and the Chinese cultures. I may know a few here and there, but by no means enough to "speak for all the people of my racial group."
>
> When McIntosh said "I can turn on the television or open the front page of the paper and see people of my race," it also made me think of how much the Asian population is still not shown on television. My mother's cousin was an actor. As for major roles in television spots, he really did not have any. He had guest appearances on shows like *Charlie's Angels*, *Silver Spoons*, and many others, but never a real leading role.

male privilege—the unearned advantages associated with being male, such as knowing that one's opinions will be respected. Women often feel that their opinions are not respected or are attributed to emotion, not sound reasoning.

White privilege—the unearned advantages associated with being White in America, such as knowing that Whiteness will be emphasized in the media. People of color are not always portrayed in the media, and when they are, they are often portrayed stereotypically rather than as multifaceted individuals.

In most of those shows he played the butler, the cook, the Japanese tourist, and roles that were very stereotypical of Japanese men. He did act in plays and was involved in other things, which supported him, but he was not really seen regularly. I think times are changing. More Asian actors and actresses are shown on television and movies, but not at a rate that is proportional to the population.

—Debbie, 20+-year-old biethnic (Japanese/Chinese American) woman

Kliman (2005) discussed how she used her European American and class privileges to demand medical attention for her husband, who may have died had he not received such attention:

> Frantic, I used class and other kinds of social privilege. I demanded immediate intervention. Did he survive at the expense of patients whose loved ones didn't share my entitlement, or of the overworked medical staff I pressed into action? . . . Race protected David, who is 6′4″ and visibly strong. Toxic with infection, he was angry, confused, and probably frightening to others. I was aggressive on his behalf. What if we had been Black or Latino, unprotected by our Whiteness? Would antibiotics, sedation, or a call to security have come first? (p. 42)

In retrospect, Kliman expresses her guilt and acknowledges her privileged status; an African American or Latinx American wife may have had to retrospectively discuss how racism took her husband's life.

Nowadays, McIntosh's (1995) article is standard reading for all graduate courses in multicultural psychology, and it is almost always included in undergraduate multicultural courses. Because one of the authors of this book is of Asian ancestry (JSM), a favorite observation is "I can turn on the television or open to the front page of the paper and see people of my race widely and positively represented." We particularly like to point out that unless one is viewing a martial arts movie, one almost never sees an Asian male on a television program or in a movie. Asian females are typically presented as the girlfriends of European American male protagonists, but Asian males are almost never seen with European American females and are rarely seen with Asian females. It is telling when we see students racking their brains trying to remember the last time they saw an Asian man together with a European American or an Asian woman on television. This seemed to have resonated with a Chinese American student, who wrote the following in one of her reaction papers:

> "Oh, look, an Asian Guy!" My husband and I have gotten used to using this phrase with each other as we watch television and look through magazines. Why, just this weekend I must have seen four or five Asian men as extras on our favorite television shows. I don't know why I was so excited to see them, because they were on the screen for less than a blink of an eye. Only one of the four or five men that I saw even had a line; the others only walked across the scene or were incidentally shot while the camera was panning onto one of the other major non-Asian actors. As we discussed in class, the incidence of seeing Asians on television is so rare that seeing three or four in a row is enough to make you wonder, "What's going on?"

—Molly, 20+-year-old Chinese American student

Like Asian males, dark-skinned African American women have a shortage of role models on television:

> This weekend I paid close attention to commercials and movies to see how many Black faces I saw. One thing that I noticed was that I did not see very many "dark" Black women. Because I am an African American woman with dark skin, I was looking to find women whom I could relate to physically.
>
> Many of the Black actresses that are well known happen to be "light-skinned"; for example, Halle Berry and Queen Latifah. I wish there were more dark-skinned Black women on television to represent role models for other children to look up to. Lighter skin has always been preferred to darker skin. This is not always the case, but it is the majority from what I have observed. Growing up I did not think I was pretty because I was dark-skinned and I went to a predominately White school, and all of the other Black students were "light-skinned." I used to wish that I was light-skinned and had what is referred to as "good hair." I have slowly grown out of this way of thinking that dark-skinned people are not as pretty as light-skinned people. However, I still have issues sometimes when it comes to my confidence level.
>
> —Sharmain, 20+-year-old African American student

For a wonderful discussion of skin color and beauty, do an Internet search for Lupita Nyong'o's speech at the 2013 Essence Awards. Nyong'o won the Academy Award for Best Supporting Actress for her role as Patsy in the film *12 Years a Slave* (McQueen, 2013). In her speech, Nyong'o talks about how desperately she wanted to be lighter skinned. However, once a dark-skinned supermodel, Alek Wek, was acclaimed by all as beautiful, Nyong'o began gaining confidence in herself. She said that her mother told her that she "could not eat beauty." What her mother meant was that beauty cannot sustain someone, but inner beauty and compassion can. More recently, the film *Black Panther* (Moore, 2018) was greeted with enthusiasm and generated multiple discussions not only about skin color, but also about identity and culture. As an example, 2018 President of the Society of the Psychological Study of Culture, Ethnicity and Race, Dr. Helen Neville wrote this in a social media post:

Asians and Latinxs have traditionally not been in positions of power. *Photographs by Tom Zasadzinski*

Lupita Nyong'o began to gain confidence in herself when she saw a dark-skinned supermodel gain acclaim.
Photograph courtesy of Joanne Davidson/Shutterstock

10 things I love about the Black Panther Movie: (1) Wakandans practice a form of African socialism; (2) Wakandans worship Bast, a goddess; (3) Shuri exemplifies #BlackGirlGenius; (4) Okoye, the general, is badass; (5) Nakia represents strength, integrity and intelligence; (6) the space the film creates for Black folks to have a discussion about Black liberation; (7) the film captures the beauty and strengths of Africa and Africans as imagined and as they currently are; (8) Wakandans are the moral compass of humanity; (9) the multiple ideological perspectives represented; and (10) the meaning this film has on our youth about what is possible.

—Helen Neville, Ph.D.,
African American Women

This issue of skin color is discussed by several students across many ethnicities:

Ximena [who is Black/Panamanian] told us a story about her niece who wanted to take only her White dolls to the park. Her niece is only two years old, and she has already noticed the difference in skin color. She did not want to take her Black dolls to the park because there are always other girls in the park, but she is the only Black girl. . . . [This reminded me of] a recent event that happened to one of my friends (Christiana), who lives in Rancho Cucamonga. Last week her eight-year-old daughter was pretending to be sick for about three days, because she did not want to go to school. The school she is attending is mostly White. Christiana got very concerned by the third day, and started confronting her daughter. Alexandria, her daughter, told her that one of her classmates was telling everybody in the class not to play with her because she is Black. She is actually Hispanic, but she has very dark skin.

—Isolda, 20+-year-old Colombian American student

Over the weekend, I had taken my two-year-old niece to the mall to buy her something for her birthday. As we perused the aisles, we handed her little toys and trinkets hoping that she would not throw them back or look in disgust. Finally, we had reached the doll aisle. She immediately tried to free herself from the cart seat that she was harnessed to and had her 1-foot arms reaching for the little baby doll—a doll that she could feed, change, and walk around in her own baby doll stroller. Her father, a Vietnamese American, had immediately noticed that the doll looked Caucasian and grabbled the Asian one and said, "Look, Nini, let's get this one!" in an excited yet frantic voice. Both dolls had no hair (because they were designed to look like babies) and the same outfit—a pink onesie. The discerning feature was their eyes: the Caucasian looking one had round blue eyes while the Asian looking one had small slanted dark brown eyes. The child refused and only wanted the doll she had in her hands. Her parents eventually gave up trying to convince their child to get the Asian looking one and instead decided to swap out the dolls when she was not looking; She eventually realized this before they even left the doll aisle and threw a tantrum. At the end of the day, we purchased Nini the doll she originally picked out.

This doll manufacturer in that particular store had a wide range of different ethnic dolls, while most other stores in that city do not, and have the same White doll with blue eyes. This means that children, at a very young age, have been exposed to racial undertones and ethnic majority. The stores that have limited inventory do not give their patrons the luxury to get to choose one doll over another, therefore, children learn racism and a preference to identify with the Caucasian majority. While this store has made an attempt to stock its shelves with dolls of many skin and eye colors, my niece has been conditioned to prefer one over the rest.

—Lau, 20+-year-old Vietnamese American student

Our class discussion of male privilege as related to White privilege resonated with one student:

I found the White privilege and the male privilege to be interesting topics to me. When reading and discussing the White privilege, I was confused and I did not quite grasp the statements that appeared on the PowerPoint. However, when the male privilege was introduced to us, everything made complete sense to me. I know that as a female my opinion is not always taken seriously. I know that the housework is always my responsibility before my brothers or my boyfriend. If they attempt at doing one load of laundry or even put their dishes in the sink they receive endless praise, [whereas] those are tasks that I am automatically expected to complete. I can never be in a bad mood without the famous question that females receive [about having my period]. I guess being on the other side (not being the privileged person) really opens your eyes to what is fair and what is not. I guess I don't really see the privileges that I receive as a White person because I have never been on the other side. These last few weeks of class have really opened my eyes to these issues and every day I see it more and more. I see the privileges that I receive as being a White person. I see the way other people, not of the White race, are treated unfairly, unjustly and the pain that must come along with it. I see the privileges that males receive just for being male. And I also see the way females are treated unfairly and unjustly and I feel the pain that goes along with it. I know the two issues of race and gender are far from different and I will never be able to understand the pain that other races feel; however, this comparison has helped me to understand it a little bit better. I feel like the issue of sexism has opened my eyes into what the world of racism must really be like.

—Alisha, 20+-year-old European American student

Yet another student made the connection of privilege to right-handed privilege:

> A girl in my class who is left-handed said no one realizes everything is made for right-handed people, even [our school] does not carry left-handed folders. While she was saying this I was thinking is it really necessary to buy a left-handed folder? How hard could it be? She said you don't think it's a problem because you do not experience it but walk around for the day using your left hand, even the doors are made for right-handed people. After that I noticed that she was right; I got in my car and realized it would be harder to drive if I was left-handed, harder to take notes in class with my folder if I was left-handed, and even harder to play video games. I had never really stopped to think to think about how being right-handed was an advantage. It made me laugh when this idea was brought up to the males in class. Men do not worry about their own safety like women do but until it was pointed out to them the men had never realized they had a little less stress in their lives. I think that privilege usually goes unnoticed by those that have it. I have heard my girl friends say a million times that it would be so easy to be a guy because they do not have to do half the things women go through to even be ready to leave the house but that thought probably never crosses a man's mind.
>
> —Allie, 20+-year-old Mexican American student

Articles such as McIntosh's (1995) help us to understand how European American people can assist in eliminating racism. Her insights help other European Americans see how society is set up to give an advantage to one class of individuals over other classes of individuals. Thus, the basis of our form of government—that all people are created equal—is not true unless we help make it true and form "a more perfect union." One step in helping to form a more perfect union is to produce more people like McIntosh—individuals who have power merely by their status but who are willing to give up some of their power to help those on the downside of power gain more equality, what writers in the field call a development of **allies** (Kivel, 1996; Mio & Roades, 2003; Roades & Mio, 2000; L. R. Rose, 1996; Tatum, 1997; Wise, 2008, 2013). Allies are those individuals on the upside of any form of unearned power and privilege—such as White privilege, male privilege, heterosexual privilege, and ability privilege—who are willing to work for social justice in giving those on the downside of power and privilege equal status. As Tatum (1997) wrote, many of her European American students feel powerless when they study racism, but when she talks about allies and how allies can help eliminate racism, her European American students suddenly feel empowered because this mindset helps them understand how they can confront this otherwise daunting issue.

allies—individuals who are on the upside of power who cross a demographic boundary to advocate for those on the downside of power.

A former student felt energized by the discovery of White privilege, and he was excited to apply it to his life:

> There are many reasons why I truly enjoy this class. The biggest reason is the fact that things are brought to my attention that were right in front of my face for as long as I can remember, but I never saw them until now. I am talking about White privilege. The fact that I am White might be the sole reason that I have never realized it until now.

The part that I enjoyed was the fact that White males are privileged enough to move away from all minorities and be entirely surrounded by other White people. A White male could move up to northern Idaho and never see a minority unless he wanted to. I never thought about this until it was brought up in class.

—Mark, 20+-year-old European American student

Here is an example of a very effective intervention by one of our students serving as an ally:

I really hate how many people in society are hom₁ phobic, especially men and especially Latino men. For instance my boyfriend, who is Mexican American [and] very smart, is about to graduate next month with his master's [degree] . . . but when it comes to homosexuality he is very ignorant and homophobic, [and] so are his friends. I know in the Latino culture, homosexuality is viewed as shameful or deviant, but I wish the younger and more educated generations would be able to get past this. For example I dragged my boyfriend to go see *Brokeback Mountain* with me when it was in the theaters. Well when his friends found out he went to go see that "gay" or "homo" movie they gave him a hard time. It really offended me that they would be so close-minded and ignorant, that I confronted their sexist and "machismo" opinions. Still today they nickname my boyfriend "Brokeback," [and] still to today I debate with them on gay and lesbian rights issues and on their ignorant statements.

I have several close gay and lesbian friends, and I am very liberal minded when it comes to gay and lesbian rights. I believe in gays and lesbians deserving to be legally married and have equality in the adoption process. So when I hear people use derogatory terms regarding gays or voicing homophobic beliefs I get really upset and usually confront them about it.

—Delinda, 20+-year-old biracial (Mexican American/European American) student

Being an ally can occur at a young age. A former student of ours told us about her brother, who was only 11 years old at the time of this event:

My little brother told me the most disturbing thing that happened in class the other day. My brother is in sixth grade and was in his Home Ec class and his teacher was giving an introduction to the sewing unit they were going to begin. She asked the class why they thought that all of the clothes we wear were made in other countries. My brother said this one boy (who happened to be Hispanic) replied in a joking manner "because people are lazy." My brother said that the teacher got really angry all of a sudden and said "So are you saying that Americans are lazy? What do you think that Mexicans are better than us? What are you, some kind of border hopper?!" My brother said that she was raising her voice and backing him in a corner (I am not sure if that was a literal or metaphorical backing into a corner) and the boy kept saying "No . . . no . . . that's not what I meant . . . I meant people in general are lazy and don't want to do it. Not that Mexicans are better than Americans" and my brother said his teacher refused to acknowledge the boy's answer and kept ranting, saying "Are your parents even American citizens? Where were they born, Mexico? Do they even have their green cards? Do you even have a green card? Where were you born!?" My brother said somehow the class went back to doing what they were supposed to but she was being really hard on the class and he thought she was being even harder on the Hispanic kids in the class. Then some student asked a question (my brother forgot what it was) but the teacher said, "Well, if you want to know about self-righteousness why don't you ask [Tracy] (the Hispanic boy she was verbally assaulting earlier)" and the boy attempted one more time by trying to defend himself saying, "I didn't mean that Americans were lazier than anyone else and if that was what I said then I would have been saying that I was lazy because I was American" and he went on to say that both of his parents were American citizens and his father was born in Chicago and his mother was born in California. To which the teacher replied, "Why did it take you like 15 minutes to say that? If it was true you would have said it in the first place" and the boy told her that he didn't say it because she scared him the way she was yelling and then the teacher got really angry saying, "Don't you accuse me of yelling at you when I was not yelling."

Well when my brother told me this I was sickened and I am actually extremely proud of my brother for what he did. After the class ended my brother went to the office and filed a formal complaint on the teacher. He sat down and wrote up what happened and then he turned it in and told me the next step is for the vice principal to read it and call my brother in for questioning. My brother told me he is doing it because he doesn't feel that anyone should be treated like that no matter what.

—Kelsey, 20+-year-old European American student

Being an ally can come at a cost, but this is the only way that society can change. One of our students discussed the difficulty of being an ally.

Becoming an ally would take a lot of courage. I think it would be very scary to stand up against injustice toward a minority group. For example, a White person speaking out against the [anti-]immigration issue that is going on today. Those in power are White and are going to ultimately make the decision of what is going to happen. A White citizen would not want to suffer the consequences of losing their job because they were marching, getting beaten up for being a "beaner lover" (I heard this term on the street the other day. It was said to a White girl who had a Mexican boyfriend), or being seen as a traitor to their own culture. . . .

We have seen in the past that the oppressed groups who have overcome their unjust situations have been those who have been allied by more powerful groups. If Martin Luther King had not appealed to White people with his message of equality and peace then perhaps many White people and White leaders would not have joined his cause. Since they did, they helped change history.

—Corina, 20+-year-old Mexican American student

Not only can *being* an ally be difficult, but also *teaching* about White privilege and social justice issues can be difficult (Boatright-Horowitz & Soeung, 2009). Boatright-Horowitz and Soeung found that professors (one European American, one Black) who taught about White privilege to European American students were rated significantly lower than the same professors who taught about social learning theory. For those of us who are committed to a just world, the consequences of teaching about these matters are worth the benefit of exposing people to such issues.

Food for Thought

You can extend Peggy McIntosh's concept of White privilege to privileges of all kinds. Men are privileged in our society over women, heterosexuals are privileged over gay and lesbian individuals, and able-bodied individuals are advantaged over individuals with disabilities. As a man (JSM), I think nothing of staying in my office late at night and then walking to my car to go home. However, my female colleagues must be concerned about doing the same thing. They can use the escort service our campus police department provides at night, but it is inconvenient. This is just one example of male privilege. We encourage you to think of other kinds of privileges from which you have benefited. In so doing, you will begin to think like an ally in working toward social justice.

Summary

Bias comes in many shapes and sizes. Some forms of bias are subtle and some are quite striking; some are unintentional and some are intentional. One of social psychology's basic theories—attribution theory—explains how bias can be revealed in our categorization of events. Ways of categorization can lead to stereotyping, prejudice, discrimination, and racism. Stereotyping and prejudice occur within ourselves and do not hurt others, whereas discrimination and racism are actions against others and consequently cause damage. This damage can be as minor as a mild irritation or a strained relationship or as serious as blatant unfairness or even death.

Ultimately, however, racism hurts everyone. The targets of racism are hurt by the racist comments or actions. The perpetrators are also hurt, because they live in fear of those whom they categorize negatively, and when someone's racist attitudes become public, that person may even lose a prestigious position. Racism can be overt and intentional and thus easily identified, but it can also be covert and unintentional and difficult to identify.

Many modern forms of racism are difficult to detect. Most individuals who hold racist views are unaware that their views are racist and would even vigorously deny that they are racist. These modern forms of racism are often unintentional, but they cannot be eliminated unless people are willing to examine their own contribution to a racist atmosphere. Racial microaggressions are forms of modern racism. They do not overtly hurt targets of racism because of the relatively minor injury they cause, but an accumulation of microaggressions can become burdensome. These microaggressions can also be applied to sexism, heterosexism, and other kinds of isms that target individuals on the downside of power. Peggy McIntosh (1995) identified the various advantages of her White privilege. These privileges are unearned and unconscious unless they are brought to light. For example, McIntosh knows that European American people will be characterized positively in almost any newspaper or television show, whereas most people of color may never see characters of their ethnicity portrayed as part of American life. By identifying these privileges, she makes herself aware of the advantages that come with her skin color and the special burden such privileges place on her to make her work harder for social justice.

Critical Thinking Questions

1. Have you ever attributed something to someone's personality but later found out it was the context that determined the person's actions? Have you ever felt that someone else unfairly attributed something you did to your personality or character when it was the situation

that determined your action? Did you get the chance to talk with the other person in either of these situations so that you could develop a better understanding?

2. If you have ever seen a television news report that a person of color has engaged in some criminal action, have you immediately attributed that action to others in that person's racioethnic group?

3. What institutional practices can you identify that unfairly disadvantage people of color? What institutional practices can you identify that unfairly disadvantage women? What institutional practices can you identify that unfairly disadvantage people of nondominant sexual orientations? What institutional practices can you identify that unfairly disadvantage people of nondominant religions? What institutional practices can you identify that unfairly disadvantage people who have physical disabilities? What institutional practices can you identify that unfairly disadvantage someone of a nondominant group?

4. What negative stereotypes can be attributed to a group to which you belong? Have you experienced stereotype threat based on these negative stereotypes?

5. What kinds of covert forms of racism can you identify around you?

6. How did Trayvon Martin and Michael Brown's cases affect you?

7. Did you think that being color-blind was something positive? If so, has your opinion changed?

8. Can you think of times when you may have committed a microaggression against someone else? If so, how might you respond now?

9. What kinds of dominant group privilege can you identify that benefit you?

10. What kinds of things related to your dominant group privilege can you do to intervene on someone else's behalf?

CHAPTER 7

Cultural Identity Development

Photograph by Marc Romanelli/Getty

A Model of Personal Identity
Racial Identity Development
> African American Identity Development
> European American Identity Development
> Chicano/Latinx Identity Development
> Asian American/Filipino American Identity Development
> American Indian Identity Development
> Multiracial Identity Development
> Gay/Lesbian Identity Development
> Racial and Cultural Identity Development Model
> Other Identities

A Critique of the Stage Models
Multiple Layering of Identities
Summary

Learning Objectives
Reading this chapter will help you to:
- understand the importance of cultural identity development;
- identify components of identity development;
- know which strategies are appropriate to apply when identity development is important;
- explain the critique of identity development models;
- recognize the differences among the cultural identity development models; and
- distinguish between European American identity development and cultural identity development.

I was talking with a colleague about her 4-year-old daughter. She said that her daughter was a very big fan of Ariel from *The Little Mermaid*. I asked her why, and she said that her daughter had red hair, and Ariel was the only main Disney character with red hair at the time.

—Jesse, 60+-year-old Asian American male

Who am I? All human beings, at some point in their lives, face that question. Erik Erikson (1950/1963) stated that one of the major developmental tasks for human beings is the establishment of an identity. Our search for an identity takes place across many domains—physical appearance, personal interests, career plans, religious beliefs, gender roles, and so on.

Although every individual struggles with identity questions, individuals from cultural diverse groups face a unique challenge. They must also resolve conflicts related to their minority status, whether that is based on race, gender, sexual orientation, physical ability, or some other trait that makes them different from the American mainstream. Society reacts to those differences, often in negative ways, and the individual must come to terms with the prejudice, discrimination, marginalization, and oppression based on his or her membership in that group. Women experience sexism, people of color experience racism, and gays and lesbians experience heterosexism. There are many more isms (e.g., ableism, classism, ageism, anti-Semitism). Individuals who hold marginalized identities struggle to make meaning of the fact that some aspect of their being is not accepted by society.

In her aptly titled book *Why Are All the Black Kids Sitting Together in the Cafeteria?*, Beverly Daniel Tatum (1997) explains what happens to African American adolescents as they experience society's negative reactions to their Blackness. When they are young, color is often not an issue for African American children who grow up in predominantly European American or mixed neighborhoods. They may make friends and interact easily with children from other racial backgrounds. African American children often have not had negative experiences associated with their race because the European American world does not yet see them as a threat.

However, as they get older, things start to change. The African American adolescent girl who goes shopping at the mall with her European American friends sees the salespeople follow her around to make sure she does not shoplift, but they do not do this to her friends. She may also notice that the salespeople rush to help her friends but ignore her. The African American adolescent boy might notice that European American women clutch their purses more tightly when he walks by, look nervous when he enters the elevator, or cross to the other side of the street to avoid him. African American young people might also notice that their friends' parents do not mind if their children have Black friends but draw the line when it comes to dating.

> Why do Black youths, in particular, think about themselves in terms of race? Because that is how the rest of the world thinks of them. Our self-perceptions are shaped by the messages that we receive from those around us, and when young Black men and women enter adolescence, the racial content of those messages intensifies. (Tatum, 1997, pp. 53–54)

When African American youths try to discuss their thoughts and feelings about racially motivated incidents with their European American (White, Caucasian, which are often used interchangeably with European American) friends, they receive little support. Their friends may respond, "Oh, I'm sure they didn't mean it like that!" or "Just forget about it. It's not a big deal." But their African American friends might say, "The same thing happened to me!" or "I know just how you feel." From their European American friends they get denial and minimization; with their African American friends, they find similarity, understanding, and support. Therefore, they gradually drift away from their European American peers and toward their African American peers.

> When feelings, rational or irrational, are invalidated, most people disengage. They not only choose to discontinue the conversation but are more likely to turn to someone who will understand their perspective. . . . Not only are Black adolescents encountering racism and reflecting on their identity, but their White peers, even when they are not the perpetrators (and sometimes they are), are unprepared to respond in supportive ways. The Black students turn to each other for the much needed support they are not likely to find anywhere else. (Tatum, 1997, pp. 59–60)

These perceptions are complicated. For example, starting at age 10, African American boys are likely to be seen as less innocent than children of other ethnic/racial groups (Goff, Jackson, Di Leone, Culotta, & DiTomasso, 2014). They are also more likely to be seen as older by both the general public and police officers (Goff et al., 2014). The latter has real implications for police actions. African American children must cope with the reality of dramatically higher incarceration rates and differential treatment within the justice system (National Council on Crime and Delinquency, 2007). They also have a greater likelihood of dying at the hands of law enforcement; one report estimated African American teenagers were 21 times more likely to be shot dead by a police officer than their European American counterparts (Gabrielson, Sagara, & Jones, 2014).

African Americans, as well as young people from other cultural minority groups, must cope with society's reactions to their otherness. This is an important part of their identity development process.

A Model of Personal Identity

An old Asian saying goes something like this: All individuals, in many respects, are (a) like no other individuals, (b) like some individuals, and (c) like all other individuals (Murray & Kluckhohn, 1953). D. W. Sue and Sue (2003) noted, "While this statement might seem confusing and contradictory, Asians believe this saying to have great wisdom and to be entirely true with

tripartite model of personal identity—the understanding that our self-perceptions are made up of unique, individual aspects, aspects of groups to which we belong, and universal aspects of human beings.

respect to human development and identity" (p. 11). D. W. Sue (2001) proposed a **tripartite model of personal identity**. The model is illustrated as three concentric circles (see Figure 7.1), which describe the individual, group, and universal levels of personal identity.

According to the adage, on the *individual level*, "all individuals are, in some respects, like no other individuals." Each person is unique in genetic makeup, personality characteristics, and personal experiences. Our individual uniqueness sets us apart from all other human beings and is an important part of our identity.

The second part of the adage says, "All individuals are, in some respects, like some other individuals." This is the *group level* of personal identity, which focuses on similarities and differences among individuals. As mentioned earlier, society divides people into groups based on demographic characteristics (e.g., gender, race, socioeconomic status, religious preference).

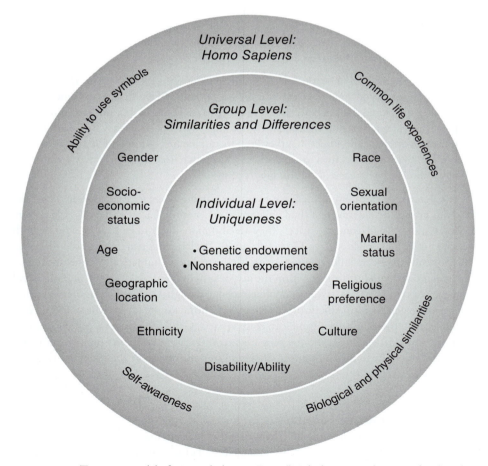

FIGURE 7.1   Tripartite model of personal identity. From "Multidimensional Facets of Cultural Competence," by D. W. Sue, 2001, *The Counseling Psychologist, 29.* (p. 793).

Therefore, a part of our identity is based on our membership in these various groups. The third part of the saying reflects the *universal level* of personal identity: "All individuals are, in some respects, like all other individuals." We all share some characteristics as members of the human race, such as biological and physical similarities, common life experiences (e.g., birth, death, love, fear), and common practices or behaviors (e.g., language).

In this chapter we focus on the second level of personal identity development: the group level. Membership in groups shapes the way we see ourselves, others in our group, and others outside our group. As we mentioned earlier, membership in some groups is valued over membership in others—men over women, Christian over Muslim, able-bodied over disabled, and White over Black. Society's reactions to our group membership influence group identity formation. A large body of literature exists on the cultural identity process, and there is no way to cover all of it, but in this chapter we will introduce you to it. The majority of this literature focuses on racial identity development, so that is where we begin.

Racial Identity Development

My memory may be a bit tainted, but I think my daughter was about 5 years old, shortly after entering kindergarten, when she began to talk about race and features. I guess before that, she was exposed to very few children. She was always with my family, wherein the subjects of race, identity, discrimination, and such topics were never discussed. When she was 5, I believe that I was still struggling with my own identity, so I really never talked about her multiracial identity. She came home and asked me why her friend's hair looked different from hers. She said that she touched it and everything, and it felt different too. I asked her "what her friend" was and she told me her friend's name. "No," I said, and I proceeded to ask about where she was from, and the color of her skin, but my daughter just concentrated on the texture of her hair, while she answered that she was from the same school and that her color was dark brown. This is going to sound amazing, but although I never had conversations with my daughter, prior to that day, about race, I thought she knew Black people from White people, Asian people from Hispanics, Whites from Asians, and so on and so forth. I believe that my assumptions were based on my own worldview and knowledge base, and I may have been projecting some feelings onto my daughter. The contradiction was that even though in my mind, I assumed that she knew the differences among different ethnic groups, I was not surprised that she couldn't tell between the racial features! How then did I think that she would know the differences between ethnic groups if she had no basis for that knowledge? I think because I assumed that a person's identity would be determined by how they looked alone, and that's how I went about defining my own ethnicity then, I assumed that my daughter and everyone else would think the same way. It was also because many people assumed that they knew exactly "what I was," based on how I looked, and for the most part, they were wrong! I was annoyed at my daughter for not knowing what I meant when I asked "what her friend was." I hated having to explain more about the one thing that I avoided all of my life. To define myself, my family, and my daughter was to justify many things that I didn't feel I should have to explain. Nowadays, I talk freely to her about ethnicity, discrimination, and such issues, because now that she is older, she too has experienced being "the other." Seeing who her friends are and how she has evolved now that I have educated myself, in turn increasing my ability to educate her, makes me feel confident that although she will continue to face obstacles along the way, she is better equipped to do so, as I am now.

—Deana, 20+-year-old Filipina/African American woman

Deana describes several phases she went through in her own identity development. At first, she saw her mixed racial background as negative; she denied it and avoided dealing with it. However, her daughter's questions about racial differences forced Deana to become comfortable with and understand her own identity. Through educating her daughter and herself, Deana gained more confidence in dealing with issues of racial identity. Although not everyone has the same experience as Deana, all individuals from diverse backgrounds face similar questions about their identity and go through similar phases in addressing those questions.

African American Identity Development

Research on cultural identity began with African Americans and can be traced back to a landmark experiment conducted by the husband-and-wife team of Kenneth and Mamie Clark, two African American psychologists, in 1939. In their study, the Clarks presented African American children with Black and White dolls and asked them a series of questions, such as which doll was the prettiest, smartest, or dirtiest. They found that African American children consistently attributed more positive traits to the White dolls and negative traits to the Black dolls.

The Clarks concluded that the results demonstrated the low self-esteem and negative self-image of Black children and attributed this to the racism, oppression, and discrimination experienced by Black children in White America. The Clark study had widespread influence in the field of psychology and beyond, and it was used as evidence in the 1954 *Brown v. Board of Education* decision by the Supreme Court that segregated schools were unconstitutional (K. B. Clark, Chein, & Cook, 2004; Pickren, 2004).

Joseph White (1970) wrote an article in *Ebony* magazine on Black identity development. He intentionally published in that source to make his ideas more accessible to the general African American community and not necessarily to researchers in psychology. An article published by William Cross in 1971 titled "The Negro-to-Black Conversion Experience" was a major influence on the study of cultural identity development professionally. Cross outlined stages that African Americans go through in moving from self-hatred to self-acceptance. He called this process *nigrescence*, or the process of becoming Black. The model contains four (originally five) stages. They are *preencounter, encounter, immersion/emersion,* and *internalization* (Worrell, Cross, & Vandiver, 2001).

preencounter stage of minority identity development—the stage or status in which one feels and accepts that the world is organized according to the dominant culture and against one's own cultural group.

encounter stage of minority identity development—the stage or status in which one is confronted with the realities of racism or other forms of devaluation of one's cultural group.

At the **preencounter stage**, individuals are programmed to think of the world as non-Black or anti-Black. They think and act in ways that devalue their Blackness and idealize Whiteness. In other words, they have internalized society's attitudes about European American superiority.

In the **encounter stage**, individuals experience some significant or startling event that forces them to reevaluate their previous ideas about race. Cross (1971) mentions the assassination of Dr. Martin Luther King Jr. as an event that forced many people in our country to reevaluate their attitudes about race.

In the third stage, **immersion/emersion**, a reversal occurs wherein people idealize Blackness, totally immerse themselves in Black culture, and reject anything that is not Black. Cross's final stage is **internalization**, wherein people feel positive and secure about their Black identity but also exhibit increased comfort with and acceptance of other cultures. Although Cross made some revisions to the original theory on the basis of subsequent research (1991, 1995), the basic structure of the model remains the same.

Mike, whom we felt was in Cross's internalization stage, was able to be self-critical in observing his own inconsistencies:

immersion/emersion stage of minority identity development—the stage or status in which one involves oneself completely within one's cultural group to the exclusion of the majority group. One emerges from this stage because one cannot meet all of one's needs if society is truly dominated by the majority group.

internalization stage of minority identity development—the stage or status in which one feels comfortable with one's identity. This allows one to express acceptance of other cultures.

> I was raised in such a way as not to be prejudiced against anyone but have other Black friends who are prejudiced against Mexicans or Asians or even non-American Blacks. I also have to admit that I have picked up some political prejudices myself. For example, I could never bring myself to purchase a German-made car because of the atrocities committed in World War II. I have owned Japanese cars almost exclusively even though I also know of similar atrocities committed by the Japanese against the Chinese. To me this just points out the irrationality of prejudice.
>
> —Mike, 40+-year-old African American man

Deana was in the preencounter stage when she avoided dealing with her multiracial background. Her daughter's questions about racial differences moved her into the encounter stage. In the end, she appears to achieve some positive resolution about her racial identity and reach the internalization stage. In the following story, see whether you can identify the different stages of racial identity development:

> It was 1963. I was only 3 years old. My family and I were sitting in the living room of our small house in East Los Angeles watching the news on television. Suddenly, the images of the civil rights protests in Birmingham, Alabama, flashed across the screen. I was stunned to see Bull Connor order the fire hoses and dogs unleashed on the African American children. My mother rushed to turn the channel, but . . . it was too late. The images were already burned in my mind. I asked her, "Why are they doing that to those children?" As my mother stood at the ironing board pressing clothes, she somberly said, "Just because they're Negroes, honey. Just because they're Negroes." I immediately responded in a chipper voice, "I'm glad I'm not a Negro!" The reaction from my family members was swift and forceful. They all immediately said together in a loud chorus, "Yes, we are!" I burst into tears as the realization flooded into my little 3-year-old mind. If those children were being treated that way just because they were Negroes, and if I was a Negro, that meant the same thing could happen to me. That was the beginning of my long journey of fear, guilt, and shame regarding my racial identity.

Moving forward a few years, my family moved to the suburbs, bought a house in a predominantly White neighborhood, and enrolled me in a predominantly White school. I was usually the only Black child in my class and one of only a handful in the whole school. I felt different from the very first day, and spent almost every day in the first grade sitting on the White teacher's lap crying. I didn't understand why, when the White girls flung their hair, it gently fell back into place. If I tried to fling my hair, it stayed standing straight up. And they laughed. I went home and told my mother that I wanted straight hair. She took me to the Black beauty shop on the other side of town and had a relaxer put in. My hair promptly fell out, leaving me bald. I ended up wearing a wig until my hair grew back. Imagine my humiliation, going to grade school, wearing a wig.

My sense of alienation, shame, fear, and guilt about my race lasted for years. It wasn't until I entered high school that I began to have some positive identification with my Blackness because there were finally more Black kids that I could relate to and hang out with. But the pain of those years still lies deep in my soul. When my sister and I recounted that and other various hair traumas with my mother, tears welled up in her eyes as she said, "We just did what we thought was best."

—Marie, 40+-year-old African American woman

Racial identity development models suggest that African Americans should develop a sense of pride about being of African descent. *Photograph by iofoto/Shutterstock*

Did you recognize any of Cross's stages as you read Marie's story? Her first encounter experience occurred when she was 3 years old. She became very aware of her race but continued to carry feelings of guilt and shame about it for many years. In high school she finally had some African American peers to "hang out with," and that helped her to develop more positive feelings about her racial identity. Perhaps that marked her entrance into the immersion/emersion phase.

Since Cross first published his stages of nigrescence in 1971, racial identity development has become one of the most widely researched topics in multicultural psychology (Parham, 2001). Parham and Helms (1981) constructed the Racial Identity Attitude Scale to measure Cross's stages (see Box 7.1 for sample items). The Racial Identity Attitude Scale has been used to explore the relationship between racial identity and a wide variety of other variables, such as self-esteem (Parham & Helms, 1985a), demographic factors (Parham & Williams, 1993), affective states (Parham & Helms, 1985b), and the counseling process (Helms, 1985). There has also been a proliferation of other cultural identity models. There are at least 11 other models for African

---

BOX 7.1 The Racial Identity Attitude Scale

Many measures have been developed to capture cultural identity. One of the most widely used, the Racial Identity Attitude Scale, was developed by Parham and Helms (1981) to measure Cross's stages of Black racial identity development. Here are some sample items from the Racial Identity Attitude Scale. Although the scale was originally designed for African Americans, we have left the race blank so that you can fill it in with your own race.

Preencounter

I believe that large numbers of _____ are untrustworthy.

I believe that White people look and express themselves better than _____ do.

I feel very uncomfortable around _____ people.

Encounter

I feel unable to involve myself in White experience, and am increasing my involvement in _____ experiences.

I find myself reading a lot of _____ literature and thinking about being _____.

I feel guilty and/or anxious about some of the things I believe about _____ people.

Immersion/Emersion

I have changed my style of life to fit my beliefs about _____ people.

I believe that everything _____ is good, and consequently, I limit myself to _____ activities.

I speak my mind regardless of the consequences (e.g., being kicked out of school, being imprisoned, being exposed to danger).

Internalization

People, regardless of their race, have strengths and limitations.

I feel good about being _____ but do not limit myself to _____ activities.

I am determined to find my _____ identity.

From *Black and White Racial Identity: Theory, Research, and Practice*, by J. E. Helms, 1990, (p.245-247). Westport, CT: Praeger.

Americans alone (Cross, Parham, & Helms, 1991; Helms, 1990). Similarly, Cross's model and its revisions (Cross, 1991, 1995; Cross, Strauss, & Fhagen-Smith, 1999; Cross & Vandiver, 2001) have stimulated a great deal of research, particularly testing the psychometric properties (see Chapter 2) of the model (Telesford, Mendoza-Denton, & Worrell, 2013; Vandiver, Cross, Worrell, & Fhagen-Smith, 2002; Vandiver, Fhagen-Smith, Cokley, Cross, & Worrell, 2001; Worrell & Gardner-Kitt, 2006; Worrell, Mendoza-Denton, Telesford, Simmons, & Martin, 2011; Worrell, Vandiver, Cross, & Fhagen-Smith, 2004; Worrell, Vandiver, Schaefer, Cross, & Fhagen-Smith, 2006; Worrell & Watson, 2008).

There are also models for Asian Americans/Filipinos (e.g., Chang & Kwan, 2009; Cheryan & Tsai, 2007; Kitano, 1982; Nadal, 2004), American Indians (e.g., Gonzalez & Bennett, 2011; Horse, 2012; Trimble, 1987, 2000; Trimble, Helms, & Root, 2002), Latinxs (e.g., Ruiz, 1990), and European Americans (e.g., Corvin & Wiggins, 1989; Helms, 1984, 1990, 1995b; Ponterotto, 1988), as well as for other identities such as gender (Kohlberg, 1966) and sexual orientation (e.g., Cass, 1979). It is beyond the scope of this chapter to describe all these models, so we will discuss three other models related to race (European American racial identity, Chicano/Latinx identity, and multiracial identity), one non-race-based identity model (homosexual identity), and one model that attempts to summarize them all. We will also briefly explain why Asian American/Filipino identity and American Indian identity development models are not specifically described.

European American Identity Development

> My wife is a woman of color. During our dating experience, I wasn't sure if we were going to marry just because I felt really stupid and ignorant sometimes. I definitely found her beautiful, but I don't think I appreciated all of her beauty until after some time.

When we first started to talk about her country, she first talked about food, dance, clothing and the indigenous aspects of her world. Then we talked more about norms and immigrating to the United States and she started to talk about racism and her hesitation to pursue our relationship because she didn't trust White people. I began to tell her that I didn't see color and that she was a human being to me, who deserved everything just like everyone else. I cringe now as I recall what I told her then. She left that night feeling reinforced about White folks. I talked with my family about it and they didn't understand why she was upset either. Why would they?! I'm not sure what I really thought at the time, but I knew that I really wanted to be with her. Initially, I wanted to learn more about discrimination and racism so that she would be with me. Then, after I paid really close attention, I saw much more, learned much more, and was humbled, embarrassed, angry, guilty, all at the same time. I saw how she was belittled next to me, and how her parents were regarded next to me. I didn't have to do a thing, and I was privileged. I know now that I will never fully understand the plight of persons of color, but I have only a view. I will advocate when I can, but I can never pretend to fully understand. She married me once she was sure that I can be at least her ally. She married me after she knew that I realized my privilege. She married me even though I am a White man.

—John, 40+-year-old European American man

Most often, cultural identity development is discussed as a minority phenomenon, in which members of minority groups struggle with the negative attitudes of and treatment by the dominant culture. What about those in the dominant group? Do they struggle with such questions as well?

John's story says that the answer is yes. By being in a relationship with an Asian American woman, John, a European American man, was forced to confront his own attitudes about race. Many multicultural psychologists have addressed the issue of European American racial identity (R. T. Carter, 1995; Corvin & Wiggins, 1989; D'Andrea, 2003; Helms, 1984, 1990, 1995b; Ponterotto, 1988). They believe that members of the dominant group must confront racism and oppression from the other side—as perpetrators rather than as recipients. Several models of European American racial identity development have been proposed (Hardiman, 1982; Ponterotto, 1988; Rowe, Bennett, & Atkinson, 1994), but the most cited and most researched was developed by Janet Helms (1984, 1990, 1995b).

Helms assumes that racist attitudes are a central part of being European American and that development of a healthy European American identity requires abandonment of racist ideas and the definition of oneself as nonracist. She delineates six stages (originally five) that European Americans go through in this process. She now uses the term *statuses* instead of *stages* to reflect the fact that individuals may exhibit attitudes and behaviors of more than one stage at the same time and that identity development is a dynamic process rather than a static condition that a person achieves or a category to which the person is assigned (Helms, 1995b).

contact—the status in which European American people are uninformed about the realities of racism and privilege.

color-blind—the stance that everyone is the same and that there is no need to acknowledge ethnic or racial differences.

In Helms's first status, **contact**, European American people are unaware of and uninformed about racism, discrimination, prejudice, and privilege. They have minimal experience with people from other backgrounds and may profess to be **color-blind** (as we discussed in Chapter 6), making such statements as "I don't see color," "People are people," and "We're all the same under our skin." Individuals in this status hold two opposing beliefs—one, that everything European American is superior and everything minority is inferior; and two, that racial and cultural differences do not matter. John was raised in an all–European American environment and had little exposure to people of color before he began to date his wife. He professed to be liberal, seeing all people as equal, and even told his wife he did not see her as different, not realizing that being a woman of color was infused into her identity.

A rather incredible illustration of this first status of contact came from popular television host Bill O'Reilly. He and the reverend Al Sharpton went to dinner in Harlem, and O'Reilly expressed surprise that there was no difference between this Black-owned restaurant and a European American–owned restaurant (Bauder, 2007).

Increased exposure to people from different backgrounds moves individuals into the second status, **disintegration**. Increased experience with people of color leads to information that is incongruent with a person's previously held notions; the contradiction causes dissonance. For example, working with an African American colleague on a project and seeing what a good job he or she

disintegration—the status in which European American people are in enough contact with people of color that their naivete about racism is shattered.

does contradicts the belief that Black people are unintelligent and incompetent. Seeing that same colleague passed over for promotions challenges the belief that everyone has an equal chance of success, regardless of color. Discovering that a loved one had to confront issues of racism challenges the idea that such things do not still happen in today's society, as John discovered when talking with his wife. The struggle to make sense of those contradictions may result in feelings of guilt, depression, anxiety, and helplessness. To reduce that conflict, European Americans may avoid members of diverse groups, try to convince others that people of color are not inferior, or convince themselves that racism does not exist or at least is not their fault.

Upon exposure to the injustices American Indians have endured throughout history, one student expressed her disappointment and guilt:

> It is disappointing that once again Americans have used another minority group and trampled all over them. It is making me ill to continue to read through the chapters only to find out how cruel we were to people who didn't look or act American enough for the government and some citizens. I am horrified that I may be associated with these low-life people just because I am not a minority. I try to contribute as a voting citizen in favor of the American Indians and other minority groups to bring justice.
>
> In last week's lecture, I learned for the first time that American Indian children were taken from their homes and put into boarding schools. The treatment and suffering those poor children went through was more than I could take for one lecture. It is just disappointing that again someone with power took advantage of those with less power . . . just because they can.
>
> —Janene, 20+-year-old European American woman

One of us was at a benefit dinner when a European American chief executive officer of a major corporation, who was married to an American Indian woman, told of his first exposure to the modern forms of racism:

> We were driving through Texas when we stopped at a restaurant for dinner. The waitress gave me a menu and I was trying to decide what to order. After a few minutes,

my wife asked me if I noticed anything "funny." I said no, but she pointed out that she did not have any silverware nor a menu. I flagged down our waitress and said, "Oh, miss, my wife doesn't have any silverware."

The waitress replied, "We don't serve Mexicans in this restaurant."

I said, "Oh, she isn't a Mexican, she is Indian."

Well, that was even worse in our waitress' eyes, and she asked us to leave.

—Harry, 50+-year-old European American man

---

reintegration—the status in which European American people retreat to their comfort zone within their European American communities.

---

pseudoindependence—the status in which European American people begin to acknowledge the realities of racism but believe that it is Blacks who should change, not European Americans.

---

immersion/emersion—the status in which European American people begin to form a more positive European American identity and to focus on changing European Americans, not African Americans.

---

autonomy—the status in which European American people are comfortable with their European American identity, understand that racism is connected with other forms of oppression, and work to address all forms of oppression.

Most likely, according to Helms (1995b), European Americans resolve the conflict by retreating to the comfort and acceptance of their own racial group and, either passively or actively, supporting European American superiority. This is the defining characteristic of the third status, **reintegration**.

The fourth status in Helms's model of European American racial identity development is **pseudoindependence**. This status marks the first phase in the development of a nonracist European American identity. European Americans begin to acknowledge some existence of racism but see the solution in changing Blacks, not European Americans. They may reach out to Blacks, wanting to help, but do so by imposing European American standards. They struggle to find a new European American identity but lack positive examples for how to do so.

In **immersion/emersion** a more positive European American identity begins to form. European Americans take time to explore their own culture, learning what it means to be European American in a diverse society. They no longer focus on changing Blacks, but instead focus on changing European Americans and understand that a central part of European American identity is letting go of one's own racist attitudes and actively fighting the racist attitudes of others.

The final status, **autonomy**, represents the accomplishment of a positive European American racial identity. European Americans feel good about their group but also find contact with individuals from other groups mutually enriching. They expand their sensitivity beyond racism to include other forms of oppression, acknowledge their privilege, and act as allies who actively seek to combat discrimination.

I am a bigot. I think I need to call myself that just as a now sober, once alcoholic person continues to call him/herself an alcoholic. I think that will always be a part of me, no matter what happens in my life now. I never thought of myself as a bigot until I met Wanda. Wanda is a beautiful, educated, and headstrong African American woman, and I fell head over heels in love with her. We worked in the same place and I initially admired her only from afar. I mean, I thought at the time that I could never date this woman because in my mind I knew I couldn't be seen with her. At the time, these were thoughts that were in my head, probably subconscious. One day, I bumped into her and that was the end of me. We had so much to talk about that we were late coming back from the break room, and I HAD to ask her to have coffee after work. We began dating, and Wanda was never shy about issues regarding racism and discrimination. She would try to get me to have discussions with her, but I told her that I completely agreed with her thoughts and that there was nothing more disgusting than racist people. She would laugh, and I would quiver with disgust at myself for the lie that I told. After about 6 months of dating, Wanda asked me to meet her parents and I happily agreed. I thought her parents lived in the same neighborhood that she did, but was I wrong! A White man going into South Central (Los Angeles) with a Black woman at 8 p.m. for dinner was not fun for me. I was scared, and I think most of the Black men who killed me with their looks knew that, too. I don't know what I expected when I entered the home. Although humble, it was clean and the smell of food was all over. Her parents were really nice people, unlike the rest of them, were my thoughts. A couple of months later, Wanda began to ask questions about my family and friends. She began to wonder why she had not met any of my friends or family members, and I didn't know what to say. One day, Wanda finally lashed out, called me a racist, and walked out. I knew that I was, but I didn't want to lose her. I tried to talk to her and tell her some of the things that I was doing in order to educate myself, but she told me that she would know if I was telling the truth. She quit the job, and stopped taking my calls. Very recently, I saw Wanda at a coffee shop that we used to frequent, and she was pleasant. I asked to talk to her, and I proceeded to tell her about all of the feelings that I had while we dated. I talked about my ignorance, denial, and racist beliefs. I said that I was confused about my attraction to her because I've never looked at a woman of color twice, but I admitted that being called a racist was the best thing that has ever happened to me. Wanda reached out and touched my hand, gave me a hug, and walked away from my life, and I haven't seen her since. I know that I have so much more to learn, but now I know that I can and will.

—Steve, 30+-year-old European American man

In Steve's story we see several aspects of Helms's model, such as his acknowledgment that he is racist and will probably always have some racist ideas, his conflicted feelings about being attracted to and dating a Black woman, and his attempts to be honest, to grow, and to educate himself. Which status do you think best describes Steve's racial identity?

If I were to distill my feelings about my ethnicity, I would say that being White, straight, and middle class puts me on an incredible footing to speak out against defamation and bigotry, because I am speaking out against my own self-interest. An interest in politics has also made me an advocate of equality for all human beings, because I have read accounts of history and see every day on the news what and who "my people" have exploited and continue to exploit to get where they are. If I were to label myself, I would say I am American, Oklahoman, and human. I sometimes feel guilty for calling myself an American because too many people have died to put me where I am today. I have come to be proud of that label though, because to me it embodies those who have willingly and unwillingly sacrificed so much.

—Bill, 20+-year-old European American man

Although the stories from Steve and Bill are powerful lessons illustrating that European Americans struggle with the issues around their own race and racial identity, sadly, many European Americans remain in the contact and color-blind statuses of Helm's model. For example, Wijeyesinghe and Jackson (2012) cite Hardiman and Keehn (2012), who interviewed European American students to get a sense of how European American students think about racial identity, privilege, and their understanding of racism in the 21st century. They asked students how they identified racially and whether they had attachment to that identity. A common theme is shared in the following response from a female European American student:

> I don't see myself as belonging to a particular racial or ethnic group . . . [I am] White, Caucasian, you know, just who I am I guess. [This] is not something that comes up in my everyday life. You know, the people I hang out with are just people I hang out with . . . everyone is just kind of "hey, we are people." (Hardiman & Keehn, 2012, as cited in, 2012, p. 125)

The work and writings of several other experts (e.g., Bonilla-Silva, 2017; Neville, Gallardo, & Sue, 2016; DiAngelo, 2016) further demonstrate this common narrative that many European Americans have in relation to their identity. These authors argue that a goal of European American identity development should be more than being *nonracist*; rather, the goal should be to be *anti-racist*, which involves being active instead of passive.

Chicano/Latinx Identity Development

Ruiz (1990) proposed a Chicano/Latinx identity development model based on four assumptions: *marginality has a high correlation with maladjustment*; *forced assimilation produces negative experiences*, which are destructive to an individual; *pride in one's own ethnic identity has a positive correlation with mental health*; and *pride in one's own ethnic identity results in freedom of choice*, especially in the acculturation process. Delgado-Romero (2001) reported that Ruiz's model was derived from case histories of Chicano, Mexican American, and other Latinx university students. We can then assume that the model may not be representative of other Latinxs, with consideration to their country of origin, socioeconomic status, acculturation, and so on. Ruiz (1990) proposed five stages of Chicano/Latinx identity development: causal, cognitive, consequence, working through, and successful resolution.

In the **causal stage**, negative messages from the environment and other individuals, which may be humiliating and traumatizing, can cause one to negate, deny, or ignore his or her Latinx heritage. Persons may fail to identify as a Latinx or with the Latinx culture. During the **cognitive stage**, because of the negative and erroneous messages from the previous stage, ethnic group membership is associated

causal stage—an emotional stage when the individual accepts the negative labels attached to a Latinx identity and feels humiliated and traumatized by these labels.

cognitive stage—the belief that maintaining a Latinx identity necessarily means being poor, that escape from poverty and prejudice can be attained only through assimilation to the mainstream culture, and that success in life is possible only through assimilation.

with prejudice and poverty, and both the only means of escape and the only road to success are to assimilate into the dominant, European American society. In the **consequence stage**, an individual may reject his or her Chicano/Latinx heritage because of ongoing and intensifying fragmentation of his or her ethnic identity. Individuals may feel significant pressure to assimilate given the negative messages and desire for acceptance from the majority culture.

consequence stage—an estrangement from the Latinx community because of the sense that negative attributes are associated with being Latinx.

I was born in Zacatecas, Mexico. I've always been told that people with lighter skin and light eyes were typically born there. Then again, many people from D.F. (Distrito Federal) seemed to also have light eyes and light skin. What I remember most after "crossing the border" is my father saying that we were "Americans now." I remember saying "Yay!," though I wasn't really sure what I was celebrating about. Then I went to school, and I was 7 years old. I spoke no English, but I looked like a *huera* (White girl). Kids didn't understand why I looked White, but I didn't understand a word that they said. I had to get "special treatment," but not in a good way because I didn't speak English. As I got older and learned more English, I remember hating having to translate for my parents. I was embarrassed of them and I was embarrassed to be Mexican. Mexicans were "beaners" and "spics" who ate lots of beans and had lots of kids. I wanted to be White. I was White. It felt good after a while and I remember that in middle school, all my friends were White and I told everyone that I was a foreign exchange student or something like that. I didn't look like my parents really, so people bought it. It really wasn't until college that I started to learn more about my culture and I really felt embarrassed for myself. I remember approaching my parents once, apologetic for my behaviors as a child. It made me feel worse that they just laughed it off and told me that they understood. I don't think they do understand. I felt as if I spat on my parents and my culture. Nowadays, when people assume I'm White, I'm not sure that I get angry, but I definitely make sure that I correct them.

—Maria Teresa, 30+-year-old Mexican American woman

In the **working-through stage**, the individual begins to struggle with the ethnic conflict, and this stage marks the beginning of a healthier and integrated Chicano/Latinx identity. The individual increases his or her ethnic consciousness and reintegrates and reconnects with his or her ethnic identity and ethnic community. In the final stage of **successful resolution**, the individual attains a greater sense of self-acceptance and acceptance of cultural and ethnic identity, believing that ethnic identity is positive and can lead one to be successful. Increased/improved self-esteem is also attained in this stage.

Ruiz's (1990) model is a stage model and follows the structure of other published models. It is also pan-ethnic, covering many subgroups that are subsumed under the umbrella of Latinx. We can assume that the model may not be representative of other Latinxs, with consideration of their country of origin, socioeconomic status,

working-through stage—a stage when the individual feels distress because of alienation from his or her Latinx community and is therefore motivated to integrate one's Latinx identity into a sense of self.

successful resolution state—the final stage when the Latinx identity is integrated into one's own identity and positive attributes of the Latinx identity are included.

acculturation, and so on. A model that takes into account the multiple Latinx subgroups and the complexities of intersecting identities was put forth by Ferdman and Gallegos (2001). The authors stressed the importance of the way Latinxs view themselves through "lenses" that capture how the individuals see themselves, how they see the broader context in which Latinxs reside, and how much they keep in or out.

Asian American/Filipino American Identity Development

Nadal (2004) explains some Asian American identity development models, but he also points out that certain models were based on Chinese Americans (S. Sue & Sue, 1971), Japanese Americans (Kitano, 1982), Asian American college students (Suinn, Ahuna, & Khoo, 1992), Filipino Americans (Nadal, 2004), and the racial and cultural identity development model (R/CID) (addressed later in this chapter). Nadal reported that Asian American models, although they make an essential contribution to Asian American literature, fail to address intragroup differences.

As much as different Asian American identity development models attempt to examine and explain ethnic identity development, there is much to say about the fact that such models cannot fully explain Asian Americans as a whole given the heterogeneity in the Asian/Pacific Islander community. Current Asian American identity development models cannot seem to describe identity development that encompasses all Asian/Pacific Islander individuals; therefore, the R/CID is most typically utilized to describe the ethnic identity development of Asian/Pacific Islanders.

> I was born in Hong Kong, but our family moved to the United States when I was about 5 years old. I speak Taiwanese, Mandarin, and English, of course. I remember attending college and talking with schoolmates who were psychology majors. They were talking about identity development and different models. I know that I felt that my identity could not be explained by models. All I know is how people wondered how I was able to learn to speak different languages. All I know is how people wondered about my "accent." All I know is how I had to translate for my parents since age 8. All I know is how I went to college, but people half-expected me to because I was born in Hong Kong and not in some obscure place in China. All I know is that I've felt more American than how some people described me to be. I'm not confused, but I'm very curious as to how these models that my schoolmates talk about describe the whole me. They didn't and I was annoyed. I don't think Chinese, Japanese, Thai, Koreans, Filipinos, and other Asian Americans need to be put in one group.
>
> —Michelle, 20+-year-old Chinese American woman

American Indian Identity Development

As with the discussion on Asian American identity models and the great heterogeneity in the Asian/Pacific Islander community, the diversity and histories of each American Indian tribe make it difficult to develop an all-encompassing identity development model for the indigenous people of North America. Having said that, a few unique characteristics in the identity development for American Indians are common. First, a primary consideration in the identity development of American Indians is political and not racial. Although American Indians are designated as a category on the Census Bureau and Equal Employment Opportunity Commission forms, the legal definition of American Indians is political and based on sovereign status through treaties signed with the federal government. As such, many American Indian individuals prefer not to be lumped together with the descriptor *people of color*. Although American Indian people recognize the struggle of oppression and marginalization that is shared with people of color, using that descriptor minimizes their indigenous and sovereign status. Second, another common factor in identity development for American Indians is related to time and space, in other words, becoming aware or gaining consciousness of their history with genocide and their connection to this land, which many tribes refer to as Turtle Island. These two aspects profoundly shape the identities of American Indians, regardless of whether they live on reservations or in urban settings, because they are reminded of it every day while living in a colonized state.

All the racial identity development models discussed thus far apply to individuals from one racial background. What about people from multiracial backgrounds? What challenges do they face in their identity development process?

Multiracial Identity Development

In 1967, the Supreme Court declared antimiscegenation laws (laws that forbade individuals from different races to marry) unconstitutional. At the time, 16 states had antimiscegenation laws on the books. Since 1967, the number of interracial marriages and multiracial births has been on the rise (Spickard, 1989). A recent Pew Center report showed that in 2010, 8.4% of marriages were interracial/interethnic compared to 3.2% in 1980 (W. Wang, 2012). The 2000 census was the first to allow individuals to mark more than one race. By 2010, more than 9 million people (2.9% of the population) identified as multiracial (N. A. Jones & Bullock, 2012). The growth in the multiracial population is also seen in the number of multiracial children. In the 2000–2010 decade, the number of multiracial children increased to 4.2 million (Saulny, 2011). With these changing demographics have come changes in attitudes. A recent Gallup poll that covered data from 1959 to 2013 showed approval of interracial marriages shifting from 4.0% to 87% (Newport, 2013).

As the number of multiracial people in the United States has risen, increased attention has been paid to their unique identity development process. Individuals from multiracial backgrounds face a more complex identity process than do those from monoracial backgrounds (Kerwin & Ponterotto, 1995). These individuals must reconcile the heritage of parents from two racial backgrounds and decide where they fit in a society that likes to pigeonhole people into a single category (Keerdoja, 1984). In addition, they may face discrimination from both groups because they are not seen as full members of either one (D. J. Johnson, 1992; D. W. Sue & Sue, 2003). Multiracial individuals may feel pressured to identify with one group over the other. Often, society's reactions are based on the person's appearance—that is, what racial group he or she looks like. Another recent study by the Pew Research Center (2015) on being multiracial in America indicated that 61% of respondents with a background that includes more than one race do not consider themselves multiracial. This multiracial gap in identity, however, differed for different groups. For example, only a quarter of adults who are biracially European American and American Indian consider themselves multiracial, whereas 70% of European and Asian biracial adults

> The country has fixated on Black–White intermarriage since the days of slavery. The prohibition on these marriages eliminated Black economic competition and Black competition for White women. Today, however racial intermarriages cover a wide spectrum of racial mixing.
>
> —Maria Root, (2001)
> multiracial researcher

self-identify as multiracial. There are varied reasons for this, but one has to do with pressure in society to identify as a single race. One biracial woman (European and American Indian) noted that it was easier to simply say she was White, because she gets tired of having to explain who she is.

> As a multiracial individual, sometimes it feels like I have no culture at all. I am Caucasian, Hispanic, and Native American. My family has lived in the United States for as long as any of us can remember. Any ethnic culture that we had seems to have gradually disappeared over time as my family members assimilated themselves into American society, leaving behind their old identities and embracing a new American culture. . . .
>
> I am very grateful for what my parents have given and sacrificed for my well-being. They've done a lot and worked hard to get where they are now and have never left me with a want or a need. Though if I could request one thing out of them, it would be to teach me more about what it means to be a Hispanic, European, and Native American.
>
> —Mona, 20+-year-old multiracial (Latinx/American Indian/
> European American) woman

We see many of the conflicts related to multiracial identity described in Mona's story: confusion about her ethnic status, the need to express gratitude to her parents to assuage her guilt, which stemmed from being angry at them for not teaching her about her multiple ethnicities, and ultimately a wish that she knew more about her heritage. Such confusion and conflict about identity has been the topic of interest among researchers in recent years (Charmaraman & Grossman, 2010; Cheng & Lee, 2009; Shih & Sanchez, 2009; Suyemoto, 2004).

Some biracial/multiracial individuals feel that their feelings and opinions are depreciated, sometimes even by their friends:

> Something that really bothered me with this was when I posted a bit of a rant on Facebook about how White individuals were privileged, and was called out for being half White by an Asian friend of mine, since he obviously could not relate to my perspective. Racism is real for me, and even though it isn't quite as bad as the racism affecting Hispanic and African American individuals, it still separates me from the pack.
>
> —Ronny, 20+-year-old biracial (European American/
> Asian) man

personal identity stage—the stage or status in which a child bases his or her identity on personal factors, such as self-esteem, instead of on race or ethnicity.

choice of group categorization stage—the stage or status in which a child is forced to choose which race or ethnicity he or she should use as the basis of his or her identity.

Many models of multiracial identity development have been proposed (J. H. Jacobs, 1992; Kerwin & Ponterotto, 1995; Kich, 1992). The first was W. S. C. Poston's (1990) five-stage model of biracial identity development. At the **personal identity stage**, a young child's sense of self is independent from his or her racial group. Identity is instead based primarily on personal factors, such as self-esteem, that develop within the context of the family. In the second stage, **choice of group categorization**, the young person feels pressure to choose one identity over the other. That pressure may come

The number of biracial and multiracial individuals has increased in recent years. *Photographs by mimagephotography/ Shutterstock and Warren Goldswain/Shutterstock*

from family members, peers, physical appearance, or society (C. C. I. Hall, 1980, 1992). In the next stage, **enmeshment/denial**, feelings of guilt and self-hatred arise from choosing one group over another. A positive multiracial identity begins to emerge in the **appreciation stage**, when the person begins to broaden his or her perspective and begins to explore the previously rejected side of his or her racial heritage. Finally, in the fifth stage, **integration**, the person sees the benefits of embracing both identities.

In his model, W. S. C. Poston (1990) suggested that healthy resolution of the multiracial experience entails integration of and appreciation for both racial backgrounds. There is an implicit assumption in his model that all biracial individuals follow the same path. Root (1990, 1998, 2004) agreed that multiracial individuals must come to terms with both sides of their heritage, but described five possible resolutions for this process. Root says that a multiracial person may choose to (a) accept the identity society assigns, (b) identify with both racial groups, (c) identify with a single racial group, (d) identify with a new *mixed-race* group, or (e) identify with the race considered the one with the higher-status culture in this country (hyperdescension as opposed to hypodescension).[1] According to Root,

enmeshment/denial stage—the stage or status in which a child feels guilty about choosing one race or ethnicity over the other, because this is an implicit rejection of the parent whose race or ethnicity was not chosen.

appreciation stage—the stage or status in which a child/adolescent begins to broaden his or her perspective to include the race or ethnicity not initially selected for his or her identity.

integration stage—the stage or status in which a child/adolescent/adult sees the benefits of embracing both races or ethnicities.

---

1   Root (2004) added this fifth resolution, which she called symbolic identity. There is typically a hypodescension of identity wherein one identifies with the lower-status culture in this country. For example, if someone is an offspring of one Black and one European American parent, the person's identity is generally considered Black. In symbolic identity, there is a hyperdescension of identity. In other words, the person identifies as being European American and consciously knows that this is a nonstandard identity. Being half Black is only symbolic to the person; the person knows he or she is half Black, but it does not have much relevance in his or her life. This is akin to the situation of someone with Irish ancestral roots who may become more aware of his or her Irish heritage on St. Patrick's Day but for whom being of Irish descent does not have much bearing on his or her day-to-day life.

each of these can represent a healthy adjustment to one's multiracial background, although accepting the identity that society assigns is passive and may not be as secure as the four other, more active, resolutions of one's identity.

However, just because someone has resolved his or her biracial identity does not mean he or she has escaped the sting of racism. This student discussed the racial tension still felt in his parents' families of origin:

> I am the product of an interracial couple—my mom's ethnic background is German American while my dad's ethnic background is African American, specifically Kenyan. I am also currently in a relationship that is very serious and interracial to an extent. My fiancée is predominantly White. What is amazing to me is the ignorance that we thought was out of our society regarding race, and how it can still [affect] our relationships today. When my parents got married, my grandfather, my mom's dad, refused to come to the wedding, much less give her away. My uncle had to give my mom away and it broke her heart that her father could not accept the fact that she was happy. It took my mom and grandfather a long time to mend the pain that was caused by that argument. My grandfather finally saw that my dad was a good man regardless of the color of his skin, and that he had no intention of leaving my mom, and my mom was finally able to forgive him for what he did to her. Also my grandfather's mom and dad never spoke to my mom again.
>
> —Jack, 20+-year-old biracial (African American/European American) man

As we have mentioned, racial identity has dominated the field of cultural identity development. However, several models address other minority identities. Here we present a model of sexual identity development as an example.

Gay/Lesbian Identity Development

> I was 7 and I think I knew I was gay. I always felt more comfortable "hanging out" with my girl cousins, playing with dolls, and watching stars on TV (all men, of course). I swooned with them over these hunks on TV, and they didn't seem to mind. I remember my dad always threatening me about how he would knock my hips back in place if I didn't learn to walk like a boy. I couldn't help it that I loved my girl cousins and the way they played pretend. I would beg for them to put makeup on me and they always did because I always had the longest eyelashes. Though, when we got a little older, my cousins began to get weird. They started to say that I was weird because I didn't like to play with the boys. People started telling my father right in front of my face that he better beat it out of me before "it" got worse. Because of all of my family members, my school friends, and even my parents' friends calling me weird, I really started to look at my behaviors and think, "Am I weird?" Especially when I started sixth grade and I always admired this boy who had black hair and green eyes. I always told myself that it was because he was "cool" and that I wanted to be cool too. While I admired this boy from afar, all the other boys bugged all of the girls. Even though deep inside I knew that I was gay from a very young age, it was not confirmed until I was in eighth grade. I was in the boy's bathroom at school and some guy kissed me . . . for a long time! He was a loner kid. I think we made out until we

heard other boys coming. I was excited! He moved away after a semester, which was probably good because I've had to maintain an image because of the years that have passed that my dad threatened me constantly. I had transformed into this stud whom all the girls wanted. Besides, I really didn't want to be different from all the boys. I even got myself a pretty girlfriend. I guess back then, looking straight and being gay was okay for me. It helped me fit in for a little while. Never mind the fact that I really had to watch out and not stare at boys too long. Never mind the fact that I was truly hiding under a stone. I had to do what I had to do to fit in.

—Rudy, 20+-year-old gay European American man

Rudy's story describes the phases he went through in his coming-out process. **Coming out**, or the process by which nonheterosexual individuals come to terms with their sexuality and share that orientation with others, is a unique aspect of their identity development. The gamut of nonheterosexual identities is broad and the current abbreviation

> **coming out**—the process by which a gay, lesbian, or bisexual individual openly expresses his or her sexual orientation.

is LGBTTQQIAAP, which stands for lesbian, gay, bisexual, transgender, transsexual, queer, questioning, intersex, asexual, ally, pansexual. For practical purposes, the label *nonheterosexual* is used in this section, although it is important to note that the length of the acronym is intended to be inclusive of the wide array of sexual identities and that an ethnic gloss such as *gay* would be inaccurate to capture the complexity of people who are not heterosexual. Nonheterosexual individuals face heterosexism in that everyone is assumed to be heterosexual. Coming out is also not a one-time event. It happens over time and in different contexts. Whenever the nonheterosexual person meets someone new, he or she must decide whether to divulge his or her sexual orientation (Israel, 2004).

Cass (1979) proposed a series of six stages that help to explain some of the thoughts and feelings Rudy had about his sexual orientation. According to Cass, the first stage that young people go through when questioning their sexual identity is **identity confusion**. This is when the first awareness of being different from same-sex peers occurs. During childhood or adolescence, the young person begins to recognize feelings, thoughts, and behaviors that are outside the norm for how their gender is socialized, such as preferring activi-

> **identity confusion**—the stage or status in which a gay, lesbian, or bisexual individual begins to question his or her sexual identity.

ties or having interests typical of another gender. Rudy noticed that he liked hanging out with his female cousins, playing with dolls, and admiring male television stars. At first that was acceptable, but soon others made fun of him because of it. Feelings and thoughts of attraction toward same-sex peers may not be apparent at this stage, but the feelings of being *the other* or different are enough to cause the child or adolescent to withdraw from family members and peers.

The next stage is **identity comparison**. In this stage, the differences are more pronounced, and a nonheterosexual child recognizes how he or she is different. Thoughts and feelings about same-sex peers become more conscious.

> **identity comparison**—the stage or status in which a gay, lesbian, or bisexual individual recognizes his or her feelings about same-sex individuals.

A girl who finds herself attracted to another girl sees that other girls talk about boys. This creates incongruence because the girl knows she's a girl and has most likely been socialized as a girl. Suddenly, things change and she has feelings that are not part of the accepted social guidelines for being a girl. She may question why she is so different. When Rudy heard the comments and questions by his family members and friends about his behavior, he began to question himself and asked, "Am I weird?" In the sixth grade he consciously noticed himself admiring another boy in his class.

identity tolerance—the stage or status in which a gay, lesbian, or bisexual individual fully recognizes his or her nonheterosexual feelings but attempts to hide them from others and from himself or herself by trying to believe, for example, that it is just a phase he or she is going through.

The third stage of sexual identity development in Cass's (1979) model is **identity tolerance**. In this stage the individual learns to walk a tightrope. The nonheterosexual person is now fully conscious that he or she has sexual feelings toward others of the same sex, but keeps the feelings hidden. Others most likely remain unaware that the individual has this orientation. This is what we typically describe as *being in the closet*. The person may work very hard to keep his or her orientation a secret, but that results in feelings of guilt, pain, anger, and self-hatred. The individual is in constant turmoil because he or she must constantly internally justify his or her actions. The individual also holds out hope that this may just be a phase. Rudy confirmed his same-sex attraction when he made out with another boy in the bathroom in the eighth grade. However, he then became the "stud" that his father wanted him to be and that all the girls desired. He even got a girlfriend and worked hard to fit in with the other boys, all the while being careful not to stare at other boys too long.

identity acceptance—the stage or status in which a gay, lesbian, or bisexual individual fully accepts his or her sexual orientation and is about to come out to others.

The fourth stage is **identity acceptance**. In this stage, the person moves one step closer to coming out. In acceptance, the individual can no longer deny his or her same-sex attraction. Nonetheless, the individual continues to live in a secret world where same-sex sexual relationships occur "underground" in limited, specific environments (e.g., gay clubs) and infrequently for fear of being discovered. The person continues to internalize society's negative views of same-sex attraction as evil, sinful, and unacceptable. This may lead to feelings of hopelessness and even suicide. The suicide rate is high for individuals who come to accept their same-sex sexual attraction as a fact but lack the social support needed to assume pride in their orientation. Specifically, lesbian, gay, and bisexual youths are 4 times more likely to attempt suicide than straight youths (Centers for Disease Control and Prevention, 2011), and lesbian, gay, and bisexual youths who come from highly rejecting families are 8.4 times more likely to attempt suicide as their lesbian, gay, or bisexual peers whose families are accepting or show low levels of rejection (Family Acceptance Project, 2009).

identity pride—the stage or status in which a gay, lesbian, or bisexual individual openly expresses his or her sexual orientation and takes pride in that identity.

The next stage in Cass's model is **identity pride**. In this stage, the person formally *comes out of the closet*. The nonheterosexual person now feels pride in his or her orientation and finds causes (e.g., rallies, clubs, walk-a-thons) to explore, express, and celebrate his or her newly found voice. Yet there is not a complete association of personal identity with same-sex attraction. For example, a man may come out to his parents and begin to join marches and rallies for gay pride, yet he may still not be out at work or with some of his friends, and he may expend a great deal of energy maintaining these multiple identities.

In the final stage, **identity synthesis**, people are able to integrate their sexual identity with their other identities (e.g., woman, African American, student). Individuals are comfortable with their orientation and no longer feel the need to justify their being. Self-acceptance provides people with the coping mechanisms needed to endure and fight the ignorance and discrimination they will face in embrac-

identity synthesis—the state or status in which a gay, lesbian, or bisexual individual is able to integrate all aspects of his or her identities, such as ethnic minority status and gender.

ing their diverse selves. This positive self-acceptance is most possible when the individual has a strong social support system to help him or her withstand societal pressures. However, that support may be difficult to obtain from family members and friends who are unwilling to accept the person's sexual orientation. It may take some time and effort to build a new support system, and this may include relocation to an environment that is more supportive (e.g., moving to a city with a large, visible nonheterosexual population).

Rudy does not describe his movement through the last two stages, but the following story describes some struggles faced by a young woman in her coming-out process.

> I wanted to be straight for a long time, but I've known that I was a lesbian for an even longer time. Anyway, when I came out to my parents, I guess I was hopeful. My dad said that he would pray for my salvation, and my mom didn't say a word. After 8 years, you'd think that one of them knew that I was not straight (I brought home my first girlfriend when I was 12). I knew I was queer before that, but I was too afraid to make any moves toward any girls. Then I turned 18, and I met the most beautiful girl in the world. I wanted to let everyone know that she was my girl. Her parents were really cool and she had been "out" for a long time. I thought it was time to come out of the closet after many years of feeling like crap and being and staying invisible. Anyway, I told my parents that I was queer, but they really reacted more violently after they found out about Michelle. I guess it was okay to say I was queer, but it wasn't okay to have proof that I am. Nowadays, Michelle and I live together. She and I go out to West Hollywood on weekends and once in a while we go to "Pride" parades, but I'm not really sure what to call us, or myself for that matter. I know that I love her, that I'm queer, but there still feels like something's missing. I remember having to write a paper in college recently, asking the question, Who are you? I wasn't sure how to answer it because being a lesbian is the most predominant identity that "rules" my life right now, but I know that I'm more.
>
> —Leticia, 20+-year-old Latinx lesbian woman

Leticia's story highlights the complexities of family interactions and sexual orientation but also invites questions about intersecting identities. What are the unique complexities of being both lesbian and Latinx? Strong arguments have been recently advanced for the importance of understanding the intersection of identities in reducing health disparities (Bowleg, 2012).

Racial and Cultural Identity Development Model
At this point you might be thinking, "I'm confused. There are too many of these identity models and they all sound alike!" It is true. There are many cultural identity development models, and we have covered only a few. They sound similar because of the influence of the original model

proposed by Cross (1971) and because all people in minority groups have the shared experience of oppression. A group of multicultural psychologists proposed a comprehensive model of cultural identity development that pulls together the common features of all the models for different groups. The first was presented by Atkinson, Morten, and Sue (1979, 1989, 1998), who called it the *minority identity development model*. The model was later revised by D. W. Sue and Sue (1990, 1999, 2003, 2008), who called it the **racial and cultural identity development model (R/CID)**. Each stage in the R/CID addresses how the individual feels about himself or herself, others of the same group, others of another minority group, and members of the majority or dominant group (D. W. Sue & Sue, 2003, 2008). The model is summarized in Table 7.1.

The first stage of the R/CID model is **conformity**. In this stage, individuals show a strong preference for the values, beliefs, and features of the dominant culture over their own. They have incorporated society's view that the dominant culture is superior. The individual has strong negative attitudes toward the self, his or her own group, and other minority groups. Members of the dominant groups are respected, admired, and emulated.

racial and cultural identity development model (R/CID)—a general model that covers all forms of cultural identity and addresses how one relates to oneself, to others of the same culture, to others of different cultures, and to the dominant cultural group.

conformity—the stage in which an individual sees the dominant culture as better and superior to all groups and sees his or her own cultural group as *less than* or inferior.

TABLE 7.1 The Racial and Cultural Identity Development Model

Stages of minority development model	Attitude toward self	Attitude toward others of the same minority	Attitude toward others of a different minority	Attitude toward the dominant group
Stage 1: Conformity	Self-depreciating or neutral because of low race salience	Group-depreciating or neutral because of low race salience	Discriminatory or neutral	Group appreciating
Stage 2: Dissonance and appreciating	Conflict between self-depreciating and group appreciating	Conflict between group-depreciating views of minority hierarchy and feelings of shared experience	Conflict between dominant held and group depreciating	Conflict between group appreciating
Stage 3: Resistance and immersion	Self-appreciating	Group-appreciating experiences and feelings of culturocentrism	Conflict between feelings of empathy for other minority	Group depreciating
Stage 4: Introspection	Concern with basis of self-appreciation	Concern with nature of unequivocal appreciation	Concern with ethnocentric basis for judging others	Concern with basis of group depreciation
Stage 5: Integrative awareness	Self-appreciating	Group appreciating	Group appreciating	Selective appreciation

Note: From *Counseling American Minorities: A Cross-cultural Perspective*, 5th ed., by D. R. Atkinson, G. Morten, and D. W. Sue, Eds., 1998, (p. 41). Dubuque, IA: Brown; and *Counseling the Culturally Diverse*, 4th and 5th eds., by D. W. Sue and D. Sue, 2003 and 2008, (p. 215). New York, NY: Wiley.

Next is the **dissonance** stage. At some point, the individual encounters information that contradicts his or her cultural values and beliefs. For example, a closeted gay man who thinks all gay men are "fairies" may meet a gay man who is very masculine. An Asian American person who thinks racism does not exist anymore may experience a racist incident. Although movement into the dissonance stage may occur suddenly with a traumatic event (as discussed in Cross's model), the developers of the R/CID model believe it occurs slowly through a gradual breakdown of denial as one questions his or her attitudes from the conformity stage. In dissonance, the person is in conflict between positive and negative views of the self, members of his or her own group, members of other minority groups, and members of the majority. One of our students discussed her transition from the conformity stage to the dissonance stage:

dissonance—the stage in which there is a sudden or gradual occurrence that challenges a person's belief that the dominant group is superior and that minority groups, including his or her own, are inferior.

> I always thought that being and acting Filipino would not allow me to have American friends because my culture is so different than Americans. I thought that I wouldn't fit in unless I acted like them. Sadly, I have sacrificed on many occasions that opportunity to teach my friends that other cultures are great if only they would give it a chance instead of making jokes about how weird other people are. I let them put me down when I would wear certain clothes or do my hair a certain way because it made me look more Asian. I have to say that I have learned that many of my so-called friends really aren't my friends. They don't want me to be who I am; they want me to be who they are, and I can't any longer. I'm not too sad to cut some of these people out of my life because I have had to deal with trying hard to be like them for so long that I just made myself exhausted. This class has taught me the beauty in understanding who I am, and where I came from. I also was able to look at other cultures' perspectives, and I have gained a lot of respect for them as well. I am choosing to become an ally for my fellow culture, as well as other minority cultures.
>
> —Celeste, 20+-year-old Filipina American woman

The third stage of the R/CID is **resistance and immersion**. In this stage, the person does an about-face and completely espouses minority views and rejects the dominant culture. The person feels guilt and shame about previously being a sellout and contributing to the oppression of his or her own group. There is anger, distrust, and dislike for the dominant group. The person is motivated to discover more about his or her own culture and builds a stronger sense of connection to his or her own group. Relationships with people belonging to other minority groups tend to be transitory and superficial.

In the **introspection** stage, the individual begins to let go of some of the intense feelings of anger toward the dominant culture and redirect that energy into greater

resistance and immersion—the stage in which the person becomes more immersed within his or her own cultural group, rejecting the dominant culture with extreme feelings of anger, guilt, and shame for his or her initial preference of the dominant culture and rejection of his or her own.

introspection—the stage in which a person becomes less angry at, as well as distrustful of, the dominant group, less immersed in his or her own group, more appreciating of other cultural groups, and more apt to educate himself or herself about his or her own identity, though the process still creates some inner conflict.

understanding of himself or herself and his or her own group. The person moves away from total immersion in his or her own group toward greater autonomy, but there is some conflict. There is also more of an attempt to understand the attitudes and experiences of other groups, including a struggle to sort out the positive and negative aspects of the dominant group.

integrative awareness—the stage in which a person finds greater balance, appreciates his or her own group as well as other cultural groups, and becomes aware of himself or herself as an individual and a cultural being, recognizing differences among cultural groups, both positive and negative.

The final stage of the R/CID is **integrative awareness**. In this stage, the person achieves an inner sense of security and appreciates the positive and the negative aspects of both his or her own culture and the dominant culture. The person has a positive sense of group pride but is also able to question group values. The person sees himself or herself as a unique individual, a member of a cultural group, and a member of the larger society. The person now reaches out to members of other minority groups to gain a greater understanding of their attitudes and experiences and expresses support for all oppressed people. The person also distinguishes between people in the dominant group in deciding whom to trust and in determining who also actively seeks to eliminate oppression.

The R/CID attempts to pull together the common characteristics of all the stage models. Do you think it is useful to have one comprehensive model of cultural identity development, or do you think each group has unique characteristics and experiences that must be taken into account? Try going back to previous stories in the chapter (e.g., Deana, Marie, Rudy, Leticia) and applying the stages of the R/CID.

Other Identities

Are there other kinds of ethnic identities? Is there an American identity that excludes people of color? Are there problems when people of color identify with American identity? Some recent studies have examined these questions.

Jiménez (2010) examined something called *affiliative ethnic identity*. This is defined as "individual identities rooted in knowledge, regular consumption and deployment of an ethnic culture that is unconnected to an individual's ethnic ancestry until that individual regards herself, and may be regarded by others, as an affiliate of a particular ethnic group" (p. 1757). Individuals who engage in affiliative ethnic identities enact their identities through dress, language, cuisine, art, music, and other cultural markers. Affiliative identities are interwoven into individuals' sense of self, so these identities are not merely ones of convenience or context.

Affiliative ethnic identity presupposes deep knowledge of the culture. Individuals do not claim ancestry in the affiliative ethnic group nor do they deny affiliation to their own ancestral group. Finally, the identity label is given by a member of the ethnic group in question (Jiménez, 2010). These characteristics are important in understanding the difference between affiliative ethnic identity and a behavior that may, at face value, appear related: cultural appropriation. Cultural appropriation occurs when people use artifacts or processes belonging to a cultural group outside their own (Rogers, 2006). The use and even ownership of artifacts and processes from a marginalized group "involve the assimilation and exploitation of marginalized and colonized cultures and in the survival of subordinated cultures and their resistance to dominant cultures" (Rogers, 2006, p. 474). Examples of cultural appropriation are ubiquitous in the music industry. Amandla Stenberg, the actress who plays Rue in *The Hunger Games*, speaks poignantly of these examples in a popular YouTube video (https://www.youtube.com/watch?v=O1KJRRSB_XA).

Devos and his colleagues (Devos, Gavin, & Quintana, 2010; Devos & Ma, 2008) wondered whether non–European Americans can ever be perceived as being as American as European Americans can be. Devos et al. (2010) discovered that Latinxs are consistently seen as being less American than are European Americans by their research participants. This was true for both Latinxs and European Americans in their samples. The authors curiously used the term *Caucasian American* as opposed to White American or European American in their study because some Latinxs considered themselves White or of European heritage. Devos and Ma (2008) found similar results when they studied Asian Americans along with their European American counterparts, even when they compared Kate Winslet with Lucy Liu, although Kate Winslet is English and Lucy Liu was born in the United States. Devos et al. (2010) concluded, "The present research suggests that a very basic right to a national identity is not equally accessible to all Americans. More precisely, the national identity is more readily granted to members of the dominant ethnic group than to members of an ethnic minority" (p. 47).

Finally, Awad (2010) discussed a dilemma for some groups in identifying with and affiliating with an American cultural group. Although Arabs and Middle Easterners who had less immersion into the dominant society experienced higher levels of discrimination,

From the early racial identity development models arose more general racial and cultural identity models, encouraging cultural pride across many groups. *Photographs by Polarpx/Shutterstock, Alina Reynbakh/Shutterstock, and Roberto Gerometta/Shutterstock*

the picture was more complicated for individuals who were Muslim. Arab Muslims experienced higher levels of discrimination than Arab Christians did, but this was true only when they were more immersed in the dominant society. Thus, although we encourage immigrants and people of color to integrate more into the broader society, Arab Muslims who do just that end up experiencing more discrimination than if they were to remain more separated from the broader society.

The more contact Muslims have with the broader society, the more discrimination they may face. *Photographs by Marie Kanger Born/Shutterstock and J. G. Domke/Demotix/Corbis*

A Critique of the Stage Models

Although cultural identity models have made a huge contribution to the field of multicultural psychology and to our understanding of human behavior and our diverse society, they are not without limitations. Most models of cultural identity development suggest a linear progression through each of the stages. In other words, it is assumed that all individuals begin at the first stage and gradually work their way through all the stages in the order described. However, that is not necessarily the case. Parham (1989) suggested that people may cycle back and forth through the stages across the life span. For example, in Cross's (1971) model, someone who has reached the final stage of internalization might have an experience that throws him or her back into the encounter or immersion/emersion stage. Helms (1995b) herself changed the term *stages* to *statuses* to reflect the idea that these identities are not static categories but represent a dynamic developmental process.

Another observation is that not all minority individuals begin their developmental process in a stage where they idealize Whiteness and denigrate their own racial minority background. For example, in Cross's (1971) model, not all African Americans begin at the preencounter stage. Children who grow up in predominantly Black environments or in homes where they are taught to have a sense of pride in their racial identity may begin at a later stage. However, negative racial experiences during adolescence (such as those described in Tatum's 1997 book) can cause them to have attitudes and behaviors more characteristic of the preencounter, encounter, and/or immersion/emersion stages of Cross's model.

Another criticism of the cultural identity models is that they assume one definition of mental health, judging the final stage of the model as the healthiest. In the final stage of most of the models, the individual achieves pride in his or her own group but also reaches out to other groups and incorporates positive aspects of the dominant group into his or her identity. However, for some individuals, immersion in their own group may be an adaptive response for their situation. The R/CID assumes that a healthy identity includes some degree of autonomy, but in some instances, sublimation of one's individual needs for the sake of the group may be a healthy choice. We must be careful in assuming that one identity outcome is the healthiest for all members of a particular group and under all circumstances (Barker-Hackett, 2003). Some critics of the stage models question the relevance of such models for different generations

(Krate, Leventhal, & Silverstein, 1974). Others criticize the models for overemphasizing reactions to racism and oppression (Akbar, 1989; Nobles, 1989) and lacking empirical evidence to support some of the stages (Behrens, 1997; Cross, 1995; Helms, 1989).

Multiple Layering of Identities

Remember Leticia, the Latinx lesbian in the preceding story? When faced with the question "Who are you?" she was not sure how to answer. She felt that her lesbian identity dominated at the time, but she also felt that she was more. Leticia is Latinx, but she does not specifically mention her ethnic identity in her story. We may wonder where she is in her ethnic identity development and how that is related to her sexual orientation identity. The emotional turmoil of the sexual identity process is painful enough, but people of color who are nonheterosexual face even more oppressive consequences. They face a unique challenge—integrating two identities, one pertaining to their ethnicity and the other to their sexual orientation—in a society that does not fully accept either one. Lesbian women of color face triple jeopardy, since they must cope with oppression occasioned by their race, their gender, and their sexual orientation (Akerlund & Cheung, 2000; Greene & Boyd-Franklin, 1996).

We may also wonder about the reaction of Leticia's family members to her sexual orientation. Was it because of their culture? Their religion? We all have multiple identities. We are not just a woman or a man, gay or straight, Catholic or Protestant; we are all these things. Membership in each of these groups shapes our experiences and our worldview. It has a powerful influence over how society views us, how we view ourselves, and how we view others (Atkinson et al., 1998; D. W. Sue & Sue, 2003, 2008).

All of us belong to more than one group (e.g., Leticia is a woman, a lesbian, a Latinx), but one of those identities may be more important to us than the others (e.g., sexual orientation over race). Characteristics of the person and characteristics of the situation interact to determine which identity is most salient at a particular time (R. M. Sellers, Smith, Shelton, Rowley, & Chavous, 1998). For example, if Leticia is at a club with all lesbian women but is the only Latinx in the room, her race may become more salient than her sexual orientation.

The work of Sellers and colleagues (Sellers et al., 1998) helps to explain this shift in the salience of identities. They examined the significance of race in the overall self-concept and defined **racial salience** as "the extent to which one's race is a relevant part of one's self-concept at a particular moment or in a particular situation" (p. 24). In other words, the significance of one's race varies across individuals and across situations. For example, being the only African American in a class may make race salient for one person but not have an impact on another African American student in the same situation because of that student's own attitudes and beliefs about his or her racial identity. The following story illustrates the multiple layering of identities and how the salience of these identities can shift.

racial salience—at a particular time or in a particular situation, the extent to which one's race is relevant in self-concept.

One summer while I was in graduate school I traveled through Europe with three girlfriends, all of whom were African Americans. It was our first time in Europe, and we were constantly amazed at the reactions we got from people. At first we couldn't understand these strange and different feelings we were experiencing. Then it dawned on us, people were reacting to us based on our culture (as Americans) and our gender (as females). At home we were used to walking in places and being ignored or having people react negatively to us simply based on our color. We were used to being on guard, ready for people to do or say something negative, hurtful, or offensive. But in Europe that wasn't happening. Or, if it did happen, it was based on something else, such as us being American or being women, not because we were Black. In fact, being Black was a positive. Our Blackness was considered beautiful. And we weren't used to that.

This realization really hit us during an incident that happened when we were in Greece. We were out on the island of Santorini. The island was full of young people from all over the world, and all the hotels were full. The only place we could find to stay was a room in a private home. Well, I'm being nice by calling it a room. It was really the unfinished upper level of a house. The floor was cement, there were no windows, no doors, and only patio lounge chairs to sleep on. During the day we thought we might be able to do it, but after dark, and after some strange men moved into the "room" next to ours, we decided we had to find another place to stay, and—thank God—we managed to find a beautiful (and complete!) room at a nearby hotel. We were so relieved and excited that we ran back to that house, packed up our things, and promptly left without telling anyone.

The next day we wanted to do some laundry, so we took our bags of dirty clothes to the only laundromat in the little seaside town where we were staying. As we approached the storefront we saw a man talking with a group of young people and overheard him say, "Well, some American girls were supposed to stay there last night, but I don't know what happened to them." I did not think their conversation had anything to do with me, but one of my girlfriends leaned over and whispered, "He's talking about us." "What?" I asked, still totally oblivious. "He's talking about us," she said a little more emphatically. "What? Really? Oh!" The light dawned. The owner of the laundromat was also the owner of the "house" we vacated the night before, and we were the "American girls" he was talking about. But, American? Me? I'd never ever identified as being American. Black, yes. But, American? No. (The term African American was not in popular usage yet.) So many negative things went along with being American. Americans were racist. Americans were the oppressors. I'm not American. But, that is how that Greek man saw us. Americans first. Girls second. Black was somewhere farther down the list. At home we would have just been "the Black girls." I was stunned. It threw me for a loop.

—LAB

In LAB's story we see that a major factor in the ordering of her identities, with race as the primary one, was the negative reactions she received from others as a Black woman in the United States. Keeping race as the top priority served as a coping strategy against racist assaults, large and small. However, in Europe the circumstances changed, and others in her environment reacted no longer primarily to her race but, rather, to her culture and gender. This forced reordering of identities was a shock for LAB.

What groups do you identify with the most? Which group identity is most salient for you? Why? Does the salience of your identities ever change? If so, how? Why?

Food for Thought

The cultural identity development models have made a huge contribution to our understanding of human behavior and our society as a whole, but perhaps the most important contribution is an increased understanding of ourselves. If you have not explored your own cultural identities, we strongly suggest that you begin such an exploration. Some people tell us, " I'm a Heinz 57—I am a mix of so many different cultures that I don't know what I am other than an American." We tell them to go home and consult with their parents and/or grandparents. They will discover that they do have some identifiable ethnicities that can be a source of interest and understanding. These students soon come back to us and say, "I was wondering where this particular characteristic came from, and then my grandmother told me that when she was growing up, she learned to behave in this manner. I guess I just picked it up from my mother, who had picked it up from my grandmother. I then looked up the country where my grandmother's parents came from, and everything began to make sense." By completing this kind of examination, you might discover how enriching it can be.

Summary

The study of identity development is one of the most popular studies in the field of multicultural psychology. Cultural minorities face unique identity challenges because of the racism, discrimination, and oppression from a society that does not value their differences. Psychologists attempt to understand how personal, social, political, and cultural factors interact to shape individuals' identities. These models began with racial and ethnic groups but quickly expanded to other groups, such as gay, lesbian, and bisexual groups, multiracial groups, and women. Many models of cultural identity development exist, reflecting the unique situations of the various groups.

The models share some common characteristics. Most assume that cultural minorities begin in a stage where they devalue their own culture and idealize the dominant culture. However, life experiences challenge that perspective and force them to reevaluate their beliefs. This moves them into a stage where they immerse themselves in their own culture and devalue the dominant culture. Resolution is achieved when the individual has a positive view of his or her own group but also identifies with and incorporates positive aspects of other groups.

All people have multiple identities, such as woman, student, daughter, and member of an ethnic minority group. At times, one of those dimensions becomes more important, and at other times another dimension becomes more important. Sometimes these dimensions can conflict. For example, if you are a woman who is a member of an ethnic minority group and the discussion turns to physical abuse, as a woman you might feel it important to speak out to put an end to the abuse, but as a member of an ethnic minority group, you might feel that your discussion of the topic may unfairly lead others to conclude that all male members of your group engage in abuse. The more secure you are in all your identities, the less these conflicts will interfere with your ability to speak your mind with confidence.

Critical Thinking Questions

1. How are you like everyone else? How are you like a group of identifiable people?
2. How are you unique?
3. How are you like others in your ethnocultural group? What similarities do you see among people of other ethnocultural groups?

4. When interacting with people of different racial and ethnic groups, have you noticed that some seem to be more connected with their groups than others are?

5. Have you noticed that some seem to reject interactions with you, whereas others seem open to interacting with you?

6. If you are multiracial, with what group or groups do you feel most comfortable? What group or groups seem to be most accepting of you? If you know people who are multiracial, with what group or groups do they feel most comfortable?

7. If you are nonheterosexual, how comfortable are you with your sexuality? If you know people who are nonheterosexual, how comfortable are they with their respective sexual orientation?

8. What other identities do you have? Do they ever come into conflict with your racioethnic identity? If so, how have you resolved those conflicts?

CHAPTER 8

Culture and Health

Photograph by Diego Cervo/Shutterstock

Learning Objectives
Reading this chapter will help you to:
- understand the relation between culture and health;
- identify components of health belief models;
- know which strategies are appropriate for approaching different health belief models;
- understand differences among ethnic groups in health outcomes;
- identify some reasons why there are differences in health outcomes across ethnic groups
- recognize the differences between groups in trust of the health-care system; and
- distinguish between the care given to groups that speak English and those that do not.

Two years ago, I was involved in a car accident, which left me in a lot of pain. My mother took me to the emergency room right away. I was expecting to be in line for a while, especially since I saw so many people waiting. To my surprise, they took me right away and began to take x-rays of my chest. After that the doctor and nurse were discussing in private. I could not help myself from being nosy with the bed next to me. The doctor stated to the nurse, "I cannot help him too much. He has no insurance and the procedure that needs to be done costs too much money. Fix him up as much as possible. Why is it that these people never have insurance?" I saw that the person was an African American male, in his late 40s. He looked as if he was in so much pain and I felt so badly. I thought that doctors and nurses should not be looking at whether an individual can pay, but get him help. It really made me upset. Everyone should receive the same health care. I told my mother and the other nurse that "we live in a great community, wherein only if you have money, will you receive help." The nurse just looked at me and said nothing. I was upset. As we were leaving, I saw the same individuals still waiting in line and then it hit me. The persons left were Hispanic/Latinx, and I couldn't believe it. I simply couldn't understand what our country has become. Individuals of different ethnicity, age, social class, and sexual orientation will always encounter some sort of inequality when dealing with health care. The new generation needs to fix that.

—Maria, 20+-year-old European American woman

An incident took place that is a prime example for discrimination between ethnic groups. A young 23-year-old Black woman came into the hospital because she had a Caesarian about 3 days prior. She complained of abdominal pain and she was not immediately treated by the facility. They had her waiting in the emergency room for 7 hours. At the same time an older White woman was complaining of abdominal pain as well—I think it was kidney stones or a urinary tract infection. But anyways they both came in at the same time and had the same chief complaint, but the White female was called in before the Black female even though she had a baby 3 days prior. The White woman was promptly treated and given antibiotics and discharged. When the Black female was called in and treated she [had to be] admitted to the hospital and immediately scheduled for surgery because the doctor who performed her C-section left part of the placenta in her stomach that was causing infection.

This incident happened on my shift and it is only one of many amazing stories that display racial discrimination within the health-care system.
—Adrian, 20+-year-old European American woman

This chapter addresses health psychology as it relates to health and health-care disparities in people of color and marginalized groups. *Marginalized groups* refers to people who are disadvantaged because of their race/ethnicity, socioeconomic status, disability, age, gender, sexual orientation, geographic location, special health-care needs, long-term care needs, or need for end-of-life care. **Health disparities** are systematic differences in health care that affect disadvantaged groups (Dehlendorf, Bryant, Huddleston, Jacoby, & Fujimoto, 2010). In the United States, disadvantage has been primarily conceptualized along racial/ethnic lines, but also includes gender, disability, sexual orientation, and income (Dehlendorf et al., 2010). Health-care disparities are defined as "differences in the quality of healthcare that are not due to access-related factors or clinical needs, preferences, and appropriateness of intervention" (Smedley, Stith, & Nelson, 2003, pp. 3–4). The Institute of Medicine focused on health-care disparities at two levels: the institutional level, where disparities are the result of structures within the health-care system, including rules and regulations, and the patient–provider level, in which discrimination affects care (Smedley et al., 2003). Although we may not be able to address the specific health and health-care requirements of each group, we will elaborate on the needs as a whole so that we begin to explore ways to make improvements in meeting those needs.

> **health disparities**—refers to different rates of health or illness that marginalized groups have in comparison with their privileged counterparts, whereas *health-care disparities* refers to the differential access to health care or treatment by health-care providers.

People of color do not receive optimal care for illnesses, whether or not those ailments can be traced primarily to nonmajority groups. The health of people of color has not historically received careful attention, so many people continue to ask the chicken-or-the-egg question: Do people of color receive suboptimal care because they do not seek medical attention and insist on self-care or "ignoring" their illnesses, or do they choose to deal with their illnesses on their own because they have continually received suboptimal care? In examining the health of people of color, it becomes clear that questions about health go hand in hand with questions about health care. We cannot discuss health without discussing health care, especially as it relates to health disparities in people of color.

First, we address definitions of health, health behaviors, and health psychology. Next, we take a look at general health problems that are more common to different minority groups than to European Americans. These health issues will help us develop a more elaborate view of health disparities, the definitions involved, possible causes, and their link to health-care disparities. Finally, we discuss goals and limitations regarding health and health-care disparities.

Health and Health Behaviors

The World Health Organization (1948) defined **health** as "a state of complete physical, mental and social well-being and not merely the absence of disease or infirmity" (p. 1). Therefore, a person is not necessarily healthy just because there is an absence of symptoms. We can argue that

> **health**—a complete state of physical, mental, and social well-being, not merely the absence of disease or infirmity.

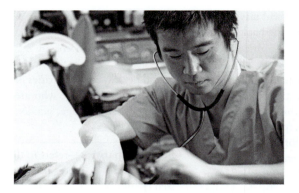

Maintaining one's health partially depends on one's access to treatment. *Photograph by James Peragine/Shutterstock*

different people of color suffer from illnesses that do not afflict the majority population as much, and the ways in which such illnesses are treated may be defined by looking at people's health behaviors. Those health behaviors are influenced by people's beliefs about their health and its treatment.

Thoughts about health and the treatment of health issues influence how people behave or seek treatment to maintain or improve their health. For example, if you feel that your health problems are caused by a chemical imbalance of some sort, you will tend to seek out a healer who will prescribe a medication. However, if you feel that your health problems are caused by a dietary imbalance, you will seek out a healer who will map out a diet program for you. People of color's thoughts about health may also be influenced by those from whom they seek treatment, such as indigenous healers, who have markedly different worldviews about the nature of disorders compared to more Western-oriented healers.

Health behaviors are behaviors undertaken by people to enhance or maintain their health. Health behaviors differ according to demographic factors. Younger, affluent, better-educated people under low levels of stress and with high levels of social support typically practice better health habits than do people under higher levels of stress with fewer resources, such as individuals in lower socioeconomic classes (S. E. Taylor, 2009). Some individuals who are not familiar with the behaviors and beliefs of people of color continue to question the need to improve health-care disparities when they observe those individuals behaving in ways that may not fit the Western conception of a healthy lifestyle. Popular press books provide excellent information for interested readers. For example, in *The Spirit Catches You and You Fall Down*, Anne Fadiman (2012) tells the story of a Hmong family and the many miscommunications between the family and Western medical providers. Lia, a child, suffered from epileptic seizures. In a poignant example, Lia's parents discarded the medications and instead used coining, a practice that prompted a call to Child Protective Services. This practice is documented in the medical literature (Tan & Mallika, 2011) but may not be easily accessible to physicians because the information may not be found in traditional medical books or U.S.-based journals. It is important to be thoughtful about people's belief systems and they ways in which these beliefs influence their health behaviors.

health behaviors—behaviors undertaken by people to enhance or maintain their well-being.

Health psychology is devoted to understanding psychological influences on how people stay healthy, why they become ill, and how they respond when they do become ill. For example, a health psychology researcher may be interested in why people continue to smoke even though they know that smoking increases their risk of cancer and

health psychology—the study of psychological influences on how people stay healthy, why they become ill, and how they respond when they do get ill.

heart disease (S. E. Taylor, 2009). On the positive side, a health psychology researcher may be interested in the factors behind why some people engage in strict regimens of good diet and exercise.

Two models are often used to predict health outcomes: the common-sense model, which taps into illness perceptions, and the health belief model. The **common-sense model** was developed specifically for medical illnesses and addresses patients' cognitive and emotional representations of illness. The **health belief model** was originally developed for preventive medicine and has been deeply studied in communications for its applicability to media and other health interventions.

The common-sense model is linear (Figure 8.1). In the model, perceptions of illness predict coping, and coping predicts the evaluations that patients use to revise their perceptions and coping. The model has been supported by individual and meta-analytic research within the United States and internationally (Dempster, Howell, & McCorry, 2015). For example, people's perceptions of their illness explain their emergency department visits (i.e., coping) regardless of the symptoms experienced (Ninou et al., 2016). Knowing this can help providers reach out to patients who either underutilize or overutilize emergency rooms. Providers can help the patients adjust their coping strategy and reduce health disparities. More recently, the common-sense model has been useful in understanding mental health outcomes for patients with significant health conditions. For example, in a systematic review of 21 studies of coronary heart disease patients, illness perceptions predicted quality of life and mood (Foxwell, Morley, & Frizelle, 2013).

The health belief model includes four main areas of analysis: **susceptibility**, **severity**, **benefits**, and **barriers** (Carpenter, 2010). The model also later specified self-efficacy, motivation, and cues to action, but these areas have little empirical support (Carpenter, 2010; C. L. Jones et al., 2015). In simple terms, the model says that when individuals perceive a health outcome to be severe (e.g., cancer),

common sense model—theoretical framework used to explain how patients perceive an illness, cope with that perception, evaluate their coping, and integrate feedback and experiences into revising their perceptions and their coping.

health belief model—a set of assumptions that suggests that one's health behavior is affected by one's perception of a personal health threat, as well as by how a particular health practice would be effective in reducing the personal health threat.

susceptibility—the likelihood of acquiring a disease or being impacted by an illness-producing stimulus.

severity—intensity of negative outcome.

benefits—advantage gained from a behavior.

barriers—obstacles that reduce the likelihood of engaging in a new behavior.

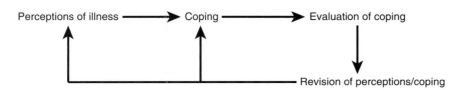

FIGURE 8.1   The Mediational Common Sense Model.

believe that they are susceptible (e.g., because they have a family history of lung cancer), perceive interventions as beneficial (e.g., smoking cessation reduces mortality), and think the barriers to adopting the new behavior are achievable (e.g., home was smoke free already because partner is allergic), then the behavior is more likely to ocurr. Researchers have not established clearly what the optimal order of these variables should be (Carpenter, 2010; C. L. Jones et al., 2015). However, the health belief model, like the common-sense model, provides important points of intervention for engaging patients in behavioral change that is likely to improve health.

Cultural beliefs and values are paramount to health beliefs, beliefs about relevant or appropriate coping/intervention strategies, and beliefs about susceptibility and severity. Indeed, medical anthropologists Kleinman, Einsenberg, and Good (1978) documented these relationships decades ago. Kleinman and colleagues recommended five key questions that continue to be used today by culturally competent health providers: (a) What do you think has caused your problem? (b) Why do you think it started when it did? (c) What do you think your sickness does to you? How does it work? (d) How severe is your sickness? Will it have a short or long course? (e) What kind of treatment do you think you should receive? It is easy to see how the tenets of the health models above map on to these questions.

> This past summer I went to Mexico to visit my uncle. He used to live here in the United States, and he told me that doctors wanted to amputate his leg. He was so upset when the doctor scheduled him for an operation, so before the surgery he took some time and left for Mexico. He went to get a second opinion and he went to a hospital in Mexico. There he felt better, because he was able to understand what was going on and, secondly, they told him that he was going to get better soon. By the time I saw him in Mexico, he was almost fully recuperated. His wound was getting better and he was able to walk and without amputating his leg.
> —Lourdes, 20+-year-old Mexican American woman

Health Disparities Defined

If a European American person suffered from a cardiovascular disease and a person of color suffered from the same illness, would they be given equal treatment? The U.S. Department of Health and Human Services (2011) defines **disparity** as "differences in health outcomes that are closely linked with social, economic, and environmental disadvantage . . . often driven by the social conditions in which individuals live, learn, work, and play" (p. 1). Synonyms for disparity include *inequity, unlikeness, disproportion,* and *difference.*

disparity—the condition or fact of being unequal.

According to the National Cancer Institute (2011), the first attempt at an official definition for *health disparities* was developed in September 1999, in response to a White House initiative. The National Institutes of Health, under the direction of then director Dr. Harold Varmus, convened a working group across the National Institutes of Health, charged with developing a strategic plan for reducing health disparities. That group developed the first National Institutes of Health definition of *health disparities*: "Health disparities are differences in the incidence, prevalence, mortality, and burden of diseases and other adverse health conditions that exist among specific population groups in the United States" (p. 123). Health disparities have also been defined as differences in health that are not only unnecessary and avoidable but also unjust and unfair (Gurung, 2010).

Before we discuss more specific causes of health disparities, let us consider some of the more common health issues faced by minority groups. Some of these health issues can be seen by comparing health problems of minority groups with health problems of the majority population, and others can be seen by comparing the health problems of ethnic minority groups.

People's health behaviors depend on their health beliefs.
Photograph by sportpoint/Shutterstock

Although health disparities have improved, there is much room for further improvement. Medical services are in high demand. In 2012, there were 929 million visits to physicians in health settings, 787 million outpatient visits to hospital settings, and 114 million visits to home health settings (Agency for Healthcare Research and Quality, 2017). Health disparities vary by race/ethnicity, gender, socioeconomic status, sexual orientation, and even geographical location. The states with the lowest health disparities may surprise some readers: Alaska, Hawaii, Idaho, Kansas, Kentucky, Maryland, North Dakota, South Dakota, Tennessee, Utah, Virginia, and Wyoming.

Notable disparities remain. In a recent report of the Kaiser Family Foundation (Artiga, Foutz, Cornachione, & Garfield, 2016), disparities are evident across racial/ethnic groups in health-care access, stable sources of care, health-care and dental visits, and preventive care. Table 8.1 shows the differences between ethnic groups across measures, reporting only on statistically significant differences. Overall, the report documents a disappointing pattern of health disparities. Across 11 measures of health access and utilization, Asian Americans (6 of 11), Latinxs (7 of 11), African Americans (7 of 11), and American Indians and Alaska Natives (6 of 11) generally fared worse than European Americans. It is important to note that this report focused predominantly on nonelderly adults, and the intersection of elder status with ethnicity may result in different disparities. Efforts are underway to acquire more information about Native Hawaiian and Other Pacific Islander populations, but insufficient data exist in the report. This is important because broad labels are applied to groups, and sometimes these **ethnic glosses** (Trimble & Dickson, 2005) can obscure issues that are significant to specific ethnic subgroups. Ethnic glosses are labels used to identify cultural groups that have great within-group heterogeneity. For example, "American Indian" is an ethnic gloss. In reality, there are 562 federally recognized Indian nations according to the National Congress of American Indians, and these varied nations have unique histories and current contexts, as well as varied histories between them. Some American Indian nations were historically at war. With regard to health outcomes, Asian American is an ethnic gloss that must be examined with caution. For example, Filipinos tend to have consistently poor health outcomes compared to Japanese American or Asian Indians, yet they are all grouped under the broad term Asian American.

ethnic glosses—labels used to identify cultural groups that have great within-group heterogeneity.

Health-care providers and society at large care about access to care and the equitable utilization of existing resources. The numbers in Table 8.1 help us understand disparities

TABLE 8.1   **Major Health Disparities in Health-Care Access and Utilization**

Area of care	Differences across racial/ethnic groups
Delayed access to care	Latinxs (24%), African Americans (21%), and American Indian/Alaska Natives (19%) were significantly more likely than European Americans (14%) to either delay or forgo medical care because of cost.
	Latinxs (28%), Black Americans (27%), and American Indian/Alaska Natives (36%) were significantly more likely than European Americans (19%) to delay medical care for reasons other than cost.
Usual source of care	Asian American (83%), Latinx (73%), and African American (81%) adults were less likely to have access to a nonemergency care provider compared to European Americans (86%).
	Children usually have greater access to care than adults. Whereas 98% of European American children had access to a regular provider, a significantly lower number of Latinx (94%), Asian American (95%), and African American (96%) children did. American Indian/Alaska Native children (98%) had the same level of access as European Americans.
	Latinx, African American, and American Indian/Alaska Native adults tend to rely on clinics more often than European Americans, who instead rely more often on a doctor's office. 77% of European Americans have a doctor's office as a typical source of care, compared to 56% of Latinxs, 71% of African Americans, and 45% of American Indian/Alaska Natives.
	A similar pattern is observed with children: 82% of European American children receive their usual care at a doctor's office compared to 55% of Latinx, 73% of African American, and 38% of American Indian/Alaska Native children.
Care in the past year	84% of European American adults reported a health-care visit in the past 12 months compared with 78% of Asian American, 70% of Latinx, and 81% of African American adults.
	66% of European American adults compared to 50% of Latinx, 55% of African American, and 53% of American Indian/Alaska Native adults reported a dental visit in the past 12 months.
	94% of European American children had a health-care visit in the past 12 months compared with 90% of Asian American, 89% of Latinx, and 87% of American Indian/Alaska Native children.
	80% of European American children compared to 74% of Asian American children reported a dental visit in the past 12 months. Notably, 87% of American Indian/Alaska Native children had a dental visit in the past 12 months, a number that is significantly higher than that of European Americans.
	Immunization rates were concerning across the board. Disparities were observed only when comparing European American children (73%) with American Indian/Alaska Native children (65%).
Health screening	In women aged 50–74, 78% of European Americans reported having a mammogram in the past 2 years. American Indian/Alaska Native women had significantly lower rates (71%), whereas African American women had higher rates (83%) than European American women.
	In women ages 21–65, 83% of European American women received a Pap smear in the past 3 years. American Indian/Alaska Native (76%) and Native Hawaiian/Other Pacific Islander women (68%) were less likely to receive the same screens. African American women (85%) were more likely than European American women to have a Pap smear.

Note: These data were obtained from Artiga et al., 2016.

in services. These numbers are also critical for understanding the consequences of underutilization of health-care resources. For example, the disparities in dental visits could be particularly problematic given research that points to low-income and ethnic minority status as predicting higher consumption of sugary drinks (Han & Powell, 2013). Sugary drinks in turn increase the risk of diabetes and other cardiac issues (Löfvenborg et al., 2016; Micha et al., 2017). Tooth decay could be an important indicator of diet choices that create other health risks. The Kaiser Family Foundation (Artiga et al., 2016) report provides us with important information regarding health outcomes across ethnic/racial groups, as summarized in Table 8.2. The report included 29 measures of health status and outcomes. Each ethnic group was compared to European Americans. Significantly poorer outcomes were documented for Latinxs in 13, African Americans in 24, and American Indian/Alaska Natives on 20 of the 29 measures. It is interesting that Asian Americans fare better than European Americans on 25 measures.

TABLE 8.2   **Major Health Disparities in Health-Care Outcomes**

Area of care	Differences across racial/ethnic groups
Self-report of health status	9% of European American adults report fair or poor health status compared with 11% of Latinxs, 15% of African Americans, and 17% of American Indian/Alaska Natives. Asian Americans have significantly better reports than European Americans; only 6% report fair/poor health.
Physical limitations	29% of European American adults reported a physical limitation compared to 39% of American Indian/Alaska Natives. In contrast, Latinxs (20%) and Asian Americans (13%) fared better than European Americans. African Americans reported the same rate as European Americans.
Unhealthy days	11% of European American adults reported 14 or more physically unhealthy days in the past month compared to 12% of Latinxs, 12% of African Americans, and 17% of American Indian/Alaska Natives. Asian American adults fared better than European Americans, at 6%.
	13% of European American adults reported 14 or more mentally unhealthy days in the past month compared to 14% of African Americans and 19% of American Indian/Alaska Natives. Asian Americans (7%) and Latinxs (11%) fared better than European Americans.
Smoking	21% of European American adults smoke compared to 32% of American Indian/Alaska Native adults. Asian Americans (9%) and Latinxs (15%) fared better than European Americans on this outcome. African Americans reported smoking at the same rate as European Americans.
Obesity	28% of European American adults are obese compared with 32% of Latinxs, 39% of African Americans, and 34% of American Indian/Alaska Natives. Only Asian Americans (9%) fared significantly better than European Americans.
	15% of European American children are obese compared with 22% of Latinx and 20% of African American children. Asian American children (9%) fare significantly better than European American children on this indicator.
Dependence on Substances	7% of European Americans ages 12 and older had alcohol dependence or abuse compared to 15% of American Indian/Alaska Natives. Asian Americans fared better (4%) and Latinxs (7%) and African Americans (6%) had similar rates to European Americans.
	2% of European Americans ages 12 and older had illicit drug dependence or abuse compared with 4% of African Americans. Only Asian Americans fared better than European Americans, at 1%.

continued

TABLE 8.2   **Major Health Disparities in Health-Care Outcomes** (*continued*)

Area of care	Differences across racial/ethnic groups
Asthma	9% of European American adults had asthma compared to significantly poorer outcomes for African Americans (11%) and American Indian/Alaska Natives (15%). Latinxs (7%) and Asian Americans (5%) fared better than European Americans on this indicator.
	African American children (17%) are significantly more likely to have asthma than European American children (10%). Asian American children (6%) fare better than European American children. Latinxs (8%) had similar rates to European Americans.
Diabetes	A greater number of Latinx (9%), African American (11%), American Indian/Alaska Native (12%), and Native Hawaiian/Other Pacific Islander (11%) adults had diabetes compared to European American adults (7%). Asian Americans (5%) fared significantly better than European Americans.
	Death rates from diabetes are significantly higher for Latinx, African American, and American Indian/Alaska Native adults when compared to European American adults. Asian Americans have significantly lower rates than European Americans.
Heart attack/heart disease	A greater number of American Indian/Alaska Natives (8%) and African Americans (5%) had been told by a physician that they had heart disease or had experienced a heart attack compared to European Americans (4%). The rates were significantly lower for Latinxs (3.6%) and Asian Americans (2%)
	Death rates from heart disease are highest for African Americans, who differed significantly from European Americans. Asian Americans, Latinxs, and American Indians fared significantly better than European Americans on this indicator.
HIV/AIDS	The HIV diagnosis rate for African Americans (13–64 years of age) is more than 8 times the rate of European Americans. The rate for Latinxs is more than 3 times that of European Americans. The AIDS diagnosis rate is much higher for Latinxs (more than 3 times) and African Americans (more than 10 times) than for European Americans. Finally, the death rate for individuals with an HIV diagnosis is higher for Latinxs (more than twice as high) and African Americans (8 times as high).
Cancer	The age-adjusted incidence of cancer is highest for African Americans, who have significantly higher rates than European Americans. Asian Americans, and American Indian/Alaska Natives have significantly lower rates than European Americans.
	Breast cancer rates are highest in European Americans and significantly lower in Asian Americans, African Americans, and American Indian/Alaska Natives.
	Colorectal cancer rates are highest in African Americans, a significant difference when compared to European Americans. Asian Americans and American Indian/Alaska Natives have significantly lower rates than European Americans.
	Lung cancer rates are highest in African Americans, a significant difference when compared to European Americans. Asian Americans and American Indian/Alaska Natives have significantly lower rates than European Americans.
	Death rates from cancer were highest for African Americans, who differed significantly from European Americans. Asian Americans, Latinxs, and American Indians/Alaska Natives fared significantly better than European Americans on this indicator.

Area of care	Differences across racial/ethnic groups
Infant mortality	African Americans have the highest infant mortality rates (11.1 per 1,000), followed by American Indian/Alaska Natives (7.7 per 1,000), both of which have significantly higher rates than European Americans (5.1 per 1,000). Asian Americans (3.9 per 1,000) have significantly lower rates than European Americans. The rate for Latinxs (5.0) is comparable to that of European Americans.
Teen births	American Indian/Alaska Native girls aged 15–19 have the highest rates of births (38.9 per 1,000), followed by Latinxs (38.0 per 1,000) and African Americans (34.7 per 1,000). All of these rates are significantly higher than that of European Americans girls (17.2 per 1,000). Asian American girls have a significantly lower rate (6.5 per 1,000) than European American girls.

Note: These data were obtained from Artiga et al., 2016.

Research on health disparities has shown the importance of taking multiple dimensions of disadvantage under consideration in understanding health disparities. A report from the Center for Medicaid Services, Office of Minority Health, and the RAND Corporation (2017) detailed health disparities in Medicare recipients using data collected in 2015 from men and women, providing a glimpse into the intersections between race/ethnicity, poverty, and gender with regard to health-care disparities. The main findings are outlined in Table 8.3. Because of the number of participants, statistical significance might not be very meaningful in a practical sense. In Table 8.3, we report on any differences that were at least 3 percentage points larger than that of the next group, a criterion that was more stringent than statistical significance.

To understand the findings of Table 8.3, it is relevant to know that people of color are much more likely to be covered by Medicaid than European Americans. In 2014, 35% of Latinxs, 37% of African Americans, 38% of American Indian/Alaska Natives, and 33% of Native Hawaiian/Other Pacific Islanders were covered by Medicaid or other public sources compared to 20% of European Americans (Kaiser Family Foundation, 2016). Only Asian Americans had rates comparable to that of European Americans (19% covered by Medicaid; Kaiser Family Foundation, 2016). It was not surprising that the rates of uninsured children and adults were highest for these groups as well, with 21% of Latinxs and American Indian/Alaska Natives and 13% of African Americans uninsured compared to 9% of European Americans. These differential rates of insurance may be strongly implicated in the differential care received across groups. It is also important to note, however, that because the European American population is larger relative to other groups, they still make up the majority of the uninsured population; specifically, of the 32.3 million uninsured individuals in 2014, 45% were European American.

Causes of Health Disparities

The notion of health disparities between African Americans (or people of color in general) and the European American population was documented as early as 1890 by W. E. B. Du Bois (Zambrana & Carter-Pokras, 2010). But what are the causes of these disparities?

Let us use the premise cited by S. E. Taylor (2009) involving the health belief model to begin exploring the causes of disparities in health and health care. An individual's perception of a health threat is influenced by at least three factors: (a) general health values, (b) specific beliefs about vulnerability to a particular disorder, and (c) beliefs about the consequences of the disorder. People's perceptions of a health threat cannot completely influence them to change health behaviors in a positive direction.

TABLE 8.3   **Health Disparities for Medicare Recipients**

Medical condition	Disparity
Flu vaccine	Received the flu vaccine: Black women, Latinx women < White women, Asian/Pacific Islander (API) women Black men, Latinx men < White men < API men
Colorectal cancer screens	Received appropriate screening (50–75 years old): Black women < White women < API women and Latinx women Black men < White men < API men and Latinx men
Diabetes	Enrollees ages 18 to 75 with diabetes (type 1 and type 2) who had an eye exam (retinal) in the past year: Black women, European American women < Latinx women, API women Black men, European American men < Latinx men, API men
	Enrollees ages 18 to 75 with diabetes (type 1 and type 2) who had medical attention for nephropathy in the past year: European American women, Black women < Latinx women, API women European American men, Black men, Latinx men < API men
	Enrollees ages 18 to 75 with diabetes (type 1 and type 2) whose most recent blood pressure was less than 140/90: Black women, European American women < Latinx women, API women Black men, European American men < Latinx men, API men
	Enrollees ages 18 to 75 with diabetes (type 1 and type 2) whose most recent HbA1c level was 9% or less: Black women < European American women < Latinx women, API women Black men < European American men, Latinx men < API men
Body mass index documented	Enrollees ages 18 to 74 who had an outpatient visit and whose body mass index was documented in the past 2 years Black women < European American women < Latinx women, API women Black men < European American men < Latinx men, API men
Beta-blockers after hospitalization	Enrollees age 18 and older who were hospitalized and discharged with a diagnosis of acute myocardial infarction and who received persistent beta-blocker treatment for 6 months after discharge: Latinx women < European American women, Black women, API women Black men, Latinx men< European American men, API men
Chronic obstructive pulmonary disease exacerbation	Enrollees age 40 and older who had an acute inpatient discharge or emergency department encounter in the past year and who were prescribed a systemic corticosteroid within 14 days of the event: Latinx women < European American women, Black women, API women Black men, Latinx men < European American men < API men
	Enrollees 40 years of age and older who had an acute inpatient discharge or emergency department encounter in the past year and who were prescribed a bronchodilator within 30 days of experiencing the event: European American women, Black women, Latinx women < API women European American men, Black men < Latinx men, API men
Rheumatoid arthritis	Enrollees who were diagnosed with rheumatoid arthritis during the past year and who were dispensed at least one ambulatory prescription for a disease-modifying antirheumatic drug: Black women, Latinx, API women, European American women Black men, Latinx, API men < European American men

Medical condition	Disparity
Chronic renal failure	Enrollees age 65 and older with chronic renal failure who were not given a prescription for a potentially harmful medication: Black women, Latinx women < European American women, API women Black men, Latinx men, API men < European American men
Dementia	Enrollees age 65 and older with dementia who were not given a prescription for a potentially harmful medication: Latinx women < European American women < Black women, API women Latinx men < European American men, API men < Black men
Prevention	Enrollees age 65 and older with a history of falls who were not given a prescription for a potentially harmful medication: European American women, Latinx women < Black women, API women Latinx men < European American men < Black men, API men
Mental Illness	Enrollees age 18 and older who were diagnosed with a new episode of major depression and remained on antidepressant medication for at least 84 days: Black women, Latinx women, API women < European American women Black men, Latinx men, API men < European American men
	Enrollees age 18 and older with a new diagnosis of major depression who were newly treated with antidepressant medication and who remained on an antidepressant medication treatment for at least 180 days: Black women, Latinx women, API women < European American women Black men, Latinx men, API men < European American men
	Enrollees age 6 and older who were hospitalized for treatment of selected mental health disorders and who had an outpatient visit, an intensive outpatient encounter, or partial hospitalization with a mental health practitioner within 7 days of discharge: Black women < European American women < Latinx women, API women Black men < European American men, Latinx men < API men
	Enrollees age 6 and older who were hospitalized for treatment of selected mental health disorders and who had an outpatient visit, an intensive outpatient encounter, or partial hospitalization with a mental health practitioner within 30 days of discharge: Black women < European American women, Latinx women < API women Black men < European American men, Latinx men, API men
Substance use	Enrollees with a new episode of alcohol or drug dependence who initiated treatment within 14 days of the diagnosis: API women, Latinx women < European American women < Black women API men, Latinx men < European American men < Black men

Note: Data were obtained from Center for Medicaid Services, Office of Minority Health, and the RAND Corporation (2017).

We should also consider whether a person believes that a health measure could reduce the threat, which involves the individual's perception of the effectiveness of the treatment as well as the cost of the treatment. For example, an individual must place a large degree of trust in the diagnosing health professional to believe that a health threat exists. The individual must also believe that treatment costs are valid and worthwhile.

According to K. O'Brien, Poat, Press, and Saha (2010), across all cultural groups, patients emphasized the importance of physicians' genuine concern for patients, physicians' competence as health professionals, and the central role of communication behaviors in proving concern and competence. In contrast, African American women often cited frustration with physicians' invalidating their perspectives, whereas Latinxs emphasized the importance of technical competence, measured by resource use and outcomes (K. O'Brien et al., 2010).

It may be hard to imagine anyone distrusting a medical professional who is supposedly trained to diagnose correctly and treat effectively, but we must look at the issue of trust from a different point of view. Through the eyes of a minority group member, health professionals do not look as reliable as they do through the eyes of a majority group member. Though we focus on the health professional as the one who is distrusted, is the health professional really the fundamental cause of health/health-care disparities?

I used to work as an independent contractor assistant social worker. Our company was contracted by home health care agencies that provided home care for predominantly senior citizens. During one of my many visits in Los Angeles, I was to provide service for an African American male, age 70. When I arrived at the home, I saw this man on the couch, lethargic and sickly thin. I approached and realized that he was blind. The man was a diabetic who had glaucoma and became legally blind. Shortly after I arrived, a neighbor came in and said that this man used to have his daughter helping him, but she recently died from cancer. I asked my questions in order to ascertain which services he needed. The man had not eaten in a day, and this was dangerous, especially for a diabetic. He had Medicaid and Medicare and earned monthly SSI [Supplemental Security Income], but was unable to acquire the needed help. Amazingly, this man was still receiving home care, which meant that a nurse visited him on a daily basis to administer the insulin injections. I immediately called the home care agency to question the staff about this particular patient. They said that the reason I was sent was to figure out what kind of help the man needed. All this time they were seeing this man, no one took the initiative to help him. Amazingly, the staff knew that he needed a caretaker and some food, but they waited awhile to contact someone to help him. We ended up having to institutionalize the man because he didn't have enough money to pay a round-the-clock caregiver and he was unable to care for himself at all. His home was not conducive for living in, since he was blind. The man died two months after being moved into a convalescent home.

Here's a similar story: I visited another man, Caucasian, age 68. This man was also a diabetic, with almost the same amount earned, but this man was on Medicare and another supplemental type of insurance. The one thing that was different was the type of care that this man received from the same home health care agency. This man was released from the hospital, and because he had more than himself to speak about his needs (he had family members), the home health care agency became more an advocate for him. He had equipment in the home to help him be more comfortable. I remember that a nurse was present during my visit with this man. She said that she wanted to make sure that I had all of the information that I needed in order to help "her" patient. After this visit, I asked the nurse about the African American man from the previous story, and this was when I found out that he died in the convalescent home. I was infuriated, and I asked her why it took their agency so long to help that man who didn't have any family members left, while they were "on top of things" with this patient who seemed to have many family members supporting him. She had no explanation for me. I told myself that this was how things were, and I began to plan my future because I know that my story might parallel that of the African American male more so than the Caucasian male patient.

—Rafael, 30+-year-old Mexican American man

Should we assume that these two stories differ because of the difference in family support? If the African American man had had more family members advocating for him, would his story have had a different ending? We can make different assumptions about these stories, but we should look at the underlying causes of the disparities in treatment and care between the two men. As in many cases, whether they involve health, finances, education, and so on, we will find that there is more than one aspect to consider in any attempt to obliterate the negative forces that make our society the unequal and disparate place that it remains today. We must look at racism, poverty, and structural barriers to obtaining health care, as well as ease of access to the health-care system. Finally, we should also look at differential treatments in health care as a continuing cause for disparities.

Racism

The United States is projected to hit some important demographic turns that will change the face of the nation. By 2060, the population of European Americans will dip to 44.3% from 61.3% in 2016 (Vespa, Armstrong, & Medina, 2018). Well before then, by 2020, fewer than 50% of children will be European Americans. These shifts in the ethnic/racial makeup of the population have been projected for years. The U.S. population is rapidly aging and by 2030 international immigration will supersede natural births as the main source of population growth in the United States. By 2035, all baby boomers will be 65 years of age or older and this age group will make up 21% of the population. Children, the elderly, people of color, and immigrants face significant health-care disparities. Should we focus primarily on health and health-care disparities? Or is there a bigger underlying factor that must be addressed to decrease disparity among minority groups in relation to the majority group?

Health-care disparities across ethnic groups are often tied to conditions related to this membership rather than to the ethnicity itself. For example, being African American does not itself cause colorectal cancer; rather, African Americans have increased rates of poverty and experiences with discrimination, past and present, which together result in systematic differences between African Americans' and European Americans' access to services and quality of services. An important variable that is heavily associated with race/ethnicity is racism. Racism operates at the individual and institutional levels. When discussing health disparities, institutional racism is most relevant. According to Brondolo, Gallo, and Myers (2009), racism has resulted in inequitable access to social, educational, and material resources, which have both direct effects on health status (i.e., through access to healthy diets and appropriate medical care) and indirect effects on health status (i.e., through their influence on stress, psychosocial resources, and positive and negative emotions).

Some may reject that idea, thinking "Are they using *that* again"? It is indeed hard to believe that research continues to reflect disparities in health and illness across ethnic groups. Many researchers have examined the relationship between experiences with discrimination and health. Instead of reviewing individual studies, we can use a meta-analysis to provide a snapshot of the literature. Paradies and a group of collaborators (Paradies et al., 2015) conducted a thorough review of the literature on racism and health between 1983 and 2013. They found 333 articles (309,687 participants) that, together, provided clear indication that self-reports of racism are associated with negative mental and physical health outcomes. Specifically, for mental health, experiences with racism were related to depression, anxiety, psychological stress, self-esteem, life satisfaction, posttraumatic stress, somatization, suicidal ideation and suicidal behaviors, well-being, and positive affect. For physical health, studies included information primarily on blood pressure and hypertension, overweight-related outcomes, heart conditions, diabetes, and cholesterol. Other health outcomes were observed, but in low quantities (e.g., asthma, cancer).

Paradies and colleagues (2015) found that the largest effect of racism was on negative mental health, followed by positive mental health and general health. The smallest effects were recorded for negative physical health. The authors also examined moderators, meaning that they looked for other variables that explained the relationship between racism and health, and they found that age, sex, place of birth, and education level did not explain the relationship. This finding is important because it means that racism operates directly on health outcomes regardless of age, sex, etc. Paradies and his colleagues did find that ethnicity was a significant moderator. More specifically, the relationship between racism and poor mental health outcomes was stronger for Asian Americans and Latinxs than it was for African Americans. For physical health, the relationship between racism and poor physical health outcomes was stronger for Latinxs than it was for African Americans. It is unfortunate that this meta-analysis included only papers published in English, 81.4% of which were published in the United States. Because discrimination and disparities in health are found globally, it is important to examine research published in languages other than English, especially given the evidence indicating that research is increasingly published in other languages (e.g., Spanish and Portuguese; VandenBos & Winkler, 2015). In their meta-analysis, Paradies et al. focused on racism itself and not on general experiences of discrimination or specific experiences of discrimination tied to other identities (e.g., gender, sexual orientation). They also excluded studies that measured racism and health outcomes together, for example, race-related stress. It is important to fill that gap.

Strong evidence indicates a relationship between racism and stress and between stress and health disparities. The APA (American Psychological Association, Working Group on Stress and Health Disparities, 2017) published an important report on stress and health. Psychological scholarship to date documents disparities in exposure to stress that are tied to institutional racism. For example, people who experience economic and social disadvantage experience greater stress and have fewer resources to respond to that stress. Stressors can be chronic, and their chronicity leads to more permanent changes, both psychologically (e.g., cognitive appraisals of threats) and physically (e.g., allostatic load). An excellent illustration of stressors is the fact that Latinx and African American men are less likely to be called for interviews or be offered employment compared to European American men who apply for low-wage jobs. This constitutes a threat to livelihood and financial stability, not only immediately but also in the long term. More important, the accumulation of stressors that result from racism and discrimination creates an exponential risk for people who experience them.

Stress and health are interconnected in important ways. The APA (American Psychological Association, 2017) report indicated four main areas that impact mental and physical health outcomes, including (a) stress reactivity/recovery, (b) health behaviors, (c) social cognitions, and (d) cognitive control processes. For example, sleep is an important component of stress reactivity and recovery. A lack of sleep can create risk for a person's ability to cope with an environmental stressor, the impact of which can affect later sleep or other physical functions (e.g., eating, substance use).

Discrimination acts as a lens through which patients appraise their experiences with health professionals, with common themes between European Americans, African Americans, and Latinxs being attributed differently in light of past experiences and expectations of racial discrimination (K. O'Brien et al., 2010). Although some people of color who have directly reported discrimination and racism that contribute to health disparities continue to utilize medical services, others refuse to entertain the idea of seeking medical help. Perceived racial or ethnic discrimination is increasingly receiving empirical attention as a class of stressors that could have consequences for health and for understanding disparities in health (D. R. Williams & Mohammed, 2009). In fact, racism and health disparities are intertwined, so much so that persons do not have to directly experience discrimination within their professional health settings for perceived discrimination to occur.

> I am not surprised that most ethnic minorities do not utilize the health-care system. Most do not use it because they do not trust the doctors, and even if they do, they do not get good treatment from them on account of their ethnicity. I have to say that I am quite apprehensive when it comes to White doctors. I prefer having a Black doctor (which I do). I used to have a White doctor, but I stopped consulting with her because we did not see eye to eye, and I felt like she did not understand me. Once I was sick, she told me that the cause of my illness is due to lack of nutrients and vitamins. I informed her that I actually took my vitamins daily and ate plenty of fruits and vegetables, so there must be another reason for my illness (she actually kept on asking me if I was sure I eat right). Also, when it came to how much I weigh, she told me I was supposed to be 20 pounds lighter and that I need to exercise and watch my food intake. I responded that I did exercise (about 5 days/week in fact) and that I always watch my calories. Although the White doctor found me to be "overweight," my Black doctor said that my weight is actually fine.
>
> —Chioma, 20+-year-old African American woman

Racism is a fundamental underlying cause of health and health-care disparities, but many researchers study it at the individual level (i.e., the individual's experience of racism and how it affects the quality and quantity of services) rather than examining the more powerful structural forces, such as social segregation and immigration policies, that likely have much stronger impacts (Gee & Ford, 2011). In Chioma's story, we can conclude that her European American physician was a racist and, thus, that eradicating the racism within her would improve her skills with other Black patients. Alternatively, and much more likely, Choima's physician was trained by people with little exposure to and knowledge of Black patients who based their knowledge in a body of scientific evidence where Blacks were not represented, thus limiting the ability for Chioma's physician to gain important knowledge. This education was perhaps obtained within a society where Blacks are over-represented among the poor and discriminated against in covert and chronic ways. This contextual examination points more clearly toward *structural racism*. Structural racism are "social forces, institutions, ideologies, and processes that interact with one another to generate and reinforce inequities among racial and ethnic groups." (Gee & Ford, 2011, p. 116)

Poverty

Poverty contributes to disparities in health care. James (2003) identified a contradiction that exists in our society: Racism is incompatible with democratic ideals, but both are deeply characteristic of U.S. society. Racism and democratic ideals coexist partly because of the moral economy of the U.S. society, which refers to the norms that govern, or should govern, economic activity in a given society and that set either tight or loose constraints on the ability of dominant groups to treat subordinated others as undeserving of the protections and privileges they accord themselves. Inequities in wealth and health result from such constraints but are publicly rationalized as logical. This was a central debate in the Obama administration health-care reform efforts, as the administration fought for greater access to the health-care system for people who were at or near the poverty level, but individuals who resisted these efforts accused the administration of attempting to provide care to undeserving people who were too lazy to work or too selfish to purchase health-care insurance.

James (2003) further added that this explanation has been uncontested and dominantly used as the reason for the nation's persistent racial/ethnic health disparities, and it has taken root in the American psyche without a shred of supporting empirical evidence. James posited that the entire argument rests on an edifice of negative moral sentiments and stereotypes about some people of color. On the one hand, the negative sentiments and stereotypes increase minorities' vulnerability to economic exploitation in the marketplace, and on the other hand, they portray minorities—subtly or overtly—as undeserving of the protections and privileges of citizenship that are readily available to others.

In a study (Harvard Mahoney Neuroscience Institute, 2009) that examined how the stress of poverty affects childhood brain development, researchers posited that parents are preoccupied with putting food on the table and providing shelter for their families, so much so that talking with their children—much less noting children's need for anything other than food and shelter—would be a near impossibility. Additionally, the authors reported that constant adversity produces **allostatic load,** or the physiological costs of chronic stress, including high blood pressure, increased heart rate, and elevated blood sugar and cortisol levels, which may help explain why the rates of hypertension, diabetes, and heart disease are higher in low-income populations.

allostatic load—the physiological cost of chronic stress.

As the distance between rich and poor continues to grow, the freshest, most nutritious foods have become luxury goods that only some can afford.
    —Lisa Miller, *Newsweek* magazine, November 29, 2010

How do people of color, especially those who have limited resources, begin to find out about health-care access? Gaining initial entry into the health-care system includes such measures as researching health professionals who are in the local area—after the minority group member acquires a way to pay for the needed medical treatment (determining whether health professionals take cash for people who are unable to acquire insurance). Many, if not most, people gain initial entry by calling around, using the Internet, and following up on referrals from other individuals.

This may seem easy enough, but if we consider the limitations of minority group members, the commonly used ways to gain entry into the health-care system may prove more troublesome. Although the digital divide has been narrowing and European Americans, African Americans, and Latinxs have similar rates of smartphone ownership, African Americans and Latinxs tend to access the Internet using their cell phones rather than a broadband connection at home (Anderson, 2015). People who live in certain neighborhoods have no reliable referrals because they live with other individuals facing similar challenges regarding the health-care system. Researchers have reported that the inability to find a physician to accept low-income women is the single largest barrier to obtaining prenatal care (Francis, Berger, Giardini, Steinman, & Kim, 2009). This issue is the same for many people of color living in urban

Poverty is related to poor health. *Photograph by Birute Vijeikiene/Shutterstock*

dwellings and low-income communities. There is an immediate need for culturally competent and affordable services for people of color who require medical services. It is interesting that more African Americans and Latinxs look for medical information online compared to their European American counterparts (Anderson, 2015). This is fitting given the argument that technology holds great promise to reduce health disparities (Corralejo & Domenech Rodríguez, 2018). Entry to the health-care system may prove more difficult for people of color than it seems to be for European Americans. Poverty hinders minorities from utilizing resources, and when we consider this along with structural barriers, it becomes clearer how disparities continue.

> I remember this time when I was at the dentist and I had to get a crown for my teeth. The dentist offered me a choice between a silver crown, and a porcelain crown (which would be a lot less noticeable). The woman next to me, who was an older Latina, who didn't speak and understood very little English, was only offered a silver crown. I asked my dentist why the lady was only offered a silver crown and he said, "Oh honey, I'm almost positive she can't afford the porcelain one, and I don't want to upset her or make her feel badly because she can't afford it." He didn't know anything about her financial situation. I didn't think much of it at the time, but when I saw my mom, I told her about the "fact" that I was special because I was getting the porcelain crown and the poor woman was going to get a silver crown because she couldn't afford the porcelain one. My mom then told me that she was talking with the woman's husband, who told my mom about a small restaurant that they opened up and that he thought business was going well. He told my mom that they were able to buy a new car. The poor woman wasn't poor after all, and was actually "better off" than our family. In this situation I was the privileged one just because I spoke English and didn't look so "Mexican," which was wrong.
>
> —Leslie, 20+-year-old Mexican American woman

Although this passage might appear to have come from times long past, the sad truth is that such experiences continue. The third author of this text (MDR) had a mammogram in 2017. While she was waiting in line, she was speaking in Spanish on the phone. She overheard the nurse offering a European American patient a higher quality mammogram. When it was her turn to check in, she was not offered the same test. MDR asked the nurse about it. The nurse said it would cost extra. MDR handed the nurse a credit card and asked to obtain the higher quality assessment.

A challenge inherent in understanding health disparities is the complex interplay between social/structural issues and personal ones. The nurse was affable and likely did not consider that she was perpetuating health disparities, but her likely implicit biases kept her from providing equitable care across patients (e.g., Spanish speaking thus must be poor). Yet the actions of one nurse do not have the power to predict disparities at the rate in which they are evidenced! Structural racism may be implicated, for example, in the form of little or no training in cultural competence in health care.

Structural Barriers

> My grandmother passed away in 1996. She suffered from diabetes, high blood pressure, cholesterol, and on top of all that, cervical cancer. What affected her most was cervical cancer. I still remember my grandmother on her death bed asking for a carnitas taco, and I remember my aunts actually bringing it to her. Everything is a blur to me, but when I read statistics in class, I couldn't help but think about all of my family members, including my grandma, who were very quick to say that doctors in the United States are "no good." They say that they only want to take your money and that the regimen that they prescribe are often a prescription toward your death bed. My grandmother refused everything except insulin. She refused surgery to remove her cancer cells, she refused to change her diet, and she refused to give in to everything a doctor had to say. So, if my grandmother did this and my family members continue this attitude toward medical care even now, I can only imagine that a lot of statistics regarding visiting doctors are majorly influenced by culture.
> —Alejanra, 20+-year-old Latinx American woman

For people of color who are limited not only by the color of their skin but also by language barriers or their immigrant/undocumented status, entry into the health-care system becomes a maze without an exit. An individual's cultural beliefs may contribute to their resistance to seeking help in the United States, but the lack of cultural competence among health professionals does not inspire people of color to be trusting of such help. Many racial and ethnic groups, as well as poor and less educated patients, are more likely to report poor communication with their physicians and to report more problems with some aspects of patient–provider relationships (Agency for Healthcare Research and Quality, 2015). For example, Asians, Latinxs, and people of lower socioeconomic status have greater difficulty accessing health-care information, including information on prescription drugs.

Furthermore, a Department of Health and Human Services report stated that geography can play an important role in health-care disparities (Centers for Disease Control and Prevention, 2017). Remote rural populations, for example, are clearly at risk for having worse access and receiving poorer quality care than their urban counterparts. People of color in rural settings are also disadvantaged in comparison to their European American counterparts (Centers for Disease Control and Prevention, 2017). African Americans, Latinxs, Asian Americans, and American Indians in rural communities reported lower health status than did

European Americans. Expense was an issue. African Americans, Latinxs, and American Indians in rural communities were more likely to report they could not afford to see a medical provider in the past year than were European Americans. These three ethnic groups were also more likely than European Americans to have high rates of obesity. However, on social determinants of health such as smoking and binge drinking, people of color generally fared better than European Americans. These data are significant when illuminating the importance of intersectionality in outcomes. Health disparities are generally observed for individuals in rural communities and for people of color. The combination of being a person of color in a rural community appears to have additive risk.

Gaining entry into the health-care system seems to require more competence from the patient, who may be linguistically, economically, and educationally challenged, than from the health professionals who are in charge of healing and advertising assistance. For most minority group members, it is easier to stay within their own community and deal with their ailments according to how it was done "where they came from" than to fight their way through a complex and perhaps unfamiliar structure.

Structural barriers can also be defined by measures of the presence or absence of specific resources that enable receipt of care within the health-care system, such as having a provider who is available at nights or on weekends or who can be contacted by telephone easily (Moy, Smith, Johasson, & Andrews, 2006). For people of color who rely on services within their own neighborhoods, because of a lack of trust for professionals, this type of availability diminishes, partly because of a lack of working professionals within rural or remote areas and also because of the cost of the resources and the number of persons who may require treatment at a time. Other structural barriers may be tied to environment risk factors. In a longitudinal analysis of pollutants in Massachusetts, although the overall levels of pollutants were reduced, inequities increased over time, especially for people of color with regard to their relative exposure to various pollutants when compared to European Americans (Rosofsky, Levy, Zanobetti, Janulewicz, & Fabian, 2018).

As readers can surmise, there are many challenges for people of color, the young, the elderly, the impoverished, and those with special needs—the "unseen people" in our society—just in considering entry into the health-care system. It is clear that certain injustices, whether within the health-care system or any other aspects of our society, are interconnected, which suggests that resolving these underlying issues could eventually put an end to discriminatory practices.

Once people of color gain entry into the health-care system, they may not be able to see their health-care professional right away. People of color must consider such issues as making appointments, transportation to the doctor's office, and referrals to specialists. Most people of color are hospitalized before they are made aware of resources that are available to them. It is interesting that one side effect of these hospitalizations is a higher rate of avoidable hospitalizations among people of color when compared to European Americans (Dalla Zuanna et al., 2017).

Most health-care providers are limited when communicating with patients of color. This limitation is either a result of the health-care professional's lack of cultural competence in dealing with individuals from different minority groups or because of language barriers. A collaboration between six hospitals accredited by the Joint Commission showed that adverse events were more likely to result in physical harm for patients with limited English proficiency when compared with English-speaking patients (Divi, Koss, Schmaltz, & Loeb, 2007).

Specifically, 49.1% of patients with limited English deficiency had physical injuries compared to 29.5% of English speakers. The harm was more likely to be moderate or severe (including death) and more likely to be the result of an error in communication (Divi et al., 2007).

Access to the Health-Care System

In most research, disparities can be organized under two headings: access to care and quality of care. According to the *National Healthcare Quality and Disparities Report* (Agency for Healthcare Research and Quality, 2017), access to health care is a prerequisite to obtaining quality care, and both are independent and additive. Therefore, we can begin by examining how access to health care can affect an individual's quality of care.

The *National Healthcare Quality and Disparities Report* (Agency for Healthcare Research and Quality, 2017) has been a leading report since 2002. Recent data indicate that most indicators of disparities have not improved significantly over time. This finding is important because it is evidence of the chronicity of health disparities. Table 8.4 includes a summary list of the measures of health-care access that are tracked at the national level. The largest amount of data are available for African American, Latinx, and Asian American groups. In Table 8.4, notice the patterns where the arrows point down across rows. Notice where the dashes do the same. Some patterns are important and are probably becoming clear over the course of reading this chapter: African Americans and Latinxs tend to have the poorest outcomes compared to European Americans. Asian Americans tend to have mixed outcomes. There are little data for American Indians/Alaska Natives and for Native Hawaiians and Other Pacific Islanders, yet the pattern of findings for the available data tend to be poor.

We have found that access to health care directly affects the quality of care that patients receive, especially people from minority groups. According to the *National Healthcare Quality and Disparities Report* (Agency for Healthcare Research and Quality, 2017), because an individual must have access to health care before quality care is acquired, we must consider multiple factors that lead to differences in health care. Such factors include different underlying rates of illness because of genetic predisposition, local environmental conditions, and lifestyle choices. The report further indicates that the differences in care-seeking behavior of patients vary because of differing cultural beliefs, linguistic barriers, degree of trust in health-care providers, or variations in the predisposition to seek timely care. If there is so much to consider when examining access to health care and care-seeking behaviors, what type of care should we expect for minority groups?

When we examine the factors that affect access to health-care services, we see many overlapping issues that must be dealt with before minority group members are able to receive quality care. For example, poverty and lack of resources leave many minority group members uninsured. People of color are less likely to be insured than are European Americans. In 2011, 13% of European Americans were uninsured compared with 18% of Asians, 21% of Blacks, 27% of American Indians, and 32% of Latinxs (Kaiser Family Foundation, 2013). Children across groups were more likely to be insured than adults were, although there were notable differences in public versus private insurance coverage. For example, 26% of European American children were publicly insured compared to 52% of Latinx and Black children and 54% of American Indian children. When children were removed from analyses, fully 41% of Latinx adults were uninsured.

TABLE 8.4　**Health Disparities Indicators: Comparison Across Ethnic Groups to European Americans**

	Latinxs	African Americans	Asian Americans	Native Hawaiians/ Other Pacific Islanders	American Indians/ Alaska Natives
Adults who had any appointments for routine health care in the past 12 months who sometimes or never got an appointment for routine care as soon as needed	↓	↓	↓		
Children who had any appointments for routine health care in the past 12 months who sometimes or never got an appointment for routine care as soon as needed	↓	↓	—		
Adults who needed care right away for an illness, injury, or condition in the past 12 months who sometimes or never got care as soon as needed	↓	↓	↓		
People under age 65 with health insurance	↓	—	↑	—	↓
People under age 65 with any private health insurance	↓	↓	↑	↓	↓
Adults age 65 and over with any private health insurance	↓	↓	↓		↓
People under age 65 who were uninsured all year	↓	—	↑		—
People under age 65 with any period of uninsurance during the year	↓	↓	↑	—	↓
People with a specific source of ongoing care	↓	↓	—	—	—
People with a usual primary care provider	↓	↓	↓	—	—
People in fair or poor health with a specific source of ongoing care	↓	—	—		
People who were unable to get or delayed in getting needed medical care in the past 12 months	↑	—	↑		
People who were unable to get or delayed in getting needed dental care in the past 12 months	—	—	↑		—
People who were unable to get or delayed in getting needed prescription medicines in the past 12 months	↑	—	↑		

continued

TABLE 8.4   **Health Disparities Indicators: Comparison Across Ethnic Groups to European Americans (*continued*)**

	Latinxs	African Americans	Asian Americans	Native Hawaiians/ Other Pacific Islanders	American Indians/ Alaska Natives
People with a usual source of care, excluding hospital emergency rooms, who has office hours at night or on weekends	—	—	↑		—
People with a usual source of care who is somewhat to very difficult to contact during regular business hours over the telephone	—	—	—		—
Adults who needed to see a specialist in the past 12 months who sometimes or never found it easy to see a specialist	↓	↓	—		
Children who needed to see a specialist in the past 12 months who sometimes or never found it easy to see a specialist	↓	—			
Adults who had a doctor's office or clinic visit in the past 12 months and needed care, tests, or treatment who sometimes or never found it easy to get the care, tests, or treatment	↓	↓	↓		
Children who had a doctor's office or clinic visit in the past 12 months and needed care, tests, or treatment who sometimes or never found it easy to get the care, tests, or treatment	↓	—			

↑ = better than the reference group (European Americans); — = same as reference group; ↓ = worse than the reference group; blank fields = no data. These data are from the *National Healthcare Quality and Disparities Report* (Agency for Healthcare Research and Quality, 2017).

Lack of health insurance limits people's ability to gain entry into the system. However, Alegria and colleagues (Alegria et al., 2012) noted that insurance coverage alone would not necessarily reduce health disparities. Practical considerations, such as making appointments, finding transportation, communicating with health-care professionals, and ensuring understanding of what they need to do to continue or maintain care can all be hindered by language barrier problems (only one of the many barriers). Language barriers (along with skin color) tend to signal minority group membership and influence patients' perceptions of how they are treated by health-care professionals. These perceptions help them eventually decide whether return, live with the illness, or continue to search for a "better" doctor or better help. This cycle continues, and meanwhile the sick get sicker and the quality of care continues to decline.

Ever since I [can] remember I've always served as an interpreter for my mom and my grandma. It all started when I was in junior high, whenever there was a parent–teacher conference I had to translate for her because some teachers did not speak Spanish. It was a difficult situation because sometimes I just couldn't find the exact word to get the right meaning across. My mom would also get frustrated but I felt that she didn't understand how troublesome it

Health disparities are related to one's access to the health-care system. *Photograph by ellenaz/Shutterstock*

was for me. I remember she would always say that she didn't know why it was so hard to translate; if I knew both languages, then there shouldn't be any problem. I would try to explain to her that I was able to understand, but I just couldn't find the appropriate translation.

Later I learned that translating for teachers was nothing compared to translating for doctors. When I would take my grandma to a doctor's appointment or whenever she was hospitalized, I had to try my best at interpreting. Sometimes it was entertaining because my grandma would just start talking without being asked anything and then the doctor would ask me what she had said. Like I mentioned earlier, it was difficult to find a good word in English to translate her conversation. There are some words that just don't have an equivalent in another language. Not only was it troublesome to paraphrase my grandma's conversation, but it was worse to translate all the scientific words that doctors use. I would always ask myself, How in the world am I going to explain this to her?

—Beatrice, 20+-year-old Mexican American woman

Patients sometimes prepare for language difficulties by bringing friends or family members to assist with communication. **Language brokers** have no translation or interpretation training and support communication between two or more people (Kam, 2011). It is common for minor children of immigrant parents to serve as language brokers. Some theories predict negative outcomes for children who broker by focusing on the negative effects of exposure to inappropriate material (e.g., a physician telling a parent through a child that they have a terminal illness). Other

language brokers—support translation or interpretation without formal training for this task.

researchers point out that brokering places children in an adult role and can negatively impact family dynamics by shifting power roles between parents and children or giving children developmentally inappropriate responsibilities. Some scholars look at the positive impact, citing an increased sense of self-efficacy and language mastery for children who broker. Another possible positive impact is that language brokering allows children to make meaningful contributions to their family, supporting interdependence.

I was watching a PBS program on health clinics in rural California. They were interviewing a 9-year-old boy about having to interpret for his monolingual Spanish-speaking mother when she went for a gynecological examination! I couldn't believe that a doctor would have such a young child interpreting for such a sensitive topic. The interviewer asked the boy how he felt about interpreting for his mother, and he just said that he was needed and he did the best he could.

—Jerry, 60+-year-old Japanese American professor

Language brokering occurs across ethnic groups, although not much is known about the frequency with which it occurs. Research is limited—meaning that many opportunities to conduct research in this area exist for our interested students! In a unique study, Kam (2011) studied language brokering among 684 Mexican American adolescents in the seventh and eighth grades. The study included positive and negative feelings about language brokering. Kam (2011) found that the frequency of language brokering was not tied to negative outcomes; in fact, language brokering frequency was associated with positive feelings, although it was also related to family-based acculturative stress. Negative brokering feelings impacted negative outcomes (alcohol use, other risky behaviors) only through family-based acculturative stress, meaning that negative brokering feelings increased stress, but it was the stress that predicted negative outcomes. The positive brokering feelings did have a direct and negative association with cigarette use. Thus, children who had positive feelings about their language brokering were less likely to smoke.

The case of language brokering is an interesting addition to our discussion on health disparities. Children may step in as language brokers to increase access of care for their parents, and this act can have important consequences for their own future health. In fact, Kam and her colleagues later studied 120 mother–adolescent pairs of varied Latinx heritage and found that both mothers and adolescents experienced benefits to language brokering, specifically greater perspective taking and empathic concern (Kam, Guntzviller, & Pines, 2017). This finding was supported whether the participants had positive or negative feelings about language brokering, suggesting the brokering itself had positive effects regardless of how adolescents or their mothers felt about it. Indeed, when children language broker for their parents, they are also shaping the parent–child relationship. In a study of 4- to 11-year-old children using direct observations of 60 parent–child pairs, Straits (2010) found that language brokering was positively related to the quality of the parent–child relationship. She also examined the impact of brokering on the parent–child power dynamic and found that the two were not significantly related.

Regardless of outcomes, it is important in health settings to have access to trained interpreters. Title VI of the Civil Rights Act prohibits discrimination on the basis of national origin. Health-care agencies must provide interpreters, yet often do not because of a lack of resources or poor access to interpreters (Tonkin, 2017). However, interpreters play a critical role in ensuring not only access to services, including proper consent and assessment, but also improved quality of care and later outcomes (Tonkin, 2017). Children have many opportunities to language broker and garner the benefits of this activity in less risky or delicate settings (e.g., working on homework together).

Differential Treatment

To reduce disparities in health/health care, individuals/practitioners must deliver culturally competent health care that focuses on risk reduction, vulnerability reduction, and promotion and protection of human rights, which involves not only information, education, diagnosis, testing, intervention, and treatment but also respect for the human rights and dignity of people who have been socially cast in inferior roles and subordinate status (Flaskerud, 2007). Researchers have noted a lack of comprehensive studies regarding health disparities and differential treatment. One point repeatedly stated in research is that individuals can become more accountable, but only when societal change occurs.

My father studied in our country and achieved a master's degree in business administration. Unfortunately, when we migrated to the U.S., his master's degree did not matter and certainly did not compete with younger students who also had a master's degree. My father, who was a very strong man back home, became ill with diabetes and high blood pressure 5 years after we moved to the U.S. My mom says that it was from all of the stress that he had to go through. My father, who held a high position back home, had to humble himself to be a door-to-door salesman. One time, I went with my dad to the doctor because he had to get some checkups done (he never said what for), but I thought it was pretty serious because he never took me to checkups before. It ended up being an extra checkup due to his diabetes and the inconsistent blood sugar levels that he was experiencing. I didn't hear any information that the doctor gave because he merely gave my dad a prescription and began to leave the room. My father called out because he had some questions, but the doctor kind of waved him off and said to try the medication first and set another appointment in two weeks. My dad didn't say a word and neither did I. We left the room and were passing by the nurses' station when we spotted the same doctor talking to a White man about this patient's exercise regimen and how it would be beneficial and so on and so forth. I thought to myself, "He couldn't answer my dad's question, but he can talk to that man about exercise?" My dad looked at me as he saw what I saw and smiled meekly.

—Priscilla, 20+-year-old Filipina American woman

It is challenging to achieve an understanding of health disparities when they are so complicated. Structural issues such as poverty play a large role, for example, in where people live, what environmental hazards they are exposed to, and what life experiences they are more likely to have. Some people might reasonably throw their hands up in the air in defeat. However, individual-level factors contribute to health disparities, and bias on the part of medical providers features prominently among these factors.

Implicit bias refers to attitudes that are unconscious or involuntary, but nonetheless influence how people feel, think, and behave. In contrast to explicit biases, which are conscious attitudes, implicit biases are hard to measure because people do not know they hold such attitudes. A clever measure for implicit bias is the Implicit Associations Test (IAT; Greenwald, McGhee, & Schwartz, 1998). The IAT measures implicit bias through response times to word–picture pairings. For example, a picture of an African American man could be presented alongside a picture of a European American man with the words *good* and *bad* over each picture. The test taker must follow an instruction in which they pair the word good with the African American or the European American picture. The ability of respondents to follow the cues as they change results in a score that provides an assessment of implicit attitudes.

implicit bias—attitudes that are unconscious or involuntary but nonetheless influence how people feel, think, and behave.

The IAT developers created Project Implicit (https://implicit.harvard.edu/implicit/), an online platform that allows individuals to take the IAT and learn what their response times suggest about their attitudes across social groups (e.g., race, gender, sexual orientation), even intersectionally (e.g., gender and race). Although Project Implicit has been operating since 2005, the first publications about implicit bias in health-care providers did not appear until 2007. Thus, this area of knowledge is relatively new. We also believe it is very exciting.

In a recent systematic review of implicit bias in health-care providers, Maina, Belton, Ginzberg, Singh, and Johnson (2018) synthesized the available knowledge gathered from 37 published reports. Health-care providers included physicians across varied areas of medicine (e.g., pediatrics, trauma surgery, emergency medicine), other providers (e.g., nurses, physician assistants, psychologists), and participants at varied levels of training (professionals, students). Most researchers (31 studies) used the Race IAT and found that health-care providers showed pro–European American and anti–African American bias that ranged from slight to strong. The same pro–European American bias was documented in fewer studies examining the Ethnicity IAT (European American/Latinx), American Indian IAT, and Skin Tone IAT. Further, a few researchers used the Race/Compliance IAT, Race/Medical Cooperation IAT, and Race/Procedural Cooperativeness IAT and found that providers saw African American patients as less compliant and less cooperative than European Americans. In contrast, researchers in studies that used the Race/Quality Care IAT showed that providers had a positive implicit association between superior quality health care in African American patients compared to European American patients. While bias was observed against people of color, the perceptions among providers was the people of color received better care.

Attitudes can be tricky. Over many years teaching multicultural psychology, we have learned that students respond negatively to receiving feedback that their implicit attitudes may be biased. In our teaching, we often stress that the nature of our automatic assumptions is not necessarily something to be ashamed of, but rather that there is power in bringing the unknown into known awareness so that we can pay attention to how our unconscious attitudes may shape our behaviors and then take steps to be more intentional about how we interact with others. Implicit attitudes matter not for their existence in someone's head, but for the impact they have on actual outcomes.

In health-care settings, implicit attitudes can result in poorer care. Indeed, in the review of the IAT literature, a striking finding was that researchers in 25 studies examined outcomes. Of the 25 studies, 12 were studies in which providers responded to vignette rather than real-world situations. Most of those 12 studies (8) did not indicate a relationship between implicit attitudes and a medical outcome. Yet of the 11 studies that involved either simulation (2) or real-world patient care (9), all but 1 documented the significant impact of implicit attitudes on outcomes, especially patient–provider communication. Although most studies have involved adult participants, the few studies with children have demonstrated the same pro–European American bias (T. J. Johnson et al., 2017; Maina et al., 2018). These are powerful findings because most people, especially in the United States, do not want to appear racist and will work diligently to project values of equality. However, many of us have been **culturally programmed** (Domenech Rodríguez, 2018) to hold biased attitudes and we have

cultural programming—The ways in which environments shape people without individuals express knowledge or awareness that this is occurring. Cultural programming can lead to implicit attitudes or biases.

been shaped to respond in ways that are biased. These realities are not personally shameful; rather, they are social realities that can be altered. What is important is what each of us does after we become aware that we hold biased attitudes and the potential they hold for shaping our actions. Few interventions to reduce implicit attitudes in medical providers exist, but some studies (Castillo, Brossart, Reyes, Conoley, & Phoummarath, 2007; Chapman et al., 2018) show promise in reducing implicit attitudes.

Differential outcomes in patients across racial/ethnic lines suggest that there is much work to be done in achieving culturally competent care. In addition to the data that have already been presented in this chapter, the *National Healthcare Quality and Disparities Report* (Agency for Healthcare Research and Quality, 2017) lists many health outcomes in their specific tables. A cursory review indicates the following:

- Latinxs fared better than European Americans on 40 outcomes, including lung cancer deaths and death from suicide. Latinxs had comparable performance on 74 outcomes. They fared worse than European Americans on 63 indicators, including lower extremity amputations resulting from diabetes, receiving care consistent with wishes while in hospice, and HIV infection deaths.
- African Americans fared better than European Americans on 24 outcomes, including home health vaccinations and suicides. They fared equally on 91 outcomes. Yet African Americans had worse outcomes in 77 areas, including low-birthweight infants, hospital admissions from home health care, and HIV mortality.
- Asian Americans fared better in 56 outcomes compared to European Americans, including suicide, adequate dialysis, and death from lung cancer. Asian Americans and European Americans has similar outcomes on 86 indicators. Asian Americans fared worse on 32 indicators, including a variety of home health indicators and obstetric trauma.
- Native Hawaiians and Other Pacific Islanders fared better on 12 indicators, including child and adult immunizations. They had 24 similar outcomes and 14 worse outcomes compared to European Americans. Worse outcomes included home health indicators and good communication about discharge medications.
- American Indians had 13 better, 62 similar, and 32 worse outcomes compared with European Americans. Better outcomes included lung cancer deaths and adequate dialysis. Worse outcomes included a variety of home health variables and infant mortality.

Overall, the trend is for the majority of indicators to be similar between people of color and European Americans; however, many indicators are worse. How many worse outcomes represent an acceptable number? Does it matter if better indicators are present as well? The answer will depend on the severity of the outcome, treatability, and other factors of interest to health-care providers. Each provider will likely be most interested in their specialty area and in outcomes that they may be able to address. For example, highly specialized findings show that African American patients are more likely to die during their first heart attack (Colantonio et al., 2017). The *Health Equity Report* (Health Resources and Services Administration, 2017) highlights important areas of disparities, specifically that American Indians/Alaska Natives are at high risk for heart disease. All major ethnic minority groups are at high risk for diabetes. American Indian/Alaska Natives and African Americans had higher rates of obesity and smoking. All of these risk factors are compounded by poverty, education, and income (Health Resources and Services Administration, 2017). The good news is that there many data to examine, which will provide information. The bad news is that there are so many data points, it can be easy to get lost.

Mistrust of the Health Care System

> I can't believe it! This is our own government! How could they do something like this? I always knew that there was some racism in our country, but I can't believe that our own government could be so cruel in its participation in this study. Before I read about this, I wanted to deny that racism was that big of a deal. This stuff happened in the days of slavery, but not today. But when I read that our own government approved of a study to simply watch people die when they knew there was a cure totally blew me away!
>
> —Darcy, 20+-year-old European American woman

This response was from a student who read about the infamous Tuskegee experiment (D. W. Sue & Sue, 2003; R. L. Williams, 1974b). In this "study," the U.S. Public Health Service recruited more than 600 African American men from rural Alabama. Approximately 400 of the men had a latent stage of syphilis, and 200 were studied as controls for people who were infected with syphilis. From 1932 until 1972, the infected men were not treated for their disease but, rather, simply observed. Ultimately, 7 of the men died directly from syphilis and 154 died of heart failure most likely connected to their untreated condition. The disclosure of this study, which was exposed only because of the Freedom of Information Act (passed because of suspicions about how the country became involved in the Vietnam War), is widely considered the impetus behind the federal government's implementation of ethical research standards for human subjects (U.S. Department of Health, Education, and Welfare, 1979). The Tuskegee experiment, along with sterilization experiments, the use of slaves as involuntary medical research subjects, and other historical experiences with the formal health-care system marked largely by disregard, disrespect, lack of access, and abuse, have affected and influenced the health preferences of African Americans (J. C. Johnson & Smith, 2002).

The Tuskegee study is one of many in a long history of what can, at best, be described as differential treatment. Harriet A. Washington (2006) published a gruesome account of the history between medical providers and African Americans in *Medical Apartheid: The Dark History of Medical Experimentation on Black Americans from Colonial Times to the Present* that would be an excellent resource for health psychologists. Among her historical accounts are grave robberies supported by medical schools that needed corpses for medical training purposes, experimental surgeries that were perfected on slaves, and the lack of use of pain killers during medical procedures because physicians believed African Americans did not experience pain in the same way European Americans did. Less violent but nonetheless ethically problematic is Skloot's (2010) account of the use of Henrietta Lack's cells in medical research without her or her family's consent. The HeLa cells continue to be used today. The long history of abuses in the service of advancing medicine provides an important context in which to understand the mistrust of the medical system that some people of color experience.

More recently, it was discovered that U.S. medical professionals not only stood by while people of color suffered from syphilis, but also attempted to give people of color syphilis and gonorrhea for purposes of studying the effects of the disease (T. Johnson, 2010). Susan Reverby, a professor of history and women's studies from Wellesley College, was interested in further information about this experiment. She had access to papers related to the Tuskegee experiment and opened a box of documents, expecting to read more about this dark history of U.S. ethics. To her surprise, she discovered that the U.S. government attempted to infect 1,500 Guatemalan prisoners with syphilis and gonorrhea between 1946 and 1948. The study was halted, not because these medical professionals felt it was unethical to conduct the research but because it was too difficult to intentionally infect the prisoners with the viruses. At first, the doctors used prostitutes who had these diseases to try to infect the prisoners. When too few prisoners contracted the diseases, the doctors attempted to directly infect the prisoners by holding infected cotton balls of the virus onto open sores on the prisoners' arms, faces, and even penises (Reverby, 2011):

> In the experiments, a doctor held the subject's penis, pulled back the foreskin, abraded the penis slightly just short of drawing blood by scraping the skin with a hypodermic needle, introduced a cotton pledget (or small dressing), and dripped drops of the syphilitic emulsion onto the pad and through to the roughed skin on the man's penis for at least an hour, sometimes two. (p. 15)

Imagine how Darcy in the previous quote would have reacted to this new discovery about U.S. medical "ethics"!

Kumanyika and associates (Kumanyika, Morssink, & Nestle, 2001) mention the ethnic minority health movement evolving as an offshoot of the civil rights struggle, with the current advocacy anchored in a 1985 federal task force report documenting excess deaths among people of color compared with the European American population. These authors further reported that disparities in some areas were seen to have persisted or worsened even in the presence of societal changes intended to improve the health-care condition of minority groups, which, according to some minority observers, is a deliberate effort to encourage the gradual disappearance of an unwanted group. There seemingly is such a deep distrust of the majority group that we cannot ignore the social explanations that stem from experiences of discrimination by the minority groups that could lead them to this type of conclusion.

How could an entire group manifest behaviors that have such underlying distrust of this society? Kumanyika and colleagues (2001) specifically address ethnic minority women's health as being fraught with vestiges of the historical relations between the European American majority and people of color. These historical relations include the stigmatization of people with dark skin, legal and de facto segregation and discrimination, and a host of painful historical associations with slavery, the Tuskegee study, involuntary sterilization, and internment in wartime relocation camps. Such historical facts describe the worst type of quality of care, if we can even refer to such events with the word *care*. We can also assume that such experiences shaped the lives not only of ethnic minority women, but also of all persons in ethnic minority groups.

Few studies have focused on how children's health and development are affected by racism and discrimination. Children of color grow into adults of color, and therefore their experiences at very early stages in their lives can shape how they view the health-care system. Pachter, Bernstein, Szalacha, and García Coll (2010) studied how perceived racism by children can potentially affect their lifetime health and development. Studies on child development and early life experiences reinforce exacerbated mistrust of the system. How should we expect the next generations to behave toward their health and health care if we do not start caring about change today?

Obscure Disparities

The bulk of this chapter has focused on disparities between people of color and European American groups. It is important that we note that there is a marginalized group of people for whom little information exists regarding health disparities: LGBTQI+ populations. A primary goal in the Healthy People 2020 initiative is to increase the capacity to monitor health outcomes of lesbian, gay, and bisexual people as well as transgender groups. However, there are not even adequate measures for assessment of sexual orientation and/or gender identity. Hughes, Camden, and Yanchen (2016) provide a good model but it's very much just a start. Indeed, in our teaching experience we find that students and even colleagues are still confused about the difference between sexual orientation and gender identity. Sexual orientation refers to a person's sexual attraction to others, and labels include lesbian, gay, bisexual, pansexual. Gender identity refers to a person's sense of self in relation to gender. When people identify with their biological sex, they are considered to be cisgender. When people are born with sex organs different from their internal sense of self, they may use the label transgender. For example, a person born with female sex organs that identifies as a man, may identify as transgender male. These distinctions are important in healthcare where approaches to treatment may be informed by biological sex characteristics and result in the invalidation, marginalization, or shaming of those that do not identify with their biological sex.

Little is known when compared to people of color. However, available data paint a bleak picture of disparities for LGBTQI+ groups. A recent review of health disparities among lesbian, gay, bisexual, and transgender (LGBT) youth revealed that LGBT youths were at higher risk for negative health outcomes such as substance use, sexually transmitted diseases, cancers, cardiovascular diseases, anxiety, depression, and obesity. These youths were also at higher risk than their non-LGBT counterparts of experiencing bullying, isolation, and rejection (Hafeez, Zeshan, Tahir, Jahan, & Naveed, 2017). LGBT youths were at higher risk of suicide (Hafeez et al., 2017), and when LGBT youths have attempted suicide, they have been found to be at dramatically higher risk for a repeated attempt (Mustanski & Liu, 2012). The Centers for Disease Control and Prevention (2016) track men who have sex with men and found that while rates of new HIV infections have remained stable for nearly two decades, Black, Latinx, and gay/bisexual men across ethnic groups are disproportionately contracting HIV infections. Importantly, the intersectionality between ethnic minority status and sexual orientation may put people of color who are LGBTQI+ at heightened risk for negative outcomes.

Why Should We Care?

Eliminating disparities in health and health care is defined as a priority in the U.S. Department of Health and Human Services' Healthy People 2020 Initiative (Office of Disease Prevention and Health Promotion, 2018).

If you receive relatively good health care or if you have reasonably good access to the health-care system, you might be tempted to ask, "Why should I care about other people not receiving adequate health care?" First, because you are reading this book on multicultural psychology, you probably already care somewhat about this issue. Second, on a broad level, persistent disparities in health care are inconsistent with American values. This country was founded on the belief that everyone is equal and that justice should apply to all. If there are systematic disparities in health care that are caused by correctable factors, we should be motivated to address those problems.

On a more pragmatic level, continued health disparities will ultimately strain our health-care system. To the extent that such persistent disparities will ultimately cause a rise in the cost of health care in our society, we will all pay for such disparities. For that reason, we must address these problems before they strain our economy beyond our capacity to pay for them.

Bringing About Change

The U.S. federal government first officially turned its attention to health disparities in 2000 when president Bill Clinton signed Senate Bill 1880, the Minority Health and Health Disparities Research and Education Act (Pub. L. No. 106-525). At the time, Clinton intended to eliminate health disparities by 2010 (Clinton, 2000), a goal that quickly proved impossible to reach and appears too elusive. The Minority Health and Health Disparities Research and Education Act amended the Public Health Act (2000) "to improve the health of minority individuals." The act established the National Center on Minority Health and Health Disparities within the National Institutes of Health with the intention of supporting new research and also supporting the diversification of the health-care workforce. The act also specified that the Agency for Healthcare Research and Quality would consistently measure disparities, that the Health Resources and Services Administration would make awards and grants to support education in the health professions to reduce disparities, and that the secretary of Health and Human Services would disseminate information and increase public awareness of health disparities. The wealth of information we have today responds to these legislative mandates.

Progress has been made in addressing health disparities, although Clinton's goal to eliminate disparities by 2010 may have been lofty. Strides have been made in the collection of data and public awareness of health disparities, but much work remains to be done in addressing access and quality of care (Institute of Medicine, 2012). In the 2000s, research was heavily focused on biological causes of disparities and moved toward social determinants of health as findings pointed to the critical importance of determinants in shaping health outcomes.

An important precursor to the Minority Health and Health Disparities Research and Education Act of 2000 was the National Institutes of Health Revitalization Act of 1993 in which federal legislation required for the first time the inclusion of women and people of color in federally funded research, especially clinical trials. Until the 1990s, people of color and women were often excluded from clinical trials or included in insufficient numbers to conduct meaningful analyses. Researchers cited the importance of controlling variables that could alter results or practical considerations in access to diverse populations. These arguments dangerously paired with a mistrust from people of color in particular toward the medical establishment and resulted in a degree of invisibility in scientific research that was so ubiquitous that published reports often did not even provide a description of the ethnicity of participants. This is no longer acceptable. A policy was instituted to reduce the likelihood that structural racism would continue to exercise its powerful impact on the base of knowledge of the health professions. However, the inclusion of women and people of color in research proved challenging. The whole research enterprise to examine health and well-being was built within a cultural context. New methods were needed. More accurately, existing community-based participatory research methods that were historically at the fringes of medical and psychological research were brought to the fore.

Community-based participatory research is an approach to generating knowledge that requires collaboration between research partners on an equal footing, at every phase of a research project. These methods respond to the long history of exploitation of vulnerable people in the name of science and seek to promote community empowerment by sharing resources and taking social action (Blumenthal, 2011). Community-based participatory research is often tied philosophically to Paolo Freire's liberation pedagogy (Berthoff, 1990). From a liberation pedagogy standpoint, a skilled teacher teaches and also facilitates self-actualization of students. Furthermore, according to Berthoff, "Freire has the audacity to believe that teachers must be learners, that they learn from students in dialogue" (p. 363). Community-based participatory research methods have been advanced in health-care research as the importance of working with communities has become increasingly clear in both understanding disparities and addressing them (Institute of Medicine, 2012). The years of unapologetically adhering to an arrogant stance of "scientist as expert "are behind us, and scientists are expected to learn from communities for knowledge to be relevant and applicable to those communities. Community-based participatory research occurs between scientists and community stakeholders and/or agencies *as equal partners*. The National Institutes of Health moved to accept proposals from community members and funds community members in leadership roles in research and demonstration projects (Institute of Medicine, 2012). A beautiful example of community engagement occurred at the 2017 Annual Sickle Cell Disease Clinical Research Meeting, hosted by the National Heart, Lung, and Blood Institute. A panel of four trial participants spoke to a standing-room-only session about the benefits of participation and their recommendations for recruitment of African American participants (National Heart, Lung, and Blood Institute, 2017).

At the practice level, health disparities have been addressed by policies such as the Affordable Care Act, by increased diversification of the health-care workforce, and by supporting the development of cultural competence in all health-care providers. The bill known as the Affordable Care Act has two parts, the original Patient Protection and Affordable Care Act and

community-based participatory research—an approach to generating knowledge that requires collaboration between research partners on an equal footing, at every phase of a research project.

the amendment titled Health Care and Education Reconciliation Act. The Affordable Care Act was signed into law in 2010 with full implementation by 2014 (Artiga, Foutz, & Damico, 2018; Rosenbaum, 2011). Since that time, access to health care has improved. The rate of uninsured persons declined from 16% in 2010 to 9.1% in 2015 (Obama, 2016). That is a dramatic shift when considering that these percentages represent 49 million (in 2010) and 29 million (in 2015) uninsured persons. Although health disparities in access continue for people of color, this group has had the largest gains in coverage since the implementation of the Affordable Care Act (Artiga et al., 2018).

The workforce diversification continues slowly, although information is difficult to ascertain. In 2014, data for physicians by ethnicity were missing for nearly 38% of the sample of 1.1 million physicians with a medical degree. However, the existing information presents a concerning picture: of those for whom data were available, the vast majority (69%) of physicians were European American, 17.5% were Asian American, 6.4% were Latinx, 6% were African American, and 0.5% were American Indian/Alaska Native (Association of American Medical Colleges, 2017). Whereas Asian Americans are over-represented relative to the general population, Latinx, African American, and American Indian physicians are grossly underrepresented relative to their numbers in the general population.

cultural competence—the ability to interact effectively with people of different cultures.

Cultural competence is "the ability to interact effectively with people of different cultures" (Substance Abuse and Mental Health Services Administration, 2016a, para. 1). Culture refers to race/ethnicity, but also to age, gender identity, sexual orientation, disability, religion, income level, education, geography, and profession (Substance Abuse and Mental Health Services Administration, 2016), para. 3). The *National Standards for Culturally and Linguistically Appropriate Services* in Health and Health Care (known as the National CLAS Standards)

Increasing the number of people of color in the health-care profession can help to overcome the distrust that many people of color have toward the system. *Photograph by bikeriderlondon/Shutterstock*

were created in 2000 and updated in 2013 to advance health equity, improve the quality of services, and support the elimination of health disparities given evidence of the effectiveness of culturally and linguistically appropriate services in improving quality of care (U.S. Department of Health and Human Services, 2013). Although the research in this area is still emerging, there are initial promising results. When examined by way of a systematic review, cultural competence training in health-care providers has been linked to improved competence in those providers (six of seven studies) and in improved patient satisfaction (five of seven studies; Govere & Govere, 2016).

Some providers not only do not possess cultural competence but also display cultural incompetence. For example, a Latinx patient we visited reported on the lack of care he received in a U.S. hospital (translated from his native Spanish language):

> I remembered things like having to use the bathroom, pressing the button for a nurse, and waiting so long that I had to "go on myself." When the nurse did show up, she became infuriated at the mess that I made, and I remember being pulled and pushed to the bathroom so hard that I threw up. This infuriated her even more and she screamed at me. Although I couldn't understand it because it was all in English, I remembered the word "stupid" once or twice. I don't want any trouble from her and I am not trying to get anyone fired. I just needed to get this off my chest, because I continue to have nightmares about it. It will be better now because I was able to "let it out."
>
> —Julio, 60+-year-old Latinx American man

After that incident was reported, a social worker was assigned to Julio's case and confirmed that his nurse had been abusive to many patients. The nurse was disciplined, and Julio was able to receive the services he needed. Can we call Julio's story one with a happy ending? The answer depends on how we want to look at things. As a health-care society, we seem to be more reactive than proactive, especially with people of color such as Julio.

How would we like to see things change? What goals should we set to improve our health-care system? Are there easy answers? Because it seems that institutionalized racism is the underlying theme within health/health-care disparities, much work must be done to document improvement in the narrowing of health/health-care disparities. We must focus on specific issues that we can directly observe, measure, and report to improve health disparities. Although there seems to be much to improve regarding health disparities in our society, we must say that all is not lost.

Summary

Health disparities exist among people of color, between groups, and between minority group members and European Americans. A look at ethnic minority groups as a whole, however, makes it easier to pay close attention to what might be involved in eliminating disparities in health and health care.

Health beliefs involve individuals' perceptions of their illness and how susceptible they are, based on their trust in the health professional who makes the diagnoses and on the cost of treatment. Health beliefs dictate the ways that minority groups maintain their health. Because health behaviors contribute to the continuation of healthy or unhealthy lifestyles, people of color who typically seek less care and receive suboptimal care compared with European Americans have a lower quality of life.

The health of minority group members depends on their ability to access care. Accessing health care in this society has proven to be more difficult for people of color than for European Americans. Gaining entry into the health-care system, structural barriers (such as transportation and getting appointments with doctors), patients' perceptions of the care they may receive or have received, and utilization of care are all categories of difficulties to consider in accessing health care. These difficulties in accessing health care ultimately determine the quality of care that people of color will receive and occur within the context of suspiciousness of the health-care system given racism that has occurred in this domain.

Because access to care and quality of care seem to go hand in hand, and may also be independent of each other, a common theme in both is institutional racism. Institutional racism dictates that health professionals remain incompetent in cultural issues (communicating with patients, understanding cultural norms when it comes to treatment, providing appropriate information and diagnoses, etc.). Racist beliefs also disempower people of color by making them fully reliant on health professionals' decisions about their treatment. People of color can remain uneducated about their health issues in critical clinical encounters.

Changes in laws and policies that govern health and health-care agencies have led to some improvements in health disparities, but disparities are still evident. Continued monitoring and improved research and practice are needed. At a broad social level, people of color are at higher risk for encountering stressors in social determinants that are tied to health outcomes. They are less likely to be insured and more likely to experience negative outcomes in other access and quality of care. The health-care workforce is sociodemographically different from the population of patients, creating opportunities for cultural misunderstandings. Some strides are evident in advancing cultural competence but there is room for much more.

Critical Thinking Questions

1. Think back to when you were growing up. Did your family have health coverage?
2. How did your family pay for visits to the doctor?
3. What kinds of healthy behaviors were around you (e.g., jogging, going to the gym)? What kinds of unhealthy behaviors were around you (e.g., smoking, drinking alcohol)? Did friends of different ethnicities have different kinds of health behaviors around them?
4. Did you have a family doctor? How easy was it for you to see your family doctor? How easy was it for you to get to a local hospital? Did your family speak the same language as your doctor, or did you need an interpreter?
5. How much did you trust your family doctor? How much did you trust other elements of the health-care system?
6. How did you feel when you read about the Tuskegee syphilis experiment and the more recent Guatemalan syphilis and gonorrhea study? Does this give you some understanding of why some groups in the United States may be suspicious of the medical profession?

CHAPTER 9

Culture and Mental Health

Photograph by TraXXXe/Shutterstock

Culture and Diagnosis
The Diagnostic and Statistical Manual of Mental Disorders:
    A Classification System
Culture and the Expression of Symptoms
Cultural Group Differences and Mental Health
    The Collaborative Psychiatric Epidemiology Studies
    National Survey on Drug Use and Health
    Ethnic/Racial Groups Not Well Represented in the Large
       Epidemiological Studies

Learning Objectives

Reading this chapter will help you to:
- understand cultural differences in definitions of mental health;
- identify diverse cultural expressions of symptoms of mental health issues;
- understand the impact of culture on the diagnosis of mental disorders;
- critically evaluate which strategies are appropriate for treating diverse groups;
- explain some cultural barriers to treatment for mental illness;
- recognize the impact of microaggressions on the diagnosis and treatment of mental disorders;
- distinguish between culture-specific approaches to treatment and general approaches
- understand the role of culture in evidence-based practice in psychology; and
- understand the role of social justice in addressing mental health issues.

Denise—a 20-year-old, African-American, lesbian college junior—was majoring in sociology at a large, predominantly White university in the southwestern United States. Denise came to the university counseling center to address feelings of depression and loneliness related to chronic difficulties with interpersonal relationships, particularly with her peers and family members, surrounding her sexual orientation.

Denise was assigned to an African American female counselor and appeared somewhat anxious during the intake session. She verbalized her ambivalence about discussing her problems in counseling because she had received numerous messages from her parents and other family members about the taboo of going to a mental health counselor to address personal things. Denise said she had trust issues and that she would feel more comfortable knowing something about the counselor. She asked the counselor about her credentials and whether she was a liberal person. After her counselor responded honestly to these questions, Denise appeared to relax.

Denise discussed some of the adjustment difficulties she was having at the university, feeling as if she was "too different from any of these people here" and as though she did not fit in. More specifically, Denise believed her interpersonal difficulties were related to her inability to deal effectively with the heterosexist attitudes of many students. She also shared that others' negative treatment of her in this regard affected her self-esteem. Although her family always fostered a sense of pride about her racial identity, they were intolerant of her sexual orientation. She stated they frequently told her that she was going to burn in hell because of her sexual orientation. She felt the African American students on campus were also judgmental and unaccepting of her sexual identity.

During the first few sessions Denise explored her feelings of sadness and anger related to feeling unsupported and oppressed by people in her social and family circles because of her sexual orientation. She also explored issues related to her internalized heterosexism, racism, and sexism. As her counselor helped her identify various cultural identities and validated her struggles to consolidate them, Denise claimed she was feeling increasingly comfortable with the idea of working to synthesize her multiple identities to formulate a more integrated sense of her being. She also stated that she was beginning to feel less depressed. Denise was able to take some responsibility for her interpersonal interactions. She came to recognize that her difficulties with trust, although warranted on many occasions because of heterosexism, sometimes contributed to her feelings of isolation and sadness. Denise traced some of her trust issues to relationships with girls in junior high who betrayed her secret of being a lesbian. She discussed at great length her feelings of disappointment and anger related to not feeling unconditionally loved by her family and was beginning to accept the fact that her family members "may never be okay with my being gay." Denise and her counselor also spent time exploring their relationship with regard to cultural differences, issues of trust, and issues of power. She also spoke about her initial fear of being rejected by her counselor, an African American woman. Denise spoke of feeling empowered by her experiences of feeling supported, validated, and challenged in counseling, and she expressed an interest in joining a lesbian support group on campus so she could obtain support and continue struggling with her issues. (adapted from D. W. Sue et al., 1996, pp. 115–117)

As we will see, Denise's case illustrates a number of issues regarding culture and mental health. A major premise of multicultural psychology is that all behavior occurs in and is shaped by only a cultural context. Therefore, mental health is influenced by culture. We can see the effect of culture on mental health in many ways, including the types of symptoms experienced, the manner in which those symptoms are expressed, and the meaning those symptoms have for the individual, his or her family, and his or her community. Culture influences how clients cope with their troubles, whether they seek help, and from whom. Culture also plays a role in the causation of mental disorders, their prevalence, and their treatment.

Culture influences not only the client but also the counselor or therapist and the institutions that provide mental health treatment. Mental health professionals bring their own culture, including their attitudes and beliefs, to the setting, which can influence their diagnosis and what strategies are used to help the client (U.S. Department of Health and Human Services, 2001).

In Denise's case, we see first a complex interaction among her symptoms of depression, loneliness, isolation, and interpersonal conflicts with her multiple identities as an African American lesbian woman. Her presenting issues went beyond her internal thoughts and feelings and were affected by her interactions with and the attitudes of other college students, particularly African American students, and her family regarding her sexual orientation. She was hesitant to go to therapy because of the negative stigma attached to it by her family but also because of her difficulties trusting others, even her African American female therapist. Denise benefited from therapy for a number of reasons, including her therapist's ability to see beyond Denise's initial presenting problems and to effectively connect her issues to the larger cultural context. In this chapter we discuss these and many other aspects of culture's impact on mental health and the diagnosis and treatment of mental health problems.

Culture and Diagnosis

We cannot discuss culture and the diagnosis of mental disorders without talking about the *Diagnostic and Statistical Manual of Mental Disorders* (*DSM*). The *DSM* is the primary manual used by health and mental health professionals in the United States to diagnose mental disorders. The *DSM* has gone through several revisions. The most current version is the *DSM-5*, the fifth edition (American Psychiatric Association, 2013).

Diagnostic and Statistical Manual of Mental Disorders—the primary reference manual used in all mental health fields to classify mental disorders. Published by the American Psychiatric Association, this manual is currently in its fifth edition (American Psychiatric Association, 2013).

Although the *DSM* is used in other countries, there are other diagnostic manuals, including one developed by the World Health Organization (2016 version), the *International Statistical Classification of Diseases and Related Health Problems,* currently in its tenth version (*ICD-10*). The *ICD-10* is an international classification system for all diseases and health problems, not just mental disorders. The developers of the *DSM-5* and the *ICD-10* worked closely together to make the two manuals compatible. Individual countries also have their own diagnostic manuals. For example, in China they use the *Chinese Classification of Mental Disorders*, third edition. This manual is also written to correspond with both the *DSM* and the *ICD;* however, it includes some cultural variations on the main diagnoses and approximately 40 culture-specific diagnoses. It is published in both Chinese and English (S. Lee, 2001; Surhone, Tennoe, & Henssonow, 2010).

The World Psychiatric Association and the World Health Organization conducted a survey of almost 5,000 psychiatrists across 44 countries regarding the cross-cultural utility of diagnostic classification systems like the *DSM* and *ICD* (Reed, Correia, Esparza, Saxena, & Maj, 2011). Most of the participating psychiatrists (70.1%) reported using the *ICD-10*, and most of the remainder (23.0%) used the *DSM-IV* (the study was conducted before the publication of *DSM-5*). A small percentage (5.6%) reported using another system (e.g., the *Chinese Classification of Mental Disorders*). The survey also included the question, "The diagnostic system I use is difficult to apply across cultures, or when the patient/service user is of a different cultural or ethnic background from my own." Overall, about 75% of the worldwide participants agreed with this statement. However, when the responses were divided by region, some differences appeared. Nearly 30% of the participants in Latin America, East Asia, and Southeast Asia agreed with this statement, whereas only 10% of participants from the United States did so. Many psychiatrists from countries such as Cuba, Russia, China, India, Japan, and France also felt there was a need for classification systems specific to their nations. In other words, a significant number of psychiatrists around the world questioned the applicability of global diagnostic systems like the *DSM* to the patients they serve.

The Diagnostic and Statistical Manual of Mental Disorders: A Classification System

Diagnostic categories in the *DSM* are based on empirical research and focus on behavioral descriptions of symptoms. Specific diagnoses represent clusters of symptoms that typically are seen together and that have some defining feature. A diagnosis is made on the basis of a set of behavioral criteria. If the person exhibits a minimum number of symptoms in the list, then a specific diagnosis is made. For example, major depressive disorder has a list of nine symptoms, including depressed mood, loss of interest or pleasure in usual activities, weight loss, and insomnia. For a diagnosis to be made, the person must experience five or more of these symptoms for at least 2 weeks. By focusing on behavioral manifestations of symptoms, the *DSM* attempts to be neutral. This enables it to be a useful communication tool for people from an array of professional backgrounds (e.g., psychologists, medical doctors, social workers), with different theoretical orientations (e.g., behavioral, psychodynamic, family/systems), in a variety of settings (e.g., hospitals, clinics, private practice; American Psychiatric Association, 2013).

The *DSM-IV* (American Psychiatric Association, 1994) was the first version of the *DSM* to systematically include cultural issues. Now, a section on cultural issues is included with each of the diagnostic categories. In addition, there is an "Outline for Cultural Formulation," a guide that helps mental health professionals systematically review the client's cultural background, the role of culture in the expression of the client's symptoms, and the role that cultural differences may play in the relationship between the client and the therapist. The outline identifies five areas that the therapist should cover in making a cultural assessment of the client and his or her presenting problems: (a) the cultural identity of the individual; (b) cultural concepts of distress, or the factors that influence how the person experiences, understands, and communicates his or her symptoms; (c) psychosocial stressors and cultural features of vulnerability and resilience, including culturally relevant social stressors and available social support; (d) cultural elements of the relationship between the individual and the clinician, including how cultural differences between the client and the therapist may affect the treatment; and (e) overall cultural assessment for diagnosis and care, in which the therapist incorporates all these cultural factors to plan the most appropriate course of treatment (American Psychiatric Association, 2013). The *DSM-5* also includes a structured interview to help clinicians cover each of these areas, called the Cultural Formulation Interview.

The *DSM-5* gives a more detailed description of the second area, cultural concepts of distress. Again, this refers to the ways in which individuals and cultural groups experience, understand, and communicate their problems. The *DSM-5* identifies three types of cultural concepts. The first are *cultural syndromes,* or clusters of symptoms that tend to occur only in specific cultural groups. These used to be referred to as culture-bound syndromes. The second are *cultural idioms* of distress, or specific ways of expressing troubling thoughts, behaviors, and emotions. Finally are *cultural explanations or perceived causes.* In other words, certain cultural groups may attach unique meanings to symptoms or have particular explanations for the etiology of illness or distress. These cultural concepts typically arise out of local folkways and may or may not correspond to specific *DSM* diagnostic categories. *DSM-5* also includes a glossary of cultural concepts of distress. We will give some examples later in the chapter.

The initial inclusion of cultural issues in *DSM-IV* was a clear step in the right direction, and some see *DSM-5* as even further improvement in making the *DSM* more inclusive (e.g., Cummings, 2013; Saville-Smith, 2013). However, there are those who believed *DSM-IV* did not go far enough (S. R. Lopez & Guarnaccia, 2000; Parham, 2002) and, despite more extensive coverage of culture in *DSM-5*, it still has critics and those who question its utility with diverse cultural groups (K. D. Jacob, 2014; K. S. Jacob et al., 2013; Reed et al., 2011).

Although the *DSM* strives to be an objective diagnostic tool, research studies repeatedly demonstrate clinician bias in applying diagnostic criteria. Clients reporting the same symptoms are given different diagnoses. For example, several studies have shown that African Americans are more likely to be diagnosed with schizophrenia and less likely to be diagnosed with a mood disorder, whereas the opposite is true for non–African Americans (e.g., Adembimpe, 1981; Neighbors, 1997; Trierweiler, Muroff, Jackson, Neighbors, & Munday, 2005). In other words, there is a tendency for therapists to give the more serious, chronic, stigmatized diagnosis of schizophrenia to African American clients and a less severe diagnosis, such as major depression, to European American clients.

Culture and the Expression of Symptoms

An accurate diagnosis depends both on the client's ability to describe his or her symptoms and on the clinician's ability to observe and accurately interpret those symptoms. Culture influences the way in which individuals express the symptoms of various disorders. People from different cultures may have the same disorder but may experience and describe their symptoms in very different ways. The manifestation of symptoms can vary with age, gender, race, ethnicity, and culture.

Let us again use the example of depression. Certain cultures might experience and express more physical symptoms than mood symptoms. This is known as **somatization**, or the expression of psychological symptoms through physical ones. For example, individuals from Latinx and Mediterranean cultures may complain of nerves or headaches, those from Middle Eastern cultures may complain of problems of the heart, and Asians may talk about weakness, tiredness, or imbalance. It is important for clinicians to be aware of such cultural differences in expression to avoid misdiagnosis. For example, some individuals may express a fear of being hexed or bewitched or may report vivid feelings of being visited by someone who has died. These may be acceptable and understood experiences in some cultures but could be mistaken by a traditional Western therapist for symptoms of psychosis.

somatization—the expression of mental disorders through physical disorders.

In addition, the expression of depressive symptoms can change with age. The symptoms described in *DSM-5* criteria typically describe how depression is experienced by adolescents and adults. Children may have somatic complaints as well as irritability and social withdrawal, and their depression often coexists with other behavioral problems, such as disruptive behavior, hyperactivity, and inattention. In contrast, depressive symptoms in the elderly may include disorientation, memory loss, and distractibility. These must be distinguished from the symptoms of dementia (American Psychiatric Association, 2013).

Chanda relocated to the United States after surviving the horrors of Pol Pot's regime in Cambodia. While living in Cambodia she lost most of the members of her extended family who were either killed by the Khmer Rouge (the ruling party) or from starvation. Chanda was married four times. Her first husband was beaten to death by the Khmer Rouge. Her second husband died of an illness while they were awaiting re-settlement in the refugee camp. Her third husband left with another woman, and she separated from her fourth husband. Chanda was pregnant 12 times. She lost 6 to miscarriages and 2 died from starvation. She has 4 surviving children—one who was the only one to survive the Pol Pot era, the second who was born in a refugee camp, and the last two that were born after she migrated to the United States. She describes the living conditions on one of the farms she worked in Cambodia:

"When the floods came we had nothing to eat at all. Living there, you know? And from working and over-exhaustion, having nothing to eat. Some months, when there was no rice at all, they would make soup out of rice peel (husk) for us to eat. There were even people who ate their own children. There was a lady who ate her dead baby, too hungry! If you don't believe me, go see for yourself, and you'll see that this village is full of skeletons. . . . We would walk around looking for food, even one little plant; we left no leaves on it."

Chanda resettled in the United States in 1983. Since then she has suffered continuously from various forms of illness, physical pain, constant coughing, feeling that something was stuck in her throat, allergies, hearing voices, and seeing spirits. Chanda describes going to the hospital where they took X-rays, but the medical people were unable to determine the cause of her problem because nothing showed up in the photos. She says:

"I told them that I had fever and things. As soon as I came down with a fever, it was like 'a hundred ghosts took over my body.' I was sick on that day. Within one hour, it was like I was sick with 10 different illnesses. I would sit there and hear ringing. I told the doctors that this hurt and that hurt, because it really did hurt inside my body. My arm hurt, to this day it hurts where I extend my arm and the pain won't go away. If I don't take painkillers I would 'sleep in tears' every night."

Chanda also experienced spirit visitations. She says these spirits keep telling her things, and she keeps seeing something from another world. Chanda's descriptions of her visitations from spirits caused her to be hospitalized for a week. (adapted from Morelli, 2005, pp. 130–134)

Although Chanda may have some physical symptoms as a result of her many years of starvation, we can also see the tendency to somaticize, or to express psychological symptoms as physical ones. We also see some symptoms that the traditional Western doctors diagnosed as psychosis (visitations from spirits), but that may represent a culturally appropriate or acceptable experience.

Cultural Group Differences and Mental Health

In the field of public health, **prevalence** is defined as the current rate of existing cases of a disorder at a given point in time. An example would be the number of people currently diagnosed with schizophrenia. Another term used often when reporting rates of various disorders is

prevalence—the current rate of a particular disorder at a given point in time.

incidence—the number of new cases of a disorder diagnosed in a given period of time.

lifetime incidence—the number of cases of a disorder that occur during one's lifetime.

incidence, which refers to the number of new cases of a disorder that occur during a given period of time, such as the number of people who are diagnosed with schizophrenia this year. **Lifetime incidence** refers to the number of cases of a disorder that occur during one's lifetime. Therefore, if an individual was diagnosed with schizophrenia 2 years ago and continues to suffer from this disorder, that person would be included in the prevalence rate, would not be included in the incidence rate in the past year, but would be included in the lifetime incidence rate.

There is a great deal of interest in comparing the incidence and prevalence rates of disorders in the different ethnic groups. The literature is mixed, with some studies showing lower rates of mental disorders in populations of color and some showing greater rates, making it difficult to draw conclusions about ethnic group differences and mental disorders. However, the results of a few large epidemiologic studies reveal some trends.

The Collaborative Psychiatric Epidemiology Studies

At the beginning of the new millennium, the National Institute of Mental Health funded three large-scale studies of mental health in the United States. The purpose was to look at the prevalence of mental disorders, associated features of the disorders, and use of mental health services. Together, these three—the National Comorbidity Survey Replication (NCS-R), the National Study of American Life, and the National Latino and Asian American Study of Mental Health—make up the Collaborative Psychiatric Epidemiology Studies (CPES; Heeringa, Wagner, Torres, Duan, Adams, & Berglund, 2004). The first study (NCS-R) was the largest and most comprehensive, the National Study of American Life focused specifically on African American and Afro-Caribbean populations, and the third focused on Latinxs and Asians. A particular focus of these studies was to investigate cultural and ethnic influences on mental health (Collaborative Psychiatric Epidemiology Surveys, n.d.). All three studies were coordinated by the University of Michigan Institute for Social Research and involved structured face-to-face interviews conducted by professional interviewers in the homes of participants across the country from 2001 to 2003. The researchers designed the studies so that data from each could easily be combined and compared (Heeringa et al., 2004). The most comprehensive of the three CPES studies is the NCS-R. The precursor to the NCS-R was the original National Comorbidity Study (NCS; Kessler et al., 1994). With the NCS-R, researchers sought to replicate the findings of the original NCS, to examine trends observed in the first study, and to get information about topics not previously covered (Kessler et al., 2004; National Comorbidity Survey, 2005). For the NCS-R, researchers interviewed approximately 10,000 U.S. English-speaking residents, ages 18 and older.

Results of the NCS-R revealed that more than half (57.4%) of U.S. residents experience a diagnosable mental disorder at some time in their life (see Table 9.1). The most common disorders are substance abuse (35.3%) and anxiety disorders (31.2%), followed by impulse control disorders (25.0%) and mood disorders (21.4%; Kessler et al., 2005).

The NCS-R included data on 5,424 Hispanics, non-Hispanic Blacks, and non-Hispanic European Americans (Breslau et al., 2006). Both Hispanics and non-Hispanic Blacks reported lower rates of depression, generalized anxiety disorder, and social phobia (see Table 9.2). Hispanics also had a lower risk for dysthymia, oppositional defiant disorder, and attention deficit hyperactivity disorder. Non-Hispanic Blacks had lower rates for panic disorder, substance

TABLE 9.1   Lifetime Prevalence Rates of *Diagnostic and Statistical Manual of Mental Disorders IV* Disorders by Sex From the National Comorbidity Survey Replication (National Comorbidity Study, 2005)

	Total sample (%)	Females (%)	Males (%)
Anxiety disorders	31.2	36.4	25.4
Mood disorders	21.4	24.9	17.5
Impulse control disorders	25.0	21.8	28.6
Substance disorders	35.3	21.6	28.6
Any disorder	57.4	56.5	58.4

Note: Adapted from Table 1, Lifetime Prevalence of DSM-IV/WMH-CIDI Disorders by Sex and Cohort. Retrieved from the National Comorbidity Survey, http://www.hcp.med.harvard.edu/ncs/index.php

use disorders, and impulse control disorders. The only instance in which a minority group had a significantly higher lifetime prevalence rate than non-Hispanic European Americans was bipolar disorder for non-Hispanic Blacks. Although Hispanics had higher rates of substance use (caused by higher rates of alcohol abuse/dependence), the number was not significantly higher than that for non-Hispanic European Americans.

In general, the numbers indicate that both minority groups had lower rates of mental disorder, with non-Hispanic Blacks experiencing the lowest rates in the most categories. No published articles were found that made direct comparisons between Asians and the other groups. However, data from the National Latino and Asian American Study of Mental Health suggested relatively low 12-month prevalence rates of mental disorder in each category for Asians, with substance use disorders showing the lowest rates, at just 1.3%, and anxiety disorders the highest, at 10% (J. Kim & Choi, 2010).

Breslau et al. (2006) noted the more recent trend in which ethnic/racial minority groups display lower rates of mental disorder than non-Hispanic European Americans. This phenomenon runs counter to the expectation that minority groups would experience higher rates of mental disorder because of the social disadvantages and stressors they experience and suggests that these groups experience some sort of protective factors against the development of mental disorders that require further investigation. Possible protective factors discussed include ethnic identification and religious participation.

TABLE 9.2   Lifetime Prevalence Rates of Mental Disorder for Hispanics, Non-Hispanic Blacks, and Non-Hispanic European Americans from the National Comorbidity Survey Replication

	Hispanic (%)	Non-Hispanic Black (%)	Non-Hispanic White (%)
Anxiety disorders	24.9	23.8	29.4
Mood disorders	18.3	16.0	21.9
Impulse control disorders	17.9	14.5	15.3
Substance disorders	16.1	10.8	14.8
Any disorder	43.7	38.5	47.6

Source: J. Breslau et al. (2006).

National Survey on Drug Use and Health

Another large epidemiologic study is the National Survey on Drug Use and Health, conducted annually since 1971 by the Substance Abuse and Mental Health Services Administration (2016b). This survey is considered the primary source of statistics on the use of illegal drugs, alcohol, and tobacco in the United States. This survey conducts face-to-face interviews with a representative sample of the noninstitutionalized general population in all 50 states and the District of Columbia. Date reported here are from the 2016 survey.

Table 9.3 summarizes results for racial/ethnic group comparisons in substance use disorders, all mental disorders, major depressive episodes, and thoughts of suicide for Asians, American Indians/Alaska Natives, Black/African Americans, Hispanics/Latinxs, and Native Hawaiian/Pacific Islanders. The overall trend shows either lower or similar rates of these mental health issues for these groups when compared with the national average. The biggest difference seems to be the higher rates of substance use disorder, any mental disorder, and major depressive episodes for American Indians/Alaska Natives. Asians exhibit the lowest rates overall. These findings are consistent with data from other epidemiologic studies.

Ethnic/Racial Groups Not Well Represented in Large Epidemiologic Studies

The large epidemiologic studies often did not include sufficient numbers of participants of color to allow firm conclusions regarding the mental health status of these populations. The CPES and National Survey on Drug Use and Health studies sought to correct this deficiency and a significant number of articles were published that give a more detailed picture of the mental health status and treatment patterns for some more diverse groups. However, there are still some groups for which more information is needed, such as Native Americans, Alaska Natives, Native Hawaiians, and Arab Americans.

The American Indian Service Utilization, Psychiatric Epidemiology, Risk and Protective Factors Project was designed to allow a comparison of findings with the results of the original NCS. This study was completed between 1997 and 1999, and diagnostic interviews were conducted based on *DSM-III-R* criteria. A total of 3,084 members, ages 15–54, from two tribes, were interviewed either on or near their home reservations. The most common lifetime diagnoses in these two groups were alcohol dependence, posttraumatic stress disorder (PTSD), and major

TABLE 9.3   **Mental Health Issues by Race/Ethnicity, 2016**

	National average[a]	Asians	American Indian/Alaska Native	Black/African American	Hispanic/ Latinx	Native Hawaiian/Pacific Islander
Substance use disorder	7.8	3.7	12.2	8.1	7.1	5.0
Any mental illness	18.3	12.1	22.8	4.5	18.7	16.7
Major depressive episode	6.7	3.9	8.7	5.0	5.6	7.3
Thoughts of suicide	4.0	2.3	3.9	3.5	3.5	2.5

[a] Percent use in past year.

Note: From *2016 NSDUH: Race and Ethnicity Summary Sheets*, by Substance Abuse and Mental Health Services Administration, 2016b, retrieved from https://www.samhsa.gov/data/report/2016-nsduh-race-and-ethnicity-summary-sheets

depressive episode. When compared with the NCS national sample, Native American tribal members were at higher risk for PTSD and alcohol dependence but at lower risk for major depressive episode. Although this is likely one of the largest samples of American Indians to date, the limitations are that the researchers surveyed only two tribes and used the older *DSM-III-R* criteria for diagnosis of mental disorders.

In contrast, Brave Heart et al. (2016) compared rates of psychiatric disorders in a national sample of American Indians, Alaska Natives, and non-Hispanic European Americans. Using *DSM-IV* diagnostic criteria, 70% of the American Indian/Alaska Native men and 63% of American Indian/Alaska Native women met the criteria for at least one lifetime mental disorder compared to non-Hispanic European Americans, for whom the rates were 62% for men and 53% for women. American Indian/Alaska Native men and women had higher rates in all eight disorder categories, including alcohol use, drug use, mood, anxiety, and personality disorders. The rates were also higher for the combined categories of any substance use and any psychiatric disorder. Adjustments for other sociodemographic characteristics accounted for some of these differences (e.g., age, education, income), but in general, these result show higher rates of mental disorders in the American Indian/Alaska Native population compared to European Americans, and these differences were more notable for women than for men.

The Centers for Disease Control and Prevention conducts random-digit-dialed telephone surveys on an ongoing basis as part of the Behavioral Risk Factor Surveillance System, asking U.S. residents a variety of questions about their health (Zahran et al., 2004). They currently survey more than 400,000 adults in all 50 states, the District of Columbia, and three U.S. territories each year (Centers for Disease Control and Prevention, 2018). One of the questions is, "Now, thinking about your mental health, which includes stress, depression, and problems with emotions, for how many days during the past 30 days was your mental health not good?" (p. 963). Zahran et al. (2004) examined the responses of over 1 million participants to this question from 1993 to 2001. Anyone who reported more than 14 days was identified as having frequent mental distress. The study is relevant here because they also made ethnic and racial group comparisons that included Native Americans and Alaska Natives. Findings revealed that Native Americans and Alaska Natives had the highest rates of frequent mental distress (14.4%) when compared with non-Hispanic European Americans (9.7%), non-Hispanic Blacks (11.3%), Asian/Pacific Islanders (6.2%), and Hispanics (10.5%). These data are limited because they are based on just one question, which measures participants' subjective ratings of their own mental health status and gives no information about specific psychiatric disorders. Nonetheless, it is a rough indicator that American Indians and Alaska Natives may struggle with more mental health issues than members of other groups. Other smaller studies confirm that alcoholism, depression, and suicide are the most common mental health problems among American Indians (Beal, Manson, Keane, & Dick, 1991; D. Johnson, 1994). In particular, suicide rates are high, at two times the national average, with the highest rate of completed suicide for any ethnic group (DeBruyn, Hymbaugh, & Valdez, 1988; Herring, 1999; Olson & Wahab, 2006).

Another neglected group in the literature is Arab Americans. Arab Americans constitute a growing ethnic group in the United States, and their presence in our society came to the forefront following the events of September 11, 2001. The large epidemiologic studies did not report on the mental health status of Arab Americans, and only a few specific studies were found that covered issues relevant to this group. These studies tended to focus on religious affiliations, immigrant status, experiences with acculturation and discrimination, and suggestions for how to address these issues in treatment (e.g., Aprahamian, Kaplan, Windham, Sutter, & Visser,

2011; Awad, 2010; Dwairy, 2006; Hakim-Larson, Kamoo, Nassar-McMillan, & Porcerelli, 2007; Moradi & Hasan, 2004; Padela & Heisler, 2010; Ramsi, Chuang, & Hennig, 2015).

Critique of the Epidemiologic Studies

The question of ethnic group differences in the prevalence of mental disorders may be a natural one to ask, but it is a complicated one to answer (Chang, 2002). The epidemiologic studies just cited represent the largest, most rigorous studies to date. However, they are not without problems. Chang (2002) discusses a number of these concerns. As mentioned previously, one problem is the lack of representation, or small sample sizes of some groups (e.g., Arab Americans, Native Americans), which leads to limited ability to make meaningful comparisons. The CPES studies sought to address some of these issues by including larger numbers of Hispanics, non-Hispanic Blacks, non-Hispanic European Americans, and Asians so that more meaningful comparisons could be made. In addition, the CPES studies examined other factors not included in the earlier studies, such as age, socioeconomic status (SES), educational level, and immigrant status, so that the impact of such factors on mental health status and help-seeking could also be explored. The CPES studies produced huge amounts of data. Studies published from these data have increased our understanding of the prevalence of mental disorders, mental health status, and related factors among various populations in the United States.

A second problem is within-group heterogeneity. Aggregate data that combine all members of an ethnic group ignore the large variation that exists within groups. For example, among immigrant groups, such as Asians and Latinxs, there is considerable variation based on generation, acculturation, linguistic ability, and SES. Many authors call for research that examines particular groups in more detail (S. Sue, Sue, Sue, & Takeuchi, 1995). Chang (2002) and others note that lumping all members of an ethnic group together ignores critical within-group differences. As already mentioned, the CPES studies included some of these factors so that within-group variation could be explored (e.g., Alegria et al., 2008; J. Kim & Choi, 2010; Woodward et al., 2009).

The differing rates of mental disorder among Latinxs illustrate this point. Several studies show that Latinxs born in the United States exhibit higher rates of mental disorders compared to Latinxs born outside the United States. For example, a study conducted with Mexican Americans living in Fresno County, California, found that about 25% of immigrants had some disorder, whereas 48% of those born in the United States did. The length of time in the United States was a factor: Immigrants who had been in the United States at least 13 years had higher prevalence rates than did those who had been in the United States less than 13 years (Vega et al., 1998). In the CPES studies, U.S.-born Mexicans had prevalence rates of mental disorders similar to those of European Americans but higher than that of individuals born in Mexico. Individuals born in Mexico had lower rates than both European Americans and U.S.-born Mexicans. Alegria et al. (2008) combined data from the NCS-R and the National Latino and Asian American Study of Mental Health studies to test this hypothesis. Their findings supported *the immigrant paradox*, in that U.S.-born Latinxs reported higher rates of psychiatric disorders when compared to their immigrant counterparts. A similar pattern was observed among Asian/Pacific Americans: Those born outside the United States showed lower rates of mental disorder and lower usage of mental health services than those born in the United States. Although Asian/Pacific Americans born in the United States had lower overall rates of mental disorder than did European Americans, their rates were still higher than those of Asian immigrants and Asians living outside the United States (Abe-Kim et al., 2007; Chang, 2002; Takeuchi et al., 2007).

This observation that the longer someone is in the United States the higher the risk of mental disorder has been called the immigrant paradox. This describes the research finding in which being born in a foreign country seemingly protects immigrants against the development of mental disorders, despite the stress associated with the experiences of being an immigrant (Burnam, Hough, Kamo, Escobar, & Telles, 1987; see Chapter 5). However, Alegria et al. (2008) found that the rates for Latinxs varied based on factors such as country of origin (e.g., Mexico versus Cuba), SES, and type of disorder. Therefore, they recommended caution in generalizing this paradox across all groups.

A third concern has to do with diagnostic accuracy. Diagnoses in the large studies were based on *DSM* criteria. The *DSM* is based on Western diagnostic concepts that may not fully recognize cultural variations in experience and expression of psychological symptoms, such as the tendency for somatization. In addition, questions may not be fully understood, respondents may not answer in a completely honest manner, and interviewers may not accurately interpret participants' responses.

Fourth, available diagnostic categories may not fully cover the range of symptoms or disorders experienced across cultural groups, such as cultural syndromes (see the discussion later in this chapter). D. R. Williams and Harris-Reid (1999) also discussed the difficulties in generalizing the findings on ethnic group differences in mental health. They cited limitations related to different research methodologies, different criteria for identifying mental disorder and minority status, the heterogeneity of minority groups, and the lack of research available on some groups.

Conclusions From Existing Data

What conclusion can be drawn from the data on mental disorder and ethnic group membership? Research indicates, with some exceptions, that people of color tend to have lower rates of mental disorders and that there is significant within-group variation based on characteristics such as gender, age, educational level, and SES.

So far, our discussion about cultural group differences and mental health has focused on differences among ethnic groups in the United States. If we look at the prevalence of mental disorders across the globe, certain disorders appear with relative consistency. Schizophrenia occurs at a rate of about 1%, bipolar disorder at 0.3–1.5%, and panic disorder at 0.4–2.9% (Weissman et al., 1994, 1996, 1997, 1998; World Health Organization, 1973). The consistency in the occurrence of these disorders across different countries, combined with the results of family and genetic studies, suggests that there is a strong genetic component to these disorders and that cultural factors play less of a role (U.S. Department of Health and Human Services, 2001). Differential rates across cultures suggest that culture plays a greater role in other disorders, such as depression, for which the rates range from 2% to 19% across countries (Weissman et al., 1996). This result suggests that cultural factors, such as poverty and violence, may play a greater role than genetics does in the causation of major depression (National Institute of Mental Health, 1998).

We can also see the influence of culture on mental disorders in the development of PTSD, a disorder that develops following exposure to a traumatic event whereby the person witnessed or experienced actual or threatened death or serious injury to him- or herself or others. Examples of traumatic experiences include rape, combat, and natural disaster. Symptoms include re-experiencing the event through, for instance, troubling or intrusive memories, dreams, or flashbacks; avoidance of situations that remind the person of the trauma; sleep disturbance; and hypervigilance (American Psychiatric Association, 2013).

Traumatic experiences are particularly common for immigrants and refugees from countries in turmoil. Aichberger (2015) reviewed the literature on the prevalence of PTSD in refugee populations. Reported overall rates vary widely, from 0% to 99%, with average rates ranging from 11% to about 40%. These differences are partially explained by demographic factors such as ethnicity, age, host country, and duration of displacement or by methodological issues such as sample size, method of diagnosis and sampling, and language. The highest rates of PTSD seemed most related to experiences with torture. Higher rates also occurred in participants from countries with ongoing conflicts and individuals who were exposed to political violence and civil unrest. For example, Steel et al. (2009) found that regions with the highest PTSD prevalence rates included 16 countries in Africa (33.5%), Kosovo (31.6%), and Cambodia (30.3%). T. S. Betancourt et al. (2017) examined trauma exposure and rates of PTSD in a sample of refugee-origin youth, immigrant-origin youth, and U.S.-origin youth. As expected, refugee youth had higher average rates of trauma exposure than either the U.S.-origin or the immigrant youth. Refugee youth also had higher rates of community violence exposure, dissociative symptoms, traumatic grief, somatization, and phobic disorder. However, refugee children exhibited lower rates of substance abuse and oppositional defiant disorder.

The diagnosis for Chanda, whose case was described earlier in this chapter, was most likely PTSD. Some people may maintain that Chanda's reactions were *normal* or *expected* given her horrific history, but in the eyes of our diagnostic system she still would be classified as suffering from PTSD.

Gender Differences

We cannot leave a discussion of group differences in mental health without talking about gender. Gender differences in the prevalence of mental disorders are fairly robust, with women reporting higher lifetime rates of mood and anxiety disorders and men reporting higher rates of substance abuse and impulse control disorders (see Table 9.1; National Comorbidity Study, 2007).

The differentiation has been described as women having higher rates of *internalizing* disorders and men having higher rates of *externalizing* disorders. What this means is that women tend to focus their feelings on the self, whereas men project their feelings outward and express them through overt behaviors. According to Rosenfeld (1999), this means that women more than men live with profound feelings of sadness, loss, low self-esteem, guilt, hopelessness, and self-blame. They suffer more anxiety, ranging from fears of specific objects or situations, to panic attacks, to free-floating anxiety and constant worry. In contrast, men consume more alcohol and drugs and do so more frequently than women. Abuse of alcohol and drugs leads to more negative physical consequences for men, such as blackouts and hallucinations, and it interferes with their lives more often, causing more problems at work, at

More therapists of color are needed in psychology.
Photograph by Tom Zasadzinski

school, or in the family. Men are more likely to exhibit aggressive and violent behavior (Mio et al., 2003). They are also more prone to criminal behavior, deceitfulness, impulsivity, irresponsibility, and recklessness.

> Ms. S. had a history of being battered by her husband, leaving that relationship and eventually marrying another man. Her own children, who were born on the reservation, had several fathers. One son was killed. Ms. S. divorced her last husband because of his repeated infidelity and moved her family, which included her mentally retarded oldest daughter and disabled mother, to a city to support them better.
>
> Ms. S. had her son arrested after he threatened her with a knife and raped her. He justified his behavior by saying that he was too drunk to know what he was doing. When he pleaded with his mother to have the authorities release him, she agreed to drop the charges. Seven months later, he was accused of sexually abusing her two granddaughters, ages 5 and 7, which he had apparently been doing since before the rape. . . .
>
> Ms. S. was referred for therapy to help her regain custody of the children. The focus of the HSD [New Mexico Human Services Department] treatment plan was to help her overcome her depression and enable her to "regain self-control, particularly with regard to defending herself from her son." She also felt abused and disempowered by the state social service and legal systems. Her family life had been completely disrupted by her son's behavior, its discovery by a foreign agency (HSD), and the interventions imposed by a hostile and alien system. (LaFramboise, Berman, & Sohi, 1994, p. 57)

This case illustrates the point that women tend to internalize their disorders, whereas men externalize their disorders. Hence, Ms. S. was diagnosed with depression, and many of the men in her life engaged in violence, alcoholism, and infidelity.

These gender differences are consistent across cultures, leading some to believe there is a biological basis. However, studies that vary the social conditions, such as wives being employed outside the home, demonstrate that differences in the rates of disorder between men and women are the same or reversed. This evidence points more to social causes than to biological causes for these differences (Rosenfeld, 1980, 1999).

Rosenfeld (1999) believed these differences are more accurately explained by life circumstances, such as women having less power (e.g., women earning less than their husbands), greater responsibility for taking care of the home and raising children, and stronger social ties. Decreased power and control and increased social responsibility and their different interpretations of those circumstances, combined with different coping strategies, lead women to have higher rates of depression and anxiety than men. For example, combining the roles of worker and parent means different things to men and women. For a man to work outside the home is consistent with his role as the breadwinner for the family. However, for a woman, providing care, nurturance, and attention for her children is more central to her role as parent than earning an income. Thus, women have higher levels of distress in combining these roles than their husbands (Simon, 1995).

There is also discussion about whether the different disorders exhibited by men and women are really in response to different circumstances or whether they are instead different reactions to the same circumstances. Norms for the acceptable expression of emotions differ drastically between men and women. These norms are socialized into boys and girls from a very young age. How many men reading this book were told, "Stop crying. Boys don't cry," "Don't be a sissy," or "Suck it up and be a man!" Men are discouraged from expressing feelings, especially feelings that are defined as feminine or weak, such as worry, fear, and helplessness—all emotions associated with anxiety and depression. Feelings such as anger are more acceptable for men. One study showed that men who come into psychiatric emergency rooms with depressive symptoms were hospitalized at a much higher rate than women with the same symptoms, whereas women who came in exhibiting antisocial symptoms or substance abuse were more likely to be hospitalized than men reporting the same problems (Rosenfeld, 1984). Men may attempt to hide or avoid the forbidden feelings related to anxiety and depression. Drinking accomplishes that goal.

Apparent gender differences may also be a result of the criteria used to diagnose depression and the way symptoms are measured. L. A. Martin, Neighbors, and Griffith (2013) examined gender differences in rates of depression when alternative symptoms were considered. They utilized two new scales that included additional symptoms beyond the typical diagnostic criteria for depression. As described earlier, they found that men reported higher rates of anger, aggression, substance abuse, and risk taking than women. When the measures included both traditional and more male-type depressive symptoms, the differences in rates of depression between men and women disappeared.

Thus, it seems that men and women have different disorders because they express different symptoms, encounter different social experiences, and have different kinds of reactions to circumstances (L. A. Martin et al., 2013; Rosenfeld, 1999).

Cultural Concepts of Distress

Earlier in the chapter we mentioned that the *DSM-5* includes a section on *cultural concepts of distress*, defined as "ways that cultural groups, experience, understand, and communicate suffering, behavioral problems, or troubling thoughts and emotions" (American Psychiatric Association, 2013, p. 758). The three types of cultural concepts include *cultural syndromes, cultural idioms of distress*, and *cultural explanations or perceived causes*. **Cultural syndromes** are mental disorders that tend to occur in specific cultural groups. They represent a unique cluster of symptoms locally recognized as a valid experience. **Cultural idioms of distress** refer to ways that specific cultural groups or communities express psychological distress. These expressions may not involve specific symptoms or disorders, but reflect a shared way of experiencing or talking about personal or social concerns. **Cultural explanations of distress or perceived causes** refers to the observation that cultural groups have different ways of explaining the causes of psychological symptoms or distress, or attach different meanings to various symptoms.

cultural syndromes—mental disorders, distinguished by unique clusters of symptoms, that only occur in specific cultures.

cultural idioms of distress—unique ways that specific cultural groups express psychological distress.

cultural explanations of distress or perceived causes—the ways in which different cultural groups explain psychological symptoms.

DSM-5 lists nine cultural syndromes with the strongest research support. One example is *ataque de nervios*. This condition is typically reported among Latinxs, especially those from the Caribbean (Guarnaccia et al., 2010; I. López et al., 2009; Lopez-Baez, 1999; Oquendo, Horwath, & Martinez, 1989). Symptoms include uncontrollable shouting, attacks of crying, trembling, heat in the chest rising to the head, fainting spells, and verbal or physical aggression. Generally, the victims report feeling out of control, and the experience often occurs in response to a stressful event, such as news of a close loved one's death.

The episodes are usually discrete, with the person quickly returning to his or her usual level of functioning (American Psychiatric Association, 2013).

Another example of a cultural syndrome is *kufungisisa,* or "thinking too much." This is an expression used by the Shona in Zimbabwe to explain anxiety, depression, and somatic complaints. For example, the person might say, "My heart hurts because I'm thinking too much." It is used as a way to express distress regarding interpersonal and social difficulties, such as marital problems or having no money to take care of one's children. Typical symptoms include excessive worry, panic attacks, depression, and irritability. Thinking too much is believed to cause damage to the mind and the body and symptoms such as headaches and dizziness. Similar expressions are used in other African cultures, such as *brain fag* in Nigeria, which is when high school and university students complain that their brains are fatigued from too much studying (American Psychiatric Association, 2013; S. Patel, Simunyu, & Gwanzura, 1995; Prince, 2000).

Yet another example of a cultural syndrome is *taijin kyofusho,* a form of social phobia observed in Japan and Korea. The individual suffers from extreme anxiety that his or her body or its functions—such as misshapen physical features, inappropriate eye contact, or body odor—are offensive to others. Although this syndrome may seem similar to social phobia or body dysmorphic disorder, the key feature is extreme fear of offending others. This makes sense if you put the symptoms in the cultural context of concerns about harmonious social interactions that characterize traditional Japanese culture (American Psychiatric Association, 2013; Atkinson, 2004; see also the discussion of individualism versus collectivism in Chapter 3).

The inclusion of cultural concepts of distress in *DSM-5* accomplishes a number of goals. First, it helps to avoid misdiagnosis. Cultural variation in the presentation and explanation of symptoms can lead clinicians to draw inaccurate conclusions. Awareness of these differences can help prevent this. Second, exploration of these cultural concepts can yield useful information and increase our understanding of the impact of culture on mental health. Third, use of these concepts can help build rapport and improve relationships between mental health providers and consumers. Clients may feel more comfortable if the therapist "speaks their language." Fourth, understanding and use of these cultural concepts can improve the effectiveness of treatment. It allows clinicians to target specific problems and apply appropriate interventions. Fifth, these concepts help guide research. As mentioned earlier, research led to the inclusion of specific cultural concepts in the *DSM.* Further research will allow expansion of this. Finally, by distinguishing these syndromes, idioms, and explanations, we can gather more accurate epidemiologic data, learn more about their incidence and prevalence, and track changes over time. All of these are reasons why the *DSM* included the section on cultural concepts of distress (American Psychiatric Association, 2013).

Although there may be some overlap, there typically is no *DSM* category that corresponds directly to a cultural syndrome. This was mentioned earlier with the similarities between social phobia and *taijin kyofusho.* Cultural syndromes may also cover a range of severity levels, with the same term used to represent a minor reaction to a single event all the way to severe pathology in need of intervention. It also may be difficult to distinguish between the three types of cultural concepts because the same term may be used to describe a syndrome, an idiom, and an explanation (American Psychiatric Association, 2013). For example, the term *kufungisisa* might be used to describe someone who exhibits clinical levels of depression or anxiety (syndrome), to express how worried a student is about an upcoming exam (idiom), or as the cause of someone's dizziness (explanation). The example given previously for *kufungisisa* in Zimbabwe also illustrates this. The statement, "My heart hurts because I'm thinking too much" represents a specific symptom. It also represents a culture-specific way of expressing that symptom (cultural idiom), as well as a cultural explanation for the symptom. These cultural concepts may also change over time in response to both local and global forces (American Psychiatric Association, 2013).

Overall, it is important to consider multiple factors when making a diagnosis; cultural, environmental, and genetic forces all interact to produce a particular disorder (U.S. Department of Health and Human Services, 2001).

Eating Disorders: An American Cultural Syndrome?

Eating disorders present an interesting example of some of the issues regarding culture and mental disorder discussed earlier. The most common eating disorders include *anorexia nervosa*, *bulimia nervosa, and binge-eating disorder.* **Anorexia nervosa** is characterized by extreme weight loss, the intense fear of gaining weight, and distorted body image. The individual continues to see her- or himself as fat even though by objective standards she or he is significantly underweight. **Bulimia nervosa** is characterized by binging and purging. The individual has episodes during which she or he consumes excessively large amounts of food; afterward, the person engages in extreme activities to avoid gaining weight, such as vomiting, excessive exercise, and the use of laxatives or diuretics. Although binge eating has been considered problematic for decades, it was not officially considered a distinct mental disorder until its inclusion in *DSM-5*. **Binge-eating disorder** is characterized by eating a larger than normal amount of food during a discrete period of time. The amount is larger than what most people would eat during that same period and under similar circumstances. For example, eating 20 hotdogs within 30 minutes would not be unusual if you were participating in a hot dog–eating contest. However, sitting at home by yourself and eating 20 hot dogs within 30 minutes would likely be considered a binge. Binge-eating disorder is also characterized by feelings of lack of control; eating more rapidly than usual; eating until one is uncomfortably full; eating large amounts when one is not physically hungry; eating alone because one is embarrassed about the amount of food being consumed; and feeling disgusted, depressed, and guilty after the binge (American Psychiatric Association, 2013). Besides simply examining full-blown eating disorders, many researchers also consider subclinical levels of disturbed eating and body image important. In other words, many people have significant issues with weight, eating behaviors, and body image who may not meet the full criteria for an eating disorder.

anorexia nervosa—an eating disorder marked by such a severe restriction of one's diet that the sufferer's weight falls far below what would be expected, given her or his height and age.

bulimia nervosa—an eating disorder marked by the consumption of a large amount of food in one sitting—called a binge—followed by the purging of that food, most typically through vomiting but also through extreme exercise or the use of laxatives.

binge-eating disorder—an eating disorder marked by consumption of large amounts of food in one sitting, accompanied by feelings of lack of control, embarrassment, disgust, depression, and guilt, along with rapid eating, eating until uncomfortably full, and eating large amounts when not hungry.

It is a commonly held belief that eating disorders are most prevalent in Western, European American, female populations (Crago, Shisslak, & Estes, 1996; Dolan, 1991; Pate, Pumariega, Hester, & Garner, 1992). Most research studies focus on this population (le Grange, Telch, & Tibbs, 1998; Thompson, 1994), but a large number of studies examine the prevalence of these disorders in different cultural groups. Some of these studies suggest that eating disorders are less common among people of color living in Western societies, but the results are inconclusive (Wildes & Emery, 2001).

For example, some studies suggest that African American women are less likely to develop anorexia and bulimia nervosa than their European American counterparts (Gray, Ford, & Kelly, 1987; Hsu, 1987). Although African American women are typically heavier than European American women, fewer African American women exhibit problematic eating behavior (Abrams, Allen, & Gray, 1993; Dolan, 1991; Rand & Kuldau, 1990), and they possess greater body satisfaction than do European American women (Harris, 1994; McCarthy, 1990). In addition, African American women have been found to have less of a discrepancy between their perceived and their ideal body size (Rucker & Cash, 1992). Some studies also show lower rates of dieting behaviors, body dissatisfaction, weight concerns, and eating disorders for Asian and Asian American women (Akan & Grilo, 1995; Dolan, 1991; Lucero, Hicks, Bramlette, Brassington, & Welter, 1992). However, Lerner and associates (Lerner, Iwawaki, Chichara, & Sorell, 1980) found that Japanese women had lower self-esteem, self-concept, and body image scores than Americans, and S. Lee (1993) found that Chinese women were similar to their Western counterparts in their desire to be thin. It is interesting that preoccupation with thinness did not lead to changing or restricting their eating behaviors. Lucero and colleagues (Lucero et al., 1992) found that Latinx American women weighed more but were less concerned with their weight than were European American women, but Fitzgibbon and associates (Fitzgibbon et al., 1998) found Latinx American women to have a greater severity of binge-eating symptoms and a lower body image ideal than African American and European American women. Liddi-Brown, Barker-Hackett, and Grizzell (2002) conducted a study with a large, multicultural college student sample that included nine measures of disordered eating and body image. They found that Latinxs had a stronger drive to be thin, and Asian/Pacific Americans and African Americans exhibited more uncontrolled overeating. Some measures of body image in their study showed that Asian/Pacific Americans and African Americans had more positive body image than did Latinx Americans and European Americans.

The CPES studies also examined the prevalence of eating disorders. Findings were reported for the overall NCS-R sample (Hudson, Hiripi, Pope, & Kessler, 2007), Asians (Nicdao, Hong, & Takeuchi, 2007), Latinxs (Alegria, Woo, et al., 2007), and Blacks (J. Y. Taylor, Caldwell, Baser, Faison, & Jackson, 2007). No data were found for non-Hispanic European Americans alone, and because of methodological limitations, no direct comparisons were made between the groups. However, results from the separate studies still reveal some trends (see Table 9.4). Lifetime prevalence of eating disorders for Asians was very low, and level of acculturation was not significantly correlated with the presence of an eating disorder (Nicdao et al., 2007). Alegria, Woo, et al. (2007) examined prevalence rates among Latinxs and concluded that Latinxs had lower rates of anorexia nervosa but elevated rates of bulimia nervosa and binge-eating disorder, equivalent to those for non-Hispanic European Americans. They noticed a trend in which U.S.-born individuals and those living in the United States for longer periods of time had higher rates than foreign-born and recent immigrants (i.e., the immigration paradox). As far as African Americans and Caribbean Blacks, results indicate that anorexia is relatively uncommon in this population, whereas bulimia nervosa occurs more frequently. No reports of anorexia nervosa were reported among Caribbean Blacks, again supporting the immigrant paradox. The rates in Table 9.4 were gleaned from separate studies. No numbers were found for non-Hispanic European Americans alone; rather, they encompassed the total NCS-R sample (Hudson et al., 2007).

TABLE 9.4   Racial/Ethnic Group Comparisons of Lifetime Prevalence Rates for Eating Disorders From Studies of the Collaborative Psychiatric Epidemiology Surveys

	Asians	Latinxs	Blacks	Total
	National Latino and Asian American Study of Mental Health	National Latino and Asian American Study of Mental Health	National Study of American Life	National Comorbidity Survey Replication
Sample	%	%	%	%
Anorexia nervosa	0.08	0.08	0.17	0.6
Bulimia nervosa	1.09	1.61	1.49	1.0
Binge-eating disorder	2.04	1.92	1.66	2.8
Any binge eating	4.35	5.61	5.08	4.5

Note: Data on Asians are from "Prevalence and Correlates of Eating Disorders Among Asian Americans: Results from the National Latino and Asian American Study," by E. G. Nicdao, S. Hong, and D. Takeuchi, 2007, *International Journal of Eating Disorders, 40*; data on Latinxs are from "Prevalence and Correlates of Eating Disorders in Latinos in the United States," by M. Alegria, M. Woo, et al., 2007, *International Journal of Eating Disorders, 40*; data on Blacks are from "Prevalence of Eating Disorders Among Blacks in the National Survey of American Life," by J. Y. Taylor, C. H. Caldwell, R. E. Baser, N. Faison, and J. S. Jackson, 2007, *International Journal of Eating Disorders, 40*, S10–S14. National Comorbidity Survey Replication data are from "The Prevalence and Correlates of Eating Disorders in the National Comorbidity Survey Replication," by J. I. Hudson, E. Hiripi, H. G. Pope, and R. C. Kessler, 2007, *Biological Psychiatry, 61.*

In addition, no study was found that directly compared data from the various CPES studies on prevalence rates of eating disorders based on race and ethnicity for apparent methodological reasons (Alegria, Woo, et al., 2007), so it is not known whether these differences are statistically significant. Nonetheless, these numbers still bear out the fact that rates of eating disorders are lower in populations of color. Comparisons suggest that anorexia nervosa occurred at slightly higher rates among Blacks than among Asians and Latinxs, whereas Latinxs had higher rates of bulimia nervosa and any binge eating. Asians had higher rates only for binge-eating disorder.

Researchers who looked specifically at binge eating found higher rates among women of color in the United States. The highest rates were seen among Latinx women when compared with African American and European American women (Bruce & Agras, 1992; Fitzgibbon et al., 1998; Smith & Krejci, 1991). African American women exhibited rates that were the same as or higher than the rates of European American women (Spitzer et al., 1993; Striegel-Moore, Wilfley, Pike, Dohm, & Fairburn, 2000; Yanovski, Gormally, Leser, Gwirtsman, & Yanovski, 1994; Yanovski, Nelson, Dubbert, & Spitzer, 1993), and the rates among Asian American women were similar to those of African Americans and European Americans (le Grange, Stone, & Brownell, 1998). No differences were observed between Native American and European American adolescents (Smith & Krejci, 1991).

As you can see, the results are mixed. Although most studies suggest lower rates of eating-related problems for women of color, a few indicated the rates were higher. To settle the controversy, Wildes and Emery (2001) conducted a meta-analytic review that involved 35 studies, with a total of more than 17,000 participants, that examined eating disturbance and body dissatisfaction in people of color and European Americans. They found that European Americans reported greater eating disturbance and body dissatisfaction than did people of color across all measures used in their study. Although African Americans had lower levels of eating disturbance than did European American women, the opposite was true for Asian/Pacific American women. The differences were greatest for subclinical levels of eating disturbance and virtually nonexistent for clinical levels, meaning that the rates of anorexia and bulimia nervosa were approximately the same for European Americans and non–European Americans. Thus, the authors concluded that European American women living in Western countries experience greater eating disturbance and body dissatisfaction than do non–European American women (Wildes & Emery, 2001).

Thus, the most consistent finding in the literature is that symptoms related to eating disorders are more prevalent in European American than in non–European American populations. This finding has led some researchers to describe eating disorders as cultural syndromes because culture clearly plays a role in their development (Crago et al., 1996; Keel & Klump, 2003; Pate et al., 1992). However, some finer distinctions may need to be made. Keel and Klump (2003) reviewed the literature looking at incidence rates and historical evidence, as well as the genetic heritability of anorexia nervosa and bulimia nervosa, and concluded that bulimia nervosa seems to be a cultural syndrome but anorexia nervosa does not. They attribute this to the fact that there seems to be a greater genetic base for anorexia nervosa.

Why do you think eating disorders might be more common among European Americans than among people of color? Most authors relate this phenomenon to cultural differences in standards of beauty, with the Western ideal being a very thin body type. Some authors believe that eating disorders are on the rise in non–European American, non-Western cultures because of increased exposure to Western standards of beauty through the media and the adoption of those standards through acculturation (Bowen, Tomayasu, & Cauce, 1991; Davis & Yager, 1992; Nasser, 1986). For example, A. E. Becker (1995) found that before 1995, Fijians had a strong admiration for robust body shapes and a tolerance for obesity. After broadcast television became widely available in Fiji in 1995, bringing American, British, and Australian programming to the island, attitudes shifted, and young Fijian women began developing a desire to be thin.

E. Lopez, Blix, and Blix (1995) found that the ideal body image was similar for European American females and Latinxs born in the United States. However, Latinxs born outside the United States who immigrated at age 17 or older tended to select a larger silhouette as their ideal body image, whereas Latinxs who were 16 or younger at immigration tended to fit within the norm of U.S.-born European American women. These findings support the notion that cultural norms in Western societies promote smaller body sizes and increased body dissatisfaction. Wildes and Emery (2001) tested the effects of acculturation in their meta-analysis, but their findings were inconclusive.

In contrast, some researchers argue that there is now adequate documentation that eating disorders are no longer exclusively a Western phenomenon. Eating disorders do exist in other countries and cultures and so should not be considered a cultural syndrome (Nasser, Katzman, & Gordon, 2001). What is the cause of this shift? As mentioned earlier, many people surmise it is a result of increased exposure to Western culture around the globe. However, Nasser et al. (2001) indicated this view is oversimplified. In their interdisciplinary critique of the issue, they examined other cultural, social, political, and economic forces that may influence the increased

Whereas eating disorders have been primarily associated with European American women, Asians are increasingly suffering from eating disorders as they are being exposed to American standards. *Photograph by Sorajack Mongkolsri/Shutterstock*

incidence and prevalence of eating disorders in non-Western cultures. For example, they noticed a rise in the rates of eating disorders in countries and groups in transition, such as among Black women in South Africa after the dismantling of apartheid and women in Russia after the fall of the Soviet Union.

This is one reason why the term *culture-bound syndromes* was dropped in *DSM-5* in exchange for *cultural concepts of distress*. It was in part because of the recognition that all forms of distress are shaped by local forces, including formal *DSM* diagnoses. Many diagnoses included in the *DSM* could have at one time been considered cultural syndromes, but as our knowledge and understanding of them grew through research and clinical practice, they became more widely accepted (American Psychiatric Association, 2013). Eating disorders were initially found to be more prevalent in Western cultures. However, as a result of actual changes in other cultures (social, cultural, economic, and political) and as a result of increased understanding stemming from research and clinical practice, we now have an expanded view of eating disorders across cultures.

In our discussion so far, we have highlighted the impact of culture on mental health. Although some variations exist in the prevalence of various disorders among groups, the current consensus seems to be that there are far more similarities than differences. You may have been surprised by the lack of group differences in the rate of mental disorders. You may have assumed that the rates would be higher for groups such as African Americans because of factors such as racism, discrimination, and poverty. These factors are important. Remember that when group differences were observed, they were most often explained by the varying circumstances of the groups. For example, some of the differences disappeared when factors such as gender, age, and SES were controlled, meaning that racial group membership was not the most important factor, but the fact that race intersects with other things, such as poverty, was. This finding points to the need to consider the context in which these disorders occur, the largest being the cultural context. D. R. Williams and Harris-Reid (1999) "emphasize the need for identifying the ways in which the mental health problems of each group emerge from the larger social context in which the group is embedded" (p. 296) and the need to examine the ways in which social economic, political, and cultural factors affect the mental health of minority groups.

In class last week, we discussed the topic of culture and mental health and I feel that I resonate with this topic very much. Over the summer, I traveled to Sri Lanka where I witnessed a lot of the cultural differences regarding mental health first hand. [The professor] mentioned in class how following the tsunami in Sri Lanka in 2004, Western psychologists and psychiatrists rushed to the people of Sri Lanka's aid, ignoring the fact that they were missing some of their fundamental needs for survival: shelter, food, and water (Watters, 2010). This was among one of the first things I noticed when I arrived in Sri Lanka, witnessing many people who were homeless, children in the orphanage that lacked a proper roof over their heads, and lacked shoes or "proper" clothing. When I shadowed psychologists that worked in the hospitals in Sri Lanka, they also mentioned the stigma around mental health in their culture, and how many believe religiously that if they are having troubling thoughts or different behavior from the norm that it is because there is a devil inside of them that needs to be freed. Many people will go to the temple, or are cared for by their families. In addition, many people do not seek help because mental illness is seen as a weakness and it would be shameful to their family it they were seen receiving help. The most interesting part of my trip was my visit to see the Buddhist monk, and my visit to see an Eastern acupuncturist and herbal doctor. In Sri Lanka, Buddhism is the primary religion and people believe that peace comes from self-awareness, self-reflection, and understanding of people's differences. If we choose to wake up in the morning and understand that people are innately good and that people's actions are a consequence of their own troubles and experience, and choose to not be affected by the unpleasantness of others, we will inevitably become more happy, understanding, and compassionate people. By doing this, we will promote world peace and conflict resolution in the world. In addition, learning about the practice of Eastern medicine in regards to mental health, including acupuncture and herbal medicine, opened my eyes to understanding a type of medicine that was unfamiliar to me, and that other countries have their own way of treating illness. Not all countries use Western medicine, and in fact, many people do not want to be educated on Western medicine because their own practices are seen by them to be just as effective, if not more so, than Western medicine. I think in order to be an effective cultural psychologist, one must not necessarily have to believe one is better than the other, but be respectful of these practices as they do have cultural significance.

—Haylee, 20+-year-old European American student

This narrative illustrates several topics related to culture and mental health. From the previous section, it illustrates how culture influences the way people define, explain, and express psychological symptoms. It also illustrates several cultural issues related to the treatment of mental disorders, such as how mental illness is perceived, willingness to seek treatment, and appropriate forms of treatment. We turn now to these topics.

Culture and the Treatment of Mental Disorders

Just as culture affects the expression and occurrence of various mental disorders, it also affects treatment of those disorders. Treatment typically refers to counseling and psychotherapy. We noted in Chapter 1 that the history of multicultural psychology is rooted in efforts to address cultural differences in counseling and psychotherapy. D. W. Sue and Sue (2016) argue that to adequately assist individuals from diverse backgrounds with mental health issues, counseling and psychotherapy must be culturally sensitive. That means mental health professionals must consciously, actively, and effectively address cultural issues in the therapeutic setting. This section covers a number of multicultural treatment issues, including underutilization of services, barriers to treatment, and various attempts at providing culturally sensitive treatments.

Underutilization of Mental Health Services

In 1978, the Special Populations Task Force of the President's Commission on Mental Health concluded that people of color are underserved or inappropriately served by the mental health system in the United States (Special Populations Task Force, 1978). More than 20 years later, in 2001, the Surgeon General's report on culture, race, and ethnicity also concluded that significant disparities exist for people of color in mental health services (U.S. Department of Health and Human Services, 2001).

> A term I hear a lot which really irks me is, "Oh, you're Asian, so you're smart. " The reason isn't because people are generalizing me and my racial group. In fact, I do feel good that people think that I am smart. However, the real reason why that statement annoys me so much is that it reminds me of my upbringing. A common cultural parenting style in Asian cultures is tiger parenting, which is how I was raised. Many hours of rigorous studying every day, seclusion from many of my friends, and extremely high expectations for academic achievement and performance were forced on me by my mother as I grew up. It was a very controlling atmosphere where I never felt comfortable with my performances and accomplishments and, as a result, I suffered from severe depression for a while.
>
> At the time, I considered going to therapy for some sort of solution. The problem is that I didn't want people to label me as a crazy person, especially my mother. It is not just my own belief either; my group of Asian American friends dealt with the same situation I was in. Being raised to follow my parents' orders made me extremely uncomfortable, and agitating them would be worse. I believe my friends felt the same way. In fact, this is one of the main reasons why many Asians like me in this situation refuse to get help from others. Nowadays, I feel much better than before. My Asian American friends and I helped each other cope with our problems. In addition, I was extremely fortunate to have my sister talk to my mother about how depressed I felt, which stopped those expectations for me. On the topic of receiving aid, I believe the style of tiger parenting has caused increased mental problems among Asian people. However, it is disgustingly effective in making extremely smart students. If this type of parenting is a bit more lax, then I am sure we could see less mental health problems and more Asians seeking help.
>
> —Karl, 20+-year-old Asian American student

> When I first started showing symptoms of depression, my mother thought that I was just being lazy, or a "bad girl." My dad was working abroad at that time. I can remember every time she talked to my dad, she would yell, "This girl is being so lazy for no reason, we've given her too much love and spoiled her." However, when I refused to go to school for weeks rather than days, refused to eat, go out with friends, watch movies, or do anything I used to enjoy, my mom's concerns deepened. I think she did not know what to do or whom to go to . . . "She can't have any mental health problem. We have given her everything she needs. I don't understand what is wrong with this girl." My mom was scared and confused. I think more than anything, she was scared to tell friends and family that her daughter was suffering from depression. I have to say, in a culture like mine, having mental health problems such as depression and anxiety was a taboo. It is not something you frequently hear about or talk about.
>
> Sudarshini, 20+-year-old South Asian student

Notice the similarities between Karl and Sudarshini's experiences. Both suffered from depression. Both attributed their depression to cultural factors and the strong pressure from parents to excel academically. Both expressed concern about the stigma attached to mental health in their culture. Neither one sought professional help, although Karl did seek help from his sister and Asian American friends. These stories illustrate several of the cultural factors that serve as barriers to mental health treatment for diverse populations.

In general, only about one in three people who need mental health services actually use them. Thus, underutilization is an issue for all segments of the population, but it is especially so for people of color (Robins & Regier, 1991). Many authors in the psychological literature have noted that people of color are less likely than European Americans to seek mental health treatment (e.g., Abe-Kim et al., 2007; Kessler et al., 1996; L. K. Sussman, Robins, & Earls, 1987; Vega et al., 1998; Zhang, Snowden, & Sue, 1998). African Americans and Asian/Pacific Americans are also more likely to delay seeking treatment until their symptoms are more severe (Chen, Sullivan, Lu, & Shibusawa, 2003; U.S. Department of Health and Human Services, 2001). Research on Asian Americans shows that about one-third of the individuals who requested an intake appointment from a mental health program failed to show up for the initial session (Akutsu, Tsuru, & Chu, 2004). For those who showed up, dropout rates after the intake session ranged from 10% to 22% (Zane, Hatanaka, Park, & Akutsu, 1994). People of color are also more likely to seek help for psychological problems from other sources, such as their primary care physician, clergy, traditional healers, family members, and friends (Buchwald, Beals, & Manson, 2000; Cooper-Patrick et al., 1999; Levin, 1986; Neighbors & Jackson, 1984; Peifer, Hu, & Vega, 2000). Woodward et al. (2009) explored the use of complementary and alternative medicine in the treatment of mental and substance use disorders among African American, Afro-Caribbean, and non-Hispanic European Americans using data from the National Study of American Life and the NCS-R. These treatments included massage, chiropractic treatment, acupuncture, herbal remedies, megavitamins, prayer or other spiritual practices, meditation, and Internet support groups. Of the participants in the sample with a *DSM* diagnosis, 34% reported using an alternative treatment in the past 12 months. In general, more non-Hispanic European Americans used such treatments when compared with both African Americans and Black Caribbeans, in that order. However, both African Americans and Black Caribbeans used prayer and other spiritual practices significantly more than non-Hispanic European Americans.

On the topic of culture and mental health, I am able to recognize that my family is not very big on seeking professional help for any health issues, but rather, they focus on Chinese medicine, herbal remedies, or even seeking out the "witch doctor" for help. It seems pretty crazy in our American society, but to my family, it is perfectly normal. Although this traditional way of thinking hasn't been passed on through our family, my mom still practices these things. When I was younger, I used to believe her when she told me, "This soup is good for your body," and basically told me it will cure me of every sickness possible, and I never questioned it. But, now, I am more hesitant to eat or drink the things she offers to me. I know it isn't bad for me, but I know it won't cure me of every sickness, either. The smell and or look of some of these things doesn't really help, either.

When my sister was visiting a couple of months ago, my mom insisted on her drinking some soup that's supposedly good for your blood and will help replenish your body. When she found out my sister has a more severe form of anemia, my mom has been coming up with many different remedies of helping my sister "get better" every time she visits. It's pretty amusing watching them fight back and forth about this. My sister is a biological science major and watching my mom try to convince my sister to drink the soup that will make her "better" is really entertaining. My mom even told me, "Drink the soup so your sister will see it's not so bad." I refused after hearing my sister say, "Look at how fatty it looks!" My sister eventually gave in and ended up drinking the soup to please my mom.

As you can see, there are some cultural differences within my own family. My mom learned about these remedies when she was growing up, but with us growing up in the U.S., it doesn't really mesh well with our society. We have been conditioned to seek professional help (visit a psychiatrist, psychologist, or physician) if anything is off balance, where as with other cultures, it is more of a taboo.

—Miriam, 20+-year-old Chinese American student

Miriam's experiences with her mother's natural remedies illustrate that some people still trust these cultural interventions more than Western medicine. Openness to such cultural practices is part of multicultural competence (D. W. Sue & Sue, 2013).

The general conclusion in the literature is that people of color underutilize mental health services (D. W. Sue & Sue, 2016). R. K. Cheung and Snowden (1990) reviewed the literature on people of color's utilization of mental health services and concluded that African Americans use services more than expected, whereas Asian Americans and Pacific Islanders use services less often. Latinx Americans', American Indians', and Alaska Natives' use of services varies according to type of service. These and other results indicate that there may be important differences in help-seeking behavior between various ethnic groups.

Although it is important to study variations in help-seeking patterns among ethnic groups, it is also important to remember that there may be significant within-group differences. Within-group differences have been observed among various Asian groups (Tracey, Leong, & Glidden, 1986), between Mexican Americans and Mexican immigrants (Keefe, 1982), and in the African American and Caribbean Black communities (Neighbors, 1984, 1985, 1988; Neighbors et al., 2007; Neighbors & Jackson, 1984).

Research shows that if ethnic minorities do go to therapy, they do not continue as long as European Americans. Several studies revealed that clients of color are much more likely to terminate therapy after just one session than are their European American counterparts (S. Sue, 1977; S. Sue, Allen, & Conaway, 1975; S. Sue et al., 1991; S. Sue & McKinney, 1974; S. Sue, McKinney, Allen, & Hall, 1974). Kearney, Draper, and Baron (2005) studied the utilization of services among students from over 40 universities nationwide. They found that European American students attended more sessions than African American, Asian, and Latinx students, although these groups demonstrated more distress at intake.

Barriers to Treatment

I remember the day that I felt really sad in high school because I had family issues, car problems, and everything seemed like it was going all wrong. I tried to talk to my counselor, who was White, but I felt like she did not understand where I was coming from. She did not understand why my parents were the way they were. I was trying to tell her that in the El Salvadorian culture parents are very strict and over protective. They don't trust anyone and they like to keep their children at home, outside of school.

She kept saying that maybe she could talk to them and convince them to give me a little more liberty. I told her no because their norms and values are different from hers. I left her office feeling the same way, but now I felt she couldn't even understand me.

—Maricella, 20+-year-old Latinx student

As discussed in the previous section, research results consistently show that people of color tend to underutilize mental health services. What are some of the barriers that prevent them from getting the services they need? Is it that they have negative attitudes toward seeking help? Toward psychotherapy? Or is it that they have negative experiences once they go to therapy? Maricella's story illustrates several of the reasons for this trend.

Mojtabai et al. (2011) explored barriers to seeking mental health treatment in the general population. They found that the majority of people with common mental disorders (e.g., anxiety, depression, substance abuse) did not seek help because of low perceived need; in other words, they did not think they needed help. Among those with a perceived need, a large portion did not seek help because they preferred to deal with problems on their own. These attitudinal and evaluative factors served to prevent help-seeking more than structural barriers, such as lack of transportation, finances, or inability to get an appointment. Mojtabai et al. found the effects of these barriers differed based on the severity of the disorder and recognized they can differ based on sociodemographic characteristics, such as race/ethnicity, gender, and SES.

It has been suggested that the negative attitudes people of color have toward psychotherapy prevent them from seeking help in the first place. For example, some authors have suggested that African Americans are reluctant to utilize mental health services because of a history of negative experiences with racism. African Americans go into a therapeutic setting viewing a European American therapist as an agent of an oppressive society who may use the information disclosed in therapy against them (Boyd-Franklin, 2003; Ridley, 1995; J. L. White & Parham, 1990). In both the NCS and the NCS-R studies, participants were asked a series of questions that assessed their attitudes toward mental health services. For example, they were asked how likely they would be, if they had a serious emotional problem, to seek help, how comfortable they would be talking to a professional about their personal problems, and how embarrassed they would be if their friends knew they were getting professional help for an emotional problem.

Using NCS data, Diala and associates (Diala et al., 2000) compared the responses of European American and African American participants to those questions. Their initial finding was surprising: Before receiving any type of professional help, African Americans had more positive attitudes about mental health services than did European Americans. However, once they received help, the attitudes of African Americans changed and became more negative. This change suggests that the African Americans' encounters with professional mental health services were negative and that something about the experience turned them off. This change, considered along with the findings mentioned previously that people of color tend not to come back after the first session, suggests that researchers must examine what happens in the therapeutic setting with people of color. Gonzalez, Alegria, Prihoda, Copeland, and Zeber (2011) used NCS-R data to explore the relationship between attitudes toward mental health treatment on service use and age, gender, ethnicity/race, and education. They observed increased use of professional mental health services by African Americans who had a stronger belief in the efficacy of treatment and increased use by Latinx and non-Latinx European Americans who expressed greater comfort levels talking to a professional.

D. W. Sue and Sue (2016) articulated what they saw as the three major barriers to effective multicultural counseling and therapy: (a) culture-bound values, (b) class-bound values, and (c) language variables (see Table 9.5).

Culture-Bound Values as Barriers

Psychotherapy is directly influenced by the culture within which it was developed. Psychotherapy was originally developed by Western Europeans (e.g., Freud); therefore, it reflects a Western perspective, and some of the central values of that perspective may be in direct conflict with the values of clients from other cultures. D. W. Sue and Sue (2016) described some of the European American values embedded in psychotherapy that may conflict with values of clients from other cultures. They refer to these values as **culture-bound values**. Culture-bound values in counseling and psychotherapy include individualism, verbal/emotional/behavioral expressiveness, insight, openness and intimacy, scientific empiricism, clear distinctions between mental and physical functioning, ambiguity, and communication patterns between client and counselor.

culture-bound values—core beliefs of one culture that relate principally to that culture and may be inappropriate for another culture.

In Chapter 3 we discussed the differences between individualism and collectivism. Psychotherapy tends to be a very *individualistic* process. If we look at the most popular theories of human development, such as those of Piaget and Erickson, we see that they emphasize individuation—the development of an autonomous, independent self—as healthy development. If we look at the goals of some of the main orientations to psychotherapy, we also see this focus on the individual. For example, Carl Rogers emphasized self-actualization, or the development of one's full potential. Alfred Adler emphasized the concept of self-esteem; how one feels about himself or herself is seen as a critical component of mental health, and a person's self-esteem is greatly influenced by his or her personal accomplishments. This concept just does not make sense in collectivistic cultures where people have an interdependent sense of the self. As

TABLE 9.5   D. W. Sue and Sue's Barriers to Multicultural Counseling and Therapy

Culture-bound values
Focus on the individual
Verbal/emotional/behavioral expressiveness
Insight
Self-disclosure (openness and intimacy)
Scientific empiricism
Distinctions between mental and physical functioning
Patterns of communication
Class-bound values
Bias toward White middle- to upper-class values
Bias against people who are poor
Lack of understanding of the stressors of poverty
Language barriers
Need for professional interpretation
Lack of bilingual therapists
Use of standard English

Source: D. W. Sue and Sue (2016).

discussed in Chapter 3, this may also be related to the difference between guilt and shame. Guilt is an individual emotion, whereas shame appears to be a group emotion, because one's behavior reflects on his or her family or group. In some cultures, too much emphasis on the self is seen as unhealthy. For example, American culture says, "The squeaky wheel gets the oil." In contrast, Japanese culture says, "The nail that sticks out gets beaten down." In American culture, the loud, assertive person gets positive attention, but in Japanese culture, assertiveness is seen as being selfish and against group standards.

> My friend is Persian and the counselor she's seeing is White. She told me that she was having trouble trying to explain to her counselor some of the cultural differences between Persian and American individuals. Persians are more collectivistic—they will sacrifice their time in order to please some family members. Also, Persians tend to be very traditional and their religion plays an important role in their everyday life.
>
> One of the things she told me was that her White counselor was unable to under-stand why she would place her brother's business before her studies and why she didn't find it easier to do her own thing in order to succeed herself. This may be easy for a White person to state, because Whites are extremely individualistic, and they fail to understand that family members in some cultures are placed before one's self.
>
> —Lana, 20+-year-old Armenian American student

The second culture-bound value described by D. W. Sue and Sue (2016) is *verbal/emotional/behavioral expressiveness.* Based on work by his mentor, Josef Breuer, Freud developed the *talking cure,* or talk therapy (Freud, 1909/1977). This therapy formed the basis for practically all modern approaches to counseling and psychotherapy (Corey, 2017). Therefore, it is expected that clients are able to verbally express their internal thoughts and feelings and engage in active dialogue with the therapist. This is viewed as an essential ingredient in effective therapy. However, not all cultures value this type of verbal expression. For example, in traditional Chinese culture, children are taught to show respect for elders and authority figures by not speaking until spoken to. In traditional therapy and counseling, therapists are trained to let the client initiate the conversation and do most of the talking during sessions. However, a Chinese client may see the therapist as an authority figure and respond with silence. A counselor or therapist who is un-aware of this cultural difference may misinterpret this silence as the client being dependent, inarticulate, or less intelligent (D. W. Sue & Sue, 2016). Different cultures place varying em-phasis on acceptable ways to express emotion. Western cultures tend to value open and outward expression of emotions, whereas other cultures, such as Asians, value emotional restraint (see our discussion of direct versus indirect expression in Chapter 4). People of color, because of mistrust, may withhold true feelings in situations in which they feel threatened, such as an African American client with a European American therapist. In the Western tradition, in which outward emotional expression is valued and expected, clients who do not express enough emotion are labeled resistant, restricted, and repressed by their therapists. With the vast popu-larity of cognitive-behavioral approaches, behavioral expressiveness has become more valued in counseling and psychotherapy (D. W. Sue & Sue, 2016). Clients are expected to be assertive, stand up for themselves, and complete assignments aimed at directly confronting problems or changing problematic behaviors. Again, some cultures value a more indirect, subtle approach (D. W. Sue & Sue, 2016). Murphy-Shigematsu (2014) explained the Japanese concept of *shikata ga nai,* which means, "It is out of my control; nothing can be done." He gave the example of

Japanese Americans placed in internment camps during World War II. Rather than resist, they chose to make the best of a bad situation. Inside the camps, they planted beautiful gardens, wrote poetry, formed baseball leagues, and so on. Some of the younger generation criticized this attitude and wondered why their elders did not fight back. Murphy-Shigematsu reframed this passivity and, rather than seeing it as a sign of weakness, interpreted it as a sign of strength. He said acceptance of one's vulnerability and helplessness takes courage and leads to new hopes and new meanings. A culturally insensitive therapist could easily misinterpret such an attitude as something negative.

The third culture-bound value described by D. W. Sue and Sue (2016) is *insight*. Many traditional forms of counseling and psychotherapy (e.g., psychoanalytic, humanistic) believe that the path to wellness lies in insight, or the client's understanding of the underlying dynamics of his or her problems. Other cultures do not see the need for such in-depth self-exploration. In fact, in some Asian cultures it is believed that thinking too much about something can make the problem worse. Asian elders advise children not to think about the problem because then you are thinking about yourself too much, instead of the family. The following story, involving a Mexican American family, illustrates a conflict over this value of insight:

> My family went to therapy once because my teenage sister was getting into a lot of trouble, and my mother didn't know how to handle her anymore. We were assigned to a White male therapist. In the first session the therapist asked my mother a lot of questions about her own feelings and actions. I could see my mother was getting a bit irritated. She didn't understand why the therapist was focusing on her and not my sister. At the end of the session the therapist suggested that my mother keep a journal, record her thoughts and feelings for the week, and bring them back to the next session. We never went back.
>
> —Belen, 20+-year-old Mexican American student

In this story, we can see the factors that resulted in this family's terminating therapy after the first session. One main factor was the clash in the culture-bound value of insight. This mother wanted practical advice on coping with her daughter's behavioral problems. Instead, the therapist told the mother to keep a journal. We can assume that the therapist had good intentions, believing that the problems lay with the interactions between the mother and the daughter and that the mother needed to become more aware of those interpersonal dynamics. However, this was not culturally sensitive intervention, and the family never went back.

The fourth culture-bound value is *self-disclosure*, or intimacy and openness. In therapy the client is supposed to share the most intimate details of his or her life. In many cultures, such personal disclosures are reserved for only the closest family members and friends. Intimate relationships are developed over time, not once a week in a 50-minute session.

> I will admit that there are times when I feel anxious, depressed, and angry. I think at some point in their lives everyone does. However, even though I've had such feelings, it has never crossed my mind, the idea of going to therapy. I guess it has a lot to do with the way I was raised. Growing up in Mexico, I only knew of one person—in my entire life over there—that was going to therapy. . . . Everyone around town would say that he was crazy because he was going to therapy. I was about ten at the time, and I felt fear towards him. I would always avoid getting close to his house because since

he was "crazy" he would probably hurt me. My family and I then migrated to the United States, and about four years ago I met him at a family wedding. Turns out we are distant relatives. Furthermore, he is a great person. I did not see any crazy in him that I won't see in any other person. I asked about the time [in Mexico] when he attended therapy. From what he told me it was nothing very out of the ordinary. Things were just not going well for him at the time and his parents misinterpreted that. However, he did tell me that he did enjoy therapy and that it did help him.

—Jaime, 20+-year-old Mexican American student

The fifth culture-bound value is *scientific empiricism*. Psychology patterns itself after the physical sciences, which emphasize objective, rational, linear thinking. In Western approaches, a therapist is supposed to be neutral, rational, and logical, like a scientist. Mental health concerns are approached through linear problem solving and quantitative evaluation through the use of tools such as psychodiagnostic tests (e.g., intelligence tests, personality tests). Instead, many cultures take a more circular, holistic, harmonious approach to the world. For example, instead of breaking nature down into its components to study it, control it, and exploit it for profit, as Western cultures do, American Indian culture emphasizes harmonious living with the world. Instead of emphasizing rational, reductionistic problem solving, they believe in the value of intuition. (Remember differences in worldview discussed in Chapter 3.)

Sixth, Western philosophy also draws a *distinction between mental and physical functioning*. In other words, the mind and the body are seen as two separate entities, and there is a distinction between mental and physical health. That distinction is not made in other cultures. Thus, in seeking help for an emotional problem, there is no difference in going to your regular physician or your priest. Just as the doctor prescribes a specific, tangible solution to the problem (e.g., medication), the counselor or therapist may be expected to do the same.

Finally, *patterns of communication* differ from one culture to another. In some cultures, such as Latinx ones, children are reared to respect their elders and authority figures, and they do not speak until they are spoken to. A therapist may be viewed as an authority figure, and a culturally different client may come in and wait for the therapist to speak first and take the lead in running the session. However, in many traditional Western therapies, the client is expected to do most of the talking and take responsibility for directing the session while the therapist takes a less active role. Therapists may misunderstand and misinterpret the behavior of a culturally different client who comes in and does not say much.

Class-Bound Values as Barriers

Effective multicultural therapy can also be hindered by **class-bound values**. According to D. W. Sue and Sue (2016), the values that underlie typical mental health practices are decidedly European American middle class and practitioners often fail to recognize the economic implications for the delivery of mental health services. D. W. Sue and Sue (2003) noted, "Class-bound factors related to socioeconomic status may place those suffering from poverty at a disadvantage and obstruct their efforts to obtain help" (p. 55). For example, poor clients may not have transportation to get to sessions and may not have the money or the insurance coverage to pay for services. A therapist who wants a poor client to openly express intimate parts of his or her life, to introspect, and to

class-bound values—core beliefs of one socioeconomic class that relate principally to that class and may be inappropriate for another level of socioeconomic status.

gain insight into the underlying dynamics of his or her behavior may be in direct conflict with a client who is more concerned about finding a job, putting food on the table, or finding adequate care for his or her child. Clients who are in survival mode, just trying to make it from day to day, may expect more tangible advice and suggestions from a therapist. It is also often difficult for a therapist who comes from a middle- to upper-class background to relate to the circumstances and hardships affecting a client who lives in poverty.

> We were in a faculty meeting discussing the final comprehensive exam for our graduate students. In part of the exam students must answer questions related to a clinical vignette. A number of faculty wrote possible vignettes, and we were trying to decide which one to use in the exam. I wrote a vignette about a 5-year-old boy who was referred for treatment for acting out at school. In the family background I mentioned that the mother lived in a small apartment where a lot of different people came in and out, many who abused drugs. One night, when the client was an infant, the mother could not get him to stop crying. One of the mother's friends, who was high on drugs, grabbed the small boy and tried to throw him off the balcony. When we got to that part of the vignette, a White male faculty member said, "We can't use that one. That would never happen in the real world." I immediately spoke up and said, "Well it does in my world. That was based on an actual case." The other faculty member turned a bit red, looked a little sheepish, but said nothing. We ended up using that vignette.
>
> —Linda, 30+-year-old African American professor

The estimated annual price tag for the treatment and consequences of juvenile psychological disorders is $250 billion.

—Jeffrey Kluger, *Time* magazine,
November 1, 2010

The inferior and biased treatment of clients of lower SES is well documented in the literature (American Psychological Association Task Force on Socioeconomic Status, 2007). For example, in a study by Garfield, Weiss, and Pollack (1973), counselors were given nearly identical descriptions of a 9-year-old boy who exhibited negative classroom behavior; the only thing that differed was his SES. Counselors who were told the boy belonged to the upper SES group expressed more of a willingness to become involved with the boy than those who were told he was from the lower SES group. Lorion (1973) found that psychiatrists more often referred clients like themselves (i.e., European American, upper SES) to therapy. These findings illustrate some of the class-bound variables that affect the provision of mental health services for members of minority groups.

---

language variables—differences in language (e.g., an English-speaking therapist and a Spanish-speaking client who may have some limited facility with English) or language usage (e.g., Ebonics or Black English).

Language Variables as a Barrier

The third barrier to effective multicultural therapy described by D. W. Sue and Sue (2016) is **language variables**. United States society is monolingual, at least in its values. The reality is that hundreds of languages are spoken within the United States, but the preferred language is English. Because psychotherapy is a "talking cure," the client and the therapist must be able to accurately and appropriately send and receive both verbal and nonverbal messages for therapy to be effective.

Individuals who do not speak English may be completely shut out from mental health services because of a lack of bilingual counselors and therapists. People who speak English as a second language may be at a disadvantage because they cannot express their thoughts, feelings, and experiences in as complex, deep, or rich a manner in English as they can in their native tongue. Those who speak nonstandard English, such as some African Americans who use Black English/Ebonics, may use words, phrases, and expressions with which a European American therapist is unfamiliar.

G. Kim et al. (2010) used data from the National Latino and Asian American Study of Mental Health to examine the impact of English language proficiency on utilization of mental health services. The sample consisted of bilingual Latinx and Asian immigrants who met the criteria for the presence of a mood, anxiety, or substance use disorder. The findings of this study corresponded to those of previous studies that confirmed that Latinx and Asian immigrants tend to seek help for mental health issues less than non-Hispanic European Americans. Less than 20% of the immigrant sample used any type of mental health service; Asian immigrants were the least likely to use services (only 13.8%). Latinxs who were proficient in English used mental health services more than those with limited English proficiency. This difference did not occur in the Asian sample. Therefore, it appears that language proficiency was more of an issue for Latinxs, but this pattern could not be confirmed for Asians.

Experience With Microaggressions

Kiana is a 34-year old multiracial bisexual woman. Her father is African American and her mother is biracial: Korean and Italian American. Kiana works as an administrative assistant at a large university while pursuing her master's degree in Fine Arts. Kiana has felt marginalized at work and also recently ended a long-term romantic relationship. She struggles with managing her work environment and with re-entering the dating scene. She has also had some trouble getting out of bed in the morning and generally feels melancholy. She asked a friend to recommend a therapist and her friend referred her to a psychoanalyst she had been seeing for years: Alan, a White male in his late 50s. Kiana had some reservations about going to therapy because her mother felt it was disgraceful and inappropriate to tell a stranger about personal problems and her father felt it was for "crazy" people.

In the first session, Kiana described her difficulties meeting single people in the city and Alan asked if her "unapproachable air" might be contributing to her inability to meet men. Kiana was surprised by his question and asked what he meant by "unapproachable"? Alan shared that his first impression of her was that her body language seemed closed and she appeared angry. Kiana paused, as this was not the first time someone perceived her as an "angry Black woman." She did not have the energy to explore this with him, so accepted his observation and tried to change the subject by pointing out she is attracted to both men and women. Alan expressed curiosity about her sexuality and offered an interpretation of Kiana's bisexuality as a phase during which a person is trying to find their sexual identity. He also expressed curiosity about her ethnicity. Kiana was familiar with this kind of curiosity, but did not want to waste her time in therapy educating Alan about her sexuality or her ethnicity. She agreed with him that identity issues were an ongoing theme in her life and moved the discussion to her workplace.

Kiana shared with Alan that in her role as an administrative assistant, she experiences persistent feelings of invisibility. She relayed multiple incidents where she would be sitting at her desk and people would look right past her, act as if she was not there, and generally treat her as unimportant. She felt she was often treated by professors and students as a "second class citizen" there to serve them. She frequently noted people's looks of surprise and shock when she revealed she was a master's student. She shared the office space with a younger White female named Michelle. Often when colleagues, delivery people, or technicians entered the office, they directed their questions toward Michelle. If Kiana was alone in the office, often people would simply walk out, as if Kiana was not there. Kiana shared with Alan that she sometimes wonders: can anybody see me? While exploring this, Alan wondered if Kiana was "making a mountain out of a molehill." For example, he asked if Michelle's desk was positioned closer to the door in the office. He also asked how Michelle greets people; was she smiling and cheerful? Alan felt it was important for Kiana to consider where these feelings of invisibility may be coming from, and invited her to consider if she felt that she was not worthy of others' attention and admiration. He then began to ask her how her relationship was with her parents as a child, with particular interest in how she felt about her father.

These questions frustrated Kiana, but she was aware that Alan was already experiencing her as closed and angry. Actually, she *was* feeling angry, and it felt very similar to the anger she experienced in her workplace. She felt caught in that moment between sharing her authentic reaction and being type cast as an angry Black woman and holding in her true feelings in order to avoid the stereotype. It was a familiar scenario. Alan interpreted Kiana's silence as resistance to the therapeutic process. Kiana responded that she had come to therapy to deepen her self-awareness: however, she could see that there were going to be too many barriers between herself and Alan for her to be able to authentically share herself. Alan expressed regret about this and asked if Kiana would consider coming to another session. He felt that Kiana's desire to terminate prematurely was a defense mechanism often exhibited by people new to therapy. This did not resonate for Kiana and she did not return for a second session (adapted from Capodilupo, 2016, pp. 180–181).

Remember the discussion on microaggressions in Chapter 6? How many microaggressions can you identify in the therapy session between Kiana and Alan? Kiana's interactions with Alan were a microcosm of her experiences in society at large. Alan relates to Kiana based on the stereotype of the angry Black woman and blames her for her feelings of invisibility while ignoring the impact of the larger environmental forces of racism, sexism, and heterocentrism. Alan unknowingly invalidates, negates, and dismisses Kiana's experiences (Capodilupo, 2016). After feeling hesitant about attending therapy in the first place, it is no surprise Kiana terminated after the first session.

Microaggressions are another significant barrier to mental health treatment for diverse populations (Capodilupo, 2016; D. W. Sue & Sue, 2003). As stated earlier, the majority of clients of color terminate after the first session. Capodilupo (2016) suggests that microaggressions may be at the core of this problem. Research results indicate that microaggressions are a common experience in therapy (Owen, Tao, Imel, Wampold, & Rodolfa, 2014) and support the conclusion that racial, gender, and sexual orientation microaggressions have a negative effect on the therapeutic alliance for members of the LGBT community (Shelton & Delgado-Romero, 2011), women (Owen, Tao, & Rodolfa, 2010), and people of color (Owen et al., 2014).

As illustrated in Kiana's case, clients may be hesitant to seek professional services because of their real and perceived negative experiences with the mental health system and other social service agencies. In addition, therapists fall prey, whether consciously or unconsciously, to their own stereotypes, biases, and prejudices. Well-meaning therapists unwittingly convey their negative attitudes to clients. They may be more resistant to seeing the harm they do and to changing their ways because they see themselves as moral, just, fair-minded, and decent (e.g., aversive racism). Also, because of their lack of familiarity and discomfort with other cultures, therapists may unconsciously do things to push culturally different clients away, such as not putting much effort into building rapport, concluding that the client is resistant or not well suited to psychotherapy, or determining that the client's needs would be better served elsewhere.

Capodilupo (2016) suggests that counselors and therapists have the opportunity to learn from their clients about microaggressions and their impact on clients' lives.

> Clients trust mental health professionals to take an intimate and deeply personal journey of self-exploration with them through the process of therapy. They grant these professionals the opportunity to look into their inner world and also invite them to walk where they live in their everyday lives. Therapists and counselors have an obligation to their clients, especially when their clients differ from them in terms of race, gender, ability, religion, and-or sexual orientation, to work to understand their experiential reality. . . . Therapists must be open to the idea that they can commit microaggressions against their clients and be willing to examine their role in this process. (Capodilupo, 2016, p. 207)

This quote applies not only to the issue of microaggressions, but also to all potential barriers to effective therapy with diverse populations. Professional counselors and therapists have a responsibility to examine all of their attitudes, beliefs, and behaviors with regard to diverse populations—whether they are related to race, ethnicity, language, gender, sexual orientation, or SES—and to take active steps to ensure that they do not interfere with their ability to work effectively toward positive outcomes in therapy.

Culturally Sensitive Therapeutic Approaches

With all these barriers to minority groups seeking and receiving appropriate mental health services, it might seem like an impossible task for members of those groups to get the help they need. Several approaches have been developed to overcome these obstacles and provide services that are more appropriate for culturally diverse groups.

Essentially, three basic approaches are described in the literature: (a) train personnel in mental health service agencies; (b) establish separate services for minority groups within existing agencies; and (c) create separate facilities for the specific purpose of providing services to culturally diverse groups (La Roche, 2013; S. Sue, 1977; Uba, 1982). Along the same lines, Rogler and associates (Rogler, Malgady, & Constantino, 1987) suggested three levels of services. The first level involves providing services in the native language of the clients, coordinating with other organizations in the ethnic community, and creating an atmosphere in the organization that is open to the cultural values of the community it serves. The second level involves selecting mainstream treatments (i.e., traditional approaches to therapy) that fit with ethnic culture. The third level involves creating interventions designed specifically for ethnic cultures. More recently, an approach known as *culturally sensitive evidence-based practice in psychology* (EBPP) seeks to incorporate these and other strategies in an effort to optimize psychotherapy outcomes for diverse populations.

In Chapter 1, we discussed the basic propositions of multicultural counseling and therapy (MCT) (D. W. Sue et al., 1996) and how these propositions formed the foundation for the basic assumptions of multicultural psychology. It is helpful to review them now as we specifically discuss the topic of therapy with diverse cultures. D. W. Sue and Sue (2016) summarized the key elements of MCT. First, MCT sees therapy as both a helping role and a process, where the role of the therapist and repertoire of helping skills are broadened to include teaching, consulting, and advocacy and are tailored to fit the cultural values and life experiences of clients. As discussed in Chapter 7, MCT recognizes that client identities are composed of individual, group, and universal dimensions. It advocates the use of both universal and culture-specific modes of helping strategies. In other words, there are universal features of helping that cut across cultures, but clients also need strategies that incorporate the values, practices, and beliefs of their particular group. Multicultural counseling and therapy incorporates both individualistic and collectivistic perspectives and strives to balance attention to unique individual characteristics with consideration for the impact of contextual factors on these individuals. This may involve a shift in focus from individual client change to altering systems (e.g., education, employment, government, business, society).

In the following sections we will discuss some of the approaches developed to provide effective mental health services to diverse populations. More specifically, we will cover the training of mental health professionals, cultural matching between clients and therapists, culture-specific approaches, and culturally sensitive evidence-based approaches.

The Training of Mental Health Professionals: Multicultural Competence

One way to overcome barriers to effective multicultural therapy is to increase the ability of mental health professionals to work with culturally diverse populations.

> It is our contention that the reasons why minority-group individuals underutilize and prematurely terminate counseling/therapy lie in the biased nature of the services themselves. The services offered are frequently antagonistic or inappropriate to the life experiences of the culturally different client; they lack sensitivity and understanding; and they are oppressive and discriminating toward minority clients. One of the major reasons for therapeutic ineffectiveness lies in the training of mental health professionals. (D. W. Sue & Sue, 1999, p. 11)

In other words, the way to effective multicultural therapy is through training and education of mental health professionals. That leads us to the issue of *multicultural competence*. In Chapter 1 we discussed the struggles associated with getting the APA to officially adopt a set of multicultural competencies and thereby set the standard for the training of professional psychologists and counselors to conduct therapy with individuals from diverse backgrounds. We now examine more closely the issue of multicultural competence and what it means.

In general, **multicultural competence** refers to effectiveness in working with people who are different from you. More specifically, Pope-Davis, Reynolds, Dings, and Ottavi (1994) define multicultural competence as

multicultural competence—the ability to work and be effective with individuals who are of a different culture from yours.

> an appreciation of and sensitivity to the history, current needs, strengths, and resources of communities and individuals who historically have been underserved and

underrepresented by psychologists. . . . Specifically, these competencies entail the following: an awareness of one's own biases and cultural assumptions, content knowledge about cultures different from one's own culture, an accurate self-assessment of one's multicultural skills and comfort level, an appropriate application of cultural knowledge to the counseling process, and an awareness of the cultural assumptions underlying the counseling process. (p. 466)

Multicultural competence is sometimes referred to as *cultural competence.* D. W. Sue & Torino (2005) offer the following definition of cultural competence:

Cultural competence is the ability to engage in actions or create conditions that maximize the optimal development of client and client systems. Multicultural counseling competence is defined as the counselor's acquisition of awareness, knowledge, and skills needed to function effectively in a pluralistic democratic society (ability to communicate, interact, negotiate, and intervene on behalf of clients from diverse backgrounds), and on an organizational/societal level, advocating effectively to develop new theories, practices, policies, and organizational structures that are more responsive to all groups. (p. 8)

Multicultural competence utilizes a broad definition of culture (see Chapter 1) whereby any kind of difference between the therapist/counselor and client is considered a cultural encounter. This includes a male therapist working with a female client, a straight therapist working with a gay client, a European American therapist working with an African American client, a Protestant therapist working with a Catholic client, and so on. Because every individual, including every therapist and client, brings his or her own unique set of cultural identities to the therapy office, all therapy could be considered multicultural therapy (Comas-Díaz, 2014; Pedersen, 1988).

The multicultural competencies were originally developed by several psychologists, most prominently Derald Wing Sue and Patricia Arredondo (Arredondo et al., 1996; D. W. Sue et al., 1982; D. W. Sue et al., 1992; D. W. Sue, Carter et al., 1998). There are three primary domains of multicultural competence: (a) the counselor's awareness of his or her own cultural assumptions, values, and biases; (b) an understanding of the client's worldview; and (c) the development of culturally appropriate intervention strategies and techniques.

One of the primary aspects of multicultural competence is self-awareness. In other words, counselors and therapists cannot be effective in working with individuals from different backgrounds unless they first understand themselves. That includes an understanding of their own cultural heritage, the impact it has on their attitudes and behaviors, and an understanding of the attitudes they have toward other groups, such as biases, prejudices, and stereotypes.

Second, effective counselors and therapists must be able to see the world through their clients' eyes. They must have basic information about the various groups they encounter, such as history of the group, current issues facing the group, and typical values held and practices followed by the group. That knowledge should not be used to formulate stereotypes or to make hasty judgments about members of particular groups, but should be used to formulate hypotheses that can be explored with the client. For example, if you are a therapist with a Latinx client, you might assume that she is Catholic and ascribes to traditional gender roles. These things may exemplify Latinx culture in general but may not hold true for an individual Latinx client in your office. These are issues that must be explored with her to see whether they apply.

Third, therapists and counselors must develop a repertoire of culturally appropriate strategies, such as the ability to assess level of acculturation and ethnic identity, comfort discussing difficult topics such as racism and sexism, and collaboration with other institutional, community, and indigenous sources of help.

See Table 9.6 for a more detailed description of the multicultural competencies. Table 9.6 elaborates the attitudes and beliefs, knowledge, and skills needed in each of the three main areas of multicultural competence.

TABLE 9.6   **Multicultural Counseling Competencies**

I. Counselor awareness of own cultural values and biases

A. With respect to *attitudes* **and** *beliefs*, **culturally competent counselors:**

- believe that cultural self-awareness and sensitivity to one's own cultural heritage are essential.
- are aware of how their own cultural background and experiences have influenced attitudes, values, and biases about psychological processes.
- are able to recognize the limits of their multicultural competencies and expertise.
- recognize their sources of discomfort with differences that exist between themselves and clients in terms of race, ethnicity, and culture.

B. With respect to *knowledge*, **culturally competent counselors:**

- have specific knowledge about their own racial and cultural heritage and how it personally and professionally affects their definitions of and biases about normality/abnormality and the process of counseling.
- possess knowledge and understanding about how oppression, racism, discrimination, and stereotyping affect them personally and in their work. This allows individuals to acknowledge their own racist attitudes, beliefs, and feelings.
- possess knowledge about their social impact on others.

C. With respect to *skills*, **culturally competent counselors:**

- seek out educational, consultative, and training experiences to improve their understanding and effectiveness in working with culturally different populations.
- are constantly seeking to understand themselves as racial and cultural beings and are actively seeking a nonracist identity.

II. Understanding the client's worldview

A. With respect to *attitudes* **and** *beliefs*, **culturally competent counselors:**

- are aware of their negative and positive emotional reactions toward other racial and ethnic groups that may prove detrimental to the counseling relationship. They are willing to contrast their own beliefs and attitudes with those of their culturally different clients in a nonjudgmental fashion.
- are aware of stereotypes and preconceived notions that they may hold toward other racial and ethnic minority groups.

B. With respect to *knowledge*, **culturally competent counselors:**

- possess specific knowledge and information about the particular client group with whom they are working.
- understand how race, culture, ethnicity, and so forth may affect personality formation, vocational choices, manifestation of psychological disorders, help-seeking behavior, and the appropriateness or inappropriateness of counseling approaches.
- understand and have knowledge about sociopolitical influences that impinge on the lives of racial and ethnic minorities.

C. With respect to *skills*, **culturally competent counselors:**

- familiarize themselves with relevant research and the latest findings regarding mental health and mental disorders that affect various ethnic and racial groups.
- become actively involved with minority individuals outside the counseling setting so that their perspective of minorities is more than an academic or helping exercise.

III. Developing culturally appropriate intervention strategies and techniques

A. With respect to *attitudes and beliefs,* culturally competent counselors:

- respect clients' religious and spiritual beliefs and values, including attributions and taboos, because they affect worldview, psychosocial functioning, and expressions of distress.
- respect indigenous helping practices and respect help-giving among communities of color.
- value bilingualism and do not view another language as an impediment to counseling.

B. With respect to *knowledge,* culturally competent counselors:

- have a clear and explicit knowledge and understanding of the generic characteristics of counseling and therapy and how they may clash with the cultural values of various cultural groups.
- are aware of institutional barriers that prevent minorities from using mental health services.
- have knowledge of the potential bias in assessment instruments and use procedures and interpret findings in a way that recognizes the cultural and linguistic characteristics of clients.
- have knowledge of family structures, hierarchies, values, and beliefs from various cultural perspectives. They are knowledgeable about the community where a particular cultural group may reside and the resources in the community.
- are aware of relevant discriminatory practices at the social and the community level that may affect the psychological welfare of the population being served.

C. With respect to *skills,* culturally competent counselors:

- are able to engage in a variety of verbal and nonverbal helping responses. They are able to send and receive both verbal and nonverbal messages accurately and appropriately. They are not tied to only one method or approach to helping but recognize that helping styles and approaches may be culture bound.
- are able to exercise institutional intervention skills on behalf of their clients. They can help clients determine whether a problem stems from racism or bias in others so that clients do not inappropriately personalize problems.
- are not averse to seeking consultation with traditional healers or religious and spiritual leaders and practitioners in the treatment of culturally different clients when appropriate.
- take responsibility for interacting in the language requested by the client and, if not feasible, make appropriate referrals.
- have training and expertise in the use of traditional assessment and testing instruments.
- attend to and work to eliminate biases, prejudices, and discriminatory contexts in conducting evaluations and providing interventions, and develop sensitivity to issues of oppression, sexism, heterosexism, elitism, and racism.
- take responsibility for educating their clients to the processes of psychological intervention, such as goals, expectations, legal rights, and the counselor's orientation.

Note: Adapted from "Operationalization of Multicultural Counseling Competencies," by P. Arredondo et al., 1996, *Journal of Multicultural Counseling and Development, 24,* 42–78; and D.W. Sure, Carter et al. (1998).

More recently, the American Counseling Association endorsed a revised version of the multicultural counseling competencies (Ratts, Singh, Nassar-McMillan, Butler, & McCullough, 2016). Emerging developments in the field and changes in the world at large highlighted the need for an update, such as increased understanding about the impact of intersecting identities (e.g., race, gender, sexual orientation, religion, SES) (see Chapter 7) and of the larger context (e.g., communities, institutions, social climates) on mental health outcomes and health disparities. According to Ratts et al. (2016), "As society evolves, multicultural competence among counselors must also evolve if the counseling profession is to continue to address the needs of culturally diverse clients and the social justice concerns that both shape and contextualize mental health and overall well-being" (p. 29). The resulting document is titled *Multicultural and Social Justice Counseling Competencies: Guidelines for the Counseling Profession* (Ratts et al., 2016).

The Multicultural and Social Justice Counseling Competencies recognize that both counselor/therapist and client bring multiple, intersecting identities to the therapeutic process. Each of these identities may be either privileged or marginalized. Remember the case of Kiana earlier in this chapter? Kiana came into that therapeutic relationship with almost all marginalized identities (female, multiracial, bisexual), whereas her therapist, Alan, had almost all privileged identities (male, European American, heterosexual). Kiana's intersecting, marginalized statuses had a significant impact on her presenting mental health issues. Alan failed to recognize the impact of these identities and statuses on both himself and Kiana. As a result, he was unable to build an effective working alliance.

The revised competencies also recognize the importance of considering the client in context, where the therapist must understand that the client is embedded in and influenced by multiple social, institutional, political, and cultural factors (remember the biopsychosocial model from Chapter 1). Alan failed to recognize the impact of Kiana's work environment on her mental health. He negated and invalidated her experience of feeling invisible. The Multicultural and Social Justice Counseling Competencies advocate a multilevel approach where individual issues are addressed in individual counseling or therapy and contextual or systemic issues are addressed in the community setting through social justice advocacy. Social justice advocacy expands the roles of mental health professionals beyond the traditional therapy office (Ratts et al., 2016). Social justice counseling and therapy is discussed in more detail later in this chapter.

Figure 9.1 summarizes the Multicultural and Social Justice Counseling Competencies. Notice that the competencies retain the primary domains of awareness, knowledge, and skills with regard to the original multicultural competencies of counselor awareness of his or her own cultural values and biases, understanding the client's worldview, and developing culturally appropriate intervention strategies and techniques. The revised competencies now also include: (a) recognition of the multiple and intersecting identities of both client and counselor that carry both privileged and marginalized statuses; and (b) action, where counselors and therapists utilize both traditional individual therapeutic interventions and social justice advocacy interventions.

The case of Denise at the beginning of the chapter illustrates several dimensions of multicultural and social justice competence. First, it might be assumed that Denise and her counselor would have an automatic rapport because they were both African American women, a marginalized identity. However, there were important differences between them, the most salient being sexual orientation. Denise was in a marginalized position, but her therapist was in a privileged one. This illustrates the point that all counseling is multicultural counseling, because we each have multiple identities. Denise and her counselor openly discussed these differences. In the beginning, Denise asked the counselor to share personal information about herself and her political attitudes. In some orientations it is taboo for the counselor to share personal information about herself, but the fact that Denise's therapist did so helped Denise to feel more comfortable and overcome some of her trust issues and some of the stigma she felt about seeing a mental health professional. Denise's counselor demonstrated a level of comfort and skill in discussing difficult and potentially conflictual issues, such as heterosexism. Denise's case also illustrates the impact of environmental forces, such as the negative attitudes of her family and religion toward her sexual orientation, and the university, which may not have demonstrated adequate support for sexual minorities. To do so effectively, Denise's counselor had to be aware of her personal attitudes on those topics. The counselor was also able to work effectively with Denise because of basic knowledge she had about the lesbian lifestyle and the

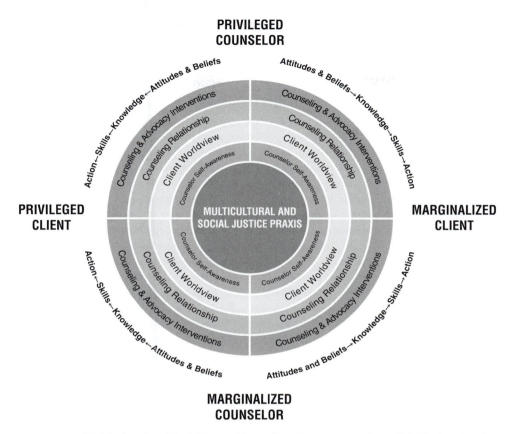

FIGURE 9.1   Multicultural and Social Justice Counseling Competencies. From "Multicultural and Social Justice Counseling Competencies," by M. J. Ratts, A. A. Singh, S. Nassar-McMillan, S. K. Butler, and J. R. McCullough, 2015, *Journal of Multicultural Counseling and Development, 44*(1), p. 4. Retrieved from https://www.counseling.org/docs/default-source/competencies/multicultural-and-social-justice-counseling-compeiencies.pdf. Copyright 2015 by M. J. Ratts, A. A. Singh, S. Nassar-McMillan, S. K. Butler, and J. R. McCullough. Reprinted with permission.

reactions of various communities to this lifestyle, as well as skill at connecting Denise with other institutional supports (e.g., the lesbian support group.) Thus, Denise's counselor was successful in helping her cope with her presenting problems by demonstrating multicultural competence—self-awareness, understanding of her client's worldview, and culturally appropriate intervention strategies. Perhaps Denise's therapist could also have engaged more actively by advocating for the university to take more steps to improve the campus environment for sexual minorities.

At my placement site, the high-risk adolescent population frequently drives away staff members. Upon starting at the school, many staff and students predicted that I would be scared away and quit in a short amount of time. However, since I am often relaxed, goofy, and occasionally unpredictable, I was able to combat attempts to intimidate me. Even though I describe myself as occasionally unpredictable, I think the main factor as to why the students tolerate me is because of my consistency in showing up.

All the students at the school are either African American or Hispanic. Being the only Asian on campus, I was met with unintentional racial and stereotypical comments from the students. On my first day at the school, several students would bow to me and greet me in Japanese or Chinese. As they bowed, another student commented, "What are you doing? What if that gets him mad and he roundhouse kicks you?" I would respond back to them in the respective language before I explained to them that I was Vietnamese. Another student would insist I looked like certain Asian characters from movies. Since I knew the characters he was referring to, I reacted by mimicking and quoting the characters. I think my reactions to these situations were unexpected and humorous enough for the students to eventually let their guard down around me.

With sensitivity to multiculturalism, I have had to adapt to the students by finding a balance between professional and approachable. Since the population does not respond well to complete professionalism, a big change for me from my first day was scaling down my dress. In addition, I had to learn all the new slang the students used. In respect to ethnic culture, I have had to become more flexible with my ideas on self-disclosure. At first, I wanted my personal life to be completely private, but I think revealing tidbits of my background has allowed them to trust me. For example, I had the most resistance from my Hispanic clients. However, when I mentioned I grew up in [name of city], which is a heavily dense Mexican neighborhood, they quickly changed their opinion about me. I am learning that clients will find strange ways to connect and build rapport. It is these small things that I often take for granted and omit, but in the end they have proven quite useful in developing my personal style and approach to therapy.

—Daniel, 20+-year-old Vietnamese student

One can see from Daniel's story that he adjusted his style to the particular population, based on age and ethnicity. Instead of being offended, he responded to the students' stereotypical comments with humor and consistency. He was also more open to disclosing some of his personal information. As a result, he was able to build strong therapeutic relationships with a challenging population through self-awareness, understanding the perspectives and experiences of the teens, and adopting culturally sensitive strategies.

Cultural Matching

When I was 15 years old I was removed from my mom's home and placed in foster care. As part of entering the system I was required to go to therapy once a week. The first therapist they sent me to was a White man in [an affluent, predominantly White neighborhood]. I immediately felt very uncomfortable. I was supposed to open up and talk about my past and what I had been through and all that, but I did not feel comfortable doing that with him. It felt very stiff and too structured. I remember him taking out these cards and laying them out on the table and asking me what the expressions meant and all that. I don't remember why he did that. I also remember him asking me about fees and how was he going to get paid. I told him I was a ward of the court and didn't know anything about that. That made me feel as if he was not there for me; he was just doing his job. After about five sessions I asked my foster mother, "Can you find me someone Black?" She talked to someone and after that I started seeing an African American male therapist in the same city. I immediately felt comfortable. It was much less structured. It felt like talking to someone I already knew. I could understand what he said and relate to the language he used. I continued to see him every week for the required amount of time, which was probably about three months.

—James, 40+-year-old African American

James's story brings up a question that naturally arises when thinking about culturally sensitive approaches to therapy: Will therapy be more effective if the client and therapist are of the same background? Like James, would you feel more comfortable talking with a therapist of the same race? The same gender? The same SES?

Karlsson (2005) reviewed the literature on ethnic matching between clients and therapists. He divided the studies into three main types—analog studies, archival studies, and process–outcome studies. Analog studies are typically conducted with college students, who are presented with a simulated therapy session and simply asked whether they would prefer an ethnically similar therapist (e.g., S. R. Lopez, Lopez, & Fong, 1991) or to place in rank order which therapist characteristics are most important to them, including ethnicity (e.g., Atkinson, Furlong, & Poston, 1986). Archival studies review clinic and hospital records to look at number of attended sessions and dropout rates. The third type of research examines what happens in actual therapy sessions. These are known as process and outcome studies.

The answer to the question of the effectiveness of ethnic matching between therapist and client is different depending on which kind of study is done. Karlsson (2005) said that the best conclusion for analog studies is that sometimes there is a preference for ethnic matching, but other therapist characteristics may be judged as more important. For example, one study found ethnic matching to be ranked higher for Native American students than for European American students, but both groups ranked similarity in attitudes and behaviors as more important than ethnic match (S. K. Bennett & BigFoot-Sipes, 1991). Attendance and dropout rates in archival studies do seem to indicate that ethnic matching is important. A large archival study was conducted by S. Sue and his colleagues (S. Sue et al., 1991) that included a sample of more than 13,000 African American, Asian American, Mexican American, and European American clients using data from the Los Angeles County outpatient mental health system. They found that a match between client and therapist in language and ethnicity predicted a decrease in dropout and an increase in the number of sessions. For clients who speak English as a second language, matching was also a predictor of treatment outcome. In contrast, studies of actual therapy process and outcome suggest that ethnic matching between the client and therapist is not important. E. E. Jones (1978, 1982) conducted experiments in which he manipulated the ethnic match between European American and African American clients and therapists. Using the therapists' assessment of treatment outcome, he found that the outcome of the therapy did not differ based on the ethnic match between clients and therapist.

After reviewing and critiquing the literature from all three types of studies on ethnic matching, Karlsson (2005) concluded that "the empirical support for ethnic matching is, at best, inconclusive and lacks a foundation of rigorous research designs" (p. 124). He calls for more and better designed studies, particularly process and outcome studies. Until then, he says "it is still unclear how mental health professionals should optimally serve ethnic minorities in a most advantageous fashion" (p. 124). In other words, research to date does not give a clear answer as to whether clients do better when they see a therapist from a similar ethnic background.

Cabral and Smith (2011) conducted a meta-analysis of racial/ethnic matching of clients and therapists. They included data from 154 studies across three categories—studies of individuals' preferences for a therapist of their own race/ethnicity, clients' perceptions of therapists across racial/ethnic match, and therapeutic outcomes across racial/ethnic match. Results indicated that clients have a moderately strong preference for a therapist of their own race/ethnicity, as well as a tendency to perceive therapists of their own race/ethnicity more positively, but there was no significant difference in treatment outcomes based on racial/ethnic matching of clients and therapists. In other words, clients tend to state a preference for and make more positive evaluations of a therapist of their own background, but research results fail to show any significant impact of the racial/ethnic match on the success of therapy. Across the three types of studies, client/therapist match had the strongest effect for African Americans. Overall, Cabral and Smith (2011) found that the effects of racial/ethnic matching are highly variable. Researchers in earlier meta-analytic studies drew similar conclusions: that individuals tend to prefer therapists of their own race/ethnicity, but this match does not improve therapeutic outcomes (Coleman, Wampold, & Casali, 1995; Maramba & Hall, 2002; Shin et al., 2005).

Is the effectiveness of cultural matching really unclear? James's story at the beginning of this section might suggest differently. In fact, James's experience is not uncommon. S. Sue and Zane (1987) concluded that therapy crucially related to how credible a therapist is. Clients of color may see an ethnically matched therapist as being credible simply because of the matching of their culture. S. Sue and Zane would call this *ascribed credibility*. Although this is only a superficial form of credibility, the therapist can earn a deeper level of trust and credibility over time, called *earned credibility*. If a therapist is not matched for ethnicity, a client may reject the therapist and not return to therapy or drop out at a higher rate. Certainly, this was the finding of S. Sue et al.'s (1991) large-scale study discussed earlier. However, *if* the client were to remain in therapy with the mismatched therapist, a good therapist can earn credibility. In E. E. Jones's (1978, 1982) studies cited above, the data collected were *therapists'* assessments of the treatment outcome. Therapists may be motivated to believe that they did a good job with any client, so this may be why matched and mismatched therapists were not different from one another when they assessed their own therapy sessions. This conclusion would have been strengthened if a measure of client assessment were also taken.

Cabral and Smith (2011) offer other possible explanations for the mixed results on client–therapist match. For example, certain client–therapist dyads may have resulted in higher drop-out rates, which may have affected the experimental results. Interpersonal similarity is also influenced by many different factors. Just because two people are of the same race/ethnicity does not mean they share the same worldview; there is substantial within-group variability. For example, people from the same racial/ethnic group may be at very different stages of racial identity development. In addition, clients and therapists of the same background may perceive more similarity than actually exists. People often make inaccurate assumptions about how similar they are. Racial/ethnic similarity also does not take into consideration other related variables, such as interracial mistrust or the therapist's level of multicultural competence. For example, this study showed that racial match was most important for African American clients who may have a higher degree of mistrust based on actual and perceived mistreatment by the system. The most optimistic explanation is that these results may demonstrate that therapists and clients have the ability to successfully navigate cultural differences to the extent that they do not have a significant impact on therapeutic outcomes. This gives hope that training in multicultural competence is worthwhile and can be effective. It also gives hope because it is often not feasible or possible to match clients with therapists of the same race/ethnicity; there are just not enough therapists of color to go around. Race and ethnicity are complex constructs, making it difficult to capture their precise impact on the therapeutic relationship and outcomes. Despite the lack of solid conclusions, the strategy of cultural matching between clients and therapists is a viable one that warrants further exploration.

Culture-Specific Therapies

Another approach to providing culturally sensitive therapy is to tailor interventions to the needs and characteristics of specific groups. The idea is that, to be effective, psychotherapy must address specific issues that members of particular groups face. Throughout this chapter and this book, we have emphasized that cultural, social, political, historical, and economic factors affect members of culturally diverse groups that make their situations, their perspective, and their behavior unique. For members of various groups to benefit from mental health services, these factors must be acknowledged and openly addressed in the therapeutic process.

Although much work has been done in developing strategies for conducting counseling and therapy from a multicultural perspective, some psychologists feel this work is too broad and leads to overgeneralizations. They call for more cultural specificity in theoretical constructs, research strategies, and treatment modalities (Boyd-Franklin, 1989; Constantine, Redington, & Graham, 2009; Nobles, 1986; Parham, 2002; Yang, 1997). In speaking about the needs of African American clients, Parham (2002) stated, "Although efforts at multicultural counseling have vastly improved over what historically existed in the profession, they are, nonetheless, limited in their utility because they lack the cultural specificity necessary to more effectively intervene with the African American population" (p. 9). Parham (2002) disagreed with the notion that a generic set of multicultural skills can be learned by all counselors and therapists that will make them effective with individuals from all different backgrounds.

A large and growing literature describes strategies for tailoring mental health services to various culturally diverse populations. Database searches reveal hundreds of articles focused on therapeutic approaches for different cultural groups. Some journals focus on particular groups (e.g., *Hispanic Journal of Behavioral Sciences, Journal of Black Psychology*). Most books on multicultural counseling include chapters that highlight the issues faced by particular groups and make suggestions for working with those groups (Atkinson, 2004; Pedersen, Draguns, Lonner, & Trimble, 2008; D. W. Sue & Sue, 2016). In addition, books dedicated to treatment issues for nearly every group are available, including gays and lesbians (Perez, DeBord, & Bieschke, 2000), women (Barret & Logan, 2002; Enns, 1997; Sechzer, Pfafflin, Denmark, Griffin, & Blumenthal, 1996), Asian/Pacific Americans (G. C. N. Hall & Okazaki, 2002; E. Lee, 1997), Latinxs (Falicov, 1998; Zea & Garcia, 1997), American Indians/Alaska Natives (Witko, 2005), and African Americans (R. L. Jones, 1998; Parham, 2002).

Example of a Culture-Specific Approach: African-Centered Psychology

African American psychologists have made great strides in developing theory, research, and methods specifically for African Americans over the past 30 years. Major theorists include Akbar (1981), Baldwin (1981), L. J. Myers (1988), Nobles (1991), Parham (2002), and Parham and Helms (1985a, 1985b). This has been called *Black psychology* or *Afrocentric, African-centered*, or *African* psychology (Grills, 2002; Parham, Ajamu, & White, 2011; J. L. White, 1972). These therapists contend that, within the Western European worldview, African Americans have been portrayed as deficient and inferior, and the use of these approaches led to the misdiagnosis and mistreatment of African Americans in the mental health system (Parham, 2002). Therefore, African psychology purports that the main problem for people of African descent is their adoption of the Western European worldview, and the key to mental health for African Americans is the renunciation of Western values and beliefs and the adoption of an African worldview (Mazama, 2001). According to Parham et al. (2011), "Mental health for Blacks requires that a person be centered in, grounded in, or otherwise in touch with one's African-American makeup, with a foundational identity, a healthy self-esteem, and a collective sense of consciousness" (p. 141). In other words, African-centered psychologists develop theories and methods based in traditional African values and philosophies, with the specific goal of helping African American clients align their ideal sense of self, or the person they wish to become, with their true African American makeup (Parham et al., 2011).

African-centered psychologists believe that, to work effectively with African American clients, a therapist must understand African culture and the basic assumptions of African psychology. The therapist must then use these principles to facilitate understanding, assessment, and treatment of his or her client (Parham & Parham, 2002). First, the therapist must understand the nature of humanity from an Afrocentric worldview, which says that all human beings are created in the image of the Creator and are therefore divine; thus, people of African descent are very spiritual. The spirit, or life force or energy, is the core of human existence, and everything on the planet is connected. This leads people of African descent to have a collective consciousness; we come to know ourselves through our relationships with others and with nature. African American spirituality is formed through individual and collective struggle and how, as a people, they have coped with the pain and suffering of their mistreatment. Another major issue for African Americans is identity, or the critical question, "Who am I?" For African Americans, the answer to this question is forged by both individual and sociocultural forces. Often, for African Americans, their sense of identity is contaminated by the racism, discrimination, and oppression present in their environment. But identity can also serve as a buffer against these negative forces, as a bond with others who share their culture, as a coping strategy that helps the individual adapt to different environments, as a means of breaking down barriers to intimacy and connection, as a sense of pride and achievement, and as a bridge that connects them to their past, present, and future (Parham & Parham, 2002). In short, Parham et al. (2011) define mental health for African Americans as "being in touch with one's spiritual essence, having knowledge of oneself as a cultural being, having favorable impressions of oneself and one's people, being able to develop and successfully navigate the dynamics of relations with others, and accessing the 'collective' for one's source of sustenance and support" (p. 141).

In African psychology the therapist's role is that of healer. Healers are individuals who give up the objective, distant, rational stance of traditional Western therapies and who demonstrate a willingness to actively engage in the healing process and to join and connect with clients on a deeper level. To achieve this, healers must be committed to their own process of transformation. Overall, the healer's role is to promote health, wholeness, and wisdom in themselves and their clients (Parham & Parham, 2002).

Once therapists understand the theory and use it to assess and build a relationship with the client, the next step in providing effective African-centered psychotherapy is the use of appropriate strategies (Parham & Parham, 2002). Some of the suggested strategies are similar to those of other therapeutic approaches, such as the importance of working with clients to set clear, specific goals; empowering clients to believe that they can effect change in their lives; helping clients recognize attitudes and behaviors that impede personal growth; and teaching clients how to problem solve. Other suggested strategies are less typical. For example, to connect with clients, Parham (2002) suggested using things such as rituals, music, poetry, and changing the setting. It is believed that the rhythms, melody, and harmony of the music stimulate the senses, emotions, and spirituality of the client and help set the proper mood for therapy. Instead of doing traditional talk therapy in a traditional office, clinicians are encouraged to find settings where other activities can take place, such as walking, running, drumming, and dancing. Therapists are encouraged to utilize clients' strengths, the attributes that have allowed clients to meet the demands placed on them by society and to overcome adversity, to understand the environmental forces that lead to client distress, and to help clients gain a balanced awareness of both the positive and the negative aspects of their experiences and the functions that their behaviors serve. Therapists who work with African American clients are encouraged to think less about what is "normal" and instead think about what might be functional or adaptive for their clients' situation or circumstances. They are also encouraged to help clients become aware of undiscovered aspects of themselves, things they are passionate about, and their spiritual energy. The use of metaphor can be helpful in these areas. The topic of identity is also important. Therapists may need to help clients become comfortable with themselves as African Americans, to develop a positive sense of their Blackness as an integral part of their self-esteem and self-worth. In accomplishing these tasks, African-centered therapists may be more directive in giving advice and counsel. Therapists may also act as advocates for their clients by connecting them to services, institutions, and agencies that can benefit them (Parham et al., 2011; Parham & Parham, 2002). Although some aspects of African-centered psychotherapy are similar to other approaches, some aspects are distinct, designed to incorporate the history, values, beliefs, and practices of African Americans.

The following case described by Parham (2002) illustrates some of the issues unique to working with clients of African descent.:

> Roland is a 29-year-old African American male (self-identified) residing in a medium-sized urban area. He has been encouraged by his wife to seek treatment because they are concerned about his recent behavior: He is constantly on edge, frequently agitated and angry, and otherwise moody. He has also begun to spend more time away from home, involving himself in assorted activities (working out, etc.). This pattern has persisted for approximately two months and seems to coincide with a change in Roland's job three months ago when he was assigned a new supervisor. Roland has been with his company for four and a half years.
>
> His new supervisor (a 44-year-old White male) exhibits a management style characterized by little encouragement, praise, or support. Instead, Roland receives constant critique, autocratic directives, and feels he is being constantly watched. Even though his work performance has been rated as "good" and he has been a steady performer, he now believes he is being targeted and unfairly treated because of his race.
>
> In addition, Roland has also begun to doubt his own sense of competence and worth, despite believing he does a reasonably good job. He is looking for help to resolve some of his emotional distress. Roland has no previous psychiatric history and denies the use of any substances (alcohol or drugs). (adapted from Parham, 2002)

From a Western European perspective, Roland's symptoms might be seen as indicative of depression, anxiety, or even psychosis. Depending on his or her theoretical orientation, a

Western therapist might suggest medication, focus on how Roland's past relationships in his family of origin are affecting his current relationships with his wife and boss, or focus on helping him change the negative thoughts he has about his work environment and his personal abilities. However, an African-centered psychologist would examine the larger forces affecting Roland, such as the institutionalized racism of the company he works for and perhaps the subtle racism expressed through the distant critical attitude and behavior of his boss. Instead of being seen as pathological, Roland's symptoms might be understood as natural reactions to these larger forces. The African-centered therapist might try to help Roland achieve greater balance between his sense of self achieved through his work (a very Western/American idea) and the more positive aspects of himself achieved in other areas, such as his relationships with his wife and other family members. An African-centered therapist might also help Roland assess his passions and whether his current job is in line with them. These are two very different ways of interpreting Roland's particular issues. Which approach do you think would be more effective?

Treatment Issues and Strategies for Sexual Minorities

In 2000, the APA published *Guidelines for Psychological Practice with Lesbian, Gay, and Bisexual Clients*, which was revised in 2012. The document includes 15 guidelines. For example, the guidelines encourage therapists to recognize that homosexuality is not a mental disorder, recognize how their own attitudes about sexual minorities influence their practice, understand the impact of social stigma on the mental health of sexual minorities and how they present in therapy, gain knowledge about and respect for homosexual relationships, understand the unique challenges faced by homosexual parents and the complex family structure for some sexual minorities, and understand the effect of an individual's sexual orientation on his or her family relationships. Several authors have suggested specific strategies for implementing these guidelines (Pachankis & Goldfried, 2013; Perez et al., 2000; Pope, 2008). The following story illustrates some of the issues unique to clients from sexual minority groups:

> It is very interesting how some people feel the need to try and impose their thoughts and "visions" on to others. They seem to have a need for those around them to "stay within the lines" of their perspective.
>
> Letting my "family" (those I have adopted as my own) know about my relationship with my partner was a very difficult decision for me. In telling those close to me I was concerned that it would change how they felt about me, that they would quite possibly see me in a different way, even to the point of no longer being part of my life.
>
> I had heard many stories from other women who chose to tell their family and friends about their same-gender relationships and lost some of those close to them in that process. In my case I am very blessed. Everyone who means much to me was very accepting of my life partner and my lifestyle with the exception of one of my friends.
>
> This individual (in my own view) has a need to have everything in its place and in the way that she sees fit. She has very specific beliefs about what's right and appropriate, especially when it comes to relationships. I had told all of my other friends about my relationship with my partner except this one. After a while it became difficult to avoid the subject in her company. I had to tell her. I did not want to because I didn't want to have to deal with whatever came out of her mouth. She can, at times, say things that are very hurtful.

Anyway, I told her about my relationship. She immediately responded with, "That's not my vision for you." She saw me married to a man with a few children. She also stated that this was just a "fad" I was going through. Never did she ask if I were happy or how I came to this decision. In future conversations she never asked about my partner. When I mentioned her she pretty much ignored what I said, but she would go on and on about her relationship with her husband. She totally and completely discounted the relationship—and in essence me—as insignificant.

For quite some time prior to telling her I had not shared very much of myself with her. I no longer trusted my inner self with her based on hurtful things she'd said to me in the past. My telling her about this very important relationship in my life, and her response further indicated to me she is not open to receive anything that is not sanctioned and approved of by her. Since then I've withdrawn from her even further.

—Kathy, 40+-year-old African American bisexual

Kathy's story illustrates some of the unique issues faced by sexual minorities (i.e., gays, lesbians, bisexual, and transgender individuals). Some of these issues include coming out, heterosexism, homophobia, reactions of family members and friends, and religious views on homosexuality. Kathy struggled with coming out to her friend.

Coming out is not something that heterosexual people and those from other minority groups, such as women, and those from physically visible racial backgrounds (e.g., African Americans, Asian/Pacific Americans) typically have to worry about. In our society, it is automatically assumed that you are heterosexual. When you walk into a room, most people form judgments about your racial group membership based on your appearance, although people from racially mixed backgrounds whose appearance is ambiguous often get the question "What are you?"

Coming out has serious risks. Being openly gay or lesbian opens the person up to potential discrimination and harassment and can even be life-threatening. (Think about what happened to Matthew Shepard, the University of Wyoming student who was beaten to death in 1998 because he was gay.) Individuals who come out to their families also risk rejection by family members. Kathy talked about the family of friends that she adopted. Sexual minorities face heterosexist attitudes or the belief that being heterosexual is normal and best (Barret & Logan, 2002). Heterosexism was evident in the lines drawn by Kathy's friend in her vision that Kathy should have a husband and children. There is a growing literature on working with sexual minority clients, and the APA published guidelines for therapists working with these groups (American Psychological Association, 2000). In short, culturally sensitive therapy with sexual minority clients requires that the therapist pay attention to these issues.

Measuring multicultural competence has been a subject of much research (Coleman, 1996; Constantine & Ladany, 2001; Owen, Leach, Wampold, & Rodolfa, 2011; Pope-Davis & Coleman, 1997). Although such general competencies have gained support, others suggest that specialized theories and techniques for specific populations be measured for the effectiveness of such approaches. This would be a natural next step and is a challenge for researchers in the next few decades. This leads us to a discussion of evidence based practice.

Evidence-Based Practice in Psychology

In Chapter 1 we briefly mentioned the three main *forces* in psychology—psychoanalysis, humanism, and behaviorism. Each of these forces developed into a form of psychotherapy with different strategies for helping individuals overcome psychological problems. For example, in psychoanalysis, Sigmund Freud believed it was necessary to uncover deep-seated, unconscious conflicts from a person's past for the individual to get better. In his humanistic approach, Carl Rogers believed that if the therapist provided the right kind of therapeutic relationship, clients would naturally grow and develop. Behaviorists, such as B. F. Skinner, believed problematic behaviors could be changed through rewards and punishments. Although these were three of the original approaches to psychotherapy, Someah, Edwards, and Beutler (2017) suggested there may currently be more than 1,200 major and minor approaches to psychotherapy. With all of these choices, which approach is the most effective overall? What about for specific disorders? Specific individuals? People from particular groups?

Psychologists have pondered these questions for decades, which led to an entire area of research on the effectiveness of counseling and psychotherapy. In other words, psychologists recognized the need to empirically identify best practices in mental health care. According to the American Psychological Association Presidential Task Force on Evidence-Based Practice in Psychology (2006), EBPP is defined as "the integration of the best available research with clinical expertise in the context of patient characteristics, culture, and preferences," and its purpose is "to promote effective psychological practice and enhance public health by applying empirically supported principles of psychological assessment, case formulation, therapeutic relationship, and intervention" (p. 273). According to the task force, effective mental health treatment involves three major components: (a) best available research, (b) clinical expertise, and (c) patient characteristics (see Figure 9.2).

First, EBPP means applying the best available research evidence when selecting and applying mental health treatments. Early studies focused on the search for *empirically supported treatments* (ESTs; also known as empirically validated treatments or research-supported treatments). These specific treatment strategies have proven effective in controlled experiments known as *randomized controlled trials* (RCTs). In RCTs, participants with a particular disorder are randomly assigned to a treatment, control, or placebo group (described in Chapter 2). Then, the specific intervention is administered to the participants in the treatment group and their response to the treatment is measured and compared with that of participants in the control or placebo group. To be labeled an EST, the treatment must be superior to a placebo in two or more RCTs, be equivalent to another well-established treatment in several RCTs, or be effective in a series of single-case controlled designs where the results for individuals are evaluated pre-and posttreatment (Chambless & Hollon, 1998). Typically, once an EST is established, a manual is published to guide individual therapists in using that

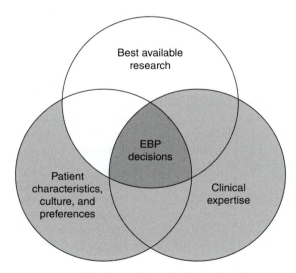

FIGURE 9.2 The three pillars of evidence-based practices. From "Evidence-Based Practices With Ethnic Minorities: Strange Bedfellows No More," by E. Morales and J. C. Norcross, 2010, *Journal of Clinical Psychology, 66*(8), p. 824.

particular treatment. This helps standardize the treatment and ensure that individual therapists administer the intervention consistently and effectively.

Results of this research have been fruitful and there are now published lists of ESTs. For example, the Society of Clinical Psychology (2016) maintains a list of ESTs on their website that can be searched by treatment or by diagnosis. Examples of some specific, well-established ESTs include cognitive therapy for depression, cognitive behavioral therapy for anorexia nervosa, exposure therapies for specific phobias, eye movement desensitization and reprocessing for PTSD, social skills training for schizophrenia, and dialectical behavior therapy for borderline personality disorder. Another list is available through the Substance Abuse and Mental Health Services Administration, National Registry of Evidence-Based Programs and Practices (2018). The purpose of this database is to provide the public with reliable information on ESTs for substance abuse and other mental health issues. Listings in the database include the title of the program, descriptions of each intervention, its intended outcomes, and the related research findings on its effectiveness. Members of the public can search the database using keywords, such as topic, type of disorder, areas of interest, and target population. As of June 2018, this registry listed 577 interventions.

The RCTs are only one form of research useful in conducting EBPP. Some psychologists have criticized the early evidence-based movement for relying too heavily on RCTs (Levant & Sperry, 2016; D. W. Sue & Sue, 2016). Currently, EBPP is viewed as a broader decision-making process that includes the integration of multiple sources of information and evidence into the intervention process (Levant & Sperry, 2016). Other types of research evidence used in EBPP include clinical observation, qualitative research, case studies, and epidemiologic research (American Psychological Association Presidential Task Force on Evidence-Based Practice, 2006).

The second critical component of EBPP is clinical expertise. In other words, mental health professionals must demonstrate competence in areas related to positive outcomes in psychotherapy. Expertise comes from both clinical and scientific education and training, an understanding of different theoretical perspectives, experience, self-reflection, knowledge of the research literature, and a commitment to continued professional education and training. Clinical expertise is demonstrated in all clinical activities, such as building the therapeutic alliance, assessment, treatment planning, goal setting, selection and implementation of treatment strategies, and monitoring patient progress (American Psychological Association Presidential Task Force on Evidence-Based Practice in Psychology, 2006).

For example, the outcome of therapy depends on more than just the specific strategies used; it also depends on the ability of the therapist to form a strong working alliance with the client. In fact, research suggests that the quality of the relationship between the therapist and the client may contribute up to 30% of the variance in therapeutic outcome (M. J. Lambert & Barley, 2001). Research in this area led to the identification of *empirically supported relationships*, or specific relationship variables that contribute to successful outcomes in therapy. Some of these empirically supported relationships include the ability to form a strong emotional bond with the client, to express empathy for the client's concerns, to work collaboratively to formulate therapeutic goals, to deal with reactions and emotions that may arise in the course of therapy, and to be genuine (Ackerman et al., 2001).

The third critical component of EBPP refers to patient (or client) characteristics. As noted previously, the task force definition states that EBPP includes responsiveness to client characteristics, culture, and personal preferences. This includes factors such as age, gender, race, and ethnicity, but also cultural values, beliefs, and practices. For example, one form of treatment may be a good fit for adults, but not for adolescents and children. Another treatment might emphasize more individualistic concerns and therefore not be a good fit for clients from more collectivistic backgrounds. A female client might prefer to see a female therapist, or a Christian client a Christian therapist, and so on. Ideally, EBPP considers all these possibilities.

Culture is most clearly addressed in the third component of EBPP; however, multicultural psychologists argue that culture should be considered in all three aspects of EBPP. The fields of evidence-based practice and multicultural psychology originated from very different sources and initially were critical of one another. Advocates of EBPP accused multicultural psychologists of being more influenced by identity politics than empirical research, and proponents of multicultural psychology accused those in EBPP of ignoring the concerns of diverse populations and having too narrow and rigid a focus on controlled experiments. In the early years of research on ESTs, few included significant numbers of ethnic group members in their samples, and they typically did not report results of group differences. In addition, few treatments were developed specifically for diverse populations (Morales & Norcross, 2010). More recently, these two fields have converged into *culturally sensitive evidence-based practice.* Morales and Norcross (2010) emphasize the importance of this interdependence and state, "Multiculturalism without strong research risks becoming an empty political value and EBP without cultural sensitivity risks irrelevancy" (p. 823). In addition, clinicians must be skilled at addressing clients' lifestyles, cultural backgrounds, linguistic backgrounds, and life circumstances. In other words, clinicians must be multiculturally competent (Zane, Bernal, & Leong, 2016).

One way to meld these two areas (EBPP and MCT) is through cultural adaptation of ESTs (D. W. Sue & Sue, 2016). As mentioned earlier, some multicultural psychologists criticized the movement toward ESTs because most of the studies did not include significant numbers of people of color in their samples and they did not specifically discuss ethnic group differences in their results. One solution to this has been to adapt ESTs for application with specific cultural groups. *Cultural adaptation* is defined as "the systematic modification of an evidence-based treatment (EBT) or intervention protocol to consider language, culture, and context in such a way that it is compatible with the client's cultural patterns, meanings, and values" (Bernal, Jimeniz-Chaffey, & Domenech Rodríguez, 2009, p. 362). In other words, cultural adaptation of an EST might include conducting therapy in the client's preferred language, matching the race/ethnicity of the client and therapist, incorporating cultural values, incorporating cultural metaphors and sayings, and considering the impact of contextual variables such as acculturation, discrimination, and SES (Bernal, Bonilla, & Bellido, 1995; T. B. Smith, Domenech Rodríguez, & Bernal, 2011; D. W. Sue & Sue, 2016). Cultural adaptation meta-analyses have verified the importance of adapting treatments for patient retention and outcomes. These meta-analyses focused on verifying the importance of cultural adaptation processes (T. B. Smith et al., 2011), the client's understanding of his or her illness (Benish, Quintana, & Wampold, 2011), and prevention contexts (Hall et al., 2016). There is also evidence that clinicians naturally adapt their treatments to individual clients and that they follow many of the same processes suggested in the research literature, with good results (Kofslofsky & Domenech Rodríguez, 2017).

An example of culturally sensitive EBPP is seen in Hwang (2016), who took an evidence-based manual for cognitive-behavioral therapy for depression and adapted it for use with Chinese Americans. The first phase of the project involved collaborating with community mental health clinics in California that primarily serviced Asian American clients. Next, the researchers generated knowledge by conducting focus groups with mental health professionals (e.g., psychologists, psychiatrists, social workers, marriage and family therapists) who worked in these agencies as individuals with expertise and insight in working with depressed Asian American clients. Other nontraditional "experts" also participated in the focus groups, including Buddhist monks and nuns, traditional Chinese medicine practitioners, and spiritual and religious Taoist masters. Participation of these indigenous healers helped ensure that cultural adaptations of the treatment accurately and adequately incorporated Chinese cultural beliefs. The second phase of the project took information obtained in the first phase and integrated this knowledge with the generic cognitive-behavioral therapy program. This resulted in a new, culturally-adapted treatment manual titled *Improving Your Mood: A Culturally Responsive and Holistic Approach to Treating Depression in Chinese Americans* (Hwang, 2008). The new manual included a variety of cultural adaptations. For example, the manual was written with various translations of Chinese in mind to facilitate comprehension across diverse Chinese groups (e.g., those from mainland China versus Taiwan or Hong Kong). The manual also incorporated Chinese metaphorical sayings, or *chengyu,* into the treatment plan. The English translation of one such chengyu says, "If a mountain is obstructing your way, then find a road around it. If there is no road around it, then you need to find or make a path of your own path. If you can't find a way around it or create a path, then you need to change the way you think and feel about the problem'" (Hwang, 2016, p. 298). This metaphor merges nicely with general cognitive-behavioral therapy problem-solving strategies, which teach clients to try their best to solve a problem, be flexible in their thinking, and tackle the problem from many different angles. If the problem cannot be solved, then clients are encouraged to change the way they think and feel about the problem, which also reduces stress. The adapted treatment also incorporated the Chinese cultural concept of *qi,* or the vital life force that flows through our bodies. In traditional Chinese medicine, imbalances in *qi* are considered the cause of most human ailments, whether physical, mental, or emotional. This program teaches clients that cognitive reframing (or changing the way they think) can help restore balance in one's *qi* and enhance intra- and interpersonal health. Therapists also incorporate discussions around issues that may contribute to depression in Chinese Americans, such as immigration, acculturation, intergenerational conflict, and family communication styles. In the third phase of the project, the same therapists who participated in the original focus groups reviewed the new treatment manual, gave feedback, and made suggestions for improvement. Phase four involved testing the new manual through a series of RCTs with Chinese American clients at community mental health centers. They assessed treatment outcome with measures of symptom reduction, treatment satisfaction, premature dropout, formation of the therapeutic alliance, and attitudes toward psychotherapy. Finally, the fifth phase involved conducting interviews with both clients and therapists about their experiences participating in the treatment program. Thus, Hwang's (2016) program specifically illustrates how ESTs can be adapted for use with diverse groups and how multiculturalism as a whole is an integral part of EBPP.

Social Justice Counseling/Psychotherapy

In traditional counseling and psychotherapy, a person who is experiencing troubling thoughts, feelings, and/or behaviors seeks help from an individual counselor or therapist. Typically, that person sees the therapist/counselor in his or her office, one time per week, for a 50-minute session. In sessions, the therapist conducts an assessment of the person's problems and then works with that individual to decrease the troubling thoughts, feelings, and behaviors and replace them with more adaptive ones. The specific strategies used to accomplish this vary depending on the therapist's theoretical orientation. Most traditional approaches to counseling and psychotherapy place primary responsibility for the cause and the solution on the individual person.

An ecological approach to counseling and psychotherapy examines the interaction between persons and their environments. In other words, instead of looking only to the individual for the cause and solution, there is a focus on environmental forces that may impact the individual and influence his or her symptoms (Bronfrenbrenner, 1979; Fouad, Gerstein, & Toporek, 2006). For example, go back to the case of Chanda earlier in this chapter. If one assesses Chanda's symptoms only from an individual point of view, she gets diagnosed with schizophrenia. However, when one considers the traumatic environmental conditions she encountered as a Cambodian refugee, the diagnosis changes to PTSD. Thus, consideration of environmental factors results in more accurate diagnosis and treatment. The impact of environmental forces is especially relevant when talking about multicultural communities. In addition to the stressors experienced by everyone else, members of these communities contend with additional stressors such as racism, sexism, homophobia, poverty, and immigrant status (Choudhuri, Santiago-Rivera, & Garrett, 2012; D. W. Sue & Sue, 2013; West-Olatunji & Conwill, 2011). A social justice perspective to counseling and psychotherapy says one must address issues at the environmental level, not just the individual level.

A social justice approach says therapists must challenge, and even reverse, traditional assumptions of therapy (D. W. Sue & Sue, 2013). For example, traditional psychology says the problem primarily resides in the individual; a social justice approach says the problem may reside in the social system. Traditional psychology says behaviors that violate social norms are unhealthy and maladaptive; social justice counseling says behaviors that violate social norms may be healthy responses to unhealthy situations. The goal of traditional psychology is remediation of the problem; social justice says prevention is a more effective solution in the long run. A traditional counselor/therapist seeks to maintain the status quo by helping the individual fit in or become a "good citizen"; a social justice counselor/therapist recognizes the need for broader organizational, institutional, and social change (D. W. Sue & Sue, 2016).

In Chapter 1 we described social justice as one of the basic values of multicultural psychology. Social justice is defined as giving "equal opportunities to all people, regardless of racial, class, sex, or ability (Moody, Ybarra, & Neighbors, 2009). Social justice involves actively working toward fairness and equity in the distribution of resources, rights, power, and opportunities for marginalized individuals and groups. What does it mean when we apply these principles to the treatment of mental health issues? D. W. Sue and Sue (2016) define *social justice counseling/ therapy* as an "active philosophy and approach" that:

1. aims to produce conditions that allow for equal access and opportunity
2. reduces or eliminates disparities in education, health care, employment, and other areas that lower the quality of life for affected populations
3. encourages mental health professionals to consider micro, meso, and macro levels in the assessment, diagnosis, and treatment of client and client systems
4. broadens the role of the helping professional to include not only counselor/therapist but advocate, consultant, psychoeducator, change agent, community worker, and so on. (p. 109)

Crethar, Torres Rivera, and Nash (2008) define social justice counseling as "a multifaceted approach to mental health care" in which clinicians work to promote both individual development and the common good. The authors noted, "Social justice counseling includes empowerment of the individual as well as active confrontation of injustice and inequality in society" (p. 270). The work of social justice counselors and therapists is guided by four main principles: *equity, access, participation,* and *harmony.* As described in Chapter 1, equity refers to the fair distribution of resources, rights, and responsibilities and the ability of individuals to access the knowledge, power, resources, and services necessary to have a certain quality of life. The principle of participation says individuals have the right to participate in and/or be consulted on decisions that affect their lives and the social systems with which they interact. An example of this is the right to vote. The fourth principle, harmony, says that individual rights must be considered within the context of the community as a whole. In other words, individual needs and wants must be balanced against the common good. In a socially just society, sometimes individuals must sacrifice personal goals to benefit society as a whole. For example, an individual person might support paying higher taxes for universal health care, even though he or she already has good private insurance, to ensure that others in society also have the same access to quality health care.

A social justice perspective urges therapists to step out of their traditional roles and become advocates for social change. They must work not only to improve the lives of individual clients, but also to improve society as a whole (Crethar et al., 2008; D. W. Sue & Sue, 2013; Vera & Speight, 2013). This means getting out of their offices and going beyond one-on-one therapy sessions to work in alternative sites (e.g., client homes, churches, community organizations), engaging in alternative activities, and playing alternative helping roles (e.g., advocate, consultant, advisor, organizational change agent, facilitator; Atkinson, Thompson, & Grant, 1993; Constantine, Hage, Kindaichi, & Bryant, 2007; Kiselica & Robinson, 2001; D. W. Sue & Sue, 2013). For example, Dr. Terrence Roberts, a psychology professor and licensed clinical psychologist and one of the "Little Rock Nine" who integrated Central High School in Little Rock, Arkansas, in 1957, returned 30 years later to Little Rock to serve as a consultant to the Little Rock school system. Thirty years later, the city of Little Rock was still under federal supervision in terms of integrating their schools. Dr. Roberts visited schools and classrooms; spoke with teachers, students, administrators, and local politicians; put together programs for training of teachers and staff; helped provide some of this training; and testified in court (T. Roberts, 2009). These are not traditional roles, settings, or activities for psychologists, and some would argue that therapists and counselors should remain neutral and not become involved in politics and social action. However, a social justice perspective and the basic values of multicultural psychology say they must.

Go back to the case of Denise at the beginning of the chapter. From a more traditional perspective, how would we explain Denise's symptoms? She came in complaining of depression, loneliness, sadness, anger, and low self-esteem. Traditional theories of counseling would suggest that she suffers from a chemical imbalance or she is interpreting her situation from a negative point of view. In terms of treatment, this would mean referring Denise to a psychiatrist for antidepressant medication and helping her learn strategies to change her negative thinking patterns to more positive ones. However, Denise's therapist took more of a social justice approach. Her therapist acknowledged the environmental forces of racism, sexism, and homophobia Denise experienced as a triple minority. In sessions, Denise said she felt oppressed by people in her family and social circle. She also talked about her own internalized racism, sexism, and homophobia. The therapist struck a balance between helping Denise take some individual responsibility for her social interactions and acknowledging that her feelings of mistrust came from the oppression she experienced. Denise's therapist could have taken an even stronger social justice stance by acting as an advocate for Denise with her family. Perhaps she could have invited the family in for a session and supported Denise in talking with them about how she appreciated the racial pride they instilled in her, but not their homophobia. The therapist could have also advocated at the university level. It appears the university had some resources, such as the lesbian support group, but perhaps more institutional-level change could help the university environment become more welcoming and comfortable for diverse students.

In sum, social justice is one of the basic values of multicultural psychology, and it can be applied to the diagnosis and treatment of mental disorders. Social justice counseling interprets mental health issues at multiple levels—the individual, social, institutional, and cultural levels. Therefore, social justice counseling says that interventions must also go beyond the individual level. This involves therapists and counselors stepping out of their traditional roles and getting involved in advocacy, public policy, and social change.

Summary

Many issues are related to culture and mental health, including the prevalence of disorders in different groups, how symptoms are expressed, and how disorders are diagnosed. The American mental health system uses the *DSM,* currently in its fifth edition (*DSM-5*). Although there are many similarities in disorders across the world, there are also some cultural syndromes. These syndromes seem to be specific expressions of disorders that are connected to cultural values and traditions. For example, although many people may not conceptualize them as such, eating disorders may be a cultural syndrome in the United States.

Treatment issues include barriers to effective multicultural treatment and efforts at overcoming those barriers, such as training mental health professionals to be multiculturally competent, providing monolingual clients with therapists able to communicate with them, cultural matching between client and therapist, and culture-specific therapies and culturally adapted evidence-based practices. One mismatch between many populations of color and mainstream modes of treatment is that modes of treatment are based on values of the majority culture, which may not resonate with the diverse populations that are being treated. In addition, effective mental health treatment of individuals from diverse backgrounds must take into consideration the social environmental forces that impact their well-being, such as poverty, racism, and immigrant status. This requires an action-oriented, social justice approach.

In conclusion, we cannot emphasize enough that, like every other aspect of human behavior, culture influences mental health. If psychotherapy is be effective in helping people from culturally diverse backgrounds, culture must be an integral part of any approach.

Food for Thought

Most of us have encountered mental health difficulties in our lives. Have you ever been so anxious before taking a test that you could not sleep the night before or concentrate on your studies for the test? Have you ever broken up with a boyfriend or a girlfriend and become very sad about it, making it difficult for you to enjoy things you usually enjoy? These are common forms of mental health difficulties, called anxiety and depression. When people encounter issues such as these, they usually can get through a brief period of discomfort and then begin feeling back to normal. However, when these problems persist, professional intervention might be needed. Some people can find appropriate mental health professionals to help them get through these periods without much difficulty. Just think how it might be if you could not find a therapist with whom you feel comfortable enough to be able to discuss your problems. Many people from backgrounds different from therapists have exactly these problems.

Critical Thinking Questions

1. Have you or anyone in your family ever needed the services of mental health professionals? If so, what was your/their experience like? Would you/they ever go again? How comfortable did you/they feel with the therapist? Was the therapist of the same racioethnic group as you or your family member, or was he or she from a different group?

2. If you have seen a mental health professional in therapy, was your therapist of the same gender as you, or was he or she of a different gender? Did you discuss issues related to gender? If so, what were they? If not, why not? If you have never seen a mental health professional, ask these questions of someone who has and who is open to discussing such matters.

3. What do you think of African-centered psychotherapy for African American clients? How might therapy be different for you if you were to be in therapy with someone who focuses on a particularly important demographic characteristic for you, for example, your gender, your religion, or your sexual orientation?

4. If you have needed to see a mental health professional, how easy or difficult was it to find such a professional? How easy or difficult was it to find a professional who spoke your preferred language? How easy or difficult was it to find transportation to this professional?

5. What do you think are the reasons for racial/ethnic group differences in the rates of mental disorders? Why do you think people of color often have lower rates of mental disorder than European Americans?

6. Which approach do you think is more important—looking for mental disorders common across cultures or looking for cultural syndromes? What are the pros and cons of each approach?

7. What do you think about social justice counseling/psychotherapy? Is it appropriate for mental health professionals to become involved in social justice issues?

8. What do you think about empirically supported treatments? Do you think only treatments that have met the criteria should be used? Do you think using a manual to provide counseling or psychotherapy is effective for every client?

CHAPTER 10

Where Do We Go From Here? Building Multicultural Competence

Photograph by ESB Professional/Shutterstock

The Three S's of Similarity
        Simple
        Safe
        Sane
Examining Your Biases, Prejudices, and Stereotypes
Learning About Your Own Culture
Understanding Other Worldviews
        Learning Key Historical Events
        Becoming Aware of Sociopolitical Issues
        Knowing Basic Values and Beliefs
        Understanding Cultural Practices
        Knowing the Dynamics of Racism, Discrimination, and Stereotyping
Development of Culturally Appropriate Interpersonal Skills
        Education and Training
        Experience and Practice
        Saying "I Don't Know" and Asking Questions
        Travel
        Speaking Up for Others: Being an Ally
        Speaking Up for Oneself: Comfort With Difficult Dialogues
        An Attitude of Discovery and Courage
        Developing Empathy
A Change in Worldview
Summary

Learning Objectives

Reading this chapter will help you to:
- define multicultural competence;
- identify components of resistances to increasing your multicultural competence;
- identify strategies for increasing your multicultural competence;
- explain how to identify your own biases;
- recognize the differences between your own and others' worldviews; and
- distinguish between a stagnant approach to multicultural competence and a dynamic approach to increasing your multicultural skills.

Today I got a job at Disneyland. I'm so excited. I think I'm glad to be part of a working society now. Well, during the interview process I was asked a few questions. During one of my responses I was able to talk about my major, GEMS (Gender, Ethnic, and Multicultural Studies), and relate the importance of multiculturalism. I told the interviewer that I was well versed in dealing with different groups of people. I said that I realize that Disney deals with all types of people from all over the world. I said that being culturally aware and being sensitive to different customs and people are useful assets to working in a diverse atmosphere such as Disneyland.

    To my surprise the gentleman truly liked my answer. He said that that was right. So I learned the value of being diverse and culturally sensitive. It made me feel good that the education that I am receiving is going to be of some value and use in the real world. I think that Disney is one of those companies that rely on people from different cultures and backgrounds as the bread and butter of their success.

—Jeannie, 20+-year-old African American student

In her story, Jeannie learned the value of multicultural competence. It illustrates the value of multicultural competence for everyone, not just counselors and therapists. In this chapter we will discuss in more detail what it means to be multiculturally competent and methods you can use to increase your personal level of multicultural competence.

Our main goal for this book is to increase your knowledge and understanding of multicultural issues and to bring those issues to life by sharing the personal stories of real people. By now you hopefully have a good understanding of the theories, concepts, and methods of multicultural psychology, and you are probably more aware of how these issues affect you and those with whom you live, study, and work every day. We hope that you are now motivated to continue learning and growing as a person living in a diverse world and that this is just one step in your journey toward multicultural competence.

What is multicultural competence? As we discussed in Chapter 9, **multicultural competence** means effectiveness in interacting with people who are different from you. It is the ability to have positive, productive, and enriching experiences with people from different backgrounds.

> **multicultural competence**—the ability to work and be effective with individuals who are of a culture different from yours.

The concept of multicultural competence originally related to the training of professional psychotherapists and counselors to work with clients from diverse backgrounds. However, multicultural competence is not just for people in the helping professions. Everyone can benefit from increasing their level of multicultural competence. In Chapter 1 we described the growing diversification and globalization of American society. Such diversity affects almost every aspect of life and increases the chances that you will interact with people who are different from you in many ways.

Right now, if you are studying in a library or some other public place, chances are you will see someone of a different background—a different race, gender, age, sexual orientation, religion, or physical ability. As you sit in your classes each day, most likely you are in rooms with people of different backgrounds. At work, there probably are coworkers, customers, clients, and supervisors from different backgrounds. What about in the building or neighborhood where you live? The stores you shop in every day? The point is that we live in a multicultural society and an increasingly diverse world.

Have you heard the term *global village*? It refers to the fact that the world is getting smaller and smaller every day because of increased mobility and technology that allow us to travel and communicate with people all over the world in an instant. We live and work in a world full of many kinds of people, and it is important to learn to interact with them effectively. For example, if you go to school with people from different backgrounds, it would benefit you to be able to study and do projects with them more effectively. When you are job hunting, it looks good to potential employers if you have skills in working with diverse groups of people. Multicultural competence is a vital skill for everyone today.

> Multicultural competence comes through: (1) academic study and reading; (2) becoming actively involved in the client's community; and (3) getting to know on a personal basis those who are different from you.
>
> (Ivey, Ivey, & Zalaquett, 2014, p. 43)

awareness of your own cultural attitudes—the part of multicultural competence that involves an individual being aware that his or her own attitudes may be heavily influenced by his or her own culture and may be different from that of a person with whom he or she is interacting.

understanding other worldviews—the part of multicultural competence that involves an individual's knowing that other cultures may have ways of seeing and interpreting the world that are markedly different from his or hers.

development of culturally appropriate interpersonal skills—the part of multicultural competence that involves an individual's knowing how to apply his or her knowledge about someone else's worldview to behaviors that appropriately take into account that knowledge, effecting positive change.

How to Increase Your Multicultural Competence: The Multicultural Competencies

In Chapter 9, we discussed the specific areas of multicultural competence for professional psychologists. The four general areas of professional multicultural competence are (a) counselor awareness of his or her own cultural values and biases, (b) an understanding of the client's worldview, (c) development of culturally appropriate intervention strategies and techniques, and (d) counseling and advocacy interventions. Each of these areas is further broken down into attitudes and beliefs, knowledge, skills, and actions (Ratts, Singh, Nassar-McMillan, Butler, & McCullough, 2015).

Although these competencies were developed for professional counselors and therapists, they can be applied to your everyday life. In other words, each person can use these guidelines to improve relationships and interact effectively with people of different backgrounds. If we apply these principles to everyday interactions, they could read as follows: (a) **awareness of your own cultural attitudes**, (b) **understanding other worldviews**, and (c) **development of culturally appropriate interpersonal skills**. Let us explore each of these areas further and see how they can be used to develop personal multicultural competence.

Awareness of Your Own Cultural Attitudes

Multicultural competence begins with awareness of your own attitudes and beliefs. An African proverb says, "Know thyself." This is an important starting point in the development of multicultural competence. Most multicultural psychologists would agree that understanding your own beliefs, values, perceptions, feelings, reactions, and so on is critical in effective interactions with others. One way to increase self-awareness is to know how you react in multicultural situations. In other words, how do you think, feel, and behave in situations with people who are different from you?

> I went out with a friend from school to celebrate the birthday of a friend of hers. After a nice dinner at [a restaurant], we decided to exercise our amazing vocal talents at a karaoke bar. We arrived at a long strip mall where the bar was located. I walked up to the door with my friend to meet the group from dinner, and we entered the building to see a small entry room connected to a long hallway. The room was painted a pale green and had off-white linoleum. The dim fluorescent lighting added to the dull setting of my surroundings. One girl from our group spoke to the Asian man at the front counter in Chinese, resulting in him leading us down the hallway to one of the doors spanning the hallway's walls. Inside we found a small room with bench seating around

a table with a small karaoke machine. A book with songs was passed around as we crammed in around the table to pick something to sing. I looked at the pages and all the words were in Chinese. I felt extremely uncomfortable as I realized not only was my friend Chinese but the rest of the group was as well and I was in a Chinese karaoke bar. Music started, showing a video on the screen with Chinese characters at the bottom. It looked like Chinese Backstreet Boys and my new friends sang along. I was extremely conscious of my Caucasian background that did not fit into the situation. I wanted to run out of there but I had no ride. I felt my face flush thinking I didn't belong. I tried but I must not have hidden my reaction well because my friend rescued me after a couple songs. My friend rescued me by asking me in a whisper if I was ready to go. I tried to hold back the enthusiasm behind my answer of "yes." She graciously took the responsibility for us leaving the fun, explaining that she had to go, giving me the opportunity to say my good-byes and a final exclamation of "happy birthday" to her friend. I felt relief flow through my body as we left the bar and drove away in the safety of her car.

—David, 20+-year-old European American student

Have you ever been in a situation like David's? What did you think? How did you feel? Did you, like David, try to make a quick escape? Chances are that you have been in a situation in which you felt very different and that, like David, you felt very uncomfortable. Such experiences are common and can help us understand the dynamics of multicultural interactions.

Dr. Shelly Harrell, a professor of psychology at Pepperdine University in California, describes the personal dynamics of difference to explain how people react in multicultural situations (1995; see also Barker-Hackett & Mio, 2000.). We can all think of times when we felt different. Perhaps as a child you were the last person picked for a dodgeball team, or were teased about being fat, or were the only person of your ethnicity in a class. Maybe you have been to a party where you felt out of place because you did not know anyone there. Maybe you were the target of taunts and prejudiced remarks for being gay. Often experiences with being different are tied to a range of negative emotions, such as fear, humiliation, rejection, alienation, sadness, and anger. Our natural tendency is to avoid such painful and uncomfortable experiences and to minimize or hide the differences.

I come from a predominately White, conservative town. The people who live there are not as open-minded as they could be. Growing up in that type of environment, then attending a school such as [school that is highly multiculturally composed] was indeed a culture shock. When I received my roommate's number whom I was supposed to live with, I was scared to call because I could not pronounce her name. I thought that it was going to be difficult to live with someone whose name I couldn't even say. When I finally called her she seemed nice, but it was hard to understand her. I had never been around an individual who had this type of accent. When it finally came to the week of moving into the dorms, I was scared. As I was moving in, I saw many types of individuals—Caucasian, African American, Asian, Peruvian. After I had lived there awhile I was used to meeting new individuals and was no longer as close-minded. Now I wish that people from my hometown could feel as I do about meeting different types of individuals and learning about their culture.

—Nina, 20+-year-old European American student

Nina's experiences going from a predominantly European American hometown to a culturally diverse college campus illustrate some of the dynamics of difference. In particular, Nina described the fear she felt at the prospect of living and interacting with her new roommate, who was obviously from a different culture. This type of fear and discomfort is normal in situations that are unfamiliar and where we feel different.

The Four F Reactions: Freeze, Flee, Fight, and Fright

Our natural human response to a situation that is unfamiliar is to interpret it as a potential threat. This activates the **freeze**, **flee**, **fight**, or **fright** response. When we interpret a situation as a potential threat, our natural instinct is to first stop and evaluate the situation (freeze). The next reaction is to try escape the danger (flee). If escape is not possible, we may become aggressive and try to fight off the danger (fight). If none of these strategies works, the next reaction may be to freeze up because we do not know what to do, because we hope we will not be noticed, or because escape is not possible and we are just waiting for the situation to be over (fright; Bracha et al., 2004). These strategies may work for a zebra being preyed upon by a lion or a cat that has been cornered by a dog. They may have also worked for human beings being chased by sabertooth tigers in the prehistoric era, but when we are talking about relationships between human beings today, these strategies may not be as effective.

freeze—to stop and try to interpret a situation that may be a potential threat.

flee—an attempt to escape an uncomfortable or potentially dangerous situation.

fight—if escape is not possible, we may attempt to be aggressive to defend against the danger we perceive.

fright—feelings of anxiety about the potentially dangerous situation.

The point is, it is natural to feel some stress, tension, or discomfort when we encounter people or situations that are different. It is even natural to feel afraid, to want to escape, to freeze up, or to even become angry and aggressive. Let's take a closer look at how people respond in situations in which they feel different.

The Five D's of Difference

Harrell (1995) uses the *Five D's of Difference* to explain people's reactions to situations in which they feel different. They are *distancing, denial, defensiveness, devaluing,* and *discovery* (Table 10.1).

Distancing

The first D of Difference is **distancing**, or avoiding situations in which we feel different. If we do not get too close to the difference, the possibility of negative experiences is minimized. Distancing can occur physically, emotionally, or intellectually. We may avoid going into situations in which we know we will be different. Many people do this by always spending time with people of similar backgrounds. Or, once we are in a situation in which we feel different, we may leave as soon as we can. David was anxious to get out of the karaoke bar and felt relief once his friend had "rescued" him. He put *physical* distance between himself and that uncomfortable situation.

distancing—avoiding situations in which one feels different. Distancing can occur physically, emotionally, or intellectually.

Harrell (1995) suggested that pity is a form of *emotional* distancing. The person feeling the pity may feel superior to the people in the other group, and the recipient of the pity may feel

TABLE 10.1   **Harrell's Five D's of Difference**

"D" term	Definition
Distancing	Avoiding situations in which one feels different
Denial	Pretending that differences do not exist
Defensiveness	Defending or protecting oneself from pain and fear
Devaluing	Evaluating a difference from oneself as unimportant or deficient
Discovery	Embracing differences and seeking opportunities to gain familiarity

Note: From *Dynamics of Difference: Personal and Sociocultural Dimensions of Intergroup Relations*, by S. P. Harrell, 1995, paper presented at the 103rd Convention of the American Psychological Association, New York.

ashamed or deviant. This emotional distancing prevents meaningful, sincere, honest interaction between the individuals as equals. (See the story analysis in Chapter 6 that asks what would have happened had Teddy Stoddard been Black.) People can also distance themselves *intellectually* and take a more scientific or objective approach to the situation:

> A student volunteered to do research with me, but she admittedly had little experience with multicultural issues, my main area of research. I suggested that she take part in the cross-cultural retreat sponsored by our campus every year to help her learn more and to develop her own level of multicultural competence. When she returned I asked her how it went. She proceeded to give me a very objective, intellectual discussion about how she observed other people and their interactions during the weekend. When she finished, I suggested to her that perhaps it was easier to take the role of observer than to actively get involved and participate where she had to experience and evaluate her own personal issues. She admitted that this was true and that she has always avoided dealing with her own ethnic background because she is very uncomfortable with the topic. She also admitted being very uncomfortable with people from other backgrounds, especially gays and lesbians, and that she'd felt "surrounded by them" at the retreat.
>
> —Linda, 30+-year-old African American professor

The student in Linda's story chose to intellectually distance herself by becoming an objective, scientific observer. That was her way of dealing with the discomfort of being around individuals whom she perceived as different from herself and with the discomfort of having to face issues regarding her own ethnic identity.

Denial

When we encounter people and situations that are different or unfamiliar, our tendency may also be to **deny** the difference. This involves pretending not to see the difference, minimizing its importance, or ignoring it altogether. Common denial statements include "People make too much out of differences. Aren't we all human beings? Don't we all have the same red blood running through our veins?"

denial—pretending that there is no difference between oneself and another, minimizing its importance, or ignoring the difference altogether.

People have said to me (LAB), "Oh, I don't see your color! You're just like everyone else to me!" I am sure the people who said that were well intentioned and thought they were paying me a compliment, but it was actually an insult. Why? Because they denied, minimized, and ignored an important part of my identity. The implication was that if they noticed I was African American, it would be negative; in reality, to me it is positive. Harrell (1995) noted that when statements are made to her such as "I don't really see you as a Black person," her internal response is, "Then you do not really see me." Would it be credible if a man said to a woman, "I don't see you as a woman; I see you only as a person"? Although it is true that many common experiences bind us together as human beings, there are also things that make us different and unique. Remember the tripartite model of personal identity (D. W. Sue, 2001) in Chapter 7? It describes the three parts of personal identity—individual, group, and universal. Although everyone has things in common, denying the differences may make others feel invisible, ignored, discounted, and unimportant, and that limits the ability to have meaningful, enriching interactions with one another.

Defensiveness

The third D of Difference is **defensiveness**. Being defensive means trying to defend or protect oneself. Remember, unfamiliar situations are often perceived as threatening, which leads to feelings of discomfort, tension, and fear. Therefore, people react by trying to protect themselves from the perceived threat. People who get defensive maintain that they are not bothered by the difference.

defensiveness—trying to protect oneself from acknowledging the difference between oneself and another to avoid the discomfort created by that difference.

A classic example of a defensive statement is "I'm not a racist!" Instead, the negative feelings associated with the difference are externalized and attributed to those other "bad, racist people." Another classic defensive statement is "I have lots of friends who are [minority group]." This again is evidence that the person is trying to prove that he or she is not bothered by the difference. This attitude may even be seen among people who are very involved in working with oppressed groups. Their involvement may be their defense against the discomfort they feel with the difference.

It is often hard for people to admit that they are bothered by difference. To admit that they do have some racist or heterosexist ideas would be a threat to their self-image as an unbiased, fair, caring individual, especially in American society, where a high value is placed on equality. These people would be classified as aversive racists (see the discussion in Chapter 6); that is, they consciously feel that racism is aversive, yet they unconsciously hold racist views. To confront their discomfort with the difference would reveal a conflict of values. Those individuals who become involved in diverse communities may feel hurt, rejected, disappointed, and confused when confronted with this contradiction. This dynamic was seen among European Americans involved in the civil rights movement during the 1960s.

In the summer of 1964 large numbers of college students, Black and White, went to Mississippi to work with SNCC (the Student Non-violent Coordinating Committee). This became known as "Freedom Summer." While Blacks and Whites previously worked side by side in the civil rights movement with few problems, many of the Blacks felt threatened because of the influx of larger numbers of Whites during that summer. "Now Black organizers were expected to welcome a bunch of cocky White kids, with advantages that African Americans could scarcely dream of, and watch them be hailed as the movement's saviors. For more than a few, it was an unbearable thought" (p. 294). As a result, some of the Black workers were cold and aloof with the White volunteers. Others took pleasure in intimidating the young, White volunteers, challenging them on everything from race to politics to sexual attitudes. On the other hand, a number of the White volunteers, oblivious to the wounded feelings of their Black co-workers, indeed had a "missionary attitude" that they were there to save the Blacks of Mississippi. Some, feeling they were more articulate and educated, aggressively told the Blacks how they thought things should be done.

Sally Belfrage, a White female volunteer, wrote about her experiences in Freedom Summer. "She and other volunteers were mesmerized by the charismatic SNCC veterans, wanted to be like them, and were deeply hurt when they realized that they would never be fully accepted by their heroes. 'And this raised the question: Why, then, am I here? If they're not grateful for my help, if we are supposed to be struggling for brotherhood and can't even find it among ourselves, why am I here?' This was each one's private battle, rarely discussed. To do so would have meant admissions, giving words to certain uncomfortable doubts" (p. 298). A White psychologist at Oxford who worked with the volunteers said the Whites were naive, believing they understood the SNCC workers because they "feel for the Mississippi Negro." But, he added, "They can't feel like the Mississippi Negro. They know it and it makes them unhappy. . . . They don't like to find out they're insensitive about anything." (adapted from Olson, 2001, pp. 298–299)

The experiences of the students during Freedom Summer illustrate some of the dynamics of distancing. Both the Black and the White volunteers engaged in distancing behaviors and attitudes. For example, some of the Black workers, feeling threatened by the larger numbers of Whites coming into the movement, distanced themselves emotionally and intellectually by becoming cold and aloof or by being outright hostile and challenging. The Whites reacted with hurt and shock, feeling that they had come to Mississippi to help and that their good intentions were not appreciated. The relationships between Black and White civil rights workers during Freedom Summer also illustrate the fourth D of Difference—devaluing.

Devaluing

As mentioned earlier, one of the first things we do when we encounter something different is evaluate it. Unfortunately, we often have the tendency to see things that are different or unfamiliar as strange, weird, or even scary. This reflects the tendency to **devalue**, which is the fourth D of Difference.

> **devaluing**—assessing the difference between oneself and another as deficient or less important.

Thomas Parham, coauthor of the book *The Psychology of Blacks* (Parham, White, & Ajamu, 1999), calls this the *difference equals deficiency* logic. In other words, we tend to see things that are different as deficient, or less than.

Think about your initial reaction when someone wants you to try a new food. You may turn your nose up at it before you have even tried it! The automatic assumption is, I'm not going to like that!

What about when you meet someone, such as a new roommate or coworker? On one level you may be excited about meeting the new person, but on another level you immediately begin to form a social hierarchy. Is this person taller than I am? More attractive? Smarter? Wealthier? You want to see how you measure up. Our natural tendency as human beings is to preserve and increase our self-esteem, so we naturally want to place ourselves higher on the scale than the other person. In other words, we find ways to devalue things about the other person to help ourselves feel more comfortable.

Another way to look at it is that to devalue is to maintain a feeling of superiority. We feel better about ourselves when we see others who are different as deviant, primitive, immoral, lazy, stupid, and so on. When we devalue people who are different, it is easier to justify our negative feelings. The fear and threat may then become anger and rage. We can justify our negative feelings about "those people" because of their bad or immoral behavior. Examples of devaluing statements are "AIDS is God's punishment on gay people for their immoral behavior" and "If Black people would just work harder, they could find jobs, do better in school, and get ahead in this world."

During Freedom Summer, the White workers devalued the Blacks living in Mississippi by taking on the *missionary attitude* and seeing them as lesser beings in need of saving. They also devalued them with their feelings that they were more articulate and educated than the Black workers and therefore had the right to tell them how to do things. They failed to recognize that the Black volunteers had been running their own movement successfully for several years before the White volunteers arrived that summer. Following is an example of devaluing:

I have to start this off by listing my "non-racist" credentials. I'm very pro–equal rights for all people of all races, genders, and orientations. I speak out against racism and other discrimination, and am committed to lowering the levels of stereotype and prejudice in my own life. However, I have noticed an uncomfortable trend in my thoughts that I wish to be rid of. Whenever I hear someone "talking Black"—that is, using urban-style slang, possessing a Southern-like accent, using "Ebonics," etc.—I sort of . . . well, have a prejudiced reaction. I tend to associate the speaker as lower economic class, probably less intelligent, and generally in the "different sort of person than me" category, unlike African Americans who do not have extremely pronounced accents. I do not negatively react in any way if I just see an African American or hear someone who is Black speaking in a more "normal" Southern California accent, but if they have a pronounced accent I've noticed I almost always jump to (quite frequently) erroneous conclusions. Case in point, one of the professors in the Sociology Department at my school is an altogether engaging and wonderful Black woman, but when I first heard her speaking I assumed she was simply an older undergrad and not a PhD. This was embarrassing to me, since I feel quite uncomfortable when I catch myself indulging in a prejudiced reaction, clearly when there is no reason I should do so.

I often actively try to correct my negative thoughts and am working on getting rid of them. Chief among the ways I am trying is simply by exposure. As I mentioned before, there were very few African Americans around when I grew up, and it may just be a familiarity thing. I'm trying to increase the number of African American friends I have (previously, the only Black friends I had used pretty normal Californian speech patterns). I figure if I make some good friends who have accents but are also obviously intelligent people, I might be able to both get used to it and prove my bad assumptions wrong. I somehow doubt I am the only person who does this—it may merely be that others are too embarrassed to talk about it. I just wanted to, well, perhaps confess a bit.

—Bob, 20+-year-old European American student

As you see from Bob's story, devaluing can be subtle. Sometimes we devalue things that are different and do not realize it. For example, sometimes people describe something or someone from a different culture as *exotic*. Often they mean that as a compliment, but to the intended recipient it can be an insult. Whereas some might see it as positive, the word *exotic* also implies "different" or "strange," and hence not understandable. At the very least, it means "something unlike me."

> This could be some form of negative stereotyping, but there have been a number of times where I have been told, "You're pretty for a Black girl." This was something I was not sure how to take at first because initially it sounds like a compliment. I questioned the wording in my head because, after thinking about it, it is sort of a back-handed compliment, because "for a Black girl" could be left out. Adding that makes me doubt their sincerity. To me, that phrase translates to: "I don't think Black girls are pretty, but you're pretty for being one." Obviously, no one can help who they like or find attractive, but it is unnecessary to directly say verbally to someone.
>
> —Brittany, 20+-year-old African American student

Thus far, the D's of Difference sound very negative, but they are natural human tendencies. It is natural to feel uncomfortable in an unfamiliar situation, and we naturally respond by trying to decrease that discomfort. As we saw in Chapter 6, it is not bad that we have stereotypes, but it is bad when we let them negatively affect our relationships with others. The same is true of the D's of Difference. We must be aware of the feelings, acknowledge them, and then take action to prevent them from negatively affecting our interactions.

Discovery

The last D of Difference is a positive experience, **discovery**. Encounters with people from different backgrounds are opportunities for discovery. Discovery means embracing and seeking greater familiarity with difference (Harrell, 1995). It involves working through the discomfort and anxiety, rather than avoiding it. It means experiencing differences as challenges and opportunities for learning and growth.

discovery—appreciating the difference between oneself and another, seeing how enriching that difference may be, and seeking out opportunities to gain familiarity.

An attitude of discovery means being willing to stretch and get outside our comfort zones. It means taking risks and feeling uncomfortable sometimes. It means keeping an open mind and being open to new experiences, new places, new things, and new people. By doing so, we enrich our own lives and the lives of others. The negative feelings associated with difference are natural. We all experience them. Their purpose is to protect us. We will not be able to eliminate those negative feelings, but with them comes the opportunity for personal growth and improved interpersonal and intergroup relations.

As we saw in Bob's story, he became aware of his tendency to negatively evaluate African Americans who speak nonstandard English. Once he became aware of it, he made a conscious effort to actively correct those negative thoughts. One method he used was to make more African American friends. His hope was that through exposure and increased familiarity, he could get rid of his prejudice. Bob took an attitude of discovery. Here is another example:

> I had the opportunity to go to a community in Mexico to fellowship with the people there. The first year I did not go, because ultimately the language barrier made me feel

uncomfortable. I kept focusing on the fact that I would be in a community of people for an entire week and I could not say anything but hola and adiós. I was scared of social situations. I did not want to have to face the "awkwardness" of not understanding someone in conversation. In the five D's of difference, I was distancing myself from a situation that was unfamiliar to me. However, the next three years in a row, I decided to go and I experienced discovery there. I realized just how quickly one could pick up a language when they are immersed in it for a period of time. I was able to make lasting friendships, and to think I never would have had the blessing of experiencing such friendships and such all because I was afraid of something that was unfamiliar to me.

I have realized and encouraged others to realize that staying in one's comfort zone is, well, comforting, but it's not nearly as rewarding as stepping out of it to find so much more about other people, and even oneself.

—Katie, 20+-year-old European American student

Experiencing other cultures can be an enriching experience. *Photograph by Tom Zasadzinski*

Katie's experience illustrates the benefits of *discovery*. She came from a predominantly European American background. At first, she distanced and turned down the opportunity to volunteer in Mexico due to her anticipated discomfort at encountering people who spoke a different language. However, the next year she worked up the courage and took on an attitude of *discovery*. She opened her mind, took a risk, got out of her comfort zone, and took advantage of the opportunity to learn and experience something new.

Discovery can also be fun if you can fight through your initial desire to distance yourself from the situation. Rayanne discovered this in a tasty way:

Since it was around Christmas and I was meeting new people I decided to get dressed up. Around the holidays my family always gets dressed up when they get together—nothing too fancy, maybe a nice sweater or blouse. Besides that, I wanted to look cute, after all I was meeting my boyfriend's family for the first time. Unfortunately I looked too nice—in fact I stood out from everyone else. Since his family was making tamales, which are very messy, his family was dressed in old jeans and sweatshirts. On top of being the new girl they looked at me funny for wearing a skirt to make tamales.

After a couple of minutes I was no longer uncomfortable by my appearance. It was a long night of making tamales but I enjoyed the time I spent with them. When we left they invited me back to eat the tamales with them on Christmas Eve. So, the next night I went back and enjoyed the food we worked so hard to make the night before.

Stepping outside one's comfort zone can lead to discovery about oneself. *Photograph by Bebeto Matthews/AP/ Shutterstock*

It was very interesting to observe his family's traditions. Every year his family does the same thing around Christmas. . . . I've discovered that other Hispanic families do the same thing around Christmas. They go to a relative's house to make tamales the day before Christmas Eve and then come back on Christmas Eve to eat them and open presents up at midnight. At first I compared my family to his and made remarks like "that's not what my family does," but now I embrace our differences.

—Rayanne, 20+-year-old European American student

Remember Nina's story at the beginning of this section? She was afraid to meet her new roommate whose name she could not pronounce, but instead of avoiding the situation and asking for a new roommate, Nina had the courage to go ahead and live with her. She also had the courage to get to know other people in the dorms from different cultures. In the end she realized how valuable it was to develop relationships with people who are different from her.

The Three S's of Similarity

Universoul Circus took me by surprise. People were standing all the way out to the parking lot, waiting to buy tickets. The enormous big top was situated in Hollywood Park off of Prairie Avenue. I have never seen a big top other than on television and I was extremely excited to go. The fact that most of the intense performances would be executed by African Americans thrilled me even more. If it wasn't for my friend's family, I would never have heard of a circus team called Universoul. Founded in 1994, the circus has expanded and has since traveled to 32 cities, including a tour in South Africa in 2001. Cedric Walker, the founder and CEO of Universoul Circus, has been quoted to say that his dream was to have "hip-hop under the big top." The vision of this circus is to find African American performers who have talents other than sports, singing, and dancing. However, the circus also searches for performers who are not of African descent to perform talents that come from their own culture. So in a sense, the circus has become a multicultural event that shows off each culture's unique talents that other cultures may have not been aware of. The big top had enough room to fit around 2,000 people and there were no empty seats. As soon as the lights went up, hip-hop music ruptured through the speakers and the performances began. From African American ice skaters dancing to hip-hop music, to an African American woman lion tamer, the talents seemed to only get better. During breaks between acts the announcer would have activities that would involve the crowd, such as naming famous 80's African American TV show song themes. There was an activity where the announcer brought up five men and women who were 25 and older and five men and women who were 18 and younger and they had a dance off to different kinds of music. The interaction with the crowd was wonderful, especially since every activity had a theme that pertained to the African American community.

It was quite a sight to see men and women of various ages interacting with each other, when usually in our culture, older men and women seem to focus more on parenting rather than socializing with younger children. But with the charming ambiance and playful atmosphere, Universoul Circus knew no boundaries when it came to interacting with the young and old. Everyone connected with each other because of each person's similar background. For example, during one of the activities, the announcer played different songs and the audience had to yell out what it was. What surprised me was how many people, young and old, knew the songs. It didn't matter when the song was made; I saw little African American kids singing, "We are Family," right along with their parents. There was a cultural connection that was shared that night because of Universoul. It targeted an audience that had similar experiences in life because of the culture they shared and gave them something they could all have fun with.

Universoul Circus was a great experience for me because it put me in a position where I was surrounded by people who were like me. I am rarely around people who share my same culture and it was surprisingly a relief to be able to easily connect with people who had similar tastes and likes. The circus is something all cultures generally enjoy in America, but Universoul Circus gave me an amazing feeling because I felt like this was something that I could personally connect with. The jokes, the music, the all-around atmosphere had me feeling very comfortable because I understood what they were trying to achieve. They wanted the audience to feel like this was dedicated to them; the whole purpose of this circus was a commitment to our community and culture as a way of saying, "This belongs to you." Universoul impacted our society because it shows the positivism of our culture rather than the expected stereotypes and stigmas.

—Alicia, 20+-year-old African American student

Alicia's story shows how comforting it can be to be around others who are similar to us. We like what is similar, or familiar. Why? One of the authors (LAB) gives three reasons, which she calls the *Three S's of Similarity*: we like things that are familiar because they are *simple*, make us feel *safe*, and help us feel *sane* (see Table 10.2).

TABLE 10.2   The Three S's of Similarity

"S" term	Term definition
Simple	It is easy to stick with the familiar.
Safe	It feels comfortable to stick with the familiar.
Sane	Being around others who are similar to us makes us feel normal or at least not unusual.

Simple

It is **simple**, or easy, to stick with what is familiar. It is more challenging to get out of our comfort zones and explore new people and new places. When we encounter something that is different, we feel uncomfortable and must work harder to function in the situation. When we stay in situations with which we are familiar, we do not have to consciously process as much information. Things are accomplished automatically without much effort or thought.

simple—things that are similar to us or our values are easy or comfortable.

> When I was in middle school a majority of my friends were Asian, but somehow one of my best friends, Nina, was Mexican. She came over to my house often and we would hang out a lot outside of school. We even took professional pictures at the mall together. As we graduated from middle school and moved on to high school, that's where we started losing touch with one another. My group of friends in high school consisted of predominantly Asians, and she started hanging around a group of friends who were predominantly Mexican. I remember thinking in high school what happened between me and Nina and would occasionally run into her at school but not really saying more than a few words. I remember asking her jokingly, "Hey, how come we never talk anymore? You were my best friend in middle school?" But there was never really an answer to my question. Now in college, I still bring out my pictures I once took with my best friend who was Mexican. It makes me sad that as we grow up and lose our innocence we start eating up what society approves and disapproves of which forces us to move into cliques of the same race because it's just easier and more comfortable to hang out with your own people whom you share the same values and culture with.
> —Amelia, 20+-year-old Asian American student

Amelia's explanation for why she and her friend drifted apart in high school was that it was easier and more comfortable to stick with others who shared the same background.

Safe

Sticking to what is familiar is also **safe**. As we have said, things that are different are often perceived as a threat. If we do not encounter them, we continue to feel safe. We do not have to risk suffering the potential negative consequences.

safe—things that are similar to us or our values are not a threat because we know how to deal with them and do not have to encounter unsettled feelings of going beyond the familiar to the unknown.

> I used to have a European American friend whom I considered to be my best friend. We met in high school, went to [community college] together and stayed close friends. One day, she went on a date with a guy. After she got back, I asked how the date went, and she said that the guy told her some interesting stuff. What the guy told her was that the reason why Asian people cannot drive is because they do not have peripheral vision since their eyes are so small. Then she went on and asked me if it was true. I have heard the stereotype of Asian people not being able to drive like a million times—which is really irritating and tiring to hear by now. I heard that the reason for that is because we do not have peripheral vision on a comedy show once. They made this old White lady say it, portraying her as an ignorant racist. But for my "best friend" to tell me that . . . I was so shocked and enraged. She had known me for

over five years before she told me this. She had seen me drive like almost every day for a few years. For her to make a stereotypical statement like Asian people cannot drive was so much worse than if it were coming from anyone else. As if that is not enough, she went on and asked me whether or not we have peripheral vision, adding insult to injury. I still cannot believe that she was dead serious about it. I really thought she was joking at first. I am not friends with her anymore, not because of this incident, but because of a lot of other differences we had. At this point of my life, I do not even have a single White friend. It's not that I am avoiding them, but many of them tend to hurt my feelings like how my friend did if I get too close to them.

—Than, 20+-year-old Vietnamese American student

Than's experience with her former friend illustrates why people have a tendency to stick with others who have similar backgrounds—it is safer because it helps them avoid such painful experiences.

Sane

We also like things that are similar because they help us feel **sane**, or at least normal or not unusual. We mentioned earlier that we have a natural tendency to preserve and build up our self-esteem. Being around people who are similar to us is validating. It affirms that we are okay if other people act, think, and feel the same way we do. When we encounter people who act, think, and feel differently, we question ourselves. Think about groups of teenagers in junior high and high school who spend time together. They dress alike, talk alike, do their hair alike, listen to the same music, and so on. We do the same thing. If you think of times when you have been in a new or unfamiliar situation, such as going to a new school, chances are the friends you made were people similar to you.

sane—things that are similar to us or our values help us feel normal because if we are like everyone else, we are not out of step; we are validated or affirmed.

> I had a teacher asking me, "Why do all of the Black kids hang out together?" I responded, "Have you noticed that all of the White kids hang out with one another, too?" Immediately, her face turned red and she tried to explain that she didn't think anything was wrong with the Black kids hanging out together, she was just curious why they felt the need to do so.
>
> —Dolly, 30+-year-old African American student

A similar issue came up in an article in one of our alumni magazines. LAB felt the need to respond to the article and write about how Black students were not trying to separate themselves, but they needed those times alone together to refuel themselves to face the many small, and sometimes large, racist insults and challenges they faced each day on a predominantly European American campus (Barker-Hackett, 1999). European American students often fail to realize that when people of color spend time with one another, it is not an insult, but perhaps it should be a message.

Beverly Daniel Tatum, in her aptly titled book *Why Are All the Black Kids Sitting Together in the Cafeteria?* (1997), says she has been asked that question hundreds of times. She discusses the coming together with others of the same background as an important step in adolescent racial identity development that reflects their response to racial messages received from the environment. As young people reach junior high and high school, race becomes more salient and they experience more racist encounters. Black youths growing up in racially mixed neighborhoods may notice that they are no longer invited to the birthday parties of their European American friends. Black girls may notice that when their European American friends start to date, they do not. When they try to discuss these things with their European American friends, they may find their friends just do not get it. As a result, "the Black students turn to each other for the much needed support they are not likely to find anywhere else" (Tatum, 1977, p. 60). Tatum says, "We need to understand that in racially mixed settings, racial grouping is a developmental process in response to an environmental stressor, racism. Joining with one's peers for support in the face of stress is a positive coping strategy" (p. 62).

> In elementary and middle school I remember having a multitude of friends from different racial groups. I remember that it was not until I got to high school that I realized that my friends were only Black. I remember as clear as day, the actual day I made the decision to start hanging out on "NIGGA HILL," which was a hill in front of this school that the Blacks named to be their hangout spot. And now that I think about it, it was probably one of the most ignorant things I have ever taken part in. It was the summer going into my freshman year, and I had heard that the school police (White) had been known to harass the Black students for silly things, but I paid the rumors no mind until one day a "friend" of mine (who was White) and I were approached by the school police while walking to class. The officer directed all questions toward me and told my friend that it would be best for his future if he didn't hang around me, and at that moment my friend walked away, leaving me there to be grilled. But at that moment some of the Black varsity football players, who knew I was also a football player, came to my rescue by telling the school police officer to quit harassing us Blacks for no reason. I realized at that moment that the only ones who would have my back were the Blacks, and that was only because they knew my pain, and [my White friend] would never have my back because he had never, and would most likely never, experience the things I had or would experience being Black. Experiencing such things at that young age shaped some of my beliefs and understanding of who I truly was, as well as what society thought about me and what they expect from me.
>
> —Calvin, 20+-year-old African American student

Calvin's story illustrates two S's of Similarity—safe and sane. First, Calvin's European American friend left him alone to be harassed by the European American police officer. His friend did not protect him. In contrast, when his fellow Black football players saw him, they immediately came to his rescue. This helped Calvin feel safe, and from then on he sought refuge with the other Black students on his high school campus. His story also illustrates how staying with those who are similar helps us feel sane. At that moment, Calvin realized that the only people who could understand his experiences and his pain were the other Black students.

Walk into a cafeteria on any high school or college campus, and chances are you will find Latinxs sitting with Latinxs, Asians with Asians, and European Americans with European Americans, although few people comment when all the European Americans sit together. On our campus the students know the areas where the Asians, Indians, Arabs, gay and lesbian students, and others tend to hang out. As seen from the foregoing stories, there are many reasons that people tend to associate with others from similar backgrounds.

Examining Your Biases, Prejudices, and Stereotypes

The D's of Difference and the S's of Similarity are useful in increasing awareness of your own attitudes and beliefs regarding multicultural issues. They help you understand your desire to stick with situations and groups that are familiar and how you react when you encounter people, things, or situations that are different or unfamiliar. You can also increase your multicultural competence by becoming more aware of your attitudes and beliefs about other cultures.

> I was riding a shuttle bus on campus one day when an African American student sat next to me. There were many available seats around us so I was immediately uncomfortable. Furthermore, he was sitting very close to me and his arm was touching my arm and side of my body. I felt violated and I was annoyed at the fact that he did not bother to leave some personal space between us. However, I immediately felt guilty and scolded myself for being so sensitive. Was I only being this way because this person was African American? I tried imagining how I would have felt if an Asian or Caucasian person sat next to me like that. Honestly, I would not have thought any more of it and would have felt rather comfortable. My ideals and values tell me that all races are equal and that stereotypes, prejudices, and racism are things that I despise. However, my physical reaction to this African American sitting next to me says that I am prejudiced because I think this man has ulterior motives in sitting so close to me when in reality, the seat next to me was probably the first seat he saw upon entering the vehicle. I attempted to rationalize my actions by stating that he was sitting too close and that his arm was touching my arm. In reality, he did not even give me a second glance and just sat there studying his notes.
>
> —Lia, 20+-year-old Chinese American student

Before taking a class in multicultural psychology, Lia may have just sat there and been annoyed and angry about the African American male student sitting so close to her on the bus. This incident may also have confirmed and strengthened a negative bias against African American men. Instead, learning about these concepts increased Lia's awareness of her own stereotypes and prejudices, which helped her identify them, challenge them, and change her response.

Increased awareness includes examining your own biases, prejudices, and stereotypes. In Chapter 6 we mentioned that biases, prejudices, and stereotypes by themselves are not necessarily bad. We naturally develop them as human beings. Stereotypes help us summarize and organize all the millions of bits of information our senses and brains are bombarded with every day. Biases and prejudices are a natural outcome of growing up in a society built on them.

The Museum of Tolerance in Los Angeles has an exhibit with two doors. One is marked *Racist* and the other *Non-Racist*. You must pass through one of these doors to continue to the next section of the museum. The only problem is that the door marked Non-Racist is locked, which forces everyone to go through the door marked Racist. The point is obvious: we all harbor racist thoughts and ideas. These thoughts and ideas become bad when we allow them to negatively affect our relationships with others. Even if we are not aware we have them, they still have an effect on us. The goal is to be aware of our racist thoughts and ideas so we can better control them, challenge them, and prevent them from negatively affecting our interactions.

Learning About Your Own Culture

Self-awareness also involves learning about your own culture and its effect on your personal attitudes and beliefs. As we discussed in Chapter 7, your personal perceptions and feelings about your own culture are an important part of your ethnic identity. These feelings may be positive, negative, or mixed. It is important to become aware of your thoughts, feelings, and behaviors as they relate to people of your own group.

I have to admit that I have never heard of Roscoe's House of Chicken and Waffles until the day my friend's family decided to eat there. The very idea of a restaurant that only served chicken with waffles (what I have always considered a breakfast food) immediately disturbed me. I was amazed as I glanced about the eatery: everyone was African American. Being a first-timer at this restaurant, I had no clue it is an African American–owned establishment and I have never eaten in a vicinity where the majority were of the same ethnicity as my own. I can specifically remember the smell because no sooner than I stepped inside, the aroma of Southern cooking took me back to the days my grandmother used to cook for my family during holidays. At that point, my apprehension became excitement because I realized that perhaps chicken and waffles weren't the only foods prepared in this restaurant.

The atmosphere was very vibrant. It was about 8 p.m. when we arrived and the place was full to capacity. Music was blasting in the corners playing 80's classics and today's hip-hop. The walls were surrounded by mirrors so everyone had their share of glances at other patrons, giving those who returned the glance a slight nod of recognition, or just to say hello. Everyone was extremely friendly, to the point of familiarity; even customers who had walked in after we had settled down would stop and talk to random customers and comment on the foods they selected. This wasn't the typical family restaurant like Denny's or Coco's; this was a home away from home. Ordering the foods looked simple enough, but being a vegetarian made it harder to choose. Every meal came with either a chicken leg or thigh. I didn't give in to the chicken leg or chicken thigh, but I did indulge in their famous greens, macaroni and cheese, cornbread and a plate of rice and beans (the plate was so big I had seconds and thirds from my leftovers the next day). I did, however, observe the main food that gives the restaurant its name. The chicken was described by my friend's family as "juicy," "crispy on the outside," "better than any other chicken you can get around here." The waffles looked so good, I had a bite. They tasted like regular waffles, but the fact that I was eating them late at night rather than early in the morning (heaven forbid my mother caught me eating breakfast food at night) made me feel extremely devious.

Towards the end of the night, not all of the customers turned out to be African American. I saw a few European American and Latino/a customers, who brought their children and grandparents. I appreciated the restaurant even more because I felt like they were giving a piece of their culture to other people who lived in and around the area. The quantity of the food, the quality of the service, and the hospitality given made me understand why it is our culture names our cooking "soul food."

That night in Roscoe's challenged me to appreciate the ordinary. In a sense, the restaurant itself was plain and not so attractive on the outside. But what I appreciated about the restaurant was the way it communicated to me through its foods. Its simplicity taught me to enjoy richness in something as trivial as to what some may consider a hole-in-the-wall restaurant. Exploring my culture through its foods was the first for me. Even when my grandmother cooked her Southern Creole foods, I never ate more than a bite. I can understand now how our food has its own significance, as do foods of other cultures. It provides comfort and togetherness with people you do not even know. For that split second, you don't mind enjoying the company of other people, because there is something in that atmosphere you can relate to. This is my culture's food, a custom that has been passed down for centuries and is still holding strong.

—Alicia, 20+-year-old African American student

Alicia deepened her understanding of her African American heritage through the experience of eating at a soul food restaurant. Students of color are not the only ones who can benefit from exploring their own culture. Some of you, especially those of you from a European American background, may be saying, "I don't have a culture." Students often say things like, "Whenever we start talking about culture in class I feel left out because I don't really have a culture." Or, "I'm boring. I'm just White." We hope you now understand that everyone has a culture. First, it is important to realize that the statement "I have no culture" is very ethnocentric. It implies that your own culture is the norm and everything else is different or abnormal. It means you use your own culture as the standard against which all others are measured. Once you do that, you risk the pitfalls described as the D's of Difference, such as devaluing other cultures.

Many of you identify with being *American*, whether that is European American, African American, Latinx American, Arab American, or Indian American—American is still part of your identity. But what does it mean to be an American?

Previously in the course, we discussed culture and its role in our daily lives. We discussed how, even though we all live in America, we still have our own customs and individual identities that we associate with through a variety of cultures. As a class, we tried to find a definition of what it meant to be an American, but everyone seemed to have a hard time in doing so. We agreed as a whole that defining what it meant to be an American is difficult because Americans do not really have a uniqueness about them that separates them from other cultures as do the Asian cultures with their traditional foods or the Middle Eastern cultures with their religious dances. It was not until the end of the class that I finally spoke up and told the class that being an American means a lot more than we know and it represents everything that we are.

When I think of being an American, I think of having the freedom to be my own person. I have the freedom to dress any way I want and to express myself through bright colors, accessories, and different sneakers. When I think of being an American, I think of being a woman who has the ability to do everything that a man can and *even more*! When I think of being an American, I think of being able to attend a four-year college and get my degree. I even think of being able to voice my opinion and vote for our United States president!

When I think of being an American, I think of walking into a classroom and seeing a bunch of students with a different skin color than mine. I think of traffic signs and city life; I think of a democracy and my constitutional rights. Being an American, we have so many privileges that thousands of people would die to have and I definitely feel lucky to be one. Being an American means having the freedom to get married to whomever you choose and have a family with as many kids as you want. Being an

American means being able to own a home, car, or business. Being an American means having a military to fight for your life and the freedom of choosing your own religion.

When I think of being an American, I think of having my own privacy and using the electricity at any hour of the day. When I think of being an American, I think of a 24-hour grocery store and access to almost any item that you could possibly think of. Growing up in the American culture, you learn how to speak English, the most commonly used language in the world!

All of these things may sound funny to someone who did not grow up as an American, or even to someone who did, but from my own experience, I think that being an American is pretty d— cool.

—Daniella, 20+-year-old Lebanese American student

Daniella came from an immigrant family, and from those experiences she gained a greater understanding of what it means to be American. Notice the things she mentioned. They relate to many of our basic American values, such as freedom, independence, equality, and democracy. They also relate to the vast opportunities—educational, economic, and social—afforded to people in our country. Other core American values include individualism, materialism, competition, and the Protestant work ethic. These concepts are specific to American culture and have an impact on all who live here—whether native born or immigrant.

> I've got to give a presentation of our family history, but ours is so boring!
> —Lisa Simpson, famous cartoon daughter

These values are so deeply woven into the fabric of everyday life in our culture that they usually go unnoticed. Only when something happens to challenge, threaten, or contradict these beliefs, values, and practices are they made explicit. For example, after the terrorist attacks of September 11, 2001, many people were talking about freedom and religious liberty. These are two of the values that distinguish American culture, even from other Western cultures. If you were born or raised in the United States, these values are part of your culture and influence your personal beliefs and behaviors. It is important to be aware of this.

An important part of multicultural competence is increasing your knowledge about your own group. How can you learn more about your own culture? Alicia's story illustrates that even something as simple as exploring the food can be a method for learning about one's culture. Another place to start is with your own family. Interview your parents, grandparents, and other relatives. Ask them to tell you about family stories, traditions, and personalities and record the interview. Begin working on a family tree. Take classes that focus on your particular group. Attend cultural events and celebrations. Read books.

My parents did a good job of instilling in me a positive ethnic identity, but your parents can take you only so far. At some point you have to explore for yourself. In high school I was involved in our Black Student Union (BSU) and helped to plan and put on Black History Month programs, but the true meaning of such things didn't really sink in. They never really had much personal significance for me. In fact, deep down I think I had some shame about it. I always had some difficulty reconciling my two worlds—the Black one and the White one. It wasn't until I was in college that I really began to explore my own ethnic identity and have some comfort with and pride about it. My self-exploration was sparked by two courses I took. The first was a sociology course on social problems I took my freshman year. I distinctly remember a film we watched in class one day on the civil rights movement. I remember watching the graphic pictures of the demonstrators being bitten by dogs and drenched with fire hoses. I felt extreme sadness, but at the same time a great sense of pride. Black people were on the move back then! I was proud of how Black people, MY people, came together to change society. The second course was one I took my junior year on African American literature. We read 11 books that semester, all by African American authors. Sad to say, I never knew there were so many books by Black people. I was enthralled as I read through the pages and saw myself, saw my people.

I read about our experiences, our thoughts, our feelings. It was amazingly powerful and sparked an interest I continue to this day. I consider African American literature a hobby and have a small but growing collection of books. About the time I graduated from college is when Spike Lee's movie *She's Gotta Have It* came out. I remember being excited to see Black people up on the big screen and feeling proud and excited when the movie was so successful and received such acclaim. Spike's success led to a sort of renaissance in Black film. I guess Hollywood finally realized that Black people pay money to go to the movies, too. And, not only that, they learned that Black films have cross-over appeal and White people will pay to see them as well. In the following years my friends and I enthusiastically went to see every Black film that came out. After a while there were too many to keep up, which was also nice.

When I was in graduate school I met a friend who was Black but did not get the same positive foundation about her identity from her family that I did. Soon after we met she said, "I want you to teach me about being Black." It was a strange request, but I understood. One of the first things I did was share with her some of my favorite books by African American authors. We also attended cultural events and celebrations, such as step shows with the Black fraternities and sororities and Martin Luther King Day parades. We threw our own Kwanzaa celebration. We also went to hear speakers who came to our campus, such as Maya Angelou and Kwame Ture (formerly Stokely Carmichael). During Black History Month each week we'd get together at my place and watch *Eyes on the Prize* on PBS (a documentary about the civil rights movement). Helping my friend explore her ethnic identity carried me further along on my journey of self-knowledge, a life-long journey I'm sure will never end.

—Lynne, 40+-year-old African American professor

The strategies used by Lynne in her personal identity development are strategies everyone can use. She took classes, read books, watched films and television programs, attended lectures, and attended cultural events and celebrations. Knowledge about your own group provides a springboard for learning about other groups. Knowing yourself gives you the confidence to go out and learn about others who are different from you.

We have spent a large portion of this chapter discussing the first area of multicultural competence—awareness of your own cultural values and biases. That is because self-awareness is arguably the most important part of multicultural competence. Knowing yourself gives you the strength and the confidence to learn about other cultures. It provides you with a foundation on which to build the other aspects of multicultural competence. Let us turn now to the second part of multicultural competence—understanding other worldviews.

Understanding Other Worldviews

Although it is vitally important to know and understand your own culture, it is also important to learn about other cultures. Part of multicultural competence is obtaining basic knowledge about different groups. Although each person within a culture is unique, there are some general facts about each cultural group that are helpful to know, such as the history of the group, current sociopolitical concerns, cultural traditions, family structure, and core values and beliefs. It is important to learn basic information, both about your own culture and about other cultures.

Learning Key Historical Events

Just as it is important to know your own history, it is important to know the key historical events that influenced other groups. For example, to truly understand African American culture, you must study the history of slavery and its continued impact on American culture. As we discussed in Chapter 6, the roots of racism in the United States go back to slavery and its aftermath, but African Americans also have a history, going back to Africa, that predates slavery. It is important to know that. It is also important to know what happened after slavery, including the civil rights movement of the 1950s and 1960s, because that had a significant impact on African American culture as well.

It is important to know the history of the different immigrant groups. As we discussed in Chapter 5, there is a difference between groups who immigrate voluntarily, such as those who come looking for a better education and better job opportunities, and refugees who come involuntarily, escaping war or political or religious persecution.

Becoming Aware of Sociopolitical Issues

It is also important to be aware of current sociopolitical issues affecting various cultural groups. For example, major events over the past few years have significantly impacted the LGBT community.

November 4, 2008, was a historic day as the United States elected Barack Obama as its first African American president. In California, the day carried mixed emotions for members of the LGBT community because on that same day, Proposition 8 passed, an amendment to the California state constitution that defined marriage as the union of one man and one woman. On the one hand, members of the community were elated and hopeful because Barack Obama was the first U.S. president to openly express support for the LGBT community (Roades, 2016). For example, he was the first president to invite an openly gay group to march in his inaugural parade. In contrast, Proposition 8 essentially made gay marriage illegal in the state of California. One lesbian woman said, "I wanted to laugh and cry at the same time. It was a difficult day" (anonymous personal communication, 2008).

The controversy over Proposition 8 illustrates the roller-coaster ride that is gay marriage. In March 2000, California voters passed Proposition 22, which stated that marriage was between a man and a woman. One week later, the California Supreme Court declared the law unconstitutional because it discriminated against gay people, opening the door for same-sex marriage. In the months following this ruling, 18,000 same-sex couples wed in California. A strong and powerful opposition group called ProtectMarriage.com rose up in the following years. This group succeeded in getting another proposition on the ballot, the "Limit on Marriage" initiative, or Proposition 8. Proposition 8 passed on November 4, 2008, by only a slim margin. Same-sex couples who wished to marry immediately filed three lawsuits with the

California Supreme Court to nullify the proposition. Between 2008 and 2013, the legal battle over Proposition 8 left those 18,000 couples in limbo. Depending on the day and the particular ruling, their marriage may or may not have been recognized. The battle went all the way to the U.S. Supreme Court, which in 2011 decided to hear the case. In February 2013, the Obama administration made an unprecedented move and filed a brief asking the Supreme Court to allow same-sex marriage in California (NBC Bay Area, 2013). On June 26, 2013, the U.S. Supreme Court did not directly rule on the constitutionality of Proposition 8, but dismissed the case on procedural grounds. This essentially accomplished the same thing and opened the door for gay marriages to resume in California. Same-sex couples lined up to get married that same day (De Vogue, Moran, & Hafenbrack, 2013). However, this ruling was limited to California. Had the Supreme Court made a broader ruling, striking down Proposition 8 as unconstitutional, same-sex marriage would have been legal across the United States.

The battle over same-sex marriage in California mirrored the situation in other states and on the federal level with the Defense of Marriage Act. By the end of 2014, 19 states had legalized same-sex marriage and 31 had bans on same-sex marriage (ProCon.org, 2014). Imagine what it would be like to live under such conditions. Legally married couples are afforded many rights and privileges denied to those who are not married. For example, if a couple is not married and one partner dies, the remaining partner is not entitled to bereavement leave from work, to receive the Social Security benefits of the loved one, or to inherit assets. Unmarried partners are not considered next of kin so are not allowed hospital visitation and cannot make emergency medical decisions. Many companies do not provide health insurance coverage for domestic partners or their children. Unmarried couples cannot file joint tax returns and are not eligible for tax benefits specific to marriage. For unmarried couples with children, the nonbiological parent is denied the right to joint parenting, joint adoption, and joint visitation. These are just a few examples of the more than 1,000 tangible benefits, rights, and protections that legally married couples receive. There are also intangible social and psychological benefits of marriage, such as security, commitment, structure, dignity, stability, and spiritual significance (Wolfson, 2004). Finally, the Supreme Court ruled on June 25, 2015, that same-sex marriages were protected by the U.S. Constitution in the *Obergefell v. Hodges* ruling (Liptak, 2015), which essentially legalized gay marriage in all 50 states. Here is a quote from that decision:

> No union is more profound than marriage, for it embodies the highest ideals of love, fidelity, devotion, sacrifice, and family. In forming a marital union, two people become something greater than once they were. As some of the petitioners in these cases demonstrate, marriage embodies a love that may endure even past death. It would misunderstand these men and women to say they disrespect the idea of marriage. Their plea is that they do respect it, respect it so deeply that they seek to find its fulfillment for themselves. Their hope is not to be condemned to live in loneliness, excluded from one of civilization's oldest institutions. They ask for equal dignity in the eyes of the law. The Constitution grants them that right. (Supreme Court of the United States, 2015, p. 28)

Despite these encouraging words from the U.S. Supreme Court, same-sex marriage remains controversial. Although many in society support marriage equality and gay rights, others still harbor strong anti-gay sentiments. Thus, even though the legality of same-sex marriage was settled by the U.S. Supreme Court, this position is strongly resisted by many people. It is important for individuals who work with the LGBT community to be aware of the impact such an atmosphere has on their daily lives.

Issues faced by the LGBT community illustrate the need to understand how current sociopolitical issues affect individuals from different backgrounds. Other examples include anti-Arab sentiments following the attacks of September 11, 2001, and controversial immigration policies, such as the proposed Dream Act, which would provide a path to citizenship for undocumented immigrants brought to the United States as minors (American Immigration Council, 2017), and the Trump administration's strict enforcement of the "zero-tolerance policy" which resulted in the separation of more than 2000 children from their parents at the U.S.-Mexico border (National Immigration Forum, 2018; Valverde, 2018). Such knowledge improves one's ability to work effectively with individuals from these groups.

In the following story, a student tells how his life changed in the aftermath of the 9/11 attacks.

My legal name, John, hasn't always been my name. My birth name meant steadfast and strong, with the hunger of a lion. It was a pretty cool name, I'm sure most people would agree after finding out the meaning, but usually the first reaction I used to get was . . . "Oh no! Terrorist."

I was born in [name of country] and came to the United States at the age of nine. I was still very VERY impressionable and boy did the next events in my life have a dramatic change in the man I would grow up to be.

Culture in the United States was insanely different from what I was used to and I experienced some culture shock; like any boy entering puberty, the curiosity in the opposite sex was raging, but even more so when it was the first time I had seen intimacy being exchanged so freely at such a young age.

September 11 followed this shock by only months and I was sent for a loop; everything that I identified with somehow now became the spotlight enemy of my peers. Islam, the Arabic language, its music, my family, my mother, and I became the monster. I had to escape to find any acceptance or belonging. At school I was consistently being socialized that anyone from the Middle East is a possible threat. This happened by the alienation that started to occur on the playground and even more so when it happened in the classroom. My fifth grade teacher, Mrs. [Name] made sure I knew I was different and didn't belong. From the consistent punishments for interacting in ways other students did with each other, but for some reason was criminal when I did so; to the time she took fifteen or so minutes going from one student to another asking them to spell the word I could not spell, making me feel so inferior; to the time she explained to my mother she did not want me in her classroom at all. My family couldn't do much about it because we were illegal then. I know different now, but then I felt like the scum, and I had to camouflage.

I tell you this story because at one point I agreed with the classroom when they spoke about us being all American, and that identifying the differences could be counterproductive. Those days the world wanted me to change and conform and any resistance to it brought along a lot of pain. But these days I disagree and understand that to conform is to act out of fear, because the differences are what make us so great. It's something we can't buy, it's something that gives you roots, it is something that SHOULD DEFINITIELY BE RECOGNIZED, and tolerated, accepted and held with sensitivity. Some second-generation minorities might disagree, but I believe they are just looking at a narrow picture. How do you know where to go if you don't know where you've been? And why do we have to see it so negatively? Differences are good; they bring diversity, different flavors and aromas to a delicious stew. We all have something different to bring to the table, no one is above or below, the equity is balanced. There is beauty to appreciate in every color, in every texture, in every shape.

—John, 20+-year-old Arab student

Knowing Basic Values and Beliefs

Aside from factual knowledge about different cultural groups, understanding other worldviews also involves knowing the basic values and beliefs of these groups. In Chapter 3 we compared and contrasted the worldviews of different cultural groups. We emphasized that although each individual is unique, there are broad concepts that characterize each group. Knowing something about an individual's culture helps you formulate hypotheses that can be explored in your interactions with that person.

For example, it is helpful to know that Latinx culture tends to be patriarchal, with more traditional gender roles. When we work with female Latinx students on our campus, we recognize that they may have more struggles being in college than other female students because they may not get the same kind of support from their families. They may have more family responsibilities at home, such as taking care of younger siblings, and these may be seen as a higher priority than their studies. One female Latinx student said, "My family is always asking me when I'm going to get married and have babies." However, we cannot assume that this is the case for all Latinx students, because it is not. It is a topic that needs further exploration.

Understanding Cultural Practices

It is also helpful to know and understand cultural practices. These are behaviors that may be normal and expected and have a particular meaning in a culture.

I happened to stop by one of the professors' offices and the professor introduced me to a visually impaired young man who was visiting him. We all chatted in the professor's office for approximately forty-five minutes and that was the last time I saw him [that quarter]. This quarter the student happened to be in my class so I thought it was appropriate to say hello; I introduced myself to him in case he did not recognize my voice from our previous meeting. After class we chatted a bit, and then I began to excuse myself because I was headed to the bookstore to buy the textbooks I needed. The student stated that he would like to come with me to the bookstore because he too was headed that way to purchase his books. My first thought was, Oh! What do I do? I did not know him that well; however, the polite thing to say was okay. We walked out of the classroom together and he suddenly stopped in the hallway and proceeded to fold his guiding cane. Suddenly there was no communication between us, I just stood there wondering why he was folding the cane at the same time I was making sure no one was going to bump into him. I looked away for a split second, he touched and grabbed my arm and then he found his way to my elbow, which was an indication that we could start walking now. It took me by surprise, and personally I was a bit uncomfortable because it was as though he was invading my space, so quickly I adjusted my arm away from my body enough to where I was comfortable and we headed out to the bookstore.

After we both purchased our books, we headed across the campus to the Starbucks coffee stand since we both had hours to spare before our next class. During our conversation I found myself not knowing where to look, since I personally like to have eye contact with the person I am conversing with. It seemed strange that these things were going through my mind, but I quickly adjusted my mentality and was able to just enjoy the conversation with this person.

The next day, I looked up on the Internet, "the blind or visually impaired culture," hoping it would provide me necessary information on what is acceptable in their culture. I felt the need to know the proper etiquette when assisting or approaching the blind or visually impaired, so that in the future I may be more sensitive or aware of what to do. I found a web page, www.afb.org American Foundation for the Blind, which listed some tips on how to approach or assist blind or visually impaired people, which are listed below.

- Identify yourself by name before you make physical contact.
- Ask if they would like *assistance* and let them tell you how you may assist them. If they say no, don't take it personally.
- When guiding them, *let them take your arm*. Do not touch the individual's cane; it is considered part of their personal space.
- Let them know when you are leaving.

If I would have had this knowledge prior to this encounter I may have avoided the awkwardness that I felt.

—Ana Maria, 30+-year-old Latinx student

Ana Maria's experience illustrates the importance of cultural differences and knowing about the values, beliefs, and practices of different groups. Knowing these things increases your level of multicultural competence.

Knowing the Dynamics of Racism, Discrimination, and Stereotyping

Another aspect of understanding other worldviews is knowledge of the dynamics of racism, oppression, discrimination, and stereotyping. We discussed each of these concepts in detail in Chapter 6, so it is not necessary to explain them again here. However, it is important to understand how these forces affect people in their everyday lives. One of our former students who was active in the gay/lesbian community on campus said that one of the main factors influencing formation of a gay/lesbian community was their response to the oppression and discrimination experienced by members of their group. They bonded because they had a common sexual orientation but also because they had a common "enemy" and came together for protection and support.

In Chapter 1, we also discussed one of the early studies by K. B. Clark and Clark (1939) in which African American children preferred White dolls to Black dolls. The researchers concluded that Black children had lower self-esteem because of the racism and discrimination experienced by their group and because of the negative portrayals of Blacks in the media. Remember our discussion of identity development in Chapter 7? Every individual from a diverse background must resolve his or her status in relation to the dominant culture and how his or her own group is perceived and treated by the dominant group. This also relates to the discussion of similarity in this chapter, in which students sought out members of their own group after having negative experiences with members of the dominant group. These examples illustrate how racism, discrimination, oppression, and stereotypes have an impact on individuals and on their development, personality, and behavior. It is important to understand these forces and their impact on your interactions with others.

Development of Culturally Appropriate Interpersonal Skills

The first two dimensions of multicultural competence involve awareness—awareness of your own cultural attitudes and awareness of other worldviews. You might be wondering, Once I become aware of all these things, what do I do? It is true that awareness is essential, but it is not enough. You must act on that awareness and take concrete steps toward building positive relationships with people from different backgrounds. That is where part three of multicultural competence comes in—developing culturally appropriate interpersonal skills (see Table 10.3).

A *skill* is the ability to do something well, or the ability to do something with accuracy and ease. Skills are developed through training, experience, and practice (Warren, 1995). Multicultural competence is an interpersonal skill. It is the ability to interact effectively with others who are different from you. To achieve this, you must have *education*, *training*, *experience*, and *practice* in working with people from different groups. This section describes specific strategies for increasing your level of multicultural competence.

Education and Training

A skill is developed through education and training. Reading this book and taking this class are significant steps toward your multicultural education and training. From them, you gained knowledge that can serve as a foundation for developing further competence. You can take more classes and attend lectures, workshops, seminars, and retreats that focus on cultural issues. For example, you can take a class that focuses on a specific cultural group, such as a women's studies course or a course on a particular religion. That will allow you to learn in more depth about

TABLE 10.3   Concrete Things to Do to Increase Your Multicultural Competence

- Take more classes and attend lectures, workshops, seminars, and retreats on multicultural issues.
- Read books, magazines, Land journals on multicultural issues.
- Watch relevant films, television shows, and videos on diverse issues.
- Listen to music and attend plays, concerts, and other cultural events and celebrations.
- Do Internet research on issues related to diversity.
- Develop relationships with people from diverse backgrounds.
- Get involved in cultural organizations.
- Develop the ability to say "I don't know" and to ask questions. You cannot possibly know everything, so allow others to help you develop your knowledge.
- Travel to experience different cultures directly.
- Be an ally and speak up on behalf of others.
- Speak up on behalf of yourself and your group.
- Develop a level of comfort discussing difficult issues.
- Have an attitude of discovery and be open to new experiences.
- Have the courage to take risks and step outside your comfort zone.
- Develop empathy for others, their experiences and perspectives.

some of the topics covered in this class. Or you can learn another language. Learning how individuals from another culture communicate is a great way to understand the culture better, and knowing another language opens the door to many opportunities.

Working with others different from oneself can be an enriching, creative activity. *Photograph by Rawpixel.com/ Shutterstock*

You can also attend lectures, seminars, and workshops offered on your campus. College and university campuses offer a wealth of opportunities for cultural education. Programs are usually available throughout the year, but a particularly good time is during cultural emphasis months, such as Black History Month, Women's Herstory Month, and LGBT Month. We shared stories about some of our experiences during the cross-cultural retreat on our campus, a weekend of experiential exercises and group discussions related to diversity. Perhaps your campus offers something similar. If not, look for organizations in your area that do. For example, the National Conference for Community and Justice (formerly the National Conference for Christians and Jews) has chapters across the country and regularly offers diversity training workshops, lectures, and seminars.

Local museums are another source for cultural education. Museums often host exhibits, lectures, and other programs related to cultural issues. Some museums focus on a particular culture. For example, in Los Angeles we have the African American Heritage Museum and the Japanese American National Museum.

You can also further your multicultural education by reading books and journals. Literature provides a wonderful window into different worlds. You gain access to the words, private thoughts, and experiences of individuals from different backgrounds.

Other suggestions for multicultural education and training include watching relevant films, television shows, or videos, doing online research, listening to music, and attending plays, concerts, and other cultural events and celebrations.

This past summer, I was given the extraordinary opportunity to study abroad in Paris, France. It was my first time traveling to Europe, which I was very excited about. I had heard Americans put down the French people and French culture countless times. They say the French are rude, that they smell, and many other preposterous comments. I made sure to prepare myself for living abroad, so I went to the bookstore and bought books about French culture; books about what to do and what not to do when living in France. I did not want to enter into their country and commit some unintentionally rude act. I wanted to blend in with the French people so I could garner more out of my stay, rather than be a perpetual tourist. I also wanted to make sure I did not misinterpret the French people and have a negative attitude about them because I did not understand their cultural mores. French people operate in a very different fashion from Americans. We should not expect everyone in the world to act just as we do, or to value the same things that we do. We need to open our eyes and realize that we are in a foreign country as guests, and we should act appropriately because we are serving as examples of our countrymen and women.

—Angela, 20+-year-old Asian American student

When preparing to study abroad, Angela resisted falling prey to the negative stereotypes Americans have about French people. Instead, she chose to educate herself about French culture by reading books and thus increase her level of competence while living in France, which would ultimately lead to a deeper and richer experience overall.

In Ana Maria's story, she was initially very uncomfortable interacting with her visually impaired classmate. However, rather than avoiding him (distancing), she chose to go online and educate herself about blind culture to improve her ability to interact with her classmate effectively.

Experience and Practice

The more *education* and *training* you get in multicultural issues, the more *experience* you accumulate and the more opportunities you have to *practice* your newfound skills. Practice is necessary to perform any new skill with accuracy and ease. You can gain more experience and practice your culturally appropriate interpersonal skills by seeking out opportunities to interact with people who are different from you. Reach out and develop relationships with people from diverse backgrounds. Start a conversation with the person sitting next to you in class. Volunteer to work with him or her on a group project, or invite him or her to study, go to lunch, or have a cup of coffee with you. Look at how much Ana Maria learned in the foregoing story, simply by having a cup of coffee with a classmate who was blind. Remember Bob, who admitted his bias against African Americans? He made an effort to develop friendships with African Americans.

You can also get involved with cultural organizations on your campus. On our campus we have multicultural centers, one for each of the major cultural groups. We encourage students to get involved with their own center, as well as others. Each of these centers puts on programs highlighting its cultural heritage, and they appreciate individuals of all cultures who are willing to serve on planning committees.

Saying "I Don't Know" and Asking Questions

Two related skills that are important to learn when reaching out to others from different cultures are the ability to say "I don't know" and the ability to ask questions. It is impossible to learn everything from taking a class or reading a book. Individual people are an invaluable source of information. Do not be afraid to admit when you do not know something about another group. People are often hesitant to admit they do not know something because they do not want to look ignorant, stupid, or insensitive, and they are afraid to ask because they do not want to offend. However, it is better to ask a question than to remain ignorant. You run a greater risk of offending someone if you interact with him or her on the basis of assumptions and stereotypes that may be incorrect, as the following story illustrates.

I was sitting in my sociology class one day, and the professor began saying something about African Americans. As often happens in classes when you are the only Black person, he turned and made a reference to me. I don't remember exactly what he said, but he implied that my family members were from the South and that I grew up in the ghetto. He was wrong on both accounts. I was offended. He assumed that all Black people come from the same background and we don't. We are all different. Here he was, a university professor, a sociologist, who claimed to know a lot about ethnic minority groups, and he was perpetuating misinformation and stereotypes.

—Beverly, 40+-year-old African American student

The professor in the story made a mistake based on his stereotypes about African Americans. It would have been nice if that professor, instead of making a faulty assumption, had asked Beverly about her background first. That would have set a more positive example for the students and sparked a more interesting and informative class discussion. Most people will not be offended if you ask questions in a respectful and caring manner. It shows them that you are genuinely interested in getting to know them and their culture. Most people will appreciate your interest and effort. Following is a more positive story about reaching out to others:

I learned to be culturally sensitive from my family. My father grew up in a small, all-White town in West Virginia. On his side of the family we can trace our roots back to the original settlers and to the Civil War. However, my father was in the military, served in Vietnam, and was stationed in Iran when I was born. I think his experience overseas taught him to appreciate other cultures. My mother's parents immigrated to the United States from Norway. I think growing up the child of immigrants influenced my mother's attitudes. My family returned to the United States from Iran when I was about one year old. My parents always made an effort to reach out to people from other cultures, and watching them taught me to do the same. For example, following the Iran hostage crisis in 1979 my mother made a special effort to talk to people she thought were from Iran. Many were afraid at that time to say where they were from, but my mother always asked and told them that we had lived there. That always surprised them and they would ask her questions, such as if she liked it. She always said yes and would tell them positive things about their country. You could tell they appreciated her kindness and openness. I remember there was an Iranian seamstress in our town who did alterations for my mother. Her face always lit up when we came in because we went out of our way to treat her with kindness and love. I learned those things from my parents. I learned we have a particular responsibility, as Americans, to be nice and to reach out to people from other cultures. It's important to be culturally aware and to be nice and welcoming, even if we make mistakes. It makes such a huge difference.

—Kathleen, 30+-year-old European American stay-at-home mom

Kathleen's story shows that positive things can happen when you reach out and build relationships with people from other cultures.

Travel

Another strategy for building culturally appropriate interpersonal skills is travel. St. Augustine wrote, "The world is a book, and those who do not travel read only one page." Traveling to other countries opens up the world to you and changes your perspective. When you travel, you interact with people from another culture. You see them in their daily lives as they work, play, and love. You experience their food, music, language, sights, and sounds.

Travel helps you learn about others as well as yourself. There are lessons learned and skills obtained when you travel that are hard to gain any other way. We cannot overstate the benefits of experiencing another culture firsthand.

> I like to travel because I learn about different cultures. I meet different kinds of people and like to see how they live and interact with one another. My travels help me learn more about people and get along with them faster. It helps me work with them more effectively. For example, we hired a guy from India whose name was "Ganesh." I said, "Ganesh! Isn't that like me being named Jesus?" (Ganesh is a Hindu God.) He looked surprised that I would know that and said, "Why, yes." Then I asked him what part of India he was from. He said, "Bombay." I asked him, "What part of Bombay?" Now he looked surprised that I would get so specific and said, "Central Bombay." I responded, "Central Bombay. Then aren't you Zoroastrian?" He almost fell out of his chair. "Why yes. How did you know that?" He was shocked that I knew what that was. That helped us to quickly establish a relationship. From then on he actively sought me out at work.
>
> I also travel a lot for work. When I have the time, I schedule a few extra days to get in some sight-seeing. When I tell the people I'm meeting with that I'll be in town a few extra days to see more of their city or country they are always surprised and impressed. They can't believe I would take the time to learn more about their culture and history. For example, the Japanese executives are amazed when I tell them I've been to Nara and saw the Buddhist temples and Shinto shrines there. It immediately gives me more credibility and improves our working relationship.
>
> —Carl, 30+-year-old European American corporate executive

Carl's story illustrates many of the benefits of travel. He gains more knowledge about other cultures and learns about the people and their way of life. That knowledge and experience help him build stronger relationships with colleagues and increase his effectiveness on the job.

You don't have to travel far to learn about another culture. Most cities have cultural centers, or neighborhoods where people of one particular culture tend to gather and live. These neighborhoods often have names that reflect that culture, such as Chinatown or Little Tokyo. You can learn a lot by visiting these cultural centers, walking the streets, eating at the restaurants, shopping at the stores, visiting the churches, and talking to the residents. With technology, we are able to travel the world and learn about other cultures without even leaving our homes. We can use the Internet to learn about and virtually experience other cultures.

Speaking Up for Others: Being an Ally

Another important interpersonal skill is learning to be an ally. (Recall our discussion in Chapter 6.) An ally is someone from a privileged group who speaks up for and supports individuals from oppressed minority groups. For example, if you are heterosexual, you can speak up when you hear someone make a negative comment about gays or lesbians. If you are in a class and hear someone make a comment based on stereotypes, you can point that out. Supporting individuals from oppressed or marginalized groups relieves them of some of the burden they carry every day. Often individuals feel the pressure of having to represent their entire race in their classes. If you see that happening in a class, you can speak up in support of that person.

When we speak up on behalf of others, we teach important lessons, as illustrated by the following story.

> I was born and raised in South Central Los Angeles. Both my parents were born in Mexico and spoke no English whatsoever. I remember when I was growing up that in our neighborhood, "Black" families also lived in the vicinity. I recall one incident when we were playing baseball out in the street and the "Black" kids approached us and asked if they could play with us. I remember we each looked at each other and we said, no. Why did I say no? Not because my parents had taught or told me not to play with them; it was because they were a different color than me. Little did I know at that moment that my mother was watching me all along. When it was time for me to go back inside my house, my mother questioned me about the incident that she had witnessed. I did tell her as to why I did not want the other kids to play with us. My mother got so angry at my response, to which she reminded me in Spanish, "When have I showed or taught you this?" I did not have a response because it was true; never had I heard my mother express herself negatively of others. That same day after dinner, my mom walked me over to the house where these children lived and embarrassingly I had to apologize. On this day, my mother taught me a lifetime lesson that I will never forget. It does not matter where each one of us is from or what language we do or do not speak, never judge anyone, and in my case, by their skin color. We are all humans and, as such, we deserve to be accepted and loved.
>
> I now have children of my own, and while they were growing up I made sure not to allow them to make the same mistake I once did, and thus far, I feel satisfied with the results. Now that I am older, I do understand that if my mother would have allowed or displayed any sort of hatred in the household, the chances of me typing this paper and describing this certain incident would not have happened.
>
> Graciela, 40+-year-old Mexican American student

Graciela's mother served as an ally by speaking up on behalf of the African American children in her neighborhood. As a result, she taught her daughter an important lesson of acceptance and respect for others who are different. When Graciela had her own children, she made a conscious effort to teach them the same lesson.

> Most people don't recognize the abilities they have to make change in this world. Power isn't just something policemen, the military, or the government are capable of possessing. Power should be seen more as a behavior or a decision. We all have the potential to make decisions that cannot only help ourselves, but others. This makes us all allies and all responsible. Much of the time individuals will choose to be silent in racial circumstances, but just because the intention isn't drawn on the self, doesn't mean we should always stay quiet. I think, "choosing your battles" is wise advice, but God gave us a voice for a reason, and we should support the struggles of others by speaking up. I plan to pay more attention to these things and do what I can to make a positive difference in someone's life.
>
> —Virginia, 20+-year-old Latinx student

Speaking Up for Oneself: Comfort With Difficult Dialogues

Part of multicultural competence is speaking up on behalf of others, or being an ally. It is also an important skill to know how to speak up for oneself.

> One evening I came home from school and my mom asked me if I wanted to go to the grocery store with her and I said, "Sure." It was a bit chilly out so I put on my yellow [name of university] sweater and hurried to the car. We walked around the grocery store and got everything we needed. As we walked down the bread aisle, I overheard a White female laugh and out of natural reaction I turned to look at her and I smiled and noticed she didn't seem too happy that I had smiled, so I turned around and walked down another aisle.
>
> Finally, once we had finished shopping we went to the register to pay and I noticed the woman from the bread aisle was in front of us paying. I tried not to look at her, not because she made me feel uncomfortable, but because I know that had she stared me down any longer I would have probably asked why she did so, and of course I did not want to cause any problems. I realized that she was staring at my sweater and really wanted to know why on earth she would be looking at me the way she did. Well, the young lady that was with her (I assume was her daughter) was talking to her and I overheard her telling her mother, "You think she actually goes there?" and the mother replying, "Yeah, right honey, she's Mexican." I was so furious I wanted to walk over to her and slap some sense into her. I don't understand how someone could want to teach their children that it is okay to stereotype someone because of their ethnic background.
>
> I am usually not someone that allows words to affect me, but they kind of did; well, they angered me more than anything. I decided as an educated Mexican that I would answer her daughter's question, so I walked up to her mother and told her, "Yes, I am Mexican, and you know what? I am also a very intelligent young lady that had the opportunity to go to other universities as well as [name of university], so you were wrong, I do attend [name of university], I'm not just some Mexican." I also advised her daughter not to be like her mother when she gets older.
>
> —Rebecca, 20+-year-old Mexican student

Despite feeling anger, Rebecca approached the mother and daughter in the supermarket in a calm and respectful manner. As a result, she hopefully educated them about stereotypes and cultural sensitivity. There are many ways to speak up for oneself. The following student illustrates that humor can also be an effective strategy.

> It took a little humor to remind myself that I did not want to become too offensive when other people commented that I spoke with an accent, even in my native language. I would jokingly reply, "Thank you for helping me learn the language in an accurate manner. I notice that it is challenging while being able to communicate in five different languages, and to read and write in four different languages."
>
> —Ang-Li, 40+-year-old Chinese student

It can be a difficult decision whether to directly address a cultural issue. In Chapter 6 we discussed the double bind that racial microaggressions cause. On the one hand, if you speak up, you take a risk regarding the reaction you get from the other person. On the other hand, if you keep silent, the internalized anger, stress, and frustration also take a toll. In fact, it is not necessary, or healthy, to speak up in every situation. Another critical skill is knowing how to pick your battles. It should also be acknowledged that some people believe speaking up is a bad thing.

> In my opinion, racism is such a big and sensitive topic because people talk about it constantly. The more people talk about it, the more apparent the divide becomes. While I understand that it does need to be talked about in order to see change, I believe that the way it is talked about is completely wrong.
>
> I recently saw a video of a *60 Minutes* interview with Morgan Freeman where the interviewer, Mike Wallace, was asking him about his opinion on Black history. Freeman replied that he found it ridiculous. He stated that Black history is American history. The interviewer then asked how we would stop racism then and Freeman replied, "Stop talking about it." He said, "I'm going to stop calling you a White man. And I'm going to ask you to stop calling me a Black man. I know you as Mike Wallace; you know me as Morgan Freeman" ("Morgan Freeman on Black History Month," www.YouTube.com).
>
> This video sums up my view quite succinctly. In class it was mentioned that people were unsure of what ethnicity they should call someone they just met because they did not want to offend them, and I found myself thinking, 'Why do you need to say they are part of such and such ethnic group?' When I first meet someone, their ethnicity never crosses my mind. I first ask their name and that's what I call them. I do not call them White person, African American person, Jewish person, Indian person, or anything else. This is how we solve racism in my opinion—stop focusing on it so much and start focusing on the people behind the color.
>
> —Lacey, 20+-year-old European American student

What do you think? On the one hand, does talking about racism, stereotypes, ethnic identity, and other cultural issues perpetuate the problem? This is one perspective. On the other hand, taking direct action by speaking up for oneself and others can be an empowering, positive outlet, and motivator for change.

It is also important to develop a level of comfort discussing difficult issues, such as racism, sexism, and heterosexism. These are emotional topics and many people are afraid to discuss them. Race, gender, sexual orientation, and religion are all core parts of a person's identity. Because these topics have such high personal relevance, people get very sensitive when they are discussed. People may also have painful experiences related to these parts of their identity, and talking about these topics brings up that pain. Others may react with anger to what they perceive to be the ignorant, insensitive, or offensive remarks of others. Those witnessing such pain or anger may feel uncomfortable or afraid. These are difficult emotions to handle, and it is easy to be overwhelmed by them, but they should not be avoided. Instead, they must be brought out in the open, acknowledged, validated, and worked through. A widely used film that deals with multicultural issues is *The Color of Fear* (M. W. Lee, 1994). At the end of the film, a European American man is able to have a breakthrough because everyone in the group took time to work through the difficult emotions experienced during their weekend together. It takes courage and skill to discuss these difficult topics in a meaningful and beneficial manner, but it is necessary to build multicultural competence.

Class this last week was interesting, if uncomfortable for me. I think one of the issues affecting White people is the fear of saying something in the wrong way and offending someone unintentionally. It almost paralyzes speech sometimes, at least for me. I have been thinking about this a lot recently, and since this is the forum for it, I will discuss it. I am beginning to think we are damned if we do, and damned if we don't. If we try to be allies, openly discuss issues, and try to lend our hand to a cause, then we are often made fun of as naive, with a bottomless pit of liberal guilt. If we just attend to our own lives, living in suburbia where we were born and raised, we are out of touch, isolationists. I believe in political correctness as a form of changing people's perception and ideas, of affording people dignity and respect, however, I think it can also paralyze discussion amongst diverse people even when all have the best intentions and hearts.

I believe that as our demographics change in this country these issues will come more and more to the forefront. I wonder what our future looks like. If White people have to pay the price for how things have been, or if over time we can together attempt to create a society where all can be afforded dignity. It will probably be a little of both, which is probably appropriate as it could ultimately make for a better all-around understanding between people, just as now I sit squirming in my seat (in my anthro/history/ethnic studies classes) as I listen to the sins of the White past. I want to know the truth of the past; I believe it's the only way to make a better future. I try to keep an open heart, even when it hurts. I do feel helpless, as it was discussed in the book. So I do what I can. I listen; I speak if I feel I can make a coherent point that is important to me. When I am with family, friends, and acquaintances and hear ideas I feel are wrong, I muster my guts and speak up, trying not to be a hypocrite by remaining silent, and I try to be an ally, for myself, even when I feel like I am probably being naive.

—Sharon, 40+-year-old African American student

An Attitude of Discovery and Courage

Perhaps the two most important skills you need to increase your level of multicultural competence are an attitude of discovery and courage. *Discovery* was defined earlier as openness to new experiences, a willingness to step out of your comfort zone. Doing that takes *courage*. As we said, encountering people and situations that are different naturally makes us feel frightened and uncomfortable. Courage is moving forward despite such negative feelings. If you do, you will reap the rewards.

When I was 21 years old, I lived in Northern California working full time at a menial job to pay the bills. I supplemented my income by playing saxophone and singing in a band. It didn't earn me a lot of money as the venues were small bars, but provided me much comfort as long hours and little pay tend to make most people feel overwhelmed. One of my musician friends that performed in a different band needed a fill-in for an evening and I agreed to help him out. He was a fantastic harmonica player and I was looking forward to performing alongside of him. He gave me the address and I set out. The location was a little bar in the middle of Oakland, California. As I parked my car and began to unload my equipment, I can tell you that I was definitely the minority in this area. I was raised in a predominantly Caucasian neighborhood during my childhood and, although I had friends of different ethnicities, I was always part of the majority. The walk from the car to the bar was a long and, quite frankly, terrifying moment. As I reached for the door, a rather large African American man stepped in front of me, laughed at me and said, "Vanilla, I think you are lost. You certainly do not belong here." I tried to explain that I was invited to play tonight with the band, thinking this would clear the way. Nope, he just looked at me and said, "Vanilla's don't play in this bar." I was very frustrated, and at the time much braver than I am now, so I said back to him, "Look, they are expecting me to play tonight. If you don't let me in, then you explain to them why they have no horn on stage tonight," and turned to leave. This made him and his friends laugh and they told me to stop. I now presumed I would be allowed in. Nope, he then proceeded to tell me that I was too small and certainly lacked any rhythm and if I was going to get into his bar, I would have to play on the street first as all great Black musicians had been forced to. In this situation, I thought that was fair, so I took out my saxophone and played a few minutes of the blues. Fortunately, music was what kept me sane at the time and playing for anyone was a treat I couldn't pass up. I guess I played okay, because when I finished, they stepped aside, patted me on the back, and wished me luck saying, "This crowd will love or kill ya, Vanilla . . . ain't gonna be no middle." The crowd took a few minutes to warm up to me, actually giving me the cold shoulder and yelling for the Vanilla to get off the stage, but Big Joe (that was the large man's name) spoke up on my behalf after a few minutes and told me to play like I did on the sidewalk. So in the angry murmuring of a small bar, with about 30 angry faces, I poured all I had into the saddest blues song I knew. I was terrified so I just closed my eyes and played. Slowly the room quieted down, then all you could hear was me playing, then the band slowly joined in, and that evening I was privileged to be on that stage, with that band, playing for a crowd that sang, danced, and enjoyed the music.

I returned to that bar on several occasions after that, always being referred to as Vanilla. No one ever asked, or cared what my real name was; I never thought to give it. After each performance, I went back to my car and drove back to my neighborhood where I was part of the majority, but I will never forget my moment of being in the minority. Living every moment terrified that any action you take will dissatisfy those around you and that it may cause them to reject or injure you would be overwhelming. I think if more people stepped out of their own life and experienced what someone else's life looks and feels like, perhaps we would have more understanding, more acceptances of our differences, more love. The best part of music is when you are happy, you hear the music and it puts a spring in your step, makes your heart pound and, if you're lucky, even prompts you to dance . . . when you're sad, you hear the lyrics and feel the emotion that is poured into every word, becoming one with song. We don't worry about how the music is packaged, just how it makes us feel and what it makes us think about. Regardless of your mood, if you just close your eyes, you can always enjoy music. Maybe, if we all just closed our eyes with the same type of acceptance for each other as we do for music, we will find a connection to each other like we do with music. Accepting the part of the other person that either connects to our heart or our mind, instead of worrying about what the packaging looks like.

—Jennie, 40+-year-old European American student

Courage is moving forward despite one's fears. Jennie admitted how scared she was as the only European American at the bar. It took courage for her to stick it out and play her saxophone in the face of such direct opposition. As a result, the experience gave her empathy for what it is like to be in the minority and have people make assumptions about her and treat her differently based only on appearance. In the end, her courage paid off and she (as well as those who enjoyed her music) was enriched by the experience.

Here is another story about courage.

It was a busy Wednesday morning in the school's parking structure. I arrived at campus around 10:40 to be here early for my 11:45 class, but there was absolutely no parking. I checked three different parking lots and found nothing. Every time I would see a student walking the opposite direction, I would ask if they were leaving and they all responded with a no. I had 15 minutes before my class was about to start and I had accepted my fate of not finding a parking spot.

I decided to take one more circle around the third floor and then I see this guy with just a paper in his hand. I assumed he was dropping the paper off at his car and then going back to class, but I still asked out of desperation, "You're not leaving, are you?" He replied with, "No, I am leaving." I was so relieved, but then I look at him again and the initial stereotypes start flowing in my head. He was a strong-built, Black guy and I couldn't help but think of the bad things that could happen to me if I let him in my car to get his parking spot. But within a second, I thought in my head that if this was a White guy or a Latino guy, I probably wouldn't react the same way, so why should I treat this stranger differently?

I quickly ignored all of those negative stereotypes and looked at the time to see I only had 10 minutes left. I asked him, "Where did you park? Can I drop you off at your car?" and then I saw the hesitation on his face. We were both looking at each other quietly for a few seconds and then he said, "Yeah sure, why not?" I realized that in the beginning while I was thinking about stereotypes of Black guys, at the same time he was probably thinking about the stereotypes about me, being a Muslim girl in the hijab. As soon as he got in my car, I started to thank him and explained to him my class was starting in 10 minutes. He was so kind and understanding, and he even offered to drop me off near my class if I wanted. It started off with the both of us having some feelings of fear towards each other but in the end, a Black man and a Muslim hijabi woman both got something positive out of it. He didn't have to walk all the way to his car and I ended up getting a parking spot and getting to class on time.

People judge all the time; it's a human characteristic. No matter how wrong you think it is or how hard you try not to judge, it's still going to happen. Stereotypes are going to get into your head. But, as long as you don't let those thoughts get into the way of how you treat someone, then it's all right. Everyone deserves respect and you can't let your judgments affect the way you treat someone.

—Aminah, 20+-year-old South Asian, Muslim student

Aminah was aware of the negative stereotypes that popped up and the accompanying fear she felt as she considered letting the young, African American male student into her car. As this happened, she recognized the irony that the young African American male student also had negative stereotypes and fears about her, a young Muslim woman wearing a hijab (head scarf). Both Aminah and the young man took a risk and had the courage to move past those stereotypes and fears. As a result, they both had a positive experience.

Putnam (2007) conducted a series of research studies that show that as communities become more diverse, people become more isolated from one another. Such diversification has the effect of increasing mistrust, even among our own ethnic group, and disrupting prosocial behaviors and community cooperation. Because of these short-term costs, it is difficult for many to see the long-term economic, cultural, and developmental benefits of diversity. However, Putnam felt that these initial obstacles can be overcome with deliberate, organized, concerted efforts on individual, organizational, societal, and cultural levels. Putnam believed the answer lies in creating *shared social identities*, or providing opportunities for lines between groups to become blurred, which fosters a sense of shared citizenship. Examples include developing programs that bring groups together at churches, schools, community centers, and athletic fields. Such local programs should receive public, national support.

Thus, Putnam (2007) believed society can be advanced if we make conscious efforts to increase meaningful interactions between diverse groups. Reaching out to others who are different from you is a critical step in this process. However, we should warn you that it will not be easy. Any time you learn a new skill you make mistakes. Remember learning to ride a bike? How many times did you fall down before you learned to stay up? Did you give up? Chances are you kept trying until you were peddling your way freely down the block. And once you learned, you never forgot how. It was automatic.

The same is true of multicultural competence. In the beginning you will have some falls, but just get up and keep trying. The more you practice, the easier it will become, and the more effective you will be at interacting with others who are different from you. After you learned to ride a bike, you probably still had a spill from time to time. The same will be true of your cultural interactions. There will always be the awkward moment, the uncomfortable situation, the statement or action that is misunderstood. Not everyone will be receptive when you reach out. Making mistakes is part of the process. As Kathleen said in her story, we still have a responsibility to reach out. Be willing to admit your mistakes and learn from them. It will only help you further along the road to multicultural competence.

Anna Deavere Smith (2000) is an actress whose life mission is to "search for American character." She travels around the country interviewing people hoping to "absorb America" and find the "doorway into the soul of a culture" (p. 12). She then turns these interviews into one-woman shows. One of her most famous plays is *Twilight: Los Angeles, 1992,* in which she portrays interviews conducted with Los Angeles residents in the wake of the unrest that followed the verdict in the Rodney King beating case (mentioned in Chapter 1). Anna Deavere Smith is someone who embodies the spirit of discovery and courage:

> I am constantly in a state of being. . . . It's actually not a bad state to be in. It might just be the best state in which to find oneself during the twenty-first century, as our culture wars continue and identity politics moves into its next phase. At such a time as this, it would be useful, I think, to have at least a cadre of people who were willing to move between cultural lines and across social strata. Globalism will require it, so we might as well practice our moves.
>
> I am prepared for difference, live in difference. My pursuit of American character is, basically, pursuit of difference. Character lives in that which is unique. What is

unique about America is the extent to which it does, from time to time, pull off being a merged culture. Finding American character is a process of looking at fragments, of looking at the un-merged. One has to do the footwork, one has to move from place to place, one has to stand outside. It's not easy. . . .

The most comfortable place to live is inside of what I call one's safe house of identity. I have observed that this is where most people live. Even if they leave a previous identity to enter another identity of choice, they often end up in another safe house, and leave behind any ambiguity that met them as they went from one house to the other. I tend to be more interested in the unsettled part of us.

I am continually leaving safe houses of identity. When you leave the house of what is familiar to you—your family, your race, your social class, your nation, your professional area of expertise—it is not likely that you will find another house that will welcome you with open arms. When you leave your safe house, you will end up standing someplace in the road. I would call these places that are without houses crossroads of ambiguity. On the one hand, they are not comfortable places. On the other hand, in them one acquires the freedom to move. In my work I have moved across many cultural boundaries. For this reason I do not suffer culture shock often. I've developed a lot of stamina for being where I don't "belong." . . .

The state of separation is what is expected. To move out of your separate place, your safe house of identity, is hard work. You have to be prepared. (Smith, 2000, pp. 23–24, 76)

We challenge you to step out of your safe house and venture along the road of discovery. Sometimes the road will be rough and at other times easy, but rich rewards await you along the way.

Developing Empathy

We have many sayings in our culture to depict empathy—walking a mile in someone's shoes, seeing the world through someone's eyes, getting inside someone's skin, and so on. Empathy means genuinely understanding another person's perspective or experience.

My mom has always said, "If you're in America, you should speak English." Often, I've found myself agreeing with her, which supports social learning theory. I always thought that one should be able to adapt to their new country in terms of language. But, last week in class, I had a total paradigm shift. Having learned the importance of culture and in turn culture's importance on language in previous class meetings, and learning about acculturation last week, I have changed my view. I asked myself, would I automatically learn and speak the language of the new culture? My answer was, "Of course not." Further, I altered the situation and made it more personal. What if my ancestors from Holland, who immigrated to the United States, had kept their native Dutch language? According to my grandmother, her Dutch parents would not speak Dutch to her or her siblings; my great-grandparents instead adopted the English language. However, if they had not adopted English, would my grandmother have learned Dutch and have learned more of the Dutch culture? In turn, would my grandmother have taught my mother and her siblings Dutch? How would my life have been changed if this chain of events had occurred? Going back to my mom's comment, I now feel differently about different peoples practicing their own language. It is sad to think of all immigrants from the early 19th century and throughout history who felt they had to completely assimilate into the American culture to fit in, thereby leaving their language, their traditions, their food, etc., behind. It is even more sad to imagine third, fourth, and fifth generations of these immigrants, who will possibly have no connection at all to their ancestors' original culture.

—Kaylah, 20+-year-old European American student

Kaylah was able to develop empathy by relating the issues of immigration, acculturation, and language to the experiences of her own family. Combined with the information she learned in class regarding these issues, this empathy helped change her perspective. Empathy makes us more sensitive to and understanding of the experiences of others and thus builds multicultural competence.

Multicultural competence involves learning about your own culture as well as other cultures. The strategies described here can be used to learn more about yourself and others. We have given only a few suggestions here for how to develop culturally appropriate interpersonal skills. If you act on these suggestions, you may find that these activities can be fun and enriching as well as important. There are many other things that you can do as well. We hope these get you started.

A Change in Worldview

Often students who take this class and read this book make statements such as "I never saw it that way," "This gave me a new perspective," and "I'm noticing things I never did before." You have read similar statements in the narratives in this chapter and throughout this book, such as Kaylah's. Perhaps you have said similar things or had similar thoughts. Such statements reflect a change in worldview.

Previously, we defined *worldview* as a psychological perception of the environment that determines how we think, behave, and feel. Worldview is influenced by past experiences and influences how we perceive, define, and interact with our environment. It is the filter through which we see and interpret the world around us. A change in worldview means you now see and understand things in a different way. As a result of taking this class and reading this book, you most likely see things in a different way. The following story depicts such a moment.

In class we watched a film called *The Color of Fear* [described earlier in this chapter], and halfway through the movie a light bulb went off inside my head, and I felt like Thomas Edison. In my mind, I thought, I get it, I get it. After I had really taken in the message and seen the emotion that every minority [in the film] was describing, I felt like a ton of bricks just hit me, and I felt sad and helpless. Sad that the message I accepted was real, and helpless because I did not know what to do to change it.

When the message hit, it was loud and clear, and I could no longer claim that racism was no longer a part of our daily lives. Even though one would like to think that in a day of progress and technological advances we have moved past that point; that we as a people have united and said we are better than that. But that is still a dream today; it is a closer dream than it was, but still a dream. Racism exists, and that is the light bulb moment. Very powerful and hard to accept, but I can no longer look the other way. Just because I do not experience racism on a day-to-day basis—actually hardly at all—does not mean it does not exist. For many White people, we live in our own world and do not get mistreated. We do not know what that feels like, so in our eyes and mind, it is not unthinkable that we would claim it is not real any more. People live in fantasy worlds they create, but the hardest thing to do is live in reality, because no one wants to live in reality; it is so ugly and hard to bear. And for many White people we have the liberty of living in a fantasy because we do not experience racism. However, for minorities, they do not have the luxury of living in a fantasy, they cannot, they will not survive this cold, hard world, and that is what is meant to be privileged. Minorities day in and day out have to be aware of everything around them. They do not get to live in the same fantasy world as White people, and they know it, and that is why they say White people are privileged, and I get it, we are.

It was so hard to accept, because it hurts. I do not want to think that people are still mistreating others based on the color of their skin. I feel like we should be past that. I feel that there are bigger problems in the world right now, and race should not be an issue. We are at war with three different countries; we should be uniting, not separating. But ultimately, because of our racist views as a country, we are Rome, trying to conquer the rest of the world and change it. We will eventually fall, and it is our privileged mind-set which will be our demise. It was hard to accept racism exists, because to me, I do not feel that way. I did not even think I was privileged, and actually hated hearing it. To me it was a cop out, blaming White people, but I am only one of my group; just because I do not mistreat others and look at race as an issue, does not mean my fellow White people do as I do. That is what is hard about accepting racism; you do not want to believe people you associate with are like that, because you are not, and they ruin it for everyone else. Which leads me to another point . . . I can truly understand why stereotypes can be so frustrating as well, because it claims a characteristic of the type of people you associate with, and you are nothing like that.

But all in all, I do understand racism exists today. But while I was watching the movie, I kept thinking in my head, but what do we do about it? I felt helpless, like it was a lost cause; it is known, but can it be changed? This country was built on a set of ideals, ideals that are imbedded into each and every one of us. We are all victims of racism. But near the end of the movie, a light was shining through. There is an answer, there is something we can do to change it, and we must, because it is not only unfair, it is not right. We need to interfere and stop those who are contributing to racism. We need to change our mind-set. If we change our mind-set, we can change the way we view each other, as well as the way we treat each other. That is what will be the key of our success as humans—the way we treat each other; to actually care about one another and not just our individual success.

We really are all humans. We must be different, and we are, and that is okay. If it was not, God would not have made us all different colors. Maybe that is God's true test to man while he is here living on Earth—to get past the shell of color and see men for who they really are, what is on the inside. Maybe then, and only then, can our souls be saved, on the Day of Judgment—that we connect as brothers and sisters as humans, not as levels of humans based on race. It is a dream, but even dreams do come true.

—Bethany, 20+-year-old European American student

Bethany describes the "light bulb moment" when she gained a deeper personal understanding of racism and White privilege. She went from believing that racism was only something people use as an excuse to understanding that it still has a very real impact on people's lives. She went from denying that she benefits from European American privilege to understanding there are unearned advantages she receives, simply based on her race. She realized that stereotypes negatively impact her personally when people assume she is racist, just because she is European American. She experienced a change in worldview.

Many other concepts you have learned describe this type of *paradigm shift*. For example, instead of imposed etics, you now understand that an accurate examination of human behavior means looking for explanations that are both culture specific (emic) and culturally universal (etic). You now understand cultural relativism, or the importance of interpreting behavior within its cultural context. These shifts signify movement away from cultural encapsulation and ethnocentrism toward *liberation of consciousness*.

In Chapter 1 we described *liberation of consciousness* as one of the primary goals of multi-cultural psychology (D. W. Sue et al., 1996). Liberation of consciousness means going beyond one's individual experience to consider underlying cultural factors that influence the situation. It means expanding your personal perspective to consider that others have differing experiences and opinions that are just as real and valid. It means breaking out of old patterns of thinking and developing new ones. It means being flexible, creative, critical, and open.

According to Freire (1973), *critical consciousness* goes beyond simply perceiving things in new ways; it also involves action. This reflects the action-oriented side of multiculturalism. Multiculturalism stands for values such as justice, equity, and sensitivity, but it also means seeing these values as goals and taking active steps to achieve these goals. In other words, when you see a wrong, you work to make it right. This is social justice. In Bethany's story, there was a moment where she felt hopeless and helpless when confronted with the stark realities of racism. Nevertheless, she found hope. She realized that with this newfound consciousness also came responsibility. She saw changing her mind-set as one step but also working to end racism as another.

We would like to close with this quote from Georgia's U.S. representative John Lewis, a major freedom fighter in the civil rights movement:

> We must not turn away from one another. We must not retreat into separate tribes of like-minded, like-looking people who worship the same god, wear the same clothes, read the same books and eat the same food as one another. This is the way of exclusion, not inclusion. We cannot afford to keep going this way. If we are to survive as a society, as a nation, we must turn toward one another and reach out in every way we can. It is not a choice; it is a necessity. We need to listen to one another, to look to open our minds, as well as our hearts. . . .
>
> Going backward will not take us where we need to go. We must push ahead, and it is not easy. We must struggle with *creating* solutions and *creating* a better society, rather than pulling down what we

U.S. Democratic Congressman and Civil Rights Icon John Lewis. *Photograph by Jim Lo Scalzo / Epa/ Shutterstock*

have built. We cannot run away, not from our problems and not from one another. This is the true meaning of integration—integrating all that we encounter around us, from problems to people, folding it all in to make us larger and stronger, rather than throwing it out, which only makes us small and weak. (Lewis, 1998, pp. 493–494)

Summary

In our increasingly diverse and global society, we come in contact with people who are different from us every day. Sometimes that makes us feel uncomfortable. Our natural tendency is to stick to what is familiar because it is easy and helps us feel good about ourselves. However, if we are to truly benefit from all the world has to offer, it is to our advantage to become skilled at interacting with people from different backgrounds. That is multicultural competence.

The three areas of multicultural competence are (a) awareness of your own culture, (b) understanding other worldviews, and (c) development of culturally appropriate interpersonal skills. Development in these three areas will help you learn to interact effectively with others from different cultural backgrounds. These are important skills in today's world.

According to Fowers and Davidov (2006), multicultural competence is characterized by *openness to the other.* This means being open to people, situations, experiences, values, and beliefs different from one's own. People who embody openness to the other embrace the basic values of multiculturalism discussed in Chapter 1, such as inclusion, sensitivity, respect, and social justice. They engage in self-exploration and self-critique, are open to differing perspectives, actively question their own, engage in meaningful dialogue with others from differing backgrounds, and are willing to be transformed by this process. This is similar to Dr. Joseph White's (2001) concept of *mutual enrichment* (also discussed in Chapter 1) where, through openness to others, both have the opportunity to learn and grow. Building multicultural competence is a lifelong educational process where individuals continuously seek knowledge and cultivate habits that make multicultural competence *second nature.*

Multicultural competence is about applying the things you have learned in this book to your life, your work, and your interactions with others. The theories, concepts, and research covered in this book should increase your self-awareness, your understanding of how your own cultural background influences you. They should increase your understanding of and empathy for people from other groups. This increased understanding of self and others should ultimately improve your interactions with others in school, at work, and in your personal life. If you open yourself up to new knowledge and new experiences, if you take the risk and accept the challenge, your life will be enriched. We are all different; no two people are alike. Our lives are enriched when we adopt an attitude of discovery, open our minds and hearts to the experiences of others, and openly share our experiences with them. If each of you reading this book takes what you have learned and applies it to your life, the world will be a better place.

> Without taking some action, learning is more difficult and less efficient because it is not grounded in real experience.
>
> (Pfeffer & Sutton, 2000, p. 7)

Food for Thought

When one of the authors (JSM) went to graduate school, it was the first time he had ever lived for an extended period of time outside his home state. He encountered people from various places of the country in an intensive environment. (Anyone who has gone to graduate school will tell you how intensive that experience really is.) He sees that time as one of the greatest periods of growth in his life. Another one of the authors (LAB) discusses how enriching it is for her to travel outside the United States. The worldviews of other cultures are quite different from the American worldview, and she learns to understand herself and her culture better through the eyes of people from other cultures. Think back to when you have met someone quite different from you. What did you learn from that person? What did that person learn from you? What you learned from one another is what Joe White calls *mutual enrichment*. Now think back to all of those who seemed quite different from you. This number may be far beyond what you can recall. However, if you conceptualize each of those interactions as being mutually enriching, you will get a sense of just how enriched your lives have become from those encounters.

Critical Thinking Questions

1. Have you ever been to a foreign country and felt out of place? Have you ever been to another part of the country and felt out of place? Have you ever been to a different area of the city you live in that made you feel out of place? How did you handle those situations?

2. Have you ever found yourself distancing yourself from the uncomfortable situations posed in the previous question? Have you ever denied that you felt uncomfortable when on reflection you actually did feel uncomfortable? Did you ever find yourself being defensive about the differences? Did you ever devalue what was different from your areas of comfort? Did you ever discover something about yourself or discover something new and exciting when you were in a situation of difference?

3. Did you ever go back to situations of comfort because they made your life simpler? Did you find such situations to be safer? Did these situations make you feel sane?

4. Has learning about the values and beliefs of others ever made you reexamine your own values and beliefs? Did that make you feel more enriched?

5. Have you ever advocated for people or groups of different demographic characteristics from yours? What were those experiences like?

6. Has anyone ever said something offensive or insensitive in front of you? Was it about you? Was it about someone else? Did you speak up and confront the person who made the offensive comment? Why or why not? What might you do the next time you hear someone make such a comment?

7. What does it mean to have empathy? What is the difference between empathy and sympathy? What are some things you can do to increase your empathy for people from backgrounds that are different from yours? What can you do to help others have more empathy?

8. How has your perspective changed since reading this book and taking this class? What are some ideas, beliefs, or opinions you had before that were challenged by what you learned? What will you do now that you have this new perspective?

Glossary

acceptance The feeling that one is accepted as an equal in the conversation.

acculturated Competent in host culture, but maintains own cultural identity as more essential.

acculturation Experiences and changes that groups and individuals undergo when they come in contact with a different culture.

acculturative stress The feelings of tension and anxiety caused by the inability to adapt in the new country.

additive bilingualism The acquisition of a second language that does not replace the native language.

ALANA Helms's acronym for African Americans, Latinxs, Asian Americans, and Native Americans.

allies Individuals who are on the upside of power and who cross a demographic boundary to advocate for those on the downside of power.

allocentrism Collectivistic tendencies that reside within an individual. Collectivism refers to the society, whereas allocentrism refers to an individual.

allostatic load The physiological cost of chronic stress.

alternation Competence in both the host culture and one's original culture such that one is able to apply the values and behaviors that are appropriate for the situation.

anorexia nervosa An eating disorder marked by such a severe restriction of one's diet that the sufferer's weight falls far below what would be expected, given her or his height and age.

appreciation stage The stage or status in which a child/adolescent begins to broaden his or her perspective to include the race or ethnicity not initially selected for his or her identity.

assimilationist An individual who blends completely into the host society, taking on the values of that society and rejecting his or her original values.

asylum seekers A special class of refugee who either already reside in the United States or are at a U.S. port of entry requesting admittance.

attribution theory A theory that attempts to determine the cause of a behavior. Two major dimensions are internal–external and stable–unstable.

authenticity Being truthful and not trying to be merely politically correct.

autonomy The status in which European American people are comfortable with their European American identity, understand that racism is connected with other forms of oppression, and work to address all forms of oppression.

availability heuristic A mental shortcut whereby the importance, frequency, or credence of something is exaggerated because it comes to mind easily.

aversive racism Covert, unintentional discriminatory behavior practiced by individuals who would deny being racist and who would be appalled to realize that they were engaging in racist acts.

awareness of your own cultural attitudes The part of multicultural competence that involves an individual's being aware that his or her own attitudes may be heavily influenced by his or her own culture and may be different from those of a person with whom he or she is interacting.

barriers Obstacles that reduce the likelihood of engaging in a new behavior.

benefits Advantage gained from a behavior.

bias in the usage A bias introduced when a test is used in an inappropriate manner, such as being administered in a language in which the test taker is not fluent.

bias of the user A bias in the interpretation of a test when the test user has a particular perspective or bias that may disadvantage a person or group.

binge-eating disorder   An eating disorder characterized by consumption of large amounts of food in one sitting, accompanied by feelings of lack of control, embarrassment, disgust, depression, and guilt, along with rapid eating, eating until uncomfortably full, and eating large amounts when not hungry.

biological concept of race   The perspective that a race is a group of people who share a specific combination of physical, genetically inherited characteristics that distinguish them from other groups.

biopsychosocial model   A model of human behavior that takes into consideration biological, cognitive-affective, social-interpersonal, social institutional, and cultural factors.

bulimia nervosa   An eating disorder marked by the consumption of a large amount of food in one sitting—called a binge—followed by the purging of that food, most typically through vomiting but also through extreme exercise or the use of laxatives.

causal stage   An emotional stage when the individual accepts the negative labels attached to a Latinx identity and feels humiliated and traumatized by these labels.

choice of group categorization stage   The stage or status in which a child is forced to choose which race or ethnicity he or she should use as the basis of his or her identity.

class-bound values   Core beliefs of one socioeconomic class that relate principally to that class and may be inappropriate for another level of socioeconomic status.

cognitive dissonance theory   When two cognitions are in conflict, a person will be motivated to change one of them to reduce the unsettled feelings caused by the discrepancy.

cognitive stage   The belief that maintaining a Latinx identity necessarily means being poor, that escape from poverty and prejudice can be attained only through assimilation to the mainstream culture, and that success in life is possible only through assimilation.

collectivism   A social pattern in which individuals tend to be motivated by the group's or collective's preferences, needs, and rights when they come into conflict with the preferences, needs, and rights of the individual.

color-blind   The stance that everyone is the same and that there is no need to acknowledge ethnic or racial differences.

color-blind racial ideology   An attempt to pretend that race and racism will not exist if people ignore race or ethnicity. This ideology has two components: color evasion and power evasion.

coming out   The process by which a gay, lesbian, or bisexual individual openly expresses his or her sexual orientation which used to be undisclosed.

community-based participatory research   An approach to generating knowledge that requires collaboration between research partners on an equal footing, at every phase of a research project.

conceptual equivalence   Refers to a term or phrase that is a culturally meaningful equivalent of the term being examined.

conformity   The stage in which an individual sees the dominant culture as better and superior to all groups and sees his or her own cultural group as *less than* or inferior.

consequence stage   An estrangement from the Latinx community because of the sense that negative attributes are associated with being Latinx.

contact   The status in which European American people are uninformed about the realities of racism and privilege.

cooperative principle   A psycholinguistic term that assumes that we strive to communicate with one another sincerely and effectively when we engage in a conversation.

countercultural individuals   Idiocentric people residing in a collectivistic culture, or allocentric people residing in an individualistic culture.

covert, intentional racism   Discriminatory behavior that is intentional but is covered up so that one can deny his or her racism.

covert, unintentional racism   Discriminatory behavior that is unintentional but serves to perpetuate ongoing racist acts or traditions.

cross-cultural psychology   The study of comparisons across cultures or countries, as opposed to comparisons of groups within one society.

cultural competence   The ability to interact effectively with people of different cultures.

cultural explanations of distress or perceived causes   The ways in which different cultural groups explain psychological symptoms.

cultural idioms of distress   Unique ways in which specific cultural groups express psychological distress.

cultural programming   The ways in which environments shape people without individuals express knowledge or awareness that this is occurring. Cultural programming can lead to implicit attitudes or biases.

cultural psychology   The study of how unique practices within a culture shape behavior, cognition, and effect.

cultural syndromes   Mental disorders, distinguished by unique clusters of symptoms, that only occur in specific cultures.

culture   The values, beliefs, and practices of a group of people, shared through symbols, and passed down from generation to generation.

culture contact   Critical incidents in which people from different cultures come into social contact with one another either (a) by living and working with one another on a daily basis or (b) through visiting other countries on a temporary basis, such as for business, tourism, or study.

culture-bound values Core beliefs of one culture that relate principally to that culture and may be inappropriate for another culture.

defensiveness Trying to protect oneself from acknowledging the difference between oneself and another to avoid the discomfort created by that difference.

delay of gratification The ability to wait for a more desirable reward instead of taking a less desirable reward immediately.

denial Pretending that there is no difference between oneself and another, minimizing its importance, or ignoring the difference altogether.

devaluing Assessing the difference between oneself and another as deficient or less important.

development of culturally appropriate interpersonal skills The part of multicultural competence that involves an individual's knowing how to apply his or her knowledge about someone else's worldview to behaviors that appropriately take into account that knowledge, effecting positive change.

Diagnostic and Statistical Manual of Mental Disorders The primary reference manual used in all mental health fields to classify mental disorders. Published by the American Psychiatric Association, this manual is currently in its fifth edition (2013).

direct communication Blunt communication that is literal and to the point.

discovery Appreciating the difference between oneself and another, seeing how enriching that difference may be, and seeking out opportunities to gain familiarity.

discrimination A negative behavior toward a group or its members based on their categorization.

disintegration The status in which European American people are in enough contact with people of color that their naivete about racism is shattered.

disparity The condition or fact of being unequal.

dissonance The stage in which there is a sudden or gradual occurrence that challenges a person's belief that the dominant group is superior and that minority groups, including his or her own, are inferior.

distancing Avoiding situations in which one feels different. Distancing can occur physically, emotionally, or intellectually.

diversity Acknowledgment of individual human differences that go beyond race, ethnicity, and nationality, such as age, gender, sexual orientation, religion, socioeconomic status, and physical ability.

ecological fit/ecological context Similarity of the social and cultural environments between an immigrant's country of origin and new host country.

emic perspective An attempt to derive meaningful concepts within one culture.

encounter stage of minority identity development The stage or status in which one is confronted with the realities of racism or other forms of devaluation of one's cultural group.

enmeshment/denial stage The stage or status in which a child feels guilty about choosing one race or ethnicity over the other, because this is an implicit rejection of the parent whose race or ethnicity was not chosen.

ethnic glosses Labels used to identify cultural groups that have great within-group heterogeneity.

ethnic minority psychology The study of issues relevant to racial and ethnic groups that have historically been marginalized, oppressed, and underserved.

ethnical psychology The study of the minds of "other races and peoples."

ethnicity A combination of race and culture.

etic perspective An attempt to build theories of human behavior by examining commonalities across many cultures.

eugenics A movement that maintains that only "good genes" should be passed from generation to generation and that "undesirable" groups should be dissuaded from reproducing.

exosystem A layer of context that includes major societal institutions, such as the media and the government.

face giving/giving face Extolling the virtues of another person in public. It would be considered boastful and individualistic if the individual did this himself/herself.

fight If escape is not possible, we may attempt to be aggressive to defend against the danger we perceive.

flee An attempt to escape an uncomfortable or potentially dangerous situation.

freeze To stop and try to interpret a situation that may be a potential threat.

fright Feelings of anxiety about the potentially dangerous situation.

functional equivalence The equating of items on a test or a survey functionally as opposed to literally.

fundamental attribution error The tendency to overestimate dispositional (internal, stable) causes of behaviors and to underestimate external causes of behaviors.

fusion The process whereby one's culture is completely dissolved into other cultures, forming a new, homogeneous culture.

goal attainment According to Ribeau and associates (Ribeau, Baldwin, & Hecht, 1999), this refers to the goal of mutual understanding between two conversational partners.

guilt   A prominent negative emotion in individualistic cultures that involves an individual's sense of personal regret for having engaged in a negative behavior.

health   A complete state of physical, mental, and social well-being, not merely the absence of disease or infirmity.

health behaviors   Undertaken by people to enhance or maintain their well-being.

health belief model   A set of assumptions that suggests that one's health behavior is affected by one's perception of a personal health threat, as well as by how a particular health practice would be effective in reducing the personal health threat.

health disparities   Refers to different rates of health or illness that marginalized groups have in comparison with their privileged counterparts, whereas *health care disparities* refers to the differential access to health care or treatment by health-care providers.

health psychology   The study of psychological influences on how people stay healthy, why they become ill, and how they respond when they do get ill.

high-context communication   Communication in which the context conveys much of the meaning.

human activity   The distinction among being, being and in becoming, and doing. Being refers to an individual's being accepted just as he or she is. Being and in becoming refers to an individual's evolving into something different and presumably better. Doing refers to an individual's being valued for the activity in which he or she is engaged.

identity acceptance   The stage or status in which a gay, lesbian, or bisexual individual fully accepts his or her sexual orientation and is about to come out to others.

identity comparison   The stage or status in which a gay, lesbian, or bisexual individual recognizes his or her feelings about same-sex individuals.

identity confusion   The stage or status in which a gay, lesbian, or bisexual individual begins to question his or her sexual identity.

identity pride   The stage or status in which a gay, lesbian, or bisexual individual openly expresses his or her sexual orientation and takes pride in that identity.

identity synthesis   The state or status in which a gay, lesbian, or bisexual individual is able to integrate all aspects of his or her identities, such as ethnic minority status and gender.

identity tolerance   The stage or status in which a gay, lesbian, or bisexual individual fully recognizes his or her nonheterosexual feelings but attempts to hide them from others and from him- or herself by trying to believe, for example, that it is just a phase he or she is going through.

idiocentrism   Individualistic tendencies that reside within an individual. Individualism refers to the society, whereas idiocentrism refers to an individual.

illusory correlation   An overestimation of the co-occurrence of two minority events.

immersion/emersion   The status in which European American people begin to form a more positive European American identity and to focus on changing European Americans, not Blacks.

immersion/emersion stage of minority identity development   The stage or status in which one involves oneself completely within one's cultural group to the exclusion of the majority group. One emerges from this stage because one cannot meet all of one's needs if society is truly dominated by the majority group.

immigrants   People who move to another country voluntarily. The decision to move can take weeks, months, or even years, which allows these people to prepare for the move and to begin the acculturation process before the move.

implicit bias   Attitudes that are unconscious or involuntary but nonetheless influence how people feel, think, and behave.

imposed etics   The forcing of one culture's worldview on another culture, assuming that one's own worldviews are universal.

incidence   The number of new cases of a disorder diagnosed in a given period of time.

indirect communication   Communication that relies on context and the receiver's ability to draw inferences.

individualism   A social pattern in which individuals tend to be motivated by their own preferences, needs, and rights when they come into conflict with the preferences, needs, and rights of a group or collective in which the individual is a member.

integrationists or biculturals   An individual who holds on to his or her original values while also learning and adopting the values of the host culture.

integration stage   The stage or status in which a child/adolescent/adult sees the benefits of embracing both races or ethnicities.

integrative awareness   The stage in which a person finds greater balance, appreciates his or her own group as well as other cultural groups, and becomes aware of him- or herself as an individual and a cultural being, recognizing differences among cultural groups, both positive and negative.

internalization stage of minority identity development   The stage or status in which one feels comfortable with one's identity. This allows one to express acceptance of other cultures.

internalized oppression   People who are colonized and/or oppressed may automatically accept the superiority of the oppressor.

intersectionality   The meaningful ways in which various social statuses interact (e.g., race, gender, social class) and result in differing experiences with oppression and privilege.

introspection   The stage in which a person becomes less angry at, as well as distrustful of, the dominant group, less immersed in his or her own group, more appreciating of other cultural groups, and more apt to educate him- or herself about his or her own identity, though the process still creates some inner conflict.

kinesics   Bodily movements in conversations, including hand gestures, facial expressions, and eye contact.

language attrition   See subtractive bilingualism.

language brokers   Support translation or interpretation but have no formal training for this task.

language variables   Differences in language (e.g., an English-speaking therapist and a Spanish-speaking client who may have some limited facility with English) or language usage (e.g., Ebonics or Black English).

lifetime incidence   The number of cases of a disorder that occur during one's lifetime.

linguistic equivalence   The translation of a term that carries with it similar meaning from one language to another.

locus of control   The focus of control over outcomes of one's life, be it internal control or external control.

locus of responsibility   The focus of responsibility for one's position in life, be it internal feelings of responsibility or external, societal responsibility.

logical positivism   Scientific approach that attempts to measure "truth" or real phenomena through methods of numbers and statistical analyses.

losing face/saving face   Loss of face involves being publicly revealed for negative behavior; face saving involves being able to protect one's public persona.

low-context communication   Language-dependent communication, in which the words carry most of the meaning and context plays a lesser role.

macrosystem   A layer of context that includes the cultural norms and societal rules that determine rules of conduct.

male privilege   The unearned advantages associated with being male, such as knowing that one's opinions will be respected. Women often feel that their opinions are not respected or are attributed to emotion, not sound reasoning.

marginal man   Stonequist's concept of how one feels when one is caught between two worlds.

marginalist   An individual who does not adopt either the host society's values or his or her original values.

masculine–feminine dimension   A continuum of authority from hierarchical (masculine) to egalitarian (feminine), also known as power distance by Hofstede (1980).

maxim of manner   A communicative presumption that suggests that we are clear in our language and that we pay attention to normal standards of conversation, such as not shouting at someone who is right in front of us.

maxim of quality   A communicative presumption that suggests that we tell each other the truth when we engage in a conversation.

maxim of quantity   A communicative presumption that suggests that we contribute an appropriate amount of talk when we engage in a conversation.

maxim of relevance   A communicative presumption that suggests that our discussion is relevant to the conversation.

mesosystem   A layer of context that includes relationships in the immediate area outside the family, such as schools, work, the extended family, and the community in which one lives.

metric equivalence   Numeric scores that are generally equivalent from one culture to another.

microaggression   A small slight or offense that may be intentional but is mostly unintentional and does not harm the target of the offenses in any major way, but can accumulate to be burdensome over time.

microassault   A blatant verbal, nonverbal, or environmental attack that is intentionally discriminatory or biased.

microinsult   An unintentional behavior or verbal comment conveying rudeness or insensitivity.

microinvalidation   An action that excludes, negates, or dismisses the perceptions of the target person.

microsystem   A layer of context that includes relationships among family members living within one household.

migration period   The period when a group is migrating from the country of origin to the host country. This includes the period immediately before the migration, when the final feelings about moving are experienced and leave is taken from family and friends from the country of origin.

multicultural competence   The ability to work and be effective with individuals who are of a culture different from yours.

multicultural perspective   The perspective that there are multiple groups within a society and all groups are mutually appreciated.

multicultural psychology   The systematic study of behavior, cognition, and affect in settings where people of different backgrounds interact.

multiculturalism as the fourth force   The idea that multicultural psychology is so important that it will fundamentally change the direction of the field of psychology, as psychoanalysis, behaviorism, and humanism did.

native bilingualism The ability to speak two languages from birth, acquired because both languages are spoken in the household.

negative cognitive triad Beck's label for the negative view depressed individuals tend to have of themselves, the world, and the future.

negative stereotyping According to Ribeau and associates (Ribeau, Baldwin, & Hecht, 1999), stereotyping that casts African Americans in a negative light or that limits discussion to "African American topics," such as athletics and music.

overt racism Discriminatory behavior in which people in the majority engage in open, hostile acts of aggression against racial minorities consciously and unapologetically.

paradigm shift A major change in the way people think about a field.

paralanguage Nonverbal vocal cues in conversation, such as loudness of voice, silences, and rates of speech.

people/nature relationship How people relate to nature, be it subjugated to nature, in harmony with nature, or mastery over nature.

personal expressiveness Speaking from the heart and not the head.

personal identity stage The stage or status in which a child bases his or her identity on personal factors, such as self-esteem, instead of on race or ethnicity.

postmigration period The period after settling into the host culture, when the stress of migration continues to be experienced and the adjustment to the new culture takes place.

power dynamics According to Ribeau and associates (Ribeau, Baldwin, & Hecht, 1999), this refers to powerlessness and assertiveness in conversations with African Americans. Sometimes, African Americans can feel powerless when conversing with European American conversational partners. In response, they may "code switch"; that is, they may switch from the mutual conversational rules to African American rules, such as Black English or the like. In code switching, African Americans can regain a sense of control over the conversation.

preencounter stage of minority identity development The stage or status in which one feels and accepts that the world is organized according to the dominant culture and against one's own cultural group.

prejudice A negative judgment about a group or its members based on their categorization.

premigration period The time before migration, when the acculturation process can begin to take place.

prevalence The current rate of a particular disorder at a given point in time.

proxemics Personal space in conversations.

pseudoindependence The status in which European American people begin to acknowledge the realities of racism but believe that it is Blacks who should change, not European Americans.

qualifiers Words or phrases that soften statements, such as "I may be wrong, but . . ."

racial and cultural identity development model (R/CID) A general model that covers all forms of cultural identity and addresses how one relates to oneself, to others of the same culture, to others of different cultures, and to the dominant cultural group.

racial salience At a particular time or in a particular situation, the extent to which one's race is relevant in self-concept.

racism Discriminatory behavior that is backed by institutional power.

refugees People who are forced to move from their homelands because of war or political oppression. The decision to move is almost immediate, taking days, hours, or even minutes, which does not allow these people to prepare for the move or to begin the acculturation process because they do not usually know which country they will finally settle in.

reintegration The status in which European American people retreat to their comfort zone within their European American communities.

relations with conversational partner A communicative presumption that suggests that we use our previous relationship with our conversational partner so that we do not have to repeat shared experiences.

resistance and immersion The stage in which the person becomes more immersed within his or her own cultural group, rejecting the dominant culture with extreme feelings of anger, guilt, and shame for his or her initial preference of the dominant culture and rejection of his or her own.

rule violations A communicative presumption that suggests that we signal our conversational partners when we are about to engage in a violation of one of the other maxims.

safe Things that are similar to us or our values are not a threat because we know how to deal with them and do not have to encounter unsettled feelings of going beyond the familiar to the unknown.

sane Things that are similar to us or our values help us feel normal because if we are like everyone else, we are not out of step; we are validated or affirmed.

separationist An individual who refuses to take on any values of the host society, hanging on to his or her original values completely.

severity Intensity of negative outcome.

shame A prominent negative emotion in collectivistic cultures that involves an individual's sense of regret for having engaged in a negative behavior that reflects badly on his or her family and/or upbringing.

simple Things that are similar to us or our values are easy or comfortable.

social relations The distinction among lineal, collateral, and individualistic. Lineal orientation is a respect for the hierarchy within one's family. Collateral orientation is essentially the same as collectivism, and individualistic orientation is the same as individualism.

sociocultural concept of race The perspective that characteristics, values, and behaviors that have been associated with groups of people who share different physical characteristics serve the social purpose of providing a way for outsiders to view another group and for members of a group to perceive themselves.

somatization The expression of mental disorders through physical disorders.

stereotype A generalization about a group or its members based on their categorization.

stereotype threat A fear that one will confirm the negative stereotype of a group to which one belongs in an area in which the individual excels.

structural introspection The method that structuralists used to examine the contents of people's minds.

structuralism The first formal approach to psychology that attempted to examine the contents of people's minds.

subtractive bilingualism The acquisition of a second language that replaces the native language.

successful resolution state The final stage when the Latinx identity is integrated into one's own identity and positive attributes of the Latinx identity are included.

susceptibility The likelihood of acquiring a disease or being impacted by an illness-producing stimulus.

symbolic racism An issue that does not overtly involve race but is used to promote racism through issues that are associated with one racial group and not the European American majority group, even if this association is not real or is exaggerated.

tag questions Questions added to a statement of assertion, such as "This is good, don't you think?"

time focus An orientation that values a particular time perspective. Some cultures value the past, some value the present, and some value the future. Although all cultures value all three, some cultures value one of these perspectives more than do other cultures.

tripartite model of personal identity The understanding that our self-perceptions are made up of unique, individual aspects, aspects of groups to which we belong, and universal aspects of human beings.

ultimate attribution error The tendency to ascribe the cause of a behavior to dispositional characteristics of the group rather than to an individual member.

understanding According to Ribeau and associates (Ribeau, Baldwin, & Hecht, 1999), the sense that a conversational partner has enough experience to truly understand the African American experience.

understanding other worldviews The part of multicultural competence that involves an individual's knowing that other cultures may have ways of seeing and interpreting the world that are markedly different from his or hers.

VREG Helms's acronym for members of visible racial/ethnic groups.

White privilege The unearned advantages associated with being White in America, such as knowing that Whiteness will be emphasized in the media. People of color are not always portrayed in the media, and when they are, they are often portrayed stereotypically rather than as multifaceted individuals.

working-through stage A stage when the individual feels distress because of alienation from his or her Latinx community and is therefore motivated to integrate one's Latinx identity into a sense of self.

worldview A psychological perception of the environment that determines how we think, behave, and feel.

References

Abe-Kim, J., Takeuchi, D. T., Hong, S., Zane, N., Sue, S., Spencer, M. S., . . . Alegria, M. (2007). Use of mental health–related services among immigrant and US-born Asian Americans: Results from the National Latino and Asian American Study. *American Journal of Public Health, 97,* 91–98.

Aprahamian, M., Kaplan, D. M., Windham, A. M., Sutter, J. A., & Visser, J. (2011). The relationship between acculturation and mental health of Arab Americans. *Journal of Mental Health Counseling, 33*(1), 80–92.

Abrams, K. K., Allen, L. R., & Gray, J. J. (1993). Disordered eating attitudes and behaviors, psychological adjustment and ethnic identity: A comparison of Black and White female college students. *International Journal of Eating Disorders, 14,* 49–57.

Acevedo-Polakovich, I. A., Reynaga-Abiko, G., Garriott, P. O., Derefinko, K. J., Winsett, M. K., Gudonis, L. C., & Brown, T. L. (2007). Beyond instrument selection: Cultural considerations in the psychological assessment of U.S. Latinas/os. *Professional Psychology: Research and Practice, 38,* 375–384.

Ackerman, S., Benjamin, L. S., Beutler, L. E., Gelso, C. J., Goldfried, M. R., Hill, C., . . . Rainer, J. (2001). Empirically supported therapy relationships: Conclusions and recommendations of the Division 29 Task Force. *Psychotherapy, 38*(4), 495–497.

Adembimpe, V. R. (1981). Overview: White norms and psychiatric diagnosis of Black patients. *American Journal of Psychiatry, 138,* 279–285.

Agency for Healthcare Research and Quality. (2015). *2014 national healthcare quality and disparities report.* Washington, DC: Agency for Healthcare Research and Quality. Retrieved from https://www.researchgate.net/profile/Edwin_Huff/publication/275099164_2014_National_Healthcare_Quality_Disparities_Report/links/55329e390cf20ea0a074b1ec.pdf

Agency for Healthcare Research and Quality. (2017. *2016 national healthcare quality and disparities report.* Washington, DC: U.S. Department of Health and Human Services. Retrieved from https://www.ahrq.gov/research/findings/nhqrdr/nhqdr16/index.html

Aichberger, M. C. (2015). The epidemiology of post-traumatic stress disorder: A focus on refugee and immigrant populations. In Schouler-Ocak, M. (Ed.), *Trauma and migration: Cultural factors in the diagnosis and treatment of traumatized immigrants* (pp. 33–37). Basel, Switzerland: Springer International.

Akan, G. E., & Grilo, C. M. (1995). Sociocultural influences on eating attitudes and behaviors, body image, and psychological functioning: A comparison of African-American, Asian-American, and Caucasian college women. *International Journal of Eating Disorders, 18,* 181–187.

Akbar, N. (1981). Mental disorder among African Americans. *Black Books Bulletin, 7,* 18–25.

Akbar, N. (1989). Nigrescence and identity: Some limitations. *The Counseling Psychologist, 17,* 258–263.

Akerlund, M., & Cheung, M. (2000). Teaching beyond the deficit model: Gay and lesbian issues among African Americans, Latinos, and Asian Americans. *Journal of Social Work Education, 36,* 279–293.

Akutsu, P. D., Tsuru, G. K., & Chu, J. P. (2004). Predictors of non-attendance of intake appointments among five Asian American client groups. *Journal of Consulting and Clinical Psychology, 72,* 891–896.

Alba, R., Deane, G., Denton, N., Disha, I., McKenzie, B., & Napierala, J. (2014). The role of immigrant enclaves for Latino residential inequalities. *Journal of Ethnic and Migration Studies, 40*(1), 1–20. doi:10.1080/1369183X.2013.831549

Albee, G. H. (2003). Confrontations and change. In D. K. Freedheim (Ed.), *History of Psychology, Vol. 1: Handbook of Psychology* (pp. 483–508). New York, NY: Wiley.

Alegria, M. A., Canino, G., Shrout, P. E., Woo, M., Duan, N., Vila, D., . . . Meng, X. (2008). Prevalence of mental illness in immigrant and non-immigrant U.S. Latino groups. *The American Journal of Psychiatry, 165*, 359–369.

Alegria, M., Lin, J., Chen, C-N., Duan, N., Cook, B., & Meng, X-L. (2012). The impact of insurance coverage in diminishing racial and ethnic disparities in behavioral health services. *Health Services Research, 47*(3 Pt. 2), 1322–1344.

Alegria, M., Mulvaney-Day, N., Torres, M., Polo, A., Zhun, C., & Canino, G. (2007). Prevalence of psychiatric disorders across Latino subgroups in the United States. *American Journal of Public Health, 97*, 68–75.

Alegria, M., Woo, M., Cao, Z., Torres, M., Meng, X., & Striegel-Moore, R. (2007). Prevalence and correlates of eating disorders in Latinos in the United States. *International Journal of Eating Disorders, 40*, S15–S21.

Alencar, A. (2017). Refugee integration and social media: A local and experiential perspective. *Information, Communication & Society*, 1–16. doi:10.1080/13691 18X.2017.1340500

Alexander, M. (2012). *The new Jim Crow* (rev. ed.). New York, NY: New Press.

Alter, A. L., Aronson, J., Darley, J. M., Rodriguez, C., & Ruble, D. N. (2010). Rising to the threat: Reducing stereotype threat by reframing the threat as a challenge. *Journal of Experimental Social Psychology, 46*, 166–171.

Alter, C. (2018, April 2). The young and the relentless: Adults have failed to stop school shootings. Now it's the kids' turn to try. *Time*, pp. 24–31.

Alter, J. (2010, September 6). "The illustrated man": Obama's enemies have painted him as an alien threat. Can he fight the flight from facts? *Newsweek*, pp. 22–29.

Alvarado, N., & Jameson, K. A. (2002). The use of modifying terms in the naming and categorization of color appearances in Vietnamese and English. *Journal of Cognition and Emotion, 2*, 53–80.

Ambrosino, B. (2017, December 6). Supreme Court hears wedding cake case: Here's what you need to know. *The Washington Post*. Retrieved from https://www.washingtonpost.com/news/acts-of-faith/wp/2017/12/05/wedding-cake-what-you-need-to-know-about-the-highly-anticipated-supreme-court-ruling/?utm_term=.45ae64cbe56a

American College of Pediatricians. (2016, November 19). *The impact of media use and screen time on children, adolescents, and families*. Retrieved from https://www.acpeds.org/?s=The+impact+of+media+use+and+screen+time+on+children%2C+adolescents%2C+and+families+&Submit.x=0&Submit.y=0

American Psychiatric Association. (1952). *Diagnostic and statistical manual of mental disorders*. Washington, DC: American Psychiatric Press.

American Psychiatric Association. (1968). *Diagnostic and statistical manual of mental disorders* (2nd ed.). Washington, DC: American Psychiatric Press.

American Psychiatric Association. (1980). *Diagnostic and statistical manual of mental disorders* (3rd ed.). Washington, DC: American Psychiatric Press.

American Psychiatric Association. (1987). *Diagnostic and statistical manual of mental disorders* (3rd ed., revised). Washington, DC: American Psychiatric Press.

American Psychiatric Association. (1994). *Diagnostic and statistical manual of mental disorders* (4th ed.). Washington, DC: Author.

American Psychiatric Association. (2000). *Diagnostic and statistical manual of mental disorders* (4th ed., text rev.). Washington, DC: Author.

American Psychiatric Association. (2013). *Diagnostic and statistical manual of mental disorders* (5th ed.). Washington, DC: American Psychiatric Association.

American Psychological Association. (2000). Guidelines for psychotherapy with lesbian, gay, and bisexual clients. *American Psychologist, 55*, 1440–1451.

American Psychological Association. (2003). Guidelines on multicultural education, training, research, practice, and organizational change for psychologists. *American Psychologist, 58*, 377–402.

American Psychological Association. (2008). *Report of the Task Force on the Implementation of the Multicultural Guidelines*. Washington, DC: American Psychological Association. Retrieved from https://www.apa.org/about/policy/multicultural.aspx

American Psychological Association. (2012). Guidelines for psychological practice with lesbians, gay, and bisexual clients. *American Psychologist, 67*(1), 10–42. doi:10.1037/a0024659

American Psychological Association. (2017a). *Ethical principles of psychologists and code of conduct, with 2010 and 2016 amendments*. Washington, DC: Author. Retrieved from http://www.apa.org/pi/oema/resources/policy/multicultural-guideline.pdf

American Psychological Association. (2017b). *Multicultural guidelines: An ecological approach to intersectionality*. Washington, DC: Author. Retrieved from http://www.apa.org/about/policy/multicultural-guidelines.pdf

American Psychological Association. (2018). *Cultural diversity and ethnic minority psychology*. Washington, DC: Author. Retrieved from http://www.apa.org/pubs/journals/cdp/

American Psychological Association, APA Working Group on Stress and Health Disparities. (2017). *Stress and health disparities: Contexts, mechanisms, and interventions among racial/ethnic minority and low-socioeconomic status populations*. Washington, DC: Author. Retrieved from http://www.apa.org/pi/health-disparities/resources/stress-report.aspx

American Psychological Association Presidential Task Force on Evidence-Based Practice. (2006). Evidence-based practice in psychology. *American Psychologist, 61*(4), 281–285.

American Psychological Association Task Force on Socioeconomic Status. (2007). *Report of the APA Task Force on Socioeconomic Status*. Washington, DC: Author. Retrieved from http://www.apa.org/pi/ses/resources/publications/task-force-2006.pdf

Americans with Disabilities Act, 42 U.S.C. Chapter 126 (1990). Retrieved from https://www.eeoc.gov/eeoc/history/35th/1990s/ada.html

Anderson, M. (2015, April 30). *Racial and ethnic differences in how people use mobile technology*. Pew Research Center. Retrieved from: http://www.pewresearch.org/fact-tank/2015/04/30/racial-and-ethnic-differences-in-how-people-use-mobile-technology/

Andersen, P. (1999). Cues of culture: The basis of intercultural differences in nonverbal communication. In L. A. Samovar & R. E. Porter (Eds.), *Intercultural communication: A reader* (8th ed., pp. 244–256). Belmont, CA: Wadsworth.

Angier, N. (2000, August 22). Do races differ? Not really, DNA shows. *The New York Times*, p. F1.

Annisette, L. E., & Lafreniere, K. D. (2017). Social media, texting, and personality: A test of the shallowing hypothesis. *Personality and Individual Differences, 115*, 154–158.

Apfelbaum, E. P., Pauker, K., Sommers, S. R., & Ambady, N. (2010). In blind pursuit of racial equality? *Psychological Science, 21*, 1587–1592.

Apfelbaum, E. P., Sommers, S. R., & Norton, M. I. (2008). Seeing race and seeming racist: Evaluating strategic colorblindness in social interaction. *Journal of Personality and Social Psychology, 93*, 918–932.

Aranda, C. (1977). *Dichos: Proverbs and sayings from the Spanish*. New York, NY: Greenwood.

Argyle, M. (1975). *Bodily communication*. New York, NY: International University Press.

Armenta, B. E. (2010). Stereotype boost and stereotype threat effects: The moderating role of ethnic identification. *Cultural Diversity and Ethnic Minority Psychology, 16*, 94–98.

Armour-Thomas, E. (2003). Assessment of psychometric intelligence for racial and ethnic minorities: Some unanswered questions. In G. Bernal, J. E. Trimble, A. K. Burlew, & F. T. L. Leong (Eds.), *Handbook of racial and ethnic minority psychology* (pp. 357–374). Thousand Oaks, CA: Sage.

Arnett, J. J. (2008). The neglected 95%: Why American psychology needs to become less American. *American Psychologist, 63*(7), 602–614.

Aronson, E. (1990, April). *The return of the repressed: Dissonance theory makes a comeback*. Presidential address presented at the 70th Annual Meeting of the Western Psychological Association, Los Angeles, CA.

Arredondo, P., Toporek, R., Brown, S., Jones, J., Locke, D., Sanchez, J., & Stadler, H. A. (1996). Operationalization of multicultural counseling competencies. *Journal of Multicultural Counseling and Development, 24*, 42–78.

Arrigoitía, M. F. (2017, October 3). *After Hurricane Maria, Trump's tweeting dredges up an ugly history for Puerto Ricans*. Retrieved from https://www.opendemocracy.net/melissa-fern-ndez-arrigoit/for-puerto-ricans-trumps-tweet-dredges-up-ugly-history

Artiga, S., Foutz, J., Cornachione, E., & Garfield, R. (2016). *Key facts on health and health care by race and ethnicity*. Kaiser Family Foundation. Retrieved from https://www.kff.org/disparities-policy/report/key-facts-on-health-and-health-care-by-race-and-ethnicity/

Artiga, S., Foutz, J., & Damico, A. (2018). *Health coverage by race and ethnicity: Changes under ACA*. Menlo Park, CA: Kaiser Family Foundation.

Associated Press. (2008, November 15). Obama election spurs race threats, crimes. *NBC News*. Retrieved from http://www.nbcnews.com/id/27738018/ns/us_news-life/t/obama-election-spurs-race-threats-crimes/

Association of American Medical Colleges. (2017). *Diversity in the physician workforce: Facts & figures 2014*. Retrieved from https://www.aamc.org/data/workforce/reports/439214/workforcediversity.html

Astor, M., Caron, C., & Victor, D. (2017, August 13). A guide to the Charlottesville aftermath. *The New York Times*. Retrieved from https://www.nytimes.com/2017/08/13/us/charlottesville-virginia-overview.html

Atkinson, D. R. (2004). *Counseling American minorities* (6th ed.). Boston, MA: McGraw–Hill.

Atkinson, D. R., Furlong, J. J., & Poston, W. C. (1986). Afro-American preferences for counselor characteristics. *Journal of Counseling Psychology, 33*, 326–330.

Atkinson, D. R., Morten, G., & Sue, D. W. (Eds.). (1979). *Counseling American minorities: A cross-cultural perspective*. Dubuque, IA: Brown.

Atkinson, D. R., Morten, G., & Sue, D. W. (1989). A minority identity development model. In D. R. Atkinson, G. Morten, & D. W. Sue (Eds.), *Counseling American minorities: A cross-cultural perspective* (3rd ed., pp. 35–52). Dubuque, IA: Brown.

Atkinson, D. R., Morten, G., & Sue, D. W. (Eds.). (1998). *Counseling American minorities: A cross-cultural perspective* (5th ed.). Dubuque, IA: Brown.

Atkinson, D. R., Thompson, C. E., & Grant, S. K. (1993). A three-dimensional model for counseling racial/ethnic minorities. *Counseling Psychologist, 21*, 257–277.

Awad, G. (2010). The impact of acculturation and religious identification on perceived discrimination for Arab/Middle Eastern Americans. *Cultural Diversity and Ethnic Minority Psychology, 16*, 59–67.

Awad, G. H., Cokley, K., & Ravitch, J. (2005). Attitudes toward affirmative action: A comparison of color-blind versus modern racist attitudes. *Journal of Applied Social Psychology, 33*, 1384–1399.

Azibo, D. A. (1989). African-centered theses on mental health and a nosology of Black/African personality disorder. *Journal of Black Psychology, 15*, 173–214.

Backenroth, G. (1998). Multiculturalism and the deaf community: Examples given from deaf people working in bicultural groups. In P. Pedersen (Ed.), *Multiculturalism as a fourth force* (pp. 111–146). Philadelphia, PA: Brunner/Mazel.

Bailey, T-K. M., Chung, Y. B., Williams, W. S., Singh, A. A., & Terrell, H. K. (2011). Development and validation of the internalized racial oppression scale for Black individuals. *Journal of Counseling Psychology, 58*, 481–493.

Baird, J. (2010, September 6). Blacks are getting happier: Whites are not. Ask your mother why. *Newsweek*, p. 20.

Baker, C. (2013). The development of theories of bilingualism and school achievement. In B. J. Irby, G. Brown, R. Laura-Alecio, & S. Jackson (Eds.), *The handbook of educational theories* (pp. 385–394). Charlotte, NC: Information Age.

Baldwin, J. A. (1981). Notes on an Africentric theory of Black personality. *The Western Journal of Black Studies, 5*, 172–179.

Ballantyne, P. J., Yang, M., & Boon, H. (2013). Interpretation in cross-language research: Tongues-tied in the health care interview? *Journal of Cross-Cultural Gerontology, 28*, 391–405.

Bandura, A. (1977). *Social learning theory.* Englewood Cliffs, NJ: Prentice Hall.

Bandura, A. (1986). *Social foundations of thought and action: A social cognitive theory.* Englewood Cliffs, NJ: Prentice Hall.

Bandura, A. (1997). *Self-efficacy: The exercise of control.* New York, NY: Freeman.

Banks, J. A. (2010). *Multicultural education: Goals and dimensions.* Seattle, WA: Center for Multicultural Education, College of Education, University of Washington. Retrieved from https://education.uw.edu/cme/view

Banks, J. A., & Banks, C. A. M. (Eds.). (2004). *Handbook of research on multicultural education* (2nd ed.). San Francisco, CA: Wiley.

Barker-Hackett, L. (1995). *The real tragedy of O. J.* Unpublished manuscript.

Barker-Hackett, L. (1999, October). Rosy or racist? *Yale Alumni Magazine*, pp. 6–8.

Barker-Hackett, L. (2003). African Americans in the new millennium: A continued search for our true identity. In J. S. Mio & G. Y. Iwamasa (Eds.), *Culturally diverse mental health: The challenges of research and resistance* (pp. 121–140). New York, NY: Brunner–Routledge.

Barker-Hackett, L., & Mio, J. S. (2000). Addressing resistance in larger group formats. In J. S. Mio & G. I. Awakuni (Eds.), *Resistance to multiculturalism: Issues and interventions* (pp. 109–127). Philadelphia: Brunner/Mazel.

Barret, B., & Logan, C. (2002). *Counseling gay men and lesbians: A primer.* Pacific Grove, CA: Brooks/Cole.

Bauder, D. (2007, November 8). Bill O'Reilly's comments about Harlem restaurant draw fire. *USA Today.* Retrieved from http://usatoday30.usatoday.com/life/people/2007-09-25-oreilly-restaurant_n.htm

Baunach, D. M. (2012). Changing same-sex marriage attitudes in America from 1988 through 2010. *Public Opinion Quarterly, 76*, 364–378.

Baye, R. (2012, December 27). Same-sex marriage faces some lingering resistance in Maryland. *The Examiner.* Retrieved from http://search.proquest.com/docview/1265830221?accountid=10357

Bayer, J. B., Ellison, N. B., Schoenebeck, S. Y., & Falk, E. B. (2016). Sharing the small moments: Ephemeral social interaction on Snapchat. *Information, Communication & Society, 19*(7), 956–977.

BBC News. (2017, July 6). *First 100 days:* Where President Trump stands on key issues. *BBC News.* Retrieved from http://www.bbc.com/news/election-us-2016-37468751

Beals, J., Manson, S. M., Keane, E., & Dick, R. W. (1991). Factorial structure of the Center for Epidemiologic Studies: Depression Scale among American Indian college students. *Psychological Assessment, 3*, 623–627.

Bearman, S., Korobov, N., & Thorne, A. (2009). The fabric of internalized sexism. *Journal of Integrated Social Sciences, 1*, 10–47.

Beck, A. T. (1967). *Depression: Causes and treatment.* Philadelphia: University of Pennsylvania Press.

Beck, A. T. (1970). Cognitive therapy: Nature and relation to behavior therapy. *Behavior Therapy, 1*, 184–200.

Becker, A. B. (2012a). Determinants of public support for same-sex marriage: Generational cohorts, social contact, and shifting attitudes. *International Journal of Public Opinion Research, 24*, 524–533.

Becker, A. B. (2012b). What's marriage (and family) got to do with it? Support for same-sex marriage, legal unions, and gay and lesbian couples raising children. *Social Science Quarterly, 93*, 1007–1029.

Becker, A. E. (1995). *Body, self and society: The view from Fiji.* Philadelphia: University of Pennsylvania Press.

Begley, S. (1995, February 13). Three is not enough: Surprising new lessons from the controversial science of race. *Newsweek,* pp. 67–69.

Begley, S. (2010, August 31). Why the belief that Obama is Muslim? People more apt to buy false claim if they focus on differences between themselves and the president, new research shows. *Newsweek.* Retrieved from http://www.newsweek.com/2010/08/31/why-the-belief-that-obama-is-muslim.htm

Behrens, J. T. (1997). Does the White Racial Identity Attitude Scale measure racial and ethnic identity? *Journal of Counseling Psychology, 44,* 3–12.

Belkin, A. (2013). The politics of paranoia. *Journal of Homosexuality, 60,* 214–218.

Belmonte, K., & Opotow, S. (2017). Archivists on archives and social justice. *Qualitative Psychology, 4*(1), 58–72.

Bendahan, S., Zehnder, C., Pralong, F. P., & Antonakis, J. (2015). Leader corruption depends on power and testosterone. *The Leadership Quarterly, 26*(2), 101–122.

Benish, S. G., Quintana, S., & Wampold, B. E. (2011). Culturally adapted psychotherapy and the legitimacy of myth: A direct-comparison meta-analysis. *Journal of Counseling Psychology, 58*(3), 279–289.

Bennett, G. (2017, August 13). Trump's reaction to Charlottesville White nationalist rally criticized by some Republicans. *NPR.* Retrieved from https://www.npr.org/2017/08/13/543197222/trumps-reaction-to-charlottesville-white-nationalist-rally-criticized-by-some-re

Bennett, S. K., & BigFoot-Sipes, D. S. (1991). American Indian and White college student preference for counselor characteristics. *Journal of Counseling Psychology, 38,* 440–445.

Bernal, G., Bonilla, J., & Bellido, C. (1995). Ecological validity and cultural sensitivity for outcome research: Issues for the cultural adaptation and development of psychosocial treatments with Hispanics. *Journal of Abnormal Child Psychology, 23*(1), 67–82.

Bernal, G., Cumba-Aviles, E., & Rodriguez-Quintana, N. (2014). Methodological challenges in research with ethnic, racial, and ethnocultural groups. In F. T. L. Leong, L. Comas-Díaz, G. C. N. Hall, V. C. McLoyd, & J. E. Trimble (Eds.), *APA handbook of multicultural psychology. Vol. 1: Theory and research* (pp. 105–123). Washington, DC: American Psychological Association.

Bernal, G., & Domenech Rodriguez, M. M. (2012). *Cultural adaptations: Tools for evidence-based practice with diverse populations.* Washington, DC: American Psychological Association.

Bernal, M. E., Knight, G. P., Ocampo, K. A., Garza, C. A., & Cota, M. K. (1993). Development of Mexican American identity. In M. E. Bernal & G. P. Knight (Eds.), *Ethnic identity: Formation and transmission among Hispanics and other minorities* (pp. 31–46). Albany: State University of New York Press.

Berry, J. (1988). *Understanding the process of acculturation for primary prevention* (Contract No. 278-85-0024 CH). Minneapolis: University of Minnesota, National Institute of Mental Health Refugee Assistance Program.

Berry, J. (1990). Psychology of acculturation: Understanding individuals moving between cultures. In R. Brislin (Ed.), *Applied cross-cultural psychology* (pp. 232–253). Newbury Park, CA: Sage.

Berry, J. (1997). Preface. In J. Berry, Y. Poortinga, & J. Pandey (Eds.), *Theory and method: Vol. 1. Handbook of cross-cultural psychology* (2nd ed., pp. x–xv). Boston, MA: Allyn & Bacon.

Berry, J. W. (1969). On cross-cultural comparability. *International Journal of Psychology, 4,* 119–128.

Berry, J. W. (1980). Acculturation as varieties of adaptation. In A. Padilla (Ed.), *Acculturation: Theory, models and some new findings.* Boulder, CO: Westview.

Berry, J. W. (1991). Managing the process of acculturation. In *Mental health services for refugees* (DHHS Publication No. ADM 91-1824, pp. 111–122). Rockville, MD: National Institute of Mental Health.

Berry, J. W., Poortinga, Y. H., Segall, M. H., & Dasen, P. R. (1992). *Cross-cultural psychology: Research and applications.* Cambridge: Cambridge University Press.

Berthoff, A. E. (1990). Paulo Freire's liberation pedagogy. *Language Arts, 67*(4), 362–369.

Betancourt, T. S., Newnham, E. A., Birman, D., Lee, R., Heidi Ellis, B., & Layne, C. M. (2017). Comparing trauma exposure, mental health needs, and service utilization across clinical samples of refugee, immigrant, and U.S.-origin children. *Journal of Traumatic Stress, 30*(3), 209–218. doi:10.1002/jts.22186

Bialystok, E., & Craik, F. I. M. (2010). Cognitive and linguistic processing in the bilingual mind. *Current Directions in Psychological Science, 19,* 19–23.

Billante, J., & Hadad, C. (2010, May 14). Study: White and Black children biased toward lighter skin. *CNN.* Retrieved from http://www.cnn.com/2010/US/05/13/doll.study/

Binet, A., & Simon, Th. (1905). Méthodes nouvelles pour le diagnostic du niveau intellectuel des anormaux. *Année psychologique, 11,* 191–244.

Bissinger, B. (2015, June 15). Caitlyn Jenner: The full story. Retrieved from https://www.vanityfair.com/hollywood/2015/06/caitlyn-jenner-bruce-cover-annie-leibovitz

Black, L. (1996). Families of African origin: An overview. In M. McGoldrick, J. Giordano, & J. K. Pearce (Eds.), *Ethnicity and family therapy* (2nd ed., pp. 57–65). New York, NY: Guilford Press.

Blaut, J. M. (1992). The theory of cultural racism. *Antipode: A Radical Journal of Geography, 23,* 289–299.

Blumenbach, J. F. (1775/1795/1865). *The anthropological treatises of Johann Friedrich Blumenbach.* London: Longman, Green, Longman, Roberts, and Green. Retrieved from http://www.archive.org/details/anthropologicaltooblumuoft

Blumenthal, D. S. (2011). Is community-based participatory research possible? *American Journal of Preventive Medicine, 40*(3), 386–389.

Boatright-Horowitz, S. L., & Soeung, S. (2009). Teaching White privilege to White students can mean saying good-bye to positive student evaluations. *American Psychologist, 64,* 574–575.

Bochner, S. (1999). Cultural diversity within and between societies: Implications for multicultural social systems: In P. Pedersen (Ed.), *Multiculturalism as a fourth force.* Philadelphia, PA: Brunner/Mazel.

Bogen, K. W., Bleiweiss, K., & Orchowski, L. M. (2018). Sexual violence is #NotOkay: Social reactions to disclosures of sexual victimization on Twitter. *Psychology of Violence.* doi:10.1037/vio0000192

Bolmont, M., Cacioppo, J. T., & Cacioppo, S. (2014). Love is in the gaze: An eye-tracking study of love and sexual desire. *Psychological Science, 25*(9), 1748–1756.

Bolzman, C., Fibbi, R., & Vial, M. (2006). What to do after retirement? Elderly migrants and the question of return. *Journal of Ethnic and Migration Studies, 32*(8), 1359–1375.

Bond, M. H., & Hwang, K.-K. (1986). The social psychology of Chinese people. In M. H. Bond (Ed.), *The psychology of the Chinese people* (pp. 213–266). Hong Kong: Oxford English Press.

Bonilla-Silva, E. (2003). *Racism without racists: Color-blind racism and the persistence of racial inequality in the United States.* Lanham, MD: Rowman & Littlefield.

Bonilla-Silva, E. (2017). *Racism without racists: Color-blind racism and the persistence of racial inequality in the United States.* Lanham, MD: Rowman & Littlefield.

Bonilla-Silva, E., & Dietrich, D. (2011). The sweet enchantment of color-blind racism in Obamerica. *Annals of the American Academy of Political and Social Science, 634,* 190–206.

Botelho, G. (2013, September 19). First Miss America of Indian descent embraces discussion of diversity. *CNN.* Retrieved from http://www.cnn.com/2013/09/18/us/miss-america-nina-davuluri/

Bowen, D., Tomoyasu, N., & Cauce, A. M. (1991). The triple threat: A discussion of gender, class, and race differences in weight. *Women and Health, 17,* 123–143.

Bowleg, L. (2012). The problem with the phrase women and minorities: Intersectionality—an important theoretical framework for Public Health. *American Journal of Public Health, 102*(7), 1267–1273.

Boyd-Franklin, N. (1989). *Black families in therapy.* New York, NY: Guilford Press.

Boyd-Franklin, N. (2003). *Black families in therapy.* New York, NY: Guilford Press.

Boylan, J. J., Jennings, J. R., & Matthews, K. A. (2016). Childhood socioeconomic status and cardiovascular reactivity and recovery among Black and White men: Mitigating effects of psychological resources. *Health Psychology, 35*(9), 957–966.

Bracha, H. S., Ralston, T. C., Matsukawa, J. M., Matsunaga, S. M., Williams, A. E., & Bracha, A. S. (2004). Does "fight or flight" need updating? *Psychosomatics, 45,* 448–449.

Brave Heart, M. Y. H., Lewis-Fernandez, R., Beals, J., Hasin, D. S., Sugaya, L., Wang, S., . . . Blanco, C. (2016). Psychiatric disorders and mental health treatment in American Indians and Alaska natives: Results of the National Epidemiologic Survey on Alcohol and Related Conditions. *Social Psychiatry and Psychiatric Epidemiology, 51*(7), 1033–1046. doi:10.1007/s00127-016-1225-4

Brenda. (2017, November 15). Youth voice: I am not your good immigrant. *Huffington Post.* Retrieved from https://www.huffingtonpost.com/entry/youth-voice-i-am-not-your-good-immigrant_us_5a0b21bee4b060fb7e59d3f0

Brennan, C., & Cook, K. (2015, September 25). Why college students aren't voting (and why it matters). *USA Today.* Retrieved from http://college.usatoday.com/2015/09/25/why-college-students-arent-voting

Brenner, C. (1982). *The mind in conflict.* New York, NY: International Universities Press.

Breslau, J., Aguilar-Gaxiola, S., Kendler, K. S., Su, M., Williams, D., & Kessler, R. C. (2006). Specifying race–ethnic differences in risk for psychiatric disorder in a U.S. national sample. *Psychological Medicine, 36,* 57–68.

Brewer, S. (2016, August 4). Huge victory for tribes: Federal courts overturn voter ID laws. *Indian Country Today.* Retrieved from https://indiancountrymedianetwork.com/news/nativ-news/huge-victory-for-tribes-federal-courts-overturn-voter-id-laws/

Brislin, R. W. (1980). Translation and content analysis of oral and written materials. In H. C. Triandis & J. W. Berry (Eds.), *Handbook of cross-cultural psychology: Vol. 2. Methodology* (pp. 389–444). Boston, MA: Allyn & Bacon.

Brislin, R. W. (1986). The wording and translation of research instruments. In W. J. Lonner & J. W. Berry (Eds.), *Field methods in cross-cultural research* (pp. 137–164). Newbury Park, CA: Sage.

Brislin, R. W. (2000). *Understanding culture's influence on behavior* (2nd ed.). Fort Worth, TX: Harcourt College.

Brislin, R. W., Lonner, W. J., & Thorndike, R. M. (1973). *Cross-cultural research methods.* New York, NY: Wiley.

Brondolo, E., Gallo, L. C., & Myers, H. F. (2009). Race, racism, and health: Disparities, mechanisms, and interventions. *Journal of Behavioral Science, 32,* 1–8.

Bronfenbrenner, U. (1979). *The ecology of human development.* Cambridge, MA: Harvard University Press.

Broverman, I., Broverman, D., Clarkson, F., Rosenkrantz, P., & Vogel, S. (1970). Sex-role stereotypes and clinical judgments of mental health. *Journal of Consulting and Clinical Psychology, 34,* 1–7.

Brower, K. A., & Dodge, C. (2010, November 5). Bush says New Orleans flyover after Katrina a "huge mistake." *Bloomberg.* Retrieved from https://www.bloomberg.com/news/articles/2010-11-05/bush-calls-new-orleans-flyover-in-wake-of-hurricane-katrina-huge-mistake-

Brown, L. S. (1986). Confronting internalized oppression in sex therapy with lesbians. *Journal of Homosexuality, 12,* 99–107.

Brown, L. S. (2011). *Queer mentoring—it's not about coming out any more (and it is).* Invited presentation at the Western Psychological Association Annual Convention, Los Angeles, CA.

Brown, P., & Levinson, S. (1978). Universals in language usage: Politeness phenomena. In E. Goody (Ed.), *Questions and politeness* (pp. 56–289). Cambridge: Cambridge University Press.

Bruce, B., & Agras, W. S. (1992). Binge eating in females: A population-based investigation. *International Journal of Eating Disorders, 12,* 365–373.

Bruder, C., Blessing, L., & Wandke, H. (2014). Adaptive training interfaces for less-experienced, elderly users of electronic devices. *Behaviour and Information Technology, 33,* 4–15.

Buchwald, D. S., Beals, J., & Manson, S. M. (2000). Use of traditional healing among Native Americans in a primary care setting. *Medical Care, 38,* 1191–1199.

Bumiller, E. (2011, July 22). Obama ends "Don't Ask, Don't Tell" policy. *The New York Times.* Retrieved from http://www.nytimes.com/2011/07/23/us/23military.html?_r=0

Burnam, M. A., Hough, R. L., Kamo, M., Escobar, J. I., & Telles, C. A. (1987). Acculturation and lifetime prevalence of psychiatric disorders among Mexican Americans in Los Angeles. *Journal of Health and Social Behavior, 28,* 89–102.

Burns, A. (2012, January 18). Romney speaking fees show he's out of touch, Santorum says. *Politico.* Retrieved from http://www.politico.com/blogs/burns-haberman/2012/01/santorum-mitt-out-of-touch-on-speaking-fees-111264.html

Burrow, A. L., & Hill, P. L. (2012). Flying the unfriendly skies? The role of forgiveness and race in the experience of racial microaggressions. *Journal of Social Psychology, 152,* 639–653.

Butcher, J. N., Dahlstrom, W. G., Graham, J. R., Tellegen, A. M., & Kaemmer, B. (1989). *Minnesota Multiphasic Personality Inventory-2 (MMPI-2): Manual for administration and scoring.* Minneapolis: University of Minnesota Press.

Cabral, R. R., & Smith, T. B. (2011). Racial/ethnic matching of clients and therapists in mental health services: A meta-analytic review of preferences, perceptions, and outcomes. *Journal of Counseling Psychology, 58*(4), 537–554. doi:10.1037/a0025266

Calvert, S. (2018, April 19). Philadelphia police chief apologizes for Starbucks incident. Commissioner Richard Ross regrets initially saying officers did nothing wrong when they arrested two African-American men. *The Wall Street Journal.* Retrieved from https://www.wsj.com/articles/philadelphia-police-chief-apologizes-for-starbucks-incident-1524169541

Camarota, S. A., & Jensenius, K. (2009, May). Trends in immigrant and native employment. *Center for Immigration Studies Backgrounder.* Retrieved from http://www.cis.org/sites/cis.org/files/articles/2009/back509.pdf

Campa, A. L. (1947). Sayings and riddles in New Mexico. *The University of New Mexico Bulletin, 15,* 5–67.

Campbell, D. T., & Stanley, J. C. (1963). *Experimental and quasi-experimental designs for research.* Chicago, IL: Rand McNally College.

Capehart, J. (2014, June 6). Time for the Supreme Court to join nation in support of gay marriage. *The Washington Post.* Retrieved from https://www.washingtonpost.com/blogs/post-partisan/wp/2014/06/06/time-for-the-supreme-court-to-join-nation-in-support-of-gay-marriage/?utm_term=.4de7a2d2b934

Capodilupo, C. M. (2016). Microaggressions in counseling and therapy. In D. W. Sue & D. Sue (Eds.), *Counseling the culturally diverse: Theory and practice* (7th ed., pp. 179–212). Hoboken, NJ: Wiley.

Carey, N. (2017). Charlottesville: A reminder of hate for upstate civil rights leaders. *Greenville Online.* Retrieved from http://www.greenvilleonline.com/story/news/2017/08/18/charlottesville-reminder-hate-upstate-civil-rights-leaders/580138001/

Carli, L. (1990). Gender, language, and influence. *Journal of Personality and Social Psychology, 59,* 941–951.

Carpenter, C. J. (2010). A meta-analysis of the effectiveness of health belief model variables in predicting behavior. *Health Communication, 25*(8), 661–669. doi:10.1080/10410236.2010.521906

Carr, D. (2008, November 9). How Obama tapped into social networks' power. *The New York Times*. Retrieved from https://www.nytimes.com/2008/11/10/business/media/10carr.html

Carrero, M. G. (2018, March 2). Puerto Rico death toll revisited. *The Los Angeles Times*, p. A6.

Carter, R. T. (1995). *The influence of race and racial identity in psychotherapy*. New York, NY: Wiley.

Casad, B. J., & Merrit, S. M. (2014). The importance of stereotype threat mechanisms in workplace outcomes. *Industrial and Organizational Psychology: Perspectives on Science and Practice, 7*, 413–419.

Casas, J. M. (1984). Policy, training, and research in counseling psychology: The racial/ethnic minority perspective. In S. D. Brown & R. W. Lent (Eds.), *Handbook of Counseling Psychology* (pp. 785–831). New York, NY: Wiley.

Cass, V. C. (1979). Homosexual identity formation: A theoretical model. *Journal of Homosexuality, 4*, 219–235.

Castellanos, J., & Gloria, A. M. (2007). Research considerations and theoretical application for best practices in higher education: Latina/os achieving success. *Journal of Hispanic Higher Education, 6*, 378–396.

Castillo, L. G., Brossart, D. F., Reyes, C. J., Conoley, C. W., & Phoummarath, M. J. (2007). The influence of multicultural training on perceived multicultural counseling competencies and implicit racial prejudice. *Journal of Multicultural Counseling and Development, 35*(4), 243–255. doi:10.1002/j.2161-1912.2007.tb00064.x

CBS News Video. (1996, October 23). *O.J. in black and white*. New York, NY: CBS News.

Ceballo, R. (2017). Passion or data points? Studying African American women's experiences with infertility. *Quantitative Psychology, 4*(3), 302–314.

Center for Medicaid Services, Office of Minority Health, and RAND Corporation. (2017). *Racial and ethnic disparities by gender in health care in Medicare advantage*. Retrieved from https://www.cms.gov/About-CMS/Agency-Information/OMH/Downloads/Health-Disparities-Racial-and-Ethnic-Disparities-by-Gender-National-Report.pdf

Centers for Disease Control and Prevention. (2011). *Sexual identity, sex of sexual contacts, and health-risk behaviors among students in grades 9–12: Youth risk behavior surveillance*. Atlanta, GA: U.S. Department of Health and Human Services. Retrieved from http://www.cdc.gov/mmwr/preview/mmwrhtml/ss6007a1.htm

Centers for Disease Control and Prevention. (2016). *Crude birth rates, fertility rates, and birth rates, by age, race, and Hispanic origin of mother: United States, selected years 1950–2015*. Retrieved from https://www.cdc.gov/nchs/data/hus/2016/003.pdf

Centers for Disease Control and Prevention (2016, February). *New HIV infections in the United States*. Retrieved from: https://www.cdc.gov/nchhstp/newsroom/docs/factsheets/new-hiv-infections-508.pdf

Centers for Disease Control and Prevention. (2017, November 17). Racial/ethnic health disparities among rural adults: United States, 2012–2015. *Morbidity and Mortality Weekly Report, 66*(23). Retrieved from https://www.cdc.gov/mmwr/volumes/66/ss/ss6623a1.htm

Centers for Disease Control and Prevention. (2018). *Behavioral risk factor surveillance system*. Retrieved from https://www.cdc.gov/brfss/index.html

Chambless, D. L., & Hollon, S. (1998). Defining empirically supported therapies. *Journal of Consulting and Clinical Psychology, 66*(1), 7–18.

Chan, C. (1989). Lesbians, gay men, and their families: Common clinical issues. *Journal of Counseling and Development, 68*, 16–20.

Chan, C. (1992). Cultural considerations in counseling Asian American lesbians and gay men. In S. Dworkin & F. Gutierrez (Eds.), *Counseling gay men and lesbians: Journey to the end of the rainbow* (pp. 115–124). Alexandria, VA: American Association for Counseling and Development.

Chang, T., & Kwan, K.-L. K. (2009). Asian American racial and ethnic identity. In N. Tewari & A. N. Alvarez (Eds.), *Asian psychology: Current perspectives* (pp. 113–133). New York, NY: Psychology Press.

Chao, M. M., Chen, J., Roisman, G. I., & Hong, Y.-Y. (2007). Essentializing race: Implications for bicultural individuals' cognition and physiological reactivity. *Psychological Science, 18*, 341–348.

Chao, R. C. L., Wei, M., Good, G. E., & Flores, L. Y. (2011). Race/ethnicity, color-blind racial attitudes, and multicultural counseling competence: The moderating effects of multicultural counseling training. *Journal of Counseling Psychology, 38*, 72–82.

Chapman, M. V., Hall, W. J., Lee, K., Colby, R., Coyne-Beasley, T., Day, S., . . . Payne, K. (2018). Making a difference in medical trainees' attitudes toward Latino patients: A pilot study of an intervention to modify implicit and explicit attitudes. *Social Science & Medicine, 199*, 202–208. doi:10.1016/j.socscimed.2017.05.013

Charmaraman, L., & Grossman, J. M. (2010). Importance of race and ethnicity: An exploration of Asian, Black, Latino, and multiracial adolescent identity. *Cultural Diversity and Ethnic Minority Psychology, 16*, 144–151.

Chen, S., Sullivan, N. Y., Lu, Y. E., & Shibusawa, T. (2003). Asian Americans and mental health services: A study of utilization patterns in the 1990s. *Journal of Ethnic & Cultural Diversity in Social Work, 12*, 19–42.

Cheng, C.-Y., & Lee, F. (2009). Multiracial identity integration: Perceptions of conflict and distance among multiracial individuals. *Journal of Social Issues, 65*, 51–68.

Cheryan, S., & Tsai, J. L. (2007). Ethnic identity. In F. T. L. Leong, A. G. Inman, A. Ebreo, L. H. Yang, L. Kinoshita, & M. Fu (Eds.), *Handbook of Asian American psychology* (2nd ed., pp. 125–139). Thousand Oaks, CA: Sage.

Chetty, R., Stepner, M., Abraham, S., Lin, S., Scuderi, B., Turner, N., . . . Cutler, D. (2016). The association between income and life expectancy in the United States, 2001–2014. *JAMA: Journal of the American Medical Association, 315*(16), 1750–1766.

Cheung, F. M. (1985). Cross-cultural consideration for the translation and adaptation of the Chinese MMPI in Hong Kong. In J. N. Butcher & C. D. Spielberger (Eds.), *Advances in personality assessment* (Vol. 4, pp. 131–158). Hillsdale, NJ: Erlbaum.

Cheung, F. M., & Halpern, D. F. (2010). Women at the top: Powerful leaders define success as work + family in a culture of gender. *American Psychologist, 65*, 182–193.

Cheung, R. K., & Snowden, L. R. (1990). Community mental health and ethnic minority populations. *Community Mental Health Journal, 26*, 277–291.

Chin, J. L., Mio, J. S., & Iwamasa, G. Y. (2006). Ethical conduct of research with Asian and Pacific Islander American populations. In J. E. Trimble & C. B. Fisher (Eds.), *The handbook of ethical research with ethnocultural populations & communities* (pp. 117–135). Thousand Oaks, CA: Sage.

Chiu, C.-Y., Gelfand, M. J., Yamagishi, T., Shteynberg, G., & Wan, C. (2010). Intersubjective culture: The role of intersubjective perceptions in cross-cultural research. *Perspectives on Psychological Science, 5*, 482–493.

Choi, I., Nisbett, R. E., & Norenzayan, A. (1999). Causal attribution across cultures: Variation and universality. *Psychological Bulletin, 125*, 47–63.

Chokshi, N., & Craighill, P. (2014, June 6). Half of Americans say gay marriage is a constitutional right. *The Washington Post.* Retrieved from http://www.washingtonpost.com/blogs/govbeat/wp/2014/06/06/half-of-americans-say-gay-marriage-is-a-constitutional-right/

Choudhuri, D. D., Santiago-Riviera, A. L., & Garrett, M. T. (2012). *Counseling and diversity.* Belmont, CA: Cengage.

Christenson, A. M., Buchanan, J. A., Houlihan, D., & Wanzek, M. (2011). Command use and compliance in staff communication with elderly residents of long-term care facilities. *Behavior Therapy, 42*, 47–58.

Cillizza, C. (2014, August 17). Obama's vision of a post-racial America looks even more distant than before. *The Washington Post.* Retrieved from http://www.washingtonpost.com/politics/obamas-vision-of-a-post-racial-america-looks-even-more-distant-than-before/2014/08/17/cdcd0fbe-261c-11e4-8593-da634b334390_story.html

Clark, A. E., D'Ambrosio, C., & Ghislandi, S. (2016). Adaptation to poverty in long-run panel data. *Review of Economics and Statistics, 98*(3), 591–600.

Clark, K. B., & Clark, M. P. (1939). The development of consciousness of self and the emergence of racial identification of Negro pre-school children. *Journal of Social Psychology, 10*, 591–599.

Clark, K. B., Chein, I., & Cook, S. W. (2004). The effects of segregation and the consequences of desegregation: A (September 1952) social science statement in the *Brown v. Board of Education of Topeka* Supreme Court Case. *American Psychologist, 59*, 495–501.

Clarke, V., Ellis, S. J., Peel, E., & Riggs, D. W. (2010). *Lesbian, gay, bisexual, trans and queer psychology: An introduction.* Cambridge: Cambridge University Press.

Clinton, W. J. (2000, November 22). *Statement on singing the Minority Health and Health Disparities Research and Education Act of 2000.* University of California: The American Presidency Project. Retrieved from http://www.presidency.ucsb.edu/ws/index.php?pid=990

Clymer, E. C. (1995). The psychology of deafness: Enhancing self-concept in the deaf and hearing impaired. *Family Therapy, 22*(2), 113–120.

Coates, T. (2017, September 14). The first White president. *The Atlantic.* Retrieved from https://www.theatlantic.com/magazine/archive/2017/10/the-first-white-president-ta-nehisi-coates/537909/

Cohen, R. J., & Swerdlik, M. E. (2002). *Psychological testing and assessment: An introduction to test and measurement* (5th ed.). Boston, MA: McGraw–Hill.

Cohn, D., & Caumont, A. (2016). *10 demographic trends that are shaping the U.S. and the world.* Washington, DC: Pew Research Center. Retrieved from http://www.pewresearch.org/fact-tank/

Colantonio, L. D., Gamboa, C. M., Richman, J. S., Levitan, E. B., Soliman, E. Z., Howard, G., & Safford, M. M. (2017). Black–White differences in incident fatal, nonfatal, and total coronary heart disease clinical perspective. *Circulation, 136*(2), 152–166. doi:10.1161/CIRCULATIONAHA.116.025848

Colapinto, J. (2004). Gender gap: What were the real reasons behind David Reimer's suicide? *Slate.* Retrieved from https://slate.com/technology/2004/06/why-did-david-reimer-commit-suicide.html

Colbow, A. J., Cannella, E., Vispoel, W., Morris, C. A., Cederberg, C., Conrad, M., . . . Liu, W. M. (2016). Development of the classism attitudinal profile (CAP). *Journal of Counseling Psychology, 63*(5), 571–585.

Cole, M., Gay, J., Glick, J., & Sharp, D. W. (1971). *The cultural context of learning and thinking.* New York, NY: Basic Books.

Coleman, H. L. K. (1996). Portfolio assessment of multicultural counseling competency. *The Counseling Psychologist, 216–229.*

Coleman, H. L. K., Wampold, B. E., & Casali, S. L. (1995). Ethnic minorities' ratings of ethnically similar and European American counselors: A meta-analysis. *Journal of Counseling Psychology, 42*(1), 55–64. doi:10.1037/0022-0167.42.1.55

Collaborative Psychiatric Epidemiology Surveys. (n.d.). Retrieved from https://www.psc.isr.umich.edu/dis/data/resource/detail/1644

Colquhoun, G. (2002). *Playing God.* Auckland, New Zealand: Publishing Press.

Comas-Díaz, L. (1990). Ethnic minority mental health: Contributions and future directions of the American Psychological Association. In F. C. Serafica, A. I. Schwebel, R. K. Russell, P. D. Isaac, & L. B. Myers (Eds.), *Mental health of ethnic minorities* (pp. 275–301). New York, NY: Praeger.

Comas-Díaz, L. (2006). Latino healing: The integration of ethnic psychology into psychotherapy. *Psychotherapy: Theory, Research, Practice, Training, 43,* 436–453.

Comas-Díaz, L. (2009). Changing psychology: History and legacy of the Society for the Psychological Study of Ethnic Minority Issues. *Cultural Diversity and Ethnic Minority Psychology, 15*(4), 400–408. doi:10.1037/a0017560

Comas-Díaz, L. (2014). Multicultural psychotherapy. In F. T. L. Leong, L. Comas-Díaz, G. C. Nagayama Hall, V. C. McLoyd, & J. E. Trimble (Eds.), *APA handbook of multicultural psychology. Vol. 2: Applications and training* (pp. 419–441). Washington, DC: American Psychological Association.

Conger, J. J. (1975). Proceedings of the American Psychological Association for the year 1974: Minutes of the annual meeting of the Council of Representatives. *American Psychologist, 30,* 620–651. doi:10.1037/h0078455

Constantine, M. G., Hage, S. M., Kindaichi, M. M., & Bryant, R. M. (2007). Social justice and multicultural issues: Implications for practice and training of counselors and counseling psychologists. *Journal of Counseling & Development, 85,* 24–29.

Constantine, M. G., & Ladany, N. (2001). New visions for defining and assessing multicultural counseling competence. In J. G. Ponterotto, J. M. Casas, L. A. Suzuki, & C. M. Alexander (Eds.), *Handbook of multicultural counseling* (2nd ed., pp. 482–498). Thousand Oaks, CA: Sage.

Constantine, M. G., Redington, R. M., & Graham, S. V. (2009). Counseling and psychotherapy with African Americans. In H. Neville, B. Tynes, & S. Utsey (Eds.), *Handbook of African American Psychology* (pp. 431–444). Thousand Oaks, CA: Sage.

Cook, D. A., & Helms, J. E. (1988). Visible racial/ethnic group supervisees' satisfaction with cross-cultural supervision as predicted by relationship characters. *Journal of Counseling Psychology, 35,* 268–273.

Cooper-Patrick, L., Gallo, J. J., Powe, N. R., Steinwachs, D. M., Eaton, W. W., & Ford, D. E. (1999). Mental health service utilization by African Americans and Whites: The Baltimore Epidemiologic Catchment Area follow-up. *Medical Care, 37,* 1034–1045.

Corey, G. (2017). *Theory and practice of counseling and psychotherapy* (10th ed.). Boston, MA: Cengage.

Corralejo, S. M., & Domenech Rodríguez, M. M. (2018). Technology in parenting programs: A systematic review of existing interventions. *Journal of Child and Family Studies.* https://doi.org/10.1007/s10826-018-1117-1

Cortés, C. E. (2000). *The children are watching: How the media teach about diversity.* New York, NY: Teachers College Press.

Corvin, S., & Wiggins, F. (1989). An antiracism training model for White professionals. *Journal of Multicultural Counseling and Development, 17,* 105–114.

Cosby, B. (2004, May 17). Address at the NAACP on the 50th anniversary of *Brown v. Board of Education.* In *American Rhetoric Online Speech Bank.* Retrieved from http://www.americanrhetoric.com/speeches/billcosbypoundcakespeech.htm

Costa, R. E., & Shimp, C. P. (2011). Methods courses and texts in psychology: "Textbook science" and "tourist brochures." *Journal of Theoretical and Philosophical Psychology, 31,* 25–43.

Cox, D., Lienesch, R., & Jones, R. P. (2017). Beyond economics: Fears of cultural displacement pushed the White working class to Trump. *PRRI/The Atlantic.* Retrieved from https://www.prri.org/research/white-working-class-attitudes-economy-trade-immigration-election-donald-trump/

Coyne, S. M., Padilla-Walker, L. M., & Holmgren, H. G. (2018). A six-year longitudinal study of texting trajectories during adolescence. *Child Development, 89*(1), 58–65.

Crago, M., Shisslak, C. J., & Estes, L. S. (1996). Eating disturbances among American minority groups: A review. *International Journal of Eating Disorders, 19,* 239–248.

Craven, J. (2017, June 21). There is no justice in America for Black people killed by cops. *The Huffington Post.* Retrieved from https://www.huffingtonpost.com/entry/philando-castile-no-justice_us_59444c46e4b0f15cd5bb6415

Crawford, M. (2003). Gender and humor in social context. *Journal of Pragmatics, 35*, 1413–1430.

Crawford, M., & Gressley, D. (1991). Creativity, caring, and context: Women's and men's accounts of humor preferences and practices. *Psychology of Women Quarterly, 15*, 217–231.

Crenshaw, K. (1989). Demarginalizing the intersection of race and sex: A Black feminist critique of anti- discrimination doctrine, feminist theory, and anti-racist politics. *University of Chicago Legal Forum, 1989*, 139–167.

Crethar, H. C., Torres Rivera, E., & Nash, S. (2008). In search of common threads: Linking multicultural, feminist, and social justice counseling paradigms. *Journal of Counseling and Development, 86*, 269–278.

Cross, W. E., Jr. (1971). The Negro-to-Black conversion experience. *Black World, 20*, 13–27.

Cross, W. E., Jr. (1991). *Shades of Black: Diversity in African American identity*. Philadelphia, PA: Temple University Press.

Cross, W. E., Jr. (1995). The psychology of nigrescence: Revisiting the Cross model. In J. G. Ponterotto, J. M. Casas, L. A. Suzuki, & D. M. Alexander (Eds.), *Handbook of multicultural counseling* (pp. 93–122). Thousand Oaks, CA: Sage.

Cross, W. E., Jr., Parham, T. A., & Helms, J. E. (1991). The stages of Black identity development: Nigrescence models. In R. L. Jones (Ed.), *Black psychology* (3rd ed., pp. 319–338). Berkeley, CA: Cobb & Henry.

Cross, W. E., Jr., Strauss, L., & Fhagen-Smith, P. E. (1999). African American identity development across the life span: Educational implications. In R. H. Sheets & E. R. Hollins (Eds.), *Racial and ethnic identity in school practices: Aspects of human development* (pp. 29–47). Mahwah, NJ: Erlbaum.

Cross, W. E., Jr., & Vandiver, B. J. (2001). Nigrescence theory and measurement: Introducing the Cross Racial Identity Scale (CRIS). In J. G. Ponterotto, J. M. Casas, L. A. Suzuki, & C. M. Alexander (Eds.), *Handbook of multicultural counseling* (2nd ed., pp. 371–393). Thousand Oaks, CA: Sage.

Cummings, C. (2013, June 27). DSM-5 on culture: A significant advance. *Thefpr.org blog*. Retrieved from https://thefprorg.wordpress.com/2013/06/27/dsm-5-on-culture-a-significant-advance/

Cushner, K., & Brislin, R. W. (1996). *Intercultural interactions: A practical guide* (2nd ed.). Thousand Oaks, CA: Sage.

Dalla Zuanna, T., Milana, M., Simonato, L., Spadea, T., Petrelli, A., Cacciani, L., & Canova, C. (2017). Avoidable hospitalization among migrants and ethnic minority groups: A systematic review. *European Journal of Public Health, 27*(5), 861–868.

Dalrymple, A. (2016, November 30). Audio: Tribe objected to pipeline nearly 2 years before lawsuit. *Bismarck Tribune*.

Retrieved from http://bismarcktribune.com/news/state-and-regional/audio-tribe-objected-to-pipeline-nearly-years-before-lawsuit/article_51f94b8b-1284-5da9-92ec-7638347fe066.html

Dana, R. H. (1993). *Multicultural assessment perspectives for professional psychology*. Needham Heights, MA: Allyn & Bacon.

D'Andrea, M. (2003). Expanding our understanding of White racism and resistance to change in the fields of counseling and psychology. In J. S. Mio & G. Y. Iwamasa (Eds.), *Culturally diverse mental health: The challenges of research and resistance* (pp. 17–37). New York, NY: Brunner–Routledge.

Darwin, C. R. (1871). *The descent of man, and selection in relation to sex*. The complete work of Charles Darwin online. Retrieved from http://darwin-online.org.uk/converted/pdf/1889_Descent_F969.pdf

David Reimer, 38, subject of the John/Joan case, dies. (2004, May 12). *The New York Times*. Retrieved from http://www.nytimes.com/2004/05/12/international/americas/12REIM.html

David, E. J. R. (2008). A colonial mentality model of depression for Filipino Americans. *Cultural Diversity and Ethnic Minority Psychology, 14*, 118–227.

David, E. J. R. (2009). Internalized oppression, psychopathology, and cognitive behavioral therapy among historically oppressed groups. *Journal of Psychological Practice, 15*, 71–103.

David, E. J. R. (2010). Testing the validity of the colonial mentality implicit association test (CMIAT) and the interactive effects of covert and overt colonial mentality on Filipino American mental health. *Asian American Journal of Psychology, 1*, 31–45.

David, E. J. R. (Ed.). (2014). *Internalized oppression: The psychology of marginalized groups*. New York, NY: Springer.

David, E. J. R., & Derthick, A. O. (2014). What is internalized oppression, and so what? In E. J. R. David (Ed.), *Internalized oppression: The psychology of marginalized groups* (pp. 1–30). New York, NY: Springer.

David, E. J. R., & Okazaki, S. (2006). Colonial mentality: A review and recommendation for Filipino American psychology. *Cultural Diversity and Ethnic Minority Psychology, 12*, 1–16.

David, E. J. R., & Okazaki, S. (2010). Activation and automaticity of colonial mentality. *Journal of Applied Social Psychology, 40*, 850–887.

David, E. J. R., Okazaki, S., & Saw, A. (2009). Bicultural self-efficacy among college students: Initial scale development and mental health correlates. *Journal of Counseling Psychology, 56*, 211–226.

Davis, C., & Yager, J. (1992). Transcultural aspects of eating disorders: A critical literature review: *Culture, Medicine, and Psychiatry, 16*, 377–394.

DeBruyn, L. M., Hymbaugh, K., & Valdez, N. (1988). Helping communities address suicide and violence: The special initiatives team of the Indian Health Service. *American Indian and Alaska Native Mental Health Research, 1*, 56–65.

de França, D. X., & Monteiro, M. B. (2013). Social norms and the expression of prejudice: The development of aversive racism in childhood. *European Journal of Social Psychology, 43*, 263–271.

Dehlendorf, C., Bryant, A. S., Huddleston, H. G., Jacoby, V. L., & Fujimoto, V. Y. (2010). Health disparities: Definitions and measurements. *American Journal of Obstetrics and Gynecology, 202*(3), 212–213. doi:10.1016/j.ajog.2009.12.003

Delgado-Romero, E. A. (2001). Counseling a Hispanic/Latino client—Mr. X. *Journal of Mental Health Counseling, 23*, 207–222.

Dempster, M., Howell, D., & McCorry, N. K. (2015). Illness perceptions and coping in physical health conditions: A meta-analysis. *Journal of Psychosomatic Research, 79*(6), 506–513. doi:10.1016/j.jpsychores.2015.10.006

Denzin, N. K., & Lincoln, Y. (Eds.). (2007a). *Collecting and interpreting qualitative materials* (3rd ed.). Thousand Oaks, CA: Sage.

Denzin, N. K., & Lincoln, Y. (Eds.). (2007b). *Strategies of qualitative inquiry* (3rd ed.). Thousand Oaks, CA: Sage.

Deters, K. A. (1997). Belonging nowhere and everywhere: Multiracial identity development. *Bulletin of the Menninger Clinic, 61*, 368–385.

De Vogue, A., Moran, T., & Hafenbrack, J. (2013). *Proposition 8: Supreme Court ruling explained*. Retrieved from http://abcnews.go.com/Politics/prop-supreme-court-ruling-explained/story?id=19439962

DeVore, C. (2015). Of the four majority-minority states in America, minorities do best in Texas. *Forbes*. Retrieved from https://www.forbes.com/sites/chuckdevore/2015/06/21/america-majority-minority-by-2044-with-four-states-already-there-minorities-do-best-in-texas/#499cd41c287c

Devos, T. (2006). Implicit bicultural identity among Mexican American and Asian American college students. *Cultural Diversity & Ethnic Minority Psychology, 12*, 381–402.

Devos, T., Gavin, K., & Quintana, F. J. (2010). Say "adios" to the American dream? The interplay between ethnic and national identity among Latino and Caucasian Americans. *Cultural Diversity and Ethnic Minority Psychology, 16*, 37–49.

Devos, T., & Ma, D. (2008). Is Kate Winslet more American than Lucy Liu? The impact of construal processes on the implicit ascription of a national identity. *British Journal of Social Psychology, 47*, 191–215.

Diala, C., Muntaner, C., Walrath, C., Nickerson, K. J., LaVeist, T. A., & Leaf, P. J. (2000). Racial differences in attitudes toward professional mental health care and in the use of services. *American Journal of Orthopsychiatry, 70*, 455–464.

DiAngelo, R. (2016). *What does it mean to be white? Developing white racial literacy*. New York: Peter Lang.

Diamond, J. (1997). *Guns, germs, and steel: The fates of human societies*. New York, NY: Norton.

Díaz Andrade, A., & Doolin, B. (2016). Information and communication technology and the social inclusion of refugees. *MIS Quarterly, 40*(2), 405–416.

Divi, C., Koss, R. G., Schmaltz, S. P., & Loeb, J. M. (2007). Language proficiency and adverse events in US hospitals: A pilot study. *International Journal for Quality in Health Care, 19*(2), 60–67. doi:10.1093/intqhc/mzl069

Docterman, E. (2017, June 19). Why Wonder Woman broke through. *Time*, p. 32.

Dolan, B. (1991). Cross-cultural aspects of anorexia nervosa and bulimia: A review. *International Journal of Eating Disorders, 10*, 67–78.

Dolphin, C. Z. (1999). Variables in the use of personal space in intercultural transactions. In L. A. Samovar & R. E. Porter (Eds.), *Intercultural communication: A reader* (8th ed., pp. 266–276). Belmont, CA: Wadsworth.

Domenech Rodríguez, M. M. (2018). Staying woke at the intersections. In L. Comas-Díaz & C. Inoa Vazquez (Eds.), *Latina psychologists: Thriving in the cultural borderlands*. New York, NY: Routledge.

Dorfman, D. D. (1978). The Cyril Burt question: New findings. *Science, 201*, 1177–1186.

Dovidio, J. F. (2001, January). *Why can't we get along? Interpersonal biases and interracial distrust*. Invited address delivered at the National Multicultural Conference and Summit II, Santa Barbara, CA.

Dovidio, J. F., & Gaertner, S. L. (2000). Aversive racism and selection decisions: 1989 and 1999. *Psychological Science, 11*, 319–323.

Dovidio, J. F., & Gaertner, S. L. (2004). Aversive racism. In M. P. Zanna (Ed.), *Advances in experimental social psychology* (Vol. 36, pp. 1–51). San Diego, CA: Academic Press.

Dovidio, J. F., & Gaertner, S. L. (2008). New directions in aversive racism research: Persistence and pervasiveness. In C. Willis-Esqueda (Ed.), *Motivational aspects of prejudice and racism* (pp. 43–67). New York, NY: Springer Science & Business Media.

Dovidio, J. F., Gaertner, S. L., Penner, L. A., Pearson, A. R., & Norton, W. E. (2009). In J. L. Chin (Ed.), *Aversive racism—How unconscious bias influences behavior: Implications for legal, employment, and health care contexts*.

Vol. 3. Social justice matters (pp. 21–35). Santa Barbara, CA: Praeger/ABC-CLIO.

Drescher, J. (2015). Queer diagnoses revisited: The past and future of homosexuality and gender diagnoses in *DSM* and *ICD*. *International Review of Psychiatry, 27*(5): 386–395.

Dubowitz, T., Ncube, C., Leuschner, K., & Tharp-Gilliam, S. (2015). A natural experiment opportunity in two low-income urban food desert communities: Research design, community engagement methods, and baseline results. *Health Education & Behavior, 42*(1, Suppl.), 87S–96S.

Duckitt, J. H. (1992). Psychology and prejudice: A historical analysis and integrative framework. *American Psychologist, 47*, 1182–1193.

Duran, E., & Duran, B. (1995). *Native American post-colonial psychology*. Albany: State University of New York Press.

Dwairy, M. (2006). *Counseling and psychotherapy with Arabs and Muslims: A culturally sensitive approach*. New York, NY: Teachers College Press.

Eagly, A. H. (2009). The his and hers of prosocial behavior: An examination of the social psychology of gender. *American Psychologist, 64*, 644–658.

Ekman, P. (1972). Universal and cultural differences in facial expression of emotion. In J. R. Cole (Ed.), *Nebraska symposium on motivation, 1971* (pp. 207–283). Lincoln: University of Nebraska Press.

Elliott, J. (2005). *Using narrative in social research: Qualitative and quantitative approaches*. Thousand Oaks, CA: Sage.

Elliot, S., Scott, M. D., Jensen, A. D., & McDonough, M. (1982). Perceptions of reticence: A cross-cultural investigation. In M. Burgoon (Ed.), *Communication yearbook 5* (pp. 591–602). New Brunswick, NJ: Transaction Books.

Ellis, R. (2017, December 4). Charlottesville protests: City officials to hear report critical of police response. *CNN*. Retrieved from https://www.cnn.com/2017/12/04/us/charlottesville-city-council-riot-report/index.html

Engel, G. L. (1977). The need for a new medical model: A challenge for biomedicine. *Science, 196*, 129–136.

Enns, C. Z. (1997). *Feminist theories and feminist psychotherapies*. New York, NY: Harrington Park.

Erigha, M. (2016). Do African Americans direct science fiction or blockbuster franchise movies? Race, genre, and contemporary Hollywood. *Journal of Black Studies, 47*(6), 550–569.

Erikson, E. H. (1950/1963). *Childhood and society* (2nd ed.). New York, NY: Norton.

Erikson, E. H. (1964). *Insight and responsibility*. New York, NY: Norton.

Eron, L. D. (2000). A psychological perspective. In V. B. Van Hasselt & M. Hersen (Eds.), *Aggression and violence: An introductory text* (pp. 23–39). Needham Heights, MA: Allyn & Bacon.

Eron, L. D., Huessman, L. R., Lefkowitz, M. M., & Walder, L. O. (1996). Does television violence cause aggression? In D. F. Greenberg (Ed.), *Criminal careers: Vol. 2. The international library of criminology, criminal justice and penology* (pp. 311–321). Brookfield, VT: Dartmouth.

Eron, L. D., Walder, L. O., & Lefkowitz, M. M. (1971). *The learning of aggression in children*. Boston, MA: Little, Brown.

Fadiman, A. (2012). *The spirit catches you and you fall down: A Hmong child, her American doctors, and the collision of two cultures* (paperback ed.). New York, NY: Farrar, Straus and Giroux.

Falicov, C. J. (1998). *Latino families in therapy: A guide to multicultural practice*. New York, NY: Guilford Press.

Falicov, C. J. (2005). Mexican families. In M. McGoldrick, J. Giordano, & N. Garcia-Preto (Eds.), *Ethnicity and family therapy* (3rd ed., pp. 229–241). New York, NY: Guilford Press.

Falicov, C. J. (2014). *Latino families in therapy* (2nd ed.). New York, NY: Guilford Press.

Family Acceptance Project. (2009). Family rejection as a predictor of negative health outcomes in White and Latino lesbian, gay, and bisexual young adults. *Pediatrics, 123*(1), 346–352.

Farley, C. J. (2004, June 3). What Bill Cosby should be talking about. *Time*. Retrieved from http://content.time.com/time/nation/article/0,8599,645801,00.html

Faucet, R., & Feuer, A. (2017). Far-right groups surge into national view in Charlottesville. *The New York Times*. Retrieved from https://www.nytimes.com/2017/08/13/us/far-right-groups-blaze-into-national-view-in-charlottesville.html

Fazio, R. H., & Dunton, B. C. (1997). Categorization by race: The impact of automatic and controlled components of racial prejudice. *Journal of Experimental Social Psychology, 33*(5), 451–470.

Fazio, R. H., & Olson, M. A. (2003). Implicit measures in social cognition research: Their meaning and use. *Annual Review of Psychology, 54*, 297–327.

Felsenthal, E. (2017, December 18). The choice. *Time*, pp. 30–33.

Ferdman, B. M., & Gallegos, P. I. (2001). Racial identity development and Latinos in the United States. In C. Wijeyesinghe & B. W. Jackson (Eds.), *New perspectives on racial identity development: A theoretical and practical anthology*. New York: New York University Press.

Fernandez, K., Boccaccini, M. T., & Noland, R. M. (2007). Professionally responsible test selection for Spanish-speaking clients: A four-step approach for identifying and selecting translated tests. *Professional Psychology: Research and Practice, 38*, 363–374.

Fernandez, M., Fausset, R., & Bidgood, J. (2018, May 18). In Texas school shooting, 10 dead, 10 hurt and many unsurprised. *The New York Times*. Retrieved from https://www.nytimes.com/2018/05/18/us/school-shooting-santa-fe-texas.html

Festinger, L. (1957). *A theory of cognitive dissonance*. Stanford, CA: Stanford University Press.

Fields, A. J. (2010). Multicultural research and practice: Theoretical issues and maximizing cultural exchange. *Professional Psychology: Research and Practice, 41*, 196–201.

Fish, J. M. (2002). A scientific approach to understanding race and intelligence. In J. J. Fish (Ed.), *Race and intelligence: Separating science from myth* (pp. 1–28). Mahwah, NJ: Erlbaum.

Fitzgibbon, M. L., Spring, B., Avellone, M. E., Blackman, L. R., Pingitore, R., & Stolley, M. R. (1998). Correlates of binge eating in Hispanic, Black, and White women. *International Journal of Eating Disorders, 24*, 43–52.

Flaskerud, J. H. (2007). Cultural competence: What effect on reducing health disparities? *Issues in Mental Health Nursing, 28*, 431–434.

Forbes, C. E., & Schmader, T. (2010). Retraining attitudes and stereotypes to affect motivation and cognitive capacity under stereotype threat. *Journal of Personality and Social Psychology, 99*, 740–754.

Ford, H., & Crowther, S. (1922). *My life and work*. New York, NY: Doubleday, Page.

Ford, T. E., Boxer, C. F., Armstrong, J., & Edel, J. J. (2008). More than "just a joke": The prejudice-releasing function of sexist humor. *Personality and Social Psychology Bulletin, 34*, 159–170.

Fortson, R., & Larson, C. (1968). The dynamics of space. An experimental study in proxemic behavior among Latin Americans and North Americans. *Journal of Communication,* 109–116.

Fouad, N. A., Gerstein, L. H., & Toporek, R. L. (2006). Social justice and counseling psychology in context. In R. L. Toporek, L. H. Gerstein, N. A. Fouad, G. Roysircar, & T. Israel (Eds.), *Handbook for social justice in counseling psychology* (pp. 1–16). Thousand Oaks, CA: Sage.

Fowers, B. J., & Davidov, B. J. (2006). The virtue of multiculturalism. *American Psychologist, 61*(6), 581–594. doi:10.1037/0003-066X.61.6.581

Foxwell, R., Morley, C., & Frizelle, D. (2013). Illness perceptions, mood and quality of life: A systematic review of coronary heart disease patients. *Journal of Psychosomatic Research, 75*(3), 211–222. doi:10.1016/j.jpsychores.2013.05.003

Francis, L. E., Berger, C. S., Giardini, M., Steinman C., & Kim, K. (2009). Pregnant and poor in the suburb: The experiences of economically disadvantaged women of color with prenatal services in a wealthy suburban county. *Journal of Sociology & Social Welfare, 36*, 133–157.

Franklin, A. J. (2009). Reflections on ethnic minority psychology: Learning from the past so the present informs our future. *Cultural Diversity and Ethnic Minority Psychology, 15*(4), 416–424. doi:10.1037/a0017560

Freedheim, D. K. (Ed.). (2003). Handbook of psychology: Vol. 1. History of psychology, in I. B. Weiner (Ed.), *Handbook of psychology*. New York, NY: Wiley.

Freire, P. (1970). *Pedagogy of the oppressed*. New York, NY: Continuum.

Freire, P. (1973). *Education for critical consciousness*. New York, NY: Continuum.

Freud, S. (1909/1977). *Five lectures on psychoanalysis*. New York, NY: Norton.

Gabrielson, R., Sagara, E., & Jones, R. G. (2014). Deadly force in Black and White. *ProPublica*. Retrieved from https://www.propublica.org/article/deadly-force-in-black-and-white

Gaertner, S. L., & Dovidio, J. F. (1986). The aversive form of racism. In J. F. Dovidio & S. L. Gaertner (Eds.), *Prejudice, discrimination and racism* (pp. 61–90). Orlando, FL: Academic Press.

Gainor, K. A. (1992). Internalized oppression as a barrier to effective group work with Black women. *Journal for Specialists in Group Work, 17*, 235–242.

Galton, F. (1883). *Inquiries into human faculty and its development*. London: Macmillan.

Gans, H. J. (2009). First generation decline: Downward mobility among refugees and immigrants. *Ethnic & Racial Studies, 32*, 1658–1670.

Garcia, M. T. (2017, October 4). Puerto Ricans deserve US support, not Trump's racist stereotype. *National Catholic Reporter*. Retrieved from https://www.ncronline.org/news/opinion/puerto-ricans-deserve-us-support-not-trumps-racist-stereotype

Garcia, O., & Kleifgen, J. A. (2010). *Educating emergent bilinguals: Policies, programs, and practices for English language learners*. New York, NY: Teachers College Press.

Garcia-Preto, N. (1996). Latino families: An overview. In M. McGoldrick, J. Giordano, & J. K. Pearce (Eds.), *Ethnicity and family therapy* (2nd ed., pp. 141–154). New York, NY: Guilford Press.

Garcia-Preto, N. (2005). Latino families: An overview. In M. McGoldrick, J. Giordano, & N. Garcia-Preto (Eds.), *Ethnicity & family therapy* (3rd ed., 153–165). New York, NY: Guilford Press.

Gardner, H. (1983). *Frames of mind: The theory of multiple intelligences*. New York, NY: Basic Books.

Gardner, H. (1993). *Multiple intelligences: The theory in practice*. New York, NY: Basic Books.

Gardner, H. (1999). *Intelligence reframed*. New York, NY: Basic Books.

Garfield, J. C., Weiss, S. L., & Pollack, E. A. (1973). Effects of the child's social class on school counselors' decision making. *Journal of Counseling Psychology, 20*, 166–168.

Garwick, A., & Auger, S. (2000). What do providers need to know about American Indian culture? Recommendations from urban Indian family caregivers. *Families, Systems & Health, 18*, 177–190.

Gay, G. (2012). Culture and communication in the classroom. In L. A. Samovar, R. E. Porter, & E. R. McDaniel (Eds.), *Intercultural communication: A reader* (13th ed., pp. 381–399). Boston, MA: Wadsworth.

Gee, G. C., & Ford, C. L. (2011). Structural racism and health inequities. *Du Bois Review: Social Science Research on Race, 8*(1), 115–132. doi:10.1017/S1742058X11000130

Georgaca, E. (2001). Rethinking qualitative methodology in psychology [Review of the book *The quality of qualitative research*]. *Contemporary Psychology: APA Review of Books, 46*, 268–270.

Ghosh, B. (2010, August 30). Islam in America. It's part of the fabric of life, but protests reveal a growing hostility to the religion of Muslims. *Time*, pp. 20–26.

Giles, H., Khajavy, G. H., & Choi, C. W. (2012). Intergenerational communication satisfaction and age boundaries: Comparative Middle Eastern data. *Journal of Cross-Cultural Gerontology, 27*, 357–371.

Gillie, D. (1977). The IQ question. *Phi Delta Kappan, 58*, 469.

Gilligan, C. (1982/1993). *In a different voice: Psychological theory and women's development*. Cambridge, MA: Harvard University Press.

Gleason, B. (2018). Thinking in hashtags: Exploring teenagers' new literacies practices on Twitter. *Learning, Media and Technology, 43*(2), 165–180.

Goff, P. A., Jackson, M. C., Di Leone, B. A. L., Culotta, C. M., & DiTomasso, N. A. (2014). The essence of innocence: Consequences of dehumanizing Black children. *Journal of Personality and Social Psychology, 106*(4), 526–545.

Goldman, M. (1980). Effect of eye contact and distance on the verbal reinforcement of attitude. *Journal of Social Psychology, 111*, 73–78.

Goldstein, E. B. (2005). *Cognitive psychology: Connecting mind, research, and everyday experience*. Belmont, CA: Wadsworth.

Gonzales, J. M., Alegria, M., Prihoda, T. J., Copeland, L. A., & Zeber, J. E. (2011). How the relationship of attitudes toward mental health treatment and service use differs by age, gender, ethnicity/race and education. *Social Psychiatry and Psychiatric Epidemiology, 46*, 45–57.

Gonzalez, J., Erickson, C., Hall, E., Lundquist, C., Showers, A., & Zamora, I. (2012, August). Microaggression experiences and the American Indian college student. Poster presented at the 120th American Psychological Association Convention, Orlando, FL.

Gonzalez, J., Simard, E. Baker-Demeray, T., Iron Eyes, C. (2014). *Internalized Oppression of North American Indigenous Peoples*. In EJR, David (Ed). The Internalized Oppression of Marginalized Groups. (pp. 31-56.) New York: Springer.

Gopaldas, A. (2013). Intersectionality 101. *Journal of Public Policy and Marketing, 23*(Special Issue), 90–94.

Goodale, G. (2012, March 20). Anti-Obama slogans with racist slants on the rise in Election 2012. *Christian Science Monitor*. Retrieved from http://www.csmonitor.com/USA/Elections/President/2012/0320/Anti-Obama-slogans-with-racist-slants-on-the-rise-in-Election-2012

Goodenough, D. R. (1978). Field dependence. In H. London & J. E. Exner (Eds.), *Dimensions of personality* (pp. 165–216). New York, NY: Wiley.

Gordon, M. M. (1964). *Assimilation in American life*. New York, NY: Oxford University Press.

Gorski, P. C. (2010). The challenge of defining multicultural education. *Multicultural Education Pavilion*. Retrieved from https://studylib.net/doc/6885865/i.-the-challenge-of-defining--multicultural-education-

Goss, S., Wade, A., Skirvin, J. P., Morris, M., Bye, K. M., & Huston, D. (2013). Effects of unauthorized immigration on the actuarial status of the social security trust funds. *Social Security Administration Actuarial Note, 151*. Retrieved from http://www.socialsecurity.gov/oact/NOTES/pdf_notes/note151.pdf

Gould, S. J. (1996). *The mismeasure of man*. New York, NY: Norton.

Govere, L., & Govere, E. M. (2016). How effective is cultural competence training of healthcare providers on improving patient satisfaction of minority groups? A systematic review of literature. *Worldviews on Evidence-Based Nursing, 13*(6), 402–410. doi:10.1111/wvn.12176

Goyette, B. (2013, May 31). Cheerios commercial featuring mixed race family gets racist backlash. *Huffington Post*. Retrieved from http://www.huffingtonpost.com/2013/05/31/cheerios-commercial-racist-backlash_n_3363507.html

Grabois, H. (1999). The convergence of sociocultural theory and cognitive linguistics: Lexical semantics and the L2 acquisition of love, fear and happiness. In G. B. Palmer & D. J. Occhi (Eds.), *Languages of sentiment: Cultural constructions of emotional substrates* (pp. 201–233). Amsterdam: John Benjamins.

Graham, G. N., & Spengler, R. F. (2009). Collaborating to end health disparities in our lifetime. *American Journal of Public Health, 99*, 1930–1932.

Gray, J. J., Ford, K., & Kelly, L. M. (1987). The prevalence of bulimia in a Black college population. *International Journal of Eating Disorders, 6,* 733–740.

Grbich, C. (2007). *Qualitative data analysis: An introduction.* Thousand Oaks, CA: Sage.

Great chain of being. (2011). Retrieved from http://en.wikipedia.org/wiki/Great_chain_of_being

Greene, B., & Boyd-Franklin, N. (1996). African American lesbian couples: Ethnocultural considerations in psychotherapy. *Women and Therapy, 19. Special Issue. Couples Therapy: Feminist Perspectives,* 49–60.

Greenson, R. R. (1967). *The technique and practice of psychoanalysis* (Vol. 1). New York, NY: International Universities Press.

Greenwald, A. G., & Banaji, M. R. (1995). Implicit social cognition: Attitudes, self-esteem, and stereotypes. *Psychological Review, 102*(1), 4–27.

Greenwald, A. G., McGhee, D. E., & Schwartz, J. L. (1998). Measuring individual differences in implicit cognition: the implicit association test. *Journal of Personality and Social Psychology, 74*(6), 1464–1480. https://doi.org/10.1037//0022-3514.74.6.1464 Greenwood, D., & Long, C. R. (2015). When movies matter: Emerging adults recall memorable movies. *Journal of Adolescent Research, 30*(5), 625–650.

Grice, H. P. (1975). Logic and conversation. In P. Cole & J. L. Morgan (Eds.), *Syntax and semantics: Vol. 3. Speech acts* (pp. 41–58). New York, NY: Seminar Press.

Grieco, E. M., & Cassidy, R. C. (2001). *Overview of race and Hispanic origin: 2000.* U.S. Census Bureau. Retrieved from https://www.census.gov/prod/2001pubs/c2kbr01-1.pdf

Grills, C. (2002). African-centered psychology: Basic principles. In T. A. Parham (Ed.), *Counseling persons of African descent: Raising the bar of practitioner competence* (pp. 10–24). Thousand Oaks, CA: Sage.

Grover, K. (2015, May 22). American Indians serve in the U.S. military in greater numbers than any ethnic group and have since the Revolution. *Huffington Post.* Retrieved from https://www.huffingtonpost.com/national-museum-of-the-american-indian/american-indians-serve-in-the-us-millitary_b_7417854.html

Guarnaccia, P., Lewis-Fernandez, R., Pincay, I. M., Shrout, P., Guo, J., Torres, M., . . . U Alegria, M. (2009). Ataques de Nervios as a marker of social and psychiatric vulnerability: Results from the NLAAS. *International Journal of Social Psychiatry, 56,* 298–309.

Guinier, L., & Torres, G. (2007). The ideology of colorblindness. In C. Gallagher (Ed.), *Rethinking the color line: Readings in race and ethnicity* (3rd ed., pp. 143–148). New York, NY: McGraw–Hill.

Gurung, R. A (2010). A sociological approach to understanding gender health disparities. *Journal of Social & Clinical Psychology, 29,* 123–125.

Guthrie, R. V. (1998). *Even the rat was White: A historical view of psychology.* Boston, MA: Allyn & Bacon.

Hackney, A. (2005). Teaching students about stereotypes, prejudice, and discrimination: An interview with Susan Fiske. *Teaching of Psychology, 32,* 196–199.

Haddon, A. C. (1910). *History of anthropology.* New York, NY: Putnam.

Hafeez, H., Zeshan, M., Tahir, M. A., Jahan, N., & Naveed, S. (2017). Health care disparities among lesbian, gay, bisexual, and transgender youth: A literature review. *Cureus.* https://doi.org/10.7759/cureus.1184

Hajnal, Z., Lajevardi, N., & Nielson, L. (2017). Voter identification laws and the suppression of minority votes. *Journal of Politics, 79*(2), 363–379.

Hakim-Larson, J., Kamoo, R., Nassar-McMillan, S. C., & Porcerelli, J. H. (2007). Counseling Arab and Chaldean American families. *Journal of Mental Health Counseling, 29,* 301–321.

Hall, C. C. I. (1980). *The ethnic identity of racially mixed people: A study of Black-Japanese* (Unpublished doctoral dissertation). University of California, Los Angeles.

Hall, C. C. I. (1992). Please choose one: Ethnic identity choices for biracial individuals. In M. P. P. Root (Ed.), *Racially mixed people in America* (pp. 250–264). Newbury Park, CA: Sage.

Hall, C. C. I. (2014). The evolution of the revolution: The successful establishment of multicultural psychology. In F. T. L. Leong, L. Comas-Díaz, G. C. N. Hall, V. C. McLoyd, & J. E. Trimble (Eds.), *APA handbook of multicultural psychology, Vol. 1. Theory and research* (pp. 3–18). Washington, DC: American Psychological Association. doi:10.1037/14189-001

Hall, E. T. (1963). A system for the notation of proxemic behavior. *American Anthropologist, 65,* 1003–1026.

Hall, E. T. (1966). *The hidden dimension.* Garden City, NY: Doubleday.

Hall, E. T. (1976). *Beyond culture: Into the cultural unconscious.* New York, NY: Anchor.

Hall, E. T. (1999). Context and meaning. In L. A. Samovar & R. E. Porter (Eds.), *Intercultural communication: A reader* (8th ed., pp. 45–54). Belmont, CA: Wadsworth.

Hall, G. C. N., & Barongan, C. (2002). *Multicultural psychology.* Upper Saddle River, NJ: Prentice Hall.

Hall, G. C. N., & Okazaki, S. (Eds.). (2002). *Asian American psychology: The science of lives in context.* Washington, DC: American Psychological Association.

Halpern, D. F., Benbow, C. P., Geary, D. C., Gur, R. C., Hyde, J. S., & Gernsbacher, M. A. (2007). The science of sex differences in science and mathematics. *Psychological Science in the Public Interest, 8* (whole issue).

Halpern, D. F., & Cheung, F. M. (2008). *Women at the top: Powerful leaders tell us how to combine work and family.* West Sussex, UK: Wiley–Blackwell.

Hamburger, C., Sturup, G. K., & Dahl-Iverson, E. (1953). Tranvestism: Hormonal, psychiatric and surgical treatment. *JAMA, 12,* 391–396.

Hamilton, D. L. (1981). *Cognitive processes in stereotyping and intergroup behavior.* Hillsdale, NJ: Erlbaum.

Hamilton, D. L., Dugan, P. M., & Trolier, T. K. (1985). The formation of stereotypic beliefs: Further evidence for distinctiveness-based illusory correlations. *Journal of Personality and Social Psychology, 48,* 5–17.

Hamilton, D. L., & Gifford, R. K. (1976). Illusory correlation in interpersonal perception: A cognitive basis of stereotypic judgments. *Journal of Experimental Social Psychology, 12,* 392–407.

Hamilton, D. L., & Rose, T. L. (1980). Illusory correlation and the maintenance of stereotypic beliefs. *Journal of Personality and Social Psychology, 39,* 832–845.

Hamilton, D. L., & Sherman, J. W. (1989). Illusory correlations: Implications for a stereotype theory and research. In D. Bar-Tal, C. F. Graumann, A. W. Kruglanski, & W. Stroebe (Eds.), *Stereotyping and prejudice: Changing conceptions* (pp. 59–82). New York, NY: Springer-Verlag.

Hamilton, D. L., & Sherman, J. W. (1994). Stereotypes. In R. S. Wyer, Jr., & T. K. Srull (Eds.), *Handbook of social cognition* (2nd ed., Vol. 2, pp. 1–68). Hillsdale, NJ: Erlbaum.

Hamilton, D. L., & Sherman, J. W. (1996). Perceiving persons and groups. *Psychological Review, 103,* 336–355.

Hamilton, D. L., & Trolier, T. K. (1986). Stereotypes and stereotyping: An overview of the cognitive approach. In J. F. Dovidio & S. L. Gaertner (Eds.), *Prejudice, discrimination, and racism* (pp. 127–163). Orlando, FL: Academic Press.

Han, E., & Powell, L. M. (2013). Consumption patterns of sugar-sweetened beverages in the United States. *Journal of the Academy of Nutrition and Dietetics, 113,* 43–53. doi:10.1016/j.jand.2012.09.016

Hancock, K. A. (2003). Lesbian, gay, and bisexual psychology: Past, present, and future directions. In J. S. Mio & G. Y. Iwamasa (Eds.), *Culturally diverse mental health: The challenges of research and resistance* (pp. 289–307). New York, NY: Brunner–Routledge.

Hanna, F. J., Talley, W. B., & Guindon, M. H. (2000). The power of perception: Toward a model of cultural oppression and liberation. *Journal of Counseling and Development, 78,* 430–446.

Hansen, E. (2017, November 13). The forgotten minority in police shootings. *CNN.* Retrieved from https://www.cnn.com/2017/11/10/us/native-lives-matter/index.html

Hardiman, R. (1982). *White identity development: A process oriented model for describing the racial consciousness of White Americans* (Unpublished doctoral dissertation). University of Massachusetts, Amherst.

Harrell, S. P. (1995, August). *Dynamics of difference: Personal and sociocultural dimensions of intergroup relations.* Paper presented at the 103rd Annual Convention of the American Psychological Association, New York.

Harris, S. M. (1994). Racial differences in predictors of college women's body image attitudes. *Women and Health, 21,* 89–103.

Harvard Mahoney Neuroscience Institute. (2009, Winter). The stress of poverty affects childhood poverty development. *On the Brain: The Harvard Mahoney Neuroscience Institute Letter, 15*(1), 3–4.

Hathaway, S. R., & McKinley, J. C. (1967). *MMPI manual* (Rev. ed.). New York, NY: Psychological Corporation.

Hawkins, D. (2016, November 21). Police defend use of water cannons on Dakota Access protesters in freezing weather. *The Washington Post.* Retrieved from https://www.washingtonpost.com/news/morning-mix/wp/2016/11/21/police-citing-ongoing-riot-use-water-cannons-on-dakota-access-protesters-in-freezing-weather/?utm_term=.41cdcbb02555

Hayashino, D. S., & Chopra, S. B. (2009). Parenting and raising families. In N. Tewari & A. N. Alvarez (Eds.), *Asian American psychology: Current perspectives* (pp. 317–336). New York, NY: Psychology Press.

Hays, P. A. (1996). Culturally responsive assessment with diverse older clients. *Professional Psychology: Research and Practice, 27,* 188–193.

Hays, P. A. (2007). *Addressing cultural complexities in practice: Assessment, diagnosis, and therapy* (2nd ed.). Washington, DC: American Psychological Association.

Hays, P. A. (2009). Integrating evidence-based practice, cognitive-behavioral therapy, and multicultural therapy: Ten steps for culturally competent practice. *Professional Psychology: Research and Practice, 40,* 354–360.

Hays, P. A. (2016). *Addressing cultural complexities in practice* (3rd ed.). Washington, DC: American Psychological Association.

Health Resources and Services Administration. (2017). *Health equity report 2017.* Washington, DC: U.S. Department of Health and Human Services. Retrieved from https://www.hrsa.gov/about/organization/bureaus/ohe/index.html

Hebert, J. G., & Lang, D. (2016, August 3). Courts are finally pointing out the racism behind voter ID laws. *The Washington Post.* Retrieved from https://www.washingtonpost.com/posteverything/wp/2016/08/03/courts-are-finally-pointing-out-the-racism-behind-voter-id-laws/?utm_term=.da6484dccd9c

Heeringa, S. G., Wagner, J., Torres, M., Duan, N., Adams, T., & Berglund, P. (2004). Sample designs and sampling methods for the Collaborative Psychiatric Epidemiology Studies (CPES). *International Journal of Methods in Psychiatric Research, 13*, 221–240.

Heim, J. (2017, August 14). How a rally of White nationalists and supremacists at the University of Virginia turned into a "tragic, tragic weekend." *The Washington Post*. Retrieved from https://www.washingtonpost.com/graphics/2017/local/charlottesville-timeline/?utm_term=.1539oc4edc2f

Heine, S., & Ruby, M. B. (2010). Cultural psychology. *Wiley Interdisciplinary Reviews: Cognitive Science, 1*(2). doi:10.1002/wcs.7

Helms, J. E. (1984). Toward a theoretical explanation of the effects of race on counseling: A Black and White model. *The Counseling Psychologist, 13*, 695–710.

Helms, J. E. (1985). Cultural identity in the treatment process. In P. Pedersen (Ed.), *Handbook of cross-cultural counseling and therapy* (pp. 239–245). Westport, CT: Greenwood.

Helms, J. E. (1989). Considering some methodological issues in racial identity research. *The Counseling Psychologist, 17*, 227–252.

Helms, J. E. (1990). *Black and White racial identity: Theory, research, and practice.* Westport, CT: Praeger.

Helms, J. E. (1992). *A race is a nice thing to have: A guide to being a White person or understanding the White persons in your life.* Topeka, KS: Content Communications.

Helms, J. E. (1995a). Why is there no study of cultural equivalence in standardized cognitive ability testing? In N. R. Goldberger & J. B. Veroff (Eds.), *The culture and psychology reader* (pp. 674–719). New York: New York University Press.

Helms, J. E. (1995b). An update of Helms's White and people of color racial identity models. In J. G. Ponterotto, J. M. Casas, L. A. Suzuki, & D. M. Alexander (Eds.), *Handbook of multicultural counseling* (pp. 181–198). Thousand Oaks, CA: Sage.

Helms, J. E. (2001). Life issues. In J. G. Ponterotto, J. M. Casas, L. A. Suzuki, & C. M. Alexander (Eds.), *Handbook of multicultural counseling* (2nd ed., pp. 22–29). Thousand Oaks, CA: Sage.

Helms, J. E., & Cook, D. A. (1999). *Using race and culture in counseling and psychotherapy: Theory and process.* Needham Heights, MA: Allyn & Bacon.

Helms, J. E., & Talleyrand, R. M. (1997). Race is not ethnicity. *American Psychologist, 52*, 1246–1247.

Henkel, K. E., Dovidio, J. F., & Gaertner, S. L. (2006). Institutional discrimination, individual racism, and Hurricane Katrina. *Analyses of Social Issues and Public Policy, 6*, 99–124.

Hennesy-Fiske, M. (2014, August 16). You have to show compassion. *The Los Angeles Times*, p. A8.

Henrich, J., Heine, S. J., & Norenzayan, A. (2010). The weirdest people in the world? *Behavioral and Brain Sciences, 33*(2–3), 61–135. doi:10.1017/S0140525X0999152X

Henrich, J., Heine, S. J., & Norenzayan, A. (2016). Most people are not WEIRD. In A. E. Kazdin (Ed.), *Methodological issues and strategies in clinical research* (pp. 113–114). Washington, DC: American Psychological Association.

Herek, G. (1995). Psychological heterosexism in the United States. In A. D'Augelli & C. Patterson (Eds.), *Lesbian, gay, and bisexual identities over the life span: Psychological perspectives* (pp. 321–346). New York, NY: Oxford University Press.

Herek, G. (2000). The psychology of sexual prejudice. *Current Directions in Psychological Science, 9*, 19–22.

Hernandez, P., Carranza, M., & Almeida, R. (2010). Mental health professionals' adaptive responses to racial microaggressions: An exploratory study. *Professional Psychology: Research and Practice, 41*, 202–209.

Herring, R. D. (1999). *Counseling with Native American Indians and Alaska Natives: Strategies for helping professionals.* Thousand Oaks, CA: Sage.

Herrnstein, R., & Murray, C. (1994). *The bell curve: Intelligence and class structure in American life.* New York, NY: Free Press.

Hesse-Biber, S. N., & Leavy, P. (Eds.). (2003). *Approaches to qualitative research: A reader on theory and practice.* London: Oxford University Press.

Hesse-Biber, S. N., & Yaiser, M. (Eds.). (2003). *Feminist perspectives on social research.* London: Oxford University Press.

Heywood, A. (2007). *Political ideologies* (4th ed.). New York, NY: Palgrave MacMillan.

Hill, C. E., Thompson, B. J., & Williams, E. N. (1997). A guide to conducting consensual qualitative research. *The Counseling Psychologist, 25*, 517–572.

Hilliard, K. M., & Iwamasa, G. Y. (2001). Japanese American older adults' conceptualization of anxiety. *Journal of Clinical Geropsychology, 7*, 53–65.

Historical definitions of race. (2011). Retrieved from http://en.wikipedia.org/wiki/Historical_definitions_of_race

Ho, M. K. (1987). *Family therapy with ethnic minorities.* Newbury Park, CA: Sage.

Hoffman, L. (1981). *Foundations of family therapy.* New York, NY: Basic Books.

Hofstede, G. (1980). *Culture's consequences.* Beverly Hills, CA: Sage.

Holder, A. M. B., Jackson, M. A., & Ponterotto, J. G. (2015). Racial microaggression experiences and coping strategies of Black women in corporate leadership. *Qualitative Psychology, 2*(2), 147–163.

Holliday, B. (2009). The history and vision of African American psychology: Multiple pathways to place, space and authority. *Cultural Diversity and Ethnic Minority Psychology, 15*(4), 317–337. doi:10.1037/a0017560

Holliday, B. G., & Holmes, A. L. (2003). A tale of challenge and change: A history and chronology of ethnic minorities in psychology in the United States. In G. Bernal, J. E. Trimble, A. K. Burlew, & F. T. L. Leong (Eds.), *Handbook of racial and ethnic minority psychology* (pp. 15–64). Thousand Oaks, CA: Sage.

Holmes, J. (2017, October 6). Trump's "Puerto Rico" accent is impressively bad. *Esquire.* Retrieved from https://www.esquire.com/news-politics/a12796828/trump-puerto-rico-accent-video/

Holoien, D. S., & Shelton, J. N. (2012). You deplete me: The cognitive costs of colorblindness on ethnic minorities. *Journal of Experimental Social Psychology, 48*, 562–565.

Hong, G. K. (1989). Application of cultural and environmental issues in family therapy with immigrant Chinese Americans. *Journal of Strategic and Systemic Therapies, 8*, 14–21.

Hong, G. K., & Ham, M. D. C. (2001). *Psychotherapy and counseling with Asian American clients: A practical guide.* Thousand Oaks, CA: Sage.

Horse, P. G. (2012). Twenty-First Century Native American consciousness: A thematic model of Indian identity. In C. L. Wijeyesinghe & B. W. Jackson III (Eds.), *New perspectives on racial identity development: Integrating emerging frameworks.* (pp. 121 – 127). New York: New York University Press.

Horton, A. (2018, April 15). Starbucks CEO apologizes after employee calls police on Black men waiting at a table. *The Washington Post.* Retrieved from https://www.washingtonpost.com/news/business/wp/2018/04/14/starbucks-apologizes-after-employee-calls-police-on-black-men-waiting-at-a-table/?utm_term=.57917c76ecb3

Hoshmand, L. L. T. (1994). *Orientation to inquiry in a reflective professional psychology.* Albany: State University of New York Press.

Hovey, J. D. (2000). Acculturative stress, depression, and suicidal ideation in Mexican immigrants. *Cultural Diversity and Ethnic Minority Psychology, 6*, 134–151.

How, P. C., Lo, P., Westervelt, M., & Ton, H. (2018). Refugees and immigrants. In J. Tse & S. Y. Volpp (Eds.), *A case-based approach to public psychiatry* (pp. 179–186). New York, NY: Oxford University Press.

Hoyenga, K. B., & Hoyenga, K. T. (1979). *The question of sex differences: Psychological, cultural, and biological issues.* Boston, MA: Little, Brown.

Hsu, L. K. (1987). Are eating disorders becoming more common among Blacks? *International Journal of Eating Disorders, 6*, 113–124.

https://www.cnn.com/videos/politics/2017/10/26/george-w-bush-hurricane-katrina-fema-michael-brown.cnn/video/playlists/president-george-w-bush/

Hudson, J. I., Hiripi, E., Pope, H. G., & Kessler, R. C. (2007). The prevalence and correlates of eating disorders in the National Comorbidity Survey Replication. *Biological Psychiatry, 61*, 348–358.

Hughes, J. L., Camden, A. A., & Yangchen, T. (2016). Rethinking and updating demographic questions: Guidance to improve descriptions of research samples. *Psi Chi Journal of Psychological Research, 21*(3), 138–151. https://doi.org/10.24839/2164-8204.JN21.3.138

Hugo Lopez, M., Passel, J., & Rohal, M. (2015, September). *Modern immigration wave brings 59 million to U.S., driving population growth and change through 265: Views of immigration's impact on U.S. society mixed.* Washington, DC: Pew Research Center. Retrieved from http://www.pewhispanic.org

Hwang, W.-C. (2008). *Improving your mood: A culturally responsive and holistic approach to treating depression in Chinese Americans.* Unpublished therapist manual.

Hwang, W.-C. (2016). Culturally adapting evidence-based practices for ethnic minority and immigrant families. In Zane, N., Bernal, G., & Leong. F. T. L. (Eds.), *Evidence-based psychological practice with ethnic minorities: Culturally informed research and clinical strategies* (pp. 289–308). Washington, DC: American Psychological Association.

Ifil, G. (2009). *The breakthrough: Politics and race in the age of Obama.* New York, NY: Doubleday.

Iijima Hall, C. C. (2014). The evolution of the revolution: The successful establishment of multicultural psychology. In F. T. L. Leong (Ed.), *APA handbook of multicultural psychology: Vol. 1. Theory and research* (pp. 3–18). Washington, DC: American Psychological Association.

Institute of Medicine. (2012). *How far we have come in reducing health disparities? Progress since 2000.* Washington, DC: National Academies Press.

Isajiw, W. W. (1990). Ethnic-identity retention. In R. Breton, W. W. Isajiw, W. E. Kalbach, & J. G. Reitz (Eds.), *Ethnic identity and equality* (pp. 34–91). Toronto: University of Toronto Press.

Israel, T. (2004). What counselors need to know about working with sexual minority clients. In D. R. Atkinson & G. Hackett (Eds.), *Counseling diverse populations* (3rd ed., pp. 347–364). Boston, MA: McGraw–Hill.

Ivey, A. E., Ivey, M. B., & Zalaquett, C. P. (2014). *International interviewing and counseling: Facilitating client development in a multicultural society* (8th ed.). Belmont, CA: Brooks/Cole.

Iwamasa, G. Y., & Bangi, A. K. (2003). Women's mental health research: History, current status, and future directions.

In J. S. Mio & G. Y. Iwamasa (Eds.), *Culturally diverse mental health: The challenges of research and resistance* (pp. 251–268). New York, NY: Brunner–Routledge.

Iwamasa, G. Y., & Sorocco, K. H. (2002). Aging and Asian Americans: Developing culturally appropriate research methodology. In G. C. N. Hall & S. Okazaki (Eds.), *Asian American psychology: The science of lives in context* (pp. 105–130). Washington, DC: American Psychological Association.

Jacobs, J. H. (1992). Identity development in biracial children. In M. P. P. Root (Ed.), *Racially mixed people in America* (pp. 190–206). Newbury Park, CA: Sage.

Jacob, K. D. (2014). *DSM-5 and culture: The need to move towards a shared model of care within a more equal patient–physician partnership. Asian Journal of Psychiatry, 7,* 89–91.

Jacob, K. S., Kallivayalil, R. A., Mallik, A. K., Gupta, N., Trivedi, J. D., Gangadhar, B. N., . . . Sathyanarayana Rao, T. S. (2013). *Diagnostic and statistical manual-5*: Position paper of the Indian Psychiatric Society. *Indian Journal of Psychiatry, 55,* 12–30.

Jahoda, G. (1982). *Psychology and anthropology: A psychological perspective.* London: Academic Press.

James, S. A. (2003). Confronting the moral economy of US racial/ethnic health disparities. *American Journal of Public Health, 93,* 189.

Jendrek, M. P. (1994). Grandparents who parent their grandchildren: Circumstances and decisions. *The Gerontologist, 34,* 206–216.

Jiménez, T. R. (2010). Affiliative ethnic identity: A more elastic link between ethnic ancestry and culture. *Ethnic and Racial Studies, 33,* 1756–1775.

Johnson, D. (1994). Stress, depression, substance abuse, and racism. *American Indian and Alaska Native Mental Health Research, 6,* 29–33.

Johnson, D. J. (1992). Developmental pathways: Toward an ecological theoretical formulation of race identity in Black–White biracial children. In M. P. P. Root (Ed.), *Racially mixed people in America* (pp. 37–49). Newbury Park, CA: Sage.

Johnson, E. P. (1995). SNAP! culture: A different kind of "reading." *Text and Performance Quarterly, 15,* 122–143.

Johnson, J. C., & Ham, C. F. (2010, November 30). *Report of the comprehensive review of the issues associated with a repeal of "Don't Ask, Don't Tell."* Retrieved December 6, 2010, from http://www.defense.gov/home/features/2010/0610gatesdadt/

Johnson, J. C., & Smith, N. H. (2002). Health and social issues associated with racial, ethnic, and cultural disparities. *Generations, 26,* 25–32.

Johnson, T. (2010, October 1). U.S. apologizes for "abhorrent" syphilis study in Guatemala. *McClatchy.* Retrieved from https://www.mcclatchydc.com/news/nation-world/world/article24595594.html

Johnson, T. (2018, February 16). Black superheroes matter: Why a *Black Panther* movie is revolutionary. *Rolling Stone.* Retrieved from https://www.rollingstone.com/movies/news/black-superheroes-matter-why-black-panther-is-revolutionary-w509105

Johnson, T. J., Winger, D. G., Hickey, R. W., Switzer, G. E., Miller, E., Nguyen, M. B., . . . Hausmann, L. R. M. (2017). Comparison of physician implicit racial bias toward adults versus children. *Academic Pediatrics, 17*(2), 120–126. doi:10.1016/j.acap.2016.08.010

Jones, C. L., Jensen, J. D., Scherr, C. L., Brown, N. R., Christy, K., & Weaver, J. (2015). The health belief model as an explanatory framework in communication research: Exploring parallel, serial, and moderated mediation. *Health Communication, 30*(6), 566–576. doi:10.1080/10410236.2013.873363

Jones, D. (2010, June 25). A WEIRD view of human nature skews psychologists' studies: Relying on undergraduates from developed nations as research subjects creates a false picture of human behavior, some psychologists argue. *Science, 328*(5986), 1627. doi:10.1126/science.328.5986.1627

Jones, E. E. (1978). Effects of race on psychotherapy process and outcome: An exploratory investigation. *Psychotherapy: Theory, Research, and Practice, 15,* 226–236.

Jones, E. E. (1982). Psychotherapists' impressions of treatment outcome as a function of race. *Clinical Psychology, 38,* 722–731.

Jones, J. (1993). The concept of race in social psychology. In L. Wheler & P. Shaver (Eds.), *Review of personality and social psychology* (Vol. 4, pp. 117–150). Newbury Park, CA: Sage.

Jones, J. M. (1997). *Prejudice and racism* (2nd ed.). New York, NY: McGraw–Hill.

Jones, J. M., & Austin-Dailey, A. T. (2009). The Minority Fellowship Program: A 30-year legacy of training psychologists of color. *Cultural Diversity and Ethnic Minority Psychology, 15*(4), 388–389. doi:10.1037/a0017560

Jones, M. L., & Galliher, R. V. (2015). Daily racial microaggressions and ethnic identification among Native American young adults. *Cultural Diversity and Ethnic Minority Psychology, 21,* 1–9.

Jones, N. A., & Bullock, J. (2012). *The two or more races population: 2010.* Retrieved from https://www.census.gov/prod/cen2010/briefs/c2010br-13.pdf

Jones, R. L. (Ed.). (1998). *African American mental health.* Hampton, VA: Cobb & Henry.

Jones, S. E. (1994). *The right touch: Understanding and using the language of physical contact.* Cresskill, NJ: Hampton Press.

Jones, V. (2015, October 26). Trump: The social media president? *CNN*. Retrieved from https://www.cnn.com/2015/10/26/opinions/jones-trump-social-media/index.html

Jorde, L. B., & Wooding, S. P. (2004). Genetic variation, classification and "race." *Nature Genetics, 36*, S28–S33.

Judkis, M. (2013, September 22). Miss America Nina Davuluri fights post-pageant racism with a beauty queen's poise. *The Washington Post*. Retrieved from http://www.washingtonpost.com/lifestyle/style/miss-america-fights-post-pageant-racism-with-a-beauty-queens-poise/2013/09/22/a90590ac-22f8-11e3-966c-9c4293c47ebe_story.html

Kaiser, C. R., Drury, B. J., Spalding, K. E., Cheryan, S., & O'Brien, L. T. (2009). The ironic consequences of Obama's election: Decreased support for social justice. *Journal of Experimental Social Psychology, 45*, 556–559.

Kaiser Family Foundation. (2013). *Health coverage by race and ethnicity: The potential impact of the Affordable Care Act*. Menlo Park, CA: Kaiser Family Foundation. Retrieved from http://kff.org/disparities-policy/issue- brief/health-coverage-by-race-and-ethnicity-the-potential-impact-of-the-affordable-care-act

Kam, J. A., Guntzviller, L. M., & Pines, R. (2017). Language brokering, prosocial capacities, and intercultural communication apprehension among Latina mothers and their adolescent children. *Journal of Cross-Cultural Psychology, 48*(2), 168–183. doi:10.1177/0022022116680480

Kamin, L. (1974). *The science and politics of IQ*. Potomac, MD: Erlbaum.

Kantor, J., & Twohey, M. (2017, October 5). Harvey Weinstein paid off sexual harassment accusers for decades. *The New York Times*. Retrieved from https://www.nytimes.com/2017/10/05/us/harvey-weinstein-harassment-allegations.html

Karlsson, R. (2005). Ethnic matching between therapist and patient in psychotherapy: An overview of findings, together with methodological and conceptual issues. *Cultural Diversity & Ethnic Minority Psychology, 11*, 113–129.

Kaslow, F. W. (Ed.). (1996). *Handbook of relational diagnosis and dysfunctional family patterns*. Oxford: Wiley.

Katriel, T. (1986). *Talking straight: Dugri speech in Israeli Sabra culture*. Cambridge: Cambridge University Press.

Kearney, L. K., Draper, M., & Baron, A. (2005). Counseling utilization of ethnic minority college students. *Cultural Diversity and Ethnic Minority Psychology, 11*, 272–285.

Keefe, S. E. (1982). Help-seeking behavior among foreign-born and native-born Mexican Americans. *Social Science and Medicine, 16*, 1467–1472.

Keel, P. K., & Klump, K. L. (2003). Are eating disorders culture-bound syndromes? Implications for conceptualizing their etiology. *Psychological Bulletin, 129*, 747–770.

Keerdoja, E. (1984, November 19). Children of the rainbow: New parent support groups help interracial kids cope. *Newsweek*, pp. 120–122.

Keib, K., Himelboim, I., & Han, J.-Y. (2018). Important tweets matter: Predicting retweets in the #BlackLivesMatter talk on Twitter. *Computers in Human Behavior, 85*, 106–115.

Keller, J., & Pierce, A. (2017). Tracking Trump's agenda step by step. *The New York Times*. Retrieved from https://www.nytimes.com/interactive/2017/us/politics/trump-agenda-tracker.html

Keller, M. D., Beardslee, W. R., Dorrer, D. J., Lavori, P. W., Samuelson, H., & Klerman, G. R. (1986). Impact of severity and chronicity of parental affective illness on adaptive functioning and psychopathology in children. *Archives of General Psychiatry, 43*, 930–937.

Kelly, H. H. (1967). Attribution theory in social psychology. In D. Levine (Ed.), *Nebraska symposium on motivation* (Vol. 15, pp. 192–240). Lincoln: University of Nebraska Press.

Kelly, H. H. (1973). The process of causal attribution. *American Psychologist, 28*, 107–128.

Keneally, M. (2017, November 22). Federal court puts stop to Trump's transgender military ban. *ABC News*. Retrieved from http://abcnews.go.com/Politics/federal-court-puts-stop-trumps-transgender-military-ban/story?id=51308499

Kerwin, C., & Ponterotto, J. G. (1995). Biracial identity development: Theory and research. In J. G. Ponterotto, J. M. Casas, L. S. Suzuki, & C. M. Alexander (Eds.), *Handbook of multicultural counseling* (pp. 199–217). Thousand Oaks, CA: Sage.

Kessler, R. C., Berglund, P. A., Chiu, W. T., Demler, O., Heeringa, S., Hiripi, E., . . . Zheng, H. (2004). The U.S. National Comorbidity Survey Replication (NCS-R): Design and field procedures. *The International Journal of Methods in Psychiatric Research, 13*, 69–92.

Kessler, R. C., Berglund, P. A., Demler, O., Jin, R., Merikangas, K. R., & Walters, E. E. (2005). Lifetime prevalence and age-of-onset distributions of *DSM-IV* disorders in the National Comorbidity Survey Replication (NCS-R). *Archives of General Psychiatry, 62*, 593–602.

Kessler, R. C., Berglund, P.A., Zhao, S., Leaf, P. J., Kouzis, A. C., Bruce, M. L., . . . Schneier, M. (1996). The 12-month prevalence and correlates of serious mental illness (SMI). In R. W. Manderscheid & M. A. Sonnenschein (Eds.), *Mental health, United States* (Pub. No. [SMA] 96-3098). Rockville, MD: Center for Mental Health Services.

Kessler, R. C., McGonagle, K. A., Zhao, S., Nelson, C. B., Hughes, M., Eshelman, S., . . . Kendler, K. S. (1994). Lifetime and 12-month prevalence of *DSM-III-R* psychiatric disorders in the United States: Results from the National Comorbidity Survey. *Archives of General Psychiatry, 51,* 8–19.

Kich, G. K. (1992). The developmental process of asserting a biracial, bicultural identity. In M. P. P. Root (Ed.), *Racially mixed people in America* (pp. 304–317). Newbury Park, CA: Sage.

Kim, B. S., & Abreu, J. M. (2001). Acculturation measurement: Theory, current instruments, and future directions. In J. G. Ponterotto, J. M. Casas, L. A. Suzuki, & C. M. Alexander (Eds.), *Handbook of multicultural counseling* (pp. 394–424). Thousand Oaks, CA: Sage.

Kim, B. S. K. (2009). Acculturation and enculturation of Asian Americans: A primer. In N. Tewari & A. N. Alvarez (Eds.), *Asian American psychology: Current perspectives* (pp. 97–112). New York, NY: Psychology Press.

Kim, B. S. K., Atkinson, D. R., & Umemoto, D. (2001). Asian cultural values and counseling process: Current knowledge and directions for future research. *Counseling Psychologist, 29,* 570–603.

Kim, B. S. K., Hill, C. E., Gelso, C. J., Goates, M. K., Asay, P. A., & Harbin, J. M. (2003). Counselor self-disclosure, East Asian American client adherence to Asian cultural values, and counseling process. *Journal of Counseling Psychology, 50,* 324–332.

Kim, G., Loi, C. X. A., Chiriboga, D. A., Jang, Y., Parmelee, P., & Allen, R. S. (2010). Limited English proficiency as a barrier to mental health service use: A study of Latino and Asian immigrants with psychiatric disorders. *Journal of Psychiatric Research, 45,* 104–110.

Kim, J., & Choi, N. G. (2010). Twelve-month prevalence of DSM-IV mental disorders among older Asian Americans: Comparison with younger groups. *Aging and Mental Health, 14,* 90–99.

Kim, S. C. (1997). Korean American families. In E. Lee (Ed.), *Working with Asians: A guide for clinicians* (pp. 125–135). New York, NY: Guilford Press.

Kim, U., & Berry, J. W. (1993). *Indigenous psychologies: Experience and research in cultural context.* Newbury Park, CA: Sage.

Kim, U., & Park, Y.-S. (2006). The scientific foundation of indigenous and cultural psychology: The transactional approach. In U. Kim, K.-S. Yang, & K.-K. Hwang (Eds.), *Indigenous and cultural psychology: Understanding people in context* (pp. 27–48). New York, NY: Springer.

Kim, U., Yang, K.-S., & Hwang, K.-K. (2006). Contributions to indigenous and cultural psychology: Understanding people in context. In U. Kim, K.-S. Yang, & K.-K. Hwang (Eds.), *Indigenous and cultural psychology: Understanding people in context* (pp. 3–25). New York, NY: Springer.

Kirmayer, L. J., Narasiah, L., Munoz, M., Rashid, M., Ryder, A. G., Guzder, J., . . . for the Canadian Collaboration

for Immigrant and Refugee Health (CCIRH). (2011). Common mental health problems in immigrants and refugees: General approach in primary care. *Canadian Medical Association Journal, 183*(12), E959–E967. doi:10.1503/cmaj.090292

Kiselica, M. S., & Robinson, M. (2001). Bringing advocacy counseling to life: The history, issues, and human dramas of social justice work in counseling. *Journal of Counseling Development, 79,* 387–397.

Kitano, H. H. L. (1982). Mental health in the Japanese American community. In E. E. Jones & S. J. Korchin (Eds.), *Minority mental health* (pp. 149–164). New York, NY: Praeger.

Kitano, H. H. L. (1999). *Race relations* (5th ed.). Upper Saddle River, NJ: Prentice Hall.

Kitayama, S., & Markus, H. R. (1999). Yin and yang of the Japanese self: The cultural psychology of personality coherence. In D. Cervone & Y. Shoda (Eds.), *The coherence of personality: Social-cognitive bases of consistency, variability, and organization* (pp. 242–302). New York, NY: Guilford Press.

Kitayama, S., & Markus, H. R. (2000). The pursuit of happiness and the realization of sympathy: Cultural patterns of self, social relations, and well-being. In E. Diener & E. M. Suh (Eds.), *Culture and subjective well-being* (pp. 113–161). Cambridge, MA: MIT Press.

Kitayama, S., Markus, H. R., Matsumoto, H., & Norasakkunkit, V. (1997). Individual and collective processes in the construction of the self: Self-enhancement in the United States and self-criticism in Japan. *Journal of Personality and Social Psychology, 72,* 1245–1267.

Kitayama, S., Snibbe, A. C., Markus, H. R., & Suzuki, T. (2004). Is there any "free" choice? Self and dissonance in two cultures. *Psychological Science, 15,* 527–533.

Kitayama, S., & Uchida, Y. (2003). Explicit self-criticism and implicit self-regard: Evaluating self and friend in two cultures. *Journal of Experimental Social Psychology, 39,* 476–482.

Kivel, P. (1996). *Uprooting racism: How White people can work for racial justice.* Philadelphia, PA: New Society.

Kleinman, A., Eisenberg, L., & Good, B. (1978). Culture, illness, and care: Clinical lessons from anthropologic and cross-cultural research. *Annals of Internal Medicine, 88*(2), 251–258.

Kliman, J. (2005). Many differences, many voices: Toward social justice in family therapy. In M. Pravder, K. L. Suyemoto, & B. F. Okun (Eds.), *Psychotherapy with women* (pp. 42–63). New York, NY: Guilford Press.

Kluckhohn, F. R., & Strodtbeck, F. L. (1961). *Variations in value orientations.* Evanston, IL: Row, Patterson.

Knowles, E. D., Lowery, B. S., Hogan, C. M., & Chow, R. M. (2009). On the malleability of ideology: Motivated construals of color blindness. *Journal of Personality and Social Psychology, 96,* 857–869.

Kohlberg, L. (1966). A cognitive developmental analysis of children's sex-role concepts and attitudes. In E. Maccoby (Ed.), *The development of sex differences* (pp. 82–172). Palo Alto, CA: Stanford University Press.

Kohlberg, L. (1968). The child as a moral philosopher. *Psychology Today, 2,* 25–30.

Kohlberg, L. (1976). Moral stage and moralization. In T. Lickona (Ed.), *Moral development and behavior* (pp. 31–53). New York, NY: Holt.

Korchin, S. J. (1980). Clinical psychology and minority problems. *American Psychologist, 35,* 262–269.

Korman, M. (1974). National conference on levels and patterns of professional training in psychology. *American Psychologist, 29,* 441–449.

Koss, M. P., Goodman, L. A., Browne, A., Fitzgerald, L. F., Keita, G. P., & Russo, N. F. (1994). *No safe haven: Male violence against women at home, at work, and in the community.* Washington, DC: American Psychological Association.

Kranich, N. (2005). Equality and equity of access: What's the difference? *American Library Association.* Retrieved from http://www.ala.org/advocacy/intfreedom/equalityequity

Krashen, S., Long, M., & Scarcella, R. (1982). Age, rate, and eventual attainment in second language acquisition. In S. Krashen, R. Scarcella, & M. Long (Eds.), *Child–adult differences in second language acquisition* (pp. 161–172). Rowley, MA: Newbury Press.

Krate, R., Leventhal, G., & Silverstein, B. (1974). Self-perceived transformation of the Negro-to-Black identity. *Psychological Reports, 35,* 1071–1075.

Kroeber, A. L., & Kluckhohn, C. (1952/1963). *Culture: A critical review of concepts and definitions.* New York, NY: Vintage Books.

Kroll, J. F., Bobb, S. C, & Hoshino, N. (2014). Two languages in mind: Bilingualism as a tool to investigate language, cognition, and the brain. *Current Directions in Psychological Science, 23,* 159–163.

Krugman, P. R. (2012). *End this depression now!* New York: Norton.

Kumanyika, S. K., Morssink, C. B., & Nestle, M. (2001). Minority women and advocacy for women's health. *American Journal of Public Health, 91,* 1383–1389.

Labouvie-Vief, G. (1985). Intelligence and cognition. In J. E. Birren & K. W. Schaie (Eds.), *Handbook of the psychology of aging* (2nd ed., pp. 500–530). New York, NY: Van Nostrand Reinhold.

LaFramboise, T. D., Berman, J. S., & Sohi, B. K. (1994). American Indian women. In L. Comas-Díaz & B. Greene (Eds.), *Women of color: Integrating ethnic and gender identities in psychotherapy* (pp. 30–71). New York, NY: Guilford Press.

LaFramboise, T. D., Coleman, H. L. K., & Gerton, J. (1993). Psychological impact of biculturalism: Evidence and theory. *Psychological Bulletin, 114,* 395–412.

LaFrance, M., & Mayo, C. (1976). Racial differences in gaze behavior during conversations: Two systematic observational studies. *Journal of Personality and Social Psychology, 33,* 547–552.

Lakoff, R. (1975). *Language and women's place.* New York, NY: Harper & Row.

Lambert, M. J., & Barley, D. E. (2001). Research summary on the therapeutic relationship and psychotherapy outcome. *Psychotherapy, 38*(4), 357–361.

Lambert, W. E. (1967). A social psychology of bilingualism. *Journal of Social Issues,* 91–109.

Lambert, W. E. (1977). The effects of bilingualism on the individual: Cognitive and sociocultural consequences. In P. A. Hornby (Ed.), *Bilingualism: Psychological, social and educational implications* (pp. 15–27). New York, NY: Academic Press.

Lambert, W. E. (1980). The social psychology of language: A perspective for the 1980s. In H. Giles, W. Robinson, & P. Smith (Eds.), *Language: Social psychological perspectives* (pp. 415–424). Oxford: Pergamon.

Lambert, W. E., & Anisfeld, E. (1969). A note on the relationship of bilingualism and intelligence. *Canadian Journal of Behavioral Science, 1,* 123–128.

Landers, A. J., Rollock, D., Rolfes, C. B., & Moore, D. L. (2011). Police contacts and stress among African American college students. *American Journal of Orthopsychiatry, 81,* 72–81.

Landrine, H., Klonoff, E. A., & Brown-Collins, A. (1995). Cultural diversity and methodology in feminist psychology: Critique, proposal, empirical example. In H. Landrine (Ed.), *Bringing cultural diversity to feminist psychology: Theory, research, and practice.* (pp. 55–75). Washington, DC: American Psychological Association.

La Roche, M. J. (2013). *Cultural psychotherapy: Theory, methods, and practice.* Thousand Oaks, CA: Sage.

Latter, B. (1980). Genetic differences within and between populations of the major human subgroups. *The American Naturalist, 116,* 220–237.

LeBlanc, P. (2017, July 2). Trump defends social media use after controversial tweets. *CNN.* Retrieved from https://www.cnn.com/2017/07/01/politics/donald-trump-tweets/index.html

Lebra, T. S. (1976). *Japanese patterns of behavior.* Honolulu: University Press of Hawaii.

Lee, E. (Ed.). (1997). *Working with Asian Americans: A guide for clinicians.* New York, NY: Guilford Press.

Lee, J. L. (2013). The Comprehensive Review Working Group and Don't Ask, Don't Tell repeal at the Department of Defense. *Journal of Homosexuality, 60,* 282–311.

Lee, M. W. (Producer and Director). (1994). *The color of fear* [Film]. Available from Stir-Fry Productions, Oakland, CA.

Lee, S. (1993). How abnormal is the desire for slimness? A survey of eating attitudes and behavior among Chinese undergraduates in Hong Kong. *Psychological Medicine, 23,* 437–451.

Lee, S. (2001). From diversity to unity: The classification of mental disorders in 21st-century China. *Psychiatric Clinics of North America, 24*(3), 421–431.

Lee, S. J., Wong, N.-W. A., & Alvarez, A. N. (2009). The model minority and the perpetual foreigner: Stereotypes of Asian Americans. In N. Tewari & A. N. Alvarez (Eds.), *Asian American psychology: Current perspectives* (pp. 69–84). New York, NY: Psychology Press.

Legal Services for Prisoners with Children. (n.d.). *People of color and the prison industrial complex: Facts and figures at a glance.* Retrieved from http://prisonerswithchildren.org/pubs/color.pdf

le Grange, D., Stone, A. A., & Brownell, K. D. (1998). Eating disturbances in White and minority female dieters. *International Journal of Eating Disorders, 24,* 395–403.

le Grange, D., Telch, C. F., & Tibbs, J. (1998). Race and eating disorders. *Harvard Mental Health Letter, 15,* 6–8.

Leong, F. T. L. (1998). Career development and vocational behaviors. In L. C. Lee & N. W. S. Zane (Eds.), *Handbook of Asian American psychology* (pp. 359–398). Thousand Oaks, CA: Sage.

Leong, F. T. L. (2001). The role of acculturation in the career adjustment of Asian American workers: A test of Leong and Chou's (1994) formulations. *Cultural Diversity and Ethnic Minority Psychology, 7,* 262–273.

Leong, F. T. L. (Ed.). (2009). History of racial and ethnic minority psychology [Special issue]. *Cultural Diversity & Ethnic Minority Psychology, 15*(4).

Leong, F. T., & Okazaki, S. (2009). History of Asian American psychology. *Cultural Diversity and Ethnic Minority Psychology, 15,* 352–362.

Lerner, R., Iwawaki, S., Chichara, T., & Sorell, G. (1980). Self-concept, self-esteem, and body attitudes among Japanese male and female adolescents. *Child Development, 51,* 847–855.

Levant, R. F., & Sperry, H. A. (2016). Components of evidence-based practice in psychology. In N. Zane, G. Bernal, & F. T. L. Leong (Eds.), *Evidence-based psychological practice with ethnic minorities: Culturally informed research and clinical strategies* (pp. 15–29). Washington, DC: American Psychological Association.

Levin, J. (1986). Roles for the Black pastor in preventive medicine. *Pastoral Psychology, 35,* 94–103.

Levitt, J. (2014, August 6). A comprehensive investigation of voter impersonation finds 31 credible incidents out of one billion ballots cast. *The Washington Post.* Retrieved from https://www.washingtonpost.com/news/wonk/wp/2014/08/06/a-comprehensive-investigation-of-voter-impersonation-finds-31-credible-incidents-out-of-one-billion-ballots-cast/

Lewin, K. (1948). *Resolving social conflicts: Selected papers on group dynamics.* New York, NY: Harper.

Lewis, J. (1998). *Walking with the wind: A memoir of the movement.* New York, NY: Simon & Schuster.

Liamputtong, P., & Ezzy, D. (2005). *Qualitative research methods* (2nd ed.). New York, NY: Oxford University Press.

Liddi-Brown, D., Barker-Hackett, L., & Grizzell, J. (2002, April). *Body image and eating disorders in a multicultural sample.* Poster presented at the 82nd Annual Meeting of the Western Psychological Association Annual Convention, Irvine, CA.

Lim, T.-S. (1994) Facework and interpersonal relationships. In S. Ting-Toomey (Ed.), *The challenge of facework* (pp. 209–229). Albany: State University of New York Press.

Lipsky, S. (1977). Internalized oppression. *Black Re-Emergence, 2,* 5–10.

Lipsky, S. (1987). *Internalized racism.* Seattle, WA: Rational Island.

Liptak, A. (2015, June 26). Supreme Court ruling makes same-sex marriage a right nationwide. *The New York Times.* Retrieved from https://www.nytimes.com/2015/06/27/us/supreme-court-same-sex-marriage.html

Liu, W. M. (2011). *Social class and classism in the helping professions: Research, theory and practice.* Thousand Oaks, CA: Sage.

Liu, W. M. (2013). Introduction to social class and classism in counseling psychology. In W. M. Liu (Ed.), *The Oxford handbook of social class in counseling* (pp. 3–20). New York, NY: Oxford University Press.

Liu, W. M., Colbow, A. J., & Rice, A. J. (2016). Social class and masculinity. In Y. J. Wong & S. R. Wester (Eds.), *APA handbook of men and masculinities* (pp. 413–432). Washington, DC: American Psychological Association.

Liu, W. M., Latino, C. A., & Loh, Y. (2017). Social class, classism, and race: Subjective worldviews and the role of rotating credit associations. In A. M. Czopp (Vol. Ed.) and A. W. Blume (Series Ed.), *Social issues in living color: Challenges and solutions from the perspective of ethnic minority psychology. Vol 2. Ethnic minority psychology: Promoting health and well-being* (pp. 123–153). Santa Barbara, CA: Praeger/ABC-CLIO.

Lluveras, L. (2017, October 18). Is racial bias driving Trump's neglect of Puerto Rico? *The Conversation.* Retrieved from https://theconversation.com/is-racial-bias-driving-trumps-neglect-of-puerto-rico-85662

Löfvenborg, J. E., Andersson, T., Carlsson, P.-O., Dorkhan, M., Groop, L., Martinell, M., . . . Carlsson, S. (2016). Sweetened beverage intake and risk of latent autoimmune diabetes in adults (LADA) and type 2 diabetes. *European Journal of Endocrinology, 175*, 605–614. doi:10.1530/EJE-16-0376

Lonner, W. J. (1979). Issues in cross-cultural psychology. In A. J. Marsella, R. Tharp, & T. Ciborowski (Eds.), *Perspectives on cross-cultural psychology* (pp. 17–45). New York, NY: Halstead Press.

Lopez, E., Blix, G. G., & Blix, A. G. (1995). Body image of Latinas compared to body image of non-Latina White women. *The Journal of Health Behavior, Education, and Promotion, 19*, 3–10.

López, I., Rivera, F., Ramirez, R., Guarnaccia, P., Canino, G., & Bird, H. (2009). *Ataques de nervios* and their psychiatric correlates in Puerto Rican children from two different contexts. *Journal of Nervous and Mental Disease, 197*, 923–929.

Lopez, S. R., & Guarnaccia, P. J. (2000). Cultural psychopathology: Uncovering the social world of mental illness. *Annual Review of Psychology, 51*, 571–598.

Lopez, S. R., Lopez, A. A., & Fong, K. T. (1991). Mexican American's initial preference for counselors: The role of ethnic factors. *Journal of Counseling Psychology, 38*, 487–496.

Lopez-Baez, S. I. (1999). *Ataque (de nervios)*. In J. S. Mio, J. E. Trimble, P. Arredondo, H. E. Cheatham, & S. Sue (Eds.), *Key words in multicultural interventions: A dictionary* (pp. 24–25). Westport, CT: Greenwood.

Lorion, R. P. (1973). Social class differences in treatment attitudes and expectations. (Doctoral dissertation). *Dissertation Abstracts International, 33*(12-B), 6084–6085.

Lott, B., & Bullock, H. E. (2007). *Psychology and economic justice: Personal, professional, and political intersections.* Washington, DC: American Psychological Association.

Louwagie, P. (2016, July 8). Falcon Heights police shooting reverberates across the nation. Gov. Dayton, seeing racial bias, calls for federal inquiry into deadly police shooting. *Star Tribune.* Retrieved from http://www.startribune.com/falcon-heights-police-shooting-reverberates-across-the-nation/385861101/

Löfvenborg, J. E., Andersson, T., Carlsson, P.-O., Dorkhan, M., Groop, L., Martinell, M., ... Carlsson, S. (2016). Sweetened beverage intake and risk of latent autoimmune diabetes in adults (LADA) and type 2 diabetes. *European Journal of Endocrinology, 175*(6), 605–614. https://doi.org/10.1530/EJE-16-0376

Lucero, K., Hicks, R., Bramlette, J., Brassington, G., & Welter, M. (1992). Frequency of eating problems among Asian and Caucasian college students. *Psychological Reports, 71*, 255–258.

Luria, A. R. (1976). *Cognitive development: Its cultural and social foundations.* Cambridge, MA: Harvard University Press.

Lusher, A. (2016). Donald Trump: All the sexist things he's said. *Independent.* Retrieved from http://www.independent.co.uk/news/world/americas/us-elections/donald-trump-sexist-quotes-comments-tweets-grab-them-by-the-pussy-when-star-you-can-do-anything-a7353006.html

Maciag, M. (2015). A state-by-state look at growing minority populations. *Governing: The States and Localities.* Retrieved from http://www.governing.com/topics/urban/gov-majority-minority-populations-in-states.html

Madej, P., Di Stefano, J. N., & Adelman, J. (2018, April 14). Black men's arrests at Philadelphia Starbucks prompt city probes amid national outcry. *Philly.com.* Retrieved from http://www2.philly.com/philly/news/starbucks-philadelphia-police-viral-video-investigation-race-20180414.html

Maina, I. W., Belton, T. D., Ginzberg, S., Singh, A., & Johnson, T. J. (2018). A decade of studying implicit racial/ethnic bias in healthcare providers using the implicit association test. *Social Science & Medicine, 199*, 219–229. doi:10.1016/j.socscimed.2017.05.009

Mann, B. (2014). Equity and equality are not equal. *The Equity Line.* Retrieved from https://edtrust.org/the-equity-line/equity-and-equality-are-not-equal/

Mannix, A. (2016, July 12). Police audio: Officer stopped Philando Castile on robbery suspicion. Police recording doesn't cover shooting itself. *Star Tribune.* Retrieved from http://www.startribune.com/police-audio-offecer-stopped-philando-castile-on-robber-suspicion/386344001/#1

Maramba, G. G., & Hall, G. C. N. (2002). Meta-analysis of ethnic match as a predictor of dropout, utilization, and level of functioning. *Cultural Diversity and Ethnic Minority Psychology, 8*(3), 290–297. doi:10.1037/10999809.8.3.290

Markus, H. R., & Kitayama, S. (1991). Culture and the self: Implications for cognition, emotion, and motivation. *Psychological Review, 98*, 224–253.

Marsella, A. J. (1980). Depressive experience and disorder across cultures. In H. C. Triandis & J. G. Draguns (Eds.), *Handbook of cross-cultural psychology, Vol. 6. Psychopathology* (pp. 237–289). Needham Heights, MA: Allyn & Bacon.

Martin, L. A., Neighbors, H. W., & Griffith, D. M. (2013). The experience of symptoms of depression in men vs. women: Analysis of the National Comorbidity Survey Replication. *JAMA Psychiatry, 70*(10), 1100–1106.

Martin, R. A. (2007). *The psychology of humor: An integrative approach*. Burlington, MA: Elsevier.

Maslow, A. (1968). *Toward a psychology of being*. New York, NY: Van Nostrand.

Maslow, A. (1970). *Motivation and personality*. New York, NY: Harper & Row.

Matsumoto, D. (1991). Cultural influences on facial expressions of emotion. *Southern Communication Journal, 56*, 128–137.

Matsumoto, D. (2000). *Culture and psychology: People around the world* (2nd ed.). Belmont, CA: Wadsworth/Thomson Learning.

Matsumoto, D., & Juang, L. (2008). *Culture and Psychology* (4th ed.). Belmont, CA: Thomson/Wadsworth.

Matsumoto, D., & Juang, L. (2012). *Culture and psychology* (5th ed.). Belmont, CA: Thomson/Wadsworth.

Matsumoto, D., Kasri, F., Milligan, E., Singh, U., & The, J. (1997). *Lay conceptions of culture: Do students and researchers understand culture in the same way?* Unpublished paper, San Francisco State University, CA.

Matthews, K. A., Boylan, J. M., Jakubowski, K. P., Cundiff, J. M., Lee, L., Pardini, D. A., & Jennings, J. R. (2017). Socioeconomic status and parenting during adolescence in relation to ideal cardiovascular health in Black and White men. *Health Psychology, 36*(7), 673–681.

Maxwell, J. A. (2004). *Qualitative research design: An interactive approach* (2nd ed.). Thousand Oaks, CA: Sage.

Mazama, A. (2001). The Afrocentric paradigm: Contours and definitions. *Journal of Black Studies, 31*, 387–405.

Mazur, A. (1977). Interpersonal spacing on public benches in contact vs. noncontact cultures. *Journal of Social Psychology, 53*–58.

McCarthy, M. (1990). The thin ideal, depression and eating disorders in women. *Behavior Research & Therapy, 28*, 205–216.

McCubbin, L. D., & Marsella, A. (2009). Native Hawaiians and psychology: The cultural and historical context of indigenous ways of knowing. *Cultural Diversity and Ethnic Minority Psychology, 15*, 374–387.

McDonald, J. D., & Chaney, J. M. (2003). Resistance to multiculturalism: The "Indian problem." In J. S. Mio & G. Y. Iwamasa (Eds.), *Culturally diverse mental health: The challenges of research and resistance* (pp. 39–53). New York, NY: Brunner–Routledge.

McGirt, E. (2016). Why "Make America Great Again" is an offensive slogan. *Fortune*. Retrieved from http://fortune.com/2016/10/21/why-make-america-great-again-is-an-offensive-slogan/

McGlone, M. S., & Neal, A. (2003, May). *Stereotype threat and the gender gap in political knowledge*. Paper presented at the 83rd Annual Meeting of the Western Psychological Association, Vancouver, Canada.

McGoldrick, M. (1982). Ethnicity and family therapy: An overview. In M. McGoldrick, J. K. Pearce, & J. Giordano (Eds.), *Ethnicity & family therapy* (pp. 3–30). New York, NY: Guilford Press.

McIntosh, P. (1988). *White privilege and male privilege: A personal account of coming to see correspondences through work in women's studies* (Working Paper No. 189). Wellesley, MA: Wellesley College.

McIntosh, P. (1995). White privilege and male privilege: A personal account of coming to see correspondences through work in women's studies. In M. L. Andersen & P. H. Collins (Eds.), *Race, class, and gender: An anthology* (pp. 76–87). Belmont, CA: Wadsworth.

McKay, V. C. (1989). The grandparent–grandchild relationship. In J. F. Nussbaum (Ed.), *Life-span communication: Normative processes* (pp. 257–282). Hillsdale, NJ: Erlbaum.

McKay, V. C. (1993). Making connections: Narrative as the expression of continuity between generations of grandparents and grandchildren. In N. Coupland & J. Nussbaum (Eds.), *Discourse and lifespan identity* (pp. 173–185). London: Sage.

McKay, V. C. (1999). Understanding the co-culture of the elderly. In L. A. Samovar & R. E. Porter (Eds.), *Intercultural communication: A reader* (8th ed., pp. 174–180). Belmont, CA: Wadsworth.

McKay, V. C., & Caverly, R. S. (1995). Relationships in later life: The nature of inter- and intragenerational ties among grandparents, grandchildren, and adult siblings. In J. Nussbaum (Ed.), *Handbook of communication and aging* (pp. 207–225). Hillsdale, NJ: Erlbaum.

McLean, G. N., & Geigi, M. (2016). The importance of worldviews on women's leadership to HRD. *Advances in Developing Human Resources, 18*(2), 260–270.

McQueen, S. (Director). (2013). *12 years a slave* [Film]. Distributed by Fox Searchlight Pictures, Los Angeles, CA,.

Media That Matters. (n.d.). *A girl like me*. Retrieved from https://www.youtube.com/watch?v=z0BxFRu_SOw

Mendoza, R. H. (1989). An empirical scale to measure type and degree of acculturation in Mexican-American adolescents and adults. *Hispanic Journal of Behavioral Sciences, 9*, 183–205.

Merida, K. (2008, May 13). Racist incidents give some Obama campaigners pause. *The Washington Post*. Retrieved from http://www.washingtonpost.com/wp-dyn/content/article/2008/05/12/AR2008051203014.html

Mestenhauser, J. A. (1983). Learning from sojourners. In D. Landis & R. W. Brislin (Eds.), *Handbook of intercultural training: Vol. 11. Issues in training and methodology* (pp. 153–185). New York, NY: Pergamon.

Micha, R., Peñalvo, J. L., Cudhea, F., Imamura, F., Rehm, C. D., & Mozaffarian, D. (2017). Association between dietary factors and mortality from heart disease, stroke, and type 2 diabetes in the United States. *JAMA, 317*(9), 912–924. doi:10.1001/jama.2017.0947

Mikkelson, D. P., & Mikkelson, B. (2005). Urban legends references pages: Glurge gallery. *Snopes.* Retrieved from https://www.snopes.com/fact-check/teddy-bared/

Miller, J., & Garran, A. M. (2008). *Racism in the United States: Implications for the helping professions.* Belmont, CA: Thomson Brooks/Cole.

Miller, L. (2010, August 16). War over Ground Zero: A proposed mosque tests the limits of American tolerance. *Newsweek,* pp. 26–33.

Mindess, A. (1999). *Reading between the signs.* Yarmouth, ME: Intercultural Press.

Mio, J. S. (2002). Narrative as exemplar: In search of culture. [Review of the book *Culture in psychology*]. *Contemporary Psychology: APA Review of Books, 47,* 506–508.

Mio, J. S. (2003). Modern forms of resistance to multiculturalism: Keeping our eyes on the prize. In J. S. Mio & G. Y. Iwamasa (Eds.), *Culturally diverse mental health: The challenges of research and resistance* (pp. 3–16). New York, NY: Brunner–Routledge.

Mio, J. S. (2008, Summer). Accepting compliments, part 2. *Asian American Psychologist: Newsletter of the Asian American Psychological Association, 3,* 9–10.

Mio, J. S. (2009). Metaphor, humor, and psychological androgyny. *Metaphor and Symbol, 24,* 174–183.

Mio, J. S. (2013). Holocultural method. In K. D. Keith (Ed.), *Encyclopedia of cross-cultural psychology* (pp. 663–664). New York, NY: Wiley.

Mio, J. S. (2016). Teaching for change: Post-racial or a different form of racism? In L. A. Barker (Ed.), *Obama on our minds: The impact of Obama on the psyche of America* (pp. 75–92). New York, NY: Oxford University Press.

Mio, J. S., & Awakuni, G. I. (2000). *Resistance to multiculturalism: Issues and interventions.* Philadelphia, PA: Brunner/Mazel.

Mio, J. S., & Barker-Hackett, L. (2003). Reaction papers and journal writing as techniques for assessing resistance in multicultural courses. *Journal of Multicultural Counseling and Development, 31,* 12–19.

Mio, J. S., & Fu, M. (2017). Poverty in the Asian/Pacific Islander American community: Social justice-related community responses. In A. W. Blume (Ed.), *Social issues in living color: Challenges and solutions from the perspective of ethnic minority psychology, Vol. 1, Overview and interpersonal issues* (pp. 75–92). Santa Barbara, CA: Praeger.

Mio, J. S., & Graesser, A. C. (1991). Humor, language, and metaphor. *Metaphor and Symbolic Activity, 6,* 87–102.

Mio, J. S., & Iwamasa, G. Y. (1993). To do, or not to do: That is the question for White cross-cultural researchers. *The Counseling Psychologist, 21,* 197–212.

Mio, J. S., Koss, M. P., Harway, M., O'Neil, J. M., Geffner, R., Murphy, B. C., & Ivey, D. C. (2003). Violence against women: A silent pandemic. In J. S. Mio & G. Y. Iwamasa (Eds.), *Culturally diverse mental health: The challenges of research and resistance* (pp. 269–287). New York, NY: Brunner–Routledge.

Mio, J. S., & Morris, D. R. (1990). Cross-cultural issues in psychology training programs: An invitation for discussion. *Professional Psychology: Research and Practice, 21,* 434–441.

Mio, J. S., Nagata, D. K., Tsai, A. H., & Tewari, N. (2007). Racism against Asian/Pacific Island Americans. In F. T. L. Leong, A. G. Inman, A. Ebreo, L. H. Yang, L. Kinoshita, & M. Fu (Eds.), *Handbook of Asian American psychology* (2nd ed., pp. 341–361). Thousand Oaks, CA: Sage.

Mio, J. S., & Roades, L. A. (2003). Building bridges in the 21st century: Allies and the power of human connection across demographic divides. In J. S. Mio & G. Y. Iwamasa (Eds.), *Culturally diverse mental health: The challenges of research and resistance* (pp. 105–117). New York, NY: Brunner–Routledge.

Mischel, W. (1958). Preference for delayed reinforcement: An experimental study of a cultural observation. *Journal of Abnormal and Social Psychology, 56,* 57–61.

Mischel, W. (1961). Delay of gratification, need for achievement, and acquiescence in another culture. *Journal of Abnormal and Social Psychology, 62,* 543–552.

Missing Migrants Project. (2017). *Migrant fatalities worldwide.* Geneva, Switzerland: International Organization for Migration. Retrieved from https://missingmigrants.iom.int/latest-global-figures

Mitchell, J. (2017). Charlottesville tragedy sparks civil rights memories. *USA Today.* Retrieved from https://www.usatoday.com/story/news/nation-now/2017/08/18/charlottesville-tragedy-sparks-civil-rights-memories/580897001/

Moberg, P. J., & Rick, J. H. (2008). Decision-making capacity and competency in the elderly: A clinical and neuropsychological perspective. *NeuroRehabilitation, 23,* 403–413.

Mojtabai, R., Olfson, M., Sampson, N. A., Jin, R., Druss, B., Wang, P. S., . . . Kessler, R. C. (2011). Barriers to mental health treatment: Results from the National Comorbidity Survey Replication (NCS-R). *Psychological Medicine, 41,* 1751–1761.

Montgomery, G. T., Arnold, B., & Orozco, S. (1990). MMPI supplemental scale performance of Mexican Americans and level of acculturation. *Journal of Personality Assessment, 54,* 328–342.

Moody, M., Ybarra, M., & Nabors, N. (2009). Social justice: Diversity in action. In J. L. Chin (Ed.), *Diversity in mind and action: Social justice matters* (Vol. 3, pp. 1–19). Santa Barbara, CA: Praeger.

Moradi, B., & Hasan, N. T. (2004). Arab American persons' reported experiences of discrimination and mental health: The mediating role of personal control. *Journal of Counseling Psychology, 51*, 418–428.

Morales, E., & Norcross, J. C. (2010). Evidence-based practices with ethnic minorities: Strange bedfellows no more. *Journal of Clinical Psychology, 66*(8), 821–829.

Moreland, K. L. (1996). Persistent issues in multicultural assessment of social and emotional functioning. In L. A. Suzuki, P. J. Meller, & J. G. Ponterotto (Eds.), *Handbook of multicultural assessment: Clinical, psychological, and educational applications* (pp. 51–76). San Francisco, CA: Jossey–Bass.

Morelli, P. T. T. (2005). Social work practice with Asian Americans. In D. Lum (Ed.), *Cultural competence, practice stages, and client systems: A case study approach.* Belmont, CA: Brooks/Cole.

Morin, R. (2013). *The most (and least) culturally diverse countries in the world.* Washington, DC: Pew Research Center. Retrieved from http://www.pewresearch.org/fact-tank/2013/07/18/the-most-and-least-culturally-diverse-countries-in-the-world/

Morrow, S. L., Rakhsha, G., & Castañeda, C. L. (2001). Qualitative research methods for multicultural counseling. In J. G. Ponterotto, J. M. Casas, L. A. Suzuki, & C. M. Alexander (Eds.), *Handbook of multicultural counseling* (2nd ed., pp. 575–603). Thousand Oaks, CA: Sage.

Morse, G. S., & Blume, A. (2013, September). *Does the APA ethics code work for us?* Communique. Washington, DC: American Psychological Association, Office of Ethnic Minority Affairs. Retrieved from https://www.apa.org/pi/oema/resources/communique/2013/09/code-ethics.aspx

Moskowitz, P. (2017). It was never going to be a normal protest. They came ready to fight. *Splinter.* Retrieved from http://splinternews.com/it-was-never-going-to-be-a-normal-protest-they-came-re-1797824445

Mossaad, N. (2016, November). *Refugees and asylees: 2015. Annual Flow Report.* Washington, DC: US Department of Homeland Security. Retrieved from https://www.dhs.gov/immigration-statistics/refugees-asylees

Moy, E., Smith, C. R., Johansson, P., & Andrews, R. (2006). Gaps in data for American Indians and Alaska Natives in the national healthcare disparities report. *American Indian & Alaska Native Mental Health Research: The Journal of the National Center, 13*, 52–69.

Mujicic, R., & Frijters, P. (2013, March). *Still not allowed on the bus: It matters if you're Black or White!* IZA Discussion Paper No. 7300.

Murphy, M. C., Steele, C. M., & Gross, J. J. (2007). Signaling threat: How situational cues affect women in math, science, and engineering settings. *Psychological Science, 18*, 879–885.

Murphy-Shigematsu, S. (2014, February). *Day of remembrance panel.* California State Polytechnic University, Pomona, CA.

Murray, H. A., & Kluckhohn, C. (1953). *Personality in nature, society, and culture.* New York, NY: Knopf.

Mustakova-Possardt, E. (1998). Critical consciousness: An alternative pathway for positive personal and social development. *Journal of Adult Development, 5*(1), 13–30.

Mustanski, B., & Liu, R. T. (2013). A longitudinal study of predictors of suicide attempts among lesbian, gay, bisexual, and transgender youth. *Archives of Sexual Behavior, 42*(3), 437–448. https://doi.org/10.1007/s10508-012-0013-9

Myers, H. F. (1986, October). *The biopsychosocial model.* Lecture presented for the first-year clinical psychology graduate students in the Psychology Department, University of California, Los Angeles.

Myers, L. J. (1988). *Understanding the Afrocentric worldview: Introduction to an optimal psychology.* Dubuque, IA: Kendall/Hunt.

Nadal, K. L. (2004). Pilipino American identity development model. *Journal of Multicultural Counseling & Development, 32*, 45–62.

Nadal, K. L. (2011). The Racial and Ethnic Microaggressions Scale (REMS): Construction, reliability, and validity. *Journal of Counseling Psychology, 58*, 470–480.

Nadal, K. L., Davidoff, K. C., Davis, L. S., Wong, Y., Marshall, D., & McKenzie, V. (2016). A qualitative approach to intersectional microaggressions: Understanding influences of race, ethnicity, gender, sexuality, and religion. *Qualitative Psychology, 3*(2), 147–163.

Nadal, K. L., Griffin, K. E., Wong, Y., Hamit, S., & Rasmus, M. (2014). The impact of racial microaggressions on mental health: Counseling implications for clients of color. *Journal of Counseling and Development, 92*, 57–66.

Nagata, D. K. (1990a). The Japanese American internment: Exploring the transgenerational consequences of traumatic stress. *Journal of Traumatic Stress, 3*, 47–69.

Nagata, D. K. (1990b). *Legacy of injustice.* New York, NY: Plenum Press.

Nagata, D. K. (1993). *Legacy of silence: Exploring the long-term effects of the Japanese American internment.* New York, NY: Plenum Press.

Nagata, D. K. (1998). Internment and intergenerational relations. In L. C. Lee & N. W. S. Zane (Eds.), *Handbook of Asian American psychology* (pp. 433–456). Thousand Oaks, CA: Sage.

Nagata, D. K., & Takeshita, Y. J. (1998). Coping and resilience across generations: Japanese Americans and the World War II internment. *Psychoanalytic Review, 85,* 587–613.

Nagourney, A. (2013, July 5). Gay marriage stirs rebellion at synagogue. *The New York Times.* Retrieved from http://www.nytimes.com/2013/07/06/us/rabbi-takes-a-stand-for-gay-marriage-and-a-segment-of-the-congregation-rebels.html

Nasser, M. (1986). Comparative study of the prevalence of abnormal eating attitudes among Arab female students of both London and Cairo universities. *Psychological Medicine, 16,* 621–625.

Nasser, M., Katzman, M. A., & Gordon, R. A. (Eds.). (2001). *Eating disorders and cultures in transition.* New York, NY: Taylor & Francis.

National Cancer Institute. (2011). *Cancer health disparities.* Retrieved from http://www.cancer.gov/cancertopics/factsheet/disparities/cancer-health-disparities

National Comorbidity Survey. (2005). *National Comorbidity Study (NCS) and National Comorbidity Survey Replication (NCS-R).* Retrieved from http://www.hcp.med.harvard.edu/ncs/

National Congress of American Indians (n.d.). *An introduction to Indian nations in the United States.* Retrieved from: http://www.ncai.org/about-tribes

National Council on Crime and Delinquency. (2007). *And justice for some: Differential treatment of youth of color in the justice system.* Oakland, CA: National Council on Crime and Delinquency. Retrieved from http://www.nccdglobal.org/sites/default/files/publication_pdf/justice-for-some.pdf

National Heart, Lung, and Blood Institute. (2017). *For diversity in clinical trials, "Include us!" patients say.* Retrieved from https://www.nhlbi.nih.gov/news/2017/diversity-clinical-trials-include-us-patients-say

National Institute of Mental Health (1998). *Genetics and mental disorders: Report of the National Institute of Mental Health's Genetics Workgroup.* Rockville, MD: Author.

National Latinx Psychological Association. (2018). *NLPA renamed the National Latinx Psychological Association name change announcement, July 2018.* Retrieved from https://www.nlpa.ws/news-events

National Multicultural Conference and Summit. (2015). *American Psychological Association.* Retrieved from http://www.apadivisions.org/multicultural-summit.aspx

National Urban League. (2014). *One nation underemployed, jobs rebuild America: 2014 state of Black America.* New York, NY: National Urban League.

Nauman, T. (2012, February 24). *Native Sun News: Sioux nation takes stand on Keyston XL.* Retrieved from http://www.indianz.com/News/2012/004715.asp

NBC Bay Area. (2013, June 25). *Timeline of California Prop. 8.* Retrieved from http://www.nbcbayarea.com/news/national-international/timeline-california-proposition-8-212382141.html

Neal-Barnett, A., Stadulis, R., Singer, N., Murray, M., & Demmings, J. (2010). Assessing the effects of experiencing the acting White accusation. *Urban Review, 42,* 102–122.

Neighbors, H. W. (1984). Professional help use among Black Americans: Implications for unmet need. *American Journal of Community Psychology, 12,* 551–566.

Neighbors, H. W. (1985). Seeking professional help for personal problems: Black Americans' use of health and mental health services. *Community Mental Health Journal, 21,* 156–166.

Neighbors, H. W. (1988). The help-seeking behavior of Black Americans: A summary of findings from the National Survey of Black Americans. *Journal of the National Medical Association, 80,* 1009–1012.

Neighbors, H. W. (1997). The (mis)diagnosis of mental disorder in African Americans. *African American Research Perspectives, 3,* 1–11.

Neighbors, H. W., Caldwell, C., Williams, D. R., Nesse, R., Taylor, R. J., Bullard, K. M., . . . Jackson, J. D. (2007). Race, ethnicity, and the use of services for mental disorders: Results from the National Survey of American Life. *Archives of General Psychiatry, 64,* 485–494.

Neighbors, H. W., & Jackson, J. S. (1984). The use of informal and formal help: Four patterns of illness behavior in the Black community. *American Journal of Community Psychology, 12,* 629–644.

Nesselroade, J. R., & Labouvie, E. W. (1985). Experimental design in research on aging. In J. E. Birren & K. W. Schaie (Eds.), *Handbook of the psychology of aging* (2nd ed., pp. 35–60). New York, NY: Van Nostrand Reinhold.

Neville, H. A., & Awad, G. H. (2014). Why racial colorblindness is myopic. *American Psychologist, 69,* 313–314.

Neville, H. A., Awad, G. H., Brooks, J. E., Flores, M. P., & Bluemel, J. (2013). Color-blind racial ideology: Theory, training, and measurement implications in psychology. *American Psychologist, 68,* 455–466.

Neville, H. A., Gallardo, M. E., & Sue, D. W. (Eds.). (2016). *The myth of racial color blindness: Manifestations, dynamics, and impact.* Washington, DC: American Psychological Association.

Neville, H. A., Spanierman, L., & Doan, B. (2006). Exploring the association between color-blind racial ideology and multicultural counseling competencies. *Cultural Diversity and Ethnic Minority Psychology, 12,* 275–290.

Newport, F. (2013, July 25). *In U.S., 87% approve of Black–White marriage vs. 4% in 1958. Gallup.* Retrieved from http://www.gallup.com/poll/163697/approve-marriage-blacks-whites.aspx

New York Times Editorial Board. (2013, November 13). Resistance to marriage equality. *The New York Times.* Retrieved from http://www.nytimes.com/2013/11/14/opinion/resistance-to-marriage-equality.html

Nicdao, E. G., Hong, S., & Takeuchi, D. (2007). Prevalence and correlates of eating disorders among Asian Americans: Results from the National Latino and Asian American Study. *International Journal of Eating Disorders, 40,* S22–S26.

Nichols, M. P., & Schwartz, R. C. (1998). *Family therapy: Concepts and methods* (2nd ed.). Boston, MA: Allyn & Bacon.

Nickerson, A., Liddell, B. J., Maccallum, F., Steel, Z., Silove, D., & Bryant, R. A. (2014). Posttraumatic stress disorder and prolonged grief in refugees exposed to trauma and loss. *BMC Psychiatry, 14*(1), 106.

Nimoy, L. (Director). (1986). *Star Trek IV: The voyage home* [Film]. Hollywood, CA: Paramount Pictures.

Ninou, A., Guthrie, E., Paika, V., Ntountoulaki, E., Tomenson, B., Tatsioni, A., . . . Hyphantis, T. (2016). Illness perceptions of people with long-term conditions are associated with frequent use of the emergency department independent of mental illness and somatic symptom burden. *Journal of Psychosomatic Research, 81,* 38–45. doi:10.1016/j.jpsychores.2016.01.001

Nobles, W. W. (1986). *African psychology: Toward its reclamation, reascension, and revitalization.* Oakland, CA: Institute for the Advanced Study of Black Family Life and Culture.

Nobles, W. W. (1989). Psychological nigrescence: An Afrocentric review. *The Counseling Psychologist, 17,* 253–257.

Nobles, W. W. (1991). African philosophy: Foundations for Black psychology. In R. L. Jones (Ed.). *Black psychology* (3rd ed., pp. 47–63). Berkeley, CA: Cobb & Henry.

Norman, D. A., & Rummelhart, D. E. (Eds.). (1975). *Explorations in cognition.* San Francisco, CA: Freeman.

Nussbaum, J., & Bettini, L. M. (1994). Shared stories of the grandparent–grandchild relationship. *International Journal of Aging and Human Development, 39,* 67–80.

Obama, B. H. (2004, July 27). Transcript: Illinois Senate candidate Barack Obama. *The Washington Post.* Retrieved from http://www.washingtonpost.com/wp-dyn/articles/A19751-2004Jul27.html

Obama, B. (2016). United States health care reform: Progress to date and next steps. *JAMA, 316*(5), 525–532. doi:10.1001/jama.2016.9797

Obasi, E. M., Flores, L. Y., & James-Myers, L. (2009). Construction and initial validation of the Worldview Analysis Scale (WAS). *Journal of Black Studies, 39,* 937–961.

O'Brien, C. (2017, August 25). Trump signs transgender military ban. *Politico.* Retrieved from https://www.politico.com/story/2017/08/25/trump-transgender-military-ban-242049

O'Brien, G. V. (2003). Indigestible food, conquering hordes, and waste materials: Metaphors of immigrants and early immigration restriction debate in the United States. *Metaphor and Symbol, 18,* 33–47.

O'Brien, K., Poat, J., Press, N., & Saha, S. (2010). *"They're looking through you": Reports from African American, Latina/Latino, and European American adults concerning experiences with doctors.* Poster presented at the first convention of the Society for the Psychological Study of Ethnic Minority Issues, Ann Arbor, MI.

O'Connor, L., & Marans, D. (2016). Here are 13 examples of Donald Trump being racist. Retrieved from https://www.huffingtonpost.com/entry/donald-trump-racist-examples_us_56d47177e4b03260bf777e83

Office of Disease Prevention and Health Promotion. (2018). *Access to health services.* Retrieved from: https://www.healthypeople.gov/2020/

O'Harra, A. (2018, March 6). I'm a high school student in Alaska. We spend more time practicing for a mass shooting than for an earthquake. *Anchorage Daily News.* Retrieved from https://www.adn.com/opinions/2018/03/06/im-a-high-school-student-in-alaska-we-spend-more-time-practicing-for-a-mass-shooting-than-for-an-earthquake/

Ohbuchi, K.-I., & Takahashi, Y. (1994). Cultural styles of conflict management in Japanese and Americans: Passivity, covertness, and effectiveness of strategies. *Journal of Applied Social Psychology, 24,* 1345–1366.

Oishi, S., & Schimmack, U. (2010). Culture and well-being: A new inquiry into the psychological wealth of nations. *Perspectives on Psychological Science, 5,* 463–471.

Okagaki, L., & Sternberg, R. J. (1991). Cultural and parental influences. In L. Okagaki & R. L. Sternberg (Eds.), *Directors of development: Influences on the development of children's thinking* (pp. 101–120). Hillsdale, NJ: Erlbaum.

Olson, L. (2001). *Freedom's daughters: The unsung heroines of the civil rights movement from 1830 to 1970.* New York, NY: Scribner.

Olson, L. M., & Wahab, S. (2006). American Indians and suicide: A neglected area of research. *Trauma, Violence, and Abuse, 7,* 19–33.

On the Issues. (n.d.). Donald Trump. *On the Issues.* Retrieved from http://www.ontheissues.org/Donald_Trump.htm

Oquendo, M., Horwath, E., & Martinez, A. (1989). *Ataque de nervios:* Proposed diagnostic criteria for a culture specific syndrome. *Culture, Medicine and Psychiatry, 16,* 367–376.

Orbe, M. P. (1999). Utilizing an inductive approach to studying African American male communication. In L. A. Samovar & R. E. Porter (Eds.), *Intercultural communication: A reader* (8th ed., pp. 227–234). Belmont, CA: Wadsworth.

Organisation for Economic Co-operation and Development. (2013). *PISA 2012 assessment and analytical framework: Mathematics, reading, science, problem solving and financial literacy.* Paris: OECD Publishing. doi:10.1787/9789264190511-en

Organisation for Economic Co-operation and Development. (2017). PISA 2015 2015 results (Volume V): Collaborative problem solving, PISA. Paris: OECD Publishing. doi:10.1787/9789264285521-en

Ortman, J. M., & Shin, H. B. (2011, August). *Language projections: 2010 to 2020.* Paper presented at the Annual Meeting of the American Sociological Association, Las Vegas, NV.

Owen, J., Leach, M. M., Wampold, B., & Rodolfa, E. (2011). Client and therapist variability in client's perceptions of their therapists' multicultural competencies. *Journal of Counseling Psychology, 58*(1), 1–9.

Owen, J., Tao, K. W., Imel, Z. E., & Wampold, B. E. (2014). Addressing racial and ethnic microaggressions in therapy. *Professional Psychology: Research and Practice, 45,* 283–290.

Pachankis, J. E., & Goldfried, M. R. (2013). Clinical issues in working with lesbian, gay, and bisexual clients. *Psychology of Sexual Orientation and Gender Diversity, 1*(S), 45–58. doi:10.1037/2329-0382.1.S.45

Pachter, L. M., Bernstein, B. A., Szalacha, L. A., & García Coll, C. (2010). Perceived racism and discrimination in children and adults: An exploratory study. *Health & Social Work, 35,* 61–70.

Padela, A. I., & Heisler, M. (2010). The association of perceived abuse and discrimination after September 11, 2001, with psychological distress, level of happiness, and health status among Arab Americans. *American Journal of Public Health, 100,* 284–291.

Padilla, A. M. (2009). A history of Latino psychology. *Cultural Diversity and Ethnic Minority Psychology, 15,* 363–373.

Padilla, L. M. (2001). "But you're not a dirty Mexican": Internalized oppression, Latinos, and law. *Texas Hispanic Journal of Law and Policy, 7,* 58–113.

Padilla, L. M. (2004). Internalized oppression and Latino/as. *Diversity Factor, 12,* 15–21.

Paludi, M. A. (1998). *The psychology of women.* Upper Saddle River, NJ: Prentice Hall.

Paniagua, F. A. (2001). *Diagnosis in a multicultural context* (2nd ed.). Thousand Oaks, CA: Sage.

Paniagua, F. A. (2014). *Assessing and treating culturally diverse clients: A practical guide* (4th ed.). Thousand Oaks, CA: Sage.

Paradies, Y., Ben, J., Denson, N., Elias, A., Priest, N., Pieterse, A., . . . Gee, G. (2015). Racism as a determinant of health: A systematic review and meta-analysis. *PLOS ONE, 10*(9), e0138511. doi:10.1371/journal.pone.0138511

Parco, J. E., & Levy, D. A. (2013). The rise and fall of DADT. *Journal of Homosexuality, 60,* 147–151.

Parekh, B. (2000). *Rethinking multiculturalism: Cultural diversity and political theory.* Great Britain: Macmillan Press.

Parham, T. A. (1989). Cycles of psychological nigrescence. *The Counseling Psychologist, 17,* 187–226.

Parham, T. A. (2001). Psychological nigrescence revisited: A foreword. *Journal of Multicultural Counseling & Development, 29,* 162–164.

Parham, T. A. (Ed.). (2002). *Counseling persons of African descent: Raising the bar of practitioner competence.* Thousand Oaks, CA: Sage.

Parham, T. A., Ajamu, A., & White, J. L. (2011). The psychology of Blacks: Centering our perspectives in the African consciousness. New York: Routledge.

Parham, T. A., & Helms, J. E. (1981). Influences of Black students' racial identity attitudes on preferences for counselor race. *Journal of Counseling Psychology, 28,* 250–256.

Parham, T. A., & Helms, J. E. (1985a). Attitudes of racial identity and self-esteem of Black students: An exploratory investigation. *Journal of College Student Personnel, 26,* 143–147.

Parham, T. A., & Helms, J. E. (1985b). Relation of racial identity attitudes to self-actualization and affective status of Black students. *Journal of Counseling Psychology, 32,* 431–440.

Parham, T. A., & Parham, W. D. (2002). Understanding African American mental health. In T. A. Parham (Ed.), *Counseling persons of African descent: Raising the bar of practitioner competence* (pp. 25–37). Thousand Oaks, CA: Sage.

Parham, T. A., White, J. L., & Ajamu, A. (1999). *The psychology of Blacks* (3rd ed.). Upper Saddle River, NJ: Prentice Hall.

Parham, T. A., & Williams, P. T. (1993). The relationship of demographic and background factors to racial identity attitudes. *Journal of Black Psychology, 19,* 7–24.

Parmer, T., Arnold, M. S., Natt, T., & Jansen, C. (2004). Physical attractiveness as a process of internalized oppression and multigenerational transmission in African American families. *Family Journal, 12,* 230–242.

Parrish, K. (2010, November 30). *DOD releases "Don't Ask" repeal implementation plan.* Retrieved from http://archive.defense.gov/news/newsarticle.aspx?id=61896

Parrish, K. (2012, May 10). *Report shows success of "Don't Ask, Don't Tell" repeal.* Retrieved from http://archive.defense.gov/news/newsarticle.aspx?id=116291

Pate, J. E., Pumariega, A. J., Hester, C., & Garner, D. M. (1992). Cross-cultural patterns in eating disorders: A review. *Journal of the American Academy of Child and Adolescent Psychiatry, 31,* 802–808.

Patel, A. (2016). "Whitelash" becomes an important word following Trump's presidency. *The Huffington Post.* Retrieved from http://www.huffingtonpost.ca/2016/11/09/whitelash-election_n_12881584.html

Patel, V., Simunyu, E., & Gwanzura, F. (1995). *Kufungisisa* (thinking too much): A *Shona* idiom for non-psychotic mental illness. *Central African Journal of Medicine, 7,* 209–215.

Patterson, C. A. (2018). Undergraduate student change in cultural competence: Impact of a multicultural psychology course. *Scholarship of Teaching and Learning in Psychology 4*(2), 81–92.

Patterson, M. L. (1983). *Nonverbal behavior: A functional perspective.* New York, NY: Springer-Verlag.

Peal, E., & Lambert, W. E. (1962). The relation of bilingualism to intelligence. *Psychological Monographs, 76,* 1–23.

Pearce, M. (2014, August 14). Protest over shooting persist. *The Los Angeles Times,* p. AA2.

Pearson, A. R., Dovidio, J. F., & Gaertner, S. L. (2009). The nature of contemporary prejudice: Insights from aversive racism. *Social and Personality Psychology Compass, 3,* 314–338.

Pearson, J. A. (2017, October 4). Donald Trump is a textbook racist. *The Los Angeles Times.* Retrieved from http://www.latimes.com/opinion/op-ed/la-oe-pearson-trumps-textbook-racism-20171004-story.html

Pearson, M., Cloud, D. S., & Armengol, R. (2017). Three dead, dozens hurt, after Virginia White nationalist rally is dispersed; Trump blames "many sides." *The Los Angeles Times.* Retrieved from http://www.latimes.com/nation/nationnow/la-na-charlottesville-white-nationalists-rally-20170812-story.html

Pedersen, P. (1988). *A handbook for developing multicultural awareness.* Alexandria, VA: American Association for Counseling and Development.

Pedersen, P. (1990). The multicultural perspective as a fourth force in counseling. *Journal of Mental Health Counseling, 12,* 93–95.

Pedersen, P. (1991). Multiculturalism as a generic approach to counseling. *Journal of Counseling Development: Special Issue on Multiculturalism as a Fourth Force, 70,* 6–12.

Pedersen, P. (1999). *Multiculturalism as a fourth force.* Philadelphia, PA: Brunner/Mazel.

Pedersen, P. B., Draguns, J. G., Lonner, W. J., & Trimble, J. E. (Eds.). (2008). *Counseling across cultures* (6th ed.). Thousand Oaks, CA: Sage.

Peifer, K. L., Hu, T. W., & Vega, W. (2000). Help seeking by persons of Mexican origin with functional impairments. *Psychiatric Services, 51,* 1293–1298.

Penner, L. A., Dovidio, J. F., West, T. V., Gaeterner, S. L., Albrecht, T. L., Dailey, R. K., & Marcova, T. (2010). *Journal of Experimental Social Psychology, 46,* 436–440.

Peralta, E. (2016, September 4). Dakota access pipeline protests in North Dakota turn violent. *NPR.* Retrieved from https://www.npr.org/sections/thetwo-way/2016/09/04/492625850/dakota-access-pipeline-protests-in-north-dakota-turn-violent

Perez, R. M., DeBord, K. A., & Bieschke, K. J. (Eds.). (2000). *Handbook of counseling and psychotherapy with lesbian, gay, and bisexual clients.* Washington, DC: American Psychological Association.

Perloff, L. S. (1983). Perceptions of vulnerability to victimization. *Journal of Social Issues, 39,* 41–61.

Pettigrew, T. F. (1979). The ultimate attribution error: Extending Allport's cognitive analysis of prejudice. *Personality and Social Psychology Bulletin, 55,* 461–476.

Pew Research Center. (2015). *Multiracial in America: Proud, diverse, and growing in numbers.* Retrieved from http://www.pewsocialtrends.org/2015/06/11/multiracial-in-america/

Pfeffer, J., & Sutton, R. (2000). *The knowing–doing gap.* Boston, MA: Harvard Business School Press.

Phillon, J., He, M. F., & Connelly, F. M. (2005). *Narrative and experience in multicultural education.* Thousand Oaks, CA: Sage.

Phinney, J. S. (1992). Multigroup ethnic identity measure. *Journal of Adolescent Research, 7,* 156–176.

Phinney, J. S. (1996). When we talk about American ethnic groups, what do we mean? *American Psychologist, 51,* 918–927.

Pickren, W. E. (2004). Fifty years on: *Brown v. Board of Education* and American psychology, 1954–2004: An introduction. *American Psychologist, 59,* 493–494.

Pike, K. L. (1967). *Language in relation to a unified theory of the structure of human behavior.* The Hague: Mouton.

Pingree, R. J., Stoycheff, E., Sui, M., & Peifer, J. T. (2018). Setting a non-agenda: Effects of a perceived lack of problems in recent news or Twitter. *Mass Communication & Society,* 555–584. doi:10.1080/15205436.2018.1451543

Plaut, V. C., Thomas, K. M., & Goren, M. J. (2009). Is multiculturalism or color blindness better for minorities? *Psychological Science, 20,* 444–446.

Poniewozik, J. (2003). October 3, 1995: Color us divided. *Time.* Retrieved from http://www.time.com/time/80days/951003.html

Ponterotto, J. G. (1988). Racial consciousness development among White counselor trainees: A stage model. *Journal of Multicultural Counseling and Development, 16*, 146–156.

Ponterotto, J. G. (2010). Learning from voices of wisdom: Reflections on multicultural life stories. In Ponterotto, J. G., Suzuki, L. A., Casas, M. J., & Alexander, C. M. (Eds.), *Handbook of multicultural psychology* (3rd ed.). Los Angeles, CA: Sage.

Pope, M. (2008). Culturally appropriate counseling considerations for lesbian and gay clients. In P. B. Pedersen, J. G. Draguns, W. E. Lonner, & J. E. Trimble (Eds.), *Counseling across cultures* (6th ed., pp. 201–222). Thousand Oaks, CA: Sage.

Pope-Davis, D. B., & Coleman, H. L. K. (Eds.). (1997). *Multicultural counseling competencies: Assessment, education and training, and supervision.* Thousand Oaks, CA: Sage.

Pope-Davis, D. B., Reynolds, A. L., Dings, J. G., & Ottavi, T. M. (1994). Multicultural competencies of doctoral interns at university counseling centers: An exploratory investigation. *Professional Psychology: Research and Practice, 25*, 466–470.

Poston, D. L., & Saenz, R. (2017). U.S. Whites will soon be the minority in number, but not in power. *The Baltimore Sun.* Retrieved from http://www.baltimoresun.com/news/opinion/oped/bs-ed-op-0809-minority-majority-20170808-story.html

Poston, W. S. C. (1990). The biracial identity development model: A needed addition. *Journal of Counseling & Development, 69*, 152–155.

Poupart, L. M. (2003). The familiar face of genocide: Internalized oppression among American Indians. *Hypatia, 18*, 86–101.

Prado, C. G. (Ed.). (2017). *Social media and your brain: Web-based communication is changing how we think and express ourselves.* Santa Barbara, CA: Praeger/ABC-CLIO.

Prado, G., Szapocznik, J., Maldonado-Molina, M. M., Schwartz, S. J., & Pantin, H. (2008). Drug use/abuse prevalence, etiology, prevention, and treatment in Hispanic adolescents: A cultural perspective. *Journal of Drug Issues, 38*, 5–36.

Prager, J. (2017). Do Black lives matter? A psychoanalytic exploration of racism and American resistance to reparations. *Political Psychology, 38*(4), 637–651. doi:10.1111/pops.12436

Price-Williams, D., & Ramirez, M., III. (1977). Divergent thinking, cultural differences, and bilingualism. *Journal of Social Psychology, 103*, 3–11.

Prilleltensky, I., & Laurier, W. (1996). Politics change, oppression remains. On the psychology and politics of oppression. *Political Psychology, 17*, 127–148.

Prince, R. H. (2000). Transcultural psychiatry: Personal experiences and Canadian perspectives. *Canadian Journal of Psychiatry, 45*, 431–437.

ProCon.org. (2014, August 21). *Gay marriage: Pros and cons.* Retrieved from http://gaymarriage.procon.org

Putnam, R. C. (2007). *E pluribus unum*: Diversity and community in the twenty-first century. The 2006 Johan Skytte Prize Lecture. *Scandinavian Political Studies, 30*, 137–174.

Pyke, K. D. (2010). What is internalized racial oppression and why don't we study it: Acknowledging racism's hidden injuries. *Sociological Perspectives, 53*, 551–572.

Queally, J., & Semuels, A. (2014, August 1). Eric Garner's death in NYPD chokehold case ruled a homicide. *The Los Angeles Times.* Retrieved from http://www.latimes.com/nation/nationnow/la-na-nn-garner-homicide-20140801-story.html

Rafferty, A., Sotomayor, M., & Arkin, D. (2017, August 16). Trump says "two sides" share blame for Charlottesville rally violence. *NBC News.* Retrieved from https://www.nbcnews.com/news/us-news/trump-defends-all-sides-comment-n793001

Ramsi, S., Chuan, S. S., & Hennig, K. (2015). The acculturation gap–distress model: Extensions and application to Arab Canadian families. *Cultural Diversity and Ethnic Minority Psychology, 21*(4), 630–642.

Rand, C. W., & Kuldau, J. M. (1990). The epidemiology of obesity and self-defined weight problems in the general population: Gender, race, age, and social class. *International Journal of Eating Disorders, 9*, 329–343.

Rappoport, L. (2005). *Punchlines: The case for racial, ethnic, and gender humor.* Westport, CT: Praeger.

Ratliff, K. A., & Nosek, B. A. (2010). Creating distinct implicit and explicit attitudes with an illusory correlation paradigm. *Journal of Experimental Social Psychology, 46*, 721–728.

Ratts, M. J., Singh, A. A., Nassar-McMillan, S., Butler, S. K., & McCullough, J. R. (2015). *Multicultural and social justice counseling competencies.* Retrieved from https://www.counseling.org/docs/default-source/competencies/multicultural-and-social-justice-counseling-competencies.pdf?sfvrsn=14

Ratts, M. J., Singh, A. A., Nassar-McMillan, S., Butler, S. K., & McCullough, J. R. (2016). Multicultural and social justice competencies. *Journal of Multicultural Counseling and Development, 44*(1), 28–48. doi:10.1002/jmcd.12035

Redding, S. G., & Ng, M. (1982). The role of "face" in the organizational perceptions of Chinese managers. *Organization Studies, 3*, 201–219.

Reed, G. M., Correia, J. M., Esparza, P., Saxena, S., & Maj, M. (2011). The WPA–WHO global survey of psychiatrists' attitudes toward mental disorders classification. *World Psychiatry, 10,* 118–131.

Regner, I, Smeding, A., Gimmig, D., Thinus-Blanc, C., Monteil, J.-M., & Huguet, P. (2010). Individual differences in working memory moderate stereotype-threat effects. *Psychological Science, 21,* 1646–1648.

Remland, M. S., Jones, T. S., & Brinkman, H. (1991). Proxemic and haptic behavior in three European countries. *Journal of Social Psychology, 135,* 215–232.

Republican Party. (1864, June 7). Republican Party platform of 1864. *The University of California: The American Presidency Project.* Retrieved from http://www.presidency.ucsb.edu/ws/index.php?pid=29621

Reverby, S. M. (2011). "Normal exposure" and inoculation syphilis: A PHS "Tuskegee" doctor in Guatemala, 1946–1948. *Journal of Policy History, 23,* 6–28.

Reyes, R. A. (2017, September 26). Trump's lack of empathy about Puerto Rico is staggering. *CNN.* Retrieved from https://www.cnn.com/2017/09/26/opinions/trumps-lack-of-empathy-about-puerto-rico-reyes/index.html

Reynolds, A. L. (1999). Etic/emic. In J. S. Mio, J. E. Trimble, P. Arredondo, H. E. Cheatham, & D. Sue (Eds.), *Key words in multicultural interventions: A dictionary* (pp. 115–116). Westport, CT: Greenwood.

Ribeau, S. A., Baldwin, J. R., & Hecht, M. L. (1999). An African American communication perspective. In L. A. Samovar & R. E. Porter (Eds.), *Intercultural communication: A reader* (8th ed., pp. 147–154). Belmont, CA: Wadsworth.

Richardson, E. H. (1981). Cultural and historical perspective in counseling American Indians. In D. W. Sue (Ed.), *Counseling the culturally different* (pp. 216–255). New York, NY: Wiley.

Ridley, C. R. (1989). Racism in counseling as an adverse behavioral process. In P. B. Pedersen, J. G. Draguns, W. J. Lonner, & J. E. Trimble (Eds.), *Counseling across cultures* (3rd ed., pp. 55–77). Honolulu: University of Hawaii Press.

Ridley, C. R. (1995). *Overcoming unintentional racism in counseling and therapy: A practitioner's guide to intentional intervention.* Thousand Oaks, CA: Sage.

Riggio, R. E. (2013). *Introduction to industrial/organizational psychology* (6th ed.). Boston, MA: Pearson.

Riggio, R. E. (2017a, November 3). The minds of powerful sexual predators: How power corrupts: Three factors that propel powerful people to outrageous behavior. *Psychology Today.* Retrieved from https://www.psychologytoday.com/blog/cutting-edge-leadership/201711/the-minds-powerful-sexual-predators-how-power-corrupts

Riggio, R. E. (2017b, December 22). 8 body language cues that can get you into trouble: The wrong nonverbal cue might even get you killed. *Psychology Today.* Retrieved from https://www.psychologytoday.com/blog/cutting-edge-leadership/201712/8-body-language-cues-can-get-you-trouble

Riley, Z. (2018, June 1). Facebook vs Snapchat vs Instagram: Which is more popular? Retrieved from https://www.valuewalk.com/2018/06/facebook-vs-snapchat-vs-instagram/

Risen, J. L., Gilovich, T., & Dunning, D. (2007). One-shot illusory correlations and stereotype formation. *Personality and Social Psychology Bulletin, 33,* 1492–1502.

Rissman, C. K. (2007). *Narrative methods for the human sciences.* Thousand Oaks, CA: Sage.

Roach, R. (2003, May 8). History's burden: After decades of neglect, an academic research agenda is being built around health disparities. *Black Issues in Higher Education, 20,* 18–23.

Roades, L. A. (2016). Barack Obama and the LGBT community: A rocky path to real progress and ongoing hopes for the future. In L. A. Barker (Ed.), *Obama on our minds: The impact of Obama on the psyche of America* (pp. 187–218). New York, NY: Oxford University Press.

Roades, L. A., & Mio, J. S. (2000). Allies: How are they created and what are their experiences? In J. S. Mio & G. I. Awakuni (Eds.), *Resistance to multiculturalism: Issues and interventions* (pp. 63–82). Philadelphia, PA: Brunner/Mazel.

Roberts, M. (2018, February 15). Parkland school shooting 208th since Columbine: The tragic list. *Westword.* Retrieved from https://www.westword.com/news/parkland-to-columbine-school-shootings-list-9993641

Roberts, T. (2009). *Lessons from Little Rock.* Little Rock, AK: Butler Center Books.

Rodenborg, N. A., & Boisen, L. A. (2013). Aversive racism and intergroup contact theories: Cultural competence in a segregated world. *Journal of Social Work Education, 49,* 564–579.

Rodriguez, C. (2013, September 17). Mexican-American boy's national anthem sparks racist comments. *CNN.* Retrieved from http://www.cnn.com/2013/06/12/us/mexican-american-boy-sings-anthem/

Rodriguez, R. (2002). *Brown: The last discovery of America.* New York, NY: Penguin Putnam.

Rogers, R. A. (2006). From cultural exchange to transculturation: A review of reconceptualization of cultural appropriation. *Communication Theory, 16*(4), 474–503.

Rogler, L. H., Malgady, R. G., & Costantino, G. (1987). What do culturally sensitive mental health services mean? The case of Hispanics. *American Psychologist, 42,* 565–570.

Root, M. P. P. (1990). Resolving "other" status: Identity development of biracial individuals. In L. S. Brown & M. P. P.

Root (Eds.), *Diversity and complexity in feminist therapy* (pp. 185–205). New York, NY: Haworth.

Root, M. P. P. (1998). Facilitating psychotherapy with Asian American clients. In D. R. Atkinson, G. Morten, & D. W. Sue (Eds.), *Counseling American minorities: A cross-cultural perspective* (6th ed., pp. 214–234). Dubuque, IA: Brown.

Root, M. P. P. (2004, August). *Mixed race identities—Theory, research, and practice implications.* Continuing education workshop presented at the 112th Annual Convention of the American Psychological Association, Honolulu, HI.

Rose, L. R. (1996). White identity and counseling White allies about racism. In B. B. Bowser & R. G. Hunt (Eds.), *Impacts of racism on White Americans* (2nd ed., pp. 24–47). Thousand Oaks, CA: Sage.

Rose, M. H. (1995). Apprehending deaf culture. *Journal of Applied Communication Research, 23*(2), 156–162.

Rosenbaum, S. (2011). The Patient Protection and Affordable Care Act: Implications for public health policy and practice. *Public Health Reports, 126*(1), 130–135. doi:10.1177/003335491112600118

Rosenfeld, S. (1980). Sex differences in depression: Do women always have higher rates? *Journal of Health and Social Behavior, 21,* 33–42.

Rosenfeld, S. (1984). Race differences in involuntary hospitalization: Psychiatric vs. labeling perspectives. *Journal of Health and Social Behavior, 25,* 14–23.

Rosenfeld, S. (1999). Gender and mental health: Do women have more psychopathology, men more, or both the same (and why)? In A. V. Horwitz & T. L. Scheid (Eds.), *A Handbook for the Study of Mental Health: Social Contexts, Theories, and Systems* (pp. 348–360). New York, NY: Cambridge University Press.

Rosenthal, R. (1991). Teacher expectancy effects: A brief update 25 years after the Pygmalion experiment. *Journal of Research in Education, 1,* 3–12.

Rosenthal, R. (1994). Interpersonal expectancy effects: A 30-year perspective. *Current Directions in Psychological Science, 3,* 176–179.

Rosenthal, R., & Jacobson, L. (1968). *Pygmalion in the classroom: Teacher expectation and pupils' intellectual development.* New York, NY: Holt, Rinehart & Winston.

Rosenwasser, P. (2002). Exploring internalized oppression and healing strategies. *New Directions for Adult and Continuing Education, 94,* 53–61.

Rosofsky, A., Levy, J. I., Zanobetti, A., Janulewicz, P., & Fabian, M. P. (2018). Temporal trends in air pollution exposure inequality in Massachusetts. *Environmental Research, 161,* 76–86. doi:10.1016/j.envres.2017.10.028

Ross, L. (1977). The intuitive psychologist and his shortcomings: Distortions in the attribution process. In L. Berkowitz (Ed.), *Advances in experimental social psychology* (Vol. 10, pp. 174–221). New York, NY: Academic Press.

Ross, L. E., Doctor, F., Dimito, A., Kuehl, D., & Armstrong, M. S. (2007). Can talking about oppression reduce depression: Modified CBT group treatment for LGBT people with depression. *Journal of Gay and Lesbian Studies, 19,* 1–15.

Rossi, E., Cheng, Hu, Kroll, J. J., Diaz, M. T., & Newman, S. D. (2017). Changes in white-matter connectivity in late second language learners: Evidence from diffusion tensor imaging. *Frontiers in Psychology, 8,* 1–15. doi:10.3389/fpsyg.2017.02040

Rowe, W., Bennett, S. K., & Atkinson, D. R. (1994). White racial identity models: A critique and alternative proposal. *The Counseling Psychologist, 22,* 129–146.

Rucker, C. E., & Cash, T. F. (1992). Body image, body size perceptions, and eating behaviors among African-American and White college women. *International Journal of Eating Disorders, 12,* 291–299.

Ruiz, A. S. (1990). Ethnic identity: Crisis and resolution. *Journal of Multicultural Counseling and Development, 18,* 29–40.

Ryan, D., Dooley, B., & Benson, C. (2008). Theoretical perspectives on post-migration adaptation and psychological well-being among refugees: Towards a resource-based model. *Journal of Refugee Studies, 21,* 1–18.

Salinas, C., Jr., & Lozano, A. (2017). Mapping and recontextualizing the evolution of the term Latinx: An environmental scanning in higher education. *Journal of Latinos and Education.* doi:10.1080/15348431.2017.1390464

Sam, D. L., & Berry, J. W. (2010). Acculturation: When individuals and groups of different cultural backgrounds meet. *Perspectives on Psychological Science, 5,* 472–481.

Sampson, R. J., & Lauritsen, J. L. (1997). Racial and ethnic disparities in crime and criminal justice in the United States. *Crime and Justice, 21,* 311–374.

Samuda, R. J. (1998). *Psychological testing of American minorities.* Thousand Oaks, CA: Sage.

Sanchez-Cao, E., Kramer, T., & Hodes, M. (2013). Psychological distress and mental health service contact of unaccompanied asylum-seeking children: Mental health service contact of asylum-seeking children. *Child: Care, Health and Development, 39*(5), 651–659.

Santos, C. E. (2017). The history, struggles, and potential of the term Latinx. *Latina/o Psychology Today 4*(2), 7–14.

Saulny, S. (2011, March 24). Census data presents rise in multiracial population of youths. *The New York Times.* Retrieved from http://www.nytimes.com/2011/03/25/us/25race.html?_r=0

Saville-Smith, R. (2013, March 27). *Releasing the spirits: The implication of cultural accommodation in DSM-5.*

Retrieved from http://www.academia.edu/3126064/ Releasing_the_Spirits_-_The_implications_of_cultural_accommodation_in_DSM5

Sawyer, P. J., Major, B., Casad, B. J., Townsend, S. S. M., & Mendes, W. B. (2012). Discrimination and the stress response: Psychological and physiological consequences of anticipating prejudice in interethnic interactions. *American Journal of Public Health, 102,* 1020–1026.

Schilling, V. (2014, May 31). Natives & the military: 10 facts you might not know. *Indian Country Today.* Retrieved from https://indiancountrymedianetwork.com/news/veterans/natives-the-millitary-10-facts-you-might-not-know/

Schock, K., Rosner, R., & Knaevelsrud, C. (2015). Impact of asylum interviews on the mental health of traumatized asylum seekers. *European Journal of Psychotraumatology, 6*(1), 26286. doi:10.3402/ejpt.v6.26286

Schwartz, G. E. (1982). Testing the biopsychosocial model: The ultimate challenge facing behavioral medicine. *Journal of Consulting and Clinical Psychology, 50,* 1040–1053.

Schwartz, S. J., Unger, J. B., Zamboanga, B. L., & Szapocznik, J. (2010). Rethinking the concept of acculturation: Implications for theory and research. *American Psychologist, 65,* 237–251.

Schwartz, S. P. (2012). *A brief history of analytic philosophy: From Russell to Rawls.* Chichester, West Sussex: Wiley–Blackwell.

Seale, C., Gobo, G., Gubrium, J. F., & Silverman, D. (Eds.). (2004). *Qualitative research practice.* Thousand Oaks, CA: Sage.

Sears, D. O. (1988). Symbolic racism. In P. A. Katz and D. A. Taylor (Eds.), *Eliminating racism: Profiles in controversy* (pp. 53–84). New York, NY: Plenum Press.

Sechzer, J. A., Pfafflin, S. M., Denmark, F. L., Griffin, A., & Blumenthal, S. J. (Eds.). (1996). *Women and mental health.* New York: New York Academy of Sciences.

Selah, M. (2013, June 5). Cheerios exec on ad featuring mixed race couple: "'We were reflecting an American family.'" *Black Enterprise.* Retrieved from https://www.blackenterprise.com/cheerios-exec-biracial-ad-american-family/

Seligman, M. E. P. (1982). *Helplessness: On depression, development and death.* San Francisco, CA: Freeman.

Sellers, J. M. (1994). *Folk wisdom of Mexico.* San Francisco, CA: Chronicle Books.

Sellers, R. M., Smith, M. A., Shelton, J. N., Rowley, S. A. J., & Chavous, R. M. (1998). Multidimensional model of racial identity: A reconceptualization of African American racial identity. *Personality and Social Psychology Review, 2,* 18–39.

Shapiro, J. R. (2013). Stereotype threat. In C. Stangor & C. S. Crandall (Eds.), *Stereotyping and prejudice* (pp. 95–117). New York, NY: Psychology Press.

Shapiro, J. R., Williams, A. M., & Hambarchyan, M. (2013). Are all interventions created equal? A multi-threat approach to tailoring stereotype threat interventions. *Journal of Personality and Social Psychology, 104,* 277–288.

Shelton, K., & Delgado-Romero, E. A. (2011). Sexual orientation microaggressions: The experience of lesbian, gay, bisexual, and queer clients in psychotherapy. *Journal of Counseling Psychology, 58*(2), 210–221.

Sherman, J. W., Kruschke, J. K., Sherman, S. J., Percy, E. J., Petrocelli, J. V., & Conrey, F. R. (2009). Attentional processes in stereotype formation: A common model for category accentuation in illusory correlation. *Journal of Personality and Social Psychology, 96,* 305–323.

Shih, M., & Sanchez, D. T. (2009). When race becomes even more complex: Toward understanding the landscape of multiracial identity and experiences. *Journal of Social Issues, 65,* 1–11.

Shin, S., Chow, C., Camacho-Gonsalves, T., Levy, R. J., Allen, I. E., & Leff, H. S. (2005). A meta-analytic review of racial–ethnic matching of African American and Caucasian American clients and clinicians. *Journal of Counseling Psychology, 52*(1), 45–56. doi:10.1037/0022-0167.52.1.45

Shon, S. P., & Ja, D. Y. (1982). Asian families. In M. McGoldrick, J. K. Pearce, & J. Giordano (Eds.), *Ethnicity & family therapy* (pp. 208–228). New York, NY: Guilford Press.

Shuter, R. (1977). A field study of nonverbal communication in Germany, Italy and the United States. *Journal of Communication, 26,* 298–305.

Silance Ballard, E. (2013, October 29). Three letters from Teddy. *Lessons Learned in Life.* Retrieved from http://lessonslearnedinlife.com/three-letters-from-teddy

Silance Ballard, E. (n.d.). Two versions of "Three Letters." *LivingLifeFully*.com. Retrieved from http://www.livinglifefully.com/flo/flothreeletters.htm

Silverman, D. (2004). *Qualitative research: Theory, method and practice* (2nd ed.). Thousand Oaks, CA: Sage.

Silverman, D., & Marvasti, A. (2008). *Doing qualitative research* (2nd ed.). Thousand Oaks, CA: Sage.

Simon, R. (1995). Gender, multiple roles, role meaning, and mental health. *Journal of Health and Social Behavior, 36,* 182–194.

Skloot, R. (2010). *The immortal life of Henrietta Lacks.* New York, NY: Random House.

Sládková, J. (2014). "The guys told us crying that they saw how they were killing her and they could not do anything": Psychosocial explorations of migrant journeys to the U.S. *Psychosocial Intervention, 23*(1), 1–9.

Smedley, B. D., Stith, A. Y., & Nelson, A. R. (2003). *Unequal treatment: Confronting racial and ethnic disparities in health care.* Washington, D.C.: National Academies Press. https://doi.org/10.17226/10260

Smiley, T. (2016). Why I fear America could enslave Black people again. *Time*. Retrieved from http://time.com/4535292/donald-trump-black-slaves/

Smith, A. D. (2000). *Talk to me: Travels in media and politics*. New York, NY: Random House.

Smith, D. (2018, February 8). The backlash against Black Lives Matter is just more evidence of injustice. *The Conversation*. Retrieved from http://theconversation.com/the-backlash-against-black-lives-matter-is-just-more-evidence-of-injustice-85587

Smith, J. E., & Krejci, J. (1991). Minorities join the majority: Eating disturbances among Hispanic and Native American youth. *International Journal of Eating Disorders, 10*, 179–186.

Smith, M. R., & Alpert, G. P. (2007). Explaining police bias: A theory of social conditioning and illusory correlation. *Criminal Justice and Behavior, 34*, 1262–1283.

Smith, P. B. (2004). Acquiescent response bias as an aspect of cultural communication style. *Journal of Cross-Cultural Psychology, 35*, 59–61.

Smith, T. B., Domenech Rodríguez, M., & Bernal, G. (2011). Culture. *Journal of Clinical Psychology, 67*(2), 166–175.

Snow, C. E. (1983). Age differences in second language acquisition: Research findings and folk psychology. In K. Bailey, M. Long, & S. Peck (Eds.), *Second language acquisition studies* (pp. 141–150). Rowley, MA: Newbury House.

Snow, C. E. (1987). Relevance of the notion of a critical period to language acquisition. In M. Bornstein (Ed.), *Sensitive periods in development: An interdisciplinary perspective* (pp. 183–209). Hillsdale, NJ: Erlbaum.

Snow, C. E. (1993). Bilingualism and second language acquisition. In J. B. Gleason & N. B. Ratner (Eds.), *Psycholinguistics* (pp. 391–416). Fort Worth, TX: Harcourt, Brace, Jovanovich.

Snow, C. E., & Hoefnagel-Höhle, M. (1978). Critical period for language acquisition: Evidence from second language learning. *Child Development, 49*, 1263–1279.

Social media case study: How Barack Obama became president. (2017, December). *Devumi*. Retrieved from https://devumi.com/2017/12/social-media-case-study-how-barack-obama-became-president

Society of Clinical Psychology. (2016). *Psychological treatments*. Retrieved from https://www.div12.org/psychological-treatments/

Sodowsky, G. R., Lai, E. W. M., & Plake, B. S. (1991). Moderating effects of sociocultural variables on acculturation variables of Hispanics and Asian Americans. *Journal of Counseling and Development, 70*, 194–204.

Someah, K., Edwards, C., & Beutler, L. E. (2017). *Schools and approaches to psychotherapy. Oxford Research Encyclopedia of Psychology*. New York, NY: Oxford University Press. doi:10.1093/acrefore/9780190236557.013.69

Spearman, C. (1927). *The abilities of man*. New York, NY: Macmillan.

Spearman, C. S. (1904). "General intelligence," objectively determined and measured. *American Journal of Psychology, 15*, 201–293.

Special Populations Task Force of the President's Commission on Mental Health. (1978). *Task panel reports submitted to the President's Commission on Mental Health* (Vol. 3). Washington, DC: U.S. Government Printing Office.

Spickard, P. R. (1989). *Mixed blood: Intermarriage and ethnic identity in twentieth-century America*. Madison: University of Wisconsin Press.

Spitzer, R. L., Yanovski, S., Wadden, T., Wing, R., Marcus, M. D., Stunkard, A., . . . Horne, R. L. (1993). Binge eating disorder: Its further validation in a multisite study. *International Journal of Eating Disorders, 13*, 137–153.

Stahl, J. (2017, June 16). Philando Castile's killer acquitted despite forensics that contradicted his case. *Slate*. Retrieved from http://www.slate.com/blogs/the_slatest/2017/06/16/philando_castile_s_killer_acquitted_despite_forensics_that_contradicted.html

Steel, Z., Chey, T., Silove, D., Marnane, C., Bryant, R. A., & van Ommeren, M. (2009). Association of torture and other potentially traumatic events with mental health outcomes among populations exposed to mass conflict and displacement: A systematic review and meta-analysis. *Journal of the American Medical Association (JAMA), 302*(5), 537–549.

Steele, C. (2012, April). *Remedying stereotype threat*. Invited address delivered at the 92nd Annual Meeting of the Western Psychological Association, San Francisco, CA.

Steele, C. M. (1997). A threat in the air: How stereotypes shape intellectual identity and performance. *American Psychologist, 52*, 613–629.

Steele, C. M. (2001). Institutional climate and stereotype threat: Enhancing educational performance and identification in the face of negative group stereotypes. Keynote address at the Second Biennial National Multicultural Conference and Summit: *The psychology of race/ethnicity, gender, sexual orientation, and disability: Intersections, divergence, and convergence*. Santa Barbara, CA.

Steele, C. M., & Aronson, J. (1995). Stereotype threat and the intellectual test performance of African Americans. *Journal of Personality and Social Psychology, 69*, 797–811.

Steele, S. (2008, November 5). Obama's post-racial promise. *The Los Angeles Times*. Retrieved from http://www.latimes.com/opinion/opinion-la/la-oe-steele5-2008nov05-story.html#page=1

Sternberg, R. J. (1985). *Beyond IQ: A triarchic theory of human intelligence*. New York, NY: Cambridge University Press.

Sternberg, R. J. (1988). *The triarchic mind*. New York, NY: Cambridge University Press.

Sternberg, R. J. (1995). For whom the bell curve tolls [Review of the book *The Bell Curve*]. *Psychological Science, 6,* 257–261.

Sternberg, R. J. (1997). *Successful intelligence.* New York, NY: Simon & Schuster.

Sternberg, R. J. (1999). The theory of successful intelligence. *Review of General Intelligence, 3,* 292–316.

Sternberg, R. J. (2002). Successful intelligence: A new approach to leadership. In R. E. Riggio, S. E. Murphy, & F. J. Pirozzolo (Eds.), *Multiple intelligences and leadership* (pp. 9–28). Mahwah, NJ: Erlbaum.

Sternberg, R. J. (2003). *Cognitive psychology* (3rd ed.). Belmont, CA: Wadsworth.

Sternberg, R. J. (2012). Intelligence in its cultural context. In M. J. Gelfand, C-Y. Ciu, & Y-Y. Hong (Eds.), *Advances in culture and psychology* (Vol. 2, pp. 205–248). New York, NY: Oxford University Press.

Sternberg, R. J. (2014). Teaching about the nature of intelligence. *Intelligence, 42,* 176–179.

Sternberg, R. J., Ferrari, M., Clinkenbeard, P. R., & Grigorenko, E. L. (1996). Identification, instruction, and assessment of gifted children: A construct validation of a triarchic model. *Gifted Child Quarterly, 40,* 129–137.

Sternberg, R. J., Grigorenko, E. L., Ferrari, M., & Clinkenbeard, P. (1999). A triarchic analysis of an aptitude-treatment interaction. *European Journal of Psychological Assessment, 15,* 1–11.

Sternberg, R. J., Rayner, S., & Zhang, L.-F. (2013). An intelligent analysis of human intelligence. *American Journal of Psychology, 126,* 505–509.

Stiglitz, J. E. (2012). *The price of inequality: How today's divided society endangers our future.* New York, NY: Norton.

Stonequist, E. V. (1937). *The marginal man.* New York, NY: Scribner.

Straits, K. J. E. (2010). Language brokering in Latino families: Direct observations of brokering patterns, parent–child interactions, and relationship quality (Doctoral dissertation). Retrieved from https://digitalcommons.usu.edu/etd/722/

Striegel-Moore, R. H., Willfley, D. E., Pike, K. M., Dohm, F., & Fairburn, C. G. (2000). Recurrent binge eating in black American women. *Archives of Family Medicine, 9,* 83–87.

Substance Abuse and Mental Health Services Administration. (2016a). *Cultural competence.* Retrieved from https://www.samhsa.gov/capt/applying-strategic-prevention/cultural-competence

Substance Abuse and Mental Health Services Administration. (2016b). *2016 NSDUH: Race and ethnicity summary sheets.* Retrieved from https://www.samhsa.gov/data/report/2016-nsduh-race-and-ethnicity-summary-sheets

Substance Abuse and Mental Health Services Administration. (2018). *National Registry of Evidence-Based Programs and Practices.* Retrieved from https://knowledge.samhsa.gov/ta-centers/national-registry-evidence-based-programs-and-practices

Sue, D. W. (1978). Eliminating cultural oppression in counseling: Toward a general theory. *Journal of Counseling Psychology, 25,* 419–428.

Sue, D. W. (1981). *Counseling the culturally different: Theory and practice.* New York, NY: Wiley.

Sue, D. W. (2001). Multidimensional facets of cultural competence. *The Counseling Psychologist, 29,* 790–821.

Sue, D. W., Arredondo, P., & McDavis, R. J. (1992). Multicultural competencies/standards: A pressing need. *Journal of Counseling and Development, 70,* 477–486.

Sue, D. W., Bernier, J. E., Durran, A., Feinberg, L., Pedersen, P., Smith, E. J., & Vasquez-Nuttall, E. (1982). Position paper: Cross-cultural counseling competencies. *The Counseling Psychologist, 10,* 45–52.

Sue, D. W., Bucceri, J., Lin, A. I., Nadal, K. L., & Torino, G. C. (2007). Racial microaggressions and the Asian American experience. *Cultural Diversity & Ethnic Minority Psychology, 13,* 72–81.

Sue, D. W., Carter, R. T., Casas, J. M., Fouad, N. A., Ivey, A. E., Jensen, M., . . . Vasquez-Nuttal, E. (1998). *Multicultural counseling competencies: Individual and organizational development.* Thousand Oaks, CA: Sage.

Sue, D. W., Capodilupo, C. M., Torino, G. C., Bucceri, J. M., Holder, A. M., Nadal, K. L., & Esquilin, M. (2007). Racial microaggressions in everyday life: Implications for clinical practice. *American Psychologist, 62,* 271–286.

Sue, D. W., Ivey, A. E., & Pedersen, P. B. (1996). *A theory of multicultural counseling and therapy.* Pacific Grove, CA: Brooks/Cole.

Sue, D. W., Lin, A. I., Torino, G. C., Capodilupo, C. M., & Rivera, D. P. (2009). Racial microaggressions and difficult dialogues on race in the classroom. *Cultural Diversity & Ethnic Minority Psychology, 15,* 183–190.

Sue, D., Mak, W. S., & Sue, D. W. (1998). Ethnic identity. In L. C. Lee & N. W. S. Zane (Eds.), *Handbook of Asian American psychology* (pp. 289–323). Thousand Oaks, CA: Sage.

Sue, D. W., Nadal, K. L., Capodilupo, C. M., Lin, A. L., Torino, G. C., & Rivera, P. (2008). Racial microaggressions against Black Americans: Implications for counseling. *Journal of Counseling and Development, 86,* 330–338.

Sue, D. W., & Sue, D. (1990). *Counseling the culturally different: Theory and practice* (2nd ed.). New York, NY: Wiley.

Sue, D. W., & Sue, D. (1999). *Counseling the culturally different: Theory and practice* (3rd ed.). New York, NY: Wiley.

Sue, D. W., & Sue, D. (2003). *Counseling the culturally diverse: Theory and practice* (4th ed.). New York, NY: Wiley.

Sue, D. W., & Sue, D. (2008). *Counseling the culturally diverse: Theory and practice* (5th ed.). New York, NY: Wiley.

Sue, D. W., & Sue, D. (2013). *Counseling the culturally diverse: Theory and practice* (6th ed.). New York, NY: Wiley.

Sue, D. W., & Sue, D. (2016). *Counseling the culturally diverse: Theory and practice* (7th ed.). Hoboken, NJ: Wiley.

Sue, D. W., & Torino, G. C. (2005). Racial-cultural competence: Awareness, knowledge and skills, In R. T. Carter (Ed.), *Handbook of racial-cultural psychology and counseling* (pp. 3–18). Hoboken, NJ: Wiley.

Sue, S. (1977). Community mental health services to minority groups: Some optimism, some pessimism. *American Psychologist, 32,* 616–624.

Sue, S. (1999). Science, ethnicity, and bias: Where have we gone wrong? *American Psychologist, 54,* 1070–1077.

Sue, S., & McKinney, H. (1974). Delivery of community health services to Black and White clients. *Journal of Consulting and Clinical Psychology, 42,* 794–801.

Sue, S., & Morishima, J. K. (1982). *The mental health of Asian Americans.* San Francisco, CA: Jossey–Bass.

Sue, S., Allen, D., & Conaway, L. (1975). The responsiveness and equality of mental health care to Chicanos and Native Americans. *American Journal of Community Psychology, 45,* 111–118.

Sue, S., Fujino, D. C., Hu, L., Takeuchi, D. T., & Zane, N. W. S. (1991). Community mental health services for ethnic minority groups: A test of the cultural responsiveness hypothesis. *Journal of Consulting and Clinical Psychology, 59,* 533–540.

Sue, S., McKinney, H., Allen, D., & Hall, J. (1974). Delivery of community health services to Black and White clients. *Journal of Consulting Psychology, 42,* 794–801.

Sue, S., & Sue, D. W. (1971). Chinese American personality and mental health. *Amerasian Journal, 1,* 35–49.

Sue, S., & Sue, D. W. (2000). Conducting psychological research with the Asian American/Pacific Islander population. In Council of National Psychological Associations for the Advancement of Ethnic Minority Interests (Ed.), *Guidelines for research in ethnic minority communities* (pp. 2–4). Washington, DC: American Psychological Association.

Sue, S., Sue, D. W., Sue, L., & Takeuchi, D. T. (1995). Psychopathology among Asian Americans: A model minority? *Cultural Diversity and Mental Health, 1,* 39–51.

Sue, S., & Zane, N. (1987). The role of culture and cultural techniques in psychotherapy: A critique and reformulation. *American Psychologist, 42,* 37–45.

Suinn, R. M., Ahuna, C., & Khoo, G. (1992). The Suinn–Lew Self-Identity Acculturation Scale: Concurrent and factorial validation. *Educational and Psychological Measurement, 47,* 401–407.

Suinn, R. M., Rickard-Figueroa, K., Lew, S., & Vigil, P. (1987). The Suinn–Lew Self-Identity Acculturation Scale: An initial report. *Educational and Psychological Measurement, 47,* 401–407.

Sullivan, T. J., & Thompson, K. S. (1994). *Introduction to social problems* (3rd ed.). New York, NY: Macmillan.

Sung, K. (1991). Family-centered informal support networks of Korean elderly: The resistance of cultural traditions. *Journal of Cross-Cultural Gerontology, 6,* 431–447.

Supreme Court of the United States. (2015). *Obergefell et al. v. Hodges, Director, Ohio Department of Health et al.* Retrieved from https://caselaw.findlaw.com/us-supreme-court/14-556.html

Surhone, L. M., Tennoe, M. T., & Henssonow, S. F. (Eds.). (2010). *The Chinese classification of mental disorders* (3rd ed.). Mauritius: Betascript.

Sussman, L. K., Robins, L. N., & Earls, F. (1987). Treatment-seeking for depression by Black and White Americans. *Social Science & Medicine, 24,* 187–196.

Sussman, N. M., & Rosenfeld, H. M. (1982). Influence of culture, language and sex on conversation distance. *Journal of Personality and Social Psychology, 42,* 66–74.

Suyemoto, K. L. (2004). Racial/ethnic identities and related attributed experiences of multiracial Japanese European Americans. *Journal of Multicultural Counseling and Development, 32,* 206–221.

Szymanski, D. M., & Kashubeck-West, S. (2008). Mediators of the relationship between internalized oppressions and lesbian and bisexual women's psychological distress. *Counseling Psychologist, 36,* 575–594.

Tafoya, N., & Del Vecchio, A. (1996). Back to the future: An examination of the Native American holocaust. In M. McGoldrick, J. Giordano, & J. K. Pearce (Eds.), *Ethnicity & family therapy* (2nd ed., pp. 45–54). New York, NY: Guilford Press.

Tafoya, N., & Del Vecchio, A. (2005). Back to the future: An examination of the Native American holocaust experience. In M. McGoldrick, J. Giordano, & N. Garcia-Preto (Eds.), *Ethnicity & family therapy* (3rd ed., pp. 55–63). New York, NY: Guilford Press.

Takeuchi, D. T., Zane, N., Hong, S., Chae, D. H., Gong, F., Gee, G. C., . . . Alegria, M. (2007). Immigration-related factors and mental disorders among Asian Americans. *American Journal of Public Health, 97,* 84–90.

Tan, A., & Mallika, P. (2011). Coining: An ancient treatment widely practiced among Asians. *Malaysian Family Physician: The Official Journal of the Academy of Family Physicians of Malaysia, 6*(2–3), 97–98.

Tan, E. S.-H., & Visch, V. (2018). Co-imagination of fictional worlds in film viewing. *Review of General Psychology, 22*(2), 230–244.

Tappan, M. B. (2006). Reframing internalized oppression and internalized domination: From the psychological to the sociocultural. *Teachers College Record, 108,* 2115–2144.

Tatum, B. D. (1997). *"Why are all the Black kids sitting together in the cafeteria?" and other conversations about race.* New York, NY: Basic Books.

Taylor, J. Y., Caldwell, C. H., Baser, R. E., Faison, N., & Jackson, J. S. (2007). Prevalence of eating disorders among Blacks in the National Survey of American Life. *International Journal of Eating Disorders, 40,* S10–S14.

Taylor, S. E. (2009). *Health psychology* (7th ed.). New York, NY: McGraw–Hill.

Telesford, J., Mendoza-Denton, R., & Worrell, F. C. (2013). Clusters of CRIS scores and psychological adjustment. *Cultural Diversity and Ethnic Minority Psychology, 19*(1), 86–91.

Telles, E. E., & Ortiz, V. (2008). *Generations of exclusion: Mexican Americans, assimilation, and race.* New York, NY: Russell Sage Foundation.

ten Have, P. (2004). *Understanding qualitative research and ethnomethodology.* Thousand Oaks, CA: Sage.

Terman, L. M. (1916). *The measurement of intelligence.* Boston, MA: Houghton Mifflin.

Thernstrom, A. (2008, November 6). Great Black hope? The reality of president-elect Obama. *National Review Online.* Retrieved from http://www.nationalreview.com/article/226264/great-black-hope-nro-symposium

Thomas, A. J., Speight, S. L., & Witherspoon, K. M. (2005). Internalized oppression among Black women. In J. L. Chin (Ed.), *The psychology of prejudice and discrimination: Bias based on gender and sexual orientation* (Vol 3., pp. 113–132). Westport, CT: Praeger/Greenwood.

Thompson, B. (1994). Food, bodies and growing up female: Childhood lessons about culture race and class. In P. Fallon, M. A. Katzman, & S. C. Wooley (Eds.), *Feminist perspectives on eating disorders* (pp. 355–378). New York, NY: Guilford Press.

Thompson, C. A., & Barker, L. A. (2016). The Obama effect on racial attitudes: A review of the research. In L. A. Barker (Ed.), *Obama on our minds: The impact of Obama on the psyche of America* (pp. 109–138). New York, NY: Oxford.

Thorndike, R. L., Hagen, E. P., & Sattler, J. M. (1986). *Technical manual for the Stanford–Binet Intelligence Scale* (4th ed.). Chicago, IL: Riverside.

Ting-Toomey, S. (1994). Face and facework: An introduction. In S. Ting-Toomey (Ed.), *The challenge of facework* (pp. 1–14). Albany: State University of New York Press.

Ting-Toomey, S. (2005). The matrix of face: An updated face-negotiation theory. In W. B. Gudykunst (Ed.), *Theorizing about intercultural communication* (pp. 71–92). Thousand Oaks, CA: Sage.

Ting-Toomey, S., & Cocroft, B.-A. (1994). Face and facework: Theoretical and research issues. In S. Ting-Toomey (Ed.), *The challenge of facework* (pp. 307–340). Albany: State University of New York Press.

Tonkin, E. (2017). The importance of medical interpreters. *American Journal of Psychiatry Residents' Journal, 12*(8), 13–13. doi:10.1176/appi.ajp-rj.2017.120806

Toppo, G. (2018, February 22). "Generation Columbine" has never known a world without school shootings. *USA Today.* Retrieved from https://www.usatoday.com/story/news/2018/02/22/generation-columbine-has-never-known-world-without-school-shootings/361656002/

Torres-Harding, S. R., Andrade, A. L., & Romero Diaz, C. E. (2012). The Racial Microaggressions Scale (RMAS): A new scale to measure experiences of racial microaggressions in people of color. *Cultural Diversity and Ethnic Minority Psychology, 18,* 153–164.

Tracey, T. J., Leong, T. L., & Glidden, C. (1986). Help seeking and problem perception among Asian Americans. *Journal of Counseling Psychology, 33,* 331–336.

Triandis, H. C. (1989). The self and social behavior in different cultural contexts. *Psychological Review, 96,* 506–520.

Triandis, H. C. (1995). *Individualism & collectivism.* Boulder, CO: Westview.

Triandis, H. C., Bontempo, R., Betancourt, H., Bond, M., Leung, K., Brenes, A., . . . de Montmollin, G. (1986). The measurement of etic aspects of individualism and collectivism across cultures. *Australian Journal of Psychology, 38,* 257–267.

Triandis, H. C., Bontempo, R., Villareal, M. J., Asai, M., & Lucca, N. (1988). Individualism and collectivism: Cross-cultural perspectives on self-ingroup relationships. *Journal of Personality and Social Psychology, 54,* 323–338.

Triandis, H., Lambert, W., Berry, J., Lonner, W., Heron, A., Brislin, R., & Draguns, J. (Eds.). (1980). *Handbook of cross-cultural psychology* (Vols. 1–6). Boston, MA: Allyn & Bacon.

Trierweiler, S. J., Muroff, J. R., Jackson, J. S., Neighbors, H. W., & Munday, C. (2005). Clinician race, situational attributions, and diagnoses of mood versus schizophrenia disorders. *Cultural Diversity and Ethnic Minority Psychology, 11,* 351–364.

Trimble, J E. (1987). Self-understanding and perceived alienation among American Indians. *Journal of Community Psychology, 15*(July), 316–333.

Trimble, J. E. (2000). Social psychological perspectives on changing self-identification among American Indians and Alaska Natives. In R. H. Dana (Ed.), *Handbook of Cross-Cultural and Multicultural Personality Assessment*, (pp. 197-222). Mahwah, NJ: Lawrence Erlbaum Associates.

Trimble, J. E. (2003). Infusing American Indian and Alaska Native topics into the psychology curriculum. In P. Bronstein and K. Quina (Eds.), *Teaching gender and multicultural awareness: Resources for the psychology classroom* (pp. 221–236). Washington, DC: American Psychological Association.

Trimble, J. E., Clearing-Sky, M., & Sapa, P. (2009). An historical profile of American Indians and Alaska Natives in psychology. *Cultural Diversity and Ethnic Minority Psychology, 15*, 338–351.

Trimble, J. E., Helms, J., & Root, M. (2002). Social and psychological perspectives on ethnic and racial identity. In G. Bernal, J. Trimble, K. Burlew, & F. Leong (Eds.), *Handbook of racial and ethnic minority psychology* (pp. 239-275). Thousand Oaks, CA: Sage.

Tsai, J. L., Ying, Y.-W., & Lee, P. A. (2001). Cultural predictors of self-esteem: A study of Chinese American female and male young adults. *Cultural Diversity and Ethnic Minority Psychology, 7*, 284–297.

Tseng, V., & Yoshikawa, H. (2008). Reconceptualizing acculturation: Ecological processes, historical contexts, and power inequities. *American Journal of Community Psychology, 42*, 355–358.

Tsukayama, H. (2015). Teens spend nearly nine hours every day consuming media. *The Washington Post*. Retrieved from https://www.washingtonpost.com/news/the-switch/wp/2015/11/03/teens-spend-nearly-nine-hours-every-day-consuming-media/?noredirect=on&utm_term=.61cc6c05bc62

Turley, J. (2009, October 13). Attorney Orly Taitz fined $20,000 for frivolous "birther" litigation. *Jonathan Turley*. Retrieved from http://jonathanturley.org/?s=orly+taitz

Tversky, A., & Kahneman, D. (1973). Availability: A heuristic for judging frequency and probability. *Cognitive Psychology, 5*, 207–302.

Tynes, B. M., & Markoe, S. L. (2010). The role of color-blind racial attitudes in reactions to racial discrimination on social network sites. *Journal of Diversity in Higher Education, 3*, 1–13.

U.S. Census. (1999, March). Table 1: Nativity of the population and place of birth of the native population: 1850–1990. Washington, DC: US Census Bureau. Retrieved from https://www.census.gov/library/working-papers/1999/demo/POP-twps0029.html

U.S. Census Bureau. (2012a). *Most children younger than age 1 are minorities, Census Bureau reports*. Washington, DC: U.S. Census Bureau. Retrieved from https://www.census.gov/newsroom/releases/archives/population/cb12-90.html

US Census Bureau. (2012b). *U.S. Census Bureau projections show a slower growing, older, more diverse nation a half a century from now*. Washington, DC: US Census Bureau. Retrieved from https://www.census.gov/newsroom/releases/archives/population/cb12-243.html

U.S. Census Bureau. (2015). *New Census Bureau report analyzes U.S. population projections*. Washington, DC: U.S. Census Bureau. Retrieved from https://www.census.gov/newsroom/press-releases/2015/cb15-tps16.html

U.S. Department of Health and Human Services. (2001). *Mental health: Culture, race, and ethnicity—A supplement to mental health: A report of the surgeon general*. Rockville, MD: U.S. Department of Health and Human Services, Public Health Service, Office of the Surgeon General.

U.S. Department of Health and Human Services. (2011). *HHS action plan to reduce racial and ethnic health disparities*. Washington, DC: T.S. Department of Health and Human Services Office of Minority Health.

U.S. Department of Health and Human Services, Office of Minority Health (2013). *National Standards for Culturally and Linguistically Appropriate Services (CLAS) in Health and Health Care*. Retrieved from: https://www.thinkculturalhealth.hhs.gov/pdfs/EnhancedNationalCLASStandards.pdf

U.S. Department of Health, Education, and Welfare. (1979). *The Belmont Report: Ethical principles and guidelines for the protection of human subjects of research*. Washington, DC: Author. Retrieved from https://videocast.nih.gov/pdf/ohrp_appendix_belmont_report_vol_2.pdf

U.S. Department of Homeland Security. (2017). *Refugees and asylees*. Retrieved from https://www.dhs.gov/immigration-statistics/refugees-asylees

U.S. General Accounting Office. (2000, March). *U.S. Customs Service: Better targeting of airline passengers for personal searches could produce better results*. Washington, DC: Author.

Uba, L. (1982). Meeting the mental health needs of Asian Americans: Mainstream vs. segregated services. *Professional Psychology: Research and Practice, 13*, 215–221.

Underwood, K. (2010). Interactive remembering: Insights into the communicative competence of older adults. *Journal of Aging Studies, 24*, 145–166.

Unger, R. K. (1995). Conclusion: Cultural diversity and the future of feminist psychology. *Bringing cultural diversity to feminist psychology: Theory, research, and practice* (pp. 413–431). Washington, DC: American Psychological Association.

United Nations High Commission for Refugees. (2015). UNCHR Global Report 2015: Every life matters.

Geneva, Switzerland: UNHCR. Retrieved from http://www.unhcr.org/574ed44c4.pdf

United Nations High Commission for Refugees. (2017). Left behind: Refugee education in crisis. Geneva, Switzerland: UNHCR. Retrieved from http://www.unhcr.org/en-us/

VandenBos, G. R., & Winkler, J. M. (2015). An analysis of the status of journals and research in psychology from Latin America. *Psicologia: Reflexão e Crítica, 28*, 82–93. doi:10.1590/1678-7153.20152840012

van Meurs, N., & Spencer-Oatey, H. (2010). Multidisciplinary perspectives on intercultural conflict: The "Bermuda Triangle" of conflict, culture, and communication. In D. Matsumoto (Ed.), *APA handbook of intercultural communication* (pp. 59–77). Washington, DC: American Psychological Association.

Van Rooy, D., Vanhoomissen, T., & Van Overwalle, F. (2013). Illusory correlation, group size and memory. *Journal of Experimental Social Psychology, 49*, 1159–1167.

Vandiver, B. J., Cross, W. E., Jr., Worrell, F. C., & Fhagen-Smith, P. E. (2002). Validating the Cross Racial Identity Scale. *Journal of Counseling Psychology, 49*(1), 71–85.

Vandiver, B. J., Fhagen-Smith, P. E., Cokley, K. O., Cross, W. E., Jr., & Worrell, F. C. (2001). Cross' nigrescence model: From theory to scale to theory. *Journal of Multicultural Counseling and Development, 29*(3), 174–200.

Varela, J. R. (2017, September 26). Puerto Rico is being treated like a colony after Hurricane Maria. *The Washington Post*. Retrieved from https://www.washingtonpost.com/news/posteverything/wp/2017/09/26/puerto-rico-may-not-be-a-colony-but-its-getting-treated-that-way/?utm_term=.7d3890655a44

Vasquez, L. (2000). *Culturally competent counseling & therapy, part III: Innovative approaches to counseling Latin/o people.* [Training videotape] Available from Microtraining Associates, Inc., Box 9641, North Amherst, MA, 01059-9641.

Vasquez, M. J. T. (2001). Reflections on unearned advantages, unearned disadvantages, and empowering experiences. In J. G. Ponterotto, J. M. Casas, L. A. Suzuki, & C. M. Alexander (Eds.), *Handbook of multicultural counseling* (2nd ed., pp. 64–77). Thousand Oaks, CA: Sage.

Vazquez-Nuttal, E., Adams, D., Carter, A. C., Boyce, C. A., Cotton, L., McDonald, A., & Ward, W. (1997). *Diversity and accreditation. American Psychological Association, Commission on Ethnic Minority Recruitment, Retention, and Training in Psychology, by the Commission's Work Group on Education and Training.* Washington, DC: American Psychological Association. Retrieved from http://www.apa.org/pi/oema/resources/brochures/accreditation.aspx

Vega, W. A., Kolody, B., Aguilar-Gaxiola, S., Alderate, E., Catalana, R., & Carveo-Anduaga, J. (1998). Lifetime prevalence of *DSM-III-R* psychiatric disorders among urban and rural Mexican Americans in California. *Archives of General Psychiatry, 156*, 928–934.

Velasquez, R. J., Callahan, W. J., & Young, R. (1993). Hispanic–White MMPI comparisons: Does psychiatric diagnosis make a difference? *Journal of Clinical Psychology, 49*, 528–534.

Verkoeijen, P. P. J. L., Bouwmeester, S., & Camp, G. (2012). A short-term testing effect in cross-language recognition. *Psychological Science, 23*, 567–571.

Vespa, J., Armstrong, D. M., & Medina, L. (2018). *Demographic turning points for the United States: Population projections for 2020 to 2060.* Retrieved from https://www.census.gov/content/dam/Census/library/publications/2018/demo/P25_1144.pdf

Vick, K. (2017, February 6). The other side. *Time*, pp. 24–33.

Vo-Jutabha, E. D., Dinh, K. T., McHale, J. P., & Valsiner, J. (2009). A qualitative analysis of Vietnamese adolescent identity exploration within and outside an ethnic enclave. *Journal of Youth and Adolescence, 38*, 672–690.

Von Drehle, D., & Altman, A. (2014, September 1). The tragedy of Ferguson. *Time*, pp. 22–27.

Wade, C., & Tavris, C. (2003). *Psychology* (7th ed.). Upper Saddle River, NJ: Prentice Hall.

Wagner, R. K. (2000). Practical intelligence. In R. J. Sternberg (Ed.), *Practical intelligence in everyday life.* New York, NY: Cambridge University Press.

Walters, K. L., & Simone, J. M. (1993). Lesbian and gay male group identity attitudes and self-esteem: Implications for counseling. *Journal of Counseling Psychology, 40*, 94–99.

Walton, G. M., & Spencer, S. J. (2009). Latent ability: Grades and test scores systematically underestimate the intellectual ability of negatively stereotyped students. *Psychological Science, 20*, 1132–1139.

Wang, J., Leu, J., & Shoda, Y. (2011). When the seemingly innocuous "stings": Racial microaggressions and their emotional consequences. *Personality and Social Psychology Bulletin, 37*, 1666–1678.

Wang, W. (2012). *The rise of intermarriage: Rates, characteristics vary by race and gender.* Retrieved from http://www.pewsocialtrends.org/2012/02/16/the-rise-of-intermarriage/

Warner, W. L., & Srole, L. (1946). *The social systems of American ethnic groups* (2nd ed.). New Haven, CT: Yale University Press.

Warren, R. (1995). *The purpose-driven church.* Grand Rapids, MI: Zondervan.

Washington, H. A. (2006). *Medical apartheid: The dark history of medical experimentation on Black Americans from colonial times to the present.* New York, NY: Harlem Moon.

Waters, M. C., & Pineau, M. G. (Eds.) (2015). *The integration of immigrants into American society*. Washington, DC: National Academies Press.

Watson, O. M., & Graves, T. D. (1966). Quantitative research in proxemic behavior. *American Anthropologist, 68*, 971–985.

Watters, E. (2010). *Crazy like us: The globalization of the American psyche*. New York, NY: Free Press.

Wead, D. (2017). *Game of thorns: The inside story of Hillary Clinton's failed campaign and Donald Trump's winning strategy*. New York, NY: Hatchett Book Group.

Wear, D. (2003). Insurgent multiculturalism: Rethinking how and why we teach culture in medical education. *Academic Medicine, 78*(6), 549–545.

Wechsler, D. (1991). *Manual for the Wechsler Intelligence Scale for Children–third edition*. San Antonio, TX: Psychological Corporation.

Weisman de Mamani, A., Gurak, K., & Sura, G. (2014). Serious mental illness. In F. T. L. Leong, L. Comas-Díaz, G. C. Nagayama Hall, V. C. McLoyd, & J. E. Trimble (Eds.), *APA handbook of multicultural psychology. Vol. 2: Applications and training* (pp. 345–359). Washington, DC: American Psychological Association.

Weissman, M. M., Bland, R. C., Canino, G. J., Faravelli, C., Greenwald, S., Hwu, H. G., . . . Yeh, E. K. (1996). Cross-national epidemiology of major depression and bipolar disorder. *Journal of the American Medical Association, 276*, 293–299.

Weissman, M. M., Bland, R. C., Canino, G. J., Faravelli, C., Greenwald, S., Hwu, H. G., . . . Yeh, E. K. (1997). The cross-national epidemiology of panic disorder. *Archives of General Psychiatry, 54*, 305–309.

Weissman, M. M., Bland, R. C., Canino, G. J., Greenwald, S., Hwu, H. G., Lee, C. K., et al. (1994). The cross-national epidemiology of obsessive compulsive disorder. The Cross National Collaborative Group. *Journal of Clinical Psychiatry, 55* (Suppl.), 5–10.

Weissman, M. M., Broadhead, W. E., Olfson, M., Sheehan, D. V., Hoven, C., Conolly, P., . . . Leon, A. C. (1998). A diagnostic aid for detecting (*DSM-IV*) mental disorders in primary care. *General Hospital Psychiatry, 20*, 1–11.

West-Olatunji, C. A., & Conwill, W. (2011). *Counseling African Americans*. Belmont, CA: Cengage.

Whitbeck, L. B., Sittner Hartshorn, K. J., & Walls, M. L. (2014). *Indigenous adolescent development: Psychological, social and historical contexts*. New York, NY: Routledge.

White, J. (2001). My story. In D. W. Sue (Chair), *Surviving racism: Lessons we have learned*. Symposium presented at the National Multicultural Conference and Summit II—The psychology of race/ethnicity, gender, sexual orientation, and disability: Intersections, divergence, and convergence, Santa Barbara, CA.

White, J. L. (1970, September). Toward a Black psychology. *Ebony*, 44–45, 48–50, 52.

White, J. L. (1972). Toward a Black psychology. In R. L. Jones (Ed.), *Black psychology* (pp. 43–50). New York, NY: Harper & Row.

White, J. L., & Parham, T. A. (1990). *The psychology of Blacks: An African American perspective* (2nd ed.). Englewood Cliffs, NJ: Prentice Hall.

Whitney, P. (1998). *The psychology of language*. Boston, MA: Houghton Mifflin.

Whitworth, R. H. (1988). Anglo- and Mexican-American performance on the MMPI administered in Spanish or English. *Journal of Clinical Psychology, 44*, 891–897.

Whyte, K. P. (2017). The Dakota access pipeline, environmental justice, and U.S. colonialism. *Red Ink, 19*, 154–169.

Wildes, J. E., & Emery, R. E. (2001). The roles of ethnicity and culture in the development of eating disturbance and body dissatisfaction: A meta-analytic review. *Clinical Psychology Review, 21*, 521–551.

Wijeyesinghe, C. L. & Jackson III, B. W. (2012). *New perspectives on racial identity development: Integrating emerging frameworks*. (pp. 121 – 127). New York: New York University Press.

Will, J., Self, P., & Datan, N. (1976). Maternal behavior and perceived sex of infant. *American Journal of Orthopsychiatry, 46*, 135–139.

Williams, D. R., & Harris-Reid, M. (1999). Race and mental health: Emerging patterns and promising approaches. In A. V. Horwitz & T. L. Scheid (Eds.), *A handbook for the study of mental health: Social contexts, theories, and systems*. New York, NY: Cambridge University Press.

Williams, D. R., & Mohammed, S. A. (2009). Discrimination and racial disparities in health: Evidence and needed research. *Journal of Behavioral Medicine, 32*(1), 20–47.

Williams, J. (1987). *Eyes on the prize: America's civil rights years. 1954–1965*. New York, NY: Viking.

Williams, J. E., & Best, D. L. (1982). *Measuring sex stereotypes: A multination study*. Beverly Hills, CA: Sage.

Williams, J. E., & Best, D. L. (1994). Cross-cultural views of woman and men. In W. Lonner & R. Malpass (Eds.), *Psychology and culture* (pp. 191–196). Boston, MA: Allyn & Bacon.

Williams, R. L. (1974b). The death of White research in the Black community. *Journal of Non-White Concerns in Personnel and Guidance, 2*, 116–132.

Winton, R., Mather, K., & Serna, J. (2014, July 31). Feds consider probe into CHP beating captured on video, sources say. *The Los Angeles Times*. Retrieved from http://www.latimes.com/local/lanow/la-me-ln-federal-probe-possible-chp-beating-20140731-story.html

Wise, T. J. (2008). *White like me: Reflections on race from a privileged son.* Brooklyn, NY: Soft Skull Press.

Wise, T. J. (Producer and Presenter). (2013). *White like me: Race, racism and white privilege in America* [Film]. Available from Media Education Foundation, Northampton, MA.

Witkin, H. A. (1949). Perception of body position and the position of the visual field. *Psychological Monographs, 63* (7, whole No. 302).

Witkin, H. A., Lewis, H. B., Hertzman, M., Machover, K., Meissner, P. B., & Wapner, S. (1954). *Personality through perception.* New York, NY: Harper.

Witko, T. (Ed.). (2005). *No longer forgotten: Addressing the mental health needs of urban Indians.* Washington, DC: American Psychological Association.

Wolfgang, A. (1985). The function and importance of non-verbal behavior in intercultural counseling. In P. B. Pedersen (Ed.), *Handbook of cross-cultural counseling and therapy* (pp. 99–105). Westport, CT: Greenwood.

Wolfson, E. (2004). *Why marriage matters: America, equality, and gay people's right to marry.* New York, NY: Simon & Schuster.

Wong, E. C., Kinzie, J. D., & Kinzie, J. M. (2009). Stress, refugees, and trauma. In N. Tewari & A. N. Alvarez (Eds.), *Asian American psychology: Current perspectives* (pp. 441–462). New York, NY: Psychology Press.

Wood, J. (1994). *Gendered lives: Communication, gender, and culture.* Belmont, CA: Wadsworth.

Wood, J. T. (1999). Gender, communication, and culture. In L. A. Samovar & R. E. Porter (Eds.), *Intercultural communication: A reader* (8th ed., pp. 164–174). Belmont, CA: Wadsworth.

Woodside, D. B., & Kennedy, S. H. (1995). Gender differences in eating disorders. In M. V. Seeman (Ed.), *Gender and psychopathology* (pp. 253–268). Washington, DC: American Psychiatric Press.

Woodward, A. T., Bullard, K. M., Taylor, R. J., Chatters, L. M., Baser, R. E., Perron, B. E., & Jackson, J. S. (2009). Complementary and alternative medicine for mental disorders among African Americans, Black Caribbeans, and Whites. *Psychiatric Services, 60,* 1342–1349.

World Health Organization. (1948). *Constitution of the World Health Organization.* Geneva: World Health Organization Basic Documents. Retrieved from http://www.who.int/about/mission/en/

World Health Organization. (1973). *Report of the International Pilot Study on Schizophrenia.* Geneva: World Health Organization.

World Health Organization. (2017, July). *Mossul crisis, Iraq. WHO special situation report.* Retrieved from http://www.who.int/hac/crises/irq/sitreps/iraq-mosul-report-17June2017.pdf

Worrell, F. C., Cross, W. E., & Vandiver, B. J. (2001). Nigrescence theory: Current status and challenges for the future. *Journal of Multicultural Counseling and Development, 19*(3), 201–213.

Worrell, F. C., & Gardner-Kitt, D. L. (2006). The relationship between racial and ethnic identity in Black adolescents: The Cross Racial Identity Scale (CRIS) and the Multigroup Ethnic Identity Measure (MEIM). *Identity: An International Journal of Theory and Research, 6*(4), 293–315.

Worrell, F. C., Mendoza-Denton, R., Telesford, J., Simmons, C., & Martin, J. F. (2011). Cross Racial Identity Scale (CRIS) scores: Stability and relationships with psychological adjustment. *Journal of Personality Assessment, 93*(6), 637–648.

Worrell, F. C., Vandiver, B. J., Cross, W. E., Jr., & Fhagen-Smith, P. E. (2004). The reliability and validity of Cross Racial Identity Scale (CRIS) scores in a sample of African American adults. *The Journal of Black Psychology, 30*(4), 489–505.

Worrell, F. C., Vandiver, B. J., Schaefer, B. A., Cross, W. E., Jr., & Fhagen-Smith, P. E. (2006). Generalizing nigrescence profiles: A cluster analysis of Cross Racial Identity Scale (CRIS) scores in three independent samples. *The Counseling Psychologist, 34*(4), 519–547.

Worrell, F. C., & Watson, S. (2008). A confirmatory factor analysis of Cross Racial Identity Scale (CRIS) scores: Testing the expanded nigrescence model. *Educational and Psychological Measurement, 68*(6), 1041–1058.

Worthington, R. L., Navarro, R. L., Loewy, M., & Hart, J. (2008). Color-blind racial attitudes, social dominance orientation, racial ethnic group membership and college students' perceptions of campus climate. *Journal of Diversity in Higher Education, 1,* 8–19.

Yan, H. (2017, June 26). "Black Lives Matter" cases: What ended up happening after police killings. *CNN.* Retrieved from https://www.cnn.com/2017/06/26/us/black-lives-matter-deaths-outcomes/index.html

Yang, K. (1997). Theories and research in Chinese personality: An indigenous approach. In H. S. R. Kao & D. Sinha (Eds.), *Asian perspectives on psychology* (pp. 236–262). Thousand Oaks, CA: Sage.

Yanovski, S. C., Gormally, J. F., Lewer, M. S., Gwirtsman, H. E., & Yanovski, J. A. (1994). Binge eating disorder affects outcome of comprehensive very low-calorie diet treatment. *Obesity Research, 2,* 205–212.

Yanovski, S. C., Nelson, J. E., Dubbert, B. K., & Spitzer, R. L. (1993). Associations of binge eating disorder and psychiatric comorbidity in obese subjects. *American Journal of Psychiatry, 150,* 1572–1479.

Yee, A., Fairchild, H., Weizmann, F., & Wyatt, G. (1993). Addressing psychology's problems with race. *American Psychologist, 48,* 1132–1140.

Yeh, C. J. (2003). Age, acculturation, cultural adjustment, and mental health symptoms of Chinese, Korean, and Japanese immigrant youths. *Cultural Diversity and Ethnic Minority Psychology, 9,* 34–48.

Yeh, C. J., & Huang, K. (1996). The collectivistic nature of ethnic identity development among Asian-American college students. *Adolescence, 31,* 645–661.

Yin, R. K. (2004). *The case study anthology.* Thousand Oaks, CA: Sage.

Yoon, E., Chang, C.-T., Kim, S., Clawson, A., Cleary, S. E., Hansen, M., . . . Gomes, A. M. (2013). A meta-analysis of acculturation/enculturation and mental health. *Journal of Counseling Psychology, 60*(1), 15–30. doi:10.1037/a0030652

Young, S. D. (2012). *Psychology at the movies.* New York, NY: Wiley–Blackwell.

Yum, J. O. (1999). The impact of Confucianism on interpersonal relationships and communication patterns in East Asia. In L. A. Samovar & R. E. Porter (Eds.), *Intercultural communication: A reader* (8th ed., pp. 78–88). Belmont, CA: Wadsworth.

Zacharek, S., Docterman, E., & Edwards, H. S. (2017, December 18). The silence breakers. *Time,* pp. 34–71.

Zahran, H. S., Kobau, R., Moriarty, D. G., Zack, M. M., Giles, W. H., & Lando, J. (2004). Self-reported frequent mental distress among adults—United States, 1993–2001. *Morbidity and Mortality Weekly Report, 53,* 963–966. Retrieved from https://www.cdc.gov/mmwr/preview/mmwrhtml/mm5341a1.htm

Zakaria, F. (2010, August 16). The real Ground Zero: Let's promote Muslim moderates right here. *Newsweek,* p. 18.

Zakaria, F. (2017). Zakaria: Why Trump won. *CNN.* Retrieved from http://www.cnn.com/2017/07/31/opinions/why-trump-won-zakaria/index.html

Zalewski, C., & Greene, R. L. (1996). Multicultural usage of the MMPI-2. In L. A. Suzuki, P. J. Meller, & J. G. Ponterotto (Eds.), *Handbook of multicultural assessment: Clinical, psychological, and educational applications.* (pp. 77–114). San Francisco, CA: Jossey–Bass.

Zambrana, R. E., & Carter-Pokras, O. (2010). Role of acculturation research in advancing science and practice in reducing health care disparities among Latinos. *American Journal of Public Health, 100,* 18–23.

Zane, N., Bernal, G., & Leong, F. T. L. (2016). Introduction. In N. Zane, G. Bernal, & F. T. L. Leong (Eds.), *Evidence-based psychological practice with ethnic minorities: Culturally informed research and clinical strategies* (pp. 3–12). Washington, DC: American Psychological Association.

Zane, N., Hatanaka, H., Park, S. S., & Akutsu, P. (1994). Ethnic-specific mental health services: Evaluation of the parallel approach for Asian-American clients. *Journal of Community Psychology, 22,* 68–81.

Zane, N., & Ku, H. (2014). Effects of ethnic match, gender match, acculturation, cultural identity, and face concern on self-disclosure in counseling for Asian Americans. *Asian American Journal of Psychology, 5,* 66–74.

Zane, N., & Yeh, M. (2002). The use of culturally-based variables in assessment: Studies on loss of face. In K. S. Kurasaki, S. Okazaki, & S. Sue (Eds.), *Asian American mental health: Assessment methods and theories* (pp. 123–138). New York, NY: Kluwer Academic/Plenum Press.

Zea, M. C., Asner-Self, K. K., Birman, D., & Buki, L. P. (2003). The abbreviated multidimensional acculturation scale: Empirical validation with two Latino/Latina samples. *Cultural Diversity and Ethnic Minority Psychology, 9,* 107–126.

Zea, M. C., & Garcia, J. (Eds.). (1997). *Psychological interventions with Latino populations.* Needham Heights, MA: Allyn & Bacon.

Zhang, A. Y., Snowden, L. R., & Sue, S. (1998). Differences between Asian- and White-Americans' help-seeking and utilization patterns in the Los Angeles area. *Journal of Community Psychology, 26,* 317–326.

Zhao, Y., Qiu, W., & Xie, N. (2012). Social networking, social gaming, texting. In D. G. Singer & J. L. Singer (Eds.), *Handbook of children and the media* (pp. 97–112). Thousand Oaks, CA: Sage.

Zong, J., & Batalova, J. (2017). *Refugees and asylees in the United States.* Washington, DC: Migration Policy Institute. Retrieved from https://www.migrationpolicy.org/article/refugees-and-asylees-united-states

Zormeier, S. M., & Samovar, L. A. (1999). Language as a mirror of reality: Mexican American proverbs. In L. A. Samovar & R. E. Porter (Eds.), *Intercultural communication: A reader* (8th ed., pp. 235–239). Belmont, CA: Wadsworth.

Zuckerman, M. (1990). Some dubious premises in research and theory on racial differences: Scientific, social, and ethical issues. *American Psychologist, 45,* 1297–1303.

Zuma, J. (2010, December 16). FOX News top source of voter misinformation, study finds. Tucson Sentinel. Retrieved from https://www.google.com/search?q=fox+news+top+source+of+voter+misinformation%2C+study+finds&ie=utf-8&oe=utf-8&client=firefox-b-1

Index

Note: Page references followed by a "*t*" indicate table; "*f*" indicate figure